Transmedia
Directors

NEW APPROACHES TO SOUND, MUSIC, AND MEDIA

Series Editors: Carol Vernallis, Holly Rogers and Lisa Perrott

Transmedia Directors

Artistry, Industry and New Audiovisual Aesthetics

EDITED BY
CAROL VERNALLIS, HOLLY ROGERS AND LISA PERROTT

BLOOMSBURY ACADEMIC
NEW YORK • LONDON • OXFORD • NEW DELHI • SYDNEY

BLOOMSBURY ACADEMIC
Bloomsbury Publishing Inc
1385 Broadway, New York, NY 10018, USA
50 Bedford Square, London, WC1B 3DP, UK

BLOOMSBURY, BLOOMSBURY ACADEMIC and the Diana logo are trademarks of
Bloomsbury Publishing Plc

First published in the United States of America 2020

Cover image: *Moonrise Kingdom*, 2012, directed by Wes Anderson / Alamy Stock Photo
Cover font: 1920's Futura Classic, by Paul Renner

Library of Congress Cataloging-in-Publication Data
Names: Vernallis, Carol, editor. | Rodgers, Holly, editor. | Perrott, Lisa, editor.
Title: Transmedia directors: artistry, industry and new audiovisual aesthetics /
edited by Carol Vernallis, Lisa Perrott, and Holly Rodgers.
Description: New York: Bloomsbury Academic, 2019. |
Series: New approaches to sound, music, and media | Includes
bibliographical references and index. |
Summary: "A look at the signature styles of well-known film and music video
directors such as David Lynch, Wes Anderson, and Baz Luhrmann in their
relationship to sound, music, and image."– Provided by publisher.
Identifiers: LCCN 2019025878 (print) | LCCN 2019025879 (ebook) |
ISBN 9781501341007 (paperback) | ISBN 9781501339271 (hardback) |
ISBN 9781501339264 (epub) | ISBN 9781501339288 (pdf)
Subjects: LCSH: Motion pictures–Production and direction. |
Television–Production and direction. | Music videos–Production and direction.
Classification: LCC PN1995.9.P7 T73 2019 (print) | LCC PN1995.9.P7 | (ebook) |
DDC 791.4302/32–dc23
LC record available at https://lccn.loc.gov/2019025878
LC ebook record available at https://lccn.loc.gov/2019025879

ISBN: HB: 978-1-5013-3927-1
PB: 978-1-5013-4100-7
ePDF: 978-1-5013-3928-8
eBook: 978-1-5013-3926-4

Series: New Approaches to Sound, Music, and Media

Typeset by Deanta Publishing Services, Chennai, India
Printed and bound in the United States of America

To find out more about our authors and books visit www.bloomsbury.com and
sign up for our newsletters.

Carol: For Margaret, Charlie and Beatrice
Holly: For Daisy, Polly and both Johns
Lisa: For Sonya, Maia, Katya and Brooklyn

CONTENTS

ACKNOWLEDGEMENTS

The editors would like to thank Leah Babb-Rosenfeld, Abteen Bagheri, Joanna Demers, Joan Friedman, Indrashish Ghosh, Joseph Kahn, Gene Kang, Jaroslaw Kapuscinski, Mathias Korsgaard, Charles Kronengold, Meredith Kurey, Bebe Lerner, Anders Aktor Liljedahl, Sean Lynch, Amy Martin, Emil Nava, Karthik Ram, Sonya Roussina, Anastasia Solovieva, Raymond Sookram, Kevin and Ryan Staake, Margaret Vernallis, Eduardo Viñuela, Paula Woods, Bevin Yeatman, John McGrath, John Rogers, Polly Rogers, Hannah Ueno, R. Lanier Anderson, Aubrey Woodiwiss, Gert Wiescher, Lea Pao, Charles Bigelow, Rennie Alphonsa, and Jessica Anderson.

The font for *Transmedia Directors* is 1920's Futura Classic, Paul Renner's first from his family of Futura fonts. Sidelined for being judged too austere for the public, it was revived recently by Gert Wiescher.

CONTRIBUTORS

Linda Badley is Professor Emerita at Middle Tennessee State University. She is widely published in film studies and popular culture, with current research interests in Nordic cinemas, Lars von Trier, transnational trends, women's cinema and American independent film. She is the author of *Film, Horror, and the Body Fantastic* (1995), *Writing Horror and the Body* (1996), *Lars von Trier* (2011) and *Lars von Trier's Depression Films* (2019), and co-editor of *Traditions in World Cinema* (2006), *Indie Reframed: Women's Filmmaking and Contemporary American Independent Cinema* (2016) and *Nordic Noir Adaptation and Appropriation* (2019). With R. Barton Palmer, she co-edits the complementary series Traditions in World Cinema and Traditions in American Cinema.

Karen Barbour is an Associate Professor in dance in the School of Arts at the University of Waikato in Aotearoa, New Zealand. Her teaching, performance and research focuses on embodied ways of knowing particularly feminist choreographic practices in dance, site-specific, digital dance and pedagogical movement contexts. Her book publications include *Dancing Across the Page: Narrative and Embodied Ways of Knowing* (2011), *(Re)positioning Site Dance: Local Acts, Global Perspectives* (2019) and *Ethnographic Worldviews: Transformations and Social Justice* (2014). Karen is Editor of the journal *Dance Research Aotearoa,* presents regularly at international conferences and performs in arts festivals, and has published her writing in a range books and journals.

Warren Buckland is Reader in Film Studies at Oxford Brookes University, UK. His recent publications include *Wes Anderson's Symbolic Storyworld* (2019), *Hollywood Puzzle Films* (ed. 2014), *Film Theory: Rational Reconstructions* (2012) and *Puzzle Films: Complex Storytelling in Contemporary Cinema* (ed. 2009).

Lori Burns is Professor of music at the University of Ottawa. Her book, *Disruptive Divas* (2002) won the 2005 Pauline Alderman Award from the International Alliance for Women in Music. She is co-editor of *The Pop Palimpsest* with Serge Lacasse (2018) and The *Bloomsbury Handbook to*

Popular Music Video Analysis with Stan Hawkins (2019) as well as series co-editor of the *Ashgate Popular and Folk Music Series*.

Theo Cateforis is an Associate Professor of music history and cultures at Syracuse University. He is the author of *Are We Not New Wave? Modern Pop at the Turn of the 1980s* (2011) and editor of *The Rock History Reader* (2007, 2013, 2019), now in its third edition. His articles and essays on popular music, American music and film studies have appeared in *American Music*, *Current Musicology*, *Journal of Popular Music Studies* and the *Journal of the Society for American Music*. He is currently president of the US Chapter of the International Association for the Study of Popular Music (IASPM-US).

Dale Chapman is an Associate Professor of music at Bates College. His research focuses on issues relating to culture, political economy and critical race theory in the context of jazz and contemporary popular music. His work has appeared in the *Journal of the Society for American Music*, *Popular Music*, the *Journal of Popular Music Studies*, the *Oxford Handbook of Sound and Image in Digital Media* and the *Grove Dictionary of American Music*, 2nd ed. He has forthcoming work in the *Oxford Handbook on Music and Advertising*, as well as a collection entitled *Cybermedia: Scientists and Humanists Face the Machines*. His book *The Jazz Bubble: Neoclassical Jazz in Neoliberal Culture* was published in 2018 with the University of California Press.

Ewan Clark is a film composer, orchestrator and lecturer based in Wellington, New Zealand. He holds a PhD from Victoria University of Wellington, the dissertation for which analyses the film scores of Alexandre Desplat. At the time of publication, Ewan lectures as a teaching fellow in film scoring at Victoria University of Wellington. He has presented at the annual meeting of the New Zealand Musicology Society in 2015 and 2018, and his research interests include film music analysis, transformational theory, semiotics and metaphor theory. As a composer, Ewan has scored the feature length docudrama *Doubt: The Scott Watson Case* (2016) and numerous short films and documentaries that have screened at film festivals around the globe. As an orchestrator, his portfolio includes David Long's score for *Beyond the Edge* (2013) and Tim Prebble's award-winning score for the feature film *One Thousand Ropes* (2016).

Kwami Coleman, PhD, is an Assistant Professor of musicology at the Gallatin School on Individualized Study at New York University. His work is focused on improvised music, aesthetics, historiography, identity and political economy. Kwami is also a pianist and composer, and released a recording called *Local Music* in 2017 of original music for trio plus field recordings captured in his home neighbourhood, Harlem. His current book project is titled *Change: The 'New Thing' and Modern Jazz.*

J. D. Connor is Associate Professor of Cinema & Media Studies in the School of Cinematic Arts at USC. His most recent book *Hollywood Math and Aftermath: The Economic Image and the Digital Recession* was published in 2018. His website is www.johnconnorlikeintheterminator.com.

Elena del Río is Professor of Film Studies at the University of Alberta. Her research on the intersections between cinema and philosophies of the body has been featured in such journals as *Camera Obscura, Chimeres, CineFiles, Discourse, Science Fiction Studies, Studies in French Cinema, Necsus, Quarterly Review of Film and Video, Film-Philosophy, The New Review of Film and Television Studies, Canadian Journal of Film Studies, SubStance* and *Deleuze Studies.* She has also contributed essays to volumes on the films of Atom Egoyan and Rainer Fassbinder, and on topics such as Asian exploitation film, cinema and cruelty, the philosophy of film and Deleuze and cinema. She is the author of *Deleuze and the Cinemas of Performance: Powers of Affection* (2008) and *The Grace of Destruction: A Vital Ethology of Extreme Cinemas* (2016).

Donald Greig began his career as a Lecturer in film studies and semiology before becoming a professional singer. Having sung with the Tallis Scholars for twenty-five years and as a founder and current member of the Orlando Consort, he is recognized as an expert in the field of early music performance. He is also a versatile session singer, appearing on countless film soundtracks and in pop music. He has recently been awarded his doctorate for his study of the various ideological and cultural constraints that inform *Voices Appeared,* his design of a live soundtrack of music composed during the lifetime of Joan of Arc to accompany screenings of Carl Theodor Dreyer's *La Passion de Jeanne d'Arc.* He has contributed articles to several journals such as *Screen* and *Early Music,* as well as several chapters for academic books, and his first novel, *Time Will Tell,* was published in 2013. Currently, he is an honorary research fellow at the University of Nottingham.

Greg Hainge is Professor of French at the University of Queensland. His most recent books *Noise Matters: Towards an Ontology of Noise* (2013) and *Philippe Grandrieux: Sonic Cinema* (2017) stray into transmedia territory. He has published widely on cinema (with multiple articles on David Lynch, including a catalogue essay for the major Lynch exhibition and retrospective that took place at the Gallery of Modern Art, Brisbane), sound, literature and philosophy. He is a fellow of the Australian Academy of the Humanities and an editor-in-chief of *Culture, Theory and Critique.*

He co-edits the Ex:Centrics book series by Bloomsbury and serves on the editorial boards of *Contemporary French Civilization*, *Studies in French Cinema*, *Corps: revue interdisciplinaire* and *Études céliniennes*.

Mark Kerins is Professor of Film & Media Arts at Southern Methodist University. As a scholar, he primarily writes on surround sound and sound design, most notably in his 2010 book *Beyond Dolby (Stereo): Cinema in the Digital Sound Age*. As a film-maker, his work has shown across the United States and internationally. *Echoes*, his most recent short, has played at over forty festivals, earned numerous award nominations and taken home festival honours including 'Best Short', 'Best Drama', 'Best Sci-Fi Short' and 'Best Director'.

Jonathan Leal is a PhD candidate in modern thought and literature at Stanford University. In recent years, his arts criticism has appeared in *The Los Angeles Times*, *The Los Angeles Review of Books*, *Huizache: The Magazine of Latino Literature* and elsewhere. In 2017, he designed sound and music for the premiere of Cherríe Moraga's *The Mathematics of Love*; in 2018, he co-produced *Wild Tongue*, a compilation album featuring new music by nine bands in the South Texas borderlands. His current research project, *Dreams in Double Time*, examines bebop's reach among youth of colour across the post-WWII United States.

John McGrath is an Irish guitarist, musicologist and a Lecturer in Music at University of Surrey. He is the author of *Samuel Beckett, Repetition and Modern Music* (2018). His music and writing has featured in The Wire and recent performances have included a solo set at Kings Place, London. He was awarded a PhD in music from University of Liverpool in 2014, which was funded by the Arts & Humanities Research Council.

Brad Osborn is Associate Professor of music theory at the University of Kansas. He is the author of the monograph *Everything in Its Right Place: Analyzing Radiohead* (2016). Osborn's other research on post-millennial rock music is published in *Music Theory Spectrum*, *Perspectives of New Music*, *Music Analysis* and *Music Theory Online*. He currently serves the Society for Music Theory as Associate Editor of the journal *Music Theory Online*. Brad writes and records shoegazey post-rock as the artist D'Archipelago.

Lisa Perrott is Senior Lecturer and Programme Convener of Screen and Media Studies at the University of Waikato. Her interests include animation, transmedia and collaborative authorship, with an emphasis on the relations between audio and visual media, popular music, music video and the avant-garde. Lisa is co-editor of *Navigating with the Blackstar: the Mediality of David Bowie* (special issue of Celebrity Studies, 2019) and the Routledge book *David Bowie and Transmedia Stardom* (2019). Her publications include *Time Is Out of Joint: the Transmedial Hauntology of David Bowie* (2019) and *Music Video's Performing Bodies: Floria Sigismondi as Gestural Animator and Puppeteer* (2015). Having completed publications on the dialogic world-building of Radiohead, Chris Hopewell, Gastón Viñas and Majid Adin, Lisa is currently writing a book on the the music videos of David Bowie.

Holly Rogers is Reader in music at Goldsmiths, University of London. Her interests include the interaction of music and image in experimental film, video art, documentary film, music video and the contemporary visual art scene. She is author of *Sounding the Gallery: Video and the Rise of Art-Music* (2013), co-author of the textbook *Twentieth Century Musics* (2020) and editor of *Music and Sound in Documentary Film* (2014) and *The Music and Sound of Experimental Film* (2017). Holly is also the founding editor of the journal *Sonic Scope: New Approaches to Audiovisual Culture*.

Gareth Schott is an Associate Professor in screen and media studies in the School of Arts at the University of Waikato, New Zealand. His current research interests are focused on personal experiences of transmedia storytelling, encompassing different forms and articulation of loss. He has published research on interactive media, music, film and graphic novels. He is the author of *Violent Games: Rules, Realism, Effect* (2016) and co-author of *Computer Games: Text, Narrative and Play* (2006). The Royal Society of New Zealand Marsden Grant (NZ), Office of Film and Literature Classification (NZ), Arts and Humanities Research Council (UK) and University for Industry (UK) have funded his research.

Jeff Smith is a Professor in the Department of Communication Arts at the University of Wisconsin-Madison and the director of the Wisconsin Center for Film and Theater Research. He is the author of two books: *The Sounds of Commerce: Marketing Popular Film Music* and *Film Criticism, The Cold War, and the Blacklist: Reading the Hollywood Reds*. He has also published many articles on music and sound in the cinema.

Bodil Marie Stavning Thomsen, PhD, is Professor at School of Communication and Culture, ARTS, Aarhus University. Her research profile includes media aesthetics and philosophy with special emphasis on fashion, film, video and interfaces. She is currently PI of the research project Affects, Interfaces, Events (2015–20) and partner in the Canadian project Immediations: Media, Art, Event, headed by Erin Manning (2013–20). She was a former leader of the Nordic project Globalizing Art (2008–11) and PI of the Danish project Reality, Realism, the Real in Visual Perspective (1999–2002). She was the Editor-in-Chief of *Journal of Aesthetics and Culture*,

Taylor & Francis (2017–19). Selected publications include *Lars von Trier's Renewal of Film 1884-2014. Signal, Pixel, Diagram* (2018); co-author of 'Affective Attunement in a Field of Catastrophe' (2015); 'Signaletic, Haptic and Real-Time Material' (2012); 'On the Spatial Construction of Time in Olafur Eliasson's Installations' (2011); and 'The Haptic Interface. On Signal Transmissions and Events' (2011).

Graig Uhlin is an Associate Professor of Screen Studies at Oklahoma State University. His essays have appeared in *Journal of Cinema & Media Studies*, *Games & Culture*, *Quarterly Review of Film & Video*, *Spectator* and *Media Fields Journal*. His scholarship has also been published in the edited collections *Affective Ecocriticism*, *The Green Thread* and *Modernism and Food Studies*. He is currently writing a book on American director David Fincher.

Carol Vernallis teaches at Stanford, and her areas of research include contemporary audiovisual aesthetics, digital technologies and popular culture. Her book *Experiencing Music Video: Aesthetics and Cultural Context* (2004) provides a theoretical account of a genre – it is the first to articulate a theory of how music, lyrics and image can be placed in relation, and also the first to provide detailed analyses of individual videos that show the parameters of sound and image at work in a temporal flow. Her second book *Unruly Media: YouTube, Music Video, and the New Digital Cinema* (2013) attempts to take account of a new mediascape that is driven by intensified audiovisual relations. She is co-editor of *The Oxford Handbook of New Audiovisual Aesthetics* and *The Oxford Handbook of Sound and Image in Digital Media* (2013).

Gabrielle Veronique is a singer, pianist and graduate student in historical musicology at UC Berkeley.

Ben Winters is Senior Lecturer in Music at the Open University, UK. He is the author of *Music, Performance, and the Realities of Film: Shared Concert Experiences in Screen Fiction* (2014) and *Erich Wolfgang Korngold's* The Adventures of Robin Hood: *A Film Score Guide* (2007); he is a co-editor of *The Routledge Companion to Screen Music and Sound* (2017). Ben co-edits the *Ashgate Screen Music* series, and is on the editorial board of *Music, Sound, and the Moving Image*.

CHAPTER 1

Introduction

Carol Vernallis, Holly Rogers and Lisa Perrott

Carol Vernallis: Intensified movements

Again, everything seems to have changed, and *Transmedia Directors* seeks to somehow capture this. Over twenty years ago, scholars like David Bordwell, Jeff Smith and Carol Vernallis began noting that directors and practitioners were producing work across multiple media – for instance, feature films, commercials, music videos and fashion photography (Smith and Vernallis have chapters in this collection).[1] It wasn't unusual for some of this work to be commissioned by production houses like Anonymous Content, Partizan and Good Company. Many of today's biggest directors, like David Fincher and Francis Lawrence, developed their styles out of these contexts. We can see their stylistic traits – hyper-control, line and glide as well as a sensitivity to audiovisual relations – as derived from these experiences.

The roles of transmedial directors and practitioners have only intensified, as have those of production houses, which serve as hubs for all kinds of media-making, including feature films, long-duration, streaming web series, mini-docs, commercials, music videos and fashion photography, Instagram and Facebook posts, and their accompanying commercial spots (now shot in batches with a range of durations, say, from fifteen seconds to seven minutes, to be distributed across multiple platforms), VR and augmented reality. Much of this is now filmed in Los Angeles (not only because talent is deep but because everyone can drive within a day's notice to almost any location – the beach, the mountains, the desert and to those that are wealthy or impoverished), but a good amount is also shot in suburbs and cities like Cape Town, Vancouver and Rio de Janeiro, because they can look American or European. For these locations, a handful of first-line talent (the director, the cinematographer and some of the performers) can be flown in, and the rest of the talent and labour can be local. Much of the work we see today isn't of anywhere specific, and only certain types of directors succeed (those who work quickly, have interpersonal skills and can survive jet lag). Jonas Åkerlund has bragged that he enjoys circulating globally and collecting experiences, as he drops into and out of micro-communities.[2]

Catching this intensified media swirl seems daunting. It involves so many strands of production, from Instagram impresario Jay Versace's thirty-second cell phone content (consumed by an audience of millions), to Michael Bay's global billion-dollar financing of his *Transformers* franchise, but it is essential. In this volume, we look at directors, drawn to the way that many seem intoxicated by the possibilities of this media swirl. Wes Anderson, Lars von Trier, Michael Bay and David Lynch (who are discussed in the chapters) have designed theme parks, restaurants, museum exhibitions, speakers, furniture, wallpaper and diamonds, as well as fashion, opera stagings, commercials, virtual reality and streaming television. We think, perhaps, that the desire to reach past every moving media format into material objects is a drive to try everything possible, or a desire to touch, finally, a material shore.

In putting together this collected volume, we had quite a few questions: What is it about these directors and practitioners? Do they have better lives than us? Can we somehow emulate them? Do they know how to negotiate neoliberalism, precarity, austerity and work speed-up in ways we can adapt and use? Were they just producing content, or did they think deeply about platforms, genres and form? Were music videos their favourite medium (because experimentation, voice and imagination could resound in these), or was it the narrative streaming series that beckoned them, because characters could be subtly and contradictorily constructed? And how did they voice their work through practitioners? Did they hold them close and adapt to them? What happened when talent changed? Because many of our directors work across the same media, might they contribute to a new style? Could we assume that films and television (with their potential for world-building and sense of the past and the future), music videos (with their audio and visual aesthetics and rhythm), commercials (with their ability to project a message quickly), the internet (with its refreshed concepts of audience and participation) and larger forms like restaurants and amusement parks (with their materiality alongside today's digital aesthetics) added up to something new? Senior directors, through their experience and influence, might project this new style, and students and younger artists would emulate it. The production houses seemed to share commonalities (i.e. what one director anonymously described as 'a wan Terrence Malick filter'?).[3] How much did they shape style? Instagram would need to be a piece. Would we wish to reassess concepts of authorship, assemblage, transmedia, audio and visual aesthetics and world-building?

There were other attractive tacks for our collection – some sort of Latourian actor network, where we would also track agents, signals and objects or an in-depth look at one or two directors from a wider range of perspectives. The term 'transmedia' (directors) in our title called for a synonym (like 'cross', 'traverse' or 'through'), because transmedia is more often defined as a franchise aimed at monetizing a concept (Henry Jenkins and others are responsible for this scholarship; we find their notions of world-building particularly helpful, but we're focused on the portability of the director and her style).[4] Our instincts, we've realized, were good. We've captured much of what we were seeking, including confirmation concerning intensified audiovisual aesthetics centrality today. All our directors and practitioners are *auteurs mélomanes* (in Claudia Gorbman's words), 'music-loving directors [who] treat music … as a key thematic element and a marker of authorial style.'[5] They seek novel realizations of the soundtrack in relation to the image. We assert that we need a new discipline, perhaps one called audiovisual studies.

Our approach – which features individual chapters and several modules on a number of today's directors and practitioners – helped us feel closer to our moment, and more aware of unfolding trends. Insights emerged as chapters came in. Our 'big' directors projected something odd in relation to scale, and we suspect their use of scale links intimately with their success: skills in modulating scale may be crucial if one wishes to span the media swirl (from the Instagram pic to the streaming web series and big-budget film). As his module shows, Wes Anderson embraces the hyper-groomed, curated and miniaturized style (though he can quickly break out of this, like *The Royal Tenenbaums*'s family friend Cash's lurid murals and extravagant car crash). Michael Bay's images on the other hand (as our author Mark Kerins notes, and he intends this as a compliment) could be seen as *advertisements for Michael Bay*. As Kerins observes, Bay's stripped-down characters and plots flatten the director's work, but they also make his products flexible and transportable. Lynch (and we're aware that this sounds impressionistic) seems to release his projects synchronized to his format; his pitched audiovisual emanations, porous and oscillating in time, are tuned so that his commercial's rhythms differ from a long-running TV show like *Twin Peaks*; both, however, feel as if they'd pre-existed as other points in the galaxy and were tied to one another – they are slices of Lynch. Barry Jenkins and his collaborators can suggest a heart-piercing humanism in one sustained shot (having African American actors directly addressing an audience is new for many), and his use of rhyme, poetic form and memory are equally important. Lars von Trier seems caught in some light/dark opposition, with works asserting greater grandeur than the forms can contain. His favourite techniques, including diagrams, plays with digital surfaces and tightly curated swatches of pop and classical music, facilitate these effects. Bowie, one of the most shape-shifting auteurs here, resembles a magpie, embracing a loose continuity; these contribute to his ability to cast a shadow even after death. Sofia Coppola's scalar visions may be the hardest to describe. Much of her work suggests an oscillation between presence and absence, with the 'now' momentarily peeking into view. An inaccessibility and timelessness beguiles through her languid figures, handsome costumes, subtle lighting and pastel colours. We'd wish to provide similar descriptions for more of our volume's subjects, such as Steve Wilson, Jess Cope, Jay Versace and Sigur Rós. These are our descriptions; you can catch your own from reading the modules. We're excited about our short chapters, which place perspectives right up against one another. Overlaps and different facets quickly emerge.

Surface features appear to connect closely to scale (director Emil Nava's and producer Calvin Harris's structures against surfaces come quickly to the fore in their module). Our directors are good at what Richard Dyer calls the intangibles of media practice: colour, light, gesture, movement and music sound.[6] Readers might keep an eye out for Wes Anderson's bright yellow, Coppola's soft pastels, Bay's 'blorange' (saturated hues, with darks skewing blue and skin skewing orange) and Lars von Trier's deep red and dull beige.

Our collection seeks to illuminate how directors work with both sound and image, and across various media. It also aims to show the ways they work in different contexts and their practices adapt over time. Uhlin's and Connor's chapters focus on auteurs and practitioners within the industry, and the ways technologies' affordances facilitate their projects. Uhlin captures David Fincher's deep ambivalence, his role's (or function's) requirement to project himself as an auteur as well as his desire to vanish, as a practitioner, from view. His recent work becomes possible not only through current, specialized forms of digital workflow (which Fincher helped design) but also through the collaboration of many specialists and their production houses. As Connor describes, Bong Joon Ho on the other hand seems transmedial not so much in the ways he works with content, as in how he crosses nations, corporations and other political, economic and social configurations. And he does this, as it seems many of our directors do, through a gesture, a concept or an image – *Snowpiercer*'s train (as a metaphor for narrative drive and capitalism), his hands making the shape of that train, and the beyond-negotiation-demand for a gimbal.

We did not write this collection to extol the great director. Instead, it's because, as Warren Buckland suggests in his chapter, we as humans desire to engage with art forms as a means to both recognize ourselves and see past ourselves. I've had a chance to talk with and meet several of the leading directors and practitioners of today, and they seem just a bit more interesting and noticeably more anxious and driven than most of us. As co-editors, we see ourselves, with varying degrees of agreement and difference, as possessing progressive politics. In more generous societies, we'd hope everyone would have the abilities and resources to produce work if they so desired, and to be seen.

Some of our commitment to this collection comes out of overlapping political work; for me, much of this is tied to audiovisual literacy, and some of it to neuroscience and new technologies. I'm co-opting Sandberg's line of 'lean in' (which Joe Tompkins has written beautifully on in relation to *The Hunger Games* series).[7] I see merit in unplugging. But there's also merit in engaging forcefully. We had long made a commitment to range and diversity, but in the interim, as we worked on our collection, #MeToo and #OscarsSoWhite unfolded. My interviews with above- and below-the-line practitioners seemed to capture the industry's new commitments to diversity and range. There's clearly an increasing engagement with showing women and people of colour before the camera (most strikingly so with advertising to millennials). And perhaps as a related corollary, there's new pressure to represent behind the camera too. I'm most moved by teams chosen by well-established production houses like Partizan (Michel Gondry's company) and Anonymous Content and Reset (David Fincher's former and current company).

This is a big volume. We've attempted to reflect gender, race, age, nationality, LGBTQ+ and disability. Some of the politics of our 'highest profile' directors are more conservative than ours (Lynch, Bay and von Trier have all expressed sentiments we can't endorse), but more are committed to social justice. We feel our collection intersects with recent thinking about the interwoven nature of individuals, community and politics, and can be turned towards progressive ends.[8]

Our directors came out of fortuitous circumstances and biological predispositions (what might be called gifts and inheritances). Wes Anderson's mother was an archaeologist and his father headed an advertising firm. Barry Jenkins and his colleagues attended Florida State University, where there was a remarkable level of energy, support and magic. Sofia Coppola's father was Francis Ford Coppola, and she has imbibed cinema since infancy. Some of it's serendipity (Bay got into trouble for blowing up his toy truck, an experience so overwhelmingly powerful he never let go of it), and some of it is biology. Von Trier and David Bowie have been forthright about being neuro-atypical, especially von Trier. But all of this is human and natural and understandable.

These artists' trajectories have been shaped by context and serendipity: it's partly a mystery (and probably some luck) how they developed, changed and persevered. Jenkins waited eight years between his *Medicine for Melancholy* (2008) and *Moonlight* (2016) films, and suddenly he's in the midst of *If Beale Street Could Talk* (2018) and the forthcoming TV series *The Underground Railroad*. It would have been hard to imagine, watching 1980s and 1990s music video directors at the time, that Dave Meyers's videos would contribute so much to the genre's potential as an art form in such surprising ways.[9]

We attempt to capture how directors' work has evolved as they've worked across media, though this can be elusive. The most in-depth descriptions are in the chapters on Michael Bay, Dave Meyers and Sophia Coppola: music videos still cast an influence on their work. Some influences can be gauged by imagining past this volume. One might speculate on the ways Wes Anderson's work will shift after his recent experiences curating a major museum exhibit (he handled thousands of art objects and whittled these down to a few – surely, given his past predilections, this would make a difference). He's just come out with wallpaper. And one wonders about the origin and development of David Fincher's meticulousness (which some claim is obsessive). Can we give music video some credit for this? Fincher has described music video as a director's sandbox, and because there isn't much dialogue, he must have spent a lot of time watching bodies within shots passing against the music, over and over again. Who wouldn't, with Fincher's inclinations, hunger for a perfect line? Traces of his early music video work appear in his recent films, like Amy Dunne's celebratory leap into the air in *Gone Girl* (2014), having successfully escaped the police. Her euphoric movement matches some of the leaps in Paula Abdul's 'Straight Up' (1988), Madonna's 'Vogue' (1990) and Justin Timberlake and Jay-Z's 'Suit & Tie' (2013). Her lacing her ballet shoes on the way to eviscerate her ex-boyfriend may draw inspiration from Abdul's 'Coldhearted Snake' (1988).

The ways directors in this collection depend on their composers and other practitioners highlight a central political point, which is that we're bound to one another: no artist makes it alone, and the same is true for ourselves. As Theo Cateforis and Ewan Clark note, it's not completely clear if Anderson had a beloved, relatively whole sound world prior to his collaborations with composer Mark Mothersbaugh, or if they co-created one together. When his next composer, Alexandre Desplat, began contributing, we don't know if he chose materials out of a respect for Mothersbaugh, to follow Anderson's taste, to maintain a house brand, or that these musical materials just seemed apt for these films' images. Still, one gets a sense how much Anderson, Mothersbaugh and Desplat became indebted to another. Perhaps similarly, Jenkins has found practitioners who beautifully augment his work, as cinematographers and sound designers, as has Nava with music producers and colour timers. Jess Cope and Steve Wilson seem intimately close. Floria Sigismondi has described her connection to Bowie as beyond the human. Schott's and Barbour's chapter on Sigur Rós shows the ways a song can carry such a clear message that no additional instructions need be included: we all want to be on the same wavelength, especially when thinking about our planet's future.

What is it about these directors and their work, and how do they get us to better lives and a better world? Dyer says that music as a part of audiovisually enlivened, popular media creates feelings of utopia, but offers no roadmap to get there. Jenkins and Meyers may provide possible paths.[10]

But these directors produce messages that are new and in sync with *always?* our time. They first capture us, as Dyer and Carl Plantinga argue, with an unpackable conundrum.[11] Buckland sketches this most fully with his description of Anderson's ironic sincerity. It's also in Lynch's and von Trier's euphoric generosity, violence and terror. And, perhaps, in Michael Bay's benevolent, extravagant figures – mechanical objects whose source remains unfathomable. And Jay Versace's desire to be king, even though he's on Instagram. These transmedia artists all stretch out to the world. (One can feel invigorated when those mechanical transformers twist their way up to an erect posture.) The directors discussed in this project project a gratitude for existence, and for coexisting with other people. Kerins captures Bay's exuberant drive, and Bodil Marie Stavning Thomsen's and Linda Badley's readings grasp a similar impulse in Trier's dark *The House That Jack Built* (2018).

The rest of this work might be done by us, and/or with us requesting more collaboration with directors and practitioners. This can be harder to facilitate today, because we're now in the era of the non-disclosure agreement, aka the NDA (though I've found many industry personnel who remained incredibly generous). One mis-quote on Twitter, and that's it. Artists and practitioners are, as Kevin Staake of Pomp&Clout notes, 'worried about the bigger, hungry fishes' mouths behind them', and many suppose we in the humanities can figure this out ourselves.[12] Letting industry personnel know how important their contributions are can make a difference.

Our project (and it can be yours) is to develop a field of audiovisual studies that's engaged with all media, and that's political. This collection attempts to contribute here in several ways. It details directors' and practitioners' engagements with sound and image (which is a relational, interpersonal affair), and dependence on one another for success. In many ways, they labour for visions that speak to us.

These directors depart from their predecessors in the ways they work with images and soundtracks. The media swirl, audiovisuality and the digital turn – and the ways these interrelate and overlap – help describe today's aesthetics. The digital turn, for example, blurs the boundaries between sound and image, for both now share an ontological ground of being code. *4* An adjustment in one medium can spur a modification in the other, and then back and forth again, nearly effortlessly. This content can then spin out into multiple forms. Sound and image relations can convey much of the work's latent meaning.[13]

Media scholars have largely focused on the image, and, while there exist film-soundtrack studies and sound studies, not enough scholarship considers the ways sound and image work together. There are three reasons for this: (1) Little theory elucidates scholars' close readings; (2) an analyst should feel comfortable working across disciplines (music and visual arts):[14] some boldness is required to attend to the soundtrack, the image, the editing, the lighting, the gesture as they unfold in both time and within the instant; (3) Academic programmes encourage neither enough crossing between disciplines nor dallying with the popular. Some of this collection's chapters closely consider audiovisual aesthetics (Holly Rogers, Lori Burns and Vernallis), and its many case studies place the soundtrack and the image side by side. These pieces' brevity and intentional juxtapositions enable new relations to emerge.

We need audiovisual studies because we live in an audiovisually intensified culture. We also need more work on brief media. It's how we consume these days, with YouTube, adverts and interrupted viewing practices. Brief media has its own aesthetic and formal shape. We have several pieces on such forms; it's our belief that if you can read a music video or short film-segment, you can also read Instagram teasers, blockbuster-film trailers, political ads and news segments (which are highly aestheticized).

This volume feels like a start. There's a moment here in our collection when Joi McMillon describes how sound can ferry a viewer across a rupture in time and space (in my interview with her, we discussed a sequence in *If Beale Street Could Talk* – a flashback in the midst of Tish's family breaking the news of her pregnancy to her in-laws – that worked beautifully in the theatre, but not, because of poorer sound quality, with my iPad and headphones).

Speaking to this disjunction, Katherine Breeden (a computer scientist at Harvey Mudd and collaborator for a study on media and eye-tracking) commented that, for neurological reasons, higher-res and more detailed sound makes the image seem richer. I've noticed that in certain news broadcasts (like Fox News) there were many devices limiting or downplaying the voices of political opponents (the newscaster's shoulder coming further forward than the guest's, in an apparent effort to edge them out; grimaces, interjections and scrolling graphics set a rhythm and help redirect attention – even the lapel pins often seem to carry semiotic meaning). I've noticed, too, that documentary footage was often recast with a green tint. And then it struck me – if these devices are already in use to undermine or discredit TV guests, what sorts of techniques might be at play in the realm of sound and image? It's important to pay attention to this, to be aware of the many ways manipulations of audiovisual media can influence or rewrite our perceptions. All forms. All practitioners. All of us.

Holly Rogers: Modules and oscillations

Above, Vernallis draws our attention to a new sensibility of media-making; one that not only complicates the emerging intensity of contemporary film but also paves the way for refreshed and extended forms of audiovisuality.

In some ways, directors, with their close engagement with scripts, editing, cinematography and sound, have always been transmedial. But here we are interested in the fresh fluidities afforded by contemporary networked and participatory culture; in the ways in which directors navigate swiftly and fluidly across forms within our post-media condition. As Vernallis remarks above, the impact on visual, sonic and audiovisual grammar has been both intense and liberating. Although all our chapters investigate the ways in which one person's voice develops through projects and across platforms while retaining a distinctive grain, most authors find an emergent mutability that embraces assemblage approaches to construction, collaborative creativity and distributed authorship.

Assemblage, collaboration and distribution. The structure of our book mirrors this dispersal of authorship by approaching topics from a variety of angles. This works in a modular way. Some sections begin with a specific idea. Our authors tackle the development of cross-medial assemblage through the work of Sofia Coppola, Michael Bay and David Fincher, for example. In other sections, transmedial possibilities for stretched or disrupted audiovisuality, colourisation, framing and rhythm take centre stage, as we see in the analyses of music videos by David Bowie, Emil Nava, Sigur Rós and Jess Cope. Modular case studies of Wes Anderson, David Lynch, Barry Jenkins and Lars von Trier form interventions into these analyses. Although each chapter within these modules operates with its own internal coherence and dynamics, when read as part of a larger project, they begin to resonate differently. Broader themes emerge; different interpretations arise. Like the directors we discuss, these chapters work transmedially.

Critics have long pointed to a music-video style that has infiltrated film-making, but we're interested in a more contemporary and richer back-and-forth movement across forms and genres guided by directors accomplished in many technologies and aesthetics. This traversal across platforms, durations, budgets, styles and teams facilitates variety while also enabling individual voices to resonate loudly across projects. At our book's centre is a collection of essays focused on this paradoxical distillation of the communal voice. Jeff Smith's identification of a feminine sensibility that runs through Sofia Coppola's work opens the discussion. Her directorial voice, evolving through the affordances of digital manipulation, can be tracked through her commercials, music videos, feature films and recent holiday special. Coppola's style can be experienced through her pastel colour schemes, soft lighting and pensive, sometimes oblique, camera flow, as well as her overarching sonic structures that afford direct access to the subjective core of her characters. These audio and visual consistencies, Smith suggests, promote moments of transcendence and bliss. Mark Kerins finds different emergent sensibilities in the work of Michael Bay. Focusing on his short-form work, Kerins reveals a cinematic approach already at play in the director's early music video and commercial projects, a process of construction and an articulation of style that informes his later feature-film construction. The pair of essays that follow deal more closely with these processes of production, concentrating in on the technological fluidity that underpins large-scale transmedial assemblage. J. D. Connor refers to interviews with South Korean Bong Joon Ho and the production history of his 2013 film *Snowpiercer* to show how a director's voice can emerge through major independent global production and digital processes that unite everything from screenwriting and design to sound, photography, editing and distribution. Graig Uhlin explores the ways in which workflow and below-the-line professionals can support the branded identity of the director through intensive forms of collaboration. David Fincher's production and post-production methods provide an example of technology and design transferability capable of forging coherence across numerous forms.

Coppola's, Bay's, Joon Ho's and Fincher's convergent, transmedial textures open spaces for vibrant forms of audiovisuality. Within today's networked interdisciplinarity of multi-platform storytelling, Claudia Gorbman's so-termed *auteurs mélomanes* that Vernallis mentions above form intense, long-lasting partnerships with composers, musicians and sound designers.[15] As Kerins shows in his work on Bay and Uhlin on Fincher, many directors began their careers in the music video industry. Skilled in cutting images to sonic rhythms and visualizing musical form, they brought unique techniques with them as they moved into feature-film production. Our three-essay module on British director Emil Nava establishes this transference of skills through close examination of his saturated audiovisual textures and intricate, experiential use of colour. Vernallis sets the scene with her interview with Nava, alighting on aspects of technology and audiovisuality and seeking his thoughts on his unusual relationship to musical form, colour and image. Building from this, Brad Osborn focuses on Nava's and Calvin Harris's collaborations across fourteen videos. Osborn combines techniques from visual and musicological scholarship to highlight an emergent style that fuses Harris's verse-chorus designs with Nava's blending of virtual and natural worlds. In his chapter, Jonathan Leal moves closer still, placing the spotlight squarely on Nava's expressive and expansive use of colour. While Smith identifies a transmedial use of pastel shades in Coppola's work, here, Leal situates Nava's work within contemporary forms of colour processing and saturation, noting how the director, working in our age of screen proliferation, app development and ubiquitous social media presence, overcomes the normalization of visual overload by defamiliarizing certain audiovisual strategies.

Following the Nava module is a section focused on music video's centrifugal forces: on the peculiar forms of visual sonicity that arise when a director moves back and forth between music video and other forms. Vernallis, in the first of three investigations of music-based transmedial projects, offers a reading of music video director Dave Meyers. Referring to work created over the last twenty-five years, she traces the ways in which his work has become more politically engaged and responsive to the song, developments stemming from his photography and film work. Lisa Perrott who coins the term 'transmedia surrealism' changes tact, homing in on the collaborative relationship between David Bowie and Floria Sigismondi to posit music video itself as a transmedial form. In her exploration of their generative and dialogic process of world-building across projects, she identifies several unfolding stylistic developments, including angular rhythms supported by stop-motion pixilation, contrasting camera movements and disorientating depths-of-field. Perrott's work draws together ideas at play in several other chapters, including hauntology and temporality, which underpin the Lynch module, and a critical engagement with *Gesamtkunstwerk* (or total artwork), an idea that flows through our chapters on von Trier. As her analysis progresses, Perrott is able to frame Bowie himself as a medium to be moulded and shaped across media.

In their close audiovisual analysis of the *Valtari Mystery Film Experiment* (2012), a group of videos – or what the authors call 'soundtrack instigated films' – by different visual artists for the sixth studio album of Icelandic post-rock band Sigur Rós, Gareth Schott and Karen Barbour find transmedia style emerging vertically, as associations and progressions are forged from sound to image, song to video. Noting the melancholy and nostalgia that underpins the band's sonic response to their homeland, the authors use the reciprocal fluidity between the structure of the post-rock songs and the human movement and gestures they evoke to develop a theory of distributed authorship for music performance and film-making.

Transmedia directors create work that demands new modes of analysis. While many of our authors deal with these demands, Lori Burns places methodology at the centre of her chapter. Through the construction of a digital storymap able to analyse, at a micro level, audiovisual gesture and rhythm, Burns proposes a new approach to music video that treads the boundary between multimodality and transmediality. Jess Cope's stop-motion animation for Steven Wilson's 'Routine' video (*Hand. Cannot. Erase.*, 2015) is used as a case study to show how a multidimensional artwork that includes video, artefacts, written texts, music and performances can offer a complex reading of human subjectivity and social experience.

Social experience and identity become the driving force for Burns's companion piece, which moves away from the fixed forms of music video and film to explore the fragmented transmediality that floods the participatory culture of social media. Here, Gabrielle Veronique investigates the confusion that arises when internet projects extend into and absorb other media forms and autobiographical events. Using Instagram celebrity Jay Versace to question the representation of queer black youth in online culture, Veronique cross-references Instagram content and the use of emojis to reveal non-normative viewing strategies. Versace's involvement with the Reebok campaign, which sees him repost photos and videos from the brand, is particularly interesting as it highlights the mediation of real life online platforms. Is this autobiography, puppetry or pure fiction?

Lying between these close investigations of transmedia directors and internet heroes are four large modules that focus on film-makers who, although not beginning life as music video directors, are nevertheless radical and progressive *auteur mélomanes*. Wes Anderson, Barry Jenkins and David Lynch have all formed long-lasting partnerships with composers, allowing audiovisual rhythms and complexities to develop across projects, while Lars von Trier, while abstaining from soundtrack music in his Dogme 95 films, later featured fragmented, culturally dissonant pre-existent music within his work. While many of our book's directors bring music video aesthetics into long-play work, in these modules we see new forms of audiovisuality begin to permeate films, internet projects, music albums and commercials; this musicalization of form and style loosens conventional narrative textures. This process of musicalization forms the basis of our four-essay David Lynch module, in which Greg Hainge argues that the director's use of granular synthesis (a process used in music production to stretch time and shift pitch) to contort temporal flow influences our experience of time by recalibrating our sense of duration. Borrowing ideas from quantum theory, and arguing that Lynch's signature style and thematic development are rooted in the specificity of his audiovisual medium, Hainge analyses moments where teleological time in Lynch's film and long-play television series appears to unravel. In my chapter, I treat this temporal fluidity more broadly. Referring to hauntological affordances similar to those that Perrott reveals in the Bowie-Sigismondi collaboration, I follow drones, room tones, acousmatic soundscapes and ruptured lip-syncs through Lynch's films, TV shows, internet projects and music videos. For me, these recurrent dissonant moments of sonic disruption operate like Mark Fischer's description of the 'eerie absence', becoming audiovisual affect able to signify significant emotional or aesthetic upheaval between and across texts.[16] John McGrath's chapter closes the module with a focus on a specific technique. For him, Lynch's unusual penchant for extreme sonic slowness, vari-speed and glitch in his work for film, television and commercials enables cinematic time to stretch out, making room for emotions to develop over long periods; these moments can be condensed and sped-up for short-form works.

Completing this module, Elena del Río develops the previous three chapters through an exploration of Lynch's aesthetics of expression. While I reveal a type of immateriality at play in Lynch's work, for del Río, the notion of the formless can be seen as a paradoxical type of consistency that draws on Gilbert Simondon's philosophy of variability, mutability and the formless, ideas that are determined by the exchange of information and differential energy between systems. For her, viewing Lynch's work evacuates fixed forms and identities and disrupts conventional concepts of individual subjectivity. Del Río calls for a new approach to transmedia based not on the recurrence of motifs, themes and objects, but on morphogenesis/ ontogenesis: 'the process that traces the emergence and mutability of forms.' Only in this way do Lynch's film simulate complex forms of reality that operate beneath formed substances.

Discussions of audiovisual temporality and speed also drive our Barry Jenkins module. Like Hainge and McGrath, Dale Chapman sees sonic slowness and slowing as processes able to disrupt traditional cinematic form. In an interview with Nicholas Britell about his time-stretched and pitch-shifted score for *Moonlight* (2016), Chapman draws our attention to the composer's appropriation of the 1990s 'chopped and screwed' aesthetic, which sees artists remixing and cutting up hip hop by slowing its tempo, dropping beats and scratching vinyl. Applying the aesthetic to his orchestral textures, which descend and deepen in both pitch and emotion, Britell allows temporal distortion to take us into the emotional heart of the story. In his companion piece, Kwami Coleman investigates how blackness, masculinity and queerness can reconfigure transmedial assemblage by directing our attention to Jenkins's next collaboration with Britell, the film *If Beale Street Could Talk* (2018). Again, temporality is key. In many ways, Jenkins's careful use of recordings, listening and physical audio devices echoes Wes Anderson's love of analogue technology (as we'll see below) and Lynch's recurrent tropes of a record stylus and scenes of listening. But here, Coleman notes how on-screen vinyl recordings of late-1950s and early-1960s jazz and rhythm and blues evoke an external, clock time that causes friction against Britell's non-diegetic leitmotivic score, which suggests a more malleable, nonlinear temporality more attuned to the interior, emotional states of the characters. Coleman reads these plural temporalities as embodying an experiential subjectivity unique to African American young adults in New York City in the early 1960s. Following these two close analyses, Vernallis gives us an insight into production practice with her interview with the editor for *Moonlight*, Joi McMillon, who became the first African American female to win an Oscar for Best Editing.

The four chapters that make up the Wes Anderson module move outwards to assess how emotion, complexity and authenticity unravel and augment not only across audiovisual work but also beyond it through fandom and cosplay. Warren Buckland kicks off with a consideration of the director's 'new sincerity', an aesthetic-affective approach to storyworld building that Buckland identifies as a 'synthetic and collective mode of knowing'. While Buckland keeps things broad, Theo Cateforis tightens the transmedial focus. For him, it is Anderson's quirky exploration of the confused and intertwined space between childhood innocence and the seriousness of adult experiences that gathers the directors' work into a coherent yet evolving style. Through an analysis of Anderson's collaborative work with composer Mark

Mothersbaugh, Cateforis draws our attention to the emergent audiovisual sensibility that ripens through their four-film collaboration. Ewan Clark uses Cateforis's analysis as the starting point for his close reading of Anderson's later films, created in collaboration with composer Alexandre Desplat. Drawing on musicological processes, Clark shows how the composer, while borrowing Mothersbaugh's instrumentation to ensure a coherent transmedial soundworld, nevertheless hones it into transmedial musical timbres that gather meaning from project to project. Drawing the section to a close, Ben Winters traces Anderson's numerous references to other medial forms, from opera, to novels, kabuki theatre and cinema itself. His focus lies on the persistent trope of analogue audio technology, which is frequently present as both sound and physical objects – record players, tapes, cassettes and telephones. Winters suggests that this technology signifies a sense of the authentic for both characters and audiences. Like Buckland, he moves beyond the frame, here using his ideas of authenticity and the analogue to explore Anderson's recent curation of a museum exhibition in Vienna.

In the book's final module, we focus on Lars von Trier, whose complex relationship to music and sound forms unique and challenging textures. First, Bodil Marie Stavning Thomsen provides us with a broad and comprehensive look at the director's transmedial borrowings across his films, from style – the mirroring of cinematic traits from film noir, horror and melodrama – technology – taking inspiration from video, digital programming and animation – and other art forms – music, visual art, theatre and literature. 'All this together has widened the spectrum for what a film can do,' explains Thomsen, as she uses comparative analysis to show how these borrowings are both undermined and extended. Drawing on recent theory of haptic affect, Thomsen shows how the materiality of Trier's films is pressed into the foreground to form a new politics of seeing.

In her chapter, Linda Badley tightens the focus. Taking the director's snippets and quotes from Wagner's work – and the Ring cycle in particular – as her starting point, she uses Wagner's conceptual *Gesamtkunstwerk* to trace the transmedial currents that course through his New Extreme Cinema films which, as Thomsen also shows, plunder traits of horror, apocalyptic disaster/ sci-fi and pornography. For Badley, von Trier's treatment of the transmedial *Gesamtkunstwerk* differs from Bowie's audiovisual work, here described by Perrott. Von Trier references numerous art forms and philosophies, and grabs attention through musical sound bites, demonstrating a paradoxical coexistence of 'Wagnerian' immersive fusion of the arts and an anti-Wagnerian, post-Brechtian form of distanciation. The audience is asked to process allusion and quotation.

Finally, Donald Greig homes in on the director's persistent penchant for early music. Eighteenth-century instrumental music, with its contrapuntal textures and intricate melodies, draws attention to itself and, perhaps for this reason, is rarely found on film soundtracks as it can disrupt conventional methods of audiovisual consumption. Von Trier, suggests Greig, delights in the possibilities of this disruption. Early music fragments, from medieval requiems to Bach's instrumental work abound through his films, yet remain at a distance from the visual events, disengaged, critical and, significantly, culturally isolated from the time and aesthetic of the images. Through the clips' opacities, Brechtian distance is often subverted.

Lisa Perrott: Transmedia, authorship and assemblage

As Vernallis and Rogers have shown, the chapters in this volume are framed by a particular context in which the past, the present and the future of transmedia are not only formative but have instilled a transformative impulse in the practice of many directors. There has recently been a flurry of scholarly energy devoted to examining transmedia storytelling, much of which has focused on how stories develop and extend across media, texts and platforms. While paving the way for vigorous dialogue about what constitutes transmedia storytelling, scholars such as David Bordwell and Henry Jenkins acknowledge the difficulties of thinking 'outside the franchise model'.[17] One pitfall of an economically overdetermined model is that the artistic motivations to work across media may be overshadowed by an emphasis upon transmedia storytelling in relation to franchise development, foundational canons and what Jenkins calls 'mothership' projects.[18] Looking beyond 'mothership' projects as transmedial progenitors, Jenkins has emphasized the role played by fans in elaborating storyworlds across diverse media and platforms. His definition of a 'transmedia story' is one that 'unfolds across multiple media platforms, with each new text making a distinctive and valuable contribution to the whole'.[19] Such a definition implies the centrality of narrative continuity and canonical world-building as essential ingredients for ensuring a coherent whole across media. The centrality of these ingredients informs the logic of several recent publications on transmedia, a context that provides a contextual springboard for this volume.

While our contributing authors have drawn usefully from this existing literature, as we have seen, the focal points of transmedia storytelling have also provided useful points of departure. Diverging from the emphasis on storytelling in the recent literature on transmedia, we invited scholars to undertake close examinations of director's artistic and collaborative process across media and to theorize these in relation to new approaches to media convergence and assemblage. As a result, the chapters in this volume reveal insights about the relations between transmedia and collaborative authorship.

While narrative continuity remains for some directors an important facet of transmedia, narrative discontinuity, audiovisual discontinuity and 'loose continuity' also provide important strategies for transmedial artists with avant-garde leanings. Just as the traditional concept of an auteur is suggested by a director's persistent continuity of style across media, singular notions of authorship are challenged by those authors who provide close examinations of dialogism, polyphony and collaborative experimentation. These authors chart the transmedial play generated within the collaborative matrix of director, artist and fan.

As such, the chapters in this volume offer alternatives and extensions to the existing literature on transmedia, authorship and assemblage. The directors and artists who are the objects of our study offer a compelling contribution to the field. While their medial crossings are in part shaped by contemporary agents such as neoliberal economics and media convergence, many are influenced by the long and rich history of transmedia. While the directors and authors in this volume speak from diverse identity positions and geographic locales, they also draw upon diverse histories of art, literature and culture, as testified by their engagement with antecedents to transmedia, such as *Gesamtkunstwerk*, 'colour music', surrealist strategies, absurdist humour, *détournement,* Baroque music, Brechtian staging, mythical archetype and psychodrama. While revealing new approaches towards technology, experimentation and assemblage, these approaches are examined in relation to the historical and cultural context in which transmedia artistry is currently practised. This book contributes a unique view of what it means to be a transmedia director in tune with the present moment, within the context of its cultural past.

PART ONE

Collaborative authorship: Wes Anderson

CHAPTER 2

The Wes Anderson brand: New sincerity across media

Warren Buckland

Wes Anderson's films are dominated by an aesthetic-affective response called 'new sincerity', a contemporary sensibility based on dynamic tension between two opposing forces: sincerity and irony. The values embodied in new sincerity are not located in sincerity or irony taken separately, or in rejecting one in favour of the other, but only emerge from their synthesis – more specifically, from their oscillation or alternation. Raymond Williams's concept of the 'structures of feeling' embodies a similar tension based on the synthesis of formal structures and transitory experiences:

> We are talking about characteristic elements of impulse, restraint and tone; specifically affective elements of consciousness and relationships: not feeling against thought, but thought as felt and feeling as thought: practical consciousness of a present kind, in a living and interrelating continuity. We are then defining these elements as a 'structure': as a set, with specific internal relations, at once interlocking and in tension.[1]

For Williams, literature constitutes a 'laboratory' of new structures of feeling, a claim we can also extend to narrative cinema, for film narratives synthesize new structures and experiences. Everyday lived experience only becomes visible when mediated through an abstract symbolic system such as writing or film, which means experience is understood retrospectively, when fixed in a symbolic structure. Everyday experience is not purely individual, private or subjective but constitutes an integral part of the collective social fabric of everyday life. Like 'structures of feeling', 'new sincerity' is a synthetic and collective mode of knowing.

In this chapter I argue that, first, Anderson creates a storyworld that elicits an aesthetic-affective response called new sincerity and, second, this response migrates across multiple (official and unofficial) media platforms and into the everyday reality of the film audience, some of whom are transformed into fans. Anderson's storyworld is therefore transmedial in that its new sincerity is not confined to his films but migrates to other media. Storyworld also influences fan behaviour like 'cosplay', a form of performative self-branding whereby fans imaginatively pretend to be film characters by dressing up in their costumes.[2] I investigate Anderson's new sincerity storyworld by analysing *The Royal Tenenbaums* (2001) and by examining the transmedial migration of this storyworld on several levels: from Anderson's extension of it in his TV advert *Come Together* (2016), to fans extending it in their own artworks (*An Unpaid Intern* (2017) by painter Matt Linares), to fans modifying their everyday behaviour via cosplay. I therefore adopt a broad definition of transmedia, one that includes the migration of a fictional storyworld not only across several media platforms but also across the fiction/nonfiction border into the practices of everyday life.

Inhabiting storyworlds

'Storyworld' names an abstract totality consisting of all the possible permutations of narrative events, only some of which are manifest in individual filmic texts. Anderson's storyworld is an abstract totality encompassing everything fictionally possible in all his films, although each film represents only part of that storyworld. Narratives create worlds, not just a sequence of divisible events; each narrative text therefore implies a larger fictional world beyond the boundaries of (or distinct from) the manifest text. Storyworld is an emergent quality arising from codes and narrative structures but is not reducible to them.

Furthermore, a storyworld is not autonomous but depends on the audience's affective and emotional response – a type of aesthetic engagement that determines whether or not they can imaginatively inhabit that storyworld. David Herman argues that 'interpreters of narrative do not merely reconstruct a sequence of events and a set of existents, but imaginatively (emotionally, viscerally) inhabit a world in which, besides happening and existing, things matter, agitate, exalt, repulse, provide grounds for laughter and grief'.[3] Inhabiting a fictional storyworld is a two-way process: imaginative projection into a film's fictional world and the expansion of that fictional storyworld across several media and into daily life, where it functions as a collective resource for structuring everyday experience. Film theorists have already developed the first idea – in the psychoanalytic theories of identification (Christin Metz) and suture (Jean-Pierre Oudart; Stephen Heath)[4] and in cognitive theories of sympathetic and empathetic engagement with characters.[5] In this chapter I work my way towards the second idea, particularly the expansion of storyworld across several media platforms.

Subsystem, system and supersystem

Systems theorists (like Mario Bunge) developed a model of reality comprised of three levels – subsystem, system and supersystem – nested inside one another.[6] Renira Rampazzo Gambarato developed a theory of transmedia storytelling from this model: 'A transmedia project can be characterized as a supersystem that incorporates a series of complex objects, its systems and subsystems, in the process of unfolding content and evolving the storyworld.'[7] Storyworld is an emergent system generated from the integration of multiple subsystems; it can in turn migrate into the realm of the supersystem. Anderson's distinctive brand identity can be understood in terms of this abstract nested model of subsystem, system and supersystem.

Subsystem

Anderson's subsystem refers to individual codes, themes and values, including the specific pattern of distributional functions that create his distinctive storylines; the indices that create idiosyncratic character traits (e.g. characters who possess quirky eccentricities based on the tension between the hypocrisy many of the male characters manifest in their public personas and the sincerity they manifest in their inner lives); and a peculiar visual style, or *mise-en-scène*.

From the numerous analyses of Anderson's visual and aural style,[8] we can identify the following eight characteristic components of Anderson's *mise-en-scène*: (1) Tableau shots: 'A static, flat-looking, medium-long or long 'planimetric' shot [...] that appears nearly geometrically even, depicting carefully arranged characters, often facing directly forward, who are made to look faintly ridiculous by virtue of a composition's rigidity (seen particularly plainly in Anderson's character introductions).'[9] The tableau shot becomes an integral part of Anderson's film-making from *The Royal Tenenbaums* onwards. Via this tableau shot, Anderson's camera develops a specific strategy – what Jeffrey Sconce calls the 'clinical observation' of eccentric characters.[10] (2) Close-ups of characters (still facing forward): The close-up typically shows the character (like Bill Murray in *Rushmore* (1998)) with a deadpan expression.[11] (3) Overhead shots in which the direction of the camera's look is perpendicular to the horizon, which is achieved when the camera points straight down – either at objects (usually on a table) or characters lying down.[12] (4) Within the tableau shots, there is a general lack of camera movement, which helps to convey a precise, static quality to the film (although this applies more to his earlier films – later films use more camera movement). When movement is introduced into a shot, it becomes noticeable: either in the form of a 90-degree whip pan or extensive tracking shots (numerous examples exist in his later films, especially the credit sequence of *Moonrise Kingdom* (2012)). (5) Anderson's early films contain at least one montage sequence. In the montage the images are unified by an abstract theme and are accompanied by a song.[13] In *Rushmore*, a montage sequence accompanied by the song 'Making Time' (1967) by The Creation depicts Max's (Jason Schwartzman) membership to many clubs; in *The Royal Tenenbaums* a montage sequence accompanied by 'Judy is a Punk' (1976) by the Ramones depicts Margot's affairs and so on. Lara Hrycaj uses Claudia Gorbman's term *auteur mélomane* to label Anderson a director with a passion for music.[14] (6) Brief slow-motion shot (in all films, except *Fantastic Mr. Fox* (2009) and *The Grand Budapest Hotel* (2014)). (7) Centred framing, or a proclivity towards symmetrical composition, which has been explored in Kogonada's exemplary video essay 'Anderson//Centered'.[15] (8) Kim Wilkins defines Anderson's dialogue as hyper-dialogue – the 'intensified, unevenly fluctuating, and often ironically inflected use of dialogue in the place of action'. She argues that hyper-dialogue 'stems from the presence of a deep, unspoken anxiety'.[16] Hyper-dialogue is new sincerity dialogue, which emphasizes the disparity 'between what is said – the dialogue – and what is felt – the anxiety'.[17]

Anderson's film style broadly serves the themes of his stories. In Adrian Martin's terms, this type of film style falls into the category of expressionist (rather than classical or mannerist) *mise-en-scène*.[18]

System

A system consists of a set of internally organized subsystem components. Anderson's storyworld combines codes, themes and values from his subsystems into an integrated system. The focus falls on the combination of subsystems manifest in all of his films. Although a storyworld is not reducible to the components in its subsystems, it is nonetheless dependent on those components. The storyworld and the new sincerity affects it generates are emergent concepts that develop out of the relation between the subsystem components, plus the audience's imaginative and affective engagement with the storyworld.

Like a select group of other contemporary transmedia directors, Anderson's storyworld has become a brand that exceeds the boundaries of his films. The codes and values embedded in and the affective responses to his films are no longer confined to the films themselves but are expanded, transformed and manifest in other media and in fan-based products. This leads to the third level: supersystem.

Supersystem

Anderson's storyworld brand is transmedial, for his storyworld extends into other media platforms: for example, his TV ads, officially sanctioned online media such as websites and trailers, the design of a café (Bar Luce) in Milan, plus unofficial fan-generated content such as fan magazines, parodies, recut trailers, merchandise (cards, posters, t-shirts and film props), cosplay and art exhibitions are based on his films. Peter Bradshaw identifies 'an online cottage industry of mini pastiches, with a Shining mashup; an X-Men spoof; a Forrest Gump skit; a State of the Union sketch from CNN's news team; and SNL's glorious quasi-horror film *The Midnight Coterie of Sinister Intruders* [Rhys Thomas, 2013]. The three-minute Anderson spoof is now almost an accepted genre.'[19] Bradshaw discusses Anderson's three-minute H&M Christmas advert *Come Together* (2016), exclaiming that it looks like an Anderson imitator made it. This, in part, is because it appears to be a mini pastiche of *The Darjeeling Limited* (2007), for both are set on a train, both involve 'coming together' (three brothers in *The Darjeeling Limited*, train passengers in the advert) and both star Adrien Brody, this time playing a train conductor who has to inform passengers that the train is delayed and will not get them home for Christmas. But, most importantly, both elicit from the viewers the same affective new sincerity response. It is the new sincerity dimension of Anderson's storyworld that migrates across to the advert. The Anderson oddball characters who inhabit his storyworld are present on the train, including a father figure (Brody) and a young orphan boy (most of Anderson's heroes are orphans). The pastiche is also evident in Anderson's exaggeration of his own film style (his tableau compositions are more stark and symmetrical and he amplifies the movements of his tracking shots); the script contains snippets of new sincerity dialogue; he adds 1970s Rock music (John Lennon's 'Happy Xmas (War Is Over)' (1971)); and he creates a 'group shot' – happy ending infused with sincere, naïve sentimentality (which was prevalent in his earlier films but less frequent in his later darker films).

Codes transition from the subsystem to the system, and storyworld transitions from the system to the supersystem. Affective and emotional processes make these transitions possible. Storyworld cannot therefore be reduced to its representational content but must also include the audience's perception of and feelings towards that storyworld, for it is the audience's perceptions and especially their feelings that make possible the transition from system (storyworld) to supersystem (transmedia). The rules of and affective responses to Anderson's storyworld need to be maintained in these other media, in order to be considered an expansion of (rather than a transformation of or deviation from) that storyworld. For Mark Wolf: 'The growth and adaptation of a world [...] goes beyond narrative and may even have very little to do with narrative. Some degree of a world's aesthetics (the sensory experience of a world) and a world's logic (how a world operates and the reasons behind the way it is structured) must be carried over from one work to another or from one medium to another.'[20] What must be carried over from Anderson's films to other media is therefore the storyworld's aesthetics, internal logic and affective (new sincerity) response, which Anderson achieves in *Come Together*, although he risks self-parody by creating a mini version of his own storyworld.

The following sections of this chapter investigate the values and affects embedded in the new sincerity and examine how they migrate to other media and to fan behaviour.

New sincerity: Sincerity + irony

The meaning of sincerity overlaps with honesty, truthfulness and integrity and is the opposite of the fake, the false, lying and the hypocritical. Sincerity strives for transparency, for taking everything at face value. Irony is the opposite; it sets up a hierarchy between deceptive surface appearance and true covert meaning and rejects received opinions located on the surface. It creates distance from the immediate engagement with appearances – a detached intellectual judgement that enables one to critique appearances. The distance irony establishes undermines the so-called transparent surface truths.

Sincerity and irony are modalities that frame the expression of emotions, as when we say that someone expressed their emotions sincerely/ironically and so on. But this example also points to the distinctive quality of sincerity, made clear by Arthur M. Melzer when he argues that sincerity is not the same as honesty: 'The latter [honesty] involves a self-disciplined adherence to the truth or to one's word, the former [sincerity] an adherence to the self.'[21] The consequences of this distinction are far ranging. The key to sincerity is self-belief and self-interest, not an abstract criterion of truth or authenticity. Echoing Richard Sennett,[22] Melzer argues that the rise of sincerity in the latter half of the twentieth century is due to the 'demotion of the public, political realm of life and the concomitant elevation of the world of the personal, the private, and the intimate'.[23] Sincerity upholds the bourgeois notion of the autonomous self, of independence and self-sufficiency (an affirmative form of humanism and individualism defined by an inner essence), and Romanticism's emphasis on self-expression, introspection and self-realization – a combination that encourages the narcissistic outpouring of the personal inner self. But sincerity can also lead to a complete withdrawal into the private realm if the public realm becomes intrusive and provokes anxiety. For these reasons, sincerity generates a sense of moral superiority, of the sincere person living an uncompromising life free from falsity and social constraints, and a withdrawal from public commitments if the realm of the personal and private is endangered.

Irony has its own form of superiority – a knowingness possessed by those who go beyond the surface meaning and reconstruct the covert opposite meaning. Irony therefore instigates a distancing or disengagement from the surface meaning; an ironic text does not mean what it says. For irony to work in a dramatic or narrative text, the audience needs to reject the literal (sincere) meaning, or at least put it in parenthesis, and instead needs to reconstruct the covert underlying opposite meaning (irony works only when the audience recognizes a dissonance between literal surface meaning and underlying covert meaning). This ironic knowingness and disengagement in turn leads to cynicism, suspicion, disbelief and mistrust of what others do and say.

'New sincerity' creates both distance and closeness; it oscillates between sincerity (closeness) and irony (distance) without being reducible to either. Sincerity undermines the cynicism and nihilism of irony, but irony undermines the earnest, transparent surface statements of sincerity. Irony and sincerity are co-present, but not harmoniously. Jay Magill argues that, in new sincerity, 'irony has the task of conveying sincerity',[24] suggesting that irony frames and incorporates sincerity, while painter Sean Landers talks about an alternation-oscillation between sincerity and irony: 'Looking for truth or purity in oneself through making art is like peeling an infinite onion. Each layer alternates between irony and sincerity. I feel more comfortable being ironic and the audience seems to dig my sincerity.'[25] Finally, Linda Hutcheon conceives of irony as 'an oscillating yet simultaneous perception' of stated (surface) and unstated (hidden) meanings.[26] In the new sincerity, sincerity and irony are at once interlocking and in dialectical tension, with the tension expressed via the continual alternation and oscillation of the two terms without resolution.

Anderson's new sincerity

Like other new sincerity texts from contemporary literature (David Foster Wallace, Dave Eggers), music, poetry, art and television, Anderson's films are organized around the tension between the two interlocking concepts of sincerity and irony. In the remainder of this chapter I examine the new sincerity in Anderson's storyworld and investigate how it migrates to other media platforms.

Sincerity and irony organize the narrative, thematic structures, style and, ultimately, the storyworld of Anderson's films. This type of organization differs from the binary oppositions embedded in classical Hollywood films and the imaginary resolution of those oppositions. In his structural analysis of John Ford's Westerns, Peter Wollen identified binary thematic oppositions, noting that 'the most relevant are garden versus wilderness, ploughshare versus sabre, settler versus nomad, European versus Indian, civilised versus savage, book versus gun, married versus unmarried, East versus West'.[27] 'Wilderness versus garden' is, according to Wollen, the 'master antinomy in Ford's films'[28] – and, in fact, one of the master antinomies of American culture, structuring its founding myth. A second related antinomy structures the relation between nomad (living in the wilderness) and settler (in the cultivated garden). Both pairs feed into the quest for the Promised Land, a major theme in Ford's films, realized through an imaginary resolution in which the settlers and their cultivated garden win out over the nomad and the wilderness.

Unlike Ford (and other classical Hollywood directors), Anderson's storyworld is organized around synthetic structures that continually juxtapose and combine oppositional terms (rather than repress one in favour of the other): the master trope of new sincerity (sincerity/irony) plus structures of feeling (structure/feeling) and intimacy/distance (rather than the Brechtian opposition between emotional engagement and distanciation-alienation). The new sincerity attempts to keep these values in balance. An imbalance in favour of sincerity can lead to naivety and sentimentality (evident in the group 'happy endings' of Anderson's early films, such as *Bottle Rocket* (1996), *Rushmore, The Royal Tenenbaums* and *The Life Aquatic with Steve Zissou* (2004), as well as his TV advert *Come Together*), while an imbalance towards irony can lead to cynicism (arguably a dominant trait of key scenes in Anderson's later films *The Grand Budapest Hotel* and *Isle of Dogs* (2018)).

Anderson's films are specific in the way these synthetic structures infiltrate and organize the themes, narratives, characters and even the style of each film, which need to be studied scene by scene, together with the viewers' affective responses to those textual features. In his 'mood cue' approach to the analysis of narrative films, Greg M. Smith identifies 'the cinematic structures that appeal to audience emotions'.[29] He sets up a hierarchy between low-level diffuse moods and high-level short bursts of emotion and argues that they sustain one another in a fiction film. New sincerity functions more like a mood in Smith's sense, although it is not continuous; instead, new sincerity's alternation or oscillation signals a dramatic change in affect and mood. Nor should new sincerity be identified with the film's boundary, which means we do not need to talk about new sincerity *films*, but new sincerity *moments*. We can therefore study Anderson's new sincerity affect in a wide variety of scenes in his films, but we can also examine how this affect migrates to other media.

The Royal Tenenbaums

Smith argues that narrative film is structured to establish the spectator's 'consistent emotional orientation toward the text'.[30] In *The Royal Tenenbaums*, this orientation is established in part by Anderson's choice of music and by the voiceover in the opening fourteen minutes of the film narrating the long expositional scenes charting the childhood and current lives of the Tenenbaum family. First, the music. Anderson's music choice consists primarily of slow ballads with an acoustic guitar accompanied by a quiet whispery voice, ranging from The Rolling Stones ('She Smiled Sweetly' (1967), 'Ruby Tuesday' (1967)) – both played within the film's diegesis – to Elliott Smith ('Needle in the Hay' (1995)), Nick Drake ('Fly' (1971)), Emitt Rhodes ('Lullaby' (1970)), John Lennon ('Look at Me' (1970)), The Velvet Underground ('Stephanie Says' (1968)) and Nico. Anderson uses the first two tracks from Nico's first album *Chelsea Girl* (1971) – 'Fairest of the Season' and 'These Days'.[31] The second song accompanies Margot (Gwyneth Paltrow) as she descends (filmed in slow motion) from the bus to meet Richie (Luke Wilson). Both characters are framed head-on, looking directly towards the camera. Carol Piechota skillfully analyses the song's relevance to the scene in terms of the mood it creates, its sincerity (especially Nico's vocal delivery) as well as the meaning of its lyrics (which express the sad melancholy that unites brother and adopted sister). Hrycaj also notes that '"These Days" was an inspiration for this scene and the film as a whole. In the audio commentary for the film, Anderson talks about how before he even had the script written, he had this scene in mind featuring a woman walking with a specific look on her face as "These Days" played on the soundtrack'.[32] Margot even looks and acts like Nico (blonde hair, never smiling, uninflected voice, liked to stay in the bath for hours). Anderson's choice of music (acoustic guitar and quiet whispery voice), which is generally interpreted as sincere and honest, acts as an emotional cue that supplements the ironical distancing created by the deadpan acting and clinical framing. In other words, the songs, in a productive tension with Anderson's visual style, create the affective state of new sincerity.

Second, the opening voiceover charts the early successes of the three Tenenbaum children as they entered the public realm as a tennis player (Richie Tenenbaum), financier (Chas Tenenbaum) and writer (Margot Tenenbaum, Richie and Chas's adopted sister) and also charts the separation of their parents, Royal and Etheline Tenenbaum. As adults, the three Tenenbaum children withdraw emotionally into themselves, for different reasons. The successful businessman Chas (Ben Stiller) is the victim of irony, the sincere individual who remains on the surface, who reads everything literally, at face value. He adheres to what David Brooks calls the 'dull, joyless, unimaginative, conformist' bourgeois individual who aims only to make a profit and keep to his schedule.[33] He is also the victim of a tragic accident, the death of his wife in a plane crash, which leaves him emotionally stunted and withdrawn. The adult Richie and Margot separately follow the Romantic lifestyle, focused on introspection, rebellion and anti-materialism, unhindered by falsity, irony and cynicism. After initial success and recognition in their careers, they both retreat from public life into themselves due to their secret undeclared love for each other. Their withdrawal takes different forms: Richie goes travelling, while Margot remains at home, locked in the bathroom; their friend Eli Cash (Owen Wilson) represents the opposite – he performs the public role of a postmodern ironic writer. Etheline Tenenbaum (Anjelica Huston) is an archaeologist, while her husband Royal Tenenbaum (Gene Hackman) is characterized by a series of traits and narrative actions that initially define him as dishonest and insincere (he is a disbarred lawyer). He lives in The Lindbergh Hotel, estranged from the rest of the family. He embodies the quintessential new sincerity character: in the first half of the film his actions are governed entirely by self-interest and are coded as cynical, but in the second half he undergoes a transformation. When he runs out of money, he pretends to be terminally ill in order to return to the family home. But his wife's new suitor, Henry Sherman (Danny Glover), an accountant and upmarket property owner, exposes his fakery. He phones up the hospital where Royal is receiving treatment. Before the telephone conversation ends, the scene shifts to Henry marching up the stairs accompanied by loud non-diegetic organ music. He gathers all the family members together next to Royal's sick bed and exposes his deception, announcing that the hospital supposedly treating Royal closed down years before. Royal gets dressed and makes a short speech before leaving:

Royal swallows one of his pills. He turns and stands in front of everyone.

ROYAL (CONT'D)
Look. I know I'm the bad guy on this one, but I just want to say that the last six days have been the best six days of, probably, my whole life.

A strange, sad expression crosses Royal's face.

NARRATOR (V.O.)
Immediately after making this statement, Royal realized that it was true.

Royal begins to gather his possessions.

INT. HALLWAY. DAY.
Royal comes out of Richie's room with his suitcases.
Etheline stands at the end of the hall.[34]

Royal gives his estranged wife Etheline (Angelica Huston) two reasons for
the deception: in a sincere voice he says he thought he could win her back,
and he ran out of money and needed a place to stay.

The new sincerity is not only evident in the characters and their
actions but also in the way Anderson films the scene. At the beginning
of the excerpt, Sherman's investigations create dramatic irony by placing
the audience in a quasi-omniscient position: his discovery is hinted at
but remains secret (the outcome of the telephone call is cut before his
discovery is disclosed to the audience). But the audience does experience an
abrupt transition, a sudden change in action and sound: a direct cut from
the motionless Sherman speaking quietly on the phone to the animated
Sherman marching purposely upstairs accompanied by loud non-diegetic
organ music sets a dramatically different mood. All intermediate action is
eliminated, making the change in mood from one shot to the next all the
more noticeable. The scene of revelation in the bedroom is standard: the
liar is exposed in front of the whole family and ejected from the house.
But the sudden return of the voiceover, the omniscient narrator expressing
Royal's thoughts, is unusual (for the voiceover has not intervened in twenty
minutes of screen time). Over the images of Royal's duplicitous actions
and a short speech he gives, the narrator expresses Royal's thoughts to
the non-diegetic audience, pointing out that his words are sincere (Figure
2.1). It is unusual that the narrator suddenly intervenes to spell out the
sincerity of a character's words. The narrator's reliability is not in doubt;

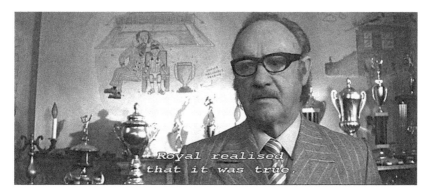

FIGURE 2.1 *Royal Tenenbaum in* The Royal Tenenbaums *(Wes Anderson, 2001).*

his voiceover functions to encourage empathy and pity towards Royal, who has been experiencing a reversal of fortunes and has reached a low point in his life. The voiceover conveys to the film audience that Royal has undergone a moment of recognition, a sincere moment of self-knowledge (the narrator is informing us that Royal believes what he just said). Later scenes in the film reinforce this impression, where we see Royal acting in a more generous and sincere manner. There is a discrepancy between Royal's previous duplicitous actions and his thoughts in this scene, a discrepancy not evident to the characters within the storyworld but shared by the director, the extra-diegetic narrator and the audience. In narrative terms, this scene represents a turning point in Royal's attitude, and the abrupt transition in mood (plus the intervention of the voiceover) makes this a powerful new sincerity moment.

The second example appears earlier in the film, when Royal first informs his estranged wife that he is terminally ill. Her response is immediate: she begins sobbing hysterically. Royal is taken aback by this display of emotion and partially retracts what he says ('I'm not dying, but I need some time'). In reaction, she changes her mood and hits him, before walking off, out of frame. He makes her return by repeating his initial assertion that he is dying. The scene ends with Etheline asking him if he is dying or not. He confirms in a weak unconvincing voice that he is in fact dying. In terms of character action and dialogue, this scene constitutes another exemplary new sincerity moment, due to the oscillation between Etheline's sincere emotional, compassionate reaction to Royal's illness and Royal's insincerity. Royal momentarily alternates from insincerity to sincerity when he experiences his wife's sudden outpouring of grief. This abrupt transition (also evident in the scenes where Sherman exposes Royal's fakery) transforms the mood of the shot, before Royal reverts back to his initial position, that he is terminally ill. At this early stage in the film, the audience is privileged into knowing that Royal is being thrown out of his hotel, but we also see him at the hospital in an inconclusive scene that suggests he is indeed ill.

But I want to focus on the way Anderson films this scene. The scene consists of four shots; the fourth one lasts ninety-eight seconds, and the camera remains locked down in a medium-long shot; it does not move (Figure 2.2). The camera is not tied to character movement or to character emotions. It does not follow Etheline as she walks away from Royal, even when she walks off screen. And there is no camera movement or cut to a close-up when she becomes upset on screen. In other words, the camera does not become close and intimate with the characters but remains still and at a distance. Anderson does not tie the camera to the characters but observes them from an aloof, detached position. (This is an example of what Jeffrey Sconce calls 'clinical observation'.) The frame is important in this type of shot; it acts as a container, delimiting on-screen space but also masking off-screen space. The stillness of the frame in shot 4 in relation to character

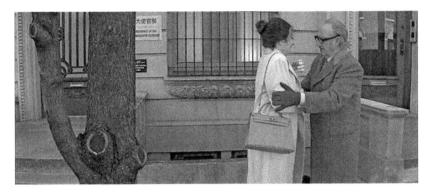

FIGURE 2.2 *Etheline and Royal in* The Royal Tenenbaums *(Wes Anderson, 2001).*

movement (walking off screen, walking on screen) draws attention to the frame and its masking of off-screen space. Drawing attention to the frame distances and detaches the viewer from the storyworld, which contains a strong, sincere emotion expressed by one of the film's central characters. Film style therefore contributes to the new sincerity affect.

The supersystem and self-modifying behaviour

We can finally work our way to Anderson's supersystem, the migration of his new sincerity affect to other media, by reviewing four ways spectators engage emotionally with films: (1) immediate evaluation of a film based on overall impression (enjoyment, pleasure and satisfaction); (2) identification with characters (especially via sympathy or empathy); (3) appreciation of film form; and (4) self-modifying behaviour.[35] The first three categories are familiar and well known; they are triggered by a film's subsystem and system (and Anderson's films are renowned for eliciting appreciations of their form and style).

The fourth category is transmedial: it operates at the same level as the supersystem and comprises of the creation of new texts and/or self-modifying behaviour. A popular activity involves producing artworks that are based on (and extend) Anderson's storyworld – including paintings, screen prints and sculpture, many of which are displayed at the 'Bad Dads' art exhibition the Spoke Art Gallery curates. In this annual exhibition, artists extract colour palettes, costumes, characters and props from Anderson's storyworld and present them in isolation (single portraits of prominent characters) or in new configurations. With regard to the latter, the pop surrealist painter Matt Linares created a painting called *An Unpaid Intern* (2017), which is ostensibly a portrait of Suzy Bishop from *Moonrise Kingdom* (2012).[36]

It condenses into one image several character traits from the film (she is dressed as a raven and her hand is bandaged), but she is also holding a box of Mendl's cakes in one hand (*The Grand Budapest Hotel*) and the seahorse in a wineglass in the other (*The Life Aquatic with Steve Zissou*). She stands in water, which contains miniatures of the shark and submarine from *The Life Aquatic*, while in the sky we see the helicopter from the same film as it crashes. A small yellow lizard rests on her bandaged hand, another reference to *The Life Aquatic*. She wears one of Margot's dresses and her iconic fur coat, plus Margot's false finger, and the falcon Mordecai is perched on her shoulder (all from *The Royal Tenenbaums*). The Darjeeling train is in the background, as is Kristofferson, the young fox from *Fantastic Mr Fox* (2007), meditating and wearing a 'bandit hat' (a tube sock). A large tree dominates the background, together with three hills (*Fantastic Mr Fox*). The title of the painting refers to the interns aboard the ship Belafonte in *The Life Aquatic*.

An Unpaid Intern creates a hierarchy of knowingness: Anderson fans recognize the elements extracted from six of his films and the way they have been reconfigured into one static image, whereas non-fans see an unusual, slightly surreal portrait of a young woman. But both types of viewer will see a sinister portrait of a conflicted woman (for Anderson fans, a fusion of two alienated female characters – Suzy Bishop and Margot Tenenbaum) with a bandaged hand and a missing finger, surrounded by elements of death and destruction (the helicopter crash that kills Ned, the shark that killed Esteban, the submarine seeking revenge on the shark, the large tree the three farmers destroy, the small lizard that Zissou carelessly flicks away) but surrounded by symbols of hope (the young, naïve but always optimistic Kristofferson, the Mendl cakes, the seahorse that the young boy Werner gives to Zissou, the falcon that signifies the deep love between Richie and his adopted sister Margot). The painting therefore condenses into one image the two sides of Anderson's new sincerity storyworld: the sincere and the sentimental framed by the darker cynical and ironical elements.[37]

The audience's involvement with Anderson's new sincerity storyworld can go deeper. The phrase 'self-modifying behaviour' refers to the internalization of a storyworld's affective and emotional values, which goes beyond the production of artworks and beyond the psychological processes of identifying/sympathizing/empathizing with characters. 'Self-modifying behaviour' results in a reconfiguring of the spectator's behaviour, feelings and beliefs. Carl Plantinga calls this 'projection', 'in which a spectator's pro attitude toward a character spills over markedly into her or his actual life, leading to emulation and fantasy'.[38] Projection and self-modifying behaviour constitute a strong affective engagement with characters and their storyworld. To react affectively to a film always involves a first-person subjective component – the film is not an entity in itself ('This is an important film') but is significant with regard to how it relates to the individual's personal world ('This film is important *to me*'). David Herman's list of the ways audiences imaginatively inhabit a storyworld – 'things matter, agitate, exalt, repulse, provide grounds for laughter and grief' – is relevant to delineating further how they react. Plantinga quotes Jackie Stacey on different types of fan behaviour, including pretending, resembling, imitating and copying.[39] Employing concepts from Judith Butler, Nicolle Lamerichs develops this idea further, arguing that cosplay, like drag, is performative.[40] Lamerichs conceives of cosplay as a performance that creates a new identity for fans – an identity that involves a crossover from fiction to physical reality. From this performative perspective, cosplay brings the fan's physical body into a closer, immersive relation to a fictional body. With projection, performativity, and self-modifying behaviour, the storyworld and fans' personal world merge.

The ideas of 'the supersystem' and of 'self-modifying behaviour' are based on the rationalist assumption that language and cognition do not passively record and reflect a pre-existing reality but that its grammar and semantics actively structure the individual's experiences and the meanings of reality. This rationalist assumption pervades cultural theory (including Raymond Williams's 'structures of feeling'), which argues that one perceives and understands reality through language, myth, fiction and fantasy (which is why cultural theorists analyse these discourses). Rationalists such as Kant argued that reality is perceived through a system of *a priori* concepts; the language analysis tradition of the twentieth century (including Saussure, Peirce and Sapir-Whorf) reworked Kantian epistemology to emphasize the role of language in structuring experience and meaning, a concept then expanded by semioticians to all systems of discourse. Claude Lévi-Strauss's important concept of symbolic efficacy demonstrates the power of language, rituals and other symbolic systems in shaping and modifying ideas and behaviour.[41] Lévi-Strauss gives the example of a Shaman helping a woman give birth via ritualistic storytelling, a notion, he points out, also prevalent in the West in the form of psychoanalysis, defined as the talking cure – a cure effected though words. Peter Berger and Thomas Luckmann expanded rationalism to sociology in their aptly titled book *The Social Construction of Reality*,[42] while Slavoj Žižek draws upon Lévi-Strauss and Lacanian psychoanalysis to argue throughout his work that perception and experience of reality are dependent upon fantasy (take away fantasy, he argues, and our sense of reality disintegrates).

Discourse, storytelling, myth and fantasy inform fan discourse surrounding Anderson's storyworld. The fans reify the imaginary fictional storyworld, turning it into their dominant reality (quite literally in terms of imitative merchandise, for the replicated objects that only exist in the storyworld become physical objects one can hold and keep in one's own world).

* * *

I have delineated three levels of Anderson's world (subsystem, system and supersystem), listed four ways the audiences engage emotionally with films and linked up the second (identification with characters) and the fourth (self-modifying behaviour), respectively, with Anderson's storyworld and the new sincerity affect it elicits. I have argued that the fictional realm of the storyworld is created via affective engagement and that the new sincerity affect is *the* vital ingredient that migrates to other media (television, video mashups and painting) and to certain practices of everyday life, such as the creation of merchandise and cosplay. The new sincerity affect involves a sudden and dramatic oscillation between the values found in sincerity and those found in irony. Both sets of values are important to the success of Anderson's storyworld and to its migration to other media platforms, for irony prevents his films from becoming too sentimental and sincerity prevents them from becoming too cynical.

CHAPTER 3

The world of Wes Anderson and Mark Mothersbaugh: Between childhood and adulthood in *The Royal Tenenbaums*

Theo Cateforis

For many years, Wes Anderson's movies have been described in terms of the director's unique and distinctive world. The press accompanying *The Grand Budapest Hotel* (2014) offered to take readers on a 'Tour of Wes Anderson's World', while *Isle of Dogs* (2018) was heralded as part of 'The Wonderful World of Wes Anderson'.[1] Pinterest, Instagram and Tumblr all have pages devoted to Wes Anderson's world, and even the long-running Wes Anderson fan site and archive 'The Rushmore Academy' is subtitled 'The World of Wes Anderson'. As Henry Jenkins has observed, worlds such as Anderson's emerge through 'compelling environments that cannot be fully explored or exhausted within a single work or even a single medium'.[2] In true transmedia fashion, Anderson has built his world not only across multiple movies but also through forays into television advertising and as a guest curator at the Viennese Kunsthistorisches Museum. Among the many links that run throughout Anderson's world are his recurring use of such actors as Bill Murray, Adrien Brody and Owen Wilson, as well as his close collaborations with the cinematographer Robert Yeoman and composer Mark Mothersbaugh. This chapter considers Anderson and Mothersbaugh's collaboration in particular, as it relates to one of the strongest unifying elements of the director's world: his fascination with childhood.

Themes of childhood have been central to Anderson's world, sometimes through the roles of children within his movies, but even more commonly through the representation of childhood itself and all its distinct signifiers. Significantly, though, Anderson views childhood not simply as a site of innocence and naïveté, but rather as something seamlessly intertwined with the seriousness and experiences of adulthood. As Peter C. Kunze has observed, Anderson's depictions of childhood are notable for the ways in which they dissolve 'any implied social separation between childhood and adulthood' and trouble the traditional child/adult binary.[3] Whether it be the adolescent Sam and Suzy in *Moonrise Kingdom* (2012), who speak with the melancholic deadpan of adults, or the title character of *The Life Aquatic with Steve Zissou* (2004), who introduces his boat, the Belafonte, through diorama-like close-ups of a toy model, Anderson's films regularly conflate the realms of childhood and adulthood.

This confusion of childhood and adulthood is a key component of Anderson's widely acknowledged 'quirky' auteur style – one that arises from the tonal tensions between artifice and authenticity, melodrama and comedy, and most of all, the combination of sincere emotional engagement and ironic detachment.[4] Consider, for example, the ways in which different childhood elements figure into two typically quirky scenes that occur back to back halfway through *The Royal Tenenbaums* (2001), the first of which has no musical underscore and the second of which features Mothersbaugh's music. In the first scene (53:48) Royal Tenenbaum (Gene Hackman) is confronted by his eldest son Chas (Ben Stiller). As we learn early in the film, Royal separated from his wife Etheline and their three children when they were adolescents. After twenty-two years away, he has returned to the family's upper crust urban home, having been evicted from his own hotel suite residence. He lies to Etheline and his children to elicit their sympathies and tells them instead that he is dying of stomach cancer. Chas, however, has never forgiven Royal for abandoning him and the family. In a heated moment, he angrily corners Royal in a cramped hallway closet filled with old board games from the Tenenbaum children's youth (see Figure 3.1). The quirky tension in this case arises, on the one hand, from our impulse to identify with Chas's sincere emotional anguish and, on the other, from the detached, absurd manner through which Anderson deliberately frames the confrontation against a precise, symmetrical backdrop of carefully stacked and arranged children's objects. The simple, nostalgic innocence of the retro board games throws into ironic relief the damaged adulthoods of the Tenenbaum children, who have never recovered from their parents' separation, and remain frozen and stunted in their adolescent states, incapable of moving forward with their lives.

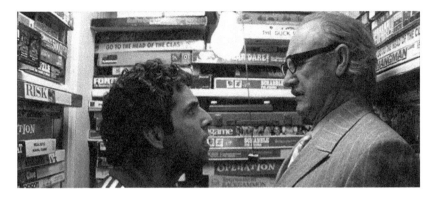

FIGURE 3.1 *Chas confronts Royal in the hallway closet* in The Royal Tenenbaums *(Wes Anderson, 2001).*

The following scene (54:21) cuts to Royal and Etheline (Anjelica Huston) strolling together in a park. Etheline expresses her concern for Royal's health, to which he responds that he is 'having a ball ... scrapping and yelling' with his family. At this point, Mothersbaugh's instrumental music enters softly underneath them (titled in the score as 'Scrapping and Yelling' after Royal's dialogue cue). The music – a lilting C major mix of plucked strings, woodwinds, brushed snare drum, glockenspiel and harpsichord – inflects different elements of the Tenenbaums' identity. The harpsichord, a fixture of the art music world, hints at the family's privileged upper middle-class standing, while the delicate strings, glockenspiel and simple tonality suggest a childlike whimsy, perhaps connected here with Royal's buoyant attitude. As the music continues, Royal compliments Etheline on her parenting, but she replies by pointedly asking him why he 'didn't ... give a damn' about his family. Despite this frank, accusatory turn in the conversation, the music remains unchanged, its oddly playful yet stately nature seemingly oblivious to the shift in tone. In its 'conspicuous indifference', the music creates what Michel Chion has referred to as an *anempathetic* effect, one 'whose studied frivolity and naiveté' ultimately invests the scene and characters with even more significance.[5] It is precisely because we are so accustomed to hearing film music as 'emotionally congruent' that Mothersbaugh's whimsical musical arrangement resituates Royal and Etheline's serious adult conversation in a more ironically incongruous, and thus quirky, light.[6]

This chapter considers the central role that childhood plays in *The Royal Tenenbaums* and also how it relates to Anderson and Mothersbaugh's broader transmedia aesthetic. More specifically, it examines the myriad ways that Anderson and Mothersbaugh explore the liminal space between childhood and adulthood. Much of this relates to the material culture of childhood that fills the screen in the form of various objects. The board games in the Tenenbaum closet – for example, Risk – are ones meant to familiarize children with the concerns of adulthood (such as warfare and power). By design their intent is to straddle and ultimately bridge the child/ adult gap. Likewise, Mothersbaugh's score draws on a mixed materiality of specific instrumental timbres that similarly cuts across this divide. In Mothersbaugh's musical world, Anderson's preferred 'high-pitched sounds' of bells, flutes and piccolos connote a childlike aesthetic that intermingles with the antiquated adult presence of the harpsichord.[7] Crucially, this mix of material culture and musical signifiers combines in *The Royal Tenenbaums* to convey not just any type of childhood but one distinguished by the privilege of social class – a theme common to many of Anderson's films such as *Rushmore* (1998) and *The Darjeeling Limited* (2007).[8] I will return to this representation of privilege and class in *The Royal Tenenbaums* later, but first it is important to understand how these filmic depictions relate to, and are rooted in, Anderson and Mothersbaugh's experiences and stylistic predilections across a variety of media.

Mark Mothersbaugh and Wes Anderson: A shared transmedia aesthetic

Anderson and Mothersbaugh's close collaboration on the director's first four films – *Bottle Rocket* (1996), *Rushmore*, *The Royal Tenenbaums* and *The Life Aquatic with Steve Zissou* – were pivotal both in establishing Anderson's recognizable auteur style and in making Mothersbaugh a highly sought out composer. As central as Mothersbaugh's scores have been to Anderson's oeuvre, however, his music has received relatively little critical or analytical attention. Much more has been written instead about Anderson's carefully curated soundtracks of pre-existing popular songs and their emotive and affective qualities.[9] This is hardly surprising given the rich extramusical connotations and connections that these songs bring to Anderson's films. Mothersbaugh's instrumental scores, by comparison, are more abstract and seemingly less inviting of interpretation. A closer examination of the composer's background, however, can provide some context for how his music relates to Anderson's cinematic vision and why the two have forged such a uniquely sympathetic collaborative process.

Mothersbaugh has built an impressive artistic world stretching across multiple media over his nearly five-decade career, ranging from his pioneering music videos as a founding member and front man of the 1970s/1980s avant-garde rock band Devo to a vast catalogue of visual art and hundreds of compositions for advertisements, video games, television shows and motion pictures. A significant portion of his music, such as his scores for the Nickelodeon television series *Rugrats* (1991–2004) and the *Hotel Transylvania* and *Lego Movie* film franchises, has been aimed primarily at a young audience, and some of it, such as his work for the live action television show *Pee-wee's Playhouse* (1986–90), has explored the ambiguities of the conflated child/adult binary. Mothersbaugh's interest in this binary stretches far back, most notably to his time with Devo when he created an alter ego named Booji Boy by donning a rubber mask of a 'little blond-haired, chubby-cheeked boy'.[10] Booji Boy became a staple both of Devo's music videos and live sets, where Mothersbaugh would emerge at the end of the show in a playpen singing in a high-pitched childlike voice. The character of a grown, adult man with the plump artificial face of a little boy was a jarring and memorable sight, one that reflected Mothersbaugh's and the band's interest in the theatrics of early-twentieth-century dada, whose masked performers adopted the irrationality and primitivism of childhood for subversive purposes. Booji Boy proved to be a key piece of Devo's conceptual performance art, a way of viscerally illustrating the band's absurdist proclamation that humanity was on a regressive descent, in this case literally devolving from man to boy.

As a composer, Mothersbaugh has pursued a correlate to Booji Boy's visual performative artifice, in all its constructed childlike innocence and naïveté, through his long-standing fascination with sonic and musical artifice. This is evident in the very title of his music production company that he founded in 1989, Mutato Muzika, with its deliberate allusion to muzak and the realm of easy listening styles.[11] During its mid-twentieth-century peak, critics roundly condemned the Muzak corporation and its generic instrumental renditions of classical, pop and jazz standards 'as the "scourge" of good music'.[12] Its repetitive musical arrangements – devoid of any wide dynamic range or harsh timbres – supposedly reduced the complexity of music to a familiar simplicity that treated its mass adult audience as if they were little more sophisticated than children. Much like the Middle-of-the-Road (MOR) music and middlebrow culture of the era, muzak was viewed as an in-between, and thus artistically compromised and artificial, style. Mothersbaugh, however, has embraced this artifice, this in-betweenness, as a perversely positive aesthetic quality, and made it a signature component of his aesthetic world.[13]

One can hear Mothersbaugh's love of artifice in his playful early 1990s score for *Rugrats*, which he composed on the (then) relatively new Fairlight CMI, Series II digital synthesizer. Like most synthesizers, the CMI had the capability to mimic traditional acoustic instruments, but it was also obvious that these sonorities were imitations and not the real things. As Mothersbaugh has explained, he deliberately approached his music with this ambiguity in mind, embracing the instrument's noticeably unreal aural approximations to create what he has called a kind of 'wood panelling' sonic aesthetic:

Gabor Csupo [*Rugrats'* producer] liked that I was using acoustic instrument sounds on the synth. Cellos, guitars, upright basses, horns; they sound more like those instruments than analogue synths, but they still kind of sound like an acoustic guitar. Like what wood paneling – that kind of plastic-coated stuff you get at Home Depot – is to real wood. It was kind of like that. And I liked the sounds because of that sort of not-here-nor-there kind of sound to them.[14]

Mothersbaugh has referred elsewhere to the CMI synthesizer's 'not-here-nor-there' aesthetic as a type of 'plastic acoustic music'.[15] In some respects, these in-between sounds are also reminiscent of the typical factory presets one finds on any number of inexpensive children's synthesizers and toy keyboards. They are a reminder of how childhood's sonic realm is often constructed as a simulation of the adult world yet to come.

Like Mothersbaugh's delight in the incongruities of 'plastic acoustic music', Anderson's appreciation for visual artifice similarly hinges on a blurred line between realism and representation. This is especially apparent in the unusual manner in which he composes his shots, staging characters and objects within the screen in meticulously detailed and unnaturally static arrangements. An entire descriptive language has emerged around this type of framing that imagines Anderson's cinematic world as if it were a 'diorama', 'dollhouse', 'shoebox' or 'model'; that is, as if it were a child's miniaturized rendition of reality. This aesthetic saturates Anderson's aesthetic, sometimes even in the form of an actual model, as with the exterior view of *The Grand Budapest Hotel* (2015). Anderson has also utilized this stylistic technique to great effect in the commercial work that he has pursued regularly throughout his directorial career, for example in two short television spots that he created in 2002 for the Swedish furniture company, Ikea. In each of these advertisements, one that takes place inside a kitchen and the other in a living room, the viewer is witness to a husband and wife in the midst of an intense domestic argument. In the middle of their squabbling, they are interrupted by an Ikea floor staff who asks them 'So, what do you think?' The camera then tracks backward to reveal that they are actually customers in a diorama-like Ikea showroom display. With the domestic setting now recontextualized as an artificial space, and the division between realism and representation jarringly confused, the couple suddenly cease their acting and happily proclaim, 'we'll take it', thus completing the advertisement's quirky, ironic inversion.

In her study of Anderson's works, Donna Kornhaber has convincingly argued that his precisely staged cinematic frames, adorned with obsessively organized objects (as one might find in an Ikea showroom display), constitute nothing less than 'a collector's cinema', and one indicative of the director's well-known personal penchant for collecting. The objects in Anderson's filmic world are never incidental or merely decorative, but rather 'brought together, carefully selected and composited from the material objects of our lived world' in a way that bears the peculiar stamp of Anderson's own collector instincts.[16] It is this collector's mentality that in many ways has served as Anderson's strongest shared aesthetic bond with Mothersbaugh, and created a fruitful meeting ground for their artistic visions. Like Anderson, Mothersbaugh is a similarly self-described 'inveterate collector', who has organized and ordered his eclectic array of acquired objects around specific themes, categories and types ranging from Mao Zedong memorabilia and Third Reich–era Hitler post cards to various 'eccentric sounds and noisemakers', including roughly 250 bird calls.[17] This includes a vast collection of vintage electronic and exotic instruments that fill the rooms of his Mutato Muzika production studio, where they have served as points of inspiration for his compositions and musical scores.

As Kornhaber describes in her analysis of Anderson's films, collecting is often an 'attempt to enact a negotiation with emotional trauma via the objects of our material world'.[18] Or to put it another way, we can consider the very act of collecting as a type of therapeutic world-building. Kornhaber points to *The Royal Tenenbaums* as an example where the 'unhealed trauma' of the broken Tenenbaum family helps explain each character's 'obsessive focus on collections'.[19] Given that Mothersbaugh and Anderson each underwent traumatic childhood events that figure prominently in their biographies, it is worth considering (if only briefly and speculatively) how this interpretive lens might apply to the artists themselves, and what it might reveal about their movies. When Mothersbaugh was eight years old he learned that he had unknowingly been legally blind for the first seven years of his life. Having barely been able to see, as if he was 'walking in a cloud', Mothersbaugh received his first pair of glasses and immediately started to draw and document the world around him, essentially collecting through his artworks everything that was now newly visible to him.[20] Anderson's parents divorced when he, like Mothersbaugh, was also eight years old. As a youth he took to collecting and before long had 'assembled his own library of carefully selected editions' and a 'cutting-edge record collection'.[21] Crucially, for both Mothersbaugh and Anderson, collecting became something imbued with taste and distinction. Theirs were not just any collections, but ones composed of select literary, musical and artistic objects from a variety of media. An activity that had perhaps begun as a response to childhood trauma, over time became a collection that accrued capital, certainly in economic terms, but more importantly of a cultural kind. If we can indeed consider Anderson's films as extensions of his collector's impulse, then it is also true that they display their collections as markers of cultural privilege and class. As the next section suggests, this is especially true of *The Royal Tenenbaums* and how it situates its collected objects as part of a cultivated childhood, and one that explores the faultlines along the child/adult binary.

The sight and sound of childhood
in *The Royal Tenenbaums*

As Whitney Crothers Dilley has observed, Anderson's films (much like those of one of his favourite directors, François Truffaut) are often autobiographical in nature, filled with copious references to his own childhood.[22] Anderson's experience of his parents' divorce clearly stands as one of the main points of inspiration for *The Royal Tenenbaums*, as does the Tenenbaums' core family structure of a mother raising her three children, which exactly mirrors that of Anderson's youth. Anderson makes this connection even stronger by investing the character of Etheline Tenenbaum with an especially high level of autobiographical detail. She shares the same occupation, an archaeologist, as Anderson's mother, and he even has Anjelica Huston wear his mother's eyeglasses.[23] As the highly educated family matriarch, Etheline plays a pivotal role in *The Royal Tenenbaums*, specifically through her parental efforts to orchestrate her children's activities and shape their development, an example of what the sociologist Annette Lareau has called 'concerted cultivation'. As Lareau explains, in this type of child-rearing practice, parents take an active part in their children's extracurricular education, cultivating their skills and talents 'in a concerted fashion' through organized, scheduled activities.[24] The film's opening flashback montage, which details Etheline's relationship to her children, is worth considering closely, as it shows this concerted cultivation at work and establishes, both visually and musically, the signature characteristics of the Tenenbaums' childhood that permeate the rest of the film.

In the montage (00:37), which is set in the children's adolescent years – presumably during the late 1970s/early 1980s – the narrator (voiced by Alec Baldwin) describes how Etheline made the children's education 'her highest priority'. An early scene shows her seated beside a chalkboard grid on which she has rigorously mapped out the children's after-school extracurricular schedule, which includes lessons in karate, Italian and ballet. The montage then introduces us one by one to the three Tenenbaum children, whose surroundings, clothing and achievements bear the signs of their specific education and talents, which have become an indelible part of their personas from an early age. Chas (Aram Aslanian-Persico), the eldest, finds success in the business and financial world, buying and selling real estate. He conducts business from his bedroom, which he has converted into an office, replete with a library of financial journals and a well-stocked wardrobe of identical business suits and ties. Margot (Irene Gorovaia), their (adopted) middle child, becomes a playwright, winning a $50,000 artistic grant in the ninth grade. We see her framed against rich, red wallpaper and in a variety of dimly lit environments – typing by lamplight, developing photos in a darkroom – all of which suggest the muted tones and ambience of a darkened theatre, suited to the performance of her plays. Richie (Amedeo Turturro), the youngest son, becomes a champion tennis player in the third grade, his athletic prowess, signified by his Björn Borg–inspired headband, striped shirt and shoulder length hair, as well as the numerous trophies adorning his bedroom. Etheline eventually documents the children's achievements and their paths to greatness in a book entitled *Family of Geniuses*.

The precociously talented Tenenbaum children are, of course, caricatures, but they resonate so strongly precisely because their concerted cultivation is an instantly recognizable sign of upper middle-class privilege, and all the advantages that come with the proper financial means to build a supplementary education. For Lareau, this type of concerted cultivation serves as a marker of America's inherent social inequality. She specifically contrasts the heavily structured and hands-on parenting of concerted cultivation with the approaches of those of working-class parents that generally lack the resources and time to attend to their children so closely. Children of these parents are more often left to their own devices, and through their free, less structured play, they achieve what Lareau calls the 'accomplishment of natural growth'.[25] Whereas these working-class children tend to recognize strict social boundaries with their parents, part of what concerted cultivation instils in middle-class children is a sense that they are on a more even footing with adults. As Lareau explains, they learn the importance of 'eye contact, firm handshakes' and articulating one's preferences, needs and opinions to adults, whether they be parents or authority figures such as doctors.[26] In short, concerted cultivation suggests a more porous space between childhood and adulthood, one that aims to empower children with the requisite social skills necessary to navigate the world of adult institutions. Part of what drives *The Royal Tenenbaums'* dark comedic effect is the Tenenbaum children's inability to achieve this goal. Despite their concertedly cultivated upbringing, the adult Tenenbaum children are isolated and can barely communicate and function properly. They return to the Tenenbaum family home, still dressed in their childhood clothes – Margot (Gwyneth Paltrow) in her striped Lacoste dress and Richie (Luke Wilson) in his tennis uniform – immobilized and stuck in an in-between state, inhabiting the realms of both childhood and adulthood. They wear the failure of their concerted cultivation in the quirky liminality of their confused childhood/adulthood state.

In his initial conception of the opening montage, Anderson had hoped to use the Beatles' original 1968 recording of 'Hey Jude' as the musical underscoring. However, when he was unable to secure George Harrison's permission, who was gravely ill and dying of cancer at the time, he decided to have Mothersbaugh arrange his own instrumental version of the song. It is easy to understand why Anderson was attracted to 'Hey Jude', for like many of the pre-existing songs that comprise *The Royal Tenenbaums'* soundtrack, it is ripe with intertextual associations that amplify the film's fracturing of the Tenenbaum family and its shattered childhoods. As Paul McCartney has explained, he originally conceived of 'Hey Jude' as 'Hey Jules', as a means to comfort five-year-old Julian Lennon, whose father had begun seeing Yoko Ono and was in the process of separating from his wife, Cynthia.[27] While the lyrics certainly suggest this interpretation ('take a sad song and make it better'), there are other lines in the song that hint at additional meanings. John Lennon, in particular, believed that lyrics like 'you have found her, now go and get her' were McCartney's sign of his approval of Yoko Ono and that the song was directed to him personally.[28] The oddly liminal form of address in 'Hey Jude' – presumably both to a child and an adult – thus neatly resonates with the jumbled state of the Tenenbaums, caught between childhood and adulthood.

In a more basic, functional sense, Mothersbaugh's chamber-sized Mutato Muzika Orchestra version of 'Hey Jude' also serves to situate the Tenenbaum family history illustrated within the montage as part of the past, and specifically a cultivated past, symbolized by the Beatles' status as one of the first 1960s 'art rock' bands to incorporate highbrow classical elements into rock's domain. Mothersbaugh's re-scoring furthers this association through its prominent use of Baroque-era instruments such as the harpsichord and piccolo trumpet. The result is a pastiche that recalls the Beatles' own use of similar Baroque stylistic elements, such as the simulated harpsichord solo (played on an electric piano) of 1965's 'In My Life' and the trumpet flourishes of 1967's 'Penny Lane' – two songs that, interestingly, deal with issues of youthful nostalgia, much as *The Royal Tenenbaums'* montage does.[29] At the same time, because Mothersbaugh confines his instrumental arrangement almost exclusively to multiple, successive repetitions of the song's relatively restrained AABA (verse/bridge) sections rather than its famed, emotionally expansive coda (which he relegates to a mere six measures at the end), his version of 'Hey Jude' assumes a slightly different character from the Beatles' original. His Mutato Muzika orchestration is more formal and mannered in tone, more suggestive of a dated, museum-like quality that emphasizes the Tenenbaum's faded glory.

Some of Mothersbaugh's other pieces for *The Royal Tenenbaums*, such as the stately Baroque pastiche of 'Mothersbaugh's Canon', follow the lead of 'Hey Jude' both in their evocations of art music and use of highly repetitious forms. One of the most notable examples is Mothersbaugh's arrangement of George Enescu's 1896 Cello Sonata No. 1 in F Minor, which underscores the film's second lengthy montage (06:41), through which we are introduced to each of the characters in the present day. Mothersbaugh takes the main subject from the Sonata's first movement (*Allegro molto moderato*) – a driving 'ostinato-like spiky cello line'[30] – and transforms it into a set of variations that changes in instrumentation and style to match each character: a trombone growl for Royal, harp for Margot, frantic bebop drums for

Chas and so on. The variations provide a template on which Mothersbaugh explores his love of artifice through a series of genre mock-ups. Richie is scored with a synthesized walking bass line and finger snaps clearly meant to suggest some type of acoustic cool jazz. For Margot's husband, the neurologist Raleigh St. Clair (Bill Murray), the walking bass line switches to an acoustic instrument, but it is now overlaid with harpsichord figuration that resembles the early 1960s fashion for Baroque jazz. By linking *The Royal Tenenbaums'* characters with different instrumental and stylistic motifs, Mothersbaugh in some respects recalls the pedagogical structure of Serge Prokofiev's symphonic children's composition, *Peter and the Wolf* (1936). Intentional or not, it is a connection that Anderson would explore more directly in *Moonrise Kingdom* with his use of Benjamin Britten's set of variations, the *Young Person's Guide to the Orchestra* (1945).

On the surface, all this repetition – whether it be the many iterations of the 'Hey Jude' verse/bridge, the variations of Enescu's Cello Sonata or the circular four-chord progression of 'Mothersbaugh's Canon' – may seem unremarkable. But this repetition takes on a greater significance within *The Royal Tenenbaums* when one considers how it mirrors the highly repetitive and ordered nature of the collected childhood material objects that fill the space of the Tenenbaum family home. On the one hand, the repetition of these objects signifies an accumulation of knowledge, a sign of the Tenenbaums' privilege and high social class standing. We see this both in Margot's carefully labelled library of plays (see Figure 3.2) and Chas's rows of hardbound financial magazines (see Figure 3.3), each of which signify the children's liminal position along the child/adult binary. More subtly, however, these repeated objects are a testament to Etheline's vision of concerted cultivation. They remind us of the repetition of scheduling, planning, practice and ritual that fosters excellence. The repetitive objects

FIGURE 3.2 *The objects of concerted cultivation: Margot's carefully organized and labelled library of plays* in The Royal Tenenbaums *(Wes Anderson, 2001).*

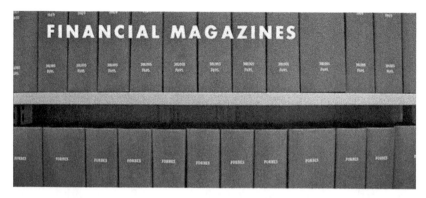

FIGURE 3.3 *The objects of concerted cultivation: Chas's neatly ordered hardbound financial magazines* in The Royal Tenenbaums *(Wes Anderson, 2001).*

and repetitive music in *The Royal Tenenbaums* stand in for the implied repetition of numerous ballet rehearsals, tennis lessons, language studies and other activities that produced a 'family of geniuses'.

Anderson deliberately contrasts the neatly ordered, repetitive rows of the Tenenbaum children's objects with the more casually arranged objects that define their father, Royal, as well as their childhood friend Eli Cash, both of whom sit noticeably outside of the Tenenbaums' elevated cultural status. As the camera pans across Royal's hotel suite (08:26), we see his most valued possession, his encyclopedia collection, crammed into various available spaces – a tabletop, a windowsill – as if to emphasize the makeshift nature of his residence. These encyclopedias, filled with generalist knowledge, lack the selective cultural hierarchy of Margot's plays or the specialized focus of Chas's financial magazines.[31] They stand apart from the types of objects that Etheline carefully curated for her children's education. The contrast with Eli Cash's objects is even stronger. As an adult, Cash (Owen Wilson) gains notoriety as a novelist of lowbrow pulp Westerns.[32] When Richie visits Cash at his apartment (40:15), we see Eli framed against a painting of weirdly violent pop art – Mexican artist Miguel Calderón's *Aggressively Mediocre/ Mentally Challenged/ Fantasy Island (Circle One of the Above)* (1998) – that hints at his decadent and debased lifestyle. More tellingly, another view reveals Cash standing alongside a hastily stacked collection of pornographic video tapes (see Figure 3.4). Cash's material setting lacks the rigour, regiment, order and good taste exhibited in the Tenenbaum's carefully cultivated material culture. As if to further emphasize his outsider status, the music that underscores Richie and Eli's visit is a recording of Erik Satie's *Gymnopédie No. 1* (1888, performed here by Aldo Ciccolini), a piece by a composer whose personal idiosyncrasies and reclusive personality made him one of the early twentieth century's most famous bohemians.

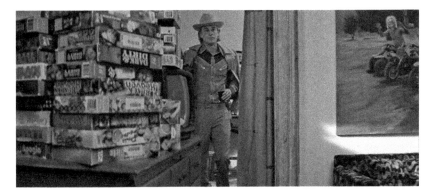

FIGURE 3.4 *Disorder and bad taste: Eli Cash stands alongside his hastily arranged stack of pornographic video tapes* in The Royal Tenenbaums *(Wes Anderson, 2001).*

In the end, however, it is ultimately Cash's supreme state of disorder that collapses the Tenenbaums' carefully constructed world and initiates a resolution to the film's various conflicts. The day that Etheline is to be married to Henry Sherman (Danny Glover), Eli, high on mescaline and his face brazenly adorned in native American warpaint, crashes his car into the Tenenbaum house, knocking over a mailbox (01:32:10). The resultant explosion unleashes a sea of letters splayed across the street and floating through air, a chaotic mess that stands in sharp contrast to the film's overriding spatial design of highly ordered material objects. A raucous scene follows as Chas chases Eli through the Tenenbaum house and into the neighbour's backyard. Exhausted, both physically and mentally, the pair collapse on the ground, and in one of Anderson's signature framing devices – the overhead close shot, which typically signals 'the moment of accepting truth' – Eli, and then Chas, both admit that they need help (01:34:41).[33] Through this simple step, they recognize their need to confront and conquer the childhood obsessions and obstructions that have prevented their successful navigation into adulthood.

On cue, Mothersbaugh's piece entitled 'Sparkplug Minuet' enters – a gentle mix of triplet piano chords, brushed snared drum and melodic celeste that is eventually joined by a floating, wordless children's choir. The emphasis on the celeste, an instrument whose bell-like timbre has long been associated with childhood innocence through such pieces as Tchaikovsky's 'Dance of the Sugar Plum Fairy' from *The Nutcracker* (1892) and the theme from the children's television show *Mr. Rogers' Neighborhood* (1968–2001) gives the piece a distinct childlike quality. Mothersbaugh has explained the significance of the celeste to his own childhood, when he regularly encountered it as part of the music for a local Cleveland children's show called *Barnaby and Me*. The host of the show would dress up in 'little pointy leprechaun ears, a straw hat and make-up that was too thick' and entertain his audience of children before weepingly bidding farewell at the end of each episode over the celeste music.[34] The idea of a childlike adult man, accompanied by an instrument – the celeste – which itself is a mixed-up version of a miniaturized piano combined with the percussive tones of a glockenspiel, seems to capture perfectly all the confusion and liminality of the Tenenbaums' adult/child binary.

As noticeable as 'Sparkplug Minuet' is for its instrumentation and delicate tone, it is also unique within *The Royal Tenenbaums* for its relative lack of overt melodic repetition. Though it begins with a brief repeating motif, the celeste soon begins to wander freely, almost as if it were improvised, suggesting a freedom of play indicative of Lareau's concept of 'natural growth' – an experience that the Tenenbaum children, with their heavily scheduled activities and cultivated upbringing, have been denied. Significantly, the scene that follows, which comprises the bulk of the three and a half minutes of 'Sparkplug Minuet', consists of a long horizontal tracking shot that moves among the various characters as the camera surveys the aftermath of the car crash. Though the shot is, of course, as purposefully and obviously staged as any of Anderson's, its freedom of motion breaks from the director's more static, symmetrically confined frames and joins with the music to provide a release from the Tenenbaums' rigidly ordered material world. The move from order to disorder thus provides the film with its necessary means of closure.

Coda: A Mark Mothersbaugh or Wes Anderson theme park?

The collaborative relationship that Anderson and Mothersbaugh established over the course of the director's first four films was central to establishing the distinctive quirky characteristics of Anderson's unique cinematic world. In the years since 2004's *The Life Aquatic with Steve Zissou*, however, Anderson has worked more closely with the composer Alexandre Desplat, turning to Mothersbaugh only once for a single piece, 'Camp Ivanhoe Cadence Medley', on the *Moonrise Kindgom* soundtrack, which is otherwise credited entirely to Desplat. Nonetheless, the two remain closely associated, a relationship that was acknowledged in 2014 when Anderson wrote the foreword to the catalogue book for Mothersbaugh's *Myopia* art exhibit. Instead of a conventional introduction, however, Anderson provided a prospectus stating that he hoped 'to soon secure the means to commission the construction of an important and sizable theme park to be conceived and designed entirely by Mark Mothersbaugh'.[35] Given both Mothersbaugh and Anderson's fascination with childhood, the idea seemed entirely plausible, at least on a conceptual level. Anderson even suggested some possibilities for the theme park, such as 'animatronic characters and creatures, rides through invented landscapes' and 'an ongoing original music score piped-in everywhere' that played on Mothersbaugh's love of both artifice and the ethereal tones of Muzak.[36] Anderson's only stipulation for the park was that all the contents be of Mothersbaugh's conception and making.

As numerous online news outlets picked up the story of the theme park, however, the headlines quickly began repositioning Anderson from his role as a producer securing funds to that of a director overseeing the project – one that seemingly promised the potential of a literal, physical realization of Anderson's virtual world-building across his many films. In short, the 'Mark Mothersbaugh Theme Park' was suddenly recast as a 'Wes Anderson Theme Park' and, as such, many of the brief news articles pondered the transmedia possibilities of various rides based on Anderson's films, such as the '*Budapest Hotel* ski chase' and the '*Darjeeling Limited*' train or 'The Life Aquatic River Adventure' and 'The Spookily Symmetrical Haunted House'.[37] Such is the force of Anderson's distinctive auteur style that Mothersbaugh virtually vanished to the margins of his own proposed theme park. In the face of such imbalance, this chapter has striven to place Mothersbaugh and Anderson on more equal footing in the roles that they have played in building the director's transmedia world. As an examination of their mutual fascination with childhood and a close analysis of *The Royal Tenenbaums* shows, Mothersbaugh and Anderson have a deep shared aesthetic that binds together their collaborative work.

CHAPTER 4

Analogue authenticity and the sound of Wes Anderson

Ben Winters

As a film-maker who appears to create worlds that are recognizably distinct from our everyday realities – and identifiable as his, not only by their colour palette and design aesthetic but also by dint of their cinematographic expression, to the point that they can be easily parodied in fan-made homages – Wes Anderson is a director who grapples with the inauthentic. In generating believable worlds, whether the transitory and small-scale fictions found in advertising campaigns or the detailed vistas of his feature films, his challenge is to root his often larger-than-life characters in a milieu that allows us, as an audience, to respond to them with genuine emotion. This is perhaps why so many of his feature films reference various forms of fictional representation – from cinema itself (*The Life Aquatic with Steve Zissou*, 2004) to plays (*Rushmore*, 1998), opera (*Moonrise Kingdom*, 2012), Kabuki (*Isle of Dogs*, 2018) and novels (*The Royal Tenenbaums*, 2001, and *The Darjeeling Limited*, 2007) – as if calling attention to the film-maker's challenge. Indeed, the plot lines and dialogue of several of these films seem to allude knowingly to the tension that exists between a search for the authentic and an acknowledgement of the artifice of cinematic fiction itself. 'You never wanted to know me; I'm just a character in your film,' says Owen Wilson's Ned Plimpton as he angrily confronts Bill Murray's Steve Zissou, the man who almost certainly isn't his father. The veracity of Zissou's film-making lies at the heart of *The Life Aquatic*, with Cate Blanchett's reporter character (Jane Winslett-Richardson) articulating the suspicion that aspects of Zissou's latest film (including the encounter with the Jaguar shark that killed his partner) 'seemed slightly fake'. It isn't, of course – and therein lies at least some measure of redemption for Zissou – yet such tensions, as explored in the films, are given added relevance in the context of Anderson's 2018 exhibition for the Kunsthistorisches Museum in Vienna.

The exhibit 'Spitzmaus Mummy in a Coffin and Other Treasures' was curated by Anderson and his partner Juman Malouf and is part of a series of exhibitions the museum has commissioned from 'remarkable creative individuals'.[1] Ignoring traditional curatorial practice, it groups like-coloured or like-shaped objects together or simply places objects in witty juxtaposition in a visual tour de force that nonetheless left some scratching their heads. As Cody Delistraty put it in the *New York Times*, 'Mr Anderson's on-screen aesthetic is all about creating narratives and moods – of yearning, of melancholy, of passion. Art curation is a fundamentally different pursuit.'[2] For Anderson's worlds to be seen as emotionally affecting, rather than merely the dry (albeit humorous) products of a postmodern bricoleur, they require something that some critics found lacking in that Viennese assemblage of objects. One way in which a sense of the authentic is created in Anderson's worlds, then, is through analogue audio recording and transmission technology – including reel-to-reel tape, vinyl, compact cassette and telephonic communication. The 'Society of the Crossed Keys' sequence in *The Grand Budapest Hotel* (2014), for instance, is partly a celebration of the timbre of mechanical telephone ringers: as Mons. Gustave's request is passed down the chain of hoteliers, the camera irises in on the act of each manager disconnecting the line and placing a new call, with the new ring heard as an insert identifying the next hotel is shown (see Figure 4.1). By celebrating analogue technology – and in

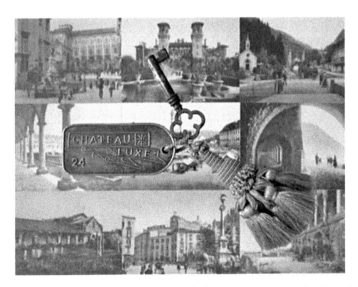

FIGURE 4.1 *Hotel names and the sound of telephone ringers in* The Grand Budapest Hotel *(Wes Anderson, 2014).*

particular the way in which his characters engage physically with its sound-producing mechanics – Anderson grants his often fantastical worlds a material physicality that I would suggest is crucial to the quality of authenticity audiences find in the characters who live in them.

In some cases, of course, uses of analogue technology are apropos to a narrative's notional historical setting (the 1960s settings of *Moonrise Kingdom* or the Stella Artois advert of 2010, which celebrates manual toggle switches, are prime examples). At other times, though, there is a certain anachronistic quality to their use. *Isle of Dogs* is set twenty years in the future, yet it appears to mix analogue and digital technologies (the 'simul-translate' device, for instance, has an audible crackle to its output and even an analogue VU metre). Likewise, the character of Badger in *Fantastic Mr Fox* (2009) uses a mechanical 'dicta-sonic' dictation machine to play a children's song while in the background there sits something that appears to be an iMac. Even the characters of *The Royal Tenenbaums* remain doggedly connected to analogue technology, whether it is Richie Tenenbaum's record player or Raleigh St Clair's impressive collection of reel-to-reel tape recorders and dictation machines (Figure 4.2).

Evidently, then, there is a certain amount of nostalgia in Anderson's use of analogue technology in his worlds, to the extent that one might invoke T. W. Adorno's critique of authenticity in his 1951 book *Minima Moralia*, wherein he challenged the basis of a philosophy of inwardness and its claims to genuineness, revealing it to be a function of the societal impulses it claimed to critique.[3] In that context, we might see Anderson's output, in its apparent celebration of the genuineness of analogue technology, as complicit in what Martin Jay characterized as a 'retreat to a prior state of allegedly plenitudinous wholeness'.[4] Moreover, the concept of authenticity – as both Adorno and Walter Benjamin recognized – only becomes relevant with the

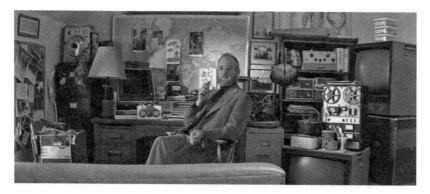

FIGURE 4.2 *Raleigh St. Clair's collection of reel-to-reel tape in* The Royal Tenenbaums *(Wes Anderson, 2001).*

advent of reproducibility. Is Anderson simply replacing – as many audiophiles might also be guilty of – the ritual veneration of the original art object with the apparent authenticity of its first-generation, pre-digital copy and the technology required to play it? Or by privileging the 'derived over the putative original' does Anderson in fact draw attention to the inauthenticity of the self in a way that both Adorno and Benjamin would have recognized?[5] Either way, it is striking that close-ups of characters engaging with analogue sound technology are common (see Figure 4.3) and that the materiality of sound is an important part of his worlds. Even in a short commercial such as the Christmas-themed *Come Together: A Fashion Picture in Motion* (2016) for clothing retailer H&M, the typically Andersonian features include not only the pastel colours, framing devices and dolly shots but also the narrative importance placed on the telephone and intercom equipment with which Adrien Brody's train conductor engages (Figure 4.4a and b). Similar intercom systems are also found in the house on Archer Avenue in *The Royal Tenenbaums* and in the echo box communication device in *The Life Aquatic*. The implied time period of the H&M commercial is ambiguous (despite the contemporary clothing range it advertises), but it is hardly surprising that there are audible signals to indicate that the 1972 John Lennon song that concludes it, and which signals the Christmas magic the conductor creates for the young boy passenger, is played on vinyl. As so often in Anderson's output, the character pulling the strings and closely controlling the environment is a stand-in for Anderson himself.[6]

Undoubtedly, though, there are specific moments in Anderson's output that celebrate the almost ritualistic act of playing sound or music on such

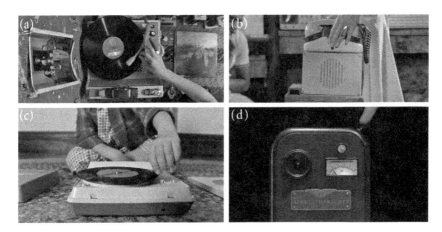

FIGURE 4.3 *Characters engaging with analogue sound technology in* The Royal Tenenbaums *(Wes Anderson, 2001) (a)*; The Life Aquatic *(Wes Anderson, 2004) (b)*; Moonrise Kingdom *(Wes Anderson, 2012) (c)*; *and* Isle of Dogs *(Wes Anderson, 2018) (d)*.

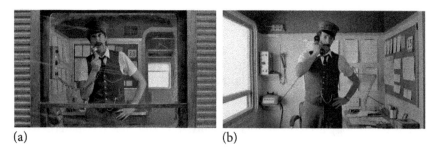

(a)   (b)

FIGURE 4.4 *Train intercom (a) and telephone (b) used in* Come Together: A Fashion Picture in Motion *(Wes Anderson, 2016).*

devices, as when Margot selects 'She Smiled Sweetly' (1967) by The Rolling Stones to play on Richie's record player in *The Royal Tenenbaums*: the moment is marked by a typical Anderson rostrum-like shot from above (see Figure 4.3a). Similarly, the climax of *Rushmore* draws attention to the physical act of playing a record, while the beginning of *Moonrise Kingdom* foregrounds the selection and playing of Benjamin Britten's 'Young Person's Guide to the Orchestra' (1945) on a portable record player (Figure 4.3c), one that accompanies runaways Suzy and Sam on their romantic adventure (Figures 4.3b and 4.3d show similar moments in *Life Aquatic* and *Isle of Dogs*). Even the final song in *Fantastic Mr Fox* ('Let Her Dance' (1966) by the Bobby Fuller Four) despite being played on a 'walk-sonic (digital)' is nonetheless activated with a foregrounded twist of a rotary knob with accompanying click. My point is that these moments do not simply celebrate the sound of the music, but the physical (and above all mechanical) actions by which characters coax the reproducing apparatus into life. It seems to represent an affirmation of their authenticity as characters in which we, as an audience, are prepared to invest emotionally. It seems all the more significant, then, that the shallow Jack Whitman, who features in the short film *Hotel Chevalier* and its feature film sibling *The Darjeeling Limited* (2007), should listen to an iPod and that his hotel room is filled with CDs. Digital technology and the ease with which it allows music to be selected and shuffled with minimum amount of physical engagement, allied with the flattened sound experience of the MP3 format, seems for Anderson to be a metaphor for the inauthenticity of the character, his brothers and their faux tourist Indian experiences – a tension with which Anderson admittedly plays and brings added nuance as *The Darjeeling Limited* plays out. Jack's iPod is playing Debussy's 'Clair De Lune' (1905) as the brothers attempt and spectacularly fail to realize their feather ceremony, the scene before the river death that is the catalyst for revealing at least some of the emotional complexity behind these spoiled and (unusually for Anderson) otherwise rather unappealing characters. The ceremony is Francis's idea of a spiritual bonding activity and involves each of them taking a peacock's feather and symbolically burying it – yet both his brothers fail to follow his instructions: Peter hangs on to his, while Jack lets his feather blow away. When the 'successful', improvised feather ceremony takes place later in the film, the iPod is nowhere in sight.

Without meaningful physical connection with analogue (and particularly audio) technology, Anderson's characters are somehow less authentically 'Andersonian'. Although his film-making style – including his attitude to music – has been described as curatorial, his foray into the world of actual museum curation in Vienna necessarily could not allow that direct physical connection with objects that his films both allow and seem to celebrate – a connection that is important for characters and, by implication, for audiences imagining themselves in the world they see and hear.[7] Is it any wonder that Delistraty found that something was missing? Such criticism points by implication to the fact that the effectiveness of Anderson's worlds is not purely visual – though that is the aspect most apparent to those seeking to capture his style through parody – but that it relies on creating in the minds of a watching audience a sense of tactility that connects them with that worlds' objects. Although the materiality of objects undoubtedly can be appreciated by viewing them in a static museum case, what Anderson's film-making can call upon in addition is the beguiling sound of mechanism activation and an audible mechanical trace on the media transmitted by such devices. Whatever the nature of the fantastical worlds Anderson creates, this plethora of audible clicks, whirrs, bells and clunks, together with the scratch of a record needle, lends these audio devices, and the characters who operate them, a material authenticity that reaches through the screen to connect with us in profound ways.

CHAPTER 5

The instrumentarium of Wes Anderson and Alexandre Desplat

Ewan Clark

Wes [Anderson's] movies are of another world. They come from Wes' world, which is a very specific and special work of his own. ... So I use my imagination in the same way that he does and try and create first an instrumentarium – a bunch of instruments that would be toys that we play together.[1]

This chapter explores the role played by instrumentation in the construction of 'Wes' world' in Alexandre Desplat's scores for Wes Anderson's last four feature films: *Fantastic Mr. Fox* (2009), *Moonrise Kingdom* (2012), *The Grand Budapest Hotel* (2014) and *Isle of Dogs* (2018). 'Wes' world' is Desplat's term for what Warren Buckland calls Anderson's 'storyworld' in Chapter 2. Buckland describes Anderson's storyworld as 'an abstract totality encompassing everything fictionally possible in all his films'; this includes the director's distinctive audiovisual style, which has become a recognizable brand. As Buckland argues, Anderson's storyworld is transmedial in that it exceeds its native medium of cinema to find robust expression in such things as TV adverts, trailers and websites promoting the films, cosplay by fans, Anderson-themed cafés and online videos parodying Anderson's style.

Anderson, Buckland notes elsewhere in this book, has been identified as an *auteur mélomane* (a director who is passionate about music) by Lara Hrycaj[2] (borrowing the term from Claudia Gorbman).[3] Consequently, Anderson's films are – among other things – an invitation to his audiences to share in that passion.

Anderson's music is also transmedial: in addition to hearing the music in the cinema, audiences can listen to soundtrack albums, attend concerts or watch interviews about the music. Some fans even make their own playlists of music they think could or should be used in an Anderson film.[4] Pastiches of Andersonian music also exist; in at least one stock music ('library music') website, it is possible to search 'Wes Anderson' and find dozens of pieces of stock music that resemble the music used in Anderson's films.[5] All of this shows that the music of Anderson's films has developed a recognizable identity and that it is integral to the transmedial expansion of the director's storyworld.

This storyworld is malleable; it accrues new elements and evolves in new directions as each new film is released. While Anderson may direct its development, it is ultimately the product of assemblage or network auteurship, in which the composer and other recurrent collaborators bring their own imaginations to support the director's vision. For Desplat, the film has three authors: 'the director, the screenwriter and the composer'.[6] With this perspective, we can understand Desplat's musical choices – including his choices of instruments – to be integral to his role as a co-auteur of the film, and as a co-auteur of Anderson's storyworld more generally.

In this chapter, I discuss recurrent approaches to instrumentation that characterize the music of Anderson's storyworld, while also pondering the symbiotic relationship between this storyworld's musical and non-musical elements. As Desplat reveals in the opening quotation, selecting a group of instruments for a score is his first creative step. Anderson and Desplat often begin discussing instrumentation before the film is shot, as was the case with *The Grand Budapest Hotel*.[7] This early prioritization of instrumentation in the discussion demonstrates the importance of timbre and texture in creating these peculiarly audible audiovisual worlds.

Before detailing Desplat's instrumentation, however, it is useful to distinguish between four broad categories of music used in Anderson's films. The first of these categories is comprised of existing popular songs, curated for the film by Anderson and his music supervisor Randall Poster, many of which are what Buckland describes as 'slow ballads with an acoustic guitar accompanied by a quiet whispery voice'.[8] Another category contains curated existing music other than popular songs, including symphonic music, choral music, jazz and folk music. In terms of original scores, there are those written by Mark Mothersbaugh for four films during 1996–2004 (our third category) and those written by Desplat for four films during 2009–18 (our fourth one).

While this chapter is primarily concerned with latter category (Desplat's scores), there are many interrelationships between the categories. Mothersbaugh and Desplat both tend to write music designed in part to complement the existing music used in the film. In Motherbaugh's case, the existing music is mostly popular song; in Desplat's case, however, it is mostly other kinds of existing music (except in *Fantastic Mr. Fox*). Consequently, Motherbaugh draws heavily on popular idioms such as rock, while Desplat draws more on the other kinds of existing music his scores sit alongside. These other kinds include Benjamin Britten's orchestral and choral music in *Moonrise Kingdom*, various European, Eastern European and Russian folk styles in *The Grand Budapest Hotel* and Japanese taiko drumming and 1950s film music in *Isle of Dogs*.

Desplat's scores also refer back to stylistic tendencies established in Mothersbaugh's scores, mingling these with some new approaches. The inherited approaches are important in that they have longevity as archetypal elements of Anderson's storyworld. These – and indeed any musical approaches used in two or more films – are musical equivalents of the eight components of Anderson's *mise-en-scène* listed by Buckland in Chapter 2. They provide a fascinating example of how the films of an *auteur mélomane* can use a distinctive musical palette that maintains a significant level of consistency, sometimes even after a change of composer. Desplat's new approaches are interesting for the opposite reason: they reveal the composer's own personal sensibilities and remind us that even a directorial style as recognizable as Anderson's can evolve in new directions when a new composer with a distinctive style becomes a co-auteur.

Instruments connoting innocence

The most important recurrent aspect of instrumentation in both composers' scores is the frequent foregrounding of high-pitched instruments that connote childhood and innocence. Mothersbaugh credits this to Anderson, saying of their first collaboration on *Bottle Rocket* (1996) that 'Wes wanted all these very high-pitched sounds. By the end of the first day, I understood that he didn't like bass sounds. He didn't like brass. He liked plucky instruments and bells and flutes and piccolos.'[9] The 'bells' in Mothersbaugh's four scores are tuned metallophones such as celeste, vibraphone, glockenspiel and untuned metal idiophones such as triangle and sleigh bells. As Cateforis writes in Chapter 3, these 'connote a childlike aesthetic', emphasizing the themes of childhood that pervade Anderson's work.[10] (Anderson's visual style, too, often seeks to portray story events as a 'child's miniaturized rendition of reality'.) Desplat said, after his third collaboration with Anderson, that the childlike element and theme of education is very strong in these films: 'It's there in *Mr. Fox*, because of the nature of the puppets, and in *Moonrise Kingdom*, because of these very young adults. … And it's there in [*The Grand Budapest Hotel*], because the heart of it is Zero is being educated by Gustave H. …you can definitely use that musically; it's something you can refer to.'[11]

Desplat was interested in connoting childhood with bell-like and plucked stringed instruments even before working with Anderson: 'The music I write generally has this childlike thing of simplicity. … I often use harps and pianos and celeste and Fender pianos and light electric guitars and little bells. It's part of my instrumentarium.'[12] It is clear that, even prior to their collaboration, Desplat and Anderson shared similar tastes in instruments, and Desplat was aware that these instruments possessed childlike associations.

But why do such sounds connote childhood? First, any high-pitched sound is suggestive of small physical size, because small objects (including children's vocal cords) resonate at higher frequencies.[13] Second, some of the instruments have well-developed associations of childhood within Western culture. For instance, the celeste has 'an association with childhood innocence, through such pieces as Tchaikovsky's "Dance of the Sugar Plum Fairy" from *The Nutcracker* (1892) and the theme from the children's television show, *Mr. Rogers' Neighborhood* (1968–2001)'.[14] The glockenspiel, possessing a very similar delicate, chiming timbre, conjures a similar association. Third, a number of the bell-like and flute-like sounds under discussion are frequently played by young children in the classroom and are therefore now associated with children and education, especially through Carl Orff's 'Schulwerk' approach to music education, best known for its use of recorders and metallophones.[15] Anderson and his composers arguably over-represent some of the 'Orff instruments' – deliberately or not – due to their association with children and education.

Importantly, none of the instruments or sounds discussed in this chapter conveys only one meaning. The recorder, for instance, might equally accrue associations from its use in early music performances. But, as Juan Chattah explains in his discussion of film music through the lens of pragmatics, 'The context in film music (i.e. visuals, narrative, or just the fact that the audience is aware of watching a movie) helps specify, or at least narrow, the meaning(s) ascribed to the music.'[16] So, for instance, when various 'Orff instruments' are present in Anderson's films – which often feature childlike imagery and characters – it is very likely that the audience will unconsciously understand that the instrumentation is part of Anderson's audiovisual exploration of innocence.

Desplat uses the celeste in all four of his Anderson scores, and it can be heard in two-thirds of the tracks on the four soundtrack albums. It usually arpeggiates chords to decorate and rhythmicize a homophonic texture and occasionally plays short melodic ideas. Sometimes, too, the use of the celeste coincides neatly with the appearance of a young, innocent character. An example of this can be found in *The Grand Budapest Hotel*, in the cue 'A Troops Barracks (Requiem for the Grand Budapest)'.[17] This accompanies an extended sequence towards the end of the film, in which the titular hotel has been overrun by a Nazi-like army in a world war, becoming a barracks. Agatha – who is seventeen but has a childlike quality (like many of the adolescents in Anderson's films) – enters the hotel, pretending to deliver pastries, while secretly retrieving a priceless painting from a safe. Much of the cue features loud, bombastic brass and percussion, emphasizing the military presence in the hotel. When the camera focus is on Agatha, however, the orchestration tends to be lighter, foregrounding the celeste delicately playing melodies or chords (spread or arpeggiated). The celeste is joined by the similarly delicate upper register harp and accompanied by pulsating chords in low woodwind.

As this example illustrates, Desplat sometimes chooses childlike instruments (celeste, glockenspiel, etc.) to support childlike moments. However, childlike instruments can accompany Anderson's adult characters, too. For instance, in *The Royal Tenenbaums* (2001), Hrycaj associates the celeste with two middle-aged characters, observing that it is associated with 'the innocence and sweetness associated with the happiness surrounding Etheline and Henry's relationship.'[18] In *The Grand Budapest Hotel*, celeste is sometimes used in moments – regardless of whether a child is involved – that are innocent in one sense but not in another, meaning the moment comes across as somewhat ironic and somewhat sincere at the same time. This creates a 'new sincerity moment' in which there is, in Buckland's words from elsewhere in this book, a 'dynamic tension between two opposing forces: sincerity and irony'.[19]

For instance, celeste arpeggios are prominently mixed with Balalaika tremolos as Gustave and Zero steal the priceless painting *Boy with Apple* from Madame D.'s wall, replacing it with another called 'Two Lesbians Masturbating'. This is more innocent than it appears, however, in that Gustave has been bequeathed the painting. The musical implication of innocence, then, registers as simultaneously ironic and sincere. There is also a sense in which Anderson's entire transmedial storyworld has a childlike aesthetic; consequently, we find childlike instruments and other elements sprinkled throughout his work, regardless of whether or not a scene explicitly emphasizes childlike or innocent subject matter.

In terms of untuned bell-like sounds, Mothersbaugh shows a particular penchant for using sleigh bells as a timekeeping instrument in his cues, especially in his scores for *Bottle Rocket* and *Rushmore* (1998). Sleigh bells can connote such interrelated concepts as sleighs, snow, Christmas, children and innocence. Hrycaj observes that in *Bottle Rocket* sleigh bells are associated with Dignan's 'innocence and the dreamer attitude',[20] while in *Rushmore* they are associated with Max Fischer's innocence.[21] She notes, too, that the innocent connotations of the instrument can be used ironically, such as when Dignan is in prison.[22] Another instance in which

Mothersbaugh ironically uses sleigh bells is in the second montage of *The Royal Tenenbaums* (analysed by Cateforis in Chapter 3). Pulsating sleigh bells are added to an already-established musical texture solely for one short shot – the one in which Royal Tenenbaum stares glumly out of a window as snow falls, heaping on the windowsill. The use of sleigh bells here is congruent with the snowy setting while at the same time ironically incongruent with Royal's body language, which exudes adult cynicism (as opposed to childlike innocence).

In *The Grand Budapest Hotel*, Desplat very clearly associates sleigh bells – or tambourines imitating sleigh bells – with hurried, adventurous travel through picturesque snowy landscapes. This invokes the original context of pulsating sleigh bells: they would jingle rhythmically on horses' harnesses as they pulled a sleigh through a snowy landscape. Desplat uses sleigh bells as a timekeeping device over the ensemble for scenes in which Gustave and Zero hurry by various means through snowy settings.[23] Before any of this, sleigh bells are used when the two begin their adventure together, when Gustave starts to interview the young Zero outside the titular Hotel, again in the snow ('The New Lobby Boy'). In the latter scene especially, the instrument's appropriateness also lies in its connotations of innocence; Zero's adventures with Gustave are, after all, being told by a middle-aged Zero looking back nostalgically on his youth. In *Isle of Dogs*, another scene involving a hurried, adventurous journey by cable car is underscored by music with pulsating sleigh bells: a swing arrangement of Prokofiev's 'Troika' (which translates as 'Sleigh Ride'). Thus, we see that the overrepresentation of an instrument in Anderson's films can promote intertextuality, contributing to the bigger picture of Anderson's transmedial storyworld.

As Cateforis has argued in his discussion of *The Royal Tenenbaums*, Anderson is concerned with the conflation of childhood and adulthood. One way in which Desplat expresses this musically is by combining signifiers of childhood with signifiers of seriousness and/or negative emotion, such as minor mode, dissonance, low register and/or slow tempo. The result is neither fully childlike nor fully adult, but a complex mixture of the two. Consider the cue twenty minutes into *Moonrise Kingdom*: 'The Heroic Weather-Conditions of the Universe, Part 1: A Veiled Mist'. This accompanies the scene in which Sam and Suzy (both twelve years old) run away together to embark on a hiking trip in which a mutual fascination burgeons into an unlikely romance. The couple show both adult and childlike behaviours. Sam, for example, speaks to Suzy like a Scout master formally briefing his troop on the journey plan (seemingly very adult, see Figure 5.1). Amusingly, though, he exudes childlike naïveté as he does so, such as when he suggests they suck on pebbles to quench their thirst, despite water being plentiful. Suzy's adult qualities include wearing make-up and perfume, although in the context of hiking these also demonstrate her naïveté, as does her choice to bring her cat and a suitcase of books.

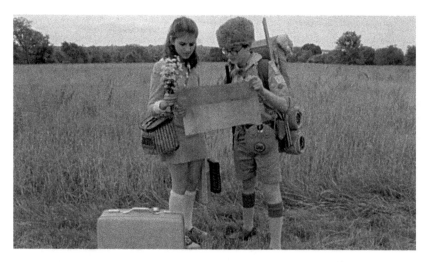

FIGURE 5.1 *Sam briefs Suzy before they begin their journey in* Moonrise Kingdom *(Wes Anderson, 2012).*

The flute, celeste and glockenspiel emphasize the pair's innocence by playing lively melodic figures with bouncy staccato notes, dotted rhythms and triplets, respectively. In a manner typical of Desplat's orchestration style, each instrument enters the texture with great clarity, without being doubled by another instrument or covered by dialogue. But the accompaniment in 'A Veiled Mist' provides a much more serious undercurrent. It lacks the bouncy rhythms and pace of the melodic figures and is rather atmospheric, with a harp providing a warm wash of sound in which each note is allowed to ring. Here, and throughout much of Desplat's music for *Moonrise Kingdom*, the accompaniment incessantly prolongs a G minor tonic chord, which contributes a sense of melancholy, despite the melodic and timbral signifiers of innocence. Desplat is, on the one hand, emphasizing that Sam and Suzy are children enacting a fun child's fantasy. On the other hand, his solemn accompaniment and tonality encourages the audience to empathize with the serious emotions they feel; their sadness and dissatisfaction with their ordinary lives has compelled them to run away. The music teeters between sincerity and irony in true 'new sincerity' fashion, in that the pervasively solemn accompaniment sounds sincere and empathetic with the character's feelings, while the contrasting musical representations of childlike fun and adult seriousness could be interpreted as ironic.

Dissonance and unconventional tonality can also combine with childlike instruments to create irony. Consider, for example, the montage early in *Isle of Dogs*, introducing us to the sick, sad and angry dogs that have been banished to Trash Island (Figure 5.2). The cue titled 'Six Months Later + Dog

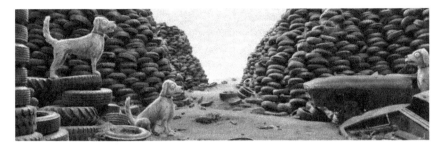

FIGURE 5.2 *An image from the montage introducing the dogs of Trash Island in* Isle of Dogs *(Wes Anderson, 2018).*

Fight' features Japanese taiko drums to connote the Japanese setting and saxophone to imitate the barking of dogs, but of interest here are the celeste arpeggios and bouncy staccato recorders.[24] These childlike instruments are congruent with the childlike visual style of the stop-motion animation. Meanwhile, the unconventional and at times dissonant pitch organization is congruent with the dogs' absurdly dire, dystopian predicament.[25] These two audiovisual strands of communication – the childlike and the dystopian – are obviously in tension with one another, and the resulting impression is ironic, even sardonic.

Instrumentation is not the only way in which Desplat achieves a sense of childlike innocence. This sense is also supported by his use of 'straightforward hypermeters and sectional durations that tend to consist of four, eight or sixteen bars'.[26] On top of this, Desplat uses simpler harmony for Anderson's films than for other films, often limiting himself to the most basic chords within a key: tonic, subdominant and dominant.[27] These combined factors allow Desplat to support Anderson's transmedial childlike aesthetic very effectively.

All that jazz

Another recurrent musical feature of Anderson's films is his use of jazz or – more frequently – music that includes jazz-like elements, especially jazz-like drumming and bass lines, usually on upright bass. Mothersbaugh and Desplat tend to layer these jazz-like elements with other elements such as classical instruments and harmonies, childlike instruments and/or elements connoting a particular setting.

To place this in a broader context, Mothersbaugh's scores for Anderson may be considered *pop scores* in that they draw on jazz and other popular musical styles (such as rock and, occasionally, electronic music). Hrycaj describes them in accordance with Jeff Smith's definition of the pop score: 'composed or compiled in one or more popular musical styles, and ... [are] formally accessible to the average moviegoer'.[28] (Smith later clarifies that the accessibility relates to stylistic familiarity and is intended to motivate moviegoers to buy the soundtrack album in large numbers).[29] Anderson certainly intended for Mothersbaugh's music to be on the soundtrack album, a fact which falls in alignment with Smith's definition of a pop score.[30] Moreover, the music was clearly intended from the outset be a transmedial product that had a life beyond the film, and this may partly explain – along with the narrative-based reasons discussed below – why the pop score approach was chosen over a more classical approach to film scoring.

Desplat's scores for Anderson also draw on popular idioms: there are elements of jazz in *The Grand Budapest Hotel* and *Isle of Dogs* and elements of bluegrass in *Fantastic Mr. Fox*. His scores have also been released on soundtrack albums. However, Smith explains that a pop score 'should use pop music as its *central* set of stylistic components'.[31] Desplat's scores do not meet this requirement to the extent that Mothersbaugh's do, in that other influences such as classical music, traditional film scoring, post-minimalism and non-Western musics often push the popular idioms to the periphery. Nevertheless, Desplat's scores have at least an element of the pop score approach in them.

Returning specifically to the use of jazz in Anderson's films, this began with the short film *Bottle Rocket* (1992) that inspired the 1996 feature of the same title. The short film had a compilation score consisting of jazz and hard bop from the 1950s, including previously released recordings by Sonny Rollins, The Horace Silver Trio and the Zoot Sims Quartet. According to Randall Poster (Anderson's music supervisor since 1996), Anderson 'seemed to take the outlaw nature of these jazz musicians and apply it to the would-be rebels in the film'.[32] In the feature version of *Bottle Rocket*, Mothersbaugh continues this association, as Hrycaj observes: 'Jazz-like cues associated with Mr. Henry link his criminal lifestyle and the life Dignan wants to achieve.'[33] Two such cues associated with Mr. Henry are 'Mr. Henry's Chop Shop' and 'You're Breaking His Heart'. The elements common to both of these cues are the brushed snare providing a swing beat, the walking jazz bass and the improvisational jazz flute. The brushed snare and jazz-like double bass are particularly noteworthy, in that these are the most consistently deployed jazz-like elements across the eight Anderson films with original scores.

One reason brushed drums may be so common is that the brushes provide a much softer sound than drum sticks; this is ideal for accompanying the relatively small ensembles that work well under dialogue, especially if the instrumentation emphasizes the delicate, childlike sounds discussed in the previous section. The brushed drumming is focused (often exclusively) on the brushed snare drum, using a technique called *stirring the pot*. The most common rhythm played is a swing or shuffle beat in a fast or very fast tempo of 140–240 beats per minute.[34]

If crime is connoted by the jazz in *Bottle Rocket*, however, it is done only in moderation. This is partly because of the relatively innocent connotations of the flute and partly because most of the jazz-like music in *Bottle Rocket* is in major mode,[35] and, according to Philip Tagg, jazz is more typically associated with crime when it is minor.[36] Minor mode or not, the association between jazz and stories about crime – including comedies about crime – dates back to the likes of Henry Mancini's score for *The Pink Panther* (1963) and Neal Hefti's theme music for *Batman* (1966).[37] Anderson is building on this tradition, but in a way that is recognizably his own.

In Desplat's work, an example of brushed snare and jazz-like double bass accompanying a criminal act is the 'Escape Concerto' from *The Grand Budapest Hotel*. As Gustave escapes jail with a group of fellow prisoners, we hear a cue scored almost entirely with untuned percussion playing driving and, at times, playfully syncopated rhythms. Much of the music is light and delicate to reflect the hushed 'tip-toed' nature of the escape, which includes crawling under the beds of sleeping guards in cartoonish fashion. In particular, there is a focus on small percussion instruments, including triangle (one of the childlike 'Orff instruments') and woodblock, whose sounds wittily imitate the sounds of the small tools used by the prisoners to escape. The childlike connotations of the triangle and woodblock are ironic in this context, because of course the escape is not an innocent act, even though one of the escapees (Gustave) has been wrongfully imprisoned. The jazz-like double bass, however, provides one clear connotation of criminality. It plays a repeated pattern of quarter notes (C–Gb–Eb–Db) in C Locrian mode, an altered form of the minor scale. According to Philip Tagg, minor-key jazz can connote crime, especially if it includes the flat fifth (Gb in this case) or other chromatic alterations (which could include the Db in this case).[38] Despite this connotation, the tone of the scene stays light and comedic through its use of high-pitched, delicate percussion.

Desplat also uses a jazz-like bass double bass line to connote criminality in *Isle of Dogs*. Here, though, there are taiko drums instead of brushed snare, and the riff played by the double bass (Figure 5.3) alludes to the same style of 1960s spy film music that inspired the well-known riff from Neal Hefti's *Batman* theme (Figure 5.4).[39] (Both bass lines have pairs of repeated eighth notes that descend and then ascend chromatically.) Desplat's riff first appears in 'Second Crash-Landing + Bath House + Beach Attack', when the dogs in the 'hero pack' fight the robotic dogs of the criminal Kobayashi regime. Desplat's allusion to a style associated with spies seems particularly apt given this subject matter.

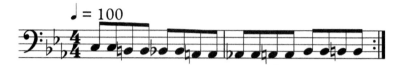

FIGURE 5.3 *Double Bass riff in* Isle of Dogs *(Wes Anderson, 2018).*

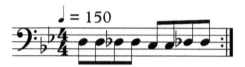

FIGURE 5.4 *Riff in Neil Hefti's* Batman *theme (TV Series, 1966).*

Although certain kinds of jazz can connote crime, jazz can, of course, also be used in non-criminal contexts. Very fast swing grooves with bass and brushed snare are also well suited to any moment of speed and/or urgency. In *Bottle Rocket*, Mothersbaugh's cue 'Rocky' illustrates this well. In this frantic scene, Anthony hurriedly proposes – through translation – that his new girlfriend Inez runs away with him. The jazzy walking bass and brushed drums not only emphasize Anthony's sense of frantic hurry but also contribute to a sense of stylistic incongruity, contrasted with the guitar melody they accompany. This melody, reminiscent of Baroque style, follows a circle of fifths progression. An additional Baroque element is provided by the use of harpsichord, playing improvisational melodic flourishes. Stylistic incongruity between the jazz rhythm section and non-jazz elements is something that both Mothersbaugh and Desplat employ to comedic effect at various times; here it emphasizes the comedic communication difficulties that can occur when two cultures collide.

Another narrative-based reason for using jazz is to help depict a setting in which one might plausibly find jazz, such as the 1930s Europe of *The Grand Budapest Hotel*, the affluent New York communities depicted in *The Royal Tenenbaums*, the swanky film premiere in *The Life Aquatic with Steve Zissou* (2004) or the private high school in which *Rushmore* is set. Occasionally, the criminal connotations of jazz require more brute force than is possible with the brushes. In these moments, the loud, rapid rhythmic pummelling of tom-toms with sticks is a common trope in Anderson's films. As Hrycaj observes, this was initially inspired by an Art Blakey drum solo featured in the short version of *Bottle Rocket*, and in Mothersbaugh's scores this is 'typically associated with moments of danger, risk, and/or criminal activity'.[40] Desplat continues this association most obviously in various robbery scenes in *Fantastic Mr. Fox*. However, in a broader sense, he continues the idea of accompanying energetic moments with percussion only, as is on display with the taiko drums that play throughout almost the entirety of *Isle of Dogs*.

Jazz-like elements have become a recurrent musical feature of Anderson's storyworld, whether the motivation is to connote crime, to evoke a setting and/or to provide a light but frantic groove to support a comedically hurried scene. The instruments that are most consistently deployed for this purpose – brushed drum kit and a single plucked double bass – have also become very typical musical elements of Anderson's storyworld in their own right, whether in the context of jazz or another popular idiom.

Desplat's reworking of Anderson's instrumentarium

Despite both composers similarly emphasizing childlike instruments and jazz rhythm sections, Desplat's instrumentarium for Anderson's films relies less on popular idioms and their instruments. Specifically, he has not continued Mothersbaugh's use of synthesizers and rock-style drumming and guitar playing. The only recognizably electric instruments he uses are old instruments dating from the 1930s: Hammond organ (in *Moonrise Kingdom* and *The Grand Budapest Hotel*), jazz electric guitar (in *Moonrise Kingdom*) and a very occasional and discreet electric bass guitar (in *The Grand Budapest Hotel*). It is significant, though, that these are old technologies, dating from the 1930s, so the sound is retro rather than contemporary. In *Moonrise Kingdom*, the only jazz-like element is the timbre (not the playing style) of the jazz guitar, and, in *Isle of Dogs*, jazz-like elements are limited to the aforementioned Batman-like bass line. Overall, the above changes represent a significant shift away from a contemporary-sounding pop score in Anderson's films.

Desplat's avoidance of contemporary sounds and idioms may be a deliberate analogy to Anderson's lo-tech and often retro visual style, in which computer-generated imagery (CGI) is largely eschewed in favour of filming physical objects. His musical background may be another cause of the shift; it is in art music, jazz and Brazilian music, as opposed to Mothersbaugh's background in avant-garde rock. Another important driver of the change is likely to be Anderson's choices of existing music: rock and other popular songs have become much less frequent in Anderson's later films.[41] In its place, Anderson and his music supervisor have curated country music for *Fantastic Mr. Fox*, orchestral and choral music by Benjamin Britten for *Moonrise Kingdom*, Russian folk music for *The Grand Budapest Hotel* and film music written or arranged in the 1950s in *Isle of Dogs*.[42] Since a degree of stylistic cohesion within each film is desirable, this changing nature of the curated existing music has likely caused the changing nature of the original music.

As well as removing certain elements from the instrumentarium, Desplat has added several new elements, reminding us that this 'Anderson sound' – just like the 'Anderson look' – is not a static entity but a transmedial collection of aesthetic choices that is alive, malleable and constantly extending in one direction or contracting in another. Desplat's approach to louder, more masculine cues is more orchestral and less reliant on popular idioms than Mothersbaugh's. French horn, timpani and/or orchestral snare drum often lead the charge in the louder moments of his scores. The clichéd convention of using French horns to connote heroism is evident, such as when Zero runs to rescue Agatha from her fall from the hotel window towards the end of *The Grand Budapest Hotel*.[43] The similarly clichéd convention of using orchestral snare drum to connote a military-like discipline is employed in the satirical portrayal of Scouts in *Moonrise Kingdom* and the police and soldiers in *The Grand Budapest Hotel*. Such clichéd associations are almost certainly deployed tongue-in-cheek; they become part of Anderson's satirical portrayal of male characters who see themselves seriously as heroes or as authority figures, but who serve, for the audience, as objects of amusement to some extent.

Desplat also uses male chorus – chanting or singing indecipherable syllables – to satirize self-important male characters. This is the most distinctive timbral element that he has added to Anderson's instrumentarium. It was first used in *Moonrise Kingdom* and retained for *The Grand Budapest Hotel* and *Isle of Dogs*. In the first two films, the chorus tends to bolster a sense of excitement in the loud, exciting, tutti sections of cues, accompanying action rather than dialogue. For example, in *The Grand Budapest Hotel*, it is used to accompany shots of Jopling (the villain) riding his motorcycle in pursuit of Serge X, of Gustave and Zero running across a field after Gustave escapes jail, and of Gustave and Zero sledding down a mountainside in pursuit of Jopling. These choral moments arguably allude to the exciting moments in an opera when the chorus joins in to comment on narrative events – often in a foreign tongue – and excitement is generated by virtue of the large number of singers involved. But it is a chamber opera that is connoted in this case – only sixteen singers are used in *Moonrise Kingdom* – and the modest scale is analogous to Anderson's miniaturized visual aesthetic. The most memorable use of chorus in *The Grand Budapest Hotel* is when one of Desplat's main themes – which has been used repeatedly throughout the film – is sung within the diegesis by monks at mass.[44] In *Isle of Dogs*, Desplat and Anderson revisit the inclusion of monk-like singing, this time in an oriental setting and at an intradiegetic level that interacts with the diegesis without having an implied sound source within it.[45]

Desplat's instrumental preferences in his collaborations with Anderson are also noteworthy in that he eschews a sound that typifies the scores of most mainstream Hollywood films, namely a symphonic string section playing emotive bowed melodies, sustained notes and chords. Bowed orchestral strings are conspicuously absent from the two most recent films (*The Grand Budapest Hotel* and *Isle of Dogs*). Desplat does use bowed strings in *Fantastic Mr. Fox*, but he only uses a string quintet – a miniature string section to compliment the miniature puppets and sets on display. This echoes Mothersbaugh's use of similarly small string ensembles in his Anderson scores. A full orchestra is used in *Moonrise Kingdom*; however, the strings only play pizzicato or short, bowed notes. Restricted budgets may have played a role in the choices of instrumentation in some films, but I suspect that association is a more important factor. Symphonic strings played in a bowed, non-staccato fashion carry associations of two things that work against Anderson's identity as a film-maker. First, they connote mainstream Hollywood cinema, and Anderson has built his career by differentiating his style from the mainstream. Second, emotive strings would arguably work against a sense of distanciation-alienation, preventing Anderson's desired balance between distanciation-alienation and emotional engagement.

All of the instrument choices I have discussed, which reoccur across at least two of Desplat's four Anderson scores, help to endow Anderson's directorial style with a consistent and recognizable brand of music. However, in addition to these cross-film continuities, Desplat explains that he and Anderson make an effort to give each score something of a unique brand all of its own: 'There's always some kind of experimentation with Wes, just to build an [instrumentation] that we haven't used before, and that we maybe haven't heard before.'[46] As Table 5.1 outlines, these tendencies of instrumentation in particular films usually relate to the film's setting and are shared with some of the other music in the film that Desplat has not written.

Conclusion

Desplat's instrumentation for these four film scores has proven to be a fertile site for analysis, in that the instrumentation serves at least four functions. First and foremost, it is an important means of articulating Wes Anderson's directorial storyworld transmedially, whether through instrumental preferences inherited from Mothersbaugh or those introduced by Desplat. Second, all of Desplat's and Mothersbaugh's instrumentation choices are meaningful both on a transmedial level and within each film, connoting and emphasizing an idea or character trait such as criminality or innocence, or an aspect of setting. Furthermore, instrumentation works with other musical elements and other aspects of the cinematic discourse to achieve typical Andersonian modes of discourse – such as a conflation of the childlike with the adult – or to achieve a sense of the 'new sincerity', carefully balancing

Table 5.1 Instrumentation tendencies particular to specific Wes Anderson films

	Instruments or ensembles whose prominent use by Desplat is particular to this film	Narrative-based motivations for the use	Other music in the film (not by Desplat) using these instruments or ensembles
Fantastic Mr. Fox	Instruments used in bluegrass, especially banjo and mandolin; small instruments	Bluegrass evokes a rural setting; small instruments imitate the smallness of the stop-motion puppets	Jarvis Cocker's 'Fantastic Mr. Fox AKA Petey's Song'
The Grand Budapest Hotel	Ensemble of Russian balalaikas (usually playing tremolo), Hungarian cimbalom	Instruments help to depict Zubrowka, which is loosely based on Eastern Europe	'The Linden Tree' and 'Kamarinskaya' by Rudolf Belov & Vitaly Gnutov
Moonrise Kingdom	Full symphony orchestra	Orchestral music is a feature of Suzy's life and a signifier of her affluence and interest in the arts	Benjamin Britten's *Young Person's Guide to the Orchestra* (1945)
Isle of Dogs	Taiko drums, saxophones usually playing staccato	Taikos evoke Japan, staccato saxophones imitate a dog's bark	Taikos: Kaoru Watanabe's 'Taiko Drumming' and 'TV Drumming'. Saxophones: Fumio Hayasaka's 'Kanbei & Katsushiro – Kikuchiyo's Mambo' from *The Seven Samurai* (1954)

sincerity with irony. Third, Desplat's instrumentation helps to provide each film with its own unique musical brand, usually by foregrounding instruments associated with the film's setting. Fourth, and finally, through comparison with Mothersbaugh's approach to Anderson's films, we have gleaned insights about Desplat's personal contribution to Anderson's style.

We have seen how he has caused the sound of Anderson's films to evolve in new directions by bringing his own innovations and personal preferences. The creative partnership of Anderson and Desplat – in which both men have brought their own personal and idiosyncratic sensibilities, each without cramping the style of the other – has yielded some wonderful music and some truly memorable cinema, and their creative output across these four films provides a rich example of audiovisual and transmedial storytelling.

PART TWO

Cross-medial assemblage and the making of the director

CHAPTER 6

Our lives in pink: Sofia Coppola as transmedia audiovisual stylist

Jeff Smith

Director Sofia Coppola was born into a family of film-makers. This ancestral legacy likely did much to shape her destiny as one of most important American directors of the new millennium. Her aunt and uncle, David and Talia Shire, both received Oscar nominations in the 1970s and made significant contributions to the 'Hollywood renaissance', the former as a composer and the latter as an actor. Her cousin, Nicolas Cage, became one of Hollywood's biggest stars, playing the lead in several blockbuster films produced by Jerry Bruckheimer and winning the Oscar for Best Actor for *Leaving Las Vegas* (1995). Her other cousin, Jason Schwartzman, made his debut in Wes Anderson's cult classic, *Rushmore* (1998), and has gone to become a featured player in films directed by Sofia, David O. Russell, Edgar Wright, Tim Burton and Alex Ross Perry. And, of course, her father is the legendary Francis Ford Coppola, the force behind *The Godfather Saga*, *The Conversation* (1974), *Apocalypse Now* (1979), *One from the Heart* (1982), *Rumble Fish* (1983), *The Cotton Club* (1984), *Peggy Sue Got Married* (1986) and *Bram Stoker's Dracula* (1992). *Pere* Coppola is widely regarded as one of the most important Hollywood directors of the post-studio era, producing an oeuvre matched by only a handful of other American film-makers during the past half-century.

For daughter Sofia, this legacy has been both a curse and a blessing. Cajoled by her father into replacing Winona Ryder in *The Godfather: Part III* (1990), she was mocked mercilessly for her performance, which critics and fans saw as an act of shameless nepotism. As a director, Sofia has lived with the burden of expectations. As she has noted in interviews, early responses to her films seemed to credit others for her success. According to Coppola, 'When I first started, people would say things like, "Oh, your casting was really well done. Did your father or your husband help you?" And that was really insulting, obviously. You wouldn't say that to a male director.'[1] At the same time, Coppola recognizes that she's had certain benefits as a result of her family's reputation. Francis Coppola's company, American Zoetrope, has provided financial backing and post-production resources on all six of Sofia's features. Her brother, Roman – a film-maker and screenwriter in his own right – has served as second unit director on several of his father's and sister's films. Still, Sofia has been keen to assert her own individuality as a visual stylist. In response to a question about Francis's influence, Sofia responded: 'I think we have very different styles, but my interest in film-making comes from him. He's always encouraged me to make things as personal as I can, to follow my heart and intuition. I get that from him, but I think I have a much more – obviously! – female point of view and approach.'[2]

Sofia's work differs from her father's in other ways that have more to do with their respective industrial and historical contexts. Francis flourished within an industry that was buffeted by change on nearly all sides. His films were produced during a period where the studios had become parts of major conglomerates and at a time where horizontal integration had replaced vertical integration. The role of ancillary revenues was considerably enhanced within this business environment as video sales and rentals, television broadcast rights and music cross-promotion all emerged as important means of managing risk.

Sofia, on the other hand, rose to prominence in the late 1990s and early 2000s. By the time she began directing, 'synergy' was already passé as an industry buzzword. Instead, the newest frontiers in the media landscape were associated with terms like 'convergence', 'e-commerce' and 'digital cinema'. Although her father dipped his toes into other media, directing an episode of Shelley Duvall's *Faerie Tale Theatre* (Season 6, Episode 1: 'Rip Van Winkle', 1987) as well as *Captain EO* (1986), the seventeen-minute Michael Jackson short film that became a Disney theme park attraction, Sofia fully embraced the brave new world of transmedia. She made music videos, ad spots and a Netflix television special alongside her feature film releases. As an audiovisual stylist, one discerns crucial continuities across Coppola's body of work, which are suggestive of her absorption and refinement of various audio and visual cultures that predominate within contemporary media.

Coppola's relationship to this broader transmedia sphere developed quite organically. Before making films, she interned at Chanel and later designed a women's clothing line called Milk Fed sold exclusively in Japan.[3] In 2001, Marc Jacobs chose Sofia to be the face of an ad campaign for his company's new fragrance.[4] Her commercials seem a natural outgrowth of her experience in the fashion world. She also appeared in music videos, including the Black Crowes's 'Sometimes Salvation' (1992), Sonic Youth's 'Mildred Pierce' (1990) and the Chemical Brothers' 'Elektrobank' (1997). After divorcing her first husband, Spike Jonze, in 2003, Sofia became romantically involved with Phoenix's lead singer, Thomas Mars. They had two children together and eventually married in 2011. The couple also collaborated on several occasions. Mars contributed music to two of Coppola's films: *Somewhere* (2010) and *The Bling Ring* (2013). Coppola, on the other hand, directed one Phoenix video, 'Chloroform' (2013) and appeared in another, 'Funky Squaredance' (2000), directed by her brother, Roman.

This chapter examines Coppola's work as a transmedia stylist, paying particular attention to the ways in which she intermingles music, editing, cinematography and design elements to produce moments of bliss or even transcendence. The director has long been noted for the care and discernment she displays in the placement of songs in her films. My concern here, however, is how music acts as a more general template for her audiovisual style, which often emphasizes rhythm, gesture, atmosphere and mood over narrative. By highlighting this dimension of Coppola's work as a transmedia artist, I contend that her style is consistent with a specific strain of contemporary cinema described by Carol Vernallis wherein 'musical structures overlay or supercede narrative ones'.[5]

Coppola is among the most prominent woman directors of the new millennium, and much previous scholarship on her films focuses on the feminine sensibility that imbues her work.[6] In interviews, Coppola has spoken eloquently on the self-consciously 'girlie' qualities she brings to her films, and there is no doubt that these qualities are important to her identity as an artist. My discussion of Coppola, however, takes its point of departure from two other authorial studies, each of which focuses more on the way her tastes in music inform her style: Tim Anderson's excellent analysis of Coppola's 'melodramatic mode' and Justin Wyatt's probing monograph on the director's first film, *The Virgin Suicides* (1999).[7]

Anderson's essay locates Coppola's work within a tradition of melodrama wherein a film's emotional qualities find expression through particular figurations of style. Music plays a particularly key role in this cinematic mode, quite literally supplying the '*melos*' to the melodrama.[8] Anderson also argues that Coppola's films share with melodrama an interest in 'momentary pleasures' that contrast with classical cinema's more linear sense of story time. For Anderson, these modalities of style and time place much greater emphasis on mood and atmosphere rather than story per se, thus enabling Coppola's films to 'center on moments of feminine revelation and change'.[9]

Wyatt's short monograph, on the other hand, takes a multidimensional look at Coppola's debut feature *The Virgin Suicides*, positioning it within a set of distinct, yet overlapping contexts. These include the rise of American independent cinema of the 1990s, Coppola's ambiguous style of narration, her use of music for mood and characterization and the film's design aesthetic, which borrowed from the look of advertisements popular during the 1970s. In his analysis of *The Virgin Suicides*, Wyatt previews several aspects of her work that I take up in more detail as trademarks within Coppola's oeuvre as a transmedia artist.

In the remainder of this chapter I look at three aspects of Coppola's style that cut across her work: (1) the distinctive look she cultivates through a combination of lighting, colour and camera position; (2) ellipsis as a dimension of her style of storytelling and editing and (3) an absurdist, sometimes mordant, humour that threads throughout her films, music videos, ads and television special. My aim is to show how these different elements combine to produce a specific variant on the 'intensified audiovisual aesthetics' found in a variety of different contemporary media.

High concept 2.0: Lighting, production design and cinematography

In his pathfinding book on 1980s Hollywood cinema, Justin Wyatt argues that a number of directors developed a high-concept visual style that derived partly from the look of advertising and music videos.[10] The directors Wyatt associated with this aesthetic, such as Adrian Lyne, Ridley Scott and Tony Scott, all cut their teeth making stylish thirty-second spots. This suggested a fairly direct line of influence where the same techniques used to make products appealing gave films a glossy visual sheen. This approach to visual style, however, was hardly confined to film-makers from the advertising milieux. Indeed, by the late 1980s, high-concept visuals could be found in the work of a former animator, like Tim Burton, or a former costume designer and screenwriter, like Joel Schumacher. Schumacher's 1990 medical potboiler, *Flatliners*, is a case in point. The staging of life and death resuscitation experiments in an empty loft furnishes compositions dominated by warm light, gothic archways and filigreed, decorative window panes – a choice that prioritizes visual flair over dramatic logic.

The high-concept visual style described by Wyatt emerged as a combination of production design elements with cinematographic techniques. Among these was a marked tendency towards hard backlighting with soft fills from the front – an approach that produced highlights on the actors' hair and sharp definition to the outline of their bodies. Cinematographers also sought ways to diffuse light within the frame. Rain-slicked surfaces bounced light to produce patterns of colour and chiaroscuro. Textural elements, such as smoke, steam and mist, make shafts of light visible as contrast to areas of darkness or shadow.

All of these elements are present in *Blade Runner* (1982) and *The Hunger* (1983), films that epitomized the high-concept visual style in the early 1980s. In interviews about *Blade Runner*, Ridley Scott famously said, 'Sometimes the design is the statement.'[11] Moreover, in a comment about the film's elaborate 'inferno' set, the director adds, 'To me, film is like a 700-layer cake.'[12] Scott's simile is particularly telling here, insofar as he acknowledges that *Blade Runner*'s depiction of futuristic urban decay nonetheless has an element of luscious decadence to it.

Although she relies on different techniques than these first-generation high-concept stylists, Coppola's films, music videos and advertisements all share a distinctive look. Indeed, this has become a conspicuous element in their reception. In a description of her commercial work, the London corporate video company, Bold Content, writes, 'Coppola has applied many of her signature film-making techniques to her commercials. This includes plenty of pastel colors, hip soundtracks, and languid camera movements.'[13] Similarly, in text accompanying a video essay, Jacob T. Swinney asks, 'What defines the Sofia Coppola aesthetic? Is it the sublime use of soft and natural lighting? Is it the subtle pastels of the color pallet? Maybe the handheld camera that dizzily floats around the characters?'[14]

Of these elements, Coppola's use of colour and soft lighting may be the most salient, unifying her visual style across a number of different forms. Indeed, some of the most iconic images in Coppola's work are defined by her use of pastels. Think of the various interior spaces of the Lisbon home in *The Virgin Suicides*. The living room is predominantly celadon in hue while the foyer and Cecelia's bedroom feature taupe and lilac walls, respectively. Or recall the pink panties Charlotte wears in the credit sequence of *Lost in Translation* (2003) and the lavender mobile she hangs in her hotel room. Consider also the pastel coloured candies and shoes on display in the famous 'I Want Candy' sequence of *Marie Antoinette* (2006). The film's palette features lots of creams and beiges that are often set off by light yellows, pinks and blues as accent colours.

The same types of colour schemes proliferate in Coppola's ads and music videos. In two of Coppola's ads for Dior – 'Miss Dior Cherie' (2008) and 'Miss Dior Blooming Bouquet' (2013) – the featured models are often draped or surrounded in various shades of pink. At one point, the star of the former, Natalie Portman, falls into a bed of roses that spans the entire spectrum of different pink tones. In the ad's final shot, Portman reclines next to a bottle of Miss Dior perfume against a light pink background. In 'Miss Cherie Dior', a pair of rhyming close-ups show Maryna Linchuk wearing virtually identical fuchsia and pale-yellow sunglasses. Another short sequence of shots shows her in a candy shop, surveying a bevy of pastel coloured bonbons. The final shot shows Linchuk rising above the Paris rooftops, carried aloft by a bunch of pink, white and light blue balloons. Lastly, in her music video for Air's 'Playground Love' (2000), Coppola uses two pieces of pastel coloured chewing gum as a motif. One is wasabi green and the other is bright pink. When shown together, they serve as metonyms for the video's two stars: Josh Hartnett and Kirsten Dunst.

Coppola's use of soft, natural light also proves to be common element across her body of work. In fact, the recurrence of this approach to lighting creates uncanny echoes between her film work and her other projects. Although their editing patterns could not be more different, the slow zooms from *Somewhere* showing Johnny Marco relaxing by the Chateau Marmont pool have the same sun-dappled quality as the pool party in Walt Mink's music video for 'Shine' (1993). Coppola's 2014 ad for Marc Jacobs, 'Daisies', shows young women in white walking through a sunlit field of daisies, their hands brushing over the tops of the flowers. Steff Yotka called it 'basically an abbreviated remake of "The Virgin Suicides", plus Sleigh Bells music'.[15] The lighting and *mise-en-scène* also recall a similar scene from *Marie Antoinette* where the young queen plays with her children on the palace grounds.

In addition to Coppola's use of colour and lighting as signature elements, I propose a third component: a tendency towards frontality in her selection of camera angles. To be sure, Coppola varies her camera angles more than some of her contemporaries, like Wes Anderson. That being said, Coppola employs a rectilinear approach for certain types of shots, especially roomy masters that resemble photographic portraiture. At such moments, Coppola often composes her shots with the subjects perfectly centred and with objects and features of décor balanced in the background *mise-en-scène*, producing a strong sense of bilateral symmetry. Consider the way this functions as a visual motif in *Marie Antoinette* in several shots showing Marie and Louis XIV, flanked by servants, enjoying royal repasts (Figure 6.1). A similar sort

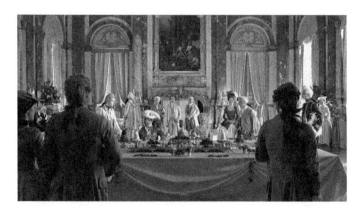

FIGURE 6.1 *Coppola's use of frontal camera positions throughout* Marie Antoinette *establishes a visual motif where royal meals are depicted in the style of eighteenth-century portraiture (*Marie Antoinette, *Sofia Coppola/Dustin O'Halloran, 2006).*

of frontality is present in several shots where Marie is dressed and groomed. The film's first shot, for example, shows Marie reclining as she receives a pedicure, the camera set at a ninety-degree angle from her supine figure.

Marie Antoinette uses this type of frontality for thematic purposes, emphasizing the sense of order and rectitude associated with the monarchy's diplomatic and social protocols. Yet Coppola also uses a suppler version of such frontality in her other films. *Lost in Translation* is a case in point. Think of certain shots of Bob and Charlotte seated at the Park Hyatt bar. Think also of the scene where Charlotte encounters a Japanese bride sheltered by an umbrella as she walks through Tokyo. The bride moves horizontally across the screen at a ninety-degree angle from the camera. Or think of Bob, dressed in his hotel robe and slippers, seated on the edge of his bed, staring out into space. The latter became the keystone image for *Lost in Translation* featured in the film's ads and poster.

Other films provide variants of this approach. Both *Marie Antoinette* and *The Bling Ring* feature montages of shoes and accessories where the camera sometimes takes an overhead position. Here Coppola mimics a style of still photography often found in fashion spreads and gourmet food magazines, intimating her apparent fascination with haute couture and haute cuisine (Figures 6.2 and 6.3). Yet, considering the dramatic contexts in which these montages are embedded, it seems more likely that Coppola is appropriating the visual language of advertising in order to critique consumerism. Tellingly, in *Marie Antoinette* the 'shoes and candy' montage occurs just after Marie's coquettish sexual advances have again been rebuffed by Louis. The sequencing of the scenes suggests that Marie sublimates her unfulfilled sexual desire in a frenzy of female hedonist excess.

The frontal positioning of the camera is a recurrent motif across Coppola's body of work, including her ads, music videos and television work. Yet, it takes on additional significance in moments that display a sense of performativity. The aforementioned scenes of royal ritual in *Marie Antoinette* illustrate this. But the shots of Bob making his Suntory Whiskey commercial in *Lost in Translation* and the long opening shot of Phoenix's 'Chloroform' video, which shows the band onstage silhouetted by a strong backlight, exhibit a similar aesthetic.

As before, the repetition of this visual motif produces continuities across different media. Coppola's presentational style figures prominently in the White Stripes' video for 'I Don't Know What to Do with Myself' (2003). Shot in black and white, the video looks like it could be outtakes from a lingerie shoot as it shows model Kate Moss writhing on a large cube and twirling and spinning around a stripper pole. The first scene of *Somewhere* not only narrativizes Moss's spectacle of feminine pulchritude but doubles the visual pleasure by showing two scantily clad twins performing on stripper poles to the Foo Fighters' 'My Hero' (1997). The frontal camera position taken to record both performances is consistent

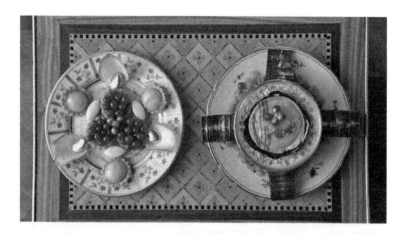

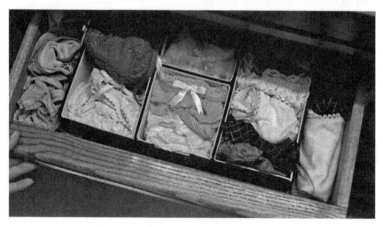

FIGURES 6.2 AND 6.3 *The use of overhead camera angles for shots of food, shoes, jewellery and accessories creates parallels across her body of work as evident in these frames from* Marie Antoinette *(Sofia Coppola/Dustin O'Halloran, 2006) and* The Bling Ring *(Sofia Coppola/Daniel Lopatin and Brian Reitzell, 2013).*

with the sorts of direct address commonly associated with a specific mode of televisuality.

As noted earlier, Coppola's use of colour, lighting and frontality situates her work within a broader turn towards 'intensified audiovisual aesthetics.' These particular stylistic motifs, though, are evident in Coppola's approach to *mise-en-scène* and cinematography considered apart from elements of editing and sound. To fully grasp the line and flow of the director's work, one needs to examine the way these motifs interact with cinema's other formal systems. It is to those aspects of Coppola's style to which I next turn my attention.

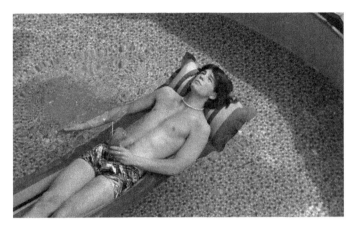

FIGURE 6.4 *This shot of Trip Fontaine is embedded in a music montage accompanied by Heart's 'Magic Man'* (The Virgin Suicides, *Sofia Coppola/Air, 1999*).

The unsaid and the space between: Coppola's use of temporal and narrative ellipsis

At the 2004 Oscar ceremony, when Coppola accepted the award for Best Original Screenplay, she thanked the many directors who inspired her, a list that included Antonioni, Wong Kar-Wai and Godard. Such acknowledgement may be the director's most forthright statement about her aesthetic sensibility, positioning *Lost in Translation* as the heir to a long-standing tradition of global art cinema. Among the various things that Coppola's work shares with these film-makers is an elliptical approach to storytelling, one that features psychologically complex characters who have difficulty expressing or even understanding their own motivations. Moreover, some Coppola films display an interest in narrative ambiguity insofar as they leave key questions in the story unresolved. *Lost in Translation* epitomizes many of these tendencies in Coppola's *oeuvre*. The film's ending shows Bob whispering something to Charlotte unheard by the audience. For years, fans of the film speculated on just what was said. Coppola refused to reveal what the line was, adding that it was unscripted and that only Bill Murray and Scarlett Johansson knew what Bob confided to Charlotte. In 2007, a YouTube video purported to use digital audio tools to reveal the dialogue buried in the audio mix: 'I have to be leaving but I won't let that come between us. Okay?' According to *Vulture*, this proved to be the most popular theory of what was said, but it was hardly definitive. Soon after, other videos came along offering completely different interpretations of the whispered line's denotative meaning.[16]

The moment is unusual in Coppola's work in the degree to which it flaunts a gap in the viewer's knowledge. But its mystery is partly preserved by a larger uncertainty about Bob and Charlotte's relationship in *Lost in Translation*. The film not only captures the characters' emotional bond but also underlines their reticence to share their feelings. Is the film a drama of unfulfilled romantic desire? A suggestion Coppola herself made by comparing *Lost in Translation* to David Lean's *Brief Encounter* (1945).[17] If so, then one wonders what prevents Bob and Charlotte from acting on those romantic impulses. In Lean's film, Laura refuses Alec's overtures in part because of her children and her reluctance to flaunt the social mores of mid-century Britain. Coppola's story eliminates such obvious impediments, thereby encouraging speculation about why Bob and Charlotte reconcile themselves to their respective unhappy marriages. This also enables viewers to posit another basis for their emotional connection. Are they simply kindred spirits cast adrift in the dreamy night life of Tokyo? Does Bob admire Charlotte's youth and independence, a proposition floated in some of the alternate theories of his whispered line at the end?[18] Or do Bob and Charlotte spend time together to simply alleviate the boredom caused by their extended stays at the Park Hyatt Tokyo?

Similar sorts of ambiguities about character motivations pop up in other Coppola films. For example, Coppola became interested in adapting Jeffrey Eugenides novel, *The Virgin Suicides*, because she saw the central story as being about 'the extraordinary power of the unfathomable'.[19] Teenage depression and even suicide is not an unusual topic in cinema. However, Coppola's film hinges on the question of why four sisters would form a suicide pact and then invite boys from the neighbourhood to witness their acts of self-destruction. As *Cinema Review* notes, Eugenides novel was conceived as a 'detective story without a solution'.[20] Offering no easy answers or pat bromides, both works dramatize our fascination with the mysteries of adolescence that Eugenides himself describes as a 'baffling, romantic, highly delusional state of yearning'.[21]

Other Coppola films create a sense of ambiguity by minimizing the kinds of backstory that is common in more conventional Hollywood films. For example, *Somewhere* offers very little information about Johnny Marco's relationship with his ex-wife, the reasons for their separation or the kinds of custody arrangements put in place for their daughter Cleo. Johnny is saddled with the sudden responsibility of caring for Cleo when his ex-wife unexpectedly takes an extended trip. Coppola cast actor Stephen Dorff because he had the aura of a 'bad boy' actor who nonetheless evinced a certain sweetness and sincerity.[22] Avoiding the scenes of conflict or crisis commonly seen in earlier Hollywood films about fatherhood, such as *To Kill a Mockingbird* (1962) or *Kramer Vs. Kramer* (1979), Coppola depicts Johnny's growing care and concern for Cleo through very mundane activities: preparing meals, playing Wii Sports and Guitar Hero, lounging by the pool, driving to school or skating practice and sampling gelato in a Milanese hotel room. Johnny's confessional breakdown proves the exception to *Somewhere*'s strategies of de-dramatization. Yet even this moment is prepared by Coppola's careful eye for detail and her ability to use the unsaid to express what Dennis Lim describes as Johnny's 'incipient identity crisis'.[23]

Coppola's interest in social ritual is occasionally recruited as a strategy for de-dramatization, offering a subtle means of conveying the emotional devastation of family tragedy. A very simple pair of scenes from *Marie Antoinette* offers a potent illustration. The birth of Marie's fourth child is commemorated in the hanging of a new family portrait. The infant's death is represented by the removal of the portrait and the subsequent hanging of an altered version of it, one in which the baby's existence is simply blotted out of the painting. The series of shots is notable both for its pithiness and for Coppola's decision to downplay such a significant narrative event. (Biopics, thy name is suffering!) Yet it also contributes to the story's development in other ways. It signals a tonal shift, introducing the sense of sorrow that suffuses the film's final twenty minutes. It also supplies motivation for Marie's decision to stay with Louis in Versailles, despite her advisors' repeated pleas that she flee to Switzerland.

Up until now, my discussion of ellipsis has centred on Coppola's approach to storytelling, which borrows from European art cinema and is sometimes indirect, allusive and dispassionate. But we might also consider Coppola's audiovisual style with regard to a more basic understanding of ellipsis – that is, the use of editing to omit stretches of story time. Coppola's films frequently alternate between fairly conventional dialogue scenes that rely on analytic editing techniques, such as shot/reverse shot, and brief montages that fragment time and space, substituting line and flow for scenic coherence.

Here again, *Marie Antoinette*'s famous 'I Want Candy' (Bow Wow Wow, 2006), sequence serves as a paradigmatic instance of Coppola's deployment of 'intensified audiovisual aesthetics'. As Tim Anderson notes, Coppola's films suspend narrative in favour of exploring character subjectivity – a cinema of heightened moments rather than straight-line stories. Popular music often bears considerable weight in these moments of audiovisual confluence, especially in giving the viewer access to subjectivity. According to Anderson, Coppola's collaboration with music supervisor Brian Reitzell enables the soundtrack to 'reveal characters' states of mind, specifically what they themselves cannot communicate'.[24] The 'I Want Candy' sequence exemplifies Coppola's ability to compose a mood, functioning as a three-minute montage set off from the more conventional dramatic moments that surround it.[25] Indeed, like some music videos, the sequence is organized as a series of temporally discontinuous shots, with the cutting patterns following the musical phrases of Bow Wow Wow's recording rather than the other way around. To heighten this sense of spatial and temporal fragmentation,

Coppola uses jump cuts in shots where the camera remains stationary as different styles of shoes and cakes are substituted one for another in an orgy of consumption. At one point, Coppola even deploys some very simple animation techniques to show a beautifully arranged platter of candies that seemingly disappear piece by piece.

'I Want Candy' might well be the clearest instance of this tendency towards ellipsis and temporal discontinuity, but similar sequences crop up throughout Coppola's film work. The introduction of Trip Fontaine in *The Virgin Suicides* fits this mould, using Heart's 'Magic Man' to accompany shots of Trip swaggering through the school's hallways, smoking pot and lounging in his pool (Figure 6.4). The 'shoes and accessories' montage in *The Bling Ring*, set to Sleigh Bells' 'Crown on the Ground', is an obvious correlate. So is Bob's cab ride to the Tokyo airport in *Lost in Translation*, which is underscored by The Jesus and Mary Chain's 'Just Like Honey'.

These are among Coppola's most iconic 'musical moments', but these patterns of audiovisual style are evident in more jejune scenes. Marie's aforementioned frolic through the field with her children is closer to a home movie than a music video, but it displays the same fragmentation of time and space. The same is true of the club scenes, party scenes and heist scenes in *The Bling Ring*. In adopting a similar audiovisual style for all of them, Coppola underlines the empty hedonism that pervades every aspect of the characters' lifestyle. On occasion, Coppola's aesthetic of discontinuity extends to scenes involving brief snatches of source music. Bob and Charlotte's night of karaoke is condensed into excerpts from their respective performances of Roxy Music's 'More than This' (1995), Elvis Costello's '(What's So Funny 'Bout) Peace, Love and Understanding' (1979) and the Pretenders' 'Brass in Pocket' (1980).

The directorial skills that Coppola displays in these 'musical moments' translate quite directly into her work for advertising spots and music videos, which display the same keen eye for detail, mastery of mood and stylistic emphasis on line and flow. Her videos for Air's 'Playground Love' and Kevin Shields's 'City Girl' (2003) reedit footage from *The Virgin Suicides* and *Lost in Translation*, respectively, functioning as music video counterparts to more conventional movie trailers. In the video for The Flaming Lips' 'This Here Giraffe' (1995) Coppola intercuts shots of the band performing with flashes of posters and flyers, brief shots of singer Wayne Coyne shaving, lateral tracking shots of a suburban neighbourhood and glimpses of the band's visit to a local zoo. Coppola's 2012 ad for H&M's Marni collection depicts a day in the life of a young woman taking a trip to Morocco. It begins with shots of the main character drowsing by a pool. It then shows a series of brief disconnected sequences of the woman driving, walking through the Moroccan desert, flirting with a well-dressed man at an elegant party and taking a nocturnal swim. The ad culminates with a romantic kiss with the man from the party. The woman awakens, though, to realize it was all a dream.

The consistency with which Coppola employs this elliptical approach demonstrates the degree to which she has absorbed the influence of MTV. Yet Coppola's identity as transmedia auteur also stems from her ability to create a unique strain within the 'audiovisual turn' described by Vernallis as a more general aesthetic shift augured by post-millennial forms and technologies. Her reliance on temporal discontinuities as a structuring element of her 'musical moments' when combined with pastels, natural light and frontal angles produce an audiovisual style that prioritizes mood and atmosphere over narrative salience, thereby creating an evanescence that mixes the observational style of the art house with the bursts of colour, rhythm and flow seen in music videos.

Pastiche, defamiliarization and absurdism: Sofia Coppola as transmedia humourist

In this section, I consider the role of humour in Coppola's work as a transmedia artist. To be sure, one would be hard-pressed to call any of Sofia Coppola's films a comedy. *The Bling Ring* may be the closest, but its mode is social satire, a far cry from the romantic comedies and raunchy *homme-coms* that comprise Hollywood's more traditional fare. Instead, Coppola's emphasis on mood and atmosphere is often keyed to her films' melancholic tone. Still, a focus solely on Coppola's cinematic output obscures a strain of humour that cuts across her advertisements, music videos and television work.

The obvious point of entry into Coppola's comic sensibility is her Netflix special, *A Very Murray Christmas* (2015), an affectionate pastiche of holiday-themed variety programmes of the 1970s and 1980s. Bill Murray is the avuncular, if mildly dyspeptic, host, updating the role played by Perry Como, Andy Williams and Bing Crosby in previous Christmas specials. Moreover, like Bob Hope's and Dean Martin's specials, which interspersed bits of comedy between the musical numbers, Coppola's programme features Amy Poehler, Chris Rock, Michael Cera and Maya Rudolph in key supporting roles, adding an element of showbiz satire to the more familiar 'saving Christmas' tropes. And, although Coppola's predecessors often mixed country musicians with pop performers, such as Jerry Reed, Mel Tillis, Crystal Gayle, Dionne Warwick and Andy Gibb, Coppola tweaks that formula by having Murray duet with talent from the indie music scene. Coppola's inspiration for this casting decision seems to be Bing Crosby's 1977 Christmas special where the elderly crooner famously sang 'The Little Drummer Boy' with David Bowie.

In an interview with *Time*, Coppola explained that she was inspired by the somewhat threadbare motivation for musical performances in those holiday specials, which 'didn't have a lot of logic to them. They were just kind of getting people together to sing holiday songs.'[26] To that end, Coppola casts several noted musicians in goofy cameo roles: David Johansen as a pompadoured bartender, Jenny Lewis as an amiable cocktail server and Phoenix as a quartet of French chefs. Yet, in keeping with the older specials' spirit, Coppola also contains musical numbers by cast members known more as actors. Playing a troubled bride and groom, Jason Schwartzman and Rashida Jones duet on Todd Rundgren's 'I Saw the Light' (1972). Maya Rudolph channels some Phil Spector–era soul on 'Christmas Baby Please Come Home' (Darlene Love, 1963). Schwartzman also plays drums on Phoenix's seemingly impromptu performance of 'Alone on Christmas Day' (Phoenix, 2015). The entire ensemble joins in on a sing-along of the Pogues's 'Fairytale of New York' (1988). This musical choice not only burnishes Coppola's credentials as a savvy *melomane* but also blends seamlessly with the show's more traditional carols.[27]

A Very Murray Christmas concludes with a dream ballet starring George Clooney and Miley Cyrus. The segment resolves an earlier dangling cause by paying off on Jackie the Talent Agent's proposal for an alternative special. It even features Cyrus in a red mini-dress, adding a bit of erotic sizzle to the otherwise solemn performance of 'Silent Night'. Its elaborate staging and set design pays homage to the production numbers beamed to American television sets in the 1970s on a weekly basis, sort of a live action version of *The Simpson Family Smile-Time Variety Hour*. Clooney smirks like a latter-day Dean Martin, and Cyrus bounces around like Juliet Prowse as a tattooed, manic pixie dream girl. Besides channelling 1970s-era glitz, the sequence also showcases Coppola's fondness for the 'strange bedfellows' oddities produced by her predecessors' mashups of different showbiz personalities.

To be sure, *A Very Murray Christmas* aims more for mirth than belly laughs. Yet its comic appeal also depends on its layered references to Bill Murray's larger star persona. On the one hand, the yuletide setting of the film invariably recalls *Scrooged* (Richard Donner, 1988), which Coppola herself calls out as a classic along with Frank Capra's *It's a Wonderful Life* (1946). On the other, the placement of Murray in the Café Carlyle invokes Nick Sands, the lounge lizard – one of the comedian's most popular characters during his run on *Saturday Night Live*. And, in a more reflexive vein, these scenes allude to the aforementioned scene of Bob performing karaoke in *Lost in Translation*. Coppola herself acknowledges that the special sprang from similar creative impulse: 'I always like to see Bill (Murray) sing'.[28]

Coppola's stated interest in making 'something joyful' tacitly acknowledges the more downbeat tone of her films. Yet she also hints at a strain of gentle humour that emerges at particular moments in her films, music videos and advertisements. In some cases, this involves the knowing citation or inversion of well-established tropes. For example, when Bob yells for assistance on the Park Hyatt's exercise bike in *Lost in Translation*, the image of him furiously pedalling recalls other sight gags involving mechanical malfunctions. Think of Charlie Chaplin on the assembly line in *Modern Times* (1936) or Jerry

Lewis's fateful encounter with a vacuum cleaner in *Who's Minding the Store?* (1962). Towards the start of the Flaming Lips' 'This Here Giraffe', Wayne Coyne is shown singing and playing his guitar while seated in his bedroom, an image of domesticity and suburbanism that upends the more customary image of male rock stars as rebellious, working-class heroes. The images of Maryna Linchuk floating above Paris in 'Miss Cherie Rose' tap into the iconography of comic fantasy, recirculating a visual trope found in films as diverse as Disney's *Mary Poppins* (1964) and Vittorio de Sica's *Miracle in Milan* (1951). Finally, scenes of American film stars appearing in foreign media outlets in *Lost in Translation* and *Somewhere* evoke the 'fish out of water' conceit that remains a dominant plotline of contemporary comedy.

Coppola's films also display elements of absurdism associated with social protocols, work routines and genre hybridity. *Marie Antoinette* offers excellent examples of the former. The presence of family members and courtiers in moments of intimacy, such as Louis and Marie's honeymoon and their first child's birth, fits traditional definitions of comic incongruity. Similarly, in *Somewhere*, Coppola sought to document the life of a working actor without actually showing him participating in a shoot. Instead, we see Johnny Marco doing promotional appearances, press junkets and the like. In one of the film's most memorable moments, Johnny undergoes the preparation of a plasticene make-up effect. He is forced to sit for hours with a layer of goop covering his face, evoking the image of a classic movie monster. Cinematographer Harris Savides underlines the tediousness of this routine by showing Johnny sitting quietly in a long, slow zoom (Figure 6.5). To heighten

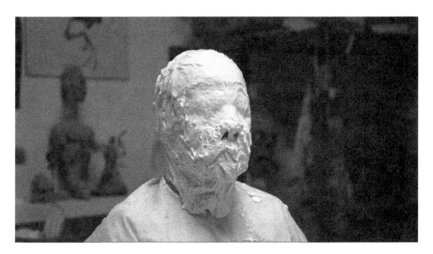

FIGURE 6.5 *This frame from a long zoom in on Johnny Marco's face encased in plasticene is typical of the absurdist humour found throughout Coppola's oeuvre (*Somewhere, Sofia Coppola/Phoenix, 2010).

the comic effect, Coppola even added the sound of a nearby phone in post-production to underline the notion that Johnny may have been forgotten.

Coppola's absurdist streak takes a slightly different form in *The Bling Ring*. Here comic incongruity is produced by the film's mixture of elements from the heist thriller with those of teen comedies. Unlike most caper films, which show teams outlining intricate plans that depend upon precise timing and careful execution, the Bling Ring's break-ins prove to be ridiculously easy. They simply monitor social media and await opportunities when their celebrity targets leave their houses vacant. Although the group's blithe ignorance of security camera footage eventually catches up with them, they mostly enter the homes they rob through open windows or doors. Adding to the film's absurdist qualities, Coppola also shows her merry band of thieves boasting about their exploits in scenes commonly associated with teen comedies: house parties, classes at school and trips to the mall. By substituting callow youth for the heist film's usual depictions of clever, sometimes hardened criminals, Coppola underlines their vacuity and stupidity. Many caper films show members of the team getting caught because they can't resist the temptation to spend their ill-gotten gains. Yet Coppola spins this generic trope by showing how Rebecca's visit to her divorced dad inadvertently implicates her in an additional federal crime when she transports stolen goods across state lines. The film closes with Nicki's talk show appearance after serving a few months of jail time. She humble-brags about the fact that her cell was next to Lindsay Lohan's. During the interview, Nicki shamelessly shills for her new website in a rather transparent attempt to capitalize on her sudden notoriety. The irony that Nicki now rubs shoulders with other tabloid celebrities may seem screamingly obvious to some viewers. Yet it is consistent with *The Bling Ring*'s broader interest in social satire, a mode activated by Coppola's absurdist collision of different genre tropes.

Finally, one also discerns an incipient absurdist tone in Coppola's video for the Flaming Lips' 'This Here Giraffe'. Admittedly, the band itself has long been known for its absurdist streak, which is especially evident in their live shows. For years, the Lips have invited fans to dress up in animal costumes and dance onstage. Similarly, as *The Register-Guard* notes, singer Wayne Coyne sometimes arrives on stage encased in a large clear plastic ball, an image reminiscent of a 'giant hamster running its wheel'.[29] Yet, the video's Spartan production values and Coppola's light-hearted treatment evoke the goofiness found in early Scopitones. Indeed, the band's trip to the zoo might be read as an allusion to the Exciters' famous short for 'Tell Him' (1963), in which shows Brenda Reid and the other vocalists make a heartfelt plea for emotional honesty to a polar bear, a lioness and a pair of swans.

A similar comic sensibility is evident in Coppola's holiday ads for The Gap, which debuted in 2014. 'Mistletoe' depicts the awkward exchange that occurs when an older teen makes a sly romantic overture to a middle-aged woman standing beneath the titular plant. To underline the irony of the situation, Coppola scores the scene with The Promise's 'I'm Not Ready for Love' (2007). 'Crooner', on the other hand, shows a young boy lip-synching Johnnie Ray's 'Cry' to a family gathering at Christmas. This spot's humour arises from the incongruity of a small child aping the poses of singer popular more than a half-century ago, perhaps the only heartthrob to perform wearing a hearing aid. It also seems oddly reminiscent of Dean Stockwell's famous rendition of 'In Dreams' from *Blue Velvet* (Lynch, 1987, discussed in Holly Rogers' chapter elsewhere in this book), albeit staged as a scene out of *Bugsy Malone* (Alan Parker, 1976).

Conclusion

As these examples indicate, Coppola's films are noted for their dark, dour tone, but they also contain moments of levity, whimsy and absurdist humour. This tendency is perhaps even more pronounced in Coppola's identity as a transmedia artist where the audiovisual forms with which she works (ads, music videos and variety shows) depend less on forward narrative movement and more on the momentary pleasures of synchronicity, line and flow. Here, as with her narrative features, music plays an especially important role, both by creating mood and atmosphere and by serving as a model of architectonic structure through which elements of colour, light, movement and editing interact to produce a unified style. Coppola's films mix dreamy visuals, evocative music and jaded social satire in ways that enable them to perform complex cultural work.

Throughout her films, Coppola focuses on characters that crave human connection, but rarely achieve it. This restlessness, though, is set off by her ability to capture the particular milieux that these characters inhabit: the suffocating probity of 1970s suburbia; the pomp and circumstance of eighteenth-century Versailles; the celebrated, if modestly decadent, luxury of the Chateau Marmont; and the bonhomie of the Café Carlyle. What perhaps unifies Coppola's transmedia artistry more than anything else is her almost ethnographic attention to details of lifestyle, her acute eye for décor, fashion, interior design and consumer goods. Her attention to these aspects of lifestyle dramatizes the ways in which her lost heroes sublimate their desires into foods and fashions. Such pleasures may be transitory and, thus, cannot completely ward off the emptiness and ennui of modern life. Yet they are pleasures nonetheless, and as Coppola's ads and films suggest, their very power rests on the lure and promise of consumer capitalism that never is completely fulfilled.

CHAPTER 7

Short-form media as style lab: The education of Michael Bay

Mark Kerins

Director Michael Bay may be the film industry's most reviled film-maker – thanks to bombastic, explosion-filled films like the *Transformers* franchise (2007–present) and the *Bad Boys* films (1995, 2003), Bay is frequently dismissed by scholars and reviewers alike as the poster child for Hollywood's emphasis on visual effects, spectacle and style at the expense of story and narrative. His films are almost reflexively panned for storytelling issues, both moment-to-moment (critics slam a disjointed visual style seemingly lacking spatial and narrative coherence) and overall (reviewers routinely catalogue the films' plot holes, unbelievable stories and stereotypical characters).

Plenty of other directors make worse, less coherent movies – Uwe Boll and McG come to mind – yet Bay occupies a unique role as the 'face' of bad Hollywood film-making. Perhaps due to his success, Bay seems more frequently targeted for critical bashing – both by serious film thinkers and by moviegoers at large – than any other film-maker. Indeed, he ranks among the few celebrity directors whose name is recognizable even to those who do not frequent his films. Consider, for instance, his appearance on *The Simpsons* (episode 'Mathlete's Feat', aired 17 May 2017) featuring elementary school students transforming then blowing up, or the *Robot Chicken* parody trailer for 'a Michael Bay film' (episode 'President Evil', aired 28 September 2008) consisting largely of random explosions – in both cases, the shows' jokes only work because everyone *knows* Michael Bay and the stereotypes about his style.

Yet his status as a household name also reflects why at least from one perspective (and an important one, given the film industry is ultimately the film *business*), these critiques of Bay miss the point: his films make money, and lots of it. In terms of sheer box office revenues, Bay is among the most successful film-makers of all time, with one of the top five cumulative grosses of any director *ever*. Moreover, he has achieved this status not through a couple of enormous hits or by making many mildly successful movies over a long career, but by *consistently* turning out highly successful and profitable films. True, the *Transformers* franchise accounts for a disproportionate share of his box office, with worldwide grosses on his five films in that series averaging over $870 million apiece (earning returns before marketing costs of more than *half a billion dollars each*). Yet even removing that entire series from his resume, Bay's remaining films have still yielded nearly two billion dollars in box office receipts on about $700 million of total budgets. His sole financial 'flop' – sci-fi thriller *The Island* (2005) – *still* ultimately grossed more than it cost to make, a boast few veteran Hollywood directors could make.

Certainly box office returns are imperfect measures of creative success or audience satisfaction (plenty of people have paid to see movies they did not particularly enjoy). Yet these numbers speak to the disconnect between Bay's films' financial success and the near-hatred of many scholars and critics for those films. This chapter offers one partial explanation for that disparity, arguing that the lens through which most film critics and scholars evaluate feature films – that of the traditional cinematic storytelling often described in film studies as Classic Hollywood Cinema – may not be the right tool for dissecting Bay's particular style.

To be sure, this is not the first piece to suggest Bay's style is not appropriately judged by the rules of classical cinema. As Bruce Bennett writes in 'The Cinema of Michael Bay: An Aesthetic of Excess', 'to understand the appeal [of Bay's films], it is necessary to employ a critical frame that is not dogmatically oriented around narrative continuity, formal unity and internal coherence and instead acknowledges the way that these films are dynamic components of a heterogeneous popular cultural field that incorporates elements of trash, kitsch and elite culture'.[1] An integral part of this 'heterogeneous popular cultural field' is the non-cinema audiovisual media, and Bennett explicitly acknowledges these forms' impact in noting that contemporary directors' styles 'have become increasingly televisual, influenced by the comparative speed and discontinuity of music videos, adverts, magazine programmes, news broadcasts and serial dramas'.[2]

While accurate overall, Bennett here paints with a broad brush; it is hardly surprising to say that any of today's feature film-makers, including Bay, have been impacted by all the other media forms that pervade contemporary society. Thus where Bennett and others note Bay has been *influenced* by other media forms, this chapter puts a much finer point on that general claim, suggesting that it is precisely Bay's history *as a transmedia artist*, cutting his directorial teeth making commercials and music videos, that explains so much of his film-making style. This background comes through in his visual approach, in his use of sound and, crucially, in the differences between the principles underlying his film-making and those on which classical character-driven narrative film is based. Criticizing Bay because his movies do not adhere to the stylistic or storytelling logic of Classic Hollywood Cinema is not just to apply the 'wrong' framework for evaluation, but to miss the effect of what he *does* do; analysis of his work in light of the norms of music videos and commercials helps illuminate both the background behind Bay's style and how that style works.

Music videos as training ground

Bay's music videos offer a clearer lens into his filmic sensibilities than his commercials due to the practical workflow differences between the two forms; in music videos the director often comes up with the concept, and almost always has free rein over its execution, while in commercials the norm is for an advertising agency to develop the concept (possibly even storyboarding the whole piece) then hire a director to execute the actual production within those tight parameters. So this piece focuses principally on his music videos, where Bay likely had far more freedom to follow his own creative impulses, with his commercials brought in where relevant.

Music video as a form is aesthetically both more flexible *and* more rigidly defined than the traditional feature film. To the former point, a music video's image track might take any number of forms: conveying a short narrative with a beginning, middle and end; creating a vague sense of story through mood and atmosphere; or having no narrative elements at all. It might incorporate concert performance footage, show the band performing in an abstract space created for the video or include no musical performance at all – and if the video does include musical performance, those shots may or may not tie into a separate narrative. This variety of forms stands in contrast to the feature film, where both fiction and documentary audiences generally expect a 'story' of some sort, with all the shots fitting together to serve that core through line.

But despite this flexibility, music video operates under some constraints other audiovisual media do not. While 'feature film' can describe everything from character studies to comedies to musicals to documentaries to action films, a music video operates within carefully prescribed limits: it's an audiovisual piece with a visual track created to complement a pre-recorded piece of music (almost invariably a radio-friendly song by a popular musical act). The length of the video is thus essentially dictated by the length of the song (with an occasional brief prologue or epilogue); while it has recently grown more acceptable for a song to stop in the middle of a music video to allow for more narrative scenes, in the late 1980s and early 1990s, when Bay was cutting his teeth, this was rarely seen. The few contemporaneous exceptions were big-budget videos for well-established stars (e.g. Michael Jackson's 'Thriller' (1983) and 'Black or White' (1991)) that were as much short films with musical interludes as they were 'music videos'.

In short, in the vast majority of cases, the music video director's job was (and usually still is) to create an interesting visual track for an existing and immutable soundtrack. It is hardly surprising that music video has proven a fertile early training ground for so many successful directors – cinema is commonly considered a visuals-centric medium, and music video directors can generally ignore the challenges of dialogue and sound design, focusing their attentions entirely on crafting images. Narrative-style music videos give film-makers the opportunity to practice telling a story *entirely* through image, without the hassle or crutch of dialogue, a skill highly regarded in feature-film directors. Yet despite this emphasis on purely visual narration, music video paradoxically remains an intrinsically audio-driven form – the project begins with the soundtrack, and the visual approach taken must somehow 'fit' the song for which the video is being made.

Sound-driven storytelling

These two aspects of music video – the visual stylistic freedom it offers and its audio-centric nature – provide a productive pair of starting points for examining how Michael Bay's early work shaped his style. Since the influence of the latter is more easily apparent in Bay's later work, it will serve as a better entry point into this exploration. As noted above, the music video is a *sound*-centric form, where the visuals have no reason to exist without the soundtrack. The goal of a music video director, then, is to create an image track that pairs well with the pre-existing music track, the combination of the two modalities ideally enhancing the experience of the song. Effective pairings result in part from finding moments of connection between the image and the soundtracks. The obvious example would be seeing a singer lip-synching the lyrics in time with the song, but any number of different connections can similarly link the two components. A change in colour, a camera movement, a cut – any of these visual elements synchronized perfectly with something in the song (a downbeat, a drum hit, a sung word) create the sense of a 'match' between the visuals and the music. One common criticism of Bay is that his movies are 'cut like music videos', which is usually shorthand for them being cut too fast (an issue discussed later in this chapter) – indeed, the very first sentence on Bay's

Wikipedia page notes his films are 'characterized by fast cutting'.[3] Yet from a music video perspective, fast cutting makes sense. Music cognition research demonstrates audiences will accept virtually *any* music/image pairing with enough 'accent points' where image and sound somehow 'match',[4] synching cuts with musical beats is one of the clearest and most common ways to create these 'accent points', and *faster* cutting allows for more cuts and hence more potential points of connection.

Bay's music videos offer numerous moments where the soundtrack drives decisions in the image track to create moments of connection between the two. Now, the same could be said of virtually any decent music video – such 'accent points' are a core component of the form, and most music videos' image tracks are shaped to help create them. But it is worth noting the rigour with which Bay employs this strategy. In particular, the times when he deviates from his trademark fast cutting are dictated by *musical*, rather than visual or narrative, demands. Some excellent illustrations can be found in Bay's 'I'd Do Anything for Love (But I Won't Do That)' (1993), one of three videos he directed for songs from Meat Loaf's *Bat Out of Hell II* album. As one would expect from Bay, most of this video is cut very quickly, starting with an opening chase sequence that crams over forty cuts into its first thirty seconds. For most of the video's entire length, cuts occur at a similar (if slightly slower) pace, about one per second. Yet in two places, this pacing slows down dramatically.

The first of these comes after the instrumental introduction, when we hear the first lyrics (Figure 7.1). Here Bay holds on a single shot of the singer for a whopping *twenty-eight seconds* – for perspective, this single shot

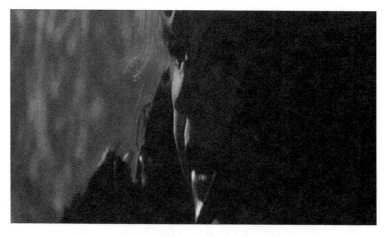

FIGURE 7.1 *Introducing Meat Loaf as the Beast, this shot holds for nearly thirty seconds. 'I'd Do Anything for Love (But I Won't Do That)' (Michael Bay, 1993, performed by Meat Loaf, written by Jim Steinman).*

thus accounts for over 6 per cent of the video's entire length. The second slowdown occurs near the end of the video, during a duet section between Meat Loaf and the object of his affections (starting ~6:36); no single shot here lasts quite as long as the twenty-eight second one near the video's start, but several successive shots each last over three seconds (an eternity in Bay time), with nine-second and seventeen-second shots among them. In this case one might argue that the visual slowdown allows us to focus on the characters' faces and emotions for their climactic duet – though this does not explain why some of the longest shots are not *of* them – but in the earlier slowdown there's no 'narrative' reason whatsoever for the change of pace. Thus a better explanation is that both these changes in *visual* rhythm are designed to parallel simultaneous *sonic* changes. Musically, these two moments are unusual within this song for their instrumentation, stripped-down to the singer(s) and a piano melody. The slower visual cutting parallels that simplicity, and this coordination is heightened after the first slowdown when the cutting pace picks back up dramatically just as the rest of the instruments – notably a strong drum track – kick back in.

Bay's videos offer plenty of other examples of such sound-driven visuals; the key point here is that Bay honed his craft in a form where visual style works in tight coordination with the soundtrack – and each is used to draw attention to certain aspects of the other. One of the intriguing results of the aforementioned research on 'accent points' is that pairing different musical stimuli with the same visual piece draws audience attentions to different aspects of the visuals, depending on where they perceive moments of matching between the two modalities.[5] Consciously or not, music video makers understand this as a key reason the form works – while some points of connection are created intentionally, others emerge unexpectedly from pairing a particular image and musical moment. Bay appears to have internalized this knowledge and brought it to his feature film-making. Often the soundtracks to his feature films convey important information about the story or the visuals; rather than playing a secondary or supporting role to the story-carrying visuals, it is the interaction *between* image and sound that points the audience to salient features of the visuals and thus guides them through the story.

I have written elsewhere about how the opening sequence of *The Rock* (1996) uses sound to add context to otherwise ambiguous images, as well as to draw viewers' attentions to key elements in the image track they might otherwise miss.[6] But this approach is not unique to *The Rock* – rather, it's a consistent component of Bay's film-making style. And perhaps nowhere is his reliance on the sound-image interaction more apparent than in his infamously chaotic action sequences. Consider as a typical example a sequence from *Transformers: Dark of the Moon* (2011) in which the heroic Autobots are escorting an ally along a highway when they are attacked by the villainous Decepticons. Visually, this sequence is classic Bay, with plenty of wanton destruction and explosions, lots of shots cut quickly together, and so much happening so quickly it is difficult to visually follow exactly where all the characters are and who is doing what. Yet the sound mix is neither overpoweringly loud nor overwhelmingly busy, as the visuals might lead one to expect. Rather, the soundtrack highlights one or two sonic elements at a time, guiding viewers' eyes to the corresponding key visual elements. When the Decepticon SUVs transform into their robot forms, the soundtrack eliminates the sounds of the dozens of other cars on the road, playing just the transforming sounds and thereby drawing our attentions to their on-screen source. Similarly, while many of the Decepticons' random acts of destruction go without accompanying sound effects, the soundtrack not only puts in but foregrounds the sound of a highway sign being knocked down – thus signalling its importance. Sure enough, a couple shots later the downed sign is used as a ramp to get a couple vehicles airborne, and the audience knows how it got there rather than wondering why there's a ramp in the middle of the highway (Figure 7.2).

Lutz Koepnick describes Bay's use of sound in part as 'compensating for certain deficits of high-velocity visibility', a perfect encapsulation of how reliant the breakneck speed of Bay's visuals is on the accompanying sounds.[7] Bay's soundtracks function like an art museum audio guide, leading our attentions one by one to different elements in a painting or particular paintings in a gallery, telling us which things are important to notice and allowing us to ignore those of less value. He also uses the soundtrack to provide information not always apparent in the image track – in the *Transformers* movies, for instance, the Autobots and Decepticons have significantly different 'transforming' sound effects (the Autobots' more electronic/pleasing, the Decepticons' more metallic/grating), so even in tight

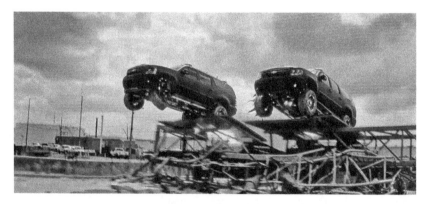

FIGURE 7.2 *Where did these ramps in the middle of the highway come from? Luckily, the soundtrack draws our attention to the signs falling over in a previous shot.* Transformers: Dark of the Moon *(Michael Bay, 2011).*

shots where the audience can't *see* exactly what's happening, the audio helps them distinguish the heroes from the villains.

This way of using the soundtrack is related to, but distinct from, the 'ultrafield' effect described in *Beyond Dolby (Stereo)*, in which responsibility for spatial information and coherence is offloaded from the image track to a multichannel soundtrack.[8] The multichannel ultrafield allows the visual track a greater freedom to dispense with conventional continuity rules in its cinematography and editing, which certainly fits with Bay's approach to action sequences. And Bay certainly makes heavy use of multichannel sound – indeed, aspects of his films have even been designed specifically to take advantage of new sound formats like Dolby Atmos.[9] But he's doing more than simply transferring some spatial responsibilities from image to sound: he's using the soundtrack as an ongoing primer for how to 'read' the visuals. And it's difficult not to interpret this reliance on audiovisual relations as an artefact of his music video roots.

Considering Bay's feature films in the light of their reliance on image-sound interactions, some common criticisms of his work read less as objective critiques and more as the results of applying image-centric analysis to works designed around a different cinematic model. Roger Ebert's review of *Transformers: Dark of the Moon*, source of the highway chase discussed above, includes several such condemnations of Bay's films, describing a battle as 'incomprehensible Autobots and Decepticons sliced up into spurts of action with no sense of the space they occupy' and lamenting 'I have a quaint notion that one of the purposes of editing is to make it clear why one shot follows another, or why several shots occur in the order that they do. *Transformers 3* has long stretches involving careless and illogical assemblies of inelegant shots.'[10] Whether Ebert's negative views on this film overall are warranted is a separate question, but implicit to these comments and others like them is a belief feature films should adhere to Classic Hollywood Cinema style, with the visuals spatially and narratively clear in and of themselves, rather than allowing for the possibility that perceived shortcomings in the visuals are intended to be filled by the soundtrack.

The importance of sound to Bay's work, and its use in his storytelling, has not gone unnoticed by the industry. Though often otherwise critically panned, his feature films have regularly been recognized for their soundtracks, earning eleven Oscar nominations and a slew of nominations and awards from the Cinema Audio Society and Motion Picture Sound Editors organizations. It is also worth noting Bay regularly works with the same sound personnel, which has allowed him to develop and hone his particular style of sound design. As long-time effects re-recording mixer Greg P. Russell (who has worked on twelve of Bay's thirteen features) notes, this includes integration of music and sound effects throughout the process – a workflow only possible when composers, sound mixers and sound editors work together often enough to learn the others' creative sensibilities.[11] To wit, Bay has usually kept the same mixers, supervising sound editors and sound designers around across multiple films – in contrast, he rarely works with the same cinematographer (usually considered one of the key personnel on a film) repeatedly, having used eight different ones on his thirteen films. Part of this may be that Bay himself is more of a visual maestro, and while he knows he can achieve what he wants visually even when working with new cinematographers, he wants to have people he trusts and who know his style handle his soundtracks. Yet if Bay's style relies on a particular relationship between sound and image, it would also make sense that he recognizes the importance of having sonic collaborators whose aural style fits his visual approach – as discussed in the next section, we see the same thing in his music video work, with Bay really hitting his stride as a music video director when working on Meat Loaf/Jim Steinman songs. True, the form of image-sound 'collaboration' possible in music video is qualitatively different than that possible in feature film, but clearly one can see how Bay's visual style naturally meshes with Meat Loaf/ Steinman's bombastic, over-the-top songs and instrumentation, and why they would work together on three videos in a row.

Developing a style through experimentation

Where the impact of Bay's training in music video shows up clearly in the role sound plays in his feature films, the import of that early work for his visual style is more subtle, and deciphering it requires a close examination of his progression as a music video director. A sampling of Bay's music videos shows the visual freedom of the form allowed Bay to experiment with a variety of techniques before honing in on what would become his signature style. Most notably, his work shows a general progression away from concert-style performance videos towards more narrative structures. His first major video (1989's 'Soldier of Love' by Donny Osmond) primarily shows the singer and his band performing in what looks like an empty bar space, with shots of dancing women occasionally interspersed, but by his next video (Richard Marx's 'Angelia' (1989)) he has already introduced a narrative component, one intercut with the full-band performance. Not long after, his video for the Divinyl's 'I Touch Myself' (1991) would still include all the band members, but appearing intermittently and spread through various locations rather than actually 'performing' as a group, and the performance elements of his videos from the following year (e.g. Lionel Richie's 'Do It To Me' (1992), Wilson Phillips's 'You Won't See Me Cry' (1992)) consist almost exclusively of the singers lip-synching in the 'narrative' spaces, with no visible bands or microphones. On the rare occasions when we do see other musicians, they're operating separately from the singer rather than performing as a group – as one commentator writes about the Richie video,

'Richie doesn't acknowledge his band. ... One quirk of Bay's choppy visual style is that even when dudes are working alongside each other, they rarely seem like they're working *together*.'[12]

Bay's final pre-*Bad Boys* music videos are a trio of songs from Meat Loaf's *Bat Out of Hell II: Back into Hell* (1993) album, and in these Bay entirely eschews traditional band performance elements, instead including only shots in service of the videos' narratives.[13] Meat Loaf may lip-sync along with his songs in all three videos, but in each it would be more accurate to describe the on-screen Meat Loaf as an *actor* singing his lines *in character* than as someone we are intended to interpret narratively as the singer Meat Loaf of the 'real world'. This is a notable change – while Richard Marx or the multiple singers of Wilson Phillips may have scenes where they are performing as characters in a narrative, these scenes are intercut with shots where we are clearly meant to interpret the artists *as themselves performing*. By his Meat Loaf trilogy, Bay has essentially jumped fully into narrative film-making, presaging his move into feature film with *Bad Boys* (1995) shortly thereafter.[14]

Along with this general progression from performance to narrative, these early videos show Bay experimenting stylistically with everything from cutting rhythms to visual effects to camerawork to colour. To be sure, some elements we would now consider 'signature Michael Bay' – constant camera movement, quick cutting, staging of multiple subjects in depth to exploit parallax when the camera moves laterally, strong (usually blue) backlights through smoke/fog, lingerie-clad beautiful women, slow-motion running, markers of (and nostalgia for) classic Americana – are visible in some of his earliest works, suggesting Bay had an innate sense from the start of what looked good to him visually. But these earlier videos also show him trying out techniques that would feel out of character for Bay as we know him from his feature-film career. It's hard to imagine a *Transformers* movie with heavy use of zooms (as we get in 'Angelia'), *Armageddon* (1998) shifting between colour and black and white (multiple videos) or *Bad Boys* resorting to a cheesy video effect like flashing back and forth between positive and negative colouration (Vanilla Ice's 'I Love You' (1991)). Watching several of Bay's early videos in succession is seeing a talented but inexperienced artist try all sorts of techniques and styles, quickly eliminating those that fail and trying variations on those that seem promising.

Bay's use of colour in his videos is a perfect illustration of this process. This is an area of experimentation from his very first video, where he removes all but one colour from each shot of the dancers in 'Soldier of Love' (an effect that would seem out of place in any mainstream feature this side of *Pleasantville* (1998)). For 'Angelia' he takes a different approach, shooting some footage in black and white (with a slight sepia tinge), some with normal colours and lighting and some with colour but strong blue-tinged lighting. This seems reasonably successful, particularly in delineating different time periods and spaces, so Bay pushes it further in 'I Touch Myself', mixing super-saturated colour footage (with production design and wardrobe in rich primary colours), blue-lit colour footage like that of 'Angelia', flickering black and white (like an old projector/camera being cranked unevenly) and smoothly shot black and white. The experimentation continues, gradually leading to the now-instantly recognizable Bay 'blorange' look (heavily saturated, with darks skewing blue and Caucasian skin skewing orange) of his feature films appearing in his Meat Loaf videos. The same sense of experimentation and progression shows up in Bay's approach to editing, camera angles and effects across Bay's music video oeuvre, with Bay taking full advantage of the aesthetic freedom the music video form provides, playing with style to discover both what works and what he himself likes.

From this perspective, 1989's 'Angelia' (his second video) and 1994's 'Objects in the Rear View Mirror May Appear Closer than They Are' (the final of his three Meat Loaf epics) provide neat near-bookends: both centre around nostalgic narratives featuring a man revisiting the site of a tragic loss in his youth and both intercut present-day footage of that visit with flashbacks to the past. Yet this same core storyline is conveyed through divergent stylistic approaches in the two videos. The Richard Marx video employs at least four visual threads – concert-style performance footage of Marx's band, flashback shots of Marx with his lover Angelia in the past, solo shots of Angelia looking seductive and/or innocent in various random locations, Marx alone in what appears to be a sparsely furnished bedroom – somewhat randomly intercut together, each with its own visual style. The Meat Loaf video, in contrast, is a largely cohesive short story, with a unity of colour palette, visual style and tone throughout the video, even as subtle differences in the camerawork (moving vs. static, width of shots) and production design differentiate between the past and the present. The overall narrative and mood comes through clearly in both, but the difference between the earlier video (which feels like a story arbitrarily intermixed with other elements) and the later one (in which every shot and stylistic decision furthers the same narrative and tonal aims) is striking, demonstrating the growth of a director who has figured out his approach to visual storytelling.

Streamlined storytelling

None of this is to say that by 1994 Bay had somehow 'perfected' narrative storytelling, or that he was making 'mini-features' – unlike, say, 'Thriller', Bay's Meat Loaf videos still feel like music videos and would never be mistaken for stand-alone dramatic shorts. But it is clear his experiments in the music video form helped Bay develop and hone his approach to visual storytelling into something recognizably akin to the style he would employ on his feature films. Put any individual shot from his Meat Loaf videos next to a shot from one of his features, and aside from catching the singer actively lip-synching in the former or recognizing an actor in the latter, one might be hard-pressed to tell which is which based on their visuals alone. Sometimes Bay directly steals from his music videos in later works: in 'Objects in the Rear View Mirror...', for instance, a low-angle shot of two boys looking up in slow motion as a plane flies overhead presages the framing and composition of a memorable shot from *Pearl Harbor* (2001), and a coffin being carried over the camera in the same video foreshadows a similar shot in the opening sequence of *The Rock* (Figure 7.3).

Yet despite their strong narrative elements and that they're built of shots that look very similar to those in Bay's feature films, Bay's Meat Loaf videos still, as mentioned above, feel *like music videos* – and it's worth considering why. Aside from the obvious music video giveaways (visible lip-synching, a song playing the whole way through), these pieces feature visual strategies not regularly seen in classical feature film. Most notable is the speed of their cutting – few shots linger more than a couple seconds, and even setting aside the anomalously fast-cut (only a couple frames per shot) plane crash in 'Objects in the Rear View Mirror...' (the speed here is clearly an attempt to create a feeling of chaos and disaster on a shoot lacking the budget to actually crash an airplane), it's not uncommon for whole sequences to feature average shot lengths well under a second. Bay, of course, hardly has a monopoly on quickly-cut music videos. Indeed, the common (usually derogatory) description of movies or shows as having an 'MTV style' is generally understood to mean first and foremost fast cutting, and secondarily that, as Carol Vernallis has argued, cutting is 'based on dislocation, free-association, flux, colour and texture'[15] rather than following conventional

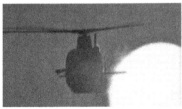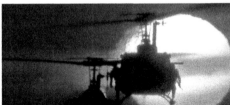

FIGURE 7.3 *By the time he was making his Meat Loaf trilogy, Bay's videos looked much like his features eventually would. The shot on the right, from* The Rock, *essentially replicates a shot from one of Bay's videos, only made 'bigger' with the second helicopter.*

left: 'I'd Do Anything for Love (But I Won't Do That.)' *(Michael Bay, 1993, performed by Meat Loaf, written by Jim Steinman).*

right: *The Rock* (Michael Bay, 1996.)

continuity rules. In a short form like the music video, quick cuts can work to provide new information quickly, at a pace that might be difficult for a viewer to process over the entirety of a feature film. Even Bay himself uses longer shots in his feature films than in his music videos, suggesting an awareness of the unsustainability of such speed over a multi-hour film.

But while short shots may be endemic to the music video form, Bay's particular approach to narrative in his music videos is more complex than just cutting fast. It is a *streamlined* method of storytelling, where narrative *efficiency* is the order of the day. Shot-to-shot continuity, backstory and detailed explanations are shunted aside wherever possible in favour of relentless forward momentum that crams as much story as possible into the time available. Given that Bay's features average close to two-and-a-half hours in length, it may seem odd to describe his style as 'streamlined'. Yet Bay's 'bigger is better' mentality dovetails neatly with this streamlined approach: he wants to put *as much stuff as possible* into each project. This means not just making bigger, longer projects, but also stripping each component of a narrative down to its core, giving the audience just enough for that element to come through before moving on to the next story beat. Consider his video for 'I'd Do Anything for Love'. Certainly this is a long music video at nearly eight minutes long. Yet that's still a shockingly short time into which Bay manages to fit the entire 'Beauty and the Beast' fable: Beauty stumbling upon Beast's castle, him watching her in the magic mirror (here a magic drinking goblet), her taking advantage of the castle's luxuries, Beauty and Beast conversing without him showing Beauty how he looks, plenty of magic, the villagers (here police) trying to find the Beast, the Beast attacking and escaping the outsiders, Beast finally revealing his monstrous face, Beauty accepting him, Beast transforming back into a regular human, and finally the 'happily ever after' (the two of them literally riding off into a sunset).

Bay's ability to cover so much ground so quickly is due in no small part to assumed audience familiarity with the well-known source fable, but he also saves time by skipping over any story detail not relevant to the *core* 'Beauty and the Beast' plot – narrative streamlining, in other words. We never find out why the police are after the Beast, how he became the Beast in the first place (a crucial plot point in every other telling of the story), or the significance of a jewelled locket that shows up repeatedly throughout the video. In a scene of Beauty in bed, two other women randomly appear (starting ~4:23), seem to be intimate with Beauty and then disappear with no clear explanation. Is this totally random, just Bay wanting to work more scantily clad women into the piece? Or a reference to similar scenes of vampire wives in the Dracula story? Or are the women perhaps conjured by (and somehow part of) the Beast, who is trying to make her happy but fears facing her himself? Careful analysis – noting the Beast lurking just outside the bedroom when the women appear, and a moment where the two lip-synch Beast's lyrics – suggests this final explanation is *likely* the intended meaning, but it's still not entirely clear, and few audiences would figure this out on a first viewing in real time (Figure 7.4).

But these questions are beside the point in Bay's model of storytelling economics: priority is given to including visually gripping or stunning shots, even at the expense of narrative clarity. In this case that means including the bedroom scene – who, Bay would likely ask, *doesn't* want to see Beauty in bed with two lingerie-clad models? – even if its narrative motivation is dubious. At other times it may mean cutting explanations or story details to make room for more striking visuals. The video's opening motorcycle/police/helicopter chase could have been given a specific backstory, time, location (it's cut too fast to get any real sense of their surroundings) and mechanics (how is the hero trying to elude them), but these would all have taken time and/or different shots, which would not have left room for all the dynamic, gorgeous close-up shots of the chase. Narrative continuity would also have meant only shooting the scene in orange golden hour light *or* blue night-time – Bay instead opts for both, giving us twice the beautiful visuals otherwise possible, with the acceptable trade-off of a time jump. It's crucial to note the point here is *not* about Bay sacrificing the *idea* of narrative or the crucial, broad-stroke beats of his story. Rather, it's that he's often willing to sacrifice continuity or the *details* of the story for momentum, larger scope and visual impact.

Bay's other two Meat Loaf videos are similarly expansive in their overall stories, and while the Meat Loaf/Jim Steinman fondness for exceptionally long songs deserves some credit as well, it's not as if either is an order of magnitude longer than most music videos: 'Rock and Roll Dreams Come

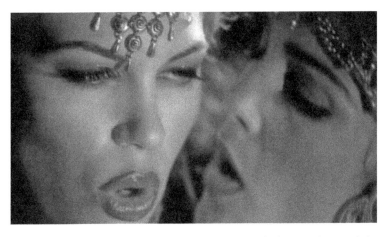

FIGURE 7.4 *Beast's perhaps-conjured women lip-synch the song lyrics while in bed with Beauty in 'I'd Do Anything for Love (But I Won't Do That)' (Michael Bay, 1993, performed by Meat Loaf, written by Jim Steinman).*

Through' (1994) is under six minutes, and even the nearly eight-minute video for 'Objects in the Rear View Mirror…' is two-and-a-half minutes shorter than the album cut of the song (meaning Bay could have had even more time to convey his story had he deemed it necessary). Rather than repeating the points made about 'I'd Do Anything for Love', let it suffice to note that both videos employ the same 'streamlined' approach, with a barrage of 'big-picture' story elements but little attention paid to story details, and an emphasis on striking visuals at the expense of total narrative coherence. In 'Rock and Roll …' Meat Loaf plays a sort of 'saviour' of characters in dire straits, bringing them music that somehow makes everything better – it's a thematic, if not literal, reworking of the song's chorus 'when you really, really need it the most, that's when rock and roll dreams come through'. Predictably, where most music videos might have focused on a single salvation story, Bay goes bigger, crowding the film with four separate characters for the singer to 'save'. The one with the most screen time is a teen runaway who first unleashes the hero from a jukebox, but Meat Loaf also rescues a youth being asked (apparently as a gang initiation) to shoot someone, a suicidal alcoholic and a blind woman frustrated with her disability. All are brought to the hero's mythical space (a fantastical forest) after being given a radio, and all seem happy at the end. Details about *how* the music saves them or changes their circumstances are missing, and two of the most striking and memorable images have no direct connection to the narrative – one features a possibly-part-cyborg woman inside a jukebox holding a glowing orb, the other an angelic white-robed woman floating peacefully over all the characters. Like the magically appearing women in the bedroom of 'I'd Do Anything For Love', neither feels entirely out of place in the world of the video, but they are certainly unexplained by and inconsequential to the narrative.

'Objects in the Rear View Mirror…', described earlier, is a nostalgic piece following an adult (Meat Loaf) returning to the place where he grew up, and flashing back through three stories that shaped him – most significantly the loss of his childhood best friend in a plane crash. Like Bay's other Meat Loaf videos, it includes a lot of big-picture story (three separate childhood incidents, plus the framing story of the adult visiting key sites of all three) but not a lot of detail. We don't know what caused the crash, much less what happened in the years between the childhood friends playing with their homemade go-kart-with-wings and the time they return to steal the plane as teenagers. We don't find out what happened with the boy's first love, whom we see only in their happier moments – Did she die? Did she break up with him? Did their relationship not survive him leaving town? Likewise with the boy's father; after the boy runs away it's unclear whether he ever returned and/or reconciled with his parent. In a tightly woven narrative script, we would likely find answers to these types of questions, probably as a reveal at the climax, but here they are omitted for the simple reason that they're unimportant to the core meat of the story. It's important – because it shaped the adult – that the main character had a good friend who died young. It's *not* important exactly *how*; the trauma would have been the same regardless.

Indeed, song lyrics and visuals actually diverge on the details of the best friend's death, with the former suggesting a drag racing accident in place of the latter's plane crash. This difference, though, is irrelevant to the impact of losing a friend as a child, so the point for Bay is what version of this tragedy allows for the best *visuals*. True, a drag race crash *could* be just as stunning to watch as a plane crash – and Michael Bay certainly has a demonstrated aptitude for shooting cars in a visually appealing way – but the change of vehicle allows Bay greater flexibility with his camera, particularly the ability to get low-angle shots with multiple levels of depth (a Bay staple). Indeed, this is probably one reason so many of Bay's movies include aerial vehicles – helicopters, planes and spaceships up in the air behind characters on the ground make it much easier to play with depth and parallax even with his characteristic extreme low-angle camera work. The 'girlfriend' flashback sequence may also have played a role in the decision to go with a plane crash; that story already features a cool convertible, so the plane would offer new and different imagery rather than duplicating something seen elsewhere in the video.

Finally, the plane crash gives the video a 'bigger' feel than a car crash. Bay's music videos not only trace a history of stylistic experimentation and gradually discovering what worked best for him but also show Bay's propensity to try to outdo his prior work with each successive new piece (a trait reviewers have also noted with his franchise films – each sequel must be somehow 'bigger' than the last in length, scope, scale of action set pieces, etc.). Having already done the 'loss in a car crash' in 'Angelia', a plane crash would mark a step forward and something more challenging. Indeed, it was apparently a big enough deal to earn Will Smith's notice and respect – the *Bad Boys* star recalls his initial impression of first-time feature director Bay as, 'he had just done the Meat Loaf video – this guy had a *plane crash* in a *music video*. I was like, *Damn*'.[16]

The irrelevance of character and narrative

Stripping narrative elements down to their core to allow more time for cool visuals represents a different film-making sensibility than usually seen in feature films, where story is ostensibly *the* fundamental attraction. Consider that all three of Bay's Meat Loaf videos rely on archetypes rather than developed or fleshed-out characters. While Disney's *Beauty and the Beast* films (1991, 2017) may not exactly be models of female empowerment, they do feature a three-dimensional heroine, the bookish, frustrated-with-small-town-life Belle who dotes on her eccentric father – she may be a beauty, but refuses to be defined by that characteristic. In 'I'd Do Anything for Love', meanwhile, we get a Beauty immediately and entirely defined by her beauty and kindness. She is paired not with a Beast who must learn to love or otherwise overcome a curse, but simply a Beast defined by his monstrous face as 'the Beast from *Beauty and the Beast*'. The same is true for the characters in the other videos: 'Rock and Roll Dreams' has 'the runaway teen girl' and 'the suicidal alcoholic', for instance, while 'Objects in the Rear View Mirror...' has 'the drunk abusive dad' and 'the teen dream girl'. In each case, we know exactly *who* the character is and their *role in the story* from the first one or two images of that character. Locations are treated similarly. From the first shot of each space – rundown family home, scary big city, idyllic small town, fantasy castle and so on – we know what that space signifies. If Bay's videos have no surprises or twists, it's because everything is exactly what it appears to be and plays out exactly as it must; the entertainment comes not from a *story* or *character* being unique, but from the *execution* of the story, the cool visuals on screen.

In Bay's award-winning 'Aaron Burr' commercial (1993) for the 'Got Milk?' ad campaign, the sole on-screen actor plays a character fully defined by a single trait – his obsession with the Alexander Hamilton/Aaron Burr duel – and the narrative is a simple ironic play on this characteristic. And this is one of Bay's more coherently narrative advertisements – his commercial work is often memorable far more for Bay's engaging visuals than for any depth of character, story or even narrative logic. Indeed, the 'stories' of ads like 'Goat Boy' (1999, for Nike) or 'Lawyers Roundup' (1993, for Miller Lite) fall apart if given the slightest thought (What are the rules of a lawyer round-up? How would a goat know where to get shoes?) – but the point isn't to think about the narrative, it's to enjoy the simple story and straightforward jokes on screen.

In music videos and commercials, of course, it's difficult to create the type of full-developed, three-dimensional characters common to television and feature film; their short length and lack of dialogue naturally lend themselves better to characters who can instantly be categorized and understood than to those with complex motivations, emotions and backstories. But Bay carries the music video approach over to his feature films. On a surface level, it's facile to note Bay's films are about *how* an age-old story is told, not about subverting the expectations of those stories. No one goes to a *Transformers* film to see whether the evil Decepticons will emerge victorious (they won't), but rather to see how the battle between them and the heroic Autobots will play out this time. In this regard Bay's films are not unusual. While audiences for an M. Night Shymalan or Christopher Nolan film might derive their enjoyment from a climactic twist or seeing how a story's puzzle pieces ultimately come together, in most cases we know the guy is going to get the girl, the spy is going to save the world and good will triumph over evil – we just want to see how *this* iteration of that classic story plays out.

But if Bay's films are similar to much of Hollywood film-making in this regard, his approach to character is not. Usually, what makes a particular film's retelling of an age-old story enjoyable or emotional is its distinctive characters. Every romantic comedy may have the same plot points at its core, for example, but a good one creates *specific* characters with their own quirks and problems to overcome, and these unique traits are what drive the narrative and initially keep the characters apart. If a particular romantic comedy is memorable, it is rarely for its plot contrivances, but rather for its precisely sketched characters, their dialogue and their relationships. Bay's feature films, on the other hand, while not necessarily *devoid* of unique characters, are rarely driven *by* or remembered *for* those characters. In many cases, even the central players are little deeper than the archetypes seen in his music videos – from the first shot of a character, we know *who* that character is and his or her *role* in the story. Bay's streamlined approach to visual storytelling places a premium on easily readable visuals: if 'who someone is' can be summed up in one or two images, this may not yield the most compelling characters, but does save a lot of exposition and development, allowing more time for cool visuals and effects. Mark Wahlberg's character in *Transformers: The Last Knight* (2017) may represent the pinnacle of Bay's hyper-efficient brand of characterization – from the first shot where he comes to the rescue of some kids, he's clearly the film's 'good guy hero'. If no more knowledge about his personality or motivations is given, it's because none is *necessary* in this approach to narrative.

Vernallis labels films whose style resembles that of a music video as the 'New Cut-Up Cinema'. She argues that when feature films employ a music video–based style, audiences (likely subconsciously) adjust their expectations to those of the music video form. Since music videos emphasize spectacle, archetypes and moment-to-moment sound/image interactions over complex narratives and characters, audiences for the 'New Cut-Up Cinema' look for the same, focusing on the entertainment of the moment rather than on broader questions of when, how or even *if* a narrative will come together. They know (thanks to years of watching movies) the plot will ultimately progress, but this is incidental to their enjoyment. As Vernallis wryly notes about one of the *Bourne* films, 'Do I care if Bourne meets Big Daddy Programmer, or Godzilla? No. The narrative pay-off is only a placeholder, a marker I know will be coming.'[17] Meanwhile, the moment-to-moment excitement of the movie's sounds and images are its *actual* purpose. In the Michael Bay episode of the video doc series 'Every Frame a Painting', narrator Tony Zhou muses that 'Bay has a need to make every image dynamic, even when it runs contrary to the theme of his own movie [. ... He] seems to think a good film is 3000 dynamic shots and no static ones.'[18] To those who consider narrative and character the most important components of a film, this sounds ludicrous, but if the narrative is really just there to give a vague *reason* for the pretty images and cool sounds we're experiencing, it actually makes a lot of sense. One writer summarizing the (apparent) narrative of 'Angelia' admits, 'It's hard to pin down exactly whether that's the story Bay's video means to tell, because, in a precursor to the scrambled narratives of Bay's later films, "Angelia" favors fleeting impressions over clarity.'[19] Audiences leave a Bay film remembering they saw something visually interesting, even if they can't always recall how it fit into the story or even what that story *was*.

Bay's famed love of musicals – calling them 'the first type of movie to really exploit film as a medium'[20] – is revealing here. What is a musical other than a feature-length series of music videos strung together between non-musical bridging segments? Classical musicals regularly disrupt narrative continuity – most lack a diegetic reason for all the characters to start singing and dancing – yet we accept their breaks from the narrative *because these films are not* about *the narrative*. A musical's story exists merely to provide a through line on which to hang the various musical numbers that are really the *point* of the film. One might read Bay's action scenes the same way – the point is not what is accomplished in terms of plot by these scenes, it is simply the spectacle of watching the scenes themselves. To quote one critic, 'Bay has always been willing to forego things like rising action or building tension to try and blast viewers to their seats from first frame to last.'[21] In Bay's music video–based style, that may be a feature, not a bug.

Audiovisual salesmanship

Before wrapping up, it's instructive to at least briefly ruminate on the fundamental *nature* of the commercials and music videos on which Bay cut his directorial teeth. Both forms are intended not simply to be enjoyed on their own, but to *promote* something else. This is obvious in the case of commercials, where the product advertised is usually clearly denoted, but is no less true in music video, where videos are intended to function as promotional vehicles for their songs (or, in some cases, more generally for the musical artist). In other words, Bay learned his craft working on media whose end goal was encouraging *consumption* of one form or another.

Music videos and commercials, of course, have long been the proving grounds of up-and-coming directors, and many of those directors have found ways to create memorable art that still serves the promotional needs inherent to these forms. When given the chance, though, most of these film-makers progress to works whose deeper narratives and characterizations are *themselves* the products designed to be consumed (e.g. feature films and television shows). Yet as discussed above, narrative and character sometimes seem of only peripheral interest to Bay. Instead, it seems that he made the move into features without ever really abandoning the core principle of his earlier works: create memorable images that make viewers want to buy or consume something.

If shots in Bay's films often resemble advertising – women are photographed as if they're in one of his Victoria's Secret commercials, while many shots of the Transformers driving could just as easily be Chevy commercials – that's because what Bay learned how to do as a young director was make things look pretty so viewers would want to buy them. Product placement aside, feature films ostensibly do not need to sell their viewers anything, but Bay's films still often essentially function as advertisements *for themselves*. Whether or not they make sense or are enjoyable as narrative feature films, Bay's movies are chock-full of cool visuals that lend themselves well to being spliced together into trailers, and thus getting audiences into theatres. The success of Bay's films at the box office is, from this perspective, not so much evidence of their quality as full-length films, but of how appealing they can be made to look when cut down into single images, commercials or trailers. Even Bay's embrace of the latest and greatest sound systems can be considered as much a business choice as an artistic one; audiences cannot replicate these systems at home, and thus know they have to *go to a theatre and buy a ticket* to experience Bay's films in all their glory.[22] As one journalist notes, a Bay film plays 'like an extended set of commercials, or a prolonged version of its own ultrasharp 1080p trailer'.[23] In the end, Bay may be the rare commercial/video-trained director who moved into feature film without ever stopping making advertisements.

Conclusion: The transmedia feature director

It's impossible to be certain whether Bay's film-making style developed the way it did because of his start in music video and commercials, or whether his aesthetic sensibilities would ultimately have led him to the same place had he somehow gone straight into feature film. What *is* clear from looking back at those early projects, though, is that by the time he did make the jump into feature film, his now-recognizable approach to film-making was already highly developed, and was ported remarkably unchanged from his short-form work into his features. While many of his peers – most notably David Fincher, who co-founded a production company with Bay in those early years[24] – also began their careers in music videos and commercials, Bay is unusual in the degree to which his feature film-making follows the same principles he developed on those short-form projects.

All of this is not to say that Bay's films lack any sort of narrative, or that he is somehow making feature-length music videos. Rather, it's that his approach to film-making owes at least as much to the commercial and music video forms as to traditional continuity-based, character-driven narrative film-making, and often people evaluate his work exclusively as the latter. Judging Bay movies by the principles of Classic Hollywood Cinema ignores that he's following a fundamentally different set of rules. In fact, Bay's features might better be thought of through as belonging to the 'cinema of attractions' of film's early years, where audiences go to a movie not to follow a narrative but simply to marvel at the images on screen.

Bay's stylistic trajectory as a feature film-maker roughly parallels the progression he made over his music video career, at least in terms of his adherence to dominant conventions. His earliest works in both forms follow conservative stylistic norms (performance-based music videos, traditional continuity-driven features), then as he gains experience he veers further from these and towards his own style. Comparing early *Transformers* films with later ones, or *The Rock* and *Pearl Harbor* with *13 Hours* (2016), one sees a move away from traditional continuity rules, visual spatial logic and character development in favour of greater numbers of dynamic moving shots, heavier reliance on the soundtrack to carry information and narrative streamlining. This may reflect the eventually waning influence of Jerry Bruckheimer (producer on Bay's first five features), or simply Bay doing the same sort of experimentation with feature film as he did with music video, embracing Classic Hollywood Cinema conventions as a safety net at first but then gradually stripping them away as he gained more experience. Visually speaking, meanwhile, Bay's work has remained remarkably consistent over a wide body of feature films ranging from action comedy to historical epic to futuristic sci-fi to war film.

Whatever the reason(s) for this evolution, it is curious that in many ways Bay's later films are *more* reminiscent of his music videos than his early ones. Commercial and music video directors who get tapped to make a feature film usually earn that chance based on demonstrating strong visual sensibilities, and the biggest challenges of their first films (e.g. Fincher with *Alien³* (1992)) tend to be story and narrative issues, which they learn how to handle better as they do more features. Bay, on the other hand, seems to have taken the opposite approach: he started with some well-made standard Hollywood fare (*The Rock*, his second film, is by most accounts his best-crafted film from a traditional narrative perspective), then gradually moved farther and farther from the narrative conventions and continuity rules on which those are built. Indeed, evaluated by its reliance on CHC principles, narrative logic or depth of characterization, *Transformers: The Last Knight* is something of a $200 million experimental film.

In the end, maybe what Bay learned through his early work is that his greatest strength is not as a *storyteller* per se, but as an *audiovisual stylist* who can create media that are *in and of themselves* worth looking at and/ or hearing whether or not they serve a story. Though unusual in mainstream contemporary film, this approach is central to music video: we accept that the visuals are there to enhance the song, do not expect that they will all add up neatly to a coherent narrative, and happily accept plot holes or leaps of logic that might be frowned upon by most feature-film audiences. Bay seems to have recognized that the Classic Hollywood Cinema style is but one of multiple directions the feature-film form could have taken, and gleefully deploys the tools of other media forms within the feature framework, sprinkling in the minimum of plot needed to string together the images. At an art museum, visitors hardly expect that every painting tells a story – they simply care that the paintings are worth looking at for one reason or another. Why, Bay seems to ask, cannot the same be true for feature films? His success thus far suggests that it can.

PART THREE

Transmedial relations and industry

CHAPTER 8

Whirled pieces: Bong Joon Ho's *Snowpiercer* and the components of global transmedia production

J. D. Connor

In July 2012, Disney's Marvel announced its production slate for Phase 2 of the Marvel Cinematic Universe. It would consist of six movies and run through 2015. Phase 3 would include ten movies and run through 2019. In 2013 Disney promised a Star Wars movie every year. In October 2014, Warner Bros. announced a competing slate of ten DC 'Extended Universe' movies running through 2020. These slates and other plans – for new Disney Princess instalments and 'live-action' remakes of animated classics; for Universal's classic-monster-centred *Dark Universe* and for the expansion of its *Fast and Furious* series – are regular features of the contemporary mediascape.[1] Those slates may be revised or abandoned, but they are used to generate fan interest, to mark out release dates and to provide a framework for the deployment of intellectual property assets across media and licensed products.

Such enormous undertakings necessarily curtail the opportunities for creative serendipity. In response, studios turn to auteur-ish directors for both unique spins on the underlying property and to manage increasingly unwieldy character rosters (Joss Whedon). That auteury cred can be deployed from the beginning of a transmedial enterprise, as it was with Duncan Jones and the videogame adaptation *Warcraft* (2016), or it can be part of a reboot strategy (Colin Trevorrow and *Jurassic World* (2015); Josh Trank and

Fantastic Four (2015)). When the aim is to control every profitable point in the value chain, then the successful transmedia auteur looks like Matthew Vaughn, screenwriter and director of *Kick-Ass* (2010, Lionsgate/Universal), *Kingsman: The Secret Service* (2010, Fox), *X-Men: First Class* (2011, Fox); and producer of *Fantastic Four* (Fox).

By contrast, *Snowpiercer* (Bong, TWC/CJ, 2013) was an indie assemblage from the beginning built around Bong Joon Ho's prior auteur status. Director Bong had built a career that combined art-house practices with a facility for crowd-pleasing genre conventions. *Memories of Murder* (2003) screened at international film festivals and went on to win South Korea's Grand Bell Award. The monster movie *The Host* (2006) both premiered at Cannes and finished the year as the most successful movie in Korean history. Yet even after his global successes, Bong regularly contributed to omnibus projects with limited market appeal. He was thus able to balance between his local-hero and transnational profiles. But where his prior projects had been set in Korea and marketed globally, *Snowpiercer* would be planetary in its story, production *and* marketing. This was a remarkable upscaling for both Bong and his underwriters. As such, the production was compelled to invent or reinvent each aspect of its passage from backlist French graphic novel to English-language action movie.[2] In that transition, it drew on the credibility and taste of Director Bong, Korean post-production infrastructure and generous Czech tax credits. Funded by an array of producers, distributors and state and quasi-state agencies, its underwriting mirrored its international cast and crew.[3] The production and distribution histories of *Snowpiercer* illustrate the possibilities and constraints of the contemporary global transmedial system. *Snowpiercer* documents the potential emergence of a globalized, multipolar cinema just outside the purview of the majors. Whether that system is durable is another question – one that Bong's follow-up, *Okja*, may partially answer.

In many ways, *Snowpiercer* constitutes the inverse of the international co-productions of the 1960s. In that earlier era, quota systems required the participation of actors from a particular country as a condition of support from various national funders. As Mark Betz demonstrates, those contractual relations were regularly figured as international romances or scenes of translation. He goes on to suggest that the foundational experience of art cinema co-production is *misrecognition*, the occlusion of the capital investments and industrial cooperation by the auteur's name above the subtitle. That signature renders the 'appearance of an actor from one nation in an art film from another ... the fortuitous meeting across national borders of a talented performer and a brilliant director'.[4] In the absence of any such quota systems today, actors and other bearers of the mark of talent *really are* artefacts of a general fortuitousness even as they *really are* instances of industrial cooperation, instances of the increasingly robust system of bilateral co-production agreements outside the ambit of the Hollywood system.[5]

In addition to a view of the edges of possibility for contemporary action cinema, *Snowpiercer* also offers a unique perspective on IP-centric transmedial production. By working through a contrasting model where the director drives the process, we are better able to understand the more general interplay of individual and systemic forces in contemporary world cinema. At the core of that interplay are the scalar differences between directors with ideas about the world, assemblages of talent and capital from across the world, global infrastructures of communication and aesthetic propagation and general systems that underpin the emergence of directors, assemblages, infrastructures and *even those systems themselves*. Those scalar differences are enacted, resisted, effaced and foregrounded only in occurrences. And those occurrences may themselves span from individual films to directorial oeuvres to strategies and on to that most evanescent of occurrences, policies.

In the contest for authoritative control over which occurrence will supervene over the enactment, resistance, effacement or foregrounding of scalar differences, we are thrown back onto cases. In the case of *Snowpiercer*, it is, I hope to show, Bong's agency – an agency that is not to be reduced to his intention – that volatilizes the possible poles of authority. That agency *configures* the transmedial and transnational totality according to a hallmark, what the older vision of the auteur criticism singled out as the overriding conviction of the work. In Bong's case, that conviction is a belief in strategic competence – a belief so strong that questions of *possibility* can be bracketed in favour of ethical questions of *consequence and entailment*. In other words, these characters are so certain that they *can* they spend all their time wondering whether they *should*. That Bong's agency is nevertheless and at the same time delimited, undermined, dissipated and so on only highlights the ways in which his authoritative competitors, those possibly contestatory vectors of determination, nevertheless conjure a place for his agency as their own occasion for activation. (As one might say, 'We want to be in the Bong Joon Ho business.')

In order to reconstruct the contours of those competing authorities, I have relied principally on interviews with crucial players in *Snowpiercer*'s production and distribution process. Those interviews are of course not self-interpreting. In particular, they register the players' strong sense of the differences between this project and others, differences they often ascribe to Bong, but which they might account for in any number of ways. Realizing that the most common agents in these histories would likely be individuals, I explicitly asked about the role other, non-individual actors might have played – corporations and regulatory bodies, pieces of software or other technologies, policies or images. Finally, I have tried to be attentive to un- and under-identified agents – mystified collectives such as 'the studio' or processes kept just outside the narrative line such as contractual negotiations. Such moments of narrative deficit are the complement to moments of narrative surplus that, in this case, revolve around Director Bong.

In an extensive French-language documentary on the making of *Snowpiercer* (*From the Blank Page to the Black Screen*, directed by Jésus Castro-Ortega, 2015), Bong recounts the moment when he first encountered *La Transperceneige*:

> The day I met this comic book, was two years ago, in the winter of 2-0-0-4. In that period I was writing the script of *The Host*. In that kind of period I need some kind of feeling and inspiration. That situation, I always visit comic book shop or cinematheque ... suddenly I discovered *La Transperceneige*. So I discover Part 1 of *Transperceneige* and I read the whole story in the bookshop. When I was reading the comic book, at the same time, I think, oh, this is just for movie. In this kind of story, the structure of the space is just at the same time the structure of narrative. That kind of integrity.[6]

Given that this interview was conducted in 2006 – half a decade before *Snowpiercer* began production in earnest – it is unlikely to be mere mythmaking. He is proclaiming his fandom and, however improbably, staking his claim on the cinematic adaptation of the book. Even then, it is already clear that a crucial feature of the text, for Bong, is the harmony between its spaces and its story. As he recounts his perception of that convergence – a perception, remember, that has yet to become anything like a design principle – he draws his spread hands together and then pushes them forward in parallel: the train and the story of the train are fused.

Let us dig deeper into that first encounter. Jerome Baron, who is in charge of foreign rights at Casterman, ascribes the complexities of foreign publication to two sources.[7] First, the French concept of the *droit d'auteur* – moral rights – gives an author continuing approval over the course of the work. By contrast, producers – particularly Hollywood producers – have long required complete authority as a matter of course, part of their efforts to centralize control. US authors may be used to such a situation, as Baron explains it, but because European authors have an expectation of continuing involvement, it is difficult to convince them to 'give up control at a level they usually don't'. Second, *whatever* the amenability of the author to adaptation, the publisher's attempts to monetize the back catalogue are thwarted by the sheer volume of work. Casterman's backlist includes some 4,000 titles, but Sophie Levie, who handles audiovisual rights, can only concentrate on five to seven per year. These she markets at specific fairs such as Shoot the Book or film markets. That work is only made possible by a prior extension of the title's reach, thus it remains the case that the key metric for the adaptability of a property is the number of prior translations, even though the print runs for those editions may range from a low of 1,500 in many territories to a high of 5,000 in the United States. In the absence of large, oligopolistic players in the European comics field, transactionality dominates: nearly every relationship is reforged anew; nearly every market extension is rebuilt from the ground up; every approval is another occasion for the process to come undone. This hand-built nature persists even though Casterman is part of Madrigall, the third largest French publisher.

Snowpiercer was, for decades, no different than its list mates. Its first translations appeared in the 1980s in Italy and Spain, then Greece. There were discussions in the mid-1980s about an adaptation with French actor-producer Robert Hossein, but Jacques Lob, who had ultimate authority, resisted.[8] Later, in roughly 1987, Lob enlisted his friend Benjamin Legrand to do the adaptation. 'Frankly it bores me,' Lob said. The two would sign a contract with an unnamed production company, then argue among themselves (about what also remains mysterious) and the project would be dropped. The result was doubly semi-ironic: the friendship frayed over the project that went nowhere, but that frustrated attempt positioned Legrand to continue the *Snowpiercer* series as its semi-authorized-legatee writer. Lob died in 1990; in 1999, Legrand and artist Jean-Marc Rochette would produce volume 2; and the next year there were again discussions with the earlier producers about re-aquiring the rights. Nothing came of them.

Already, one can see why Baron's account began with the complexities introduced by the *droit d'auteur* system. The long history of failed attempts to film *Transperceneige* emerged not from a fundamental unwillingness but from the proliferation of frustrating conditions. But Baron's account also expresses his frustrations with the limits placed on adaptability by the small amount of attention each title can receive and the difficulties in properly sequencing the expansion of a title's availability, hence its adaptability.

That adaptation logjam was broken five years later. Alongside the balky system of piecemeal property extension through translation and fitful adaptation through extensive negotiations lies a far more flexible system of piracy and happenstance. In the case of *Snowpiercer*, a Korean publisher issued an unauthorized version in 2004. It may, or may not, have been based on an authorized serialization agreed to in 2000 – Casterman's records are sketchy.[9] It was undertaken as part of 'the first wave of translations of European material to Japan and Korea', in the early 2000s as Baron describes it.[10] Here, again, we see the small-scale expansion of the model: more territories improve the intermedial adaptability of the text. But if adaptability is a possibility on the horizon, the actuality of the system behind it is a semi-regular process of translation in which a constellation of intermediary institutions (that is, similar publishers and bookshops) feeds a niche market (that is, college kids and genre film-makers). That configuration affirms the reliability of a market for semi-unauthorized entrants (the translation). The appearance of an object, then, regardless of its legitimacy, becomes the crucial occasion for the operation of intraindustrial capital: Bong's *taste* confirms the suitability of the object for adaptation and that confirmation can be leveraged into the proffering of actual capital necessary to begin the process.

In the ordinary telling, Bong is immediately taken with *Transperceneige* and decides that it will be his next project – or the project after that since *Mother* was already in development. Still, such moments of effective affection require the mobilization of any number of ancillary systems. Here, those systems are routed through director Park Chan-wook, who has a production company and a development fund that will allow *him* to serve as an even more direct vehicle between capital and cinematic development. In keeping with the usual protocols of career management among successful creative workers, Park asks Bong whether he has any idea of what he will work on next. Park's company then makes inquiries about the rights to the book, and, as *Histoires du Transperceneige*, a making-of coffee-table book, describes it, the Korean publisher and Casterman 'intelligently' 'normalize their relations: the "pirate" translation … is transformed into an official edition. No more anomalies in the landscape: *Everything is back in line so that Bong Joon Ho is able to take control of his project.'* The *'traduction sauvage'* is legalized.[11] Now, the object can become part of a regular system of contract. Here we find the characteristic alignment of serendipity, taste and borderline illegality that gives rise to an aura of indie auteurism. We also find that the public story crowds out the decidedly less hip process of retroactively negotiating for the rights to the underlying work. Finally, we see in the immediate recourse to train-talk ('back in line' 'take control') a principle of production discourse: when systems reinforce each other, the allegorical becomes irresistible.

With the legal mechanics of the adaptability of the text taken care of, and with the promise of access to some degree of financing, those systems can assume an ancillary position. Now Bong's own credibility as an auteur constitutes a countervailing figure of creativity that can serve as real capital's proxy in the negotiations. *He* can impress Legrand and Rochette; he can be the one to solicit their participation. Their authors' rights can be transferred in part because within that transfer there is no weakening of the *notion* of authorship. The moral principle is maintained. Thus, to dial out a bit, the ethical seriousness that Bong's oeuvre carried even at that point can function as the stalking horse in an indie production strategy. The Frenchmen wouldn't have sold out for a mere payday; they know Bong isn't just buying.

In practice – again, this is the emergence of the allegorical in situations of systemic reinforcement – this will mean enlisting both Legrand and Rochette as silent-witness extras on the movie. Moreover, Rochette will serve as the on-set artist, drawing the images that are attributed to the character of The Painter (Clark Middleton). Authorship thus survives not only through the proxy of Bong but in metonym. That surplussive, happy relationship is then – as always – seized upon by the publicity apparatus and plugged back into the distribution process. In the extensive making-of documentary, Rochette in particular becomes a sympathetic figure, a thorny artist-for-hire whose career is revitalized by the *Snowpiercer* deal. From his work on set to his trips to the Korean premieres to shots of him in his new Berlin studio, Rochette's story is one where the global system of transmediation has not only been *fair* but where the pursuit of cinematic art has had other beneficial effects (Figure 8.1). Furthermore, as the aesthetic conscience of the property, Rochette solidifies the idea that what independent production offers is the chance at multivalent authorship, distributed according to desert. But if *Snowpiercer*'s origin story is imagined as the fortuitous tale of authorial or artistic talent finding and fostering itself across the globe, the infrastory of the production shifts the register of that globalism towards a more modular and more regularized approach.

A bit of background: the world has frozen. All that remains of humanity lives aboard a thousand-car train, a nearly perpetual motion machine that loops, endlessly, around the planet. The first volume of the graphic novel tells the story of one man's movement forward from the nightmarish cars at the tail of the train to the upper-class carriages towards the front. And

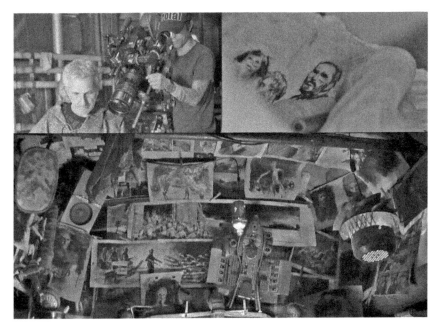

FIGURE 8.1 *Images of Marc Rochette: drawing for the camera; drawing on camera; and the array of drawings decorating the painter's bunk. By connecting Rochette's work on the graphic novel with his work on set, the production was able to finesse the questions of artistry at the heart of the adaptation:* 'Le Transperceneige: From the Blank Page to the Black Screen' *(dir. Jésus Castro-Ortega, 2015), on* Snowpiercer *(RadiusTWC/Starz/Anchor Bay, 2015; Blu-Ray).*

while there are similarities in his affect, the progress is entirely different. In the graphic novel, he sneaks around the outside of the train before ducking back inside. In the movie, he leads a collective from the tail as they fight their way forward. The adaptation also adds a vast array of characters; a history of revolts and the cold instrumentalization of those conflicts; Mason, a managerial figure played by Tilda Swinton; a religious cult of personality centering on Thomas Wilford (Ed Harris), the train's inventor; a legacy of anthropophagy in the tail cars; and drug-induced telepathy that helps the insurgents reach the front.

Unlike the Bong's initial discovery of the book, which was a material collision, the adaptation process was spatially dispersed and digitized. In that sense, *Snowpiercer* offers a window into ordinary screenwriting processes as a result of its specifiable differences. 'Screenplay studies' is still an emerging field of inquiry. On the one hand, there is a robust history of attention to the collaborative effort that goes into a screenplay and to the ways in which, as a document, the screenplay exerts a disciplining force over the production once it is put into action. On the other hand, screenplay studies, as of now, lacks the long-standing traditions of attention to digital textuality one finds in literary criticism (this trend is charted in Matthew Kirschenbaum's book *Track Changes*, for instance).[12] There are, to be sure, fragmentary accounts of the consequences of screenwriting software such as Final Draft, for example, Julian Hoxter's essay on screenwriting in the 1980s and 1990s. As Hoxter explains, these programmes 'facilitated online collaboration and moved a project more seamlessly all the way from first draft through production. ... Built into the design of these new programs was an assumption that the screenwriting process was not a solitary endeavor.'[13]

In the case of *Snowpiercer*, that collaborative flow could not rest on the screenwriting software alone. Initially Bong generated a thirty-page, fleshed story outline in Korea that was then translated and sent (digitally) to Kelly Masterson, then in New Jersey.[14] At the same time, Masterson was also sent a hastily prepared English version of the graphic novel (Figure 8.2). The JPEGs of individual pages show that dialogue in the word balloons has simply been obscured and then English text in comic sans has been entered over it. (The translation and lettering are not the same as the version published to coincide with the movie's release.) Masterson converted Bong's outline into standard Hollywood screenplay form. That version was then translated back into Korean for Bong's contributions, then back into English and so on. Such translations, as well as the on-set translation once the movie entered production, were usually handled by fresh-out-of-film-school Koreans or Korean-Americans.[15] Thus while the script would eventually take its standard place as a production reference document for budgeting and dialogue, and while it would be broken into smaller chunks for storyboarding, at this early stage it did far more. Its iterations set the pattern for the marshalling

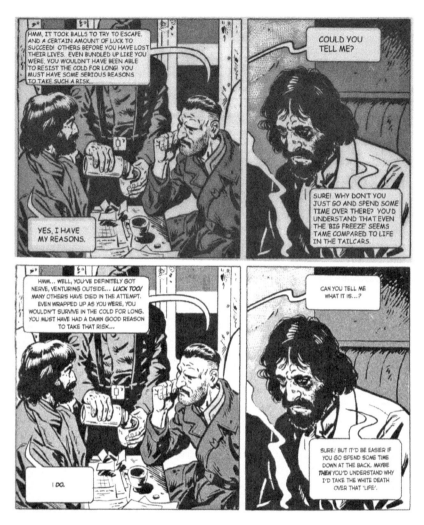

FIGURE 8.2 *The materiality of global exchange. The upper image shows the quickie translation provided to screenwriter Kelly Masterson early in the process. The English dialogue is jammed into the balloons. The lower image is the same page from the published English translation, more idiomatic and better positioned (Production document courtesy Kelly Masterson; Jacques Lob and Jean-Marc Rochette,* Snowpiercer, Vol. 1 *[Titan Comics, 2014], 11).*

of additional labour (translation). That labour would prototype the transmediations the movie both relied on and would market.

Scripts are also central objects in the provision of 'notes' – that ritualized feedback process that allows for both the maximum delegation of authority and, in theory, the maintenance of executive oversight. But in contrast to typical studio film-making, *Snowpiercer*'s script meetings were held entirely via videoconference (Skype) and between Masterson and Bong *alone*, without the participation of studio execs or producers and without extensive written exchanges. Masterson attributed these departures from the norm to Bong's influence, not the studio's modesty. He and Bong had their first interaction on 31 August 2010. In May 2011 they had reached agreement; by July they had a first draft. Three passes later, the script was ready to shoot. The heavily digital adaptation process was discursively configured around Bong's unique status which in turn insulated the project from outside interference and reduced the lines of authority dramatically.

The Korean studio infrastructure was more traditional. Park Chan-wook's Moho Films have a production/distribution deal with CJ Entertainment, which, along with Lotte, Orion and Next World, dominate the Korean industry, with over 90 per cent of the market. CJ in particular is the largest theatre owner in South Korea (nearly half of all cinemas) which for years helped it maintain its position at the top of annual market share rankings.[16] Korea's massive diversified conglomerates (*chaebols*) have also been at the forefront of the effort to rationalize production in the country. Bong's deal with Moho guaranteed him sufficient funds to go forward. Casting followed, and principal photography took place in the spring and summer of 2012.[17]

In the lead up to production in 2012, the crucial factor shifted away from the adaptation of the property or a budget guarantee to the actual mechanics of the set and the orchestration of principal photography. Again, labour and material concerns dovetailed. Even before Czech production designer Ondrej Nekvasil was hired, Bong knew that he wanted a studio where a vast section of the train could be built. In particular, for the breakout sequence, the production would need four cars on separate gimbals. The crucial term is 'need'. Here, need does not mean something like 'must have if the project is to be complete at all', but rather 'would be required to complete the project in a way up to Bong's preferred standard', a standard that would, of course, be subject to negotiation and, of course, evolve. How that need would interact with the budget is a crucial question. For example, instead of gimbals, the production might have relied on the 'poor man's process' where the camera tilts and the actors sway like the crew of the Starship Enterprise when it takes a blast from a photon torpedo. Such a workaround is always an option, but it is a cheap-looking option. Saving that money and reducing the movie's production values at the early stages can interact negatively with the production's ability to attract its preferred talent mix, including both below-the-line technicians and actors, and that weakness can in turn hinder the production's ability to generate publicity and its presales profile, thus further dampening the budget overall. Again, these chains of value-interaction are hand-built in the case of *Snowpiercer*, not set in advance as part of a slate budget. At CJ or Mojo there were likely models for forecasting potential revenue, but because this was budgeted as the most expensive 'Korean' production to date, those comps were necessarily slightly speculative. So while there is remarkable coherence to the production, it is nevertheless contingent at each decision point.

While the primary production constraint is the need for a very long soundstage, at the same time, every large production is also eager to shoot in a jurisdiction that will provide a substantial production incentive. Given that the global system of production incentives is largely mature, the production likely only needed to *find* that studio because the odds were that it would be located in a jurisdiction where motion pictures enjoy favourable tax status. As a result, the production's *discourse* could be shaped around the material circumstances necessary to realize Bong's vision, and the production's desire to find the best deal could take a backseat. In this case, Barrandov studios in Prague is large enough to accommodate the train, and the Czech Film Commission incentive is 20 per cent of Czech spend, with an additional bonus for VFX work undertaken in-country.[18] Bong got his stage; the production got its subsidy.

That incentive structure was the outcome of a continent-wide scramble for film and video production. The Czech Republic had in the post–Cold War 1990s enjoyed the advantages of historically preserved locations, highly skilled labour and a convenient central European location. Subsequently Hungary and Germany both managed to lure away productions through aggressive tax policy changes. In the Republic, Ludmila Claussova was the point person in convincing the legislature to support a Czech Film Commission that would rebalance the production landscape; the CFC was launched in 2004. The overall effect was a race to the bottom: each jurisdiction touted the size of its incentives and the ease with which expenses could be recouped. That incentive structure stabilized at 20–25 per cent of overall, in-country spending. While production tax credits have not been increasing, they have proven remarkably resistant to reduction even in periods of stark austerity (Table 8.1). Such credits were firmly in place in 2012 even as the Czech Republic ran up record budget deficits in the wake of the Great Recession. Currently, each year the Republic hosts more than a dozen German films and TV shows, several Scandinavian period subjects, a few marquee US/UK productions, and an increasing number of global streaming series. 'It's a good mixture,' Claussova feels.[19] *Snowpiercer* took its place at the more expensive end of the non-Hollywood productions.

These taxation regimes are not only insulated from macroeconomic cycles, they function almost autonomously. State-sanctioned agencies play less of a role in certifying foreign productions than one might expect. While tax incentives throughout the European Union are contingent upon a 'cultural test' in which the project must pass muster, in practice, that test is simply a way of distinguishing between film-and-television and commercials. As Claussova explained, 'You don't need to give it so much importance because the cultural test for the film fund is just an instrument. ... Once it passes it

Table 8.1 Comparison of global film and television production tax credits

	California	Louisiana	Czech Republic	UK	Canada	New Zealand	South Korea
Organization	California Film Commission	Louisiana Entertainment	Czech Film Fund	British Film Commission / British Film Institute	Canadian Heritage + provincial organizations	New Zealand Film Commission	KOFIC (Korean Film Council)
Annual Budget	$330m	$180m	€31 production; €14 'selective support'	No cap / ~£100m	No cap	No cap / $12m	No cap
% Refunded	20% + 5% Uplift (25% for indie and relocation)	25% + 10% for Louisiana Screenplay + 5% outside New Orleans	20% on Czech spend	25% / n/a	16% on Canadian labor; 20% in Quebec; 35% in British Columbia	20% + 5% Uplift / n/a	25%
Form	Non-Transferrable Tax Credit	Tax Credit, transferrable to state at 88%	Cash Rebate	Cash Rebate / Recoverable Grant	Refundable Tax Credit (usually)	Cash Grant / Cash grant	Cash Grant

Test							
Allocation via 'Jobs Ratio' with bonuses for VFX, shooting outside Los Angeles, etc.	None	European Union cultural test and production criteria points system	Cultural Test or co-production / Grantmaking Committee	None	Test for Uplift / Grantmaking Committee	Committee Evaluation (Tourism, Film Industry, Engagement)	

California: http://film.ca.gov/tax-credit/the-basics-2-0/
Louisiana: https://louisianaentertainment.gov/film/motion-picture-production-tax-credit
Czech: http://www.filmcommission.cz/en/incentives/cultural-test/
UK BFI: https://www.bfi.org.uk/2022/financial_plan.html
Canada: https://www.canada.ca/en/canadian-heritage/services/funding/cavco-tax-credits/film-video-production-services.html
Quebec: http://www.qftc.ca/tax-incentives/information/
BC: https://www.creativebc.com/programs/tax-credits/film-incentive-bc/
NZ: https://www.nzfilm.co.nz/international/screen-incentives
ROK: http://www.koreanfilm.or.kr/eng/coProduction/locIncentive.jsp

passes. [The] criteria are so broad that somehow any project can pass.'[20] Most larger productions make initial contact with the facility (Barrandov) or local production service companies with a track-record of handling major motion pictures. In this case, Stillking is the crucial partner, and they worked with *Snowpiercer* from the start. Thus while the production received the fourth largest incentive in the half-decade of austerity from 2010 to 2015 (on a $39 million budget), the Film Fund played little role in linking it to its key Czech talent – its production designer, VFX firms, studio or production services company.[21] The state is along for the ride.

When national or local subsidy schemes 'succeed', they not only efface the active intervention of the state – converting state endorsements into 'neutral' tax policies – they also leave behind institutional, technological, material and labour resources for future productions in roughly the same location.[22] That geographic convergence reinforces the temporal disruption of the production process under new digital regimes. The formerly linear vision of sequential phases of production – development, pre-production focusing on design and casting, principal photography and post-production focusing on editing, sound and visual effects – has been all but replaced by a vision of coincident phases spread across multiple *sites*.[23] With *Snowpiercer*, and as a result of the Czech tax credits, many of those sites are collocated in the Republic.[24]

That constellation of sites continues into the-phase-formerly-known-as-post-production, where VFX firms in both Korea and the Czech Republic (UPP) worked in concert. But without the extra subsidy, both editing and sound were principally located in Korea. In contrast to the separated but rather linear writing process, production and post-production were wildly dispersed spatially *and* temporally. Sound, for example, was a Pacific Rim operation overseen by Bong's long-standing sound partners in Korea, Live Tone. Live Tone's work was supplemented in three ways. First, legendary New Zealand sound designer Dave Whitehead produced novel train sounds. Second, Whitehead drew on a new commercially available library of train sounds from Boom Library. Third, the final sound mix was done at Technicolor at Paramount in Los Angeles.

If that spatial dispersal is typical of the current global system, Bong's relationship with Live Tone is not. As Nikki Y. Lee and Julian Stringer have demonstrated, Bong and Live Tone have a unique partnership. Over time, their working relationship has tightened, and Bong has brought the sound studio into his projects earlier and earlier. By the time he was making *Snowpiercer*, Live Tone was providing Bong with 'film sound maps' – 'a full-service written document detailing all manner of conceptual and logistical arrangements at the earliest stage of pre-production'.[25] Lee and Stringer argue this document is a unique instantiation of Randy Thom's contention that productions should engage in 'screenwriting for sound', and it surely seems to be. But even Live Tone's CEO Ralph Tae-young Choi concedes that the company finds its way into the earliest stages of Bong's projects because he is 'the only person who has a clear concept about the sound from the pre-production process'.[26] The digitally driven disarticulation of the production/post-production processes has allowed for the rearrangement of both their sequencing and, to a degree, a reshuffling of their hierarchical relations. In most cases, the system restabilizes around an economically rational allocation of work by site and quality (large soundstages; good VFX talent). But the relative openness of the hierarchy allows for auteurist reshaping; in this case, a rare prioritization of sound design.

At the same time, though, the early and meaningful involvement of the sound studio is in keeping with a discourse one finds in virtually every craft: bring us on board earlier. Whether production or costume design, cinematography or visual effects, sound or music, all argue for the importance of early participation.[27] What the digital turns in craftwork have allowed for is a contingent reshuffling of the order in which those crafts are engaged. That is, the ability to reconfigure separable aspects of the division of cinematic labour may be digitally enabled, but because such aspects revolve around shifting constellations of material and digital facture, they benefit from regular consultation. While a craft might be temporally shifted or spatially dispersed, the overlapping of what had been linear phases of the process has now become a production model.

Or, rather, it has become the ground for a set of possible production models. In the one I have been tracing, that model is able to foster and sustain a broad consensus – among craft workers, cast members, funders, marketers and audiences – in which the director not only meaningfully shapes the story we see and hear but also the order and intensity with which the forces of production are brought to bear. In Director Bong's case, a process of simultaneous engagement with the range of technical and aesthetic dimensions of the movie helps cultivate his reputation for attention to detail – 'Bong-tail' – while at the same time giving rise to a unique preeminence to the soundtrack. By contrast, in a major Hollywood studio production, a similar convergent process serves as a guarantor of the progress of the production as a corporate-sanctioned – even corporate-authored – endeavour. So, as Marvel producer Kevin Feige explains, beginning with *Iron Man* it became standard practice to gather department heads for weekly design meetings during 'pre-production'. Those conferences in turn served as the model for both the Marvel Cinematic Universe from then on and for director Jon Favreau's work on Disney digital live-action movies beginning with *Jungle Book*.[28]

It is time to bring to the fore a final crucial aspect of *Snowpiercer*'s articulation of its conditions of production with its continuing status as a lucky convergence of possibilities: how the modularity of the indie production struggle is figured in the modular progress through the train. The linear globalism of the train's path seems to be a particular key that unlocks the figurative heart of the system. In the case of *Snowpiercer*, Bong is hooked by the allegory. He is, as I discussed above, taken with the idea that the progress of the train in space is the progress of the narrative. In the climactic confrontation, Wilford will praise the story we have just seen as 'the great Curtis revolution: a blockbuster production with a devilishly unpredictable plot'. Yet that spatio-temporal convergence is only part of what draws him: 'What I found so interesting [is] that social segmentation, behind the wagons at the head for the privileged classes. ... There are survivors, but they are divided into different classes. And the division of the classes finds an echo in the structure of the train itself. That is certainly what most attracted me to this story.'[29] Thus the structure of the train allegorizes the class structure while the progress of the train allegorizes the narrative form.

One might push that doubled convergence even further. What attracts Bong is not one single allegory or a simple chain that would link allegories of social stratification to spatial progress to narrative form. Rather, what lies at the core of *Snowpiercer*'s figurative power is the fungibility of the allegory as such, its deployability across scales. Those scales span the individual story of Curtis fighting his way from one paternal figure to another, to the design language of the train cars, to the looping route the train – and the movie – take through the global circuits of production and distribution that link the movie's facture to its exhibition, circuits that ultimately run through the homes of key actors – Korean, British, American and French. The train movie is thus an emblem *for* Bong but also an emblem of the translatability of this movie *for* others.[30] And just as the territory-by-territory expansion-via-translation process undergirded *Snowpiercer*'s adaptability, so the successful conclusion of territory-by-territory distribution deals is necessary for its profitability. In each of those negotiations, the decision that matters is not whether to advance but whether that advance will be joined or resisted.

As complex or malleable as those further dimensions of Director Bong's investment in the story are, and as powerful as they were in enlisting others, there is still another, competing imaginary. If trains are modular, linear, vectorized, path-dependent, scheduled and so forth, train movies routinely instantiate direct contrasts to those aspects: the passage from car to car that links the modules; the separability of cars that breaks the unity of the train as such; the station stop and the crash which undercut the train's ability to figure momentum; the slow curve which foregrounds the limitations of its linearity; the moment when the train is thrown into reverse which highlights the strongly vectorized nature of the engine; those stretches when the train is running late giving lie to the train's inevitability. *Snowpiercer* holds in abeyance some of the usual aspects – the separability and crashability of the train appear only very late in the movie – while it alters the nature of a train's schedule, reconfiguring it as a matter of cycles and geography, a lap a year, with anniversaries celebrated at the Ykaterina Bridge and Tunnel. But whether held in abeyance or reconfigured, these are the usual versions of the train.

What trains are not is instantaneous and nonlinear. Those versions of space-time require a different figuration. For most of the production, Bong imagines the nonlinear in the modular, artisanal form of the drawing. Such drawings can be ordered and reordered, as in the storyboard; or arrayed, as in the production design images that surround Nekvasil. Further, those images can be searched, swiped through in an easy succession (Figure 8.3). Those versions of the nonlinear, though, can be betrayed. Curtis's passage from the tail to the engine turns out not to be a tale of moral declension. What looks like a journey from the nurturing father Gilliam (John Hurt) to the bad dad (Ed Harris) turns out not to be an ethical journey at all. Gilliam is not the source of resistance to the technocratic calculations of the engineer but rather his *supplier*. The great betrayal of the film is the discovery that the eruption of the revolution is itself part of a plan, scheduled not according to a temporal cycle but to a Malthusian one in which 'individual units kill off other units'. And what makes that schedule possible is the instantaneous, telephonic communication of the head and the tail.

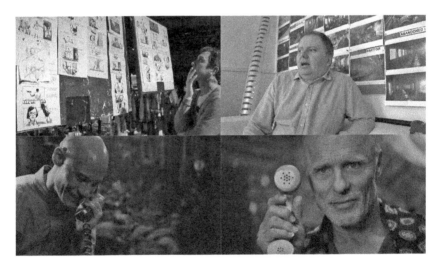

FIGURE 8.3 *Images of nonlinearity appear throughout the production. Like the array of Rochette drawings in Figure 8.2, the upper images can be shuffled in time. On the left, the storyboards; on the right, production designer Ondrej Nekvasil discusses the revolutionary plot in front of key design images. The lower images capture the instantaneous connection of engine and tail: 'Le Transperceneige: From the Blank Page to the Black Screen' (dir. Jésus Castro-Ortega, 2015), on* Snowpiercer *(RadiusTWC/Starz/Anchor Bay, 2015; Blu-Ray).*

This, I want to say, is the movie's understanding of the dependence of its indie globalism on a mode that is not modular and artisanal, but instantaneous. As producer Dooho Choi explained:

> We like to joke that without Skype we couldn't have made *Snowpiercer*. Credit to Skype. At the time it was really just Skype. Most of the development I was in LA and Bong was in Seoul … it was really about doing a lot of Skyping … that's really how we were able to do this global project if you will … even during our postproduction VFX reviews Bong was editing in Seoul; post-production was in Los Angeles, Prague, South Korea, London, Germany, Los Angeles, Vancouver.[31]

When the film was looking for American distribution at the American Film Market in 2012, CJ, the Korean major, negotiated with The Weinstein Company. Choi and Bong read Peter Biskind's *Down and Dirty Pictures* as preparation, in an effort not to get screwed.[32] They pretty much got screwed. Presented with Bong's final version, Weinstein demanded twenty minutes be cut; Bong resisted and apparently prevailed – not on contractual grounds but based on an unsuccessful preview screening of the shortened version. Nevertheless Weinstein moved the distribution from the flagship studio to Radius-TWC, the VOD arm of the company. In the United States, then, *Snowpiercer* was only released in a few theatres for a brief window before being pushed to streaming. It received no theatrical release at all in other major Anglophone territories. And while it performed very well *as a VOD feature*, and while there was a great deal of trade press coverage of this 'new mode' of distribution, it seems certain that the Weinsteins left money on the table.

What made the sacrifice of the Anglophone markets a plausible option for CJ and Bong was the combination of their reduced financial interest – the title had been presold – and the movie's runaway success elsewhere. In Korea it was the third most successful film of 2013, and it performed very well in France and China.[33] However improvised and compromised, then, the result of this piecemeal negotiation looks like an arrangement of sufficient systematicity that we might say that it is the emerging norm for indie and streaming service alike: A movie with sufficient theatrical potential will be screened, or perhaps not, territory by territory, more or less at the same time around the globe. That system was novel enough with *Snowpiercer* that the serious arguments between Bong, Choi and the Weinsteins could be reprocessed in Slatepitch contrarianism as an innovative model: 'What the Economics of "Snowpiercer" Say about the Future of Film.'[34]

Following this trainwreck of distribution, it is no surprise that Bong's next movie, *Okja*, was distributed by Netflix. Nor is it a surprise that its socio-industrial allegory turned *not* on the disruption of a looped, linear process (cinematic rollout) but on the simultaneous development of independent life forms – Super Pigs – in strategically chosen locations around the globe (simultaneous distribution). No longer required to line up and pull together (the indie train), each of *Okja*'s Super Pigs is left to grow on its own. Such a complex process requires explication. Where *Snowpiercer* divides its exposition between opening titles and an animated documentary played for schoolchildren much later in the movie, *Okja* combines the two into its opening. Tilda Swinton explains the impending Super Pig competition while slick graphics play behind her. As the backstory unrolls, Swinton's tale of hand-selected local farmers is punctuated by the various producers' credits, announcing an allegory where the 'livestock industry' stands in for our contemporary global digital distribution system for movies and television and in which Netflix boss Ted Sarandos is able to stand out as 'the expert'.

Neither the conclusion of *Snowpiercer*'s production and initial distribution nor the continuing evolution of director Bong's career constitutes the end of this story. It is tempting to regard the production as a redoubt of the sort of creative serendipity that is often eradicated from major studio moviemaking. If one makes such a mistake, then the existence of a range of diligent lawyers, agents, producers and others looms threateningly over Bong's authorship or even art more generally. To conceive instead those contingencies as nevertheless a part of the system that seems to oppose studio movie making at every turn requires that the supporting systems reinforce each other. That reinforcement, in turn, allows Bong's unique agency to span the production, from the discovery of the graphic novel to the renegotiation of a distribution agreement.

Yet even that configuration misplaces the industrial significance of *Snowpiercer*. As with Bong's other movies, *Snowpiercer* dwells on questions of consequence and entailment. Ultimately, its significance lies outside its own history, in the ways it revealed to its participants and might reveal to us the contingencies already present in the global production system. The train may wreck, the audience may be unnecessarily limited, but such events seem contingent. For those involved in the project such contingencies also include their negations: happy accidents, possibilities for innovative creative practices enabled by various digital turns and spillover effects from the enlistment of other artists in meaningful work. As a result of the manifold ways in which *Snowpiercer* takes its distance from other global cinematic endeavours, it conveys to its participants, and perhaps to us, a sense that however things are they might be otherwise.

CHAPTER 9

David Fincher's righteous workflow: Design and the transmedial director

Graig Uhlin

The 1995 film *Se7en* did much to establish David Fincher's reputation as a talented, if provocative, director of feature films. Prior to filming this dark serial killer narrative, Fincher primarily directed commercials and music videos. Then came the highly contentious production of the third instalment of the *ALIEN* franchise. The making of *ALIEN³* (1992) is now fabled for its clashes between the young film-maker and executives at 20th Century Fox over cost and schedule overruns, and these tales from the set (not to mention Fincher's subsequent disowning of the film) positioned Fincher within the conventional frame of the auteur film-maker as an embattled artist protecting his vision against studio constraints. Fincher has sometimes encouraged this perception of himself as a rebel against studio authority – as when, a few years later, he got 20th Century Fox to bankroll a film (*Fight Club* (1999)) that concluded with the controlled demolition of the studio's headquarters. This combative reputation, however, obscures another mode of auteurism that characterizes Fincher's approach to transmedial production beyond film direction. This alternative model of auteurism emphasizes collaboration and post-production workflow, recasting the director as more closely aligned to below-the-line craftsmanship than to notions of authorship derived from literature or the fine arts. As this chapter will argue, transmedial production places central importance on practices of design, and Fincher's creative output – encompassing feature films, television shows, music videos and commercials – is rooted in production methods that sustain creative autonomy in a fragmented media landscape.

Gesturing towards this other mode of auteurism, the opening titles of *Se7en*, beyond their narrative function of introducing the film's serial killer John Doe (Kevin Spacey), reintroduced Fincher to audiences after the disastrous production of *ALIEN*[3]. Even as the industrial task of opening credits is to assign authorship and apportion credit, the film's title sequence, both textually and meta-textually, places authorship under erasure. Designed by Kyle Cooper, it opens with a lateral view of the pages of a journal in close-up, as a silhouetted hand turns a page. These journals, handwritten by Doe, 'as though it was [his] job to prepare them', provide a framing device for the sequence.[1] This bit of handicraft involving an assemblage of voluminous prose and collaged photographs (many taken from medical literature) provides Doe's justification for his murders, the rationale for his 'work'. Though he seeks maximum publicity for his crimes, he nonetheless must cloak his identity. Extreme close-ups show fingertips being shorn of their skin with a razor blade, to remove identifying fingerprints. Nor do we see his face. Doe's labour is therefore anonymous, but his is not the only 'uncredited' work in this sequence: both Spacey and Cooper are not credited until the end of the film. In Spacey's case, the actor agreed to defer credit so as to not clue audiences in early to Doe's identity. Cooper's name meanwhile appears in the scroll of the closing credits ('Main and end titles designed and executed by Kyle Cooper'), where the use of 'executed', the 'u' flipped in a typographic inversion, links Cooper's relatively anonymous labour to Doe's vocation of serial killing, as two craftsmen toiling away without public recognition. Like Doe, Cooper utilizes a handcrafted aesthetic: while job titles are presented in Helvetica, the standard font of corporate branding, cast and crew names appear in a hand-etched scrawl (Figures 9.1–9.3). Cooper created them by scratching the emulsion of the film, borrowing

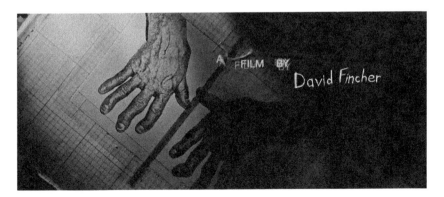

FIGURE 9.1 *David Fincher's possessory credit in* Se7en *(1995).*

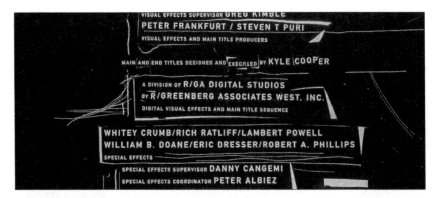

FIGURE 9.2 *Kyle Cooper's credit in the end titles of* Se7en *(David Fincher, 1995).*

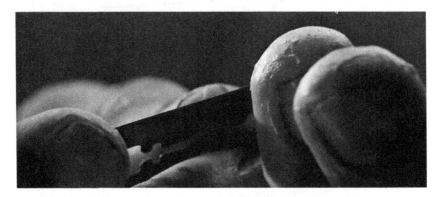

FIGURE 9.3 *Anonymous labour in* Se7en's *opening title sequence (David Fincher, 1995).*

a technique used by avant-garde film-makers such as Len Lye (cited by Cooper as an influence). Ben Radatz, writing for *Art of the Title*, notes that this scrawled text risked running afoul of guild rules about the legibility of credits.[2] Typographic design, like the intrusive '7' of the film's title, is thereby used to signal Fincher's disaffection with film-making as a corporate art, even as he continues to make studio-backed films.

Though the opening titles anonymize the labour performed by Doe, Cooper and Spacey, Fincher's name appears twice – as a possessory credit ('A film by David Fincher') and as the film's director ('Directed by David Fincher'). The arrogation of credit to a single individual, whose imprimatur subsumes the work of others, is a standard feature of auteurism. Yet Fincher has been quick to disclaim his own status as an auteur. The value of making commercials, as he sees it, is that there is no such attribution, and he refers to the transition to explicitly naming the director of a music video as 'a horrible day': 'I just thought it was so cool that you could try out this stuff and no one would ever – you know, they'd blame it on Michael Jackson.'[3] Fincher may identify with the image of self-effacement presented in *Se7en*'s title sequence, with the idea of a director as the designer of so much 'anonymous content', to borrow the name of one of his later production outfits, but anonymity has limited value in an industry that depends on credits. It is the work of building a reliable brand that underwrites future work. In short, Fincher prizes anonymity but depends on credit. However, this is not Fincher trying to have it both ways, by disclaiming the very privileges of auteurism while leveraging them to his advantage. Rather, this contradiction is a structural feature of how auteurism is being reshaped by transmediality, and what makes Fincher representative of these contemporary currents.

As the name brand, Fincher's auteur status can sponsor and promote the work of his relatively anonymous collaborators. Here again, the opening title sequence of *Se7en* is instructive. Its outsized influence allowed Cooper to stake out his independence. Cooper directed the sequence while employed at R/Greenberg Associates. Founded by Robert and Richard Greenberg in 1977, R/Greenberg (now R/GA) was among the freelance design firms that, as Jan-Christopher Horak notes, began replacing in-house titling operations at the studios throughout the 1960s and 1970s.[4] The company created, as some of its first notable projects, the opening titles for *Superman* (Richard Donner, 1978) and *ALIEN* (Ridley Scott, 1979), and Cooper worked there as a titles specialist from 1988 to 1996. That year, following *Se7en*, he co-founded Imaginary Forces, a design firm dedicated to title sequences, corporate branding and commercials. Under this imprint, Cooper designed titles for films such as *Donnie Brasco* (Mike Newell, 1997), *Sphere* (Barry Levinson, 1998) and *Arlington Road* (Mark Pellington, 1999). In 2003, he co-founded Prologue Films, with Kimberley Cooper, in order to keep his operations small and to stay involved on the creative side. There, Cooper created the animated logo for Marvel Studios, a flipbook animation of comic book pages that precedes every film of the Marvel Cinematic Universe.

In Cooper's career trajectory, we can see Hollywood's own recent history – charting a path from a brash, stylistic indie with handcrafted visuals to the branded intellectual property of contemporary franchise film-making. The demand for design has correspondingly risen in that intervening period. Once peripheral to the operations of the film industry, the subcontracted firms that execute branding strategies and visual effects sequences for media conglomerates are now integral to modes of cultural production organized along post-Fordist lines. Just as the creative industries more generally rely on the cultural capital of design to compete in a crowded marketplace, a cottage industry of boutique firms – including Cooper's Imaginary Forces and Fincher's Propaganda Films – emerged to service the need for branded content, underlining the close integration of art and marketing in design cultures.

While it figured in important ways to the history of mass production and modernism, design's cultural and economic ascendancy has accelerated since the 1980s, evidenced in part by the substantial growth in design professions across the creative industries. Design historian Guy Julier indicates that we have now reached 'a point of "critical mass" whereby [design] now takes a prominent public and commercial role'.[5] Julier attributes the proliferation of design to deindustrialization, especially as economies have shifted to cultural goods and services. The offshoring and outsourcing of manufacturing, enabled by aggressive deregulation, facilitated a split between the immaterial and material components of production, as planning and design are often cordoned off from the site of manufacture. Distinct from the era of uniform mass production, the flexible specialization of post-Fordism targets a 'lifestyle' consumer, and necessitates the use of marketing techniques and product packaging to reinforce the identity-shaping nature of consumption (especially for a buyer for whom the modifier 'designer' signals cultural capital). Because it generates value, design is now more thoroughly integrated into every phase of product's life cycle, organizing the spaces of consumption as much as production.

Design became an important factor as industries privatized or conglomerated. Julier points to the rise of design consultancies in the deregulated 1980s of Thatcherite Britain. As corporations merged, design firms were contracted to develop a corporate identity that would unify diverse acquisitions. These transformations took root somewhat earlier in the United States, but for the film industry, the 1980s was a key decade for its commitment to design. For instance, design played a role in the corporate takeover of Hollywood film studios, as they became one component of larger media conglomerates. For film historian J. D. Connor, the pendulum swing in studio film-making from the auteurist 1970s to the high-concept 1980s is clarified by the central place accorded to design (in practical terms, by the prominence of production design, and in industrial terms, by the reassertion of control by the studios in response to New Hollywood's auteurist renaissance). The development of high concept at Paramount, by the team of executives under Barry Diller known as the 'Killer Dillers', is central to Connor's account of this transformation. As its parent company Gulf + Western streamlined its diversified holdings into an entertainment and financial services conglomerate, Paramount functioned as the flagship entity for this synergistic reorganization. This corporate restructuring, Connor argues, redounded to the films themselves, which could model (or allegorize) the channelling of synergy under an all-encompassing design. High concept is the name for this total integration of the elements of a film under a singular look, and the subordination of aesthetics to the demands of marketing. It entailed, Connor writes, 'a reduction in narrative complexity in favor of an assertion of stylistic control'.[6]

Fincher came of age in this period of the studios' retrenchment, but as his sympathies were allied with the New Hollywood auteurs, when he turned to feature film-making in the early 1990s, his aim was to throw some grit into high concept's polish. While the beleaguered production of *ALIEN³* might be seen as a first salvo against high concept's smooth operations, it was *Se7en* and its thematically abrasive and visually abraded opening titles that effectively announced that Fincher would establish his own brand within the industry. It is only by doing so that he would be able to sponsor the activity of his various collaborators, who might subsequently position themselves to attain creative autonomy for their own work, as Cooper did. Fincher's career traced a similar path to Cooper's, having worked on the visual effects team at George Lucas's Industrial Light & Magic before co-founding Propaganda in 1983. And others would follow: Tim Miller of Blur Studio (founded in 1995) worked in visual effects for years, including designing the opening title sequence for Fincher's *The Girl with the Dragon Tattoo* (2011), before directing *Deadpool* (2016). Fincher is now collaborating with Miller on an animated anthology series (*Love, Death & Robots*) for Netflix. Fincher's creative output has been consistently divided between feature films, television shows (whether for premium cable or streaming sites), music videos, commercials and other types of branded content – and therefore he never fully 'graduated' into film-making.

The transmedial aspects of Fincher's work can be productively distinguished from the transmedial practices of media conglomerates, such as the creation of cinematic 'universes' that depend on the maximal exploitation of intellectual property across media platforms. His choice to take a possessory credit, for instance, cuts against his alliance with the relative anonymity of below-the-line labourers, but that choice is made with the recognition that establishing a brand as an auteur is what licences future work. Classical auteurism, in other words, is its own form of intellectual property, establishing ownership over cultural products and subsuming the labour of many under a single signature. Contemporary transmedia production has renewed the proprietary tensions between the auteur and the studio, especially as franchise film-making tends to privilege the latter. While Marvel Studios has more recently turned to recognizable directors to re-energize the superhero genre, the Marvel Cinematic Universe, especially in its early years, nonetheless considered directors and stars to be more or less replaceable.[7] Their labour is in service to marketable characters and recognizable fictional worlds. Fincher's residual auteurism thereby positions one form of intellectual property against another, increasingly ascendant form. However, as much as Fincher's auteurism designates a signature style, it more importantly specifies a set of production practices, rooted in digital workflow methods drawn from the once-peripheral domain of visual effects. It is these production methods that unify Fincher's transmedial work, and which are intended, though not always successfully, to insulate his creative activity and the work of those he sponsors from being wholly subsumed by the type of labour on offer by media conglomerates chasing valuable IP.

The difference hinges on the matter of scale. Fincher has proved not to be a good fit for franchises, as indicated by *ALIEN*[3], *The Girl with the Dragon Tattoo* and the recently cancelled sequel to *World War Z* (Marc Forster, 2013). He is more commonly associated with the sort of mid-budget film targeted at adults that is no longer a Hollywood mainstay, in part because these stand-alone projects do not iterate out well into multi-platform content creation. It is precisely this type of auteur-director that has migrated to television in recent years, as Fincher himself has done as producer and director of Netflix's first original scripted series *House of Cards* (2013–18) and *Mindhunter* (2017–), as well as a couple of stalled projects at HBO. By remaining somewhat agnostic about what medium he labours in (whether commercials, TV or film) and scaling his productions accordingly, Fincher has managed to sustain an increasingly outmoded form of auteurism that had reached its heights in the New Hollywood era. We can attribute this to how Fincher has downscaled studio-level production through the use of digital technologies, from his early adoption of digital image capture to his reorganization of post-production workflow. Just as like-minded directors such as Michael Mann and especially Steven Soderbergh have done, Fincher has leveraged these affordable but sophisticated technologies to create a craft-oriented, collaborative environment that can flexibly adapt as needed to a diversified media landscape. In a transmedia era, the scale of productions across media has effectively converged. For example, Fincher was involved in the formation of the production and management company Anonymous Content, whose portfolio transitions between feature films and prestige television shows, not to mention branded content for luxury products. The company's approach to packaging a TV show bears little difference from how they package a film project, and in fact, the former was modelled on the latter. In this convergence of film and television, just as in the 1990s when music video directors transitioned to film, Fincher represents one model for maintaining creative autonomy and uses that autonomy to sponsor the work of below-the-line professionals.

Foregrounding workflow processes, particularly as a practice of design, highlights Fincher's collaborative efforts and his redistribution of credit downward to below-the-line crew. Workflow is central to digital film production, which is no longer dependent on expensive laboratory processing and linear editing systems. Ignatiy Vishnevetsky has emphasized that workflow describes a process akin to the classical notion of *découpage* and its primary importance entails its blurring of the boundaries between production and post-production.[8] A maximally efficient workflow is designed, he notes, to quickly transfer and organize the digital information recorded by cameras from the set to the post-production facilities where editors manage their assembly. As Julier indicates, the collapse of above-the-line and below-the-line work in the creative industries is a feature of 'concurrent design' practices. Rather than having product output dependent on hierarchical and linear processes, in concurrent design, 'teams from different departments work simultaneously on the development of products, continuously interchanging information and the results of development', allowing for iterative methods to inform product design.[9] Julier cites concurrent design as one aspect of the post-Fordist reorganization of the design industry in the 1990s. In what he notes has been called the 'third wave' in advertising, the large design consultancies of the previous decade disaggregated into the growing ranks of 'small-scale but well-known design groups … operating within flexible networks working for a multinationalized corporate infrastructure'.[10] Production became dependent on subcontracted peripheral entities that serviced corporate branding strategies previously executed in-house. This transition dovetails with the proliferation across the film industry of visual effects firms and post-production houses that met the rising demand from studios and advertising companies for digital animation and laboratory services. Though these firms would increasingly founder and self-cannibalize when forced to chase smaller and smaller margins for effects work, their ascendancy in the industry set the conditions for Kyle Cooper to transition from a relatively anonymous title designer to having the status sufficient to provide the brand for Marvel Studios films. Moreover, as the centre of the industry has shifted from production to post-production, these peripheral firms have mastered core competencies that can scale in different directions, with their creative personnel moving easily between client-service work such as commercials and effects sequences and more 'respectable' film and television productions.

Underlying this transmedial flexibility, workflow is a design process that organizes and integrates production and post-production practices. John Pavlus has proposed that Fincher embodies the idea of 'director-as-designer', since although all directors are essentially designers, broadly conceived as creative professionals responsible for the look of a consumer product, Fincher's film-making exhibits distinct qualities – among them, an obsessive attention to detail and a streamlined efficiency – that suggest more of a design ethos that might said of other film-makers. Fincher's films, Pavlus says, are 'exquisitely designed machines', and he draws a comparison to Apple's chief design officer Jonathan Ive, whose sleek product designs, like Fincher's, 'just work – with style to burn'.[11] Design's relevance for film, however, should not be limited to questions of style. The comparison to Ive, for instance, might be more apt for how Fincher's production workflow aspires to the same type of end-to-end control that Apple exerts over its product designs. A consideration of workflow, moreover, emphasizes that post-Fordist design encompasses more than the production of objects to include immaterial processes. The remainder of this chapter will outline Fincher's use of development of a 'tapeless' workflow as a collaborative effort with below-the-line professionals and in consultation with Adobe, whose suite of software products provide the basis for an integrated system of information flows on set and in post-production. I argue that this tapeless workflow constitutes a 'protocological' reorganization of film production, following Alexander Galloway's understanding of protocols as instruments of control within a decentralized network.[12]

Since *Zodiac* (2005), Fincher has reorganized his production methods around an exclusively digital workflow. Previously, images recorded on film were transferred to a digital intermediate for assembly, for compositing and other effects shots and for colour correction. This intermediate was then outputted back to film for exhibition prints. In a tapeless workflow, there is no point in the film's work cycle where it resides on some form of physical (i.e. non-digital) media. Fincher has called this type of workflow 'righteous', given its efficiencies and time-saving benefits – responsible, for instance, for shaving a few days off the shooting schedule for *The Social Network* (2010).[13] Fincher has explained his adoption of digital image capture as rooted in considerations about workflow: 'It's not the camera. There are certain things that digital doesn't do well – but it's more about the workflow to me. It's about the way that I'm able to make my movie.'[14] A digital camera, for instance, provides more flexibility and choice in shot composition through an expanded range of the frame. Beginning on *The Social Network*, images were recorded with extra space on all four edges, that is, beyond the parameters of the final aspect ratio. This practice continued on *The Girl with the Dragon Tattoo* and *Gone Girl* (2014), which were shot on the Red One and Red Dragon cameras, respectively. On *Gone Girl*, scenes were recorded at 6K but framed for a 5K centre extraction. What this spatial latitude allowed for was any stabilization or repositioning that Fincher might want during the editorial process. 'David was able to come into the DI suite, look at a shot and then say, "zoom in a little bit" or "pan left" without any resolution penalty,' according to Ian Vertovec, co-founder of Light Iron, who built the real-time 5K workflow for *Dragon Tattoo*.[15] Stabilization would smooth out or eliminate 'imperfections' in camerawork – either a slightly shaking frame or inconsistent speed in a camera movement.

Fincher prizes the immediacy of digital image capture, since it permits the director to make continual adjustments rather than wait for dailies to be processed. Of his switch to digital, he has said:

The thing for me – I love film: I think it looks beautiful. And in the right hands, to me, there are maybe 10 guys in the world that make a difference. But when it comes to that gnawing, horrible, 24-hour period between having shot something and seeing it in dailies, and going, 'What the f... you don't have one take that's in sharp focus?' I will trade four or five stops of high-end shoulder exposure for the ability to have a 23" HD monitor that allows me to go: 'See this thing right here? You can see his ears end and his eyes are out.' I can't stand it when movies are out of focus – it just bugs.[16]

The HD monitor ensures that members of the crew – 'from the boom operator to the make-up artist to the actors to the dolly grip' – see the same image from which to make judgements and suggestions. A similarly non-hierarchical process operates in the distribution of dailies via Fincher's use of the web-based Pix system. Starting with *Panic Room* (2002), Fincher has used this interface, which allows for tiered and remote access to footage among the post-production team. By enabling remote collaboration between different departments, Fincher can provide, through notes appended to each take, immediate feedback to the editorial or effects departments. Crew members can view the same set of images simultaneously without any loss of quality. These affordances of remote collaboration and live updating are characteristic of the concurrent design practices that Julier points to in the post-Fordist reorganization of design.

Also characteristic is the collapse of previously linear and autonomous processes. Fincher's collaboration with Adobe on the production of *Gone Girl* exemplifies the virtuous circle created by standardization and uniformity. On that film, all editing and post-production effects were achieved using the Adobe Creative Suite (Premiere Pro for editing, After Effects for compositing and other effects). Fincher's crew worked closely with Adobe to modify the production workflow for maximum efficiency – decreasing the loading times for high-resolution images, for instance. The most significant advance, however, concerned the reciprocal communication established between Premiere and After Effects, which allowed for simultaneous procedures to be run among the post-production team. As editor Kirk Baxter explains, the choice to use the Adobe platform

> was made because it was the best tool for us to use to bring a lot of the effects in-house, to be doing a lot of After Effects work and for that to be seamlessly integrated into the process of editing. If somebody updated a visual effects shot in the building it just went straight through into my timeline. It was more about workflow than it was about what I prefer to work with.[17]

The tapeless workflow thereby represents a convergence of previously separate domains. Moreover, by using digital cameras and software available and affordable to even amateur film-makers, Fincher's workflow downscales studio film production to the level of a small, collaborative team akin to a design firm, which maintain the flexibility for and responsiveness to the specific demands of transmedia production.

While this mode of production opposes the arrogation of credit to the director as in standard models of auteurism, it does not wholly democratize production either. It has, rather, an ambivalent relation to authorial control, since it both empowers collaborators while retaining authority for the director. As indicated by Alexander Galloway, protocol names the organizational principle of distributed networks, such as the parallel processes of Fincher's decentralized production workflow. Galloway provides a corrective to utopian appraisals of the internet, emphasizing that its non-hierarchical architecture depends on a set of standardized conventions and technical specifications (i.e. protocols) that run counter to the anarchic potential of the network. Protocols allow for freedom yet enforce standardization, hence the diagrammatic structure of the Web as a 'regulated flow': 'Information does flow, but it does so in a highly regulated manner.'[18] Accordingly, when the moving image in an era of media convergence becomes data, then film-making becomes data management. The networked nature of Fincher's digital workflow allows for multiple points of entry for feedback and modification, whether on set or in post-production, granting relative autonomy to individuals within the production. Yet these same procedures only heighten Fincher's authority, which now has a capillary reach into aspects of the production process, extending the same scalpel-like control given to film-makers by the digital manipulation of images. Consider two changes Fincher insisted on in the procedures for digital image capture: auto-slating and deletion of takes.[19] Auto-slating automatically records all relevant metadata for future reference in assembly in the initial frames of each take. This enables Fincher, already known for multiple takes on set, to move quickly from one take to the next with minimal interruption. The other change permits Fincher to delete takes on set, which the specifications of the delivery from camera to storage magazine originally disallowed since it risks losing valuable data. Fincher's seamless workflow is based then on the automation and integration of processes across the pipeline, coupled with the selective ability to interrupt these processes. Authorial control is protocological, then, in the sense it can design a set of procedures around its stated preferences, while also maintaining the privilege to suspend those procedures.

As Fincher has developed it, workflow entails the reorganization of production around collaborative authorship, particularly with below-the-line crew and subcontracted personnel such as title designers. This working environment decentres film as a privileged site of moving image production, since the workflow's skills and procedures are transportable across different types of production. Indeed, Fincher often utilizes his commercial shoots as test-runs or experimental playgrounds for the exploration and refinement of new technologies, such as the face-replacement effects in *The Curious Case of Benjamin Button* (2007). Lacking the resources of other blockbuster film-makers such as Steven Spielberg, Fincher had to shoot a couple commercials to fund the development of that technique. While the commercials and music videos offer opportunities to beta-test technological innovations, Fincher's work in television demonstrates the subsequent application of his workflow to other media. According to editor Tyler Nelson, *Mindhunter* utilized Adobe Premiere and After Effects for compositing and shot stabilization, just as previously done on Fincher's feature-film productions.[20] Nelson himself was promoted to one of the series editors after having worked as an apprentice and assistant editor on *Curious Case* and other Fincher projects. Fincher's production workflow thus involves the recruitment of personnel and the scaling up of methods developed in the peripheral domains of film-making, which in actuality are no longer peripheral in an era of convergence.

In considering these production methods, I have thus far largely bracketed questions of visual style, but in closing, I will briefly indicate how Fincher's seamless workflow ramifies to an aesthetic practice that blur boundaries across media. His transposable set of production practices yields continuities of style regardless of media format. Given his start as a music video director, one aspect of this style involves the percussive or rhythmic coordination of image and sound. Consider the Henley Royal Regatta sequence of *The Social Network*, where the crew team of the Winklevoss twins (Armie Hammer and Josh Pence) finishes second in a race, just as they lose to Mark Zuckerberg (Jesse Eisenberg) in creating a social networking site. The sequence is somewhat extraneous to the narrative; its inclusion stems from the slim narrative pretext that the Winklevoss twins can discover that Facebook has spread to Europe. Its superfluity, however, allows for some formal play, and the self-contained sequence channels music video aesthetics, particularly in its rhythmic use of editing. Fincher has affirmed as much in a 2010 interview with *Pitchfork*. In that interview, moreover, he specifies that he cut the scene to the music, 'a Wendy Carlos version of [Edvard Grieg's] "In the Hall of the Mountain King"'.[21] Sound designer Ren Klyce had suggested Grieg after Fincher requested an example of an Edwardian composer, and composers Atticus Ross and Trent Reznor provided the electronic version of the classical piece. The music accelerates in its pacing across the sequence, and the editing responds accordingly. As the race approaches its finish line, framing gets progressively tighter, focusing ultimately on the strained faces of the rowers. Throughout the scene, Fincher maintains symmetry in his shots of the two boats. For example, a medium shot of two rowers angled to the right riverbank, followed by a shot of the oars from the same angle, is matched by the same series of shots, this time of the other boat and its oars, and angled towards the other riverbank. Moments later, a head-on close-up of one rower is mirrored by the same framing of a competing rower. This symmetry is ultimately broken towards the end of the race, when the victory of one team is assured. This sequence is also distinct from the rest of the film in that its very narrow depth of field produces a somewhat unreal effect that resembles the look of tilt-shift photography, bringing it therefore into close relation to the stylized imagery of Fincher's music videos.

The Henley Regatta sequence can be compared to a notable montage sequence from the Fincher-directed second episode of *Mindhunter*. This montage scene features a similarly percussive use of editing, done by frequent Fincher collaborator Kirk Baxter, in narrating the dull routines of life on the road for FBI agents Holden Ford (Jonathan Groff) and Bill Tench (Holt McCallany). Set to Steve Miller's jaunty 'Fly Like an Eagle', the montage relies on several series of match cuts (coffee cups being filled, throwing suitcases on motel beds, car doors being closed, etc.) in which actions repeat at different times and locations, providing a condensed impression of the tedium of travelling. The visuals exhibit a few sly jokes – two successive images of diner food are followed by the plop of an Alka-Seltzer in a glass of water – but their effect is more readily felt in their rhythmic timing. For instance, there are three successive beats of coffee cups being filled, following by a longer shot of Tench pouring an excessive amount of sugar into his cup. The pouring of the sugar has the feel of a slow release following the staccato pulses of the preceding shots. Whereas the Henley Regatta sequence vectorizes time in a strongly linear fashion, *Mindhunter*'s travel montage emphasizes circularity and repetition – beginning and ending, for instance, on the same shot from inside the trunk of a car.

Like the elaborate title sequences in some of Fincher's films, such as in *Se7en* and *The Girl with the Dragon Tattoo*, these scenes demonstrate the continuing influence of music video and commercial aesthetics into film-making. This influence also runs in the other direction, as evidenced not just by Fritz Lang's *Metropolis* (1927) serving as a template for Madonna's 'Express Yourself' video but also by Fincher's use of his lead actors in commercial spots (Brad Pitt for Heineken, Rooney Mara for Calvin Klein and the music video for Justin Timberlake's 'Suit & Tie'). Through this cross-pollination of media formats, Fincher has developed an audiovisual aesthetic that resembles his tapeless workflow. Just as the aim of the digital workflow is to provide for the 'frictionless' transmission of data by not relying on physical media, analogously Fincher's visual style utilizes a 'weightless' digital image that is as malleable and free-floating as musical form. Relevant here are his use of digital compositing in *Panic Room* (2002) and *Fight Club* to execute 'impossible' camera movements (i.e. through the floor or into a keyhole), since the digital image is unrestricted by physical architecture. However, a more succinct example, and one that underlines the transmediality of his work, comes from a commercial Fincher directed for Hewlett-Packard in 2004. Set to the opening strains of the Who's 'Baba O'Reilly', the spot titled 'Constant Change' features an employee in an office workplace walking from his office to the elevator. As he walks, everything in the surrounding environment, including the clothes he wears, changes. With each pulse of the music, background details alter: day turns to night, the office layout shifts, employees pop in and out of the frame and so on. His face remains the same, however, as the primary unchanging element in the shot. The advertisement's tagline – 'solutions for the adaptive enterprise' – could double as a description for Fincher's own flexible workflow. Given that what is being sold is less a durable consumer product than a new organization of work around an integrated set of computer technologies, it is the flashy visuals of the commercial that function as 'proof of concept'. Fincher creates a plastic image that transforms as effortlessly as the site of production that manufactures it; the image's fluidity is an analogue of the adaptive potential of the designed environment. The commercial legitimates both Fincher's stylistic choices and his production methods.

Fincher's transmediality is rooted in the proliferation of post-production houses and design firms that, on the one hand, reside at the margins of the industry, dependent on a competitive market for digital animation, and, on the other hand, have established a lean and flexible cottage industry that service a range of clients across multiple media platforms. Fincher's own recurring group of collaborators are often drawn from this world – he has few such collaborations with above-the-line talent – and he has thus played a significant role in establishing a craft-based network for content creation. This media ecosystem runs counter to narrow specialization of labour; Fincher works consistently with people who, like himself, are skilled across Hollywood's standard division of labour. It also seeks to consolidate previously autonomous aspects of production in-house under the post-production and editorial departments. Fincher aims, in other words, to restage studio-level production on a smaller scale. This is a version of synergy that is distinct from the one deployed in the transmedia storytelling of media conglomerates, which tends to aggrandize authorship under the studio label (i.e. Marvel), rather than with the director or other above-the-line talent. Fincher's transmedial production instead places downward pressure on the attribution of credit. This redistribution of credit, however, still depends on the brand identity of the auteur-director, whose status in the industry licenses the work of others, and as I indicated earlier, the collapse of Hollywood's division of labour in Fincher's comparatively non-hierarchical workflow nonetheless still extends the authorial control of the director.

PART FOUR

Music video's forms, genres and surfaces

CHAPTER 10

A conversation with Emil Nava

Carol Vernallis

Carol: Hi Emil! Can you tell me how you got into music video?

Emil: We noted earlier that I love colours. So much of it is through feeling. I didn't go to film school and I didn't study film. I started as a PA runner to get coffee, so everything I know is based on emotion and feeling, and for me, colours are a huge part of that, whether I'm going dark, or with lighter colour palettes. So I guess injecting big punches of colour is like injecting big punches of feeling.

I was making tea and coffee, and I quickly became, back in the early 2000s – in playback, like when you record from the cameras to watch back. I would sit next to the director and I would record the shot. And then he would say 'oh, can you play it back to me?' And then I would hear the conversations he was having. And I'd be on the set and I was watching the monitor because I would have to record. So I was very much, for a good year, just by the monitors, watching and breaking them down. I had a lot of musician friends. I knew several people in the industry because I was running – I got a camera deal. Funnily enough, the person who graded my first-ever film was this kid. I walked into the Mill in London and I said, 'Who's your new assistant?' They said, 'Yeah, this guy Aubrey Woodiwiss.' He's been my grader forever. He won the Black Pencil. He's the biggest grader in the world.[1]

Carol: Before your experiences in the industry, I heard you first worked as a cook; did you study formally? Isn't video-making kind of like cooking, like adding a punch of chilli, or adding a little corn starch, swirling?

Emil: I left school at 16. I wanted to be an actor, but I wasn't ready to act. I think I had some really crazy chefs I worked with and it was intense. When you're in the middle of a cooking service, nothing else matters. It's the same as a shoot. You're working with multiple personalities and you don't have time to think about anything except what is right in front of you. And you're creating by mixing. I say about films and music videos. I try to film something one time, and I try it again and it doesn't work. When I try to cook one dish, and I try it again and it doesn't work. It's like there's an element of magic.

Carol: I noticed you were, at one point, doing the very dense overlays, and the image was kind of milky, like with Pharrell's 'Feels'. I guess your training comes back to you?

Emil: I love layers; I always joke with the editors. I love where the clip becomes slightly dreamy and you can get lost. You can get so lost in a moment, you're just in it.

Carol: Can I note something about your work? There's often a pinpoint of focus but also a lot of energy or freneticism, and then a second anchor point as well. You've got really dramatic changes in colours. You use music video's classic techniques, for example, that one should build out – start small and expand upon it, while gradually bringing in new things. You're very good at building to a peak musical moment, which can be exciting near a clip's end.

Emil: Thank you. I don't analyse my own work very much, but I know singular characters are important to me, which in my life have been artists and performers. I've managed to keep such long-standing relationships with artists, because my focus is always on the central character, the song and their performance. I feel I can then go crazy with ideas, colours and frenetic shots.

Carol: In your Eminem video 'River', he's the centre of a cyclone.

Emil: Yeah, definitely, and that's like the epitome of it. It's like him being in the centre of the ground, of this full cyclone in the middle of a bedroom. And in a way it's weird, I guess if I think about the conversations I have with my therapist … isolation, loneliness, the chaos that surrounds me. I just shot my first movie, *Snorkeling*, at the beginning of the year.

Carol: Cool!

Emil: We're editing it in the next room right here! Similarly to the Eminem clip, it's about one young male character and the mayhem of his life. A focus on a singular character has been what's always worked for me. I'm quite ADD and I'll get bored quite quickly. I like to have it constantly changing, which I guess is very similar to my life.

Carol: What's it like to work in commercials?

Emil: I find commercials limiting. You have no creative input. You're just turning up and doing what someone tells you. There's no magic there. Though we just did my favourite commercial I've ever done, for the new Gap Christmas campaign. I also just set up a company called Ammolite. We offer a kind of 360 creative, beyond video, into visuals, photography and so on. We represent videographers, photographers, graphic designers, we even have an architect.

Carol: These cross-medial techniques are in everything. Even with your Sam Smith 'Promises' video, the opening might be considered a kind of doc?

Emil: Yeah, and actually we're just trying to figure this out. I think we're going to release a long form version of the video, which is a documentary about the mock.

Carol: Can you tell me about editing?

Emil: I think you have to reedit. I edit a mad version, I edit a simple version, I edit every version until I'm like, that's the one! I think you've got to go so far one way, and then so far the other, for you to see the polarizing differences and then work out what's the magic mix, you know? We did that with my film *Snorkeling*. We did a really mad edit, and it was so mad that you couldn't imagine anyone watching it. And then we did a really simple version, and now we're marrying the two together.

Carol: Let's watch a little of your 'This Is What We Came For!' – through Skype!

Emil: Yeah, let's do that, okay.

Carol: It looks like you've got real smoke crossing in, and real leaves. And then I love – you've got your glitter, your tiny stuff. These are within your arsenal of techniques. It'd be great to make a catalogue.

Emil: I had a lot of other ideas. Obviously when it comes down to time, you're limited. I was trying to bring as much nature and realism into a space that essentially wasn't real. So we created a 360 projection. We had a 360 VR camera which we took to all the locations, and filmed 360. Then we stitched all of the footage into one video, and we projected it onto the cube.

Carol: Okay, wonderful. Here we are.

Emil: Wow, over 2 billion views now. I didn't see that it'd crossed that mark.

Carol: I'm impressed that you didn't dress Rihanna in a way to accentuate her body. She's wearing a moonsuit.

Emil: Yeah, that was definitely down to her. We went over the idea, and I think she knew the visuals. This was what she wanted to bring to it.

Carol: And she's wearing very shiny beautiful things in her hair. It picks up the glitter.

Emil: Kind of rave-y. Calvin is known for slightly rave music.

Carol: Were the lasers live?

Emil: The lasers were live in the space, and they were also in the 360. So everything that we shot from our side of the cube on the 360 camera, we also did for real in the cube.

Carol: You get the illusion that there really are dancers behind the cube. It's very convincing, right?

Emil: The feeling is that she's being transported through these spaces, and they're inside her mind, I guess. I think we wanted it to feel like at moments as if it's vast and endless and we're in locations like the desert, yet in the next minute she's in a cube, and the next minute she's in a warehouse, and then in a rave. It was definitely about playing with perspective.

Carol: That red.

Emil: Yeah, there's the red. Love that red.

Carol: And you popped that in in real time?

Emil: Yeah, that's all happening in camera right there and then.

Carol: You digitize the dress a bit.

Emil: We actually very carefully chose really tiny little moments in the beginning to just hint at the madness that's about to come. Same with the colours, we wanted to start in a very stark, empty space – a bare cube.

Carol: How much time did you devote to the shoot, pre-production and post?

Emil: We prepped for a couple of weeks, and then we did a two-day shoot in Los Angeles. Like the horses, the car, the warehouse, the desert. Then we had a week's prep, where we built the set and the 3D models out of the footage in New York. And then we did a one-day shoot. This wasn't a long day. The post-production was just an edit. We didn't do any CGI. It was probably only a week after we edited and then it was out.

Carol: And then you just drop it, right?

Emil: Just drop it, exactly.

Carol: Lovely. That's a very pretty purple. And you've got some smoke here, right? Or fog?

Emil: Yeah. That's real smoke happening in camera in the cube.

Carol: It feels as if it's in a real time.

Emil: Rihanna got to watch the videos before we shot it, so she knew how to play with it; she knew then to turn around in the door, as the dancers moved around her. All of it. Every take was a full one. We didn't do many because we wanted it to feel like it was real.

Carol: Wow! How much do the lyrics, like 'lightning,' play a role?

Emil: Lots. I think lightning, flashes, strobes and energy were a huge part of the idea. In the screens, the edits, everything really.

Carol: Who is Rihanna's 'you?'

Emil: Rihanna's performing just to the camera – she would look, almost straight through the camera at you watching.

Carol: So it's me.

Emil: Yeah, it's you, definitely.

Carol: This moment is nice because it's not a one-to-one connection, the shift to green, 'we go fast...' But there are also big sync points.

Emil: I really like big bold markers, where it feels like everything changes. Because I feel like when the music changes, I want everything to change. In the same way you have an Act 1, Act 2 and Act 3 in a movie, I want my videos to have stamps like that, so you almost reset your emotion.

Carol: Here, the dust of the car is entering the dust in the cube. How'd you do that technically? Did you have a dust blower?

Emil: As the car moved, we powered it in.

Carol: Did you have four or five people, each responsible for one effect?

Emil: Yeah, we had a big art department team and they were all outside of the cube. So they were throwing in the leaves, the glitter and then the smoke. There's a photo of me, and I'm pushing the smoke into the cube.

Carol: Where's this location of the cube in the field?

Emil: This was in the mountains towards Big Bear. We carried that cube a great distance and assembled it there. We added smoke, but there was actually this crazy fog that came over at one point, so we had a double effect.

Carol: You often have Calvin as a totem, just standing there, like in 'One Kiss'. Is this about personality?

Emil: Calvin's a producer, a writer and a musician. I think he's like, to me, I always see him in the music. He's not an upfront and centre kind of guy.

Carol: This is nice. You feel the car comes in.

Emil: This is one of the few times we cut inside the projector. This is a real shot of the car, filmed not by a 360, but rather a normal camera. It was meant to feel like we were coming through the real world, through the screen and then even through that world as well. We're constantly going through – it's like worlds on worlds in worlds, you know?

Carol: Oh, I like this hologram, Tron-like moment. A good moment of sync – perhaps all you need is one, late in the video, an element that really punches it, right? Something like this.

Emil: Yeah, definitely.

Carol: Or the kiss in the Charlie Puth, 'Promises' video. Yeah, you just need one.

Emil: One big moment.

Carol: Oh yes, the *Tron*. That's star behaviour, yeah.

Emil: But I also love when Rihanna's neck and the leaves are falling down. I think whenever I get really lost and I wonder where I am, it's my favourite bit. Because then it feels like the concept of the video is working, you know.

Carol: Yeah. Wow. Well thank you, Emil. That's lovely.

Emil: Good stuff.

CHAPTER 11

Risers, drops and a fourteen-foot cube: A transmedia analysis of Emil Nava, Calvin Harris and Rihanna's 'This Is What You Came For'

Brad Osborn

British director Emil Nava has directed over one hundred music videos, several of which have won MTV Music Video Awards. Scottish musician Calvin Harris started out as a DJ and singer but has quickly grown into one of the most sought after electronic dance music (EDM) producers of the last decade. The two have collaborated on fourteen music videos since 2013. Table 11.1 shows these fourteen videos in chronological order.

Watching these fourteen videos in chronological order reveals several distinct changes in style in both cinematography and musical design. Here, I begin by describing what I see as the broadest continuities and changes in these clips. Though Harris's oeuvre suggests two broad phases while Nava's suggests three, each artist enters into a distinctly new phase after Rihanna's 'This Is What You Came For' (2016). After this, I move to a close reading of Rihanna's video in order to show how both Nava and Harris begin to adapt their previous styles in order to better respond to each others' changing style, focusing specifically on the ways in which Nava's changes in setting either align or do not align with Harris's sectional changes in musical form. Since the specific musical form

Table 11.1 Nava/Harris Collaborative Music Videos

Year	Title	Singer(s)	Nava Phase	Harris Phase
2013	I Need Your Love	Ellie Goulding		
2014	Outside	Ellie Goulding		
2014	Blame	John Newman	1	
2014	Slow Acid	(none)		
2014	Summer	Calvin Harris		1
2015	Pray to God	HAIM		
2015	How Deep Is Your Love	Disciples		
2016	My Way	Calvin Harris	2	
2016	This Is What You Came For	Rihanna		
2017	Feels	Pharrell, Katy Perry and Big Sean		
2018	Nuh Ready, Nuh Ready	PARTYNEXTDOOR		
2018	One Kiss	Dua Lipa	3	2
2018	Promises	Sam Smith		
2019	Giant	Rag'n'Bone Man		

Nava had become accustomed to accommodating in Harris's music since 2013 (what I will call *EDM form*) was beginning to change around this time, it is interesting to note the ways in which Nava's particular rhythm of introducing and cutting between settings adapts to this change.

Continuity and change in Nava, Harris and their collaborations

Cars, motorcycles and horses run throughout Nava's output, but in his early videos with Harris these are mere symbols of luxury, acting as signifiers for excessive wealth, partying and hedonism. Harris's song forms in this period are what I call *EDM forms*, in which songs are built from one or more rotations of a *verse*, a tension-building *riser* (usually featuring the song title), and a massive, climactic *drop* – the moment of ecstatic dancing to a four-on-the-floor house beat. Nava's video for 'Blame' (2014) shows Harris performing these EDM forms in opulent clubs. Indeed, Harris was for six consecutive years (2013–18) the highest-paid EDM musician in the world, and held standing gigs at elite Las Vegas casinos.[1]

From 2015 onwards, most of Nava's videos with Harris centre on the construction of virtual worlds, but through two different techniques. In the four videos from his second phase (2015–16), Nava creates expansive, open, often 'natural' sets that nevertheless bear a strange relationship to reality. 'Pray to God' (2015) features the three members of HAIM in simulated nature scenes with real exotic beasts but unreal backdrops. 'My Way' (2016) foregrounds this virtual aesthetic through extended scenes of VR goggles and extensive visual glitching, blurring the line between reality and the virtual. Harris' EDM forms in this era always save their loudest, most bombastic drop for the end, which Nava responds to by cycling through most if not all previously introduced settings with blinding speed and virtuosity. Harris's process of cycling through the same samples in different arrangements (a hallmark of EDM) is thus remarkably akin to Nava's approach to temporality. In 'How Deep Is Your Love' (2015), for example, Nava introduces several distinct settings each at the on-set of Harris's sections – a club (drop, 1:04), yacht (riser, 1:20) rooftop pool (drop, 1:35), hydroponic farm (drop, 2:05) and tattoo parlour (riser, 2:24) – before revisiting each of them in the final drop from 3:40 on.

The 2017 video for 'Feels' (featuring an all-star cast of singers) represents a palpable change for both artists. Moving away from EDM forms with huge drop sections, Harris begins adopting standard *verse/chorus forms* to highlight the contributions of the singers he's now collaborating with. Verse/chorus forms consist of one or more rotations of familiar *verse*, *pre-chorus* and *chorus* sections. Instead of the four-on-the-floor drop being the climactic highpoint (as in EDM forms), from 2017 onward we now hear three or four memorable sung choruses (usually featuring the song title) with Harris providing less bombastic beats beneath. This is part of a larger trend in EDM-pop to move away from the hard-hitting house beats – made popular almost a decade ago by hits from David Guetta such as 'Titanium' – towards softer beats that showcase vocal hooks.

Figure 11.1 shows the differences between Harris's two formal designs side by side. In EDM forms like 'Outside' (2014) the verse (0:10) advances a narrative story; the riser (0:38) begins quietly without a beat, gradually builds rhythmic propulsion and presents the title lyric; and the drop (1:09) features a powerful four-on-the-floor dance beat.[2] In verse/chorus forms like 'One Kiss' (2018) the verse (0:31) still advances a story, but the pre-chorus (0:46) presents a contrasting vocal hook that prepares for the memorable sung chorus (1:02) prominently featuring the title lyric. Harris uses EDM forms in nearly every video in his first phase ('Pray to God' is the

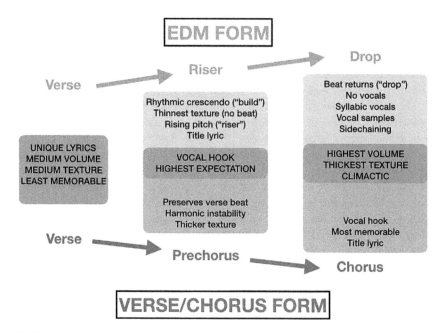

FIGURE 11.1 *Comparison of formal functions of EDM and verse/chorus forms.*

exception), then begins using verse/chorus forms exclusively in his second (2017 onwards). In these later songs and music videos, verse and chorus forms combine their moment of greatest sonic intensity with their moment of greatest lyrical-melodic memorability (the chorus), while the earlier EDM videos separate these two functions, with the memorability occurring in the title-containing riser and the sonic intensity waiting until the drop.[3] So then the question arises: How does Nava respond to this change in song form?

As if responding to Harris's use of a 'throwback' form (verse/chorus has been a hallmark of pop music since the 1960s), 'Nuh Ready Nuh Ready' resurrects many of the same techniques seen in hip-hop videos of the early 1990s.[4] The post-production animation overlaid onto several of the video's dancing scenes recalls PM Dawn's 'Set Adrift on Memory Bliss', while the black light used to accentuate the dancers' make-up borrows from Monie Love's 'It's a Shame'. Nava's virtual sets in his third phase (2017 onwards) become shallower, less expansive and full of two-dimensional artifice. Pastel colours dominate 'Feels' and 'One Kiss'. Hung tapestries act as artificial backdrops of 'Promises' (a cityscape) and 'One Kiss' (a pool), both of which reveal to the viewer the rigging used to hang these sets, essentially breaking the fourth wall and making the artifice a focal point.

Having given an overview of the evolution of these collaborations between Nava and Harris, I will now focus on a video that I see as a turning point for both, 'This Is What You Came For' (featuring Rihanna). It is here that Harris begins infusing EDM forms with verse/chorus attributes, neatly synthesizing the two in a way that foregrounds both his production skills and Rihanna's infectious melodies. For Nava, this video is the last of his Harris collaborations to feature expansive worlds that contra-pose large physical spaces with virtual artifice. In examining this pivotal video, I hope to demonstrate each artist's flexibility in adapting to each others' changing style. Throughout the analysis, I will also draw the reader's attention to threads of continuity in the other thirteen videos by Nava and Harris, which might be seen as hallmarks of their personal style(s).

Close reading: 'This Is What You Came For' (Nava, Harris and Rihanna)

'This Is What You Came For' is a collaboration between artists Nava, Harris and Rihanna. At the time of this writing, the video has received over two billion hits on YouTube. We encounter at the very on-set a multitude of spaces, including a desert, a clearing in the Cascadian forest, and a massive white cube, closed on all sides except one. Roughly two-and-a-half times Rihanna's height on all sides, I estimate it to be over 14 feet tall with a volume of nearly 3,000 cubic feet. A remarkably similar cube opens 'My Way' from the same year.

The video was filmed near Big Bear Lake in California. Forest settings are common in several of these videos, including 'Blame', 'Pray to God', 'My Way' and 'Giant' (2019). But the video is just as notable for its virtual spaces. Using an innovative 360-degree camera technology and projection mapping, Nava is able to project realistic environments into the cube which are captured entirely in-camera (i.e. no post-production, no CGI). Such virtual spaces, which include dance clubs, desert scenes and even a simulacrum of the aforementioned forest, are so convincing that the viewer sees Rihanna, the video's constant focal point, to be interacting with them in real time.

Several scholars have suggested breaking down a music video into its component parts (cinematography, music, lyrics, etc.) before interpreting the artwork as a whole.[5] In measuring several different parameters, we might deem such an approach 'parametric'. Building on this approach, Table 11.2 shows what I call the parametric form of the video.[6] By demonstrating how the onsets of each section of the song either do or do not align temporally with shifts in the video's setting, the parametric form graph enables us to compare how song form interacts with visual form. In this particular graph I have also included the visual–musical–lyrical text-paintings that occur throughout (to be discussed shortly). Parametric form allows us to better appreciate what I see as the two crucial aspects of setting in 'This Is

What You Came For': (1) the distinction between the physical cube and the projections mapped onto it; and (2) Rihanna's interaction with the cube (and its virtual augmentations), expressed both through her movements and her lyrics.

What makes 'This Is What You Came For' so interesting formally is how Harris seamlessly blends compositional techniques derived from EDM form (phase one) and verse/chorus form (phase two). This results in some rather idiosyncratic section names in Table 11.2.[7] Harris's climactic drop sections (1:01, 2:18 and 3:20) exemplify what Charlie Harding has called the *popdrop* – a type of drop that is less hard hitting than the massive side-chained house drop heard in earlier EDM tracks (e.g. 'Summer' (2014) at 1:01). Crucially, a standard EDM drop, unlike the chorus, does *not* contain a memorable vocal hook, and frequently contains only chopped up, sampled vocals (if it contains vocals at all). But according to Harding, the popdrop functions as 'the new climax of the song, right where you would *expect* to hear the chorus'

Table 11.2 Parametric Form in 'This Is What You Came For'

Time	Section	Setting	Text Painting
0:01	Video intro	*Mise-en-scène*: cube in desert–soundstage–nature	
0:16	Chorus	R inside cube, virtual colours	'she moves'
0:30	Post-chorus	R looks at us, cube goes black	'you', filter sweep
0:46	Riser-chorus	Virtual dance party, lasers	'what you came for' (party)
1:01	Popdrop	R leaves cube; soundstage, lasers, dancers	Claps=sampled claps
1:32	Verse	R in cube; virtual nature versus actual nature	'when we meet'
		Car, desert projection; soundstage, Harris cameo	
2:03	Riser-chorus	Horse, dancers, desert	
2:18	Popdrop	Car on road (projected and real); R at edge of box	
2:49	Riser-chorus	Album cover projection	'lightning'
3:06		lights coming on with riser, shattering panes right before drop	Riser=lights come on
3:20	Popdrop	Accumulative, cycling through all the things that were introduced	Drop=tiles dropping

(emphasis his).[8] Contrast this with what I've called the *riser-chorus*, which is where we actually hear the song title (a function of the chorus), but combined with the sonic characteristics of an EDM riser, in which a rising pitch and building rhythm produce tension leading up to the drop.[9]

So, which section draws viewers in the most? Is it the quiet riser-chorus on the song title (0:46) or is it the energetic popdrop (1:01), which *also* features memorable vocals (albeit monosyllabic and sampled)?[10] The former blends riser and chorus function, building up tension yet containing the title lyric, while the latter blends chorus and drop functions by combining somewhat memorable lyrics with a popdrop. Why this matters for the analysis of music video is simple. A section that piques our auditory interest is likely to, consequently, attract our visual attention as well, and may even lead to the formation of distinct audiovisual memories.[11] A listener anticipating the syntactical highpoint (sung vocal hook and song title) in the riser-chorus at 2:03 is likely to perceive the corresponding change in scenery (desert and horse) more saliently than a listener who is still waiting until 2:18 for the beat to drop.

One utility of the parametric form chart is its ability to show the moments in which musical timing (e.g. when a section changes) and cinematic timing (e.g. when a setting changes) either do or do not line up.[12] Several of Nava's cuts occur mid-section in this video. He does tend to align big changes in scenery with Harris's changes in formal sections (e.g. the sports car arrives with the on-set of the popdrop at 2:18), but others are introduced mid-section (e.g. the car and desert arrive in the middle of the verse). Nava's particular rhythm of introducing these settings does have an interesting parallel to EDM production. Harris, like most EDM producers, begins a track by introducing only a handful of samples, adds additional samples slowly as the song unfolds, then combines them more freely in at the end.[13]

In several of these videos, Nava reserves this celebratory moment – cycling through virtually all previously introduced settings – for the final drop. Here, the cuts move so quickly that they occur not only mid-section but also mid-phrase, providing a syncopated counterpoint to the regular four-on-the-floor beat. For example, there are six cuts lasting, on average, less than a second from 3:47–3:52, cycling through the forest, the cube, the desert and the dance party settings. We might also understand Nava's increase in the speed of cuts near the end of the video as giving the viewer 'what they came for' – namely the so-called 'quick MTV cut' that Emily Caston describes as a hallmark of music video.[14]

Throughout all of these setting changes, Nava's unequivocal focus is on Rihanna's performance.[15] Ellie Goulding takes up a similarly centred role in 'Outside', in which the space she occupies, which, though centred in the frame is notably 'outside' of the home she used to share with her lover, is essential to the video's meaning. Understanding Rihanna's constantly changing relationship to the cube, both its physical and virtual space(s), is similarly essential to understanding this video. Nava describes Rihanna as being 'transported' through these spaces. I would like to argue that she also acts as a guide for us, the viewers, as we visually navigate the same spaces. Gillian Rose suggests an image such as this, with complex geometrical perspective, 'offer[s] a particular position to its viewers'.[16] Her relationship to the physical edges of the cube and her interactions with the virtual projections help us to appreciate the complexity of the real and the virtual in the video, and also help the viewer position ourself in relation to the space.

Rihanna begins the video fully encased in the cube. During the intro we see the cube in three different settings: the desert, the soundstage and the forest. So, where is Rihanna?

A remarkably long cut that takes up nearly an entire section (0:34–0:57) helps the viewer to understand her relationship to the cube. The dark background focuses our attention on the flashing neon lights of a dance club behind her. But why is the doorway to this club getting closer (or at least bigger)? Just as she appears to turn and walk through the doorway, we realize that the dance party is virtual – a 360-degree projection onto the cube. The doorway wasn't getting closer, and Rihanna didn't walk through it. She now walks towards the back of the cube until 0:56 when we see a projection of the soundstage, giving the viewer a curious *misunderstanding* of the space: the cube must be translucent, and it's sitting in the soundstage. This turns out to be half true. Just before the drop, Rihanna walks out the front of the cube for the first time and we realize that, while she (and the cube) *are* in the soundstage, the cube is not translucent, and all of the spaces we have experienced thus far have been virtual projections inside of it.

In the analysis of song, 'text painting' connotes the use of musical gestures to reflect the meaning of a word of phrase.[17] But in music video we can also interpret a video's visuals in concert with the song's lyrics. Surely Rihanna's gentle sway at 0:23 must be interpreted as animating the lyrics 'she moves' just like her eye contact with the camera at 0:33 relates to the lyric 'you', the viewer now suddenly feeling put on the spot, especially given the simultaneous dimming of the background. These changing spaces also give deeper meaning to the song's title. In the beginning, we might assume that Rihanna herself is 'what (we) came for', but when she walks into the club at 0:48, glancing over her shoulder at the viewer as she does so, we might assume that it's the *party* we came for.

The possibilities for text painting in music videos are not limited to utterances involving lyrics. If we understand music video as a synthesis of three media (lyrics, visuals and music),[18] then a cross-domain mapping between any two or more of these 'texts' becomes text painting. Harris applies a filter sweep to text paint Nava's gradual zoom on the dancing crowd from 0:40 to 0:47. The filter sweep, which gradually introduces higher frequencies into the mix, is the sonic analogue of walking into a dance club. Because of the occlusion principle you can initially only hear the deep bass notes – the full frequency range is only revealed once you have fully entered the space. Nava similarly text paints the rising pitch (riser) at 2:17 with a left-to-right camera pan that mimics turning the volume and/or tone knobs on a radio clockwise. Carol Vernallis suggests that such connections between camera and musical motion – in this case a panning shot that follows the same curve as the track's volume profile – help to establish continuity in music videos.[19]

At the first popdrop we finally fully understand the relationship between Rihanna, the cube, the soundstage and the projections. Distinguishing between the physical and the virtual is now less taxing, and we celebrate with flashing lights and confetti. Rihanna finally joins the dancers in this celebration (ironic, because she's now outside of their space), her visual handclap at 1:17 aligning with Harris's sampled handclap in the track at precisely the right moment, what Michel Chion would describe as a *synch point.*[20]

The relationship between song form and video form gets more complex at the on-set of the verse. Rihanna looks somewhat surprised at 1:35 when the projected party changes abruptly to a forest projection. This reinforces the explanation given by Nava that these virtual spaces are outward projections of Rihanna's inner imagination,[21] and, after all Nava used a similar technique to portray a disoriented central subject (Gigi Hadid) in 'How Deep Is Your Love?' from the previous year.

At 1:43 we see the cube in the Cascadian forest clearing. Are we now to assume that Rihanna is in that box? Swapping the falling confetti from the dance scenes with falling green leaves suggests so. Indeed, floating particulate matter helps establish settings in several of Nava's videos, especially the snow in both 'Pray to God' and 'Giant'. Halfway through the verse the projections change again, this time to a sports car in the desert. Then we're back to the soundstage for Calvin Harris's cameo. In several of his early videos (especially 'I Need Your Love') Harris is quite animated, smiling frequently and interacting with other characters. But when Rihanna sings 'your place when we meet' the stoic, reserved stance he takes in this and later videos makes it unclear if she's actually *meeting* Harris, or if he too is a projection. Perhaps the car speeding down the road simply text paints 'fast' in the lyrics, but then again perhaps it's a date, or even a road trip.

The third chorus adds a horse and rider to the aforementioned desert scene. With the exception of a single live shot (the sports car driving down a highway), the rest of the video cycles through previous settings. Though horses, desert and cars are all well-worn tropes from Nava's phase one, here they take on different meaning in relation to Harris's form. Nava text paints Harris's final riser-to-drop sequence brilliantly starting at 3:15 (riser) with pairs of lights that turn on row by row, rising upwards through the frame, followed by the projected panes shattering and dropping to the floor at 3:22 (drop). This final popdrop delights in visual excess, combining nearly all previously seen settings with quick cuts, lasers and even a projection of the duo's album artwork (Figure 11.2).

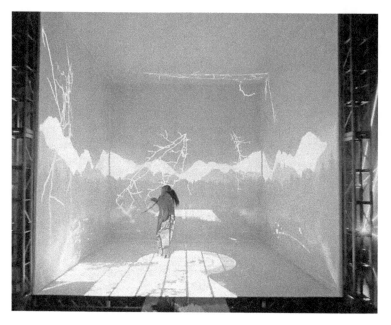

FIGURE 11.2 *Album cover projection in 'This Is What You Came For' (Emil Nava, Calvin Harris, Rihanna: 2016, 3:24).*

Conclusion

A close reading of a video like 'This Is What You Came For' may be, on its own, a worthy exercise in audiovisual analysis, but the analysis is surely enriched by contextualizing the rich interpretive moves each artist makes within a larger history of their collaborations. Sectional boundaries, largely the provenance of producer Calvin Harris, tend to align with changes in scenery orchestrated by director Emil Nava. Rihanna plays a pivotal role throughout the video in adding further meaning to the overall formal design by animating – both with her lyrics and her movements – aspects of both. Adapting the techniques of formal analysis to the audiovisual medium, while also drawing upon established visual analytical methods from scholars such as Vernallis, Caston, Chion and Rose, allows us to appreciate the video's form in visual and musical domains simultaneously. Music video analysts who adopt and further adapt these tools will likely find them helpful for analysing all three of these domains first separately, then together.

CHAPTER 12

On colour magic: Emil Nava's 'Feels' and 'Nuh Ready Nuh Ready'

Jonathan Leal

Thirty seconds into House of Fraser's 2016 Christmas ad – amid Laura Mvula's bombastic take on the Fugees's 'Ready or Not', amid a series of potent glitter bombs, amid a flood of fuchsia fog – there is a bolt of strange lightning (Figure 12.1). Lasting just a few frames, appearing by an excited dancer, the lightning shocks not only for its contrast against a midnight screen but also for its hyper-colouration: a pink and violet vine hanging from a superchromatic heaven. The colours, impossible yet clearly visible, estrange the lightning, injecting it with a new and uncanny energy. Gone in a flash, the colours make one wonder what the eerie glow signified, its afterimage a lingering question.

Indeed, the questions raised by this kind of colour processing – the most basic of which being, 'What did I just see?' – are what I'm after here. They are also what transmedia director Emil Nava has been after in recent projects, working in music video, advertising and film. Nava, an acclaimed, London-raised artist, has thus far completed hundreds of music videos in collaboration with musicians including Ed Sheeran, Dua Lipa, Eminem, Jennifer Lopez, Selena Gomez, AlunaGeorge and others. While some videos, including Kwabs's 'Wrong or Right' (2015) use dance and gesture as a primary means of exploring visual metaphor – and while still others, including Elli Ingram's 'Mad Love' (2013), Sheeran's 'Give Me Love' (2011) and Folly Rae's 'Karma Club' (2018), exhibit filmic narrative aspirations,

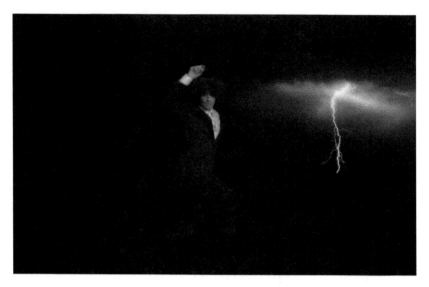

FIGURE 12.1 *Strange lightning in House of Fraser's Christmas advertisement (Emil Nava, 2016) (0:36).*

playing with classic character types to tell complete stories – what has been common across his body of work thus far has been *colour magic*: chromatic studies in saturation and replacement, removal and recombination.

Colour magic is a still-growing suite of contemporary post-processing effects made possible by digital intermediate and emergent techniques like datamoshing, a practice described by William Brown and Mectali Kutty as a process that enables 'audiovisual artists [to] actively downgrade the quality of digital images in order to render a more "raw" aesthetic on screen' (165).[1] In the context of film, advertisement and music video, colour magic not only evokes the corrupted, the surreal and the impossible by interrupting expectations of photorealism, but also does so artfully, extending and contesting sound, text, shape and movement. In effect, colour magic in the post-internet age performs a familiar gesture: it highlights visual images *as data*, heightening contemporary viewers' awareness of popular video as shaped and shapeable information. Such gestures feel important today for at least one reason: in a digital contemporary in which experiences of connectivity, alienation and mediation are heightened and consolidated by pocket-sized devices many of us use daily, efforts to defamiliarize this present – to make the contemporary freshly available for representation – have ameliorative potential. Nava's work, I suggest, is part of this fold.

When, as YouTube counts attest, Nava's music videos have garnered many billions of views worldwide; when, as social media posts highlight, his commercial and film works have attracted important attention; and when, as our screens make clear, a number of his major projects have pushed for new spectral possibilities, one is thus invited to ask: What is Nava helping us see? In this short essay, I take this question up in two ways: first, by sitting briefly with today's colour processing and second, by turning to two recent videos that highlight Nava's defining colour sensitivities: 'Feels' (2017) and 'Nuh Ready Nuh Ready' (2018).

Colour magic

Intense colour processing is a core vocabulary of today's popular visual media. Recent examples include many of the sequences in Marvel Studios' *Dr. Strange* (2016) and *Infinity War* (2018); older cases certainly include Gary Ross's *Pleasantville* (1998), about which film scholar John Belton has written wonderfully.[2] As a broad idea, colour manipulation has rich and diffuse histories in experimental art, including the chromatic studies and synesthetic films of Oskar Fischinger and the boundary pushing visual narratives of Peter Greenaway (for instance, *Prospero's Books* in 1991).[3] Scholar Maura McDonnell has described how artists including Walter Ruttmann, Léopold Survage and the Whitney brothers worked out new visual possibilities in analogical relation to musical structures, techniques and performance practices, pushing medial and technological boundaries by striving to transfer sonic procedures into unprecedented visual works.[4] Theorist Lisa Perrott, writing on artist Len Lye, has articulated the importance of Lye's kinesthetic and material-expressive experiments in addition to his synesthetic thinking, further pushing experiential boundaries for viewers and artists alike.[5] And yet what I am here calling *colour magic* feels like a differentiable extension from such previous experiments (and much aligned with, say, Dave Meyers and Travis Scott's work on 'Sicko Mode ft. Drake' in 2018) in at least one key respect: with colour magic, the digital and the surreal are interlaced with the seemingly 'untouched' and 'natural', effectively highlighting the digitality not only of photorealistic video sequences but also of contemporary life.[6] (This, as opposed to dazzling light displays that work almost entirely by abstraction – or, as with some of Fischinger's work, functions as videographic musical notation.)[7] Today's colour magic, which Nava's work demonstrates, foregrounds the *integration* of the allegedly photoreal and the wondrously luminous; one of its broader functions, I suggest, is to draw new attention to our sparkling screens.

For this all comes at a time when colour manipulation has spread beyond the realm of specialist practice. With the last decade of screen proliferation, app development and social media evolution, far more people are manipulating their own images and videos on a daily basis. And while technical democratization in the arts is, in the long view, very much a good thing, in the present, it has resulted in what some viewers consider a desensitizing visual homogeneity. As writer-photographer Teju Cole has argued of the photography of social media: 'Postprocessing is [now] easy and rampant: beautiful light is added after the fact, depth of field is manipulated, nostalgia is drizzled on in unctuous tints of orange and green. The result is briefly beguiling to the sense but ultimately annoying to the soul.'[8] As he continues (with slightly less salt), we are

> seeing images all the time, millions of them, billions, many of which are manipulated with the same easy algorithms, the same tiresome vignetting, the same dark green wash. ... The problem is not that images are being altered – it's that they're all being altered in the same way: high contrast, dewy focus, oversaturation, a skewing of the RBG curve in fairly predictable ways. Correspondingly, the range of subjects is also peculiarly narrow: pets, pretty girlfriends, sunsets, lunch. In other words, the photographic function, which should properly be the domain of the eye and the mind, is being outsourced to the camera and an algorithm.[9]

By contrast, Nava isn't manufacturing nostalgia; instead, he is pushing to imagine new visions within the frame of pop products. Indeed, in contrast to the 'outsource[ing]' of energy 'to the camera and an algorithm', part of what makes Nava's videos so relevant and arresting – and part of what has made his career trajectory so meteoric – has been that his colour experiments in advertising, music video and documentary film have all been ad hoc and intentional. Each instance has been a sign of interpretation and collaboration, of insight and agency; each effort has been fundamentally human focused, using advanced tools and techniques to bring artists' unnamed thoughts and feelings into view for the first time. And this intentionality and specificity – every project having its own unique chemistry and thus not relying on stale templates – is, as he has stated, at the forefront of his collaborations: 'Sometimes, I feel like directors make videos for themselves, not for the artists. For me, I want to make music videos for the artists, films for the characters, documentaries for the people ... I want to make them for other people and for the viewers, but I also have my own goals and views of things I want to inject into the world.'[10] For Nava, the cinematographic 'domain of the eye and the mind' need not be at odds with the camera or the algorithm.

Additionally, the sticking power of Nava's visual experiments can be partially explained by their coincidence with the rise of new visual technologies and outputs, all of which are changing how we see, as Bruce Sterling has identified, 'information visualization. Satellite views. Parametric architecture. Surveillance cameras. Digital image processing. Data-mashed video frames. Glitches and corruption artifacts. Voxelated 3D pixels in real-world geometries. Dazzle camou, Augments, Render ghosts.'[11] In some cases, Nava's purposeful experiments look markedly different from these algorithmic half-accidents, as in Harris, Kehlani and Lil Yachty's 'Faking It' (2017). In others, as with Harris and Dua Lipa's 'One Kiss' (2017), Harris and Rihanna's 'This Is What You Came For' (2016) and, as we shall see, 'Feels' and 'Nuh Ready Nuh Ready', Nava's work visually rhymes with glitch art, participating in the new, post-internet information aesthetics. Yet in every project, across different film genres, Nava's engagements with new, proximate technologies and their machine gazes are methodical, practised, even *magical*, completed in pursuit of two braided, meaningful goals: an immediate desire to realize a collaborator's vision and a more lasting push to foster that rare gift of visual art – the 'double take of seeing'.[12] Colour magic, as a means to achieve these goals, thus possesses some nominative and defamiliarizing potential in our increasingly informational life worlds. And in the two music video examples that follow, I shall work to show how.

'Feels' and 'Nuh Ready Nuh Ready'

In Nava's video for 'Feels', a song born of a collaboration between Harris, Pharrell Williams, Katy Perry and Big Sean, colour is paramount. In its opening moments, the video introduces each artist and their corresponding built environments: Perry in a lush meadow, donning gold hair and sunflower dress; Williams on a faux beach, standing upright in a small rowboat and surrounded by fake palms; Big Sean in an artificial rainforest, seated between two living, grooving parrots. The colours of each space arrest: verdant, rich and floral. They also soon begin to shift: the meadow's sun changes hues, drifting from yellow to orange; the beach's water transforms, shifting from blue to purple to teal; the rainforest's parrots shimmer, flying clear across the colour wheel. And yet as intriguing as these flourishes are – invoking, alongside the guitar chucking, the downbeat-heavy bass lines and the clean percussion, some 1970s funk fashions – they're all simply set-up.

For at 1:28, in a moment of subtle convergence – after Perry's syrupy vocal hook ends with the lyric 'I know you ain't scared to catch feels with me' – the extant palette of soft lavender, yellow-gold, forest green and feather red warps into a nuclear emerald-ultramarine (Figure 12.2).

What makes this colour shift interesting – aside from the ample motion trails, the overlaid ocean footage and the subsequent burst of bubbly verse from Williams – is that it is motivated by a lyric: 'I know you ain't scared to catch feels with me.' For Nava here, a new, uncanny palette becomes an interpretive gesture; for Nava, colour magic becomes a way of finding visual expression for attraction and levity: 'feels', a rush of high frequency.

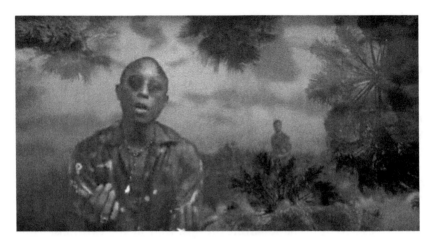

FIGURE 12.2 *A sudden palette shift in 'Feels' (Emil Nava, 2017) (1:28).*

Nava later contrasts this idea with another visual shift at 2:56 (Figure 12.3), nearer the end of the video; more subtle than his 'feels' shift (though equally arresting), it, too, is motivated by a lyric, arriving just after Big Sean's line: 'If I put you on my phone and upload it it'd get maximum views.'

At this moment, Perry's face is framed, mediated by a machine gaze: glitchy, multiple, partially corrupted. Minute facial details crumble into algorithmic dust. Silhouettes of teal and yellow overlap the principal picture, invoking the image capture errors of satellite photography. Her one visible eye becomes a stabilizing singularity at the centre of the frame. And in this instant, audiences are invited to consider what 'maximum views' might mean within Nava's visual language, beyond the phrase's immediate denotation within social media: Do the layered images and colour-rich shadows allow a view of one's own multitudes? Or, does digital sight squish them into flattened data? When this 'you' is uploaded, alchemized into an 'it', whose 'views' – of life, of art – are maximized? And what does digital Perry see?

This moment, embedded in an infectious groove space, creates a small though noticeable rift between two colourful ideas and their related concepts: 'feels' and 'views'. 'Feels': washy and RBG colour shifted; 'views': crystalline yet corruptible. 'Feels': emotional and aqueous; 'views': vibrant yet glassy. This subtle differentiation, asserted with grace, is effectively an argument about different ways of seeing in the digital now – a visual thesis born of Nava's careful reading. And as with other similar experiments, it begets the driving questions: What in the world did I just see? And why did it make me catch feels?

Another good example of Nava's colour magic is the bulk of his video for 'Nuh Ready Nuh Ready' (2018), a musical collaboration between Harris

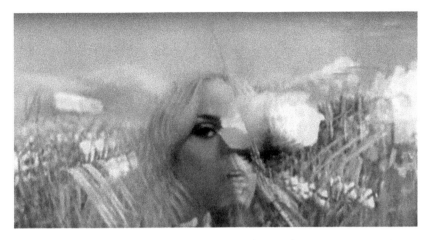

FIGURE 12.3 *Evoking the digital present in 'Feels' (Emil Nava, 2017) (2:56).*

and PartyNextDoor. In this video, set to a spare UK house-style rhythm track that features bitcrushed bass, ethereal synth pads and artificial brass, colour – as process and data – helps convey a sense of dislocation, unease and, in particular, male unreadiness.

After opening with a helicopter shot of night-time London, the video crossfades into the interior of a checkerboard cube; inside the cube is a three-dimensional amoebic mirror, warping the walls' black and white tiles as it undulates (Figure 12.4). The room spins. Black tiles become speckled with nebulae and galaxies, rhyming with the London city lights. A moonstone iridescence covers all.

Suddenly, a woman dancer materializes, her video layered atop the previous shot. Her shirt is rendered completely invisible, the geometric patterns of the background filling the negative space; all one can see of her is her face and floating arms. While her movements are animated, her gaze is absent. A moment later, she is replaced by another figure, dancing before tessellating metallic gold, teal, purple and white squares; soon after, this dancer recedes to clear the way for PartyNextDoor, who appears as he delivers his defining opening line: 'me and di mandem, we haffi run from half of di gyal dem'. The resulting combo of subdued music, lyrical fronting, spare choreography, unbroken stare and kaleidoscopic geometry quickly creates an uncanny chord: hetero-male normalcy converging with site-specific issues of race, class and youth culture, all mediated through the self-estranging technologies of the digital contemporary. And as per this video's signature density, all of this happens in the first twenty seconds.

In the minutes that follow, Nava utilizes all manner of advanced CGI, DI and datamoshing techniques to elaborate this too-muchness: colour

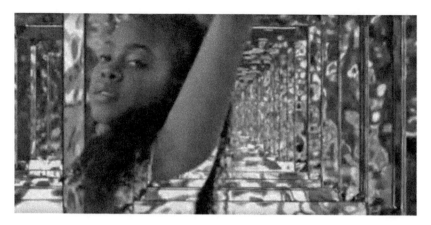

FIGURE 12.4 *Kaleidophonia in 'Nuh Ready Nuh Ready' (Emil Nava, 2018) (0:14).*

mapping, data corruption, pixel sorting and RBG channel shifting. To bring calm to otherwise feverish sequences, Nava concentrates motional energy at the centre of the frame, giving the visuals a feeling of balance, symmetry. An effect of this gesture: viewers are invited to replicate the dancers' unbroken stare: to peer uninterrupted through a keyhole, into a world of a radiant collision (Figure 12.5).

Eventually, at 1:50, one of the opening visual ideas returns. One of the video's four women dancers stands before a stark white background, recorded by a lone cameraperson. After, in a previous shot, being doused with colour-shifting paint, the entirety of her skin becomes replaced by the earlier video of kaleidoscopic metals. She becomes an outline, a digital spectre; her interiority becomes represented (or better, *replaced*) by graphic twisting, by Euclidean fantasy. The visual makes productive trouble for PartyNextDoor's accompanying lyric – 'Cause I need to know where you are'. The takeaway: the song's persona, dizzied by his hyper-city and his own puffed-up imaginings, can't see what's right in front of him.

The visual density of 'Nuh Ready Nuh Ready' thus elaborates an instrumental reserve and a lyrical unease. And as with 'Feels', this video's exploration of shape, motion and superimposition (depth) again renders colour a primary means of expression. Colour, here and elsewhere in Nava's work, is about revelation, delight and critical comment. It remains deeply linked to the directorial practices of careful reading and open dialogue by living firmly in the realm of the *verb*, what Charles Baudelaire once called the 'angel of motion'.[13] As a verb in our 'present tense', colour is addition and subtraction, modification and repurposing, and persuasion and personal testimony. In the context of 'Nuh Ready Nuh Ready', colour, as unfolding

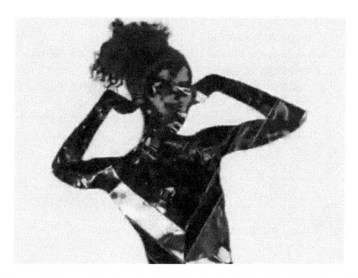

FIGURE 12.5 *Projected interiors in 'Nuh Ready Nuh Ready' (Emil Nava, 2018) (1:52).*

patterns of glitched-out dissociation, names the deeper anxiety in the tune's grooves: it is all too much and 'I'm not ready.'

Double take

Nava's colour magic is certainly not limited to these two examples nor is it to his often-experimental collaborations with Calvin Harris; there are, across Nava's videography, dozens of videos with colour as a crucial poetic device: L Devine's 'Peer Pressure' (2018), Burns's 'Beauty Queen' (2016), 'Ne-Yo and Juicy J's "She Knows" (2015), Pusha T's 'Lunch Money' (2014). (Too, in social media promo for his upcoming documentary film, *Snorkeling*, Nava uses intense colour modifications on an otherwise photorealistic image; among his hashtags: '#snorkeling', '#Ammolite' and '#colour').[14] In each of them, the notion of colour as an injection of feeling, as a temporal process and as a magical act is ever present.[15] Colour, for Nava, is at once a focus of attention and a means of estrangement; it's the visible truth outpacing our descriptions.[16]

Today, in a crowded directorial field, Nava's knack for colour is a welcome one. Our hypermodern geographies are being shaped by more screens than we can track; the techniques and qualities of meaningful formal representation are changing as our world modulates. In this environment, Nava's use of colour is inviting new ways of seeing. His approach is to use the affordances of new media to expand the 'domain of the eye and the mind'.[17] And while it is certainly possible to read Nava's experiments as embedded in a totalizing industry logic – better displays for richer colour, crisper attention-engineering for maximized engagement, accelerated invention for increased profit – it is equally possible to see them in a warmer light. As one watches, absorbed by strange lightning, it is possible – and, I suggest, rewarding – to track this transmedia director's feel for our current moment, for the magic still possible.

PART FIVE

Music video's centrifugal forces

CHAPTER 13

Dave Meyers's moments of audiovisual bliss

Carol Vernallis

Many of today's transmedia directors have developed techniques and approaches from working across music videos, commercials and films. Capturing what influenced them and how their styles have changed across several decades feels challenging. This chapter focuses on director Dave Meyers, whom I interviewed and wrote about in 2008. Then as now, he was a preeminent music video and commercial director. I'll focus on two of his recent videos, Kendrick Lamar's 'All the Stars' (2018) and Maroon 5's 'Wait' (2018), with glances at earlier projects. I'll characterize what has changed and make suppositions about the director's influences. In the 1990s and early 2000s I was able to interview several members of his cohort – up-and-coming music-video directors who've since become even more successful (including Francis Lawrence, Jonas Åkerlund, Floria Sigismondi, Marcus Nispel and David Fincher). Looking at their work now shows that some of these directors have blossomed while others have maintained a consistent voice. I'm surprised that it's Meyers's work that moves me; I think of it as the very best in the music video canon.

Meyers's 'All the Stars' (a music video for the film *Black Panther*, 2018) possesses a beauty that comes from its audiovisual relations, the ways its sound and image work together. Describing the clip's audiovisual aesthetics may seem a bit ephemeral. As abstract as these phenomena may sound, their traces can still be shown. I'll begin with the ways sound permeates performers, objects, settings and spaces, because these are some of the most structurally important features of 'All the Stars' (Figure 13.1). First, I'd

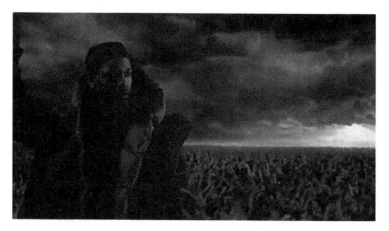

FIGURE 13.1 *Sound permeates the image's ether in 'All the Stars' (Kendrick Lamar and Dave Meyers, 2018).*

like to claim that the song, at the far distance, penetrates the image's ether. Second, it envelops the human figures, giving the air a different weight. And third, it resonates within bodies, its musical features felt.

(1) In the distance. In the clip's first shot, Kendrick Lamar stands as the skiff's guide, ferried by a sea of waving hands that form rivulet-patterns. As his craft zigzags towards us, we see, in the distance, lightning bolts breaking through dark clouds seemingly triggering synths in the high register. Thunder and lightning make good subject matter for music videos, because they raise questions about cause and effect. Thunder and lightning happen simultaneously, but while we say thunder first, light travels more quickly to us than does sound. Perhaps there's an uncertainty for us, for why would our language confuse these phenomena? In 'All the Stars', the synths appear after the lightning bolts within a long enough interval to make us unsure about whether we should link these events (and thus we're not sure how we might begin to forge connections between sound and image) (See Figure 13.1). Some other playful cognitive challenges that 'All the Stars' presents include the following: Lamar, later, gazing from a rooftop, raises his arm towards fireworks resembling bursts of dark dustclouds, synchronized by what we might hear as sonic pops. (Why dustclouds in the sky?). Images of stars, and the camera, too, will circle singer SZA as she emerges from a pinpoint, materializing within a studio space depicting galaxies (her emergence is accompanied by a loud whoosh). SZA will reach forward and grab a phantom (or is it a real?) star and Lamar, as he walks towards us, will suddenly produce a cigar interlaced among his fingertips (Figure 13.2).

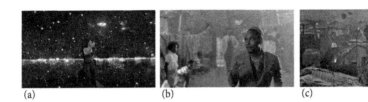

(a)   (b)   (c)

FIGURE 13.2 *A visual rhyme in 'All the Stars' (Kendrick Lamar and Dave Meyers, 2018).*

The above gestures form a rhyming structure about reaching. They could all be described as holes in the video's audiovisual fabric. The sudden materialization and animacy of sounds and images is a favoured technique of Meyers's, but here they take on a higher function – they could be called auratic. Drawing on the same techniques (where sounds and images pierce spaces) the director used for 'All the Stars', Maroon 5's 'Wait' shows unspooling strings passing through the video's environs and, later, meteors falling while trails of fire arc back up towards the sky. Here again, there's the forging of audiovisual sync (the former, linked with a reiterating sixteenth-note rim shot, and the latter, rising synth glissandi).

(2)   It's harder to show how sounds envelop figures. Listeners tend to bind a song's musical elements to objects within a clip's frames.[1] Even more, we start projecting audiovisual trajectories for both figures and sound. This video's characters walk, turn and twirl, and as their limbs gracefully glance along the sides of their bodies, we sense the air and sound pressing in on them, carrying them aloft.

(3)   And within the body. The clip's foregrounded dancers press deeply into the ground, with their heels stamping out the song's rhythms so vigorously we might guess the song's pulse resounds within the performers. Each performer seemingly nurtures a private trajectory that traces a unique feature of the song (Figure 13.3). And another example about sounds within bodies is one drawn from the director's favoured techniques. Even in his earliest videos Meyers often placed children at the beginning. I took this as a means for enhancing charm or reassuring viewers about music video's often fraught representations; they'd then intuit that the clip unfolded within a privileged space. But now, raising a child, I'm aware that Meyers's engagements might reflect something different (he too is a family person and now has a changed relation to children). A child's consciousness differs in some marked way from an adult's; children take in the world differently. A child offers a connection to a song apart from the video's other characters (Figure 13.4).

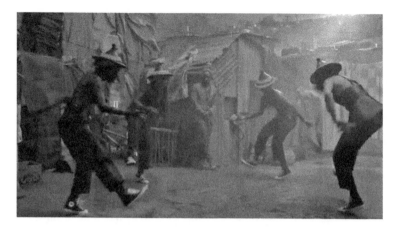

FIGURE 13.3 *Sound resonates within performers in 'All the Stars' (Kendrick Lamar and Dave Meyers, 2018).*

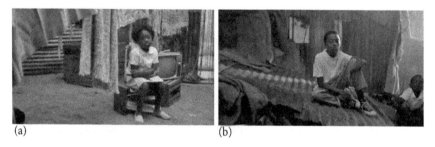

(a)　　　　　　　　　　　　　　　　　　(b)

FIGURE 13.4 *A child offers new connections to a song in 'All the Stars' (Kendrick Lamar and Dave Meyers, 2018).*

The ways sound permeates all aspects of 'All the Stars' may be its most significant feature, but many other aspects contribute to the video's beauty as well. The clip's opening shot resembles a kōan, a poetic metaphor for the song and image in their entirety. Like Lamar, we're ferried by – as the video's titling notes – 'Meyers and his homies', as if we and they were on a journey, buoyed by the sea of waving hands; even when the song's tempo or direction appears to shift, we can count on this not-quite-locatable but continuous progression. I'd like to say that this forward gesture offers an uncanny sense of movement resembling an airport's moving walkway. Lamar and we seem to search without a clear goal. Is he a kind of Moses? Who are the totemic figures? Are they connected with biblical figures? The video comprises patterned layers of sound and image that cross edits; each layer, like the video's performers, possesses its own trajectory. One can think of these swathes of aural and visual material as tectonic plates, sliding over one another, and, as they extend across shots and musical phrases, at least one plate, even as it drifts forward or reveals a gap, still offers a sense of ground. How is this effect achieved? The song's high-register synth pad has an insistent tremolo that might suggest a bath in which other materials can slide. The bass line, doubled at the octave, with harmonically inflected pitches schematically filled in, suggests big chunky sonorous chords, like heavy moving objects. The heavily processed bass drum and handclap sounds suggest forward motion as well as depth. The rhythm arrangement has a lot of detail, like a reverbed, flanged click that immediately precedes the bass drum's articulations. The rich, bass-heavy rhythm arrangement thickens our relation to the song.

The image also foregrounds features that suggest change within an unceasing flow. When SZA dances within a galaxy of stars, she first performs big gestures, with her arms thrust out and her body twirling. Later, her gestures become miniaturized, her hands placed before her face: she pantomimes something resembling windows and doors opening and closing. Here, musical material can be carried forth across domains. A shock of recognition may thrum later, when SZA, perched higher in the frame, overlooks her dancers circling with great assertiveness. The performers seem to carry forth the deep-blue gestural weight of the previous section, as if they'd heard what unfolded and could carry it forward into new contexts (Figure 13.5).

All the video's characters seem to have their own arcs. Lamar sometimes seems sadder, slower and more introspective than the visual and musical elements surrounding him. (In the song he comes across as angrier, at least in his verses.) The image is generous in the ways that some of its fastest rhythms (the dancers with bent knees and kicked out feet) and some of its slowest (the planes of water, boat and Lamar drifting upon it) provide an expansive upper and lower limit, which cradles the song. And in fact, for all of the lyrics' anger, the song also presents a rocking figure.

Over time, Meyers has learned to free himself from the ground, and to deploy complex spatial configurations. In 'All the Stars', buildings, people and telephone poles tilt. The horizontal plane through which SZA and the

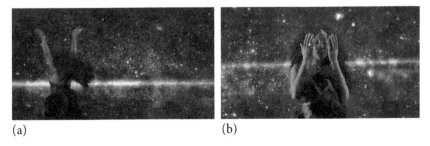

(a) (b)

FIGURE 13.5 *Performers carry material into new contexts in 'All the Stars'*
(Kendrick Lamar and Dave Meyers, 2018).

other dancers move shifts periodically from higher to lower in the frame (Figure 13.6). Perhaps this helps to highlight the distance between Lamar's and SZA's vocal registers, as when the melody vollies up while SZA sings 'all of the stars'. The voices' cresting helps to underscore the lyrics 'All the stars are closer' (the frame's placement of performers and objects also dovetails with other visual materials: for example, Lamar's reaching towards the dust-firework bursting patterns in the sky that echoes and helps to chart a distance from the earlier, ferrying hands that form a kind of sea: see Figure 13.2).

'All the Stars' showcases other spatial deformations. We don't expect Lamar to turn away or drop his gaze from and then once again reconnect with us at such surprising moments, or for SZA's dancing to play so much at the frame's edges, with sudden sweeps towards and away from the camera. The video's totemic figures are also distorted. A giant goddess appears near the clip's beginning; while her head has dimensionality, her chest seems rendered in 2D, forming a kind of paper cut out of a tent. The goddesses at the clip's end whom Lamar looks up to seem both elongated and gigantic. All of Africa, rendered as points of light, is framed within SZA's hair.

Maroon 5's 'Wait' has similar deformations. Lead singer Adam Levine twists his head and shoulders back and forth, as he seeks his lover at several hallways' juncture from the ground floor of a modernist glass house. The lover, who comes in and out through various stairways, hallways and an atrium, encourages Levine's continual pivot, and the space seems as complicated as an Escher drawing. Part of our confusion derives from a piling up of visual rhymes, now realized in the black paisley patterns on Levine's white shirt. (Earlier, his mother-in-law had worn a black, lacey butterfly-like pop-up accessory off her shoulder, and Levine had dropped a similarly shaped black scorpion onto his girlfriend as she lay in her wake's coffin – most likely to revive her so she could confront him about his role in her death.) The reiterations of the patterns on Levine's shirt is too subtle to be unpacked on first viewings, yet its piling up, along with other audiovisual materials, carries weight. This sense of accrued detail is made

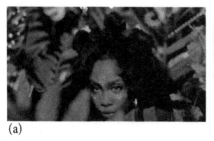 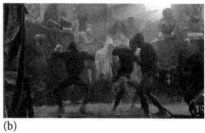

(a)   (b)

FIGURE 13.6 *Dancers shift from low to high in the frame in 'All the Stars'* *(Kendrick Lamar and Dave Meyers, 2018).*

good on later. Levine will soon be immersed underwater, surrounded by hundreds of iterations of his girlfriend, at first glance looking mermaid-tailed (Figure 13.7). He'll then be trapped within his car underwater, and next, as the car door opens, he and water unspools into an oil field (a birthing image!) with his girlfriend seated, waiting for him on an abandoned mattress. 'Wait' shows a puzzling and impressive trajectory of settings. What, we might wonder, does the working-class bungalow in front of which Levine's girlfriend and what most likely are previous girlfriends, all in solidarity, wielding baseball bats and bottles at him have to do with the earlier appearing modernist, wealthy home? Is this Levine's return to earlier relationships or to childhood memories? And other threads make matters denser. Some are tied to questions of vision. Realistic blinking eyelids suggest Levine's or our occluded vision. Levine also wears thick glasses at one point, and his girlfriend sometimes flickers in and out, and at other times is visible behind a gossamer veil. There are also the unspooling strings, falling meteors and rising lines of fireworks to make sense of. (And in the Ariana Grande video, 'No Tears Left to Cry', Meyers takes a hallway, a building, a waterfall and the sky and rotates them like panels on a Rubik's cube.)

All of this is wonderful, but perhaps not an unexpected shift in technique and style. Meyers has long specialized in fantastical imagery. Limp Bizkit's 'Boiler' (2000) had a delirious sequence with pod-women succubuses, for example. So if not this, what has changed? Perhaps it's that in Meyers's earlier videos the musicians seemed to be consciously assuming the mantle of performers inserted into music-video scenarios, and they often seemed somewhat bemused by their situation. Now, they are actor/performers who don't need to be singing or playing instruments, and they belong to their environments. They hold backstories and futures that we have less access to. They belong here, and what happens matters; but we have only a small window into their larger world.

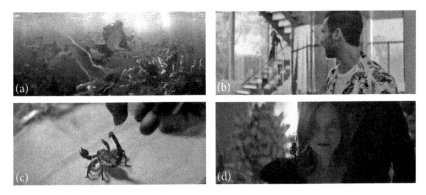

FIGURE 13.7 *Visual rhymes start piling up in 'Wait' (Maroon 5 and Dave Meyers, 2018).*

It's not entirely clear where Meyers's new approach to characterization comes from. Fully inflected characters are rare in music video; videos are brief, lack dialogue and have difficulty suggesting futures and pasts. My guess is that Meyers studied the handful of videos best able to depict characters and their worlds, such as Francis Lawrence's and Justin Timberlake's 'Cry Me a River' (2002) and the videos of Mark Romanek. His work in commercials has surely played a role. His website shows recent work, and YouTube playlists can help give us a sense of his earlier oeuvre. It's not surprising that they're all fast-paced. This is something Meyers has an affinity for – he was responsible for the dancing silhouette for the iPod. In the last few years, however, the amount of time Meyers allotted to present a person seems to have telescoped to a third of a second. Meyers has a long-standing interest in photography – how to capture the sense of a person in an instant must have remained a question for him. A good example of how the director engages with an instant occurs in Janet Jackson's 'Made for Now' (2018). Note the gaze of a potential paramour in a kind of Virginia Reel line of dancers. The potential lover seems to intuit that he has less than a millisecond to kiss Janet Jackson's hand and project the intensity of his ardour. Meyers also wants to direct more Hollywood films. His film *The Hitcher* (2007) feels like a B-movie noir that a 1940s and 1950s studio would have been proud to have cranked out (and it's a remake of Ida Lupino's famous noir, *The Hitch-Hiker* from 1953). The script isn't compelling, but the villain is strong, and the directing – its visual scape and pacing – is well done. I didn't notice a direct shift in style after Meyers made the film, but effects can be far-reaching. (This is probably a question best answered by the director.) A brief side note. Michael Bay produced the film, and perhaps at that point he was trying to build a stable of directors. Perhaps this film was a try-out to consider Michael Meyers as one of a group? Or was it a way to fill out a production quota? Bay has said that he likes to keep his favourite production practitioners employed, and this film may also have been a way to hold onto his crew or to try out new talent. In conversation, Meyers told me that he reached out for Bay's help only in the instances when it was really needed, which may also provide a glimpse into the film's production context.

These three media, commercials, music videos and Hollywood film, would offer Meyers a new variety of approaches. And there most likely are others. Documentary is its own mode, and Meyers has made a wonderful short of Ice Cube showing off his favourite LA locations for the Getty.[2] Being able to separate how much narrative and documentary film-making has shaped Meyers's experience, as opposed to photography, commercials, music videos and so on would help present a richer picture. Like the other music video directors I've spoken with, I've gotten the sense that for-hire directing can be a growth experience, but not that rewarding. Meyers still very much wishes to make another film, this one, hopefully more personal. And this drive surely shapes his music video making and his commercials.

I also like to think that Meyers (like hopefully me) has grown up. He now has a family, and people and interpersonal relations may now matter even more deeply. He's long worked with remarkably talented artists, and in his interviews he's mentioned how inspirational these collaborations have been to him. He's claimed P!nk and Missy Elliott were especially important. (I'd love to know – what do their influences look like?) Wanting to do well by so many people surely must have an effect.

Meyers is also working with songs within genres that he feels a debt to and a respect for. I think he's aware that his relation to hip hop is one that isn't seamless, but rather complicated. A white person who makes hip-hop videos has many responsibilities. It's probably intentional that many of the songs that he chooses recently are 'woke', and I assume that his careful depictions are partly a way of expressing gratitude. And this leads me to wonder about the rough and tumble stars Meyers used to work with (Ludacris, Kid Rock and so on). Did they offer different possibilities?

Keeping with this line of thought, here's another supposition about changes in Meyers's work. Do the songs today provide richer affordances? In other words, is there something more three dimensional, narratively inflected and humanistic about the songs today than in the 1990s? It's possible. The cartoonish ornamental surfaces in which Britney and P!nk move in 'Lucky' (2000) and 'Get the Party Started' (2001) seem to fit their songs well (and I wonder if this is just as true for a song like Jennifer Lopez's 'I'm Gonna Be Alright' from 2001). Since Meyers has often worked with the same stars over a long period, we might be able to make some comparisons. One could argue that there's something deeper about Janet Jackson's 'Made for Now' (2018), with its embrace of 'an African edge to an already bouncy mix of Latin and Caribbean vibes' than 'All for You' (2001) which has a breezy '90s feel to it. Though 'All for You' is a lovely song and a lovely video, it's hard to imagine what more one could do with it.

And there are broader effects like the media swirl, and larger social contexts, as they rub against the development of the music video genre, which we should take account of as well. It's one thing to make a video in the 1980s and the 1990s for a very young artist, with you as a well-known director, knowing that because of your reputation, MTV will most likely play this video or another. And it's another thing to make a video for a seasoned artist today who possesses a whole history of music video production behind her. Even if record companies helped boost viewership on YouTube, there must be a sense that you can't be sure an audience will be there for you. Now, the media landscape is different, and competition may feel steep. The time that can be granted to and what people need from their media surely carries weight as well. Capitalist America has always been difficult, but somehow with Black Lives Matter, MeToo, Trump, enormous income disparities, work speed-up, the gig economy, affective labour, global warming, the degradation of the planet, and so on, we may need something much more from our media, and some artists may be more sensitized to this fact than others.

I've claimed that the chance to work across various media has been crucial for transmedial directors today. Though I want to argue for the relevance of Meyers's practising many forms and drawing on other directors who do the same, I also have the intuition that Meyers's receptivity to, knowledge about and playfulness with popular music has also had shaping influences. Over time, Meyers has discovered new ways of drawing attention to a song's elements and to give them meaning in a visual context. 'All the Stars' 's emotional weight comes partly from Meyers's underscoring moments within the vocal performance, as when SZA sings the first word in her sweeping melodic line '*maybe* the stars', or Lamar's opening rap – '*tell me*'. There's a quality of a raw heartbreak at these moments, a tear (and I'd like to use 'tear' in a doubly inflected sense, both as a painful injury and as weeping), and yet the singer and the rapper continue, following through with the phrase and making good on the line.

This sense of vulnerability and heart shows up visually in 'All the Stars'. The orange glow emerging from within the tent (at the outskirts of the city) resembles a cloaked but visible beating heart. A first goddess, with a hollowed-out chest, possibly made of paper, links to notions of the heart's intimacy and vulnerability. The solemn cluster of youths, wearing bright, soft red hats and traditional wax-dyed shirts who gather around Lamar in what we might guess is a spiritual context, do too. There's Lamar's constant look away, which is emotionally affecting (perhaps some thoughts are too private) (Figure 13.8). Meyers once told me that he wished to make videos everyday people could relate to, which sometimes meant showing the star in a down position. In Maroon 5's 'Wait', Adam Levine's girlfriend aggressively attacks him (she wields a bottle of booze as if it were her penis, pouring its liquid on him like urine; soon, we assume, she'll throw down a lit match. She also threatens him with a baseball bat), but her rage feels warranted. It's an inference that must be drawn from outside the video's diegesis, but a viewer who rearranges the images might assume that Levine was unable to stop her after a fight, which led to her death. I think we take seriously that the threads' unspooling becomes Levine's unravelling. And the fraught distance

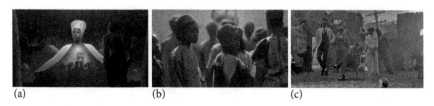

(a)　　　　　　　(b)　　　　　　　(c)

FIGURE 13.8 *Affectively rich imagery in 'All the Stars' (Kendrick Lamar and Dave Meyers, 2018).*

between the couple is set meticulously as roughly four inches between the couple's two faces, recurrently faced off and profiled. The song seems to foreground exactly that gap too. In the chorus, Levine sings and there's a pause – no music, 'Wait' (Figure 13.9).

It would take a scholar's devotion (perhaps at the level of Tag Gallagher's monumental book on John Ford) to track moments of change as they unfold through Meyers's work – and some of the difficulties might derive from inventorying the director's work across various media. Here are two instances to be identified and followed. Directors like Meyers often become enamoured with a motif, technique or parameter, extending, reworking and possibly denaturing it. Recently Meyers has been working closely with some admired choreographers to sharpen gesture, and dance is much richer in his recent videos than previously. Meyers has also had an interest in skies since his earliest videos (in the 1990s, his skies were often lurid, with intense sherbet coloured sunsets, and Britney Spears's 'Lucky' was full of glittery stars and a moon). 'All the Stars' 's depiction of stars may have reverberated for Meyers in a way that he couldn't quite let go of. In Ariana Grande's 'No Tears Left to Cry' (2018), she's nestled in a cocoon-like web of star-like lights, and in Camila Cabello's 'Consequences' (2018), stars surround the ghostly characters like fireflies.

I once claimed Meyers takes us on picaresque journeys. We travelled from one wondrous tableau-like setting to another, as aural and visual motifs came forward and back. He was a song's devoted tracker and he often found ways to direct attention to an often unloved portion of a song that other directors might have overlooked, perhaps a brief break, as in Missy Elliott's 'Get Ur Freak On' (2001). And his attention to musical sound was striking – we couldn't help but notice that suddenly sounding, luminous, silvered trumpet! Now, however, Meyers brings forward sonic elements in a different way, so that they seem to drill more deeply into the video's space.

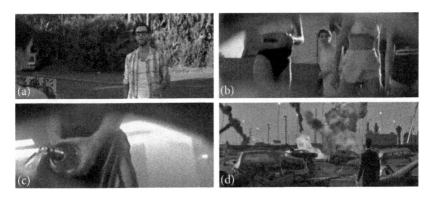

FIGURE 13.9 *Meyers working through a visual motif in 'Wait' (Maroon 5 and Dave Meyers, 2018).*

It doesn't mean that the videos have necessarily become more narrative; it seems, however, that they carry more weight.

Let me show what I mean, returning again to 'All the Stars'. At first, we hear something in the low bass. Is it a heartbeat? What, we might wonder, at some not-quite-voiced level, is keeping everything flowing? We try to follow. This sense of being brought forward is underscored in one tableau as Lamar walks through an expanse of blackened tree trunks, with black panthers pacing before and behind him. Suddenly, one rushes forward as if pressed on by the rhythms of Lamar's rap, 'tell me what you *do* for me', and we suddenly turn our attention for an instant to Lamar's poetry.[3] But what's unfolding doesn't make narrative sense. The panthers don't seem to be listening to Lamar's rapping. But once again, it's one of those weird events in a music video's cosmology. I think this is one of the things viewers at some pre-conscious level wonder about. What encouraged the panther to rush at this moment? Is it the music? It almost surely can't be, but what else can we assume? (See Figure 13.8). As the clip draws to a close, and a male voice (Lamar's?) and SZA sing a duet, suddenly we're in a field of bronze-goldish, hanging African-designed motifs, layered over and spangled, from the fore to the background (against beautiful women stoically and perhaps hopefully posed in costumes of bronze and gold). It has a bit of a Klimt look to it. Kendrick drags himself through this field of glory, relatively unmoved. But for the first time, our experience may fork dramatically from his. We've been following along partly because of the sense of his heartbeat; at this moment, however, we may feel suddenly hopeful. If we continue and hold on to what we believe in, if we can raise our voices, being flexible enough to shift up or down as the video has done this far, to trust passage and to participate in at least one line of the vocal duct, we can happen upon something as glorious as this (Figure 13.10). A similar technique tied to the accruing of meaning through audiovisual motifs occurs in 'Wait'. The song's rimshots 'tick tick tick' gradually become slowly identified with the spool of unwinding twine, Levine's goldfish-like girlfriend's wiggling tails and then finally Levine's unravelling. These come late in the video.

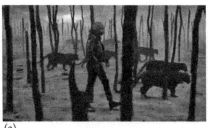
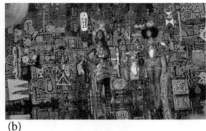

(a)   (b)

FIGURE 13.10 *What are the panthers listening to? The viewer's identification splits – a field of glory in 'All the Stars' (Kendrick Lamar and Dave Meyers, 2018).*

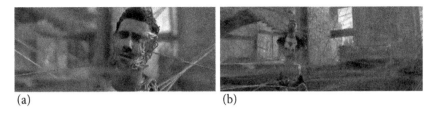

(a)　　　　　　　　　　　　　　　　　　(b)

FIGURE 13.11 *Sound and image relations begin to accrue meaning: Adam Levine's unravelling and our relationships in 'Wait' (Maroon 5 and Dave Meyers, 2018).*

There's much more about these videos that I'd like to note. For example, they show us that sound can be discovered and understood, and if we're a bit more attentive than Levine (who admits he might have been a bad guy) we might be able to rescue our relationships through attention and care (Figure 13.11).

These powerful, fleeting moments show how music videos carry meaning. Before closing, I'd like to note a few more aspects of the clip, for example, the moments when SZA spins and twirls, arms over head and we can't tell whether she's on water or ice. She forms the role of a female Rodin sculpture, and the next shot is a match cut to Lamar in a contemplative sitting position too. This sense of contemplation seems to spread out in 'All the Stars' to the handsomely dressed high-cheeked woman in a West African green dress and later to what we might assume is her similarly regal male partner, dressed in blue, as well as the sombre children. The tempo for these senses of contemplation start forming a continuum with other events, objects and people expressing different types of awareness.

I'd also like to talk about several of the settings, for example one which is very faithful to the African residents and housing at the outskirts of cities, with their clay walls, imported tin roofs, and men dressed up as fancily as princes, yet the dancing is probably more American. The children most likely couldn't afford the shoes and starched shirts. In 'All the Star' 's bridge, SZA lies in a field of pink water surrounded by African designs cut out like puzzle pieces, and a circle of women dance vigorously around her, cloaked in feathered wings and headdresses, which may have some traditional roots, but the pink feels, at least for American audiences, probably closer to Broadway or Las Vegas. Yet, though this sounds jarring, this setting feels fully integrated. What does this mélange tell us? Is the clip partly aspirational? I noted earlier that the Maroon 5 'Wait' video had similar discongruities. We should turn to both videos and compare, but also to discontinuities in earlier instances in Meyers's work. What's the same and what's new? What I'd like to do is a slow process, and most helped by thoughts shared from the director, fellow practitioners and audiences. To do this with many directors might tell us how we all find ourselves in a new moment.

CHAPTER 14

The alchemical union of David Bowie and Floria Sigismondi: 'Transmedia surrealism' and 'loose continuity'

Lisa Perrott

> Exactly when did poetry become subsumed by rock 'n' roll? When was experimental film swallowed and digested by music videos? My generation of artists held a starry-eyed belief in the notion of crossing over; of leaving the elitism of the white cube for other media and venues: video, performance, audio, music. (Tony Oursler)[1]

It is fitting to open this chapter with the words of an artist who was not only David Bowie's friend and muse but a collaborator who was interstitially involved with the music videos Bowie created with Floria Sigismondi. A significant transmedia artist in his own right, Tony Oursler understood the artistic magnetism that drew Bowie and Sigismondi into a creative partnership. Oursler's 'starry-eyed belief in the notion of crossing over' and resistance to elitism sum up an approach that has been neglected by much of the literature on transmedia. The creative motivations of an artist to 'cross over' have tended to be eclipsed by a scholarly emphasis upon transmedia storytelling in relation to franchise development, foundational canons and what Henry Jenkins calls 'mothership' projects.[2] With the aim of redistributing light onto the artistry, mediality and temporality of transmedia, this chapter examines the 'starry-eyed' transmediality of Bowie and Sigismondi in two steps. First, by exploring how Bowie developed his own approach to working across media and tracing how this has come to distinguish his oeuvre. Secondly, by examining how Bowie and Sigismondi's distinctive approaches to transmedia have manifested collaboratively across the music videos they created together. While the first part establishes the context and motivation for their media crossings, the second part draws upon my analysis of three music videos to explicate a complex network of connective threads and signature traits woven across media, texts, oeuvres and time.

Through a close examination of these medial and authorial crossings, I argue that studying transmedia from the perspective of artistic collaboration can uncover insights about the potential for 'dialogic world-building' as a generative artistic process.[3] Drawing on Mikhail Bakhtin's concept of 'dialogism',[4] I define this form of world-building as a reciprocal process of creative dialogue, interaction and contradiction between artists, authors and their collaborators, often involving the reworking of world components derived from other artists. As a collaborative team, Bowie and Sigismondi exemplify this process, since they engaged in a dialogic process to build elaborate worlds. Beyond the authorship they shared with each other, their dialogic process extended to re-interpreting world components derived from ancient mythology, esoteric philosophy, popular culture and the avant-garde, all of which are reimagined across a variety of media.

Transmedia through and beyond narrative

Much of the existing literature on transmedia is concerned with transmedia storytelling, particularly the way in which stories and narrative elements travel across media, texts and platforms. Scholars such as David Bordwell and Jenkins have established useful theoretical frameworks for considering the idea of transmedia storytelling, primarily in relation to film, television and franchise. Aware of the limitations of prioritizing film and franchise as central to the discussion on transmedia, Bordwell acknowledges, 'It's hard to think outside the franchise model, even if we want to denounce Hollywood for being stuck in an outdated commitment to the theatrical feature as foundational "content"'.[5] Encouraging researchers to consider the role played by fans in elaborating canonical storyworlds, Jenkins defined a 'transmedia story' as one that 'unfolds across multiple media platforms, with each new text making a distinctive and valuable contribution to the whole'.[6] Arguing that 'world-building' and 'seriality' are the 'aesthetic properties of texts that lend themselves to transmedia experience', Jenkins adds that transmedia texts 'rely on open ended and serialized structures', where the hope is 'for a certain level of integrity and continuity between the pieces which allows us to find the coherent whole from which the many parts must have once broken adrift'.[7] While Jenkins's definition has been predominantly applied to film, television and franchise development, its flexibility is most apparent when theorized in relation to a broader range of media, and may therefore provide a lens through which to consider artists such as Bowie, whose transmedial work is not centred upon this triad. However, Bowie's 'story' is not quite as straightforward or as continuous as Jenkins's theory suggests, and the depth of field captured by the lens of 'transmedia storytelling' doesn't extend to the broad field of aesthetics, objects, archetypes and intangibles that Bowie refracted across media.

[If] [we cast ou]r eyes across Bowie's oeuvre and consider his lifelong [work as an] artist, it would appear to be marked by discontinuity. [Born] [...] out of a restless drive for experimentation, this discontinuity [inv]olved frequent chameleon-like changes in appearance, death and re-birth of personae, and shifts in musical style and visual aesthetic. However, his oeuvre is also distinguished by 'loose continuity', a concept developed by the painter Paul Klee to allude to 'those vague patterns, random encounters and tangential connections that are only revealed in hindsight after a long passage of time'.[8] For scholars and fans who have paid close attention to Bowie's work, what is revealed 'after a long passage of time' is a veritable toy-box full of characters, archetypes and ideas, all of which provide threads of 'loose continuity'. As with the tropes of the puppet, the mask and the alien, the figures of Pierrot, Major Tom, Thomas Newton and The Thin White Duke exemplify resilient threads of continuity that persistently weave their way through and across mediums, texts and time. Bowie is distinctive as a transmedia artist partly because of this very paradox; his work across media simultaneously exhibits loose continuity and discontinuity. Just as Bowie constructs imaginary world components that develop over time, their development is marked by incoherence, instability, transformation and temporal disjuncture. If it is possible to discern a story unfolding across Bowie's oeuvre, it unfolds not with narrative coherence, but more akin to the surrealist subversion of narrative convention achieved by the film *Un Chien Andalou* (Luis Buñuel and Salvador Dalí, 1929). Bowie's surrealist approach to transmedia doesn't fit neatly into the framework already drawn around transmedia storytelling and world-building, with its emphasis on narrative continuity and the coherency of canonical worlds.[9] I therefore draw attention to two foundational antecedents to the transmedia practice of Bowie, Sigismondi, Oursler and David Lynch: *Gesamtkunstwerk* and surrealism. Since the word 'surreal' has been liberally applied to a broad array of phenomena, it is necessary to define my use of the term 'surrealism', as the avant-garde movement in art and literature which (though often relegated to the 1920–30s), continues to provide conceptual and methodological tools for artists to release the creative potential of the unconscious psyche.

Transmedial surrealists such as Jan Švankmajer endeavour to create sensorially provocative artworks through the irrational juxtaposition of images, along with the estrangement of everyday objects.[10] Such uncanny provocations are achieved by strategies such as aleatory and alchemical process, automatism, analogical composition, temporal disjuncture and *détournement*.[11] These strategies undergird the creative process of Bowie and Sigismondi, as will be revealed in the following analyses.

Another important antecedent to contemporary transmedia practice is *Gesamtkunstwerk*,[12] which has been translated as 'total work of art' or 'synthesis of arts'.[13] In her article on Richard Wagner's theories on *Gesamtkunstwerk* and theatre as an ideal medium, Krisztina Lajosi suggests the concept 'might also be rendered as "communal or collective artwork of the future"'.[14] Contemporary proponents of *Gesamtkunstwerk* strive for a multisensory synthesis of art forms, often involving the communal and/ or integrated performance of music, literature, theatre, dance, painting and sculpture.[15]

A transmedia star, a navigator, a medium

It was Bowie's affinity for the tenets of surrealism and *Gesamtkunstwerk* that led to him being considered as a vanguard and innovator of transmedia, or as Mehdi Derfoufi describes him, 'a star of the transmedia era'.[16] Such lofty evaluations find support in recently published research examining the nature of Bowie's mediality in relation to his 'navigational' role in illuminating pathways to new knowledge and alternative identities.[17] Even as early as 1976, Bowie was beginning to perceive himself as a transmedia navigator:

> I thought, 'Well, here I am, I'm a bit mixed up creatively, I've got all these things I like doing at once on stage ... I'm not quite sure if I'm a mime or a songwriter or a singer, or do I want to go back to painting again. Why am I doing any of these things anyway ...' and I realised it was because I wanted to be well known [...] I wanted to be the instigator of new ideas, I wanted to turn people on to new things and new perspectives ... I always wanted to be that sort of catalytic kind of thing.[18]

With this 'catalytic' impulse and his natural inclination to move across media, Bowie not only modelled his own transmedial practice but also shone a torch on the many ways in which transmedia has been done in the past and how it could be done with a difference in the future. When interviewed in 1976, he suggested that one of these ways was to *become* a medium: *or a brand?*

> I ... decided to use the easiest medium to start off with which was rock 'n' roll, and then to add pieces to it over the years and so that really by the

end of it I was my own medium ... I mean hopefully that'll happen one day ... that's really why I do it ... to become a medium ... I guess I was one of the first to come out and say I'm using rock n roll, it's not my life ... I'm only using it as a medium.[19]

What is significant about this interview is that Bowie appears to be theorizing his own approach to transmedia, an approach that entailed considering himself as a particular type of medium: a canvas. As he stated in another interview that same year, 'I'm using myself as a canvas and trying to paint the truth of our time on it.'[20] Just as a painter would apply different textures and hues of paint to a canvas, Bowie would apply different media to himself as a canvas, according to the specific affordances of each medium. Beyond expressing this as an abstract notion in interviews, Bowie reiterated this idea in his work so insistently that scholars are now able to reflect back on his body of work and examine the figure of Bowie, as a medium. For example, Katherine Johnson suggests that Bowie's creative process can be 'interpreted as part of the process of becoming a "medium"'.[21] In a similar vein, Will Brooker examines, 'Bowie's work not as a linear evolution ... but as a matrix, a dialogue, a network of ideas that echo back and forth across the five decades of his career, interacting with each other and with the surrounding culture'.[22] Also understanding Bowie as a developing medium within a matrix, Dene October explores Bowie's identity as 'seriously instantiated through and across media'.[23] This notion of an artist's identity developing across media confounds those conceptions of authorship that rely on identity stability, and takes the concept of transmedia through and beyond the realm of storytelling. Reading Bowie's 'story through a transmedia lens', October observes how the character Thomas Newton 'survives the film *The Man Who Fell to Earth* (Roeg 1976) to appear in adaptations, music videos and the play *Lazarus* (2015). Like David Bowie he can be understood as a serial figure, one who exists as a series across media.'[24] Describing this phenomenon as the 'Bowie-Newton matrix', October shows how the serial figures of Bowie and Newton are medial agents interlocked in a dialogic relationship, serially weaving their way through texts and across media.[25] In addition to the examples mentioned above, intertextual references to Newton and *The Man Who Fell to Earth (TMWFTE)* (Nicolas Roeg, 1976) appear in the music and cover designs for Bowie's albums *Station to Station* (1976) and *Low* (1977), in the music videos for 'Lazarus' (Johan Renck, 2015) and 'No Plan' (Tom Hingston, 2017), in the *Vittel* commercial (Andrew Douglas, 2003) and in the duffle coat worn by Bowie/Newton in *TMWFTE*, which was provocatively referenced by *Doctor Who* actress Jodie Whittaker,[26] and emulated in the fashion of the Liverpool subculture known as the 'Football Casuals' during 1976–9. Examining the medial transit of Newton's duffle coat, Mairi McKenzie points out how 'Bowie reconfigured and advanced the meanings inherent in this material object, transcending the weight of its history, and activating a process of transmedial cultural transit'.[27] Music videos provide a particularly suitable vehicle for the cultural transit of such material objects and their convergence with other media. As was hauntingly demonstrated by the posthumous release of the video for 'No Plan', the serial figures of Bowie and Newton outlive the terminus typically instigated by the death of the physical actor in a televised serial narrative. In order to contemplate the significance of Bowie's serial development, we must first trace the broad brush strokes that illustrate how this serial narrative unfolded across media and time.

Performing across stage and screen

While most prominently lauded for his extensive contributions to rock and popular music, music constitutes only one strand of the many artistic threads Bowie wove together. During his teenage years he began a lifelong pursuit of traversing and synthesizing the sonic, visual and performing arts. While learning to play musical instruments, singing and generating marketing ideas for his bands, Bowie studied art and design at Bromley Technical High School after which he developed his promotional and branding strategies as a junior visualizer/paste-up artist for *Nevin D Hirst Advertising*.[28] Under the tutelage of Lindsay Kemp, he honed his skills in live stage performance, dance and mime. These skills were then transferred to the medium of film for *The Mask* (1969, Malcolm Thomson),[29] a five-minute mime performance in which Bowie presciently and 'ominously depicts his future stardom and the subsequent near-madness it caused him', concluding with the destruction of the mask-wearer.[30] Transferring his musical and mime performance from stage to screen gave him a taste for platform crossing. In 1968 he acted as 'Cloud', performing alongside Kemp in the pantomime *Pierrot in Turquoise or the Looking Glass Murders*.[31] Initially staged at the London Mercury Theatre, it was re-performed as a television short in 1970, enabling Bowie to consider the different affordances of theatre and televisual media and potential expansion of audience enabled by acting on screen.[32]

Entwined with his prolific creative production as a musician, visual artist and performance artist, Bowie practised the craft of acting, moving with relative ease across stage, film and television. When considering the diverse roles he played holistically, a sense of loose continuity develops. As posited by Toija Cinque, Angela Ndalianis and Sean Redmond, Bowie's screen performances are 'loosely bound by a profound alterity – a signification of difference'.[33]

Entangled with alterity, Bowie's work is also loosely bound by a transmedial engagement with hauntology. 'The time is out of joint', a line from William Shakespeare's play *Hamlet*, was appropriated by Jacques Derrida in 1994 to describe a state of haunting whereby 'revenants' (spirits, spectres and ghosts) reappear in a different time, giving rise to a sense of untimeliness and ontological uncertainty.[34] While Derrida coined the term 'hauntology' with reference to the apparitional workings of political discourse, this concept has since been developed as a means of examining how mediated cultural forms trigger a sense of temporal disjuncture. Extending upon Derrida's theory, Mark Fisher has demonstrated how music and screen media can produce a nostalgic engagement with the past and future, along with an eerie sense of dyschronia.[35] Propelled by Fisher's acute attention to the specific temporal and cultural affordances of music and audiovisual media, I have examined Bowie's engagement with hauntology, thus demonstrating the concept's utility as a tool for transmedial analysis.[36] An early example of his engagement with hauntology can be observed in *The Image* (1969, Michael Armstrong), a short film in which Bowie plays a ghostly character who metaphorically acts out his penchant for traversing media and for considering himself as a canvas, as well as his interest in the shifting agency between artist and artwork. The artist who creates him is haunted by Bowie's character, who appears to step out from the painted canvas, morphing from a painted form into an illusionary human form, whose omnipresence torments the artist until he repeatedly attempts to kill-off his creation, thus giving rise to a sense of ontological instability.

A similar sense of instability and shifting agency is carried over into Bowie's alter ego Ziggy Stardust, the alien 'leper messiah' who lands on Earth amid stardust and fame, only to be 'killed-off' onstage, due to the persona having tormented Bowie, consuming his creative agency and psychic well-being. On 3 July 1973, London's Hammersmith Odeon teemed with throngs of fans adorned with platform boots, space-age copper mullets and mask-like faces painted with lightning bolts and forehead patches. To this idolatry audience, Ziggy performed onstage and backstage for Don Pannebaker's documentary film *Ziggy Stardust and the Spiders from Mars* (1973). Eerily referencing the mime-artist's demise in *The Mask*, and the artist's killing-off of his painted creation in *The Image*, Bowie used this performance to document the moment he killed-off the all-consuming Ziggy persona. In the process, he moved closer to achieving the *Gesamtkunstwerk* that would again be realized with his stage shows for *Diamond Dogs* (1974), *The Glass Spider* (1987) and *Lazarus* (2015 onwards). Through Ziggy, Bowie and his collaborators synthesized the kinetic art form of mime with rock music, together with visual aesthetics drawn from *kabuki* theatre, the *noh* mask tradition and the fashion design of Kansai Yamamoto.[37] This dialogic cultural canvas was further hybridized by his performance of ambiguously gendered gestural signifiers, seemingly channelling Marlene Dietrich and Romy Haag.[38] While this synthesis of intertextual references, art forms and mediums achieved *Gesamtkunstwerk*, the different layers of performance were filmed by Pannebaker, forming yet another permanent record of Bowie's traverse of stage and screen. With its intimate capturing of Ziggy's onstage sexual ambiguity, backstage dressing room performance, fan adulation and emulation, the resulting film serves not only as a historic record of the emergence of 'Direct Cinema' but also as a cultural and ethnographic record of the performativity of gender and sexuality.[39]

Considering the string of personas that followed Ziggy, Bowie's legacy to the realms of fashion, art and subculture can be credited in part to the inspiration he gleaned from the Italian performance troupe *Commedia del'arte*, which provided rich material for Bowie's allegorical use of the figure of Pierrot across his oeuvre.[40] Another important cultural antecedent to the realms of performance art and fashion was the Dandy, for which Oscar Wilde has been cited as a significant influence to Bowie.[41] Inspiration was also drawn from sci-fi themes and aesthetics plucked from the films of Stanley Kubrick and the literature of William Burroughs and George Orwell, all of which have been observed by Angela Ndalianis as inspirations for Bowie's 'science fictionality', a particularly resilient strand of Bowie's transmediality that has 'contagiously filtered into popular culture, forming a logic of its own. In the process, Bowie as science fiction has become a stable memetic complex, spreading its memes and becoming its own distinctive form of science fiction thinking.'[42] Providing a cultural and material palette for Bowie's stage and music video performances, his contributions to the worlds of costume design and fashion can be understood as dialogic world-building components, generated by his magpie approach to mimicry and his collaborations with an array of renowned costume designers.[43] Bowie's vast repertoire of costumes, masks and bodily adornments constitutes an elaborate sign system, furnishing his world and connoting his performing body with a sensibility of alterity.

This sense of alterity was reiterated by Bowie's performing body across several of his acting roles. Reflecting on Bowie's performance as the alien Thomas Newton in *TMWFTE*, Roeg recollected that 'he really came to believe that Bowie was a man who had come to Earth from another Galaxy'.[44] The transmedial flow of Bowie's alienness is charted by October, who suggests the possibility of the character 'Newton exhorting Bowie's performance in Yentob's *Cracked Actor*. The documentary for BBC's *Omnibus* strand was so admired by Roeg, it convinced him Bowie was already Newton and should not be required to act.'[45] For his role as John Merrick in the Broadway production *The Elephant Man* (Jack Hofsiss, 1980–1),[46] Bowie tapped into his deep sense of otherness to deliver an extremely compelling performance, imparting extreme disfigurement through his bodily, facial and vocal contortion.[47] His innate sense of difference also made him eminently suited to play the role of vampire John Blaylock in the film *The Hunger* (Tony Scott, 1983), the ambiguously sexualized role of the goblin king Jareth in *Labyrinth* (Jim Henson, 1986), and to channel the eccentric mannerisms of Andy Warhol in *Basquiat* (Julian Schnabel, 1996).

These strands of loose continuity (alterity, alienation, persona as allegory and hauntology) weave across Bowie's acting performances in music videos and commercials. In the *Vittel* water commercial,[48] Bowie performs alongside his impersonator David Brighton, acting out several of his personas in a playfully ironic scenario in which Bowie finds himself annoyed by the ubiquitous presence of his younger personas who eat his food, drink his water and occupy his personal space, all set to Bowie's song 'Never Get Old' (2003). Like a disgruntled father, Bowie enters the bathroom to find Ziggy preening in front of the mirror, a scene that intertextually references the recurring trope of the mirror image of Bowie, which moves fluidly across film, music video and art photography. As he descends the stairs, it seems fitting that he should stumble upon Newton from *TMWFTE*, a mnemonic fixture upon the staircase, who looks up momentarily with a melancholic glance of recognition at his actor/other self. Bowie continues to step down this Jungian 'path to the unconscious', moving aside to make way for Halloween Jack as he struts energetically up the stairs in glamorous platform boots, turning to look down condescendingly upon the older, plainer looking Bowie. Entering his kitchen, Bowie encounters a gathering of his personas sharing a meal and giving each other knowing glances. With a slice of toast in one hand, The Thin White Duke poses with hand on hip, a feminized pose that has become synonymous with Bowie's early personas. Opening his fridge and dismayed by the remains of his *Vittel* water, Bowie fires a quizzical look at the three personas eating at his table. Enacting his mime skills, Pierrot from 'Ashes to Ashes' raises his arms in a gesture of disavowal. Just as Bowie is about to escape this Jungian house with his *Vittel* bottle securely tucked inside his pocket, his attention is drawn to the top of the stairs by the bark of a reclining Diamond Dog, only to see that he's being watched by Alladin Sane from the mezzanine floor above.

As we shall see, Bowie engages in similarly playful performances with his past personas in music videos directed by Sigismondi, as well as his self-directed video for 'Love Is Lost' (2013). An examination of the audiovisual composition of this video reveals other persistent threads of continuity across his oeuvre. For instance, temporal dissonance is evoked by James Murphy's palimpsestuous remix of the song, as unpacked by Chris O'Leary:

> To a track already freighted with the past, Murphy layered in more callbacks, scribbled more lines upon the palimpsest. Most notably Steve Reich's 'Clapping Music'..., which becomes the fulcrum of the new beat,

and … Roy Bittan's keyboard line from 'Ashes to Ashes', which appears as a special guest on a variety show, entering at a peak moment to rounds of applause.[49]

Perfectly complementing these sonic callbacks, Bowie pulls from his toy-box reoccurring tropes of the puppet and mask, reiterated via his collaborations with Klaus Nomi ('Boys Keep Swinging', performed on *Saturday Night Live*, 1979), Jim Henson (*Labyrinth*, 1986), Oursler ('Where Are We Now?', 2013) and Sigismondi ('Little Wonder'). Having employed Henson's Creature Shop in 1999 to create two of his personas as life-size wooden puppets for the aborted video 'The Pretty Things Are Going to Hell' (1999),[50] Bowie was able to breathe new life into these dormant *Faustian* puppets.[51] Casting them as archetypal characters in yet another Jungian psychodrama, his ageing self is represented via a disembodied mask, haunted by The Thin White Duke's omnipresent gaze; a scenario that reoccurs in 'The Stars' (2013) (Figures 14.1 and 14.4). Animated with the sentient gestures of an older sibling, this puppetized persona cradles the ailing, faceless form of his progeny persona Pierrot, whose stolen face is projected onto Bowie's fabric mask; creating a disembodied hybrid of the ageing Bowie singing as a 'sad clown' (Figures 14.1 and 14.2). This facial transference appears to signify the shifting of agency and blurring of identity between an artist and his creations, akin to the artist/creation relationship performed in *The Image* and by the multilayered performance of Ziggy Stardust. For Tom Hawking, 'the implication seems to be that behind all the characters, there's a blank canvas.'[52]

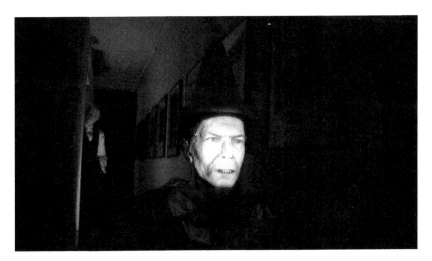

FIGURE 14.1 *The Thin White Duke watches Bowie. 'Love Is Lost' (David Bowie, 2013).*

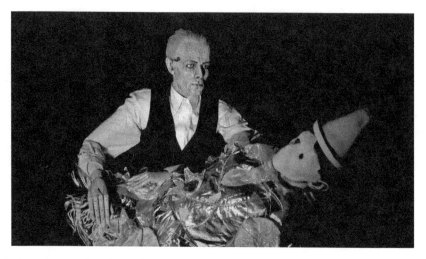

FIGURE 14.2 *The Thin White Duke cradles his progeny persona Pierrot. 'Love Is Lost' (David Bowie, 2013).*

Visual art, voice and collaboration

Onto his canvas, Bowie projected not only personas and performativity but the dialogic textures of visual, vocal and musical media. He painted, drew storyboards, sketched designs for album covers and elaborate stage sets, and designed multi-platform story worlds and wallpaper. Portraying an extensive knowledge of art history and an expressionistic soul, his paintings materialize his intention to become a medium, as a canvas.[53] An art collector, curator and publisher, he also served as editor, art critic and writer for *Modern Painters*.[54] These activities were integral to his traverse of fine art and popular culture, as vividly exemplified by Bowie's collaborative approach to designing his album cover art, for which he often provided his designers with elaborate sketches and distinctive branding ideas. His cover art, paintings, storyboard sketches and set designs portray his synthesis of references to popular culture, Hollywood cinema, surrealist, expressionist and outsider art, along with dystopian themes and science-fiction aesthetics, thus exemplifying how transmedia can engender new forms of foraging.[55] Bowie's iconic pose on the album cover for *Heroes* (1977) has come to signify the pinnacle of his innovative conjunction of avant-garde aesthetics and popular music.[56] His distinctive angular arm gesture intertextually references Erich Heckel's painting *Roquairol* (1917) exemplifying Bowie's migration of gestures across mediums.[57] Serializing this act of remediation, the *Heroes* cover is *détourned* for *The Next Day* (2013) album cover, where Bowie's iconic pose is eclipsed by a white square. As a two-step act of remediation and self-*détournement*, this altered signification asserts Bowie's playful encounter with his own past, along with his transformative engagement with celebrity and his conjunction of popular culture and fine art.

Bowie collected a broad array of art, including German expressionist paintings, modern British art, contemporary African art, sculptural assemblages of found objects, postmodernist furniture and an Italian designed radiophonograph. His collection included works by Jean-Michel Basquiat, Pablo Picasso and Frank Auerbach.[58] He held long-standing collaborative friendships with contemporary artists; with Oursler he collaborated on music videos and engaged in dialogue about the artistic significance of Jung's ideas, and the crossing over between visual art and music. When Oursler asked Bowie how he related to visual artworks by Jaqueline Humphries, he replied: 'It's very similar to the way I think about constructing music. Overlapping patterns and layers scraped away to reveal other patterns.'[59] With fellow art critic William Boyd, Bowie plotted and published a copiously illustrated 'haux' biography written by Boyd about a fictitious 'dead' artist named Nat Tate.[60] With Damien Hirst, Bowie discussed the agency and presence of the artist, chance composition, the value of play[61] and of an artist relinquishing final control 'to the universe'.[62] This approach to creativity is consistent with the aleatory compositional methods utilized during Bowie's collaborations with Brian Eno, and can be observed as a continuous thread reiterated in different ways across Bowie's sonic and visual compositions. This aspect of Bowie and Eno's collaboration is best illustrated in the YouTube video animated by the Brothers McLeod and voiced by Adam Buxton, which parodies the nerdy eccentricity of their 'oblique strategies'.[63] Taking its place alongside the *Flight of the Conchords* episode *Bowie* and its spin-off video 'Bowie's in Space', these fan-made texts serve as elaborations of Bowie's idiosyncratic vocality and sense of humour.[64] As do the vocals of the Conchords comedy duo, Buxton's close emulation of Bowie's distinctive voice serves as a trans-authorial addition to the continuity of Bowie's voice across media and time.

The continuity and variation of Bowie's voice has a dramaturgical context, in which vocal character is a performative aspect of personae and archetype. Bowie's use of studio production techniques such as pitch shifting, vari-speed, flanging and filtering 'often served a *dramaturgical* purpose, imparting a *character* to the vocal', which is particularly apparent in his songs 'The Laughing Gnome', 'Scream Like a Baby' and 'the swirling spectral vocals of "The Man Who Sold the World"'.[65] Connected to these compositional strategies, Bowie's voice is also recognizable for its distinctive tremulous quality, broad range and playful lilt.[66] He also conjured vocal traces of performers he admired.[67] Such hauntological affordances play an important part in the creation and extension of a transmedia universe.

Hauntology, extending transmedia

Bowie's engagement with hauntology through and across media exemplifies how we are haunted not only by figures from the past appearing in the present but also by the eerie vacillation between presence and absence. Ontological dissonance is provoked when cinematic images are set in motion and visualized by the flickering light of a projector; when there is an audiovisual mis-match, like when a strong vocal presence is accompanied with images that visually reinforce the absence of the singer (as in the video 'No Plan'), and when human motion is fragmented by pixilation, a stop-motion technique used by Sigismondi and Lynch to accentuate the unsettling oscillation between stasis/motion, life/death and absence/presence.

Bowie's absence is sometimes eerily highlighted by his apparitional presence, mediated through other actors.[68] His apparitional presence moves across many mediums, sometimes merely implied by reiterated gestures or associations with past performances. Twenty-five years after Bowie played Phillip Jeffries in *Twin Peaks: Fire Walk with Me* (1992), Lynch taunted his cult audience in *Twin Peaks: The Return* (2017) with constant reminders of Bowie's absence by way of Jeffries's absence. After much speculation from fans, Dale Cooper's doppelganger searches incessantly for Jeffries for fifteen episodes, only to find him (ironically) in the form of a 'tin machine'.[69]

Denis Flannery observes how Bowie often deftly employed an 'aesthetics of absence' as a generative energy and mode of resistance.[70] This strategy has manifested in powerful ways since Bowie's death, such as with the posthumous release of the music video for 'No Plan' in 2017. Director Tom Hingston tapped into Bowie's generative energy by mediating his absent-presence through a wall of anthropomorphic television screens, performing what feels like a spiritual séance. Situated within the shop window of 'Newton Electrical', this scenario intertextually references the wall of television screens in an iconic scene in *TMWSTW*. Animated with the bygone sensation of television static, the screens illuminate the raindrops on the window and haunt the audience with the eerie presence of a spectre seeking transmission through layers of static. It feels as though Bowie has tuned in from some liminal non-place: the intimate sentience of his voice communicating through an interface of dead screen technology. An analogous sense of Bowie's apparitional presence mediated through screens was also poignantly alluded to in James Murphy and LCD Soundsystem's song 'Black Screen' (2017). The referential music and epistolic lyrics of this tributary song evoke a haunting sensation of Murphy communicating necromantically with the ghost of his friend and collaborator.

Highlighting the absence of Bowie's physical body, his voice and music have been used in numerous television productions, films and commercials to provide affective resonance. In episode 3.5 of the television series *Peaky*

Blinders (2016) Bowie's absent-presence is conjured by his song 'Lazarus' (2015). Laden with the vertiginous sonic space created by the saxophone's gravitational 'fall to earth', together with the raw vulnerability of Bowie's vocality and sense of gravitas associated with his terminal illness, this song provides a therapeutic sonic bedrock to the scene, affectively reanimating lead character Tommy Shelby as he lies as a slain corpse on his own deathbed, and then miraculously rises from his near-death experience. Given the song and music video's biblical references to the raising of Lazarus from the dead, and the serialized conjuncture of this biblical mythology with the 'Newton-Bowie matrix', this transmedial crossing contributes yet another extension to Bowie's serial development across media.[71] These conjurings of Bowie's apparitional presence extend upon his vast cultural repository of hauntological world components, as does the performative reiteration of gestural signification by fans.

Bowie's death triggered an abundance of tributes; numerous fan-made artworks, music videos, short films, animated vignettes and memes spread virally across the internet, assuring the open-ended and dialogic nature of Bowie's transmedial universe. His gesturing image leapt from mobile digital screens to the animation of urban space, appearing in the form of ephemeral street art palimpsestuously layered over historic architecture and the remnants of prior street art.[72] The spirit of Bowie is also kept alive by numerous tributes in the form of sonic compositions, theatrical and televised performances by Lorde, Amanda Palmer and Cowboy Junkies, and by lesser-known artists who participate in a cycle of performativity inspired by Bowie.[73] Particularly relevant transmedial extensions include screenwriter Todd Alcott's reimagining of Bowie songs as book covers;[74] and the persona-puppets created by Tanja Stark, whose artworks converge with her extensive writing on Bowie's engagement with Carl Jung.[75] The spectral presence of Bowie also began haunting the Soho *Hotel Café Royal*, where Bowie retired his Ziggy Stardust alter ego in 1973. Located within this restaurant, *Ziggy's* opened in 2018 as a themed cocktail bar where fans and devotees can experience Ziggy-inspired cocktails, furniture and décor. While the cocktail titles reference pertinent song lyrics, photographs of Ziggy Stardust taken by Mick Rock adorn the walls of the bar, thus conjuring the spectral presence of Bowie and further enriching the intermedia experience of this tribute.[76]

These extensions to Bowie's universe show how artists and fans have utilized a variety of media to performatively extend the threads of loose continuity woven through and across his canvas. What began as a blank canvas has become a rich tapestry comprised of persistent threads of alterity, alienation and hauntology, and tropes of the persona, the mask and the puppet, intersecting with aleatory strategies that play with temporal disjuncture and Jungian archetypes. These broad brush strokes portray the serialized texture of Bowie's transmedia canvas, thereby framing the following examination of his collaborative work with Sigismondi.

Stirring the Cauldron with Floria

Bowie's collaborative relationship with Sigismondi provides a vital window into the alchemical process related to transmedia surrealism. While it is neither ethical nor desirable to undertake a forensic examination of such an intimate relationship, the following section provides a respectful glimpse through this window in order to better understand the dialogic nature of their collaborative process. The deeply personal nature of this collaborative relationship is poignantly expressed by Sigismondi in this statement posted on her official Facebook page after Bowie's death in 2016:

> The passing of David Bowie has affected me in ways I have never experienced. He channelled something supernatural in his music and art that made him otherworldly, that transcended trends, genres and time. He reached in and took out the unseen and brought it to us as art, so we can look, dissect and dive deeper to discover who we are. He paved the way for gender transgression and androgyny. My numerous video collaborations with David have changed the course of my art forever. He taught me to be fearless, the most important thing for an artist.[77]

Underpinned by a mutual understanding of art and its capacity for transcendence, Sigismondi and Bowie shared many transformative collaborative experiences. In a 1997 interview, Bowie mused, 'The texture part is what draws me to Floria's work. She moves away from narrative to a certain extent. Narrative that she does put in is generally pretty abstract, and I like that aspect of working with her.'[78] Integral to the working process of both artists are these capacities to move beyond narrative and to apply painterly techniques such as texture and abstraction across a variety of media. Sigismondi has carried her distinctive visual and kinetic aesthetics across painting, fine art and fashion photography, sculpture, music video, installation art, film, television, commercials and her audiovisual and set designs for live performance. In an interview for *Variety* in 2017, Sigismondi explained that while 'painting is my first love', time itself is a very significant medium, and directing is what 'encompasses all the forms of media' that she loves, including

> sculpture, fashion, sound, tone, lighting, mood and *time*. We demand time of people which is like no other medium, except for music or a painting of a photograph, where someone can give you three or four seconds. But

there's something interesting about asking someone of time. That's the most fulfilling medium.[79]

This notion of time as a medium is not only a distinctive signature trait across Sigismondi's work, but it also weaves its way across Bowie's oeuvre.[80] While Bowie achieved temporal disjuncture through strategies such as sonic and visual mimicry, gestural animation and studio production techniques such as pitch shifting, Sigismondi achieved temporal dissonance through cinematic strategies of time manipulation. Fundamental to kinetic art forms such as mime, puppetry, photography and animation, the medium of time underpins the directorial approach of both artists. For Bowie, puppetry and gestural animation were frequently incorporated into his bodily movement and performance strategies. Sharing a similar understanding of the signification of the puppet as an avant-garde strategy, Sigismondi's methods complement those practised by Bowie. I describe her as a 'gestural animator and puppeteer' to emphasize the distinctive way in which she directs the performers in her music videos, at times puppetizing their bodies.[81] By metaphorically manipulating imagined marionette strings as she animates performers' gesturing bodies, Sigismondi vivifies the time-space in between the still and moving image. In addition to her gestural direction, she uses cinematic methods such as time-lapse photography, speed-ramping and the stop-motion technique of pixilation to punctuate and momentarily disturb the viewer's perception of 'normal' human motion. This manipulation of animated time in relation to bodily movement creates a sense of temporal dissonance that persists across her work as a distinctive visual-kinetic 'time signature', a signature that complements Bowie's treatment of time as a medium.

Having directed music videos for many enduring figures of the music industry, Sigismondi has developed a formidable reputation as a director who challenges audiences with her beautifully macabre imagery. Primed by her childhood exposure to the opulence of theatrical sets and costumes, her films and music videos are distinctive for their cinematic virtuosity. Her understanding of art history, painting and photography was developed through her art school education followed by her work as a fashion photographer.[82] The professional step from photography into directing music video enabled Sigismondi to explore the relationship between the still and moving image using a medium well suited to experimenting with the commute and contrast of affordances across media.

Through such experimentation, her work has become distinctive for the way in which it pushes beyond conventional expectations about what constitutes a music video.[83] Incorporating intertextual references to photography, sculpture, silent film, avant-garde art, theatre and cinema, her music videos blur the boundaries between forms and genres, while also drawing inspiration from artists such as Lynch, Stephen and Timothy Quay,

Cindy Sherman, Sarah Moon, Hans Bellmer and Francis Bacon.[84] Specific attributes of these artists are conjured by the way in which Sigismondi's videos portray a painterly treatment of lighting, colour and depth of field, a close visual relationship with musical rhythm and timbre, and a haunting evocation of the spectral character of settings and environments. Populated by performing objects, mythical archetypes and puppetized humans interacting with strangely familiar other-worlds, her work across media embodies a congruence of imagery that is simultaneously familiar and beautiful, yet strange and macabre. Establishing a sense of continuity in the imagery she moves across media, Sigismondi reiterates particular textures, colours and motifs, such as dolls, mannequins, estranged eyeballs, bathtubs, mirrors, beds, blood, lipstick and unusual interpretations of bodily beauty. Her work is distinctive for her haptic use of rich colours, luxurious fabrics and opulent costumes that call up the sensory experience of specific time periods.

Just as Bowie's work is marked by alterity, Sigismondi is drawn to working with people who don't fit into conventionally coded notions of beauty and gender. Sigismondi continuously transcends normative boundaries, just as she explores similar themes such as alienation, death, vitalism, age, time travel, psychosis, beauty and gender ambiguity. While Bowie was an expert in the art of posing as an object to be gazed upon, Sigismondi complemented this 'poseur' with her expertise in the art of photographing the pose. Her experience as a fashion photographer informs her cinematic representations of the posed body as an object of desire *and* abjection. Conceptualizing pose in relation to objectification and agency, Bowie and Sigismondi shared an acute awareness of 'the gaze' within visual culture, and of the archetype within mythology and artistry. Sigismondi recalls how their mutual interest in art became apparent at their first meeting:

> We ended up spending five hours talking about art, so it was so great. I remember he had some ideas that he wanted to do. Since they were coming from him I took them very seriously but didn't know what to do with them. And then I remember getting this amazing message on my answering machine where he just went like, do your own thing or create your own thing. He was giving me permission to be the artist that I was or that he respected. So we met in an artist-to-artist way.[85]

The openness by which Bowie invited Sigismondi to 'create her own thing' shows continuity with his earlier collaborations with Eno and Hirst, which were underpinned by chance composition and relinquishing control to 'the universe'. Bowie and Sigismondi shared a mutual appreciation with the transcendental capacity of art, surrealism and its association with dream states, all of which underpin their openness to aleatory composition and alchemical process. As we shall see, surrealist strategies, hauntological gestures, temporal disjunctures, archetypes and allusions to dream states travel across their music videos in ways that relinquish control to the universe. Revealing the results of such playful alchemy, the following analyses explicate the weave of loose continuity across Bowie and Sigismondi's intersecting oeuvres.

'Little Wonder' (1997)

In the music video for 'Little Wonder', Bowie's occasional direct address to camera winks to the audience as he plays the persona of middle-aged Bowie attempting to make a connection with his younger self. Bowie's prior personas are present via costume and make-up, including a 'Halloween Jack' eye-patch, a 'Ziggy' bodysuit, platform shoes and forehead patch and alien eyes resembling those revealed when Newton plucked out his human eyes with tweezers in *TMWFTE*.

A narrative of time travel is established as the younger and older versions of Bowie communicate by sending anthropomorphic body parts between time zones.[86] While Bowie's personas connect seamlessly across time, their body movement is temporally dislocated. Along with the temporal dissonance created by pixilation, the motion-blurred bodies of the passers-by shape-shift between human forms, transparent shadows and eyeless ghosts. Their slippage between presence and absence engenders them as fluid apparitions. Estranged motion, 'reverberating space',[87] colour and costume suggest shifting temporal zones and a sense of alienation. These cues exemplify Sigismondi's use of painterly texture and time as mediums, complementing Bowie's sonic manipulation of texture and time.

The musical and lyrical composition of 'Little Wonder' is consistent with Bowie's prior use of aleatory strategies: his 'dramaturgical' use of studio production techniques and his use of the Burroughs cut-up technique to compose song lyrics.[88] When writing the lyrics for 'Little Wonder', Bowie found novel ways to include all the names of the Seven Dwarfs.[89] While this playful compositional strategy contributes a melodic liveliness, 'Little Wonder' was not only an exercise in lyric composition but also an experiment with semi-random sonic sampling and rhythmic dissonance.[90] The song's production incorporated a spontaneously playful 'studio *vérité*' sampling process, resulting in a rhythmically complicated composition characterized by abrupt stops and starts, sudden speed ups, slowdowns and unresolved chord arrangements.[91] Utilizing elements of the Jungle drum and bass genre, such as stop-time break-beats, syncopated percussive loops, samples, synthesized effects, fast tempos and snare rolls, Bowie experimented with creating temporal dissonance between the mismatched rhythm of the bass and the drums. The frenetic energy and stop-time of the music is visually complemented by Sigismondi's use of stop-motion pixilation, alternating camera speeds, time-lapse photography, restless camera movement and shifting depth of field. This unsettling combination of audiovisual jitter, syncopated movement and spatial reverberation is accentuated by abruptly shifting sets as well as the composited layering of the imagery. Thus, 'Little Wonder' served as an ideal temporal experiment for two artists obsessed with the medium of time as an essential facet of art.

As with 'Dead Man Walking' (1997), for 'Little Wonder', Bowie and Sigismondi incorporated visual imagery inspired by Francis Bacon's paintings and the puppet animations of the Quay Brothers.[92] The expressionist and surrealist affordances of this imagery are knitted together with artworks created by Tony Oursler. Appearing as absurd caricatures resembling Bacon's distorted painted figures, Oursler's dolls are anthropomorphized creatures and disembodied body parts. One of the most unsettling images in the video depicts an assortment of dolls hanging limply from strings, much like an infant's mobile. Although predominantly static, the dolls are animated by their sentient facial gestures, a life force that is paradoxically extinguished by the image of limp bodies hung by nooses. This macabre suggestion of death is further complicated, since the hanging dolls conjure memories of mobiles dangling above a baby's cot.

Early in the video the younger Bowie plucks an eyeball from a coffee cup. An alien-like mother kisses her baby's head, which falls off and rolls along the floor, the only visible feature being a projected mouth. These eyeball and mouth motifs reappear in the older Bowie's time zone as a large sphere, humanized by a projected eye and mouth. This bizarre combination of bodily fragmentation and anthropomorphized facial gesture accentuates the resemblance between Oursler's animated dolls and Bowie's puppetized movement. The techniques of pixilation and speed-ramping estrange Bowie's body, making it appear jerked and controlled by an off-screen agent. This point is driven home by the final shot. After having wriggled, jerked, danced and flapped his arms like wings, Bowie's body flops limply in time with the song's ending; as a marionette kept alive by an off-screen puppeteer. Having finished playing with her puppet, Sigismondi releases the strings and leaves him to droop lifelessly (Figure 14.3).

The music video for 'Little Wonder' illustrates the key threads of Bowie's loose continuity. Inhabiting an imaginary world characterized by estranged figuration and temporal dissonance, Bowie's puppetized form acts out his conception of himself 'as a medium' – his fragmented identity travelling across time and media. In dialogic collaboration, Bowie, Sigismondi and Oursler have drawn upon surrealist strategies to create a hauntological artefact of reverberating space and disjointed time.

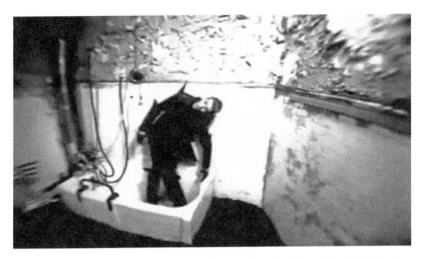

FIGURE 14.3 *Bowie's puppetized body droops lifelessly. 'Little Wonder' (Floria Sigismondi, 1997).*

'The Stars (Are Out Tonight)' (2013)

For 'The Stars', Bowie and Sigismondi engaged in another allegorical play with personas. While intertextual references, performative role-play and cinematic strategies create an uncanny sense of time travel and temporal disjuncture, discomfort is also provoked by the intersection of gender transgression and ontological estrangement. Consistent with the signification of difference woven across Bowie's oeuvre, a powerful sense of alterity is produced by the meta-drag-performance vicariously performed by his co-actors. While Bowie plays a subdued, 'normalized' figure of himself, his prior personae are recast through four androgynous stars. The Thin White Duke is embodied by Iselin Steiro, and Tilda Swinton morphs from a middle-aged housewife into a Bowie-Newton look-alike. Acting out a Jungian 'conjunction of opposites',[93] models Saskia de Brauw and Andreja Pejić play a 'celebrity couple', who shape-shift between sycophantic fans, seductive succubae and younger versions of Bowie and Swinton. Swinton's presence as Bowie's wife generates further layers of performative complexity. While she has developed a cult reputation as Bowie's doppelganger,[94] Swinton casts the shadow of a distinctive repertoire of ambiguously gendered, otherworldly roles, whereby she has developed 'the capacity to move across, to embody the mobility of temporal flux'.[95] Enriching the co-presence of past/present and death/life within and across personae and performers are references to cinema's gendered archetypes, including neurotic kitsch housewife, glamourous starlet and hysterical actress. Plucking their personae from a toy-box, Bowie and Swinton channel these archetypes through imaginative play. Such playful engagement with archetypal figures is also apparent in Sigismondi's work across media. In her horror film vignettes for the *New York Times 'Great Performers'* series (2017), Sigismondi utilized the codified imagery associated with archetypal characters in order to create disturbing horror scenes.[96] According to Jung, imagery depicting archetypal figures may engender profoundly affective responses due to our primordial recognition of archetypes circulating via the collective unconscious.[97] Given the persistent reference to archetypes, dream states and other Jungian ideas across Bowie and Sigismondi's oeuvres, 'The Stars' appears as a complex Jungian psychodrama.

This capacity to stretch the music video form to serve as therapeutic psychodrama is in keeping with Sigismondi's knack for expanding music video's form and function. Possibilities for identity liberation are suggested in this video by the interplay of archetypes and through the performativity of gesture and pose. Through her gestural performance, Steiro channels the androgynous posture and foppish attitude of The Thin White Duke, ironically haunting Bowie with the apparitional presence of his persona. When an intimate moment between Bowie and his wife is interrupted by the band playing next door, he knocks at his neighbour's door to complain. How ironic that Bowie's annoyance at hearing his own song leads to a face-to-face confrontation with his (mediated) younger self. By choreographing a discomforting reunion of younger and older personas, Sigismondi and Bowie allude to the multiplicity and integration of identity. In her analysis of 'The Stars', Stark proposes that the doppelgangers 'dwelling in the house next door, possessing the wife and replacing domestic reality with eccentric orgiastic passions ... was virtually a poetic retelling of Jung's warning on the danger of ignoring the repressed energy of an unconscious shadow'.[98] As an archetypal element of Bowie's unconscious shadow, his Thin White Duke persona haunts him sonically and visually, much like his puppetized form did in 'Love Is Lost'.

Under the surveillance of his apparitional persona, Bowie's psyche is threatened by a crouching succubus attempting to seduce him in his sleep (Figures 14.4a and 14.4b). Remediating mythical artworks of crouching succubi,[99] this scene also enacts Jung's description of the anima: 'She comes upon us just as a nixie might; she sits on top of us like a succubus; she changes into all sorts of shapes like a witch ... she is a mischievous being who crosses our path in numerous transformations and disguises.'[100] Unaffected by this attempt to possess his soul, Bowie watches as his writhing wife becomes seduced by the succubus under the bed. Seemingly under the possession of an off-screen agent or puppeteer, Swinton becomes a gesturing hysteric in a macabre dinner scene played out like a 1920s surrealist film. Waving an electric knife in a frenzy, Swinton carves up a raw chicken carcass and

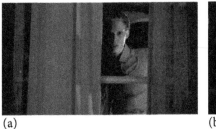 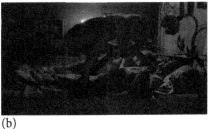

(a)   (b)

FIGURE 14.4 *(a) Iselin Steiro, as the Thin White Duke, watches over Bowie as he sleeps. 'The Stars (Are Out Tonight)' (Floria Sigismondi, 2013). (b) Andreja Pejić as a succubus crouches upon Bowie as he sleeps. 'The Stars (Are Out Tonight)' (Floria Sigismondi, 2013).*

accompanies the celebrity couple as they jerk towards Bowie like reanimated ghosts from his past, moving in to take possession of his soul.

As spectres of Bowie's 'dead' personae, the gestures performed by these puppetized stars are like 'wandering homeless ghosts', reanimated to haunt and taunt him.[101] This kinetic spectrality is enhanced by Sigismondi's skill in exploiting the temporal affordances of audiovisual media. Alternating frame rates, stop-motion techniques and the gestural language of early cinema create the illusion of involuntary, syncopated movement closely associated with early film projection. When we experience cinematic time as 'out of joint' and androgynous actors morphing between human subjects and controlled objects, we're invited to link the notion of gender fluidity to a broader ontological uncertainty. As though offering some semblance of resolution to this psychodrama of uncertainty, Swinton transforms into a Bowie-Newton persona, showering Bowie with lipstick kisses. Since Bowie's appearance (with hooded duffle-style coat) references the 'Bowie-Newton matrix',[102] a Jungian interpretation may suggest that Swinton's lipstick kisses signify 'syzygy', which for Jung meant the 'balanced union' of anima and animus, bringing about integration within the Self.[103]

Extending the perceived forms and functions of music video, 'The Stars' challenges its audience to tap into the collective unconscious and to engage with identity fluidity and the persona complex. This confluence of music video and psychodrama is one way in which Sigismondi permeates the borders between music video, cinema and theatre. These intermedial borders are further traversed by her insistent creation of a film feel. In 'The Stars', the establishing shots are overlaid with a title sequence, followed by 'A FILM BY FLORIA SIGISMONDI'. The sense of watching the opening to a film is further reinforced by the use of spoken dialogue and diegetic sounds. Bookending this 'film feel' with a playful transmedial twist, the final scene leaves the audience with a sense of having watched a film – which turns out to be the same film the actors are watching on television. The four characters have exchanged places with their younger and older selves and are now watching themselves inside the television screen, their faces distorted by television static, and overlaid with the end-title 'FIN'. Remediating the hauntological affordances of cinema, television, gesture and historical images of mythical archetypes, 'The Stars' is interlaced with intertextual references to past and future media. Prefiguring the haunting television static of 'No Plan' and recalling The Thin White Duke, Newton and the significance of television watching in *TMWFTE*, this video palimpsestuously extends upon the loose continuity of Bowie's development across media and time.

The Next Day (2013)

Just as diegetic sound and spoken dialogue establish a 'film feel' in 'The Stars', these devices are again used to create a similar cinematic feel in Sigismondi's video for *The Next Day* (2013). The beginning of the video feels familiarly like the opening scene of a narrative film. The first shot establishes the Italian catholic significance of the setting by signposting the bar's name, 'THE DECAMERON'. Sonically alluding to the ten-day significance of Giovanni Boccaccio's literary work *Decameron* (c. 1350–3),[104] the opening shots are accompanied with the sound of a church bell tolling ten times. Establishing tone, the sanctity associated with the toll of church bells helps set the scene for the desecration that follows. There's a scuffle between a scantily clad door-girl and a beggar, who is knocked out by a priest played by Garry Oldman. Not the type of actor who would typically appear in a music video, Oldman's cinema credentials add to this filmic set-up. As the tracking shot follows Oldman and his veiled companion through doors and down stairs, the amplification of the sound is cleverly adjusted to create the filmic experience of diegetic music emanating from the bar below. The song is muffled until Oldman opens the second set of doors, enabling us to hear and see that the music is being played by a band in the corner of the bar.

Dressed as Christ and performing as a prophet, Bowie plays lead singer of this resident band, thus making a firm connection between religion and celebrity. If this den of iniquity is an allegory for the church of Catholicism, then it is also an allegory for the church of celebrity. Channelling her cultural understanding of the theatre of Catholicism, Sigismondi directs a sacrilegious psychodrama, all under the prophetic watch of Bowie. Reminiscent of the analogical structure of *Un Chien Andalou*, *The Next Day* sets up, and then subverts audience expectations. While the set-up anticipates the conventions of narrative film, continuity editing then establishes the characters within the spatial dimensions of the den. But this familiar flow of shot continuity is interrupted by images of estranged beauty and remediations of the iconography associated with Italian Catholicism (Figure 14.5).

With Bowie performing in a spectacular costume 'on stage', this filmic music video crosses over into theatre, biblical mythology and surrealist allegory. This convergence of platforms, texts and genres is reinforced by a gathering of archetypal figures drawn from the histories of art and literature. A freshly scarred self-flagellator hovers guiltily with whip at the ready, and an armour-cloaked Joan of Arc kisses the ring of the creepy looking cardinal. An albino-esque Swan Bride sits at the bar wearing little more than a wedding veil along with nipple and fingernail adornments. With macabre black eyes and beautiful eyelashes flowing like locks of hair from her lower eyelids down her cheeks, the eyeless *Saint Lucy* holds a plate containing her disembodied eyes, a clear reference to the many paintings of *Saint Lucy* located in the repositories of Catholic art history (Figures 14.5a, 14.5b and 14.5c).[105]

Having arrived with *Saint Lucy* on his arm, Garry Oldman proceeds to perform as a debauched priest, bestowing perverse attention upon Marion Cotillard, who plays a Magdelline-esque figure. No sooner are we invited to gaze upon Cotillard's slow-motion dancing body when she is stricken by a stigmata. Blood spurts violently from her wrists, horrifying the sleazy priests and splattering the pure white veil and alabaster skin of the Swan Bride. What makes these grotesque images even more discomforting is the

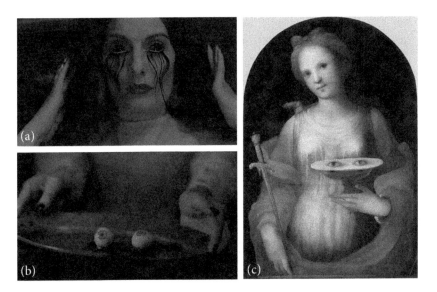

FIGURE 14.5 *(a) Megan Neal Bodul as the eyeless St. Lucy.* The Next Day *(Floria Sigismondi, 2013). (b) Remediating the eyeless St. Lucy.* The Next Day *(Floria Sigismondi, 2013). (c)* Saint Lucy *(1521) [Painting] Artist: Domenico Beccafumi.*

macabre imagery derived from art history that estrange the ubiquitous codes of beauty and glamour. This Sigismondi signature aesthetic crosses over into her fashion photography and commercials. For instance, in the Cinderella-themed commercial for GHD, *At the Stroke of Midnight* (2010),[106] the archetypal characters are uncannily striking for their glamorous yet bizarre hair arrangements and unusual make-up, including overly long false eyelashes. This remediation of imagery derived from art history exemplifies Sigismondi's reiteration of the surrealist strategy of estrangement as a cohesive thread across media, mythology and time.

The Next Day concludes with another reminder of how Sigismondi's distinctive aesthetics flow across commercials and music videos, this time calling up her use of high-angle shafted light in the *ALIEN* perfume commercial for Thierry Mugler (2014).[107] While Sigismondi has a particular ability to craft light in order to achieve a transcendental affect, she also has a special understanding of the steep-angled natural light shafts that create drama in Italian churches such as The Pantheon. Just as it gives life to the statue in the *ALIEN* commercial, this shaft of 'God-light' appears to immortalize Bowie as a prophet. In hindsight, this turns out to be the set-up for an existential joke. Playing with cinematic codes and temporal disjuncture, this surrealist psychodrama culminates with a moment of Monty Python-esque absurdist humour (a trait that can be traced across Bowie's oeuvre). Bowie smirks as he thanks his cast of celebrities, then with the final toll of the church bell and the simplest stop-motion trick, he disappears. As he did with the album cover for *The Next Day*, Bowie forces us to be aware of his presence, through his absence.

My analysis of *The Next Day* video illustrates Bowie and Sigismondi's dialogic engagement with hauntology, archetype and surrealist strategies of estrangement. Both the video and the album cover are treated as mediums through which to de-proselytize celebrity. In light of Marshall McLuhan's conceit 'the medium is the message', Bowie *as medium and message* warns his fans to beware of the illusory nature of celebrity and deification. He may look like a prophet, but he's only a medium.[108]

Serial theatre and transmedia surrealism

This chapter demonstrates how Sigsimondi stretches the formal and functional conventions of music video, how she carries signature traits and generic codes across media and how she and Bowie use time as a medium in a complementary way. When considered in relation to my preliminary discussion of Bowie's unique approach to transmediality, these analyses show how the figure of Bowie *as* a medium develops serially across media. In this light, O'Leary astutely observes how the sequence of music videos for *The Next Day* album unfolds as serial theatre, incrementally revealing a transmedia story of Bowie's position as a performer off-and-on stage:

> It's all a bit of theatre. But the main joke is about Bowie. The sequence of Next Day videos is a storyline. 'Where are we now' is the returned 'Bowie' as a mummified museum exhibit, supervised by the 'real' Bowie who keeps off stage. 'The Stars are Out Tonight' is Bowie playing himself as a senior citizen. And 'The Next Day' is his big, vulgar Cinescope resurrection, with Bowie howling, jumping around, cursing, performing 'live' again. 'The normalisation', as the blogger How Upsetting described it. 'Bowie performs. He hams it up. The curtain is pulled back. The deity figure is snuffed out at the end.'[109]

While each of these videos is a work of theatre in its own right, this notion of Bowie unfolding as serial theatre is not only applicable to the videos for *The Next Day* album but to his entire oeuvre. In addition to off- and onstage theatrical performance, what develops across the videos examined in this chapter is a shifting sense of Bowie's agency in relation to persona and archetype. In 'Love Is Lost' Bowie's shifting agency is represented by the transposition of Pierrot's mask and the apparitional agency of puppetized personas. Controlled by imaginary marionette strings in 'Little Wonder', Bowie's jittery movement emulates Oursler's dolls, along with the temporal dissonance of his own music. In 'The Stars', Bowie's fragmented agency shifts between personas and archetypes. And in the finale of *The Next Day*, Bowie finally exhibits the onstage agency of a 'howling' gesticulating prophet with jazz hands, God-light and a gathering of remediated archetypes. In accordance with this surrealist 'joke', his agency is presciently 'snuffed out' by an off-screen agent.

Situating this serial theatre of music videos within the broader context of Bowie and Sigismondi's oeuvres, their unique approaches to transmedia exemplify the world-building integrity and seriality outlined by current definitions of transmedia storytelling. Seeking alternative defining criteria for transmedia artistry, I argue that Bowie and Sigismondi's work may be usefully examined through the lens of 'transmedia surrealism'. This term describes my approach to examining transmedia through and beyond narrative, so as to focus on the less rational facets of cross-media cohesion, such as temporality, analogy, mythical signifiers, archetype and persona. Consequently, this chapter points to the value of historical concepts such as *Gesamtkunstwerk*, loose continuity and hauntology as tools for tracing those less tangible threads of continuity that may escape a lens focused primarily on narrative cohesion and storytelling.

Another reason for adopting such a conceptual lens is to divert attention away from the currently popular 'franchise' rationale for building transmedia storyworlds as commercial commodities, instead elucidating artist's creative motivations to 'cross over'. As vehicles for their media crossings, Sigismondi and Bowie drew upon the surrealist strategies of estrangement and analogical composition to transgress the limitations of normative identity, narrative coherence and celebrity culture. These strategies link to a broader alchemical process that Bowie alluded to when he said 'I like putting together interesting ideas and seeing how they, stir them up and see how they come out.'[110] Bowie's tendency for putting ideas together randomly and stirring them up alludes to the productive capacity of dialogism and the psychic transcendence of alchemy apparent in his collaborations with Sigismondi.[111] As Bowie's collaborator Derek Boshier observes, 'We know [David's] a chameleon, but he's also an alchemist, one who can conjure magic – whether it be words, music, postures, or spaces – from thin air.'[112] Though seemingly produced from thin air, Bowie's magic was conjured through dialogic collaboration with other artists. A very magical alchemy occurred when Bowie stirred the cauldron with Floria.

CHAPTER 15

Filmic resonance and dispersed authorship in Sigur Rós's transmedial *Valtari Mystery Film Experiment*

Gareth Schott and Karen Barbour

The alternative guitar genre of post-rock is often appraised as a sonic mode of cartography, for it fashions a sense of space via its vast extended song structures and the tone, and colour and intensity of its sonic layering, producing soundscapes that veer between the sparse and delicate and the dense and powerful. The music of Icelandic post-rock band Sigur Rós (1994–present) is often interpreted as an auditory reflection of the vast natural beauty of their homeland. This commonly applied interpretation of their music is used to distinguish them from the geographic imagination stimulated by other renowned post-rock groups like Godspeed You! Black Emperor (GY!BE) whose work is more overtly aligned with urban politics. However, in his discussion of Sigur Rós's music as an elegy for place, Lawson Fletcher has sought to broaden the customary categorization of their music as simply a romanticized representation of the Icelandic landscape.[1] In the band's 2007 tour documentary film *Heima*, a tour film with a difference, the group is documented performing in different locations and spaces in their homeland, ranging from abandoned and disused industrial spaces to areas of natural beauty that are scheduled to be erased by flooding for new hydro dams. Fletcher argues that the film displays deliberate critique, melancholy and nostalgia for lost actions, habitation and industrial practices. This chapter seeks to reinforce and extend Fletcher's observation through an analysis of the subject matter produced under the *Valtari Mystery Film Experiment* (2012),[2] a project instigated by Sigur Rós in which they invited a select group of visual artists to respond freely to the delicate, tranquil, poignant, epic and dramatic compositions that comprised the band's sixth studio album *Valtari* (also 2012).[3] In this chapter, it is argued that the resulting films extend the ethos of post-rock as a democratic, cooperative mode of music production and performance into film, successfully distributing authorship to create a transmedia extension of the resonance of their music into film.

While this chapter adds to a growing scholarly interest in Sigur Rós as a group that continues to evolve post-rock, a genre of guitar music that challenges the conventional structures of rock music and rock music instrumentation, in new and innovative ways, our discussion of the *Valtari Mystery Film Experiment* is symptomatic of the broader way that the band operates at the forefront of musical and artistic innovation and collaboration in their desire to expand the nature of audience engagement with their music. It is possible to cite an assortment of projects in which the band has variously trialled social media and new technologies in order to extend the application of, and encounters with their music both in its absolute form (completed works such as mastered songs that typically comprise an album) and as formless and unstructured sounds, pieces or parts via adaptive and interactive musical systems. Starting with the former, prior to the official release of *Valtari* the album was first streamed in a global listening event titled the Valtari Hour in which the communal nature of first experiencing the album was further enriched by inviting fans to post their response to the album on Instagram using #valtarihour. Turning to new formats, uses and applications of their music, in 2016 Sigur Rós embarked a twenty-four-hour journey around their home country's ring road, Route 1 (1,332 kilometres). Not only did the band live stream the entire journey on YouTube, but they also used generative software to create a soundtrack for the journey, fashioned from the stems (individual tracks) from their song 'Óveður' (2016). More recently, details of the band's sustained collaboration with tech company Magic Leap have emerged, teasing fans with a mixed (augmented and virtual) reality app titled Tónandi (or sound spirit) that once more represents Sigur Rós's continual endeavours to modify the structures and nature of music and widen listening experiences. When released, Tónandi promises to give users the ability to physically interact with sounds that comprise Sigur Rós's music to participate in both its construction and deconstruction. Finally, continuing their reevaluation of the music recording process beyond the linear process of releasing infrangible finished creations, the band have also created a new and ongoing body of work titled *Liminal* (2018). As their website explains:

> liminal sees sigur rós as an eco-system. it identifies the connections and blurs the boundaries between work done and work to come; between new music and ideas barely yet born; between songs written 20 years ago and collaborations to be made tomorrow. in bringing together these collaborations and commissions – for choreographers, visual artists and new technologies – with solo work and remixes, film score and generative music, as well as friends in the wider sigur rós 'family', liminal aims to take the listener to a place neither here nor there, a 'liminal' space. liminal will live as an 'endless' mixtape, always growing but never done. [*lowercase as it appears on the* website https://liminal.la/][4]

Drawing on the reference to 'friends in the wider sigur rós "family"' in the above description, this chapter focuses exclusively on the *Valtari Mystery Film Experiment*, a project that initiated a transmedial visual rendering of the inherent metaphorical and formal qualities of Sigur Rós's music in a filmic space. In doing so, the project performs what Henry Jenkins has described as a mode of media consolidation and horizontal integration associated with now mainstream modes of transmedia production.[5] In the context of the *Valtari Mystery Film Experiment*, a broad range of visual (and performance) artists known to and admired by Sigur Rós, many of whom also had a prior role in constructing the visual aesthetic associated with the band and their body of work (e.g. album covers, website and stage design), were invited to translate their practice and extend the narratives embedded in and conveyed by the band's music. The term 'filmic resonance' used in the title of this chapter refers to the dispersal of the themes contained within the music in film form, rather than the use of music video to simply expand the delivery of music via screen-based media. Thus, the *Valtari Mystery Film Experiment* is presented as a transmedia project creating 'music > videos' or 'soundtrack instigated films' that have an intended connection, association and progression from song to film, distinct from other applications of music video, for example, as cadenced expression of music (e.g. the relationship created between Michel Gondry's 'bullet camera' technique and the rhythm of the White Stripes' 'Hardest Button to Button' (2003) in his music video).

This chapter seeks to demonstrate how the *Valtari Mystery Film Experiment* reflects transmedia storytelling as defined by Jenkins as a 'story that unfolds across multiple media platforms, with each new text making a distinctive and valuable contribution to the whole'.[6] In announcing the film project online, Sigur Rós declared: 'We never meant our music to come with a pre-programmed emotional response. We don't want to tell anyone how to feel and what to take from it. With the films, we have literally no idea what the directors are going to come back with. None of them know what the others are doing, so hopefully it could be interesting.'[7] The project engaged visual and performance artists 'known' to the band but allowed each 'director' to respond to whatever track or tracks they wished from the album *Valtari* in a manner that drew on their own artistic methods. By virtue of working from the music or their listening experience of the album, what emerged was a great deal of correspondence and 'additive comprehension' (Jenkins crediting Young)[8] of *Valtari*'s subtext among the resulting films, irrespective of their distinct visual execution and style. Crucially, reflection on a project of this nature serves to shift scholarly emphasis on transmedia storytelling and production away from conservative notions and constructions of 'single' authorship. Indeed, O'Meara and Bevan make a similar argument in their assertion that 'transmedia theory works to construct patriarchal ideals of individual authorship to the detriment of alternative conceptions of transmediality'.[9] The *Valtari Mystery Film Experiment* exemplifies how the dispersal of theme and narrative can operate through the transferal of authorship and praxis and yet still produce a coordinated and connected media experience that enhances and reveals the complex themes of the worlds present in Sigur Rós's aesthetic.

From the sixteen films that were eventually released as a DVD collection in 2013 representing the *Valtari Mystery Film Experiment*, this chapter will provide close readings of four films and the artists who opted to construct a filmic response to the same song – 'Varúð'. These are film #2 by Ingibjörk Birgisdóttir, film #6 by Ryan McGinley, film #14 by Christian Larson and film #15 by Björn Flóki. While each of the films lengthened the reach, and articulate the sentiment of 'Varúð' in a distinctive manner, examined together the responses reveal a concern with apparitional traces or vestiges of human presence in selected locales and spaces. That is, the works address what Anna Tsing et al. describe as the 'overlaid arrangements of human and non-human living spaces, which we call "landscapes"'.[10] These are layers in which past and present collide, as industrial and urban ecologies either discarded or still thriving continue to shape human action, connection and potential. We argue that the themes evident in films #2, #6, #14 and #15 were activated by the ethereal presence of unfamiliar, forgotten, discarded sounds from the past that commingle with Sigur Rós's compositions within their atmospheric textural layering. Thus, the *subject* of transmedia storytelling evident in the filmic treatments of 'Varúð' is derived from a *process* of layering, mirroring the musical style and construction methods employed by Sigur Rós. Together both music and film reflect a concern with our current geological age, the anthropocene – an acknowledgment of the way human activity has had an irreversible impact on the climate and the environment.[11] We argue that the 'Varúð' films function to populate the spaces embodied within Sigur Rós's music, giving particular attention to placing individuals in openings that display the scars of a post-industrial landscape.[12] In this way, the films constitute a form of filmic resonance, in which a decoding of the themes encoded in sonic form is evident, signifying an 'auditory drift' from one medium into a new hybrid form.

Transmedia architecture

The process of Sigur Rós handing over creative freedom and responsibility to a group of visual artists meant that the *Valtari Mystery Film Experiment* gives the impression of a non-commercial approach to the production of, what otherwise serve as, promotional videos for marketing music. The resultant films were not necessarily (or intended to be) oppositional to the music video format. Many of the creatives invited to contribute to the project work evenly across both commercial (advertising and promotion) and art sectors. Furthermore, a number of the responses to the *Valtari Mystery Film Experiment* opted to partner the music with its most established affect – movement and dance. Some of the most memorable and acclaimed music promotional videos in the genre's short history have effectively used body movement to access and translate the emotional resonance of a composition, noise, melody or refrain. Notable recent examples include looping and repetition of movement in The xx's 'Islands', the fragmented and sinuously fluid movement of Wayne McGregor's choreography (e.g. for Radiohead's 'Lotus Flower' (2011)) or *Valtari Mystery Film Experiment* contributor ('Fjögur Píanó') Ryan Heffington's award-winning choreography of Sia's 'Chandelier', a tour de force in virtuosic gestures and movement.

According to Jenkins, the development of transmedia storytelling practices has produced 'gifted transmedia artists' that are able to surf effortlessly across media conglomerates.[13] Indeed, shifting the emphasis from adaptable industry structures to creative proficiency, the majority of the creatives solicited to respond to *Valtari* were required to shift into film directing as they were more commonly associated with a different range of practices and art forms, including graphic novels (Dash Shaw), video installation and performance art (Ragnar Kjartansson), mixed-media art (Inga Birgisdóttir), photography (Ryan McGinley) and documentary film-making (Alma Har'el, Henry Jun Wah Lee). As a result, some of the films inevitably permitted art practices such as installation, performance and sculpture to effectively cross over into the music video genre. In Film #1 'Ég Anda', for example, performance artist Ragnar Kjartansson opted to employ a public service announcement format. The film details how to save various people (man, pregnant lady and baby) from choking, complete with graphic enactments captioned with placards held up by a straight-faced narrator. Kjartansson describes 'Ég Anda' as the 'first useful pop video in history. File under: educational'.[14] In adopting the role of film-makers, contributing visual artists provided an alternative platform, use and outlet for the source material, redolent of its multilayered nature. At the same time, as an enhancement of viewer experience, transmediality also serves to open up audience experience from familiar and known media experiences to alternative media platforms.[15] In this instance Sigur Rós also created entry points to a range of artists and their work through the *Valtari Mystery Film Experiment.* In a curatorial fashion Sigur Rós applied a great tradition in music, in which a music artist's influences are invariably transferred onto their fan base via lyrical references (e.g. from Morrissey to Oscar Wilde and other literary references), artwork (e.g. Stone Roses use of Jackson Pollock's action painting), political viewpoints (e.g. U2 placing links to Amnesty International on album sleeves) and fashion (e.g. punk's direct route to the fashion of Vivienne Westwood).

'Varúð'

In order to outline how the song 'Varúð' functions as a transmedia object, forming the nucleus for different filmic expressions, it is first necessary to introduce the instrumentation, arrangement and sentiment of the song. As the third track on the album *Valtari,* the song 'Varúð' commences with the comforting familiarity of an echo-laden upright piano that delivers sparse piano chords that possess the quality of an aged recording unearthed from yester-year. The dissonant lightly distressed sound is equally suggestive of a forgotten out-of-tune piano, rarely played or used. While sonically the piano chords provide a stable platform upon which the song slowly builds over its six and a half minutes playing time, the confident attributes of the chords are counterbalanced by the sound quality which conjures the uncertainty of a player nonchalantly sitting at the instrument maybe for the first time in a while – slowly feeling their way back into the instrument. The simplicity is deceptive, a pensive foundation for a layering process that eventually pinnacles in an upsurge and swelling of emotion.

Accompanying the piano in the song's opening moments are atmospheric notes that resemble the trailing off of sounds that have been carried across a wide expanse. Haunting wisps reach the listener, seemingly just in time, before they fade or are overlaid by the arrival of further distant echoes or reverberated tones. Together, the distorted undulations from Birgisson's bowed guitar and the tail end of reverberated violin notes encircle the piano chords in anticipation of the song's eventual melody and ascent. Post-rock typically provides an embodied experience of music that 'moves' listeners affectively through a musical landscape comprising of otherworldly resonance and dislocated sounds that construct a new relationship between sound and space (both real and implied). In particular, the application of reverb as 'sonic space-making device'[16] produces an aural depth that is capable of transporting listeners to imagined spaces and vistas.

As the first minute of the song elapses Birgisson's voice enters the song. Contributing to the mosaic nature of the song's construction, Birgisson's Icelandic lyrics create an abstract picture of a wilderness beset by a wintriness that necessitates a gathering around bonfires for light, warmth, hope and connection. Indeed, the song's title translates to 'caution' or 'warning'. For most listeners Birgisson's words aren't discernable, but contribute to the mood of the overall piece. The quality of Birgisson's falsetto voice is often described as ethereal and mournful, occupying attention not for its message but its spirit, both tangible and elusive in equal measure, giving focus to the band's often minimal and largo compositions that are often constructed piece by piece for the listener as an accretion of tone colours. In discussing Birgisson's voice, Edward Miller explains that his falsetto voice serves to extend the 'male's voice, moving beyond restraints, harking back to a boy's voice, and reaching forward to a woman's range, without ever sounding female',[17] thus contributing to the curiosity it produces and its inimitability. In 'Varúð', Birgisson's eventual vocal chorus refrain of the word 'varúð' is backed with a choir adding power and a spiritual overtone to the song, while also serving as a literal coming together with other voices. Indeed, the choir serves to connect the music to past rites, traditions and communal acts that the song appears to be longing for. The quasi-religious chorus of 'Varúð' represents one of *Valtari's* rare melodies. A burgeoning drum pulse eventually enters the track around the four-minute mark, cueing a gradual increase in pace and the song's encasement in a cloud of distortion that carries it to its eventual apotheosis. The song's epic finale completes the transformation of the mournful intoning of its opening into a celebratory convergence of various players responsible for the song's rise, momentum and drive, while also presenting a figurative sense of a collective assembling in response to an individual plea.

In keeping with the sentiments conveyed within 'Varúð', the following sections outline how visual artists Ingibjörk Birgisdóttir, Ryan McGinley, Christian Larson and Björn Flóki variously commute the transmedial affordances of Sigur Rós's music, and the way they invite listeners into a world betwixt and between in which transgenerational encounters occur between the past, the present and the future. These encounters cued creative artists to create augmented realities in which various injunctions are placed on the intrusion of human activity on the world, pausing to reveal its impact and allowing other possibilities of existence to reveal themselves. The spectrality inherent in all the works serve to 'reveal something hidden or forgotten, to right a wrong or to deliver a message that might otherwise have gone unheeded'.[18] The following sections also chronicle the visual artists whose creative praxis corresponds with the post-rock methods and philosophy employed and practised by Sigur Rós.

Film #2 by Ingibjörk Birgisdóttir

'Varúð', the first film to feature in the *Valtari Mystery Film Experiment*, constituted a family affair produced by lead singer Jonsi Birgisson's younger sister, who is a prominent visual artist. Film #2 possesses a Roy Anderson-esque feel due its use of a static (virtual) camera in front of a painterly landscape, unmoved for the duration of the song (Figure 15.1). In the mid-ground of the image, cliff faces undulate from the left to the right side of the frame. A connected land mass is arranged in a valley formation – a steep, craggy rock formation rises and falls on the left across to a sheer cliff face on the right side of the frame. The foreground is comprised of a rocky waterbed in which the viewer assumes a position at the bottom of the cliffs. Between the spectacular ascent of the cliff faces we see in the distance broad outlines of mountains. The landscape image of Film #2 is revealed slowly only once a thick snowstorm clears. The illusion of a static pictorial scene rendered in paint is then presented to the audience, only broken as the eye moves across the canvas/screen to reveal pockets of movement, such as light catching on flowing water. Like Film #6 (discussed below) Birgisdóttir opts to play with time and space keeping some aspects of the image frozen in its painterly form, while others shimmer and change. A sense of depth is first expressed traditionally via the materiality of the image, its appearance creating the impression that it has been constructed and built up from its imprimitura layer. The atmospheric vista captures elements that one would otherwise

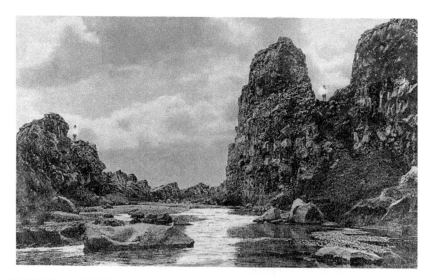

FIGURE 15.1 *Still from Film #2 by Ingibjörk Birgisdóttir,* Valtari Mystery Film Experiment (2012).

expect to see moving, such as the cumulus clouds in the background. Yet, in this moment they are frozen in time. Film #2's technique has since been re-produced in other acclaimed animated painting projects such as Rino Stefano Tagliafierro's 2013 short film *Beauty* in which he animated masterpieces of Western art by William Adolphe Bouguereau, John William Godward, Michelangelo and Rembrandt among others, to imbue familiar suspended scenes with gentle movement in order to bring the subjects of paintings to life.

The landscape image of Film #2 also provides an aesthetic connection to the album cover art for *Valtari* – the result of a collaboration between sisters Ingibjörk and Lilja Birgisdóttir. The album cover depicts a colourized photographic image of a fishing vessel floating over a grass-green ocean. In this image, shot off the coast of Grótta, a small island connected to Reykjavík by a narrow isthmus, no landmarks are depicted. In discussing the cover, Lilja Birgisdóttir has stated: 'We wanted it to be timeless and not connected to a specific location – just everywhere, everywhere and nowhere.'[19] Film #2 offers a continuation of that narrative by bringing it inland. 'Varúð', as stated above, suggests caution or warning, and so connecting the cover art to Film #2 are visual emanates for signals of danger or vulnerability. As Lilja comments, 'Ship horns are a method for ships to communicate on sea, it's a language, and they all have a meaning',[20] while on shore, the narrative of Film #2 unfolds gradually in unison with the pace of the song with the measured introduction of silhouetted figures atop the cliffs on both sides of the valley 'making warning signs with a flashlight' (I. Birgisdóttir).[21] Both imaginings depict human presence in nature in ways that communicate susceptibility outside the perceived safety of the infrastructures of city ecosystems. With the appearance of humans comes a sense of danger as we 'have no idea who they are or what they are warning us about'.[22] Film #2 draws on the emotional and psychological spirit of the music in a manner that preserves its mysterious and equivocal nature. Sighting or detecting human presence in the vastness of nature is both comforting and daunting. We are left uncertain as to whether human presence reflects hope or warning in this instance.

The landscape employed as a setting for the human story of Film #2 is itself a remediated postcard that depicts the Öxará River in Iceland's Þingvellir National Park. Connecting this output with Sigur Rós's methodology and the artists broader body of work, the Icelandic Art Centre describes Birgisdóttir's art as 'a game of layers ... as everywhere in her imagery one will find a mixture of old national emblems, waterfalls, mountains, and animals. Nowhere does Ingibjörg leave an empty space, evoking a Baroque-era fear of emptiness.'[23] As an artefact, the humble postcard offers historical representation of landscapes that pre-date the use of sequential aerial photographs or satellite images as a means of monitoring landscape changes.[24] Yet, postcards also represent idealized images of places and seek to present them at their most picturesque. As Carol Sawyer and David Butler state, 'This would often involve removing, adding, or otherwise changing features on a landscape and colourisation of images.'[25] To a large degree, Birgisdóttir employs the postcard as it was initially presented, combining 'the realism of colour photograph with the imaginative license' of paint.[26] Lilja Birgisdóttir employed a similar method for the album cover. As she explained: 'Instead of trying to copy reality, I'm using the colours as a layer on top of the image to bring something surreal to it.'[27] In doing so, this approach exploits the postcard in the way it comprises an alternate world not always congruent with reality.[28] As Nicolas Whybrow states, the postcard 'is an anachronism, a "ruinous artefact" clung to by visitors as an essential feature of a romantic ideal. But it also serves crucially as the comparative barometer for the tourist of a mediated beauty.'[29]

By employing the human figures issuing warnings on the cliff tops of an otherwise idealized image of a natural landscape, Birgisdóttir presents past idealism while effectively stressing impending threats. As Brian Massumi maintains, the very nature of threats is that they come from the future – 'It is what might come next.'[30] Adding to the poignancy of Film #2 is how slow the audience might be to respond to the presence of the figures on the ridge of the cliff as it occurs in an open frame where gaze is not directed. Uncertainty as to the nature of the forewarning, and our possible delay in registering it, works as a metaphor for consciousness of climate change and our eventual ability to be able to adapt to changes in temperature, water cycles and other environmental conditions that will affect life on Earth. Indeed, Robert Kirkman has argued, 'The effects of climate change are dispersed in time,'[31] thus rendering it a future threat that for many is theoretical, as it sits outside the immediate orbit of our current living conditions.

Film #6 by Ryan McGinley

Ryan McGinley is an American photographer whose work rose to prominence for his representation of the street culture of his adolescence in which he documented skateboarders, club kids, graffiti artists, queer-identified youths in New Jersey and downtown Manhattan at the turn of the last century. What began as candid images of his and his friends' lifestyles are (like the postcard example above) now considered iconic documents of a particular generation. The Guggenheim Museum have characterized the subject matter of McGinley's early photographs as candidly representing 'androgynous, often-nude youths raving, hanging precariously from rooftops, shoplifting, running, falling, cavorting, and living with hedonistic abandon, exuberance, and rebellion'.[32] At the age of twenty-five, McGinley holds the honour of being the youngest photographer to hold a solo show entitled *The Kids*

Are Alright at the Whitney Museum in New York City. For the cover artwork for their 2008 album *Með suð í eyrum við spilum endalaust,* Sigur Rós used McGinley's image of wonderlust hipsters running naked across a highway taken from his 2007 exhibition *I Know Where the Summer Goes.* For this particular body of work, McGinley orchestrated a specific itinerary that took his models through a range of American landscapes. As the Team Gallery in New York states, 'The resultant pictures of nude young men and women playing and living in the great outdoors are innocent yet erotic, casual yet calculated.'[33] The same exhibition also inspired the music video for the album's lead single 'Gobbledigook', directed by long-term collaborators Stefán Árni Þorgeirsson and Sigurður Kjartansson, known as Árni and Kinski ('Viðrar vel til loftárása', 'Glósóli' and Film #4 'Rembihnútur' in the *Valtari Mystery Film Experiment*).

Like Ingibjörg Birgisdóttir's art (discussed above), the very nature of McGinley's images and his creative process play with notions of spontaneity and control in order to highlight the ambivalence of reality.[34] Aligned with the modest and unassuming ethos of post-rock, Rory Satran describes McGinley's subject matter as capturing youth 'without the outfits, the posturing, the comedown'.[35] The subjects of his photographs exhibit a sense of ease and comfort around their observer. McGinley attributes his capacity to be able to capture 'happenings' to the locations he selects for his shoots: 'As they go to a place that is freeing and I access something in them that's a bit childlike.'[36] Tying his work to the illusionary dreamlike nature of Sigur Rós's music, the essence of McGinley's photography also rests in the sentiment that what he captures is genuine but not real life. As he states: 'You want to be in that world all the time. But it's not a place that you can live in.'[37]

The film that McGinley created to accompany the song 'Varúð' possesses comparable themes to those found in his photographic work. It features a young girl skipping barefoot through the median of traffic-congested avenues and the organized charge along the sidewalks of New York (Figure 15.2). Both her uninhibitedness and attire appear at odds with her surroundings, for she playfully skips through a metropolis clothed only in a casual oversized T-shirt and a gold lamé wig, as if she were playfully kicking about in the privacy of her own backyard. She appears as an apparition as the traffic continues to flow and the surrounding city-goers appear resolute in their purpose. She skips a straight line through the conurbation as if its myriad of dangers and hazards are non-existent. The film constitutes a dreamlike collision between youthful exuberance and the bustling abrasive city streets. McGinley's fondness for using effects in his photographic practice in order to craft a magical mood is delicately evident in the film, as the cheap gold wig emanates traces of little golden specks that continue to float once the skipping girl has passed by.

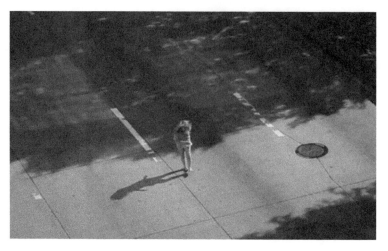

FIGURE 15.2 *Still from Film #6 by Ryan McGinley,* Valtari Mystery Film Experiment (2012).

For much of the film the viewer floats above the scene, assuming a bird's eye view of the girl and the city. The floating sensations evoked by the music and perspective are contrasted by what we see, as we look down on the different forms of detritus either discarded or spilling out of the compact commercial and residential spaces of America's densest city. We observe the city-strata of the anthropocene, what Jan Zalasiewicz et al. describe as a 'complex assemblage of novel, human-made minerals and rocks such as steel, glass, plastics, concrete, brick, and ceramics'.[38] In this act of de-familiarization the eye is drawn to aspects of the city that are hidden from street-level, such as the bright red chair cushions strewn over a building overhang (0:46), unknown to those walking on the sidewalk below. In describing his intent for the film McGinley wrote: 'This piece is my poem to New York city. I wanted to bring a childhood innocence to the streets, through a character whose own light and wonder effects [*sic*] the world around her. I'm always interested in an atmosphere where dreams and reality mingle on equal term.'[39] To this effect, McGinley's film employs a similar strategy to Birgisdóttir's film as the cityscape is altered and petrified. The skipping girl's effortless passage through the compact city and its moving objects is aided by freeze-framing the otherwise unstoppable activity and commotion of the city around her. The film depicts a subjective perception of time, which suggests that the delectation of the skipping girl's playful abandon causes the linear march of time to collapse. Indeed, in this respect Film #6 encapsulates how music and play embody a separate temporal experience capable of distorting or negating clock time. In these nested temporal worlds we are prone to lose ourselves, or at least to lose all semblance of objective time.[40] The constant rhythm of the skipping girl creates its own time signature distinct from the tempo of the music and the city. The girl eventually fades into a wash of light and the fleetingly frozen pedestrians once again find their rhythm.

While Films #2 and #6 portray spaces wherein humans are not quite able to come together, either due to the contours of an unforgiving landscape or from suffering the effects of urban disconnectivity, films #14 and #15 look beyond the intended relationship between space, architecture and social design to present human connectivity that defies architectural design and purpose (#14), and a recognition of the temporal nature of human occupation and command over nature (#15).

Film #14 by Christian Larson

In Film #14, Swedish director Christian Larson's fascination with movement of bodies, objects and places as seen in his commercials for brands Absolut, Mercedes Benz and Roche Bobois, his 2010 documentary *Take One* about Swedish House Mafia and various music videos is extended into a riveting filmic response to Sigur Rós's music. Collaborating with Antwerp-born choreographer Sidi Larbi Cherkaoui (known for award-winning work with Les Ballets C. de la B., the Royal Ballet of Flanders and his own company Eastman), Film #14 utilizes sections of tracks from 'Ekki Múkk', 'Valtari' and 'Rembihnútur' before settling on 'Varúð'. The shared fascination of Larson and Cherkaoui with movement produces a dance film exploring the intensity of human relationships[41] in the current era, in which the affective qualities of the music are heightened through the dancers' embodiment.

Two characters (Australian dancers Nicola Leahey and James O'Hara) are introduced independently, one walking across a field towards large seemingly uninhabited buildings. The other is engrossed in an aching and contorting solo, like Film #6 bare feet and skin rasp over cold, gritty concrete this time within the harsh environs of a derelict building. The spacious aural landscape of the music heightens the sense of individual isolation of the two characters. Hands sliding over flaking wall paint (repeated in Film #15 discussed below), the woman ventures into the building creating a sense of anticipation that the two will meet. The degraded open interior of the building, concrete structures, steel girders, peeling paint and leaking pipes, looms large, becoming a third character as this narrative of nostalgia and transcendence in the anthropocentric age unfolds. The performer-site relationship locates this work clearly in the genre of site dance film.[42]

Across the emptiness of the degraded interior of the building, the woman encounters and observes the man. Responding herself to the arching, kneeling man, the woman arches backwards in an effort to mirror him. The dancers' twisting endeavours are kinetically absorbing, turning and suspending. Choreographer Cherkaoui suggests that one person may provide a mirror for the other,[43] literally represented in the reflected movement and longing of the dancer's gaze, and further reinforced with the gaze of the camera. Rolling, sliding, arching, twisting and spiralling, the sinewy and flowing physicality of both dancers' bodies dramatically contrasts with the cold, dirty building (Figure 15.3). The curious complexity of the dancers' contortions potentially serves to free the viewer's imagination, in parallel to the manner in which the lengthy Sigur Rós's composition 'Varúð' frees the listener's imagination and breaks away from the conventions of the rock music genre, tools and performativity. Site dance film too, frees viewers from the conventional structures, tools and performativity of the theatre, and questions where dance occurs, redefining and recontextualizing it.[44]

Close-up details of feet, hands, legs and torsos moving through the site stimulate the viewer's kinesthetic response, the cold surface of the concrete seeming to abrasively affect the viewer. Described as a 'de-territorialization' of the body in dance film, such close-up shots of the body allow feet, hands or torsos to convey dramatic emphasis as much as the face often does, 'so that any part of the corporeal whole can operate as a site for dance and, thus, meaning production and expression'.[45] These close-ups heighten the distance between the dancers, and contrast with the use of long shots, zooms and occasional slow-motion shots. The choreography and the editing function together to simultaneously locate the viewer in the narrative and also to create a sense of embodied disorientation. Melanie Kloetzel argues that the use of long shots in dance film reminds the viewer of the fragility of the dancer's body in the site and also 'attempt[s] to highlight the environment as a key contributor to the work'.[46]

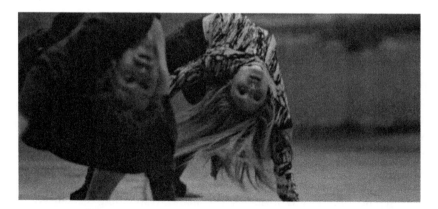

FIGURE 15.3 *Still from Film #14 by Christian Larson,* Valtari Mystery Film Experiment (2012).

As the two dancers appear closer and closer in subsequent shots, some shots linger on the woman watching while others 'jump' into detail of the derelict structures, and the choreographic narrative moves towards realizing the dancers' longing for connection. The choreographic form of the duet allows for all the possibilities of tension and drama in relationship, as well as for desire, romance and union. In this anticipated duet, the dancers face each other. As Cherkaoui states, they then 'copy each other's movements and flow into one another'.[47] An excess of contorting movement evolves into unison choreography as the dancers synchronize, repetitions and dynamic developments grow with the musical ascension. With the upswelling of the music, the duet morphs into more and more intimate and emotionally expressive movement. Moving in, through and over each other's bodies in contact partnering, the duet becomes increasingly sensuous, spiralling and arching bodies rising with the music evoking emotional and physical intensity as they claim each other's bodies, skin to skin. Entwined as lovers, layers of clothing are removed and the tumbling choreography builds to a climax, resolving as the dancers repeatedly replace each other in mid-shot while the camera whirls around their stationary, half-naked bodies. In this dynamic intensity the viewer is offered a release, a revelation of the beauty of human intimacy even in the crumbling desolation of human structures.

Thus, despite destructive human actions in the anthropocentric era, there remains a sense of hope conveyed in the fragile beauty and harmony of the organic human intimacy expressed in this site dance film. In the longing to see the other, in the desire for relationship with another human and with environment, the potential for transience remains. As a consequence, the sense of foreboding in the opening shots of Film #14 and the warning conveyed in 'Varúð' transforms in this work as an expression of hope for the transformative affect of deeply felt relationships between people and place.

Film #15 by Björn Flóki

Digital designer and producer Björn Flóki is the director of Film #15, having previously been responsible for Sigur Rós's online web-presence. In his film the anthropocene again constitutes a playground, this time for a climate resilient and nostalgic protagonist. Flóki's film is the most direct reflection of the current epoch, which acknowledges how human domination of the Earth's surface geology, via the production of long-lasting human-made materials, has left the surface of the planet noticeably altered. In this way, Flóki's response to 'Varúð' connects with the 2009 short film *Plastic Bag* by American independent director and scriptwriter Ramin Bahrani, who also contributed to the *Valtari Mystery Film Experiment* with Film #5. Bahrani's short film, which featured a soundtrack by Sigur Rós's multi-instrumentalist

Kjartan Sveinsson, tells the story of the epic journey of a single plastic bag. Plastics are destined to have long-lasting impact on the planet's geology as they are inert and problematic to degrade. As a result, plastics endure past their use to travel afar as they get caught up in the 'great oceanic garbage patches' or sink to the sea floor where they become a part of the strata. As Matt Edgeworth states, plastics should be considered archaeological and geological materials despite being so new.[48] Flóki too draws on the planet's transfiguration and its associated destruction by placing his film in the midst of the fragments and debris of human production.

Flóki's 'Varúð' appears to chronicle one individual's efforts to escape solastalgia,[49] a portmanteau of the words 'solace' and 'nostalgia' that describes environment-induced stress from witnessing the transformation and deterioration of a landscape within a single lifetime. While the pain of solastalgia arises from staying put and enduring environmental transfiguration, the protagonist in Film #15 seeks to mitigate its impact by cognitively and emotionally escaping the reality in which she lives. She does this by fashioning what can best be described as a mock-augmented reality helmet from the discarded debris in and around an abandoned building (Figure 15.4). In donning the helmet, she is transported to an imaginary lush green space in nature, bathed in light. The imaginative exercise then becomes a mixed-media experience of bio-mimicry as the touch of peeling paint acts as a substitute for tree bark and building beams are used to mimic the sensation of swinging from tree branches. Following the ascension of the music, our fantasist works her way up to the upper floors of her abandoned and dilapidated playground so that she looks out over the natural surrounds from a cliff top, of what could conceivably be the Holocene. The film

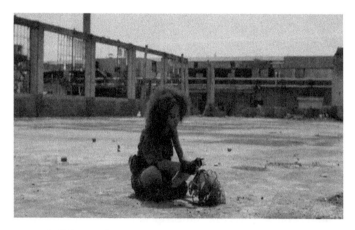

FIGURE 15.4 *Still from Film #15 by Björn Flóki,* Valtari Mystery Film Experiment (2012).

culminates in her eventual discarding of her protective footwear and her helmet to submerge herself in her imaginings of a lost world, leaving behind our irreversible transformation of the landscape. While escapism is the protagonist's deliverance from the ubiquity of modern waste, it also possesses a somewhat negative connotation as it suggests an inability to face facts[50] and, in this case, address the current trajectory and permanence of change to our ecosystem.

Conclusion

The *Valtari Mystery Film Experiment* provided an opportunity for visual artists to enter the dreamlike ethereal nature of Sigur Rós's compositions to forage and grasp impressions and images. The Icelandic post-rock group apply rock instrumentation in the production of incidental, sprawling compositions that dismantle the conventional rock song structure, delighting instead in repetition, measured swells and upsurges, alongside experimentation in timbre, dynamics and texture. In a similar manner, the filmic responses to 'Varúð' breakdown and meditate on the stratigraphic elements of human existence, accentuating different modes of spatial syntax. Like the transformational properties associated with the praxis of post-rock, the 'Varúð' films take representation of waking life and infuse it with reverie in the nostalgia and unwanted beauty[51] of human-initiated desolation, devastation and our insignificant attention to our obligations to nature. The films considered in this chapter contemplate life and existence in, around and away from the detritus caused by the land use of one species. Indeed, sites such as tumbledown or antiquated built environments proved ripe for reevaluation and reinterpretation leading to their unanticipated uses that sit beyond the initial design intent or imagination of their architects. The absence of purpose and function leaves haunting traces of past energies, resolve, industriousness that have failed, been discarded or forced to move on. Rather than take human presence for granted the 'Varúð' films de-familiarize human presence or actions, making them appear aberrant. In doing so, the films muse on the way humans continue to exist in disharmony with nature irrespective of the fact that nature is capable of surviving without humans, if not unaffected by human-induced ecological crises.

The practice of *dismantling* offers a childlike rebellious pleasure, brings new opportunities for the reuse of constituent elements and can foster a deeper understanding of how aspects of a disassembled object operate. This playful stance is evident in the compositional approach of the post-rock genre and was further explored by the *Valtari Mystery Film Experiment,* which developed existing inter-art relationships with the band, inviting visual thinkers and creators from a range of associated mediums to work with and from their soundscape music within a moving-image format. In this context, neither prior experience nor renown as a music video director was a requirement for inclusion in the project, creating an opportunity for participating individuals to translate and expand their existing visual practices and further their association with fashioning the band's visual aesthetic. Like the themes of the resulting films, individuals were placed in an unusual creative space and encouraged to move, think, play and work differently. The transmedia directors responsible for the *Valtari Mystery Film Experiment* were Sigur Rós themselves, the evocative and beguiling nature of their music which occupies its own space, not subjugated or dominated by presence of the performer, thus enabling it to exhort its conceptual meaning more freely. The allusive techniques employed by Sigur Rós in creating their spatial music evade 'technological listening',[52] where the listener is able to perceive the technology or musical technique behind the music, thus encouraging the individual directors of the *Valtari Mystery Film Experiment* films to embrace the embodied and affective dimensions of the music's meaning in a transmedia storytelling process.

PART SIX

Audiovisual emanations: David Lynch

CHAPTER 16

The audiovisual eerie: Transmediating thresholds in the work of David Lynch

Holly Rogers

David Lynch's sonic resonances echo through projects and media. Pulsating room tone, eerie *acousmêtre*, electronic wash, static drones, thwarted resolutions and remediated retro textures frequently trouble the image, while imploding lip-syncs violently tear sound from sight and disembodied noises lead attention beyond the edge of the screen. Lynch's soundscapes point beyond themselves. They are disruptive, bleeding between film, television, internet and music video work, resonating in the unseen spaces that surround each narrative centre before overflowing into ancillary worlds. These liminal spaces are occupied by sound alone and mark the threshold not only between projects but also between music and image, inside and out, real and imagined. Where are the sounds going and should we follow? Who or what is listening and what is heard?

I suggest that Lynch's production of a consistent sonic space across genres and platforms amounts to more than stylistic cohesion. In fact, his distinctive aural textures enable a peculiarly eerie form of transmedia to arise based not on the augmenting strategies of world-building but on its opposite: on the displacement and deconstruction of knowledge. As we have seen throughout this book, the success of a transmedial extension is predicated on a duality: if the broadening is to be truly 'symbiotic', explains David Bordwell, the principal project must simultaneously provide enough narrative core to build on yet leave ample space for imaginative enhancement.[1] Although the enhancement of a film usually develops through posthumous paratexts in the form of sequels, spin-offs, novels, comics and so on, world-building can also begin before the host project drops, something eloquently accomplished through the pre-screening flyers, adverts and billboards that paved the way for the premieres of *The Blair Witch Project* (Daniel Myrick and Eduardo Sánchez, 1999) and *District 9* (Neill Blomkamp, 2009). In both cases, the paraphernalia blurred the boundaries between real and filmed worlds even before screenings took place. Such extensions underpin Henry Jenkins' formative understanding of a transmedia story as that which 'unfolds across multiple media platforms, with each new text making a distinctive and valuable contribution to the whole'.[2] With an emphasis on the creation of backstory, he suggests that this 'shifts our identifications and investments in characters and thus helps us to re-watch the scenes again with different emotional resonance. More often, it is about picking up on a detail seeded in the original film and using it as a point of entry into a different story or a portal into exploring another aspect of the world.'[3] Yet Bordwell reminds us that

> gap-filling isn't the only rationale for spreading the story across platforms, of course. Parallel worlds can be built, secondary characters can be promoted, the story can be presented through a minor character's eyes. If these ancillary stories become not parasitic but symbiotic, we expect them to engage us on their own terms, and this requires creativity of an extraordinarily high order.[4]

On the surface, Lynch's collaborative work offers just this. For all its enigmatic charm, surrealist twists and loose-ends, for instance, the *Twin Peaks* project (1990–2017) nevertheless works around a core crime-drama and its ramifications to offer what Mark Fisher refers to as 'a superficial coherence'.[5] This coherence, however fragile and easily de-stabilized, nevertheless provides enough of a framework for parallel world-building to manifest between official moving image forms (TV and film), diegetic augmentations (diaries, books, transcriptions and maps) and sonic extensions (soundtrack albums and previously unreleased music), while fan-based 'gap-filling' in the form of internet community building, collaborative twitter literature and sampled, remediated songs deal in specific ways with distinct pockets of the enigma. All make 'a distinctive and valuable contribution to the whole', as we shall see below.

Other forms of intertextual fluidity across platforms are more seamless, as individual components are encouraged to morph into each other almost imperceptibly. This is particularly apparent in works that stem from, or reside in, online culture. In her work on contemporary media, Anne Friedberg suggests that 'the movie screen, the home television screen, and the computer screen retain their separate locations, yet the types of images you see on each of them are losing their medium-based specificity'.[6] Along similar lines, Jenkins has argued that 'because digital media potentially incorporate all previous media, it no longer makes sense to think in medium-specific terms'.[7] In Lynch's work, different forms of screen media frequently merge, a fusion particularly apparent in his first digital film *Inland Empire* (2007), which seeps beyond its feature borders to remediate not just content but also the form and structure of media culture more generally. *Rabbits*, an eight-episode web-based 'sitcom' (2002; davidlynch. com) that uses a predominantly static shot to show a domestic living room in which actors in rabbit suits speak in non-sequiturs, randomly punctuated by canned laughter, later became integrated into *Inland Empire*, with some changes in the dialogue and several new scenes. Within their new setting, the low-fi internet quality of the cameo-like segments promotes just such a deconstructed specificity, as they spread out into the film thanks to Lynch's preference for commercial-grade digital cameras: 'High-def is a little bit too much information,' he explains.[8] Drawing attention to the numerous loops, side-slips, echoes, repetitions and mirroring that infuse and confound the film's narrative, Dennis Lim takes the idea of undoing 'medium specificity' further, noting that 'not only does *Inland Empire* often look like it belongs on the Internet, it also progresses with the darting, associative logic of hyperlinks'.[9] While *Inland Empire* appears to connect and consume the form *and* the content of other media forms, Lynch's more recent internet work exposes the physical 'associative logic' of interactive media. Some projects are available exclusively on his website davidlynch.com (such as the animation *DumbLand*, 2002), but others embrace the mosaic possibilities of cross-referencing and nonlinearity that the internet affords. *Interview Project* (2009), for instance, offers 121 brief interviews constructed during 'a 20,000-mile road trip over 70 days across and back the United States', directed and edited by Lynch's son Austin Lynch with Jason S.[10] Taken separately, each mini-documentary gives a fleeting glimpse into the lives of various people met along the route, but when placed together, in any order the user chooses, a larger and surprisingly cohesive narrative arises about rural contemporary American life (Figure 16.1). Other projects use the internet as a conduit between forms in a more transmedial way: before his collaboration with Lykke Li for his second studio album *The Big Dream* (2013) was released, for instance, he dropped 'TBD716', a mysterious forty-three-second video, to his YouTube and Vine accounts (the latter as a six-second version).[11]

However, the 'darting associative logic' of Lynch's cross-medial work also problematizes traditional notions of transmedia, built on gap-filling, world-building and the undoing of medium specificity. While the unique combination of narrative core and mysterious diffusion that drives the *Twin Peaks* project can also be found in many of Lynch's earlier works from

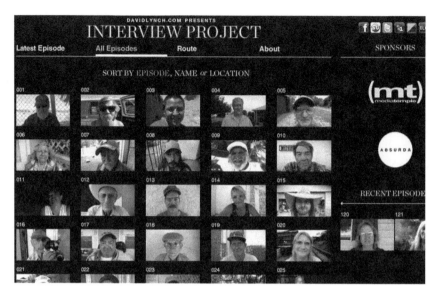

FIGURE 16.1 *David Lynch, front page of* Interview Project *(2009).*

Eraserhead (1977) – which Michel Chion understands as 'a narrative film with dialogue, a hero and a linear story' – through to *The Elephant Man* (1980) and *Dune* (1984), some of his later films embrace more surrealistic forms.[12] In her analysis of *Lost Highway* (1997), for instance, Marina Warner identifies a plot that 'binds time's arrow into time's loop, forcing Euclidian space into Einsteinian curves where events lapse and pulse at different rates and everything might return eternally'.[13] By the time we get to *Mulholland Drive* (2002) and *Inland Empire*, linear progression and coherent forms of causality have been almost entirely replaced by oneiric, labyrinthine loops and curvaceous simulacra, which results in what Brian Jarvis refers to as an 'a-destinationality'; a 'failure to go anywhere'.[14] As time and plot slip and slide around one other, traditional processes of transmedial story-building are troubled. What to latch onto when things are continually undermined?

It is within this web of contradiction and confusion that Lynch's particular and unique form of transmedia arises, one enabled not only by character exploration or narrative continuity but also – and often simultaneously – by a tangled form of *dis*continuity. Within this discontinuity, music and sound assume a vital role. Despite hyperlinking and 'Einsteinian curves', Lynch's worlds embody an immediately recognizable aesthetic that forges a distinctive sensory continuity within and between his works, with visual tropes including, surreal objects, doppelgängers, tunnel-vision night shots, deserted streets, doors and curtains, fever dreams, closed-eye vision, and sonic resonances comprising heightened room tone, drone-based synths, ethereal female voices, reimagined 1950s songs and a resistance to resolution. Lynch's visual tropes in particular have encouraged much critical interest. Chion has devoted a chapter of his book on Lynch to these visual recurrences, for instance, offering a 'Lynch-kit' that identifies the director's intertextual zeal for objects such as scissors, chairs, ears, curtains and stages and the atmospheric interferences of wind and smoke.[15] But while Chion hypothesizes certain semantic stabilities that drive these recurrences, he doesn't treat the echoes as a form of transmedial extension between texts. What do these intertextual correlations signify? Do they also gather and develop signification between and through projects, or are they simply stylistic echoes across the void? Zoran Samardzija builds on Chion's 'Lynch-kit' in her reading of *Inland Empire* to more explicitly acknowledge the snakes-and-ladders-like connectivity between his projects. Like Lim, she constructs her reading on the metaphor of the hyperlink:

> It is neither a Möbius strip that endlessly circles around itself, nor is it divisible into sections of fantasy and reality. Its structure is more akin to a web where individual moments hyperlink to each other and other Lynch films – hence the musical number that closes the film which contains obvious allusions to everything from *Blue Velvet* to *Twin Peaks*.[16]

While she stops short of tracing the actual hyperlinks themselves beyond the above acknowledgement of possible allusions, Samardzija's idea more concretely suggests tangible links between projects. In fact, the hyperlink metaphor is a significant one for an understanding of Lynch's strain of transmedia not only in terms of cross-platform storytelling but also as an allegory for a threshold or portal into spaces that lie beyond substantiating 'allusion'. These spaces are the key to Lynch's unique form of transmedia. As distinct and original texts, many of his films and internet projects are not immediately relatable to the traditional concepts of transmedia outlined by Jenkins and Bordwell above. Apart from *Twin Peaks*, his films are discrete narratological forms that offer original plots rather than back story or secondary character augmentation. And yet, although most projects come with distinct locations, protagonists and scenarios, there exist stylistic echoes and resonances strong enough to suggest that there is more at play in and between his work than is attributable simply to the distinctive style that drives auteurism.

Many of these echoes are sonic. Sound design and music stitch many of Lynch's transmedial components together and have formed an integral – even driving – part of his idiosyncratic style from the outset. The director has often spoken of sound as the catalyst in his early progression from static art into the moving image, for instance. Referring to his painting, he explained, 'As I looked at what I'd done, I heard a noise. Like a gust of wind. And it came all at once. I imagined a world in which painting would be in perpetual motion.'[17] As a driving force for his subsequent work with the moving image, sound is a frequent component of the early film-making process, often coming before principle photography to assume influence over visual pace and rhythm during filming (he famously plays music on set and wears headphones while directing).[18] The result, he says, are 'films [which] are 50 percent visual and 50 percent sound. Sometimes sound even overplays the visual.'[19]

Building on Chion's identification of Lynch's intertextual echoes, and pressing further into Samardzija's hyperlink metaphor of visual 'allusion', I suggest that, if we seek not only visual but also sonic resonances and remediations between projects and platforms, a broader, yet paradoxical understanding of *audio*visual transmedia can arise. The other authors in this module react to Lynch's audiovisuality through the coexistent forms of duration that determine quantum theory (Greg Hainge), the aesthetics of slowing, slowness and vari-speed (John McGrath) and a sense of formlessness derived from Simondon's theory of individuation and in-formation (Elena del Río). Although working along similar lines, I focus in on moments of audiovisual rupture, arguing that Lynch's undoing of traditional transmedial forms operates in direct opposition to the gap-filling, or 'parallel' world-building role often played by ancillary or paratextual projects.[20] In Lynch's work this is achieved through an undoing of conventional audiovisual practice, particularly in the moments when the sonic 'overplays the visual' or rather undermines or contradicts what we are seeing. As we shall see, his on screen music often violently ruptures audiovisual synchronicity, while his soundscapes coalesce from myriad disembodied sources. The holes between what is seen and what is heard release sound from the grip of the diegesis and allow it to overspill its boundaries, as our attention is constantly drawn to what is beyond the frame: where are the sources of these sounds, and what is it that we are hearing? Significantly, many of Lynch's soundscapes outstrip their visual containers without linking to anything that supports, explains or bolsters what Jenkins calls the 'mothership' project.[21] In fact, audiovisual ruptures and disembodied sounds do not lead to substantiated worlds or knowledge but rather to greater uncertainty, hovering beyond the limit of sight, and reverberating between platforms, worlds and dreams. Such sonic emphasis on what is beyond the frame initiates a type of augmentation that troubles Bordwell's notion of 'gap-filling'. However, certain sonic gestures, particularly those that produce an audiovisual dissonance, frequently reappear in different texts, often at moments of significant emotional or aesthetic upheaval. This suggests a form of sustained aesthetic development that manifests not at the level of plot, but rather transmedially, through and across different, seemingly unrelated, texts. By embracing audio and visual fissures, Lynch's cross-project transmedia arises through absences and echoes; or what Mark Fischer has described as an 'eerie absence'.[22] It offers an obscuration of linearity and causality; it operates through diffusion and blockage; and it leads us further and further away from the familiar. Lynch's transmedia does not fill gaps; in other words, it extends and promotes them.

Twin Peaks and the undoing of transmedial auteurism

Although often touted as an exemplar auteur, Lynch opts for a creative process that is openly collaborative. Working with the same actors, cinematographers, editors, costume designers and casting directors across projects, his team-based, assemblage approach to creativity forges transmedial flow through many voices: 'while rooted in Hollywood production practice', argues Annette Davison, he also 'offers a radical reconfiguration of it'.[23] This reconfiguration begins to undo the classic concept of the auteur as a singular force reliant on what Andrew Sarris understood, in his seminal article, as 'the distinguishable personality of the director' which manifests over several films to produce 'certain recurrent characteristics of style, which serve as his signature'.[24] Looking further into the 'recurrent characteristics' across a director's work, Timothy Corrigan identifies a shift the 1980s, in which the auteur became commodified, a star in his/her own right and a marker of meaning that audiences recognize and use to interpret a film (or other text) before and after experiencing it: during this time, auteurism evolved into 'a way of viewing and receiving [...] rather than as a mode of production', he writes.[25] While Corrigan acknowledges signature style as a tool for reception as much as production, authorship also needs to be considered vertically in order to acknowledge the multifaceted, assemblage approach to creativity required for film-making. Despite working with several composers in his early work (for instance, Peter Ivers's original song 'In Heaven' for *Eraserhead*, John Morris's score for *The Elephant Man* or Toto's music and Brian Eno's 'Prophecy Theme' for *Dune*), Lynch's connection with composer Angelo Badalamenti was instant, and the duo worked together on *Blue Velvet* (2001), *Wild at Heart* (1990), *Twin Peaks: Fire Walk with Me* (1992), *The Straight Story* (1999), *Lost Highway* and *Mulholland Drive*, on television shows *Twin Peaks*, *On the Air* (1992) and *Hotel Room* (1993; Lynch did the sound design), the theatre project *Industrial Symphony No 1: The Dream of the Broken Hearted* (1990) and the internet series *Rabbits*. Lynch's noise-based soundscapes are similarly collaborative, crafted at first in conjunction with Alan Splet (for the films *The Grandmother* (1970), *Eraserhead*, *Dune* and *Blue Velvet*), before a less-successful partnership with Randy Thom (*Lost Highway*) prompted him to take over the sound-design role himself.[26] These two long-standing collaborations had a profound impact on what has become known as the director's 'signature style'. As we shall see, when Lynch broke with Badalamenti to write his own music for *Inland Empire*, the soundtrack remains awash with the composer's drone-based, throbbing textures; likewise, the soundscapes crafted by Lynch since Splet's early death retain their noisy and ambiguous grain.

When combined with the power of expectation, an assemblage approach to construction can forge a distinctive voice strong enough to withstand – or integrate – substantial intervention. This is certainly true of Lynch's 'signature' which not only develops through multiple close collaborations but also provides the space for sustained directorial intervention and fan augmentation. In fact, he is a useful example of what Roberta Pearson calls a 'hyphenate-auteur', a type of practitioner that emerged during late 1990s television projects able to fulfil several meta roles – director, writer, creator, producer, composer – while reliant on teams of writers to mobilize things at a local level.[27] Joss Whedon (*Buffy the Vampire Slayer*, 1997–2003; *Angel*, 1999–2004), for instance, embraces a flexi-narrative format in which his responsibility for large-scale framing storylines is balanced by writers who work closely on discrete episodes. This team-driven process befuddles the idea of authorship, although a strong 'signature style' can hold things together at the level of reception.

Lynch's engagement with transparent transmedial play and assemblage authorship can be seen in and around the world of *Twin Peaks*, co-created with Mark Frost, which manifested through two original series (1990–1) and a prequel film (*Twin Peaks: Fire Walk with Me,* 1992) before returning to the small screen for a third series (*Twin Peaks: The Return,* 2017). Many of the episodes from the first two series were directed by others, according to a carefully prepared plan overseen by the co-creators. And yet, the style is largely consistent, persuasive and overflows its boundaries in myriad ways. Initially, the world bled into a series of tie-in thirty-second adverts for Georgia Coffee (1992), made for Japanese television and including many of the main cast members and snippets of Badalamenti's score, before extending beyond moving image media altogether. With the original series, there also came the opportunity to buy several transmedial texts that form what Jason Mittell refers to as 'a *diegetic extension*' to the filmed world, including *The Secret Diary of Laura Palmer* (Jennifer Lynch, 1990), a reproduction that included details about characters and events that would later reappear in the prequel films; *The Autobiography of F.B.I. Special Agent Dale Cooper: My Life, My Tapes* (Scott Frost, 1991) which operates as the transcripts of Cooper's Dictaphone; and *Twin Peaks: An Access Guide to the Town* (Lynch and Frost, 1991), which acts as a tour guide to the fictional area, with maps and histories, as well as information on local wildlife, diners and culture.[28] Significantly, some of these diegetic extensions emerged independently of Lynch. Frost provided two epistolary novels that straddled the release of the third series, for instance.[29] These blurrings between real and fictional worlds extend to other artefacts: available to buy were Black Lodge candles, pillows from the Red Room and coffee cups from the Diner. Then there are the actual physical recreations in the form of yearly *Twin Peaks* conventions that allow fans to meet the actors and the recreation of specific spaces, such as the pop-up Road House Bar on LA's Melrose Avenue (8 December 2017–1 January 2018), that served Cherry Pie and specially named cocktails. These physical spaces fused Lynch and Frost's fictional world with the real one.

The sound and music of *Twin Peaks* – in its original and ancillary forms – is one of the most consistent elements of the world's transmedial percolation. As with many other components of the project, they developed through close collaborative processes. In preparation for the first series of *Twin Peaks*, Lynch and Badalamenti, together with singer Julee Cruise and a band of carefully picked musicians, including guitarist Vinnie Bell and jazz drummer Grady Tate, set up in a New York studio to work on three closely linked ventures: Cruise's first album, *Floating Into the Night* (1989), the soundtrack for *Twin Peaks* and *Industrial Symphony No 1*. Although distinct products, the transmedial resonances are clear to see. The album's second track, 'Falling', morphed into the iconic 'Twin Peaks Theme', while most of the other songs made an appearance in the series either as dramatic music or performed by Cruise in person at the Roadhouse. Similarly, four songs from the album were woven into *Industrial Symphony*, which also saw Cruise cast as The Dreamself of the Heartbroken Woman. The transmedial blurring of these projects extended further when components of the theatre plot later morphed into elements of *Wild at Heart*.

While Cruise's album acted as a pivot point in the transmedial flow between several of Lynch's projects then, *Twin Peaks* subsequently produced an extensive array of responsive sonic paratexts, including five official soundtrack albums.[30] While a few unreleased Badalamenti compositions were included on these albums, the most powerful sonic form of world-extension was found on davidlynch.com as *The Twin Peaks Archive* (2011–12), a collection of 212 previously unreleased, unused or rare tracks from the television and film worlds, available for digital download. This limited time-release resource allowed people to imagine un-visualized scenarios, extended storylines and emotional augmentations through sound alone. But while these sounds extended the Twin Peak's world through aurality, Lynch stretched music more concretely beyond the series in several ways, most notably through his organization of 'The Music of David Lynch Benefit Concert', where Karen O, Duran Duran, Moby and Lykke Li joined Chrysta Bell and Badalamenti to perform music from Lynch's films at the Theatre at Ace Hotel, Los Angeles (1 April 2015, Figure 16.2). Through television serials, a film and adverts to diaries, maps, cherry pies, records and concerts, then, the audiovisual worlds of *Twin Peaks* flow from closely authored moving image media to extensive and participatory activities that open wide the idea of storytelling and authorship. This has important ramifications for the idea of transmedia in the digital age.

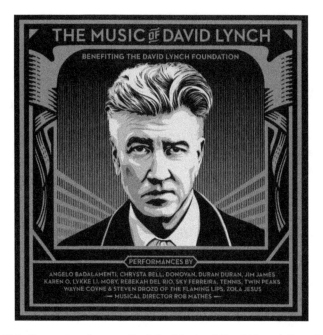

FIGURE 16.2 *Promotional poster for 'The Music of David Lynch Benefit Concert'* *(Ace Hotel Los Angeles, 1 April 2015).*

Fandom and transmedial flow beyond the auteur

In much of his work, Jenkins has sought to liberate our understanding of transmedial storytelling as both a narratological and a technological process by repositioning emphasis onto the new and emancipating strategies of 'work – and play'. The merging of media, he suggests, encourages spectators to perform unique interpretative strategies as they navigate between and through platforms: 'Convergence represents a cultural shift as consumers are encouraged to seek out new information and make connections among dispersed media content.'[31] Within this emergent networked culture, argues Jenkins, 'the meanderings of multimedia browsing can't be described with the confidence we can ascribe to a film's developing organization. Facing multiple points of access, no two consumers are likely to encounter story information in the same order.'[32] While we can see this happening in the *Twin Peaks* universe, it is also more than this: when fan contributions are taken into account, the world augments and multiplies in unpredictable and uncontainable ways, with the spaces between cross-medial elements becoming a vital part of the connective fluidity.

The mysteries surrounding the murder of Laura Palmer and the strangeness of *Twin Peaks* and its occupants, for instance, provided ample opportunity for what Matt Hill refers to as 'endlessly deferred narratives'.[33] It wasn't long before the officially sanctioned extensions to *Twin Peaks* splintered into a bewildering array of fan-based and participatory extensions that sought not only to fill the strategic gaps in the enigma but also to actively promote and extend them. Fan fiction, internet hunting, discussion pages and twitter groups diffused and 'endlessly deferred' the project, which quickly took on a life of its own. Producing a post-medial, post-cinematic example of viral 'spreadability', a concept proposed by Jenkins that operates in 'contrast to older models of stickiness which emphasize centralized control over distribution and attempts to maintain "purity" of message', fan-produced storytelling decentred both text and its authors.[34] This is most apparent in the 2014 enterprise '@Enter the Lodge' which self-identifies as 'a fan-made work of Twin Peaks Twitter fiction'.[35] Here, over fifty characters from the original series, each with their own Twitter account, recreated events from March 1989 – the date of the penultimate episode – before extending into an imagined Series 3 (Figure 16.3). Twitter storytelling, as an example of the intersecting platforms of the post-cinematic, can here be seen both as an attempt to grapple with the ambiguities of *Twin Peaks* and collectively to invent and play with the very nature of its abstruse forms. In this sense, the open-ended databases being used to explore and flesh out the fictional world resemble the endless pluralities of that world itself.

Digital platforms have also impacted on the remediation of the *Twin Peaks* soundworlds, which have undergone radical configuration through

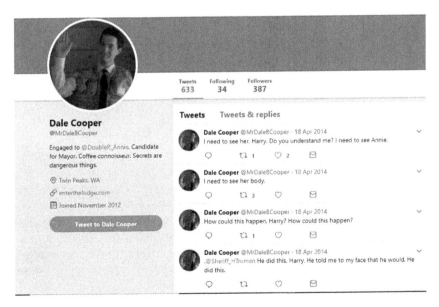

FIGURE 16.3 *Agent Dale Cooper's Twitter page ('@Enter the Lodge', 2014).*

sampling, quotation and variation, including Moby's career-launching rave reworking of 'Laura Palmer's Theme' for 'GO (Woodtick Mix)' (1990), Xiu Xiu's experimental cover album in 2016, *Xiu Xiu Plays the Music of Twin Peaks*, a cover of 'Sycamore Trees' (Badalamenti/Lynch, *Fire Walk with Me*) by Niitch (2016) and Chrysta Bell's 2017 cover of 'Falling', which offered an uncanny interconnection through her concurrent appearance as Special FBI Agent Tamara Preston in *Twin Peaks: The Return*. Others have extended the sonic worlds in more clearly transmedial ways. Mount Eerie's 'Between Two Mysteries' (*Wind Poem*, 2009) samples Badalamenti's 'Laura Palmer theme' to weave a lyrical evocation around the mythical location: 'The town rests in the valley beneath Twin Peaks / Buried in Space / What goes up there in the night / In that dark, blurry place?' Bastille's 'Laura Palmer' (*Bad Blood*, 2013) offers a different response, with no musical allusions to the world, but a close engagement with the protagonist, as singer Dan Smith explains, 'On "Laura Palmer", I wanted to capture the urgency of the image of her coming off a motorbike and running through the forest.'[36]

While the official 'diegetic extensions' of *Twin Peaks* demonstrate traditional forms of transmedial world-building, then, fan-driven extensions fracture off in volatile ways. Speaking about the reception of his song among his British indie-pop fans, Smith remarked: 'I enjoyed fans asking, "Who's Laura Palmer? Is it your ex-girlfriend?" I still get people saying, "Thank you for introducing me to *Twin Peaks*."'[37] Returning to Jenkins's observation that multimedia browsing opens up 'multiple points of access', we can see that the porosity of *Twin Peaks* enables just this. Already replete with enigmatic gaps, the world troubles traditional and discrete forms of storytelling by activating audiences in two complimentary ways: the first by asking us to 'work' in order to fill in the gaps in a story that is open ended and enigmatic; and second, by inviting us to 'play' through physical participation in the form of interactive internet sites and Twitter discussions.

The wrongness of the weird and the absence of the eerie

While the many worlds of *Twin Peaks* demonstrate myriad possibilities for transmedia and assemblage auteurism, when visual and sonic tropes link across different projects, the concept of world-building morphs into something more nebulous. Rather than the substantiation of specific character, plot or specific event, connections between works can manifest at a more elusive, conceptual level. Predicated on fissure and absence, ethereal forms of transmedia can open a space for the eerie to arise. In his critical evaluation of the concept, Fisher positioned the eerie in close but oppositional relation to the weird, or that which arises through the intrusion of the outside into our world. Such incursion 'involves a sensation of *wrongness*: a weird entity or object is so strange that it makes us feel that it should not exist, or at least it should not exist here'.[38] Speaking in relation to H. P. Lovecraft's fiction, Fisher notes that 'the weird is constituted by a presence – the presence of *that which does not belong*. In some cases of the weird … the weird is marked by an exorbitant presence, a teeming which exceeds our capacity to represent it.'[39] Situated beyond comprehension, yet utterly compelling, the weird occupies a transgressive position within extant modes of understanding, opening up what Herbert Graves calls a 'third aesthetic' that sits between the traditional categories of Beauty and Sublimity: this liminal realm, he argues, is the place where the uncanny gives rise to unsettled states governed by uncertainty and incomprehension.[40] Weird intrusions recur (in moderated form) throughout Lynch's work, from the frequent appearance of supranatural characters – the Mystery Man in *Lost Highway*, Bob and the Giant in *Twin Peaks* and Phantom in *Inland Empire* – to those, like *Twin Peaks*' Log Lady, who are able to manifest weird conjunctions.[41] Referring to *Twin Peaks*, Chion writes of 'characters who belong to the parallel dimensions, who appear in fantasies and dream, loom up among the gaps in the tissue of reality or communicate with other forces'.[42] The fractured tissues of reality also give rise to psychological disturbances such as dreams and illusions that encourage and generate transmogrification: Fred becomes Pete in *Lost Highway*, Sandy and Dorothy assume a parallel existence in *Blue Velvet*, Betty morphs into Diane in *Mulholland Drive*, Sue incorporates Nikki in *Inland Empire*, the White Lodge transitions to its black version in *Twin Peaks* and Dale Cooper assumes an evil doppelgänger and his tulpa Dougie Jones in *The Return*.[43]

Fundamental to all these weird collocations is the notion of the threshold. Intrusion, coexistence, morphing and transition require movement between one's state – or one reality – and another. Within Lynch's work, these physical and psychological transitions are signalled by several different forms of liminality. The recurring trope of heavy curtains, which appear when narrative cohesion is at its most vulnerable, for example, clearly signals confusion: is it night or day; what is behind, a window or a door; who, what or where lies beyond the folds? The velvet curtains of The Red Room in *Twin Peaks* (Figure 16.4a), with their dual function to conceal and reveal, designate the threshold that divides worlds and times, a visual motive that echoes both within this world – Nadine Hurley's fervent desire for 'silent drape runners' – and between projects: the curtains that partially conceal the protagonist in the opening scenes of *The Elephant Man* for example (Figure 16.4b). 'I don't know where it came from, but I love curtains. There is something so incredibly cosmically magical about curtains opening and revealing a new world,' explains Lynch.[44] Notably, however, curtains frequently form the backdrop of music performance, as if to signal the power of sound to move the audience between states. They hang heavily

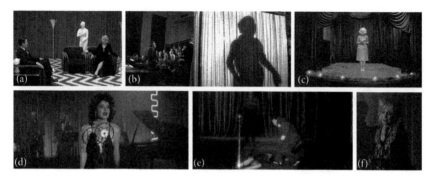

FIGURE 16.4 *(a) The Red Room in* Twin Peaks *(David Lynch, 1990–1); (b) the opening scene of* The Elephant Man *(David Lynch, 1980); (c) the Lady in the Radiator performs 'In Heaven' (David Lynch,* Eraserhead, *1977); (d) Dorothy Vallens performs 'Blue Velvet' (David Lynch,* Blue Velvet, *2001); (e) Rebekah del Rio performs 'Crying' (David Lynch,* Mulholland Drive, *2002); (f) Julee Cruise performs at the Bang Bang Club (David Lynch,* Twin Peaks: The Return, *Part 17, 2017).*

behind the Lady in the Radiator's performance of 'In Heaven' (*Eraserhead*, Figure 16.4c), Dorothy Vallens' version of 'Blue Velvet' (Bobby Vinton, 1963, Figure 16.4d) at the Slow Club in the eponymous film, Rebekah del Rio's Spanish a cappella rendition of Roy Orbison's 1962 hit 'Crying' (*Mulholland Drive*, Figure 16.4e), through to the guest performances, heard in their entirety, in the Bang Bang Club, that close each episode of *The Return* (Figure 16.4f). Echoing Lynch's own sentiment, Fisher, who situates curtains and thresholds firmly within the weird as they demarcate the juxtaposition of worlds, points out that curtains 'do not only mark a threshold; they constitute one: an egress to the outside'.[45] This is significant here. For Lynch, curtains do not simply denote a clashing of physical or ontological states, but signify the presence of the 'outside'. This is particularly apparent in the endless gateways and passageways that drive what Fisher describes as the 'labyrinthine, rabbit-warren anarchitecture' of *Inland Empire*: in a way reminiscent of Lim's hyperlink metaphor, Fisher explains that 'each corridor in the film ... is potentially the threshold to another world'.[46]

While curtains symbolize the transition between dream world and reality, the doors of *Inland Empire* signify in a less ambiguous way. *Axxon N* is one of the clearest examples of Lynch's thresholds, and can be read as a metaphor for networked culture and its endless linking to other portals. Originally intended as a nine-episode mini-series for Lynch's website (2002), *Axxon N* was never made. However, it became a shifting lynchpin for *Inland Empire*; acting as a portal into other realities, the name appears on various doors, inviting protagonist Nikki/Sue to pass through into the twilight zones of altered consciousness and ambiguous locations. The first time she passes through a door with *Axxon N* inscribed on it, she finds herself first on Stage 4, where *On High in Blue Tomorrows* is being shot; the next time, on Hollywood Boulevard, it initiates a physical split as she spies herself across the street; and the third time she finds herself in Sue's house where she shoots the Phantom. Greg Hainge surmises that the appearance of the word initiates 'an aporia, a point at which we are required to relinquish our normal modes of understanding and find new connections that are not so obviously causal'. These aporetic moments, he writes, 'force[sic] different spatiotemporal realities to inhabit the same space'.[47] A film within a film, a play continually in the process of becoming and awash with a confusion of ontological and televized spaces, *Inland Empire* can be read as a commentary on the weird transmedial ability for art to constantly consume and remediate itself.

Alongside the strangeness of a weird presence, explains Fisher, lies a disquieting absence:

> The eerie, by contrast, is constituted by a *failure of absence* or by a *failure of presence*. The sensation of the eerie occurs either when there is something present where there should be nothing, or is there is [sic] nothing present when there should be something.[48]

While a failure of presence often arises in desolate landscapes and ruins that give the sense that something significant has left the space, Fisher posits the 'eerie cry' of a bird as an example of the failure of absence, a sound that suggests a motivation more elusive than simple avian impulse.[49] But what? Vital to the eerie is the feeling of otherness and the realization that resolution will require an understanding that lies outside of the normal state of things, as Fisher explains:

> Such speculations are intrinsic to the eerie, and once the questions and enigmas are resolved, the eerie immediately dissipates. ... It must be stressed at this point that not all mysteries generate the eerie. There must also be a sense of alterity, a feeling that the enigma might involve forms of knowledge, subjectivity and sensation that lie beyond common experience.[50]

Unresolved absences pulse through Lynch's work: deserted corridors, deserts, forests and endless empty roads that throb with the sense that someone, or something, has just departed, are countered by spaces pregnant with artifice, illusion and theatricality that, writes Philip Brophy, 'are fixed at the borders of towns, the edge of night, the precipice of morality'.[51] The combination of these locational borders, edges and precipices with the murky visibility of Lynch's tunnel vision, chiaroscuro, unusual camera angles and regular focus on unfolding weather conditions – mist billowing down a mountain side, branches slowly blowing in the wind – leaves the edges of the frame, and the narrative, open. Although Fisher situates Lynch's obsession with thresholds firmly within the weird, these perforations nevertheless also conjure up both types of eerie: as Isabella van Elferen asks, these are 'doors to *what* or *where*?'[52] But absence also invades the transfigurations of the characters outlined above: as they merge and reform, an eerie absence or void is revealed – where did the original go? Where are we now? And where is everyone else?

In Lynch's work, moments of visual desolation are often compounded by an abundance of sound. Yet while initially this may seem to restore some plenitude to the eerie void, Lynch's soundscapes are themselves infused with both the failure of absence *and* the failure of presence: as The Man from Another Place explains as he dances to Badalamenti's noirish 'Dance of the Dream Man' (*Twin Peaks*, 1990) in the Red Room, 'Where we come from ... there is always music in the air'. Lynch's worlds – which sound to David Toop 'like the resonating chambers of multiple nightmares' – evoke the eerie through both audio (dis)placement and sonic composition.[53] Sound that hovers 'in the air' without apparent source constantly displaces our attention and allows an eerie alterity to seep into the diegesis: Who is making this disembodied sound? Which image does it connect to? What is just beyond the frame? Withholding the source can produce an unsettling sense that there 'is something present where there should be nothing', while a sudden rupture to a well-established audiovisual connection can reveal the illusion behind traditional cinematic forms of representation. Such troubled audiovisuality can be further compounded by a sonic texture that is also ambiguous. In Lynch's worlds, then, the aural eerie can arise through abstruse sound design, ruptured synchronicity, mysterious nostalgia and unusual stylistic juxtapositions. Significantly, these distinctive moments of audiovisual disruption recur across projects.

The audiovisual eerie

(a) Audiovisual rupture

Within Lynch's worlds, things are often not as they seem. The troubling of expectation is at its most lucid when audiovisual synchronicity is destabilized or broken altogether. While such moments result in an audiovisual rupture at the local level, they can, paradoxically, also operate as a cohesive trope able to connect disparate projects in a sonic equivalent to Chion's visual 'Lynch-kit'. This can happen in several ways. First, interference can occur when things sound but not in the way that we would expect – the transmogrification of voice in *Twin Peaks'* Red Room is a good example, where The Man from Another Place and a Laura Palmer look-alike speak what appears to be backwards – or when previously secure audiovisual connections are pulled apart. Unlike a dramatic music track, which has become such a customary addition to a mainstream film's world that audiences rarely seek the source of the non-diegetic music, real-world sounds are often used to give a film space an illusory sense of fidelity through tight audiovisual synchronicity. Walter Murch, for instance, has famously asserted that the re-association of image and sound during postproduction – and the resultant audiovisual synchronicity – is the 'fundamental pillar upon which the creative use of sound rests, and without which it would collapse'.[54] There are many instances in Lynch's work when an apparently reliable bond between sound and image proves deceptive, as van Elferen has noted:

> Extra diegetic music or white noise often suddenly appears to be diegetic when a shot of a jukebox, radiator, or lamp explains the source of the sound, but when this alleged source suddenly gets turned off, or the film proceeds to another scene, the sound is still there, and the viewer is left wondering whether it was extra-diegetic after all.[55]

Chion points to several of these moments, including one in *Twin Peaks: Fire Walk with Me*, where he identifies the beat of a ceiling fan in the Palmer house that Leyland turns on when about to possess Laura as one of the main, and most consistent, sound effects, yet one that eventually significantly outstrips its visual source as it is later present at the scene of Laura's murder.

Other examples are more consistent and bleed between texts. Close-up shots of a record stylus form a clear transmedial echo across projects, for instance, and yet the relationship of image to sound is often awkward. The audiovisual trope gathers signification until its suggestion that all is not as it seems – that what we are being shown may not be the whole truth, or that we are hearing somewhere different from the place we are seeing – manifests a persistent form of eerie absence. The trope can first be found in Henry's use of the gramophone in *Eraserhead*, Lynch's first film (Figure 16.5a). At times we see the protagonist placing the needle on the grooves just long enough for a snippet of jazz to burst forth before the stylus is moved to another strain.[56] The music is disjointed but the audiovisual synchronicity is tight. At other times in the film, however, this correspondence is less clear, as Hainge has pointed out: the record player 'seems to produce the exact same vinyl hiss and rhythmic pop no matter what the sonic content of the vinyl platter the needle reads – noises which, in some scenes, also continue long after the song itself has stopped playing'.[57] That the rupture involves the hissing of a record stylus is significant. Speaking of 'the metaphysics of crackle', Fisher finds complex nostalgia-ridden hauntological reverberations in materiality of vinyl play.[58] As the crackle is wrestled from the image in *Eraserhead*, it is

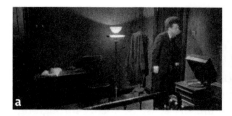 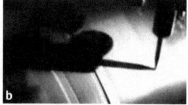

FIGURE 16.5 *(a) Henry puts on his gramophone in* Eraserhead *(David Lynch, 1977); (b) A record stylus opens* Inland Empire *(David Lynch, 2006).*

allowed to take on a hauntological life of its own; or rather, we are asked to question whether this life was ever dependent on the physical apparatus at all. A similar situation arises at the beginning of *Inland Empire*. Opening with sound, it is a while before the hissing and crackle of vinyl is located in a black-and-white close-up of a gramophone needle illuminated by what seems to be the beam of an old movie projector (Figure 16.5b). Once located, the sounds continue over a series of fuzzy shots of a couple speaking Polish before cutting to a lady crying in front of a television playing *Rabbits*. And yet these things are not as embodied as they first seem, as they constantly point towards an absence. At the start of the film, the gramophone produces an announcement about a radio play that openly references the threshold transmedial play of the film's origins, a play, moreover, that is never realized: 'Axxon N, the longest running radio play in history, tonight, continuing in the Baltic region, a grey winter day in an old hotel'; similarly, the television screen points out of the film to Lynch's website.

It is significant that the audiovisual rupture of the gramophone trope is signalled by the materiality of music-making. We are given an unequivocal moment of synchronicity – this is where the sound is coming from – before the comfort of a unified gesture is profoundly disturbed. In both films, then, the ruptured audiovisuality of the record stylus signifies the beginning of a journey from relative stability to narrative, oneiric and emotional upheaval; the moment when events begin to outstrip not only the characters' control but also rational understanding. In *Eraserhead*, the protagonist takes control of the vinyl himself, before the sounds eventually break from their visual container. This creates a confusion between on-screen and off-screen music and sound – between what Henry can hear and what lies beyond his acoustic realm – and initiates a sonic shift into the realm of the eerie, as we shall see below. The vinyl-drenched opening of *Inland Empire* operates more emphatically. We do not see the agency behind the gramophone and the dislocation of sound from image happens not only immediately but also at a fundamental, filmic level. The initial rupture is never forgotten and the film quickly spirals into an ontological confusion that is nearly impossible to untangle, a privileging of the formless that del Río interrogates in her chapter. In both examples, the audiovisual rupture marks the start of an emotional undoing and, like the visual trope of curtains and doors, represents a character teetering on the threshold of 'alterity'. Here, a specific sound travels across Lynch's works, accumulating resonances of rupture and transgression as it weaves in and out of aesthetic echoes.

By the time we get to *Interview Project*, the trope of displacement is so ingrained in Lynch's style that we are given the sound of vinyl with no corresponding image. With a soundtrack by Lynch's long-term collaborator Dean Hurley, together with Stoll Vaughan, and with additional music by Eugene Wasserman and Oto Gillen, each interview contains a vocal or instrumental song; all, however, are infused with eerie sonic resonance. The segments open to the sound of a jumping record stylus, before a low-resolution image of Lynch appears, producing an undoing of medium specificity similar to that found in *Inland Empire*, mentioned above. Here, however, the poor quality image is accompanied by the sound of static, which morphs into noisy, throbbing room tone as the interviewee appears on screen. In Jeremie's video (episode 31, 30 August 2009), we hear the needle skipping with vinyl noise and a low drone before we see Jeremie sitting on a hotel bed talking above a constant room tone that heightens with the appearance of intertitles. An acoustic guitar track plays the segment out, before again fading into a strong Lynchian noise that crescendos to what might be a distorted human scream as the credits appear: 'Absurda'. Introducing each segment, the vinyl operates as title music that draws out the parallels between each separate interview; yet, with its accumulated resonances of rupture and transgression from previous projects, it also emphasizes the transitory nature of each segment, the information and backstory we are not given and the gaps in our knowledge of each person's history and future. In a sense, then, it signifies the threshold moment when their histories will be taken from them, fragmented and juxtaposed with those of other people; the moment when these disparate stories are manipulated into new combinations by the website's user.

While the gramophone's recurrent trope of audiovisual fissure is relatively subtle, the most devastating ruptures occur during scenes of singing and technological mediation, in which a dramatic breakdown in synchronicity calls into question the agency behind the sound. This can initiate a viewing strategy at odds with the effacing of medium specificity noted by Friedberg and Jenkins above by revealing the film's technological materiality: as the compère of *Mulholland Drive*'s Club Silencio reminds us, 'There is no band. It is all recorded. It is all a tape. It is an illusion.' This illusion is most lucidly revealed during scenes in which characters ventriloquize someone else's voice: Ben's (Dean Stockwell) theatrical lipsyncing of Roy Orbison's 'In Dreams' (1963) in *Blue Velvet*, for example, or del Rio's catastrophic collapse while performing 'Crying' during *Mulholland Drive* that operates as the pivot point of the film.

Both moments are arresting, but operate in different ways. In *Blue Velvet*, sound and image play against each other, yet are both located within the diegesis. The music erupts during the first close altercation between Jeffrey (Kyle MacLachlan) and Frank (Dennis Hopper), which occurs in the apartment of Frank's crime partner, Ben shortly after Frank catches Jeffrey with Dorothy. In a scene of unusual visual stasis (as all actors remain inert, listening) and significantly staged between two hanging curtains, Ben theatrically mimes to Orbison's well-known voice, his underlit face heightening the dramatic artifice of the moment. A double displacement occurs when Frank joins in, mouthing along with such emotional sincerity that it is as though the lyrics were revelatory (Figure 16.6). His intensely thoughtful and almost motionless consumption of the song contrasts with the flamboyance of Ben's performance, particularly when both actors are in shot for the chorus; 'In Dreams I Walk with You'. Just before Frank presses stop and removes the tape, Ben stops miming and lowers his microphone. Similarly, when the music restarts after the joyride, Frank asks for 'candy-coloured clown' (the song's opening lyrics) to be put on the car stereo. Again, the music's materiality is in the foreground, and Frank contemplates each lyric, underlit in a way reminiscent of Ben's earlier performance. Although this scene presents a strange reading of the music, it does not present a moment of fractured audiovisuality at a material level; there is no deceit here. And yet it does initiate a narrative upheaval; Jeffrey receives a vicious and sinister beating which prompts his decision to go to the police station.

By contrast, del Rio's performance is shocking; when she falls to the floor and the song continues, we feel tricked. Until then, her performance is convincing and emotionally arresting, so when the image rips apart from the music with such force, the materiality of the film is laid bare, the fundamental pillar catastrophically collapsed. But it is more than this. Already embodied

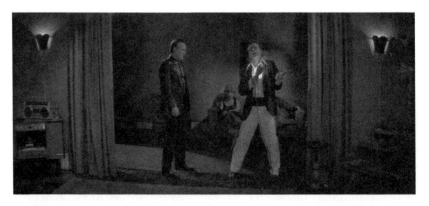

FIGURE 16.6 *Ben (Dean Stockwell) mimes to 'In Dreams' in* Blue Velvet *(David Lynch, 1986).*

in the recorded voice is an absence; by their very nature, recordings point to a bygone time and place. Not only does the audiovisual rupture make us re-evaluate the fidelity of what we are seeing and hearing, then; it also adds a second layer of dislocation as it transpires that the voice singing to us is from the past. As in the previous examples, this double displacement initiates a fundamental shift in the film. Betty finds a blue box in her bag that matches Rita's mysterious blue key; when Rita opens it, the film's inversion begins. Diane Selwyn now looks like Betty and her successful ex-lover, Camilla Rhodes, has turned into Rita. Like the rupture initiated by the gramophone trope, the visual wrenching of del Rio from her voice marks the start of a fundamental change in the film's trajectory.

It is deeply significant that this moment of eerie rupture is performed in front of curtains, a reiterated Lynchean symbol that, appearing within specific contexts, and in connection with eerie sounds, has become codified to serve a peculiarly ontological aesthetic, as we have seen; the mobile threshold between entities, worlds and texts. On the one hand, then, we can say that del Rio's ventriloquized performance reveals an audiovisual gash in the film's material sign system, but on the other, it is aesthetically united as the sonic absence resonates with the curtains which act as 'an egress to the outside'. Both sound and image, in other words, point elsewhere. Such a shocking fissure in the audiovisual fabric, based on an already absent source, is deeply eerie. To return to Fisher, in taking our attention beyond the frame they generate 'a sense of alterity, a feeling that the enigma might involve forms of knowledge, subjectivity and sensation that lie beyond common experience' not only of film consumption but also of the biological process of sensory integration.

(b) The eerie acousmêtre

Related to these instances of rupture is a second form of dissonance that manifests through noises that have no obvious connection to the diegesis at all. Like broken synchronicity, these disembodied sounds can de-emphasize what we are seeing and place attention beyond the screen. Here, there is not so much an audiovisual rupture, but rather an audiovisual incompatibility, or, as I have called it elsewhere, an aporia.[59] Whereas in normal practice, presence or room tone is a unifying form of 'silence' used during dialogue editing to suggest a realistic ambience, Lynch's atmospheres throb, hum, click and wheeze with rarely identifiable sounds. To a certain extent, the unique texture of these soundscapes formed as a result of Lynch's close collaborative – and eventually solo – work on both the sound and music of his films: 'there are sound effects, there are abstract sound effects', then 'music turns into sounds, and sounds turn into music', he explains.[60] Elsewhere he articulates this transition even more clearly: 'The borderline between sound effects and music is the most *beautiful* area.'[61] This borderline is explored through the compositional method, in terms of both ambient sound and music. From the outset, the collaborative process between Splet and Lynch emerged through *musique concrète* methods, a compositional approach replete with an eerie absence, which abstracts real-world noise from its source and reconfigures it as autonomous sound objects. Speaking about gathering the sound for the short film *The Grandmother*, for instance, Splet recalls that 'we'd start scouring the company for things to make sounds with – you know, like crushing a plastic box, or in one case we used a pencil sharpener, and in another case we used a staple gun'.[62] Here, real-world sounds were abstracted into musical textures. For other projects, the process worked the other way around and traditional musical sounds were de-familiarized: the recording of Badalamenti's music for *Lost Highway* involved the unusual placement of microphones – inside plastic piping and bottles – to disrupt the easy identification of the source.[63] These processes of defamiliarization are significant. According to Pierre Schaeffer, *musique concrète* produces an *acousmêtre* – 'a sound that one hears without seeing what causes it' – which encourages a process of 'reduced listening'.[64] In an audiovisual setting, this process can induce great anxiety.

Reduced or indirect listening is extremely difficult to achieve in an audiovisual medium, particularly one predicated on audiovisual fidelity. In his repurposing of the term 'acousmatic' to the audiovisual medium of film, Chion identified two distinct processes. 'Embodied' sounds are first heard in clear conjunction with either a visual or plausible on-screen source before continuing when the camera moves away. Their initial 'visualized' utterance locks together the audiovisuality and ensures against semantic instability, even when the images are no longer shown. When sounds are first heard from within the acousmatic space, on the other hand, and are only later synchronized with a visual source, a process of de-mythologization – or what Chion calls 'de-acousmaticization' – occurs. The tension and release generated 'between visualised and acousmatic provides a basis for the fundamental audiovisual notion of offscreen space', he writes.[65] The compulsion to locate a source for a sound-effect is a powerful one; not only do we seek a clarity of audiovisual articulation, but we also strive to substantiate – and thus embody – a film's diegesis through the unseen spaces that lurk just beyond the frame. These spaces can be rendered concrete through editing techniques (like shot-reverse-shot), but are often the domain of sound. When sounds refuse a visual connection or the process of de-acousmaticization, the result can be extremely disquieting.

The form of *concrète* created by Lynch and his collaborators embraces the ambiguity of the unresolved *acousmêtre* through both its method of creation and its placement within the audiovisual whole. Many of these soundscapes are animated by loud noises that remain in a de-visualized state throughout, a sonic texture whose prolonged distance from the images confounds the traditionally conceived 'audiovisual notion of offscreen space' by drawing our attention beyond the frame altogether. The sense that something hovers just out of sight clearly animates many of Lynch's projects: a 'constant rush of boiler sounds, whirlpools, electronic organ chords, and the like' (Chion) vibrate through *The Elephant Man*, while unresolved *acousmêtre* dominates the soundscape of *Twin Peaks* and *Fire Walk with Me*, phases in and out of *Blue Velvet* and rises to prominence when thresholds are crossed in *Inland Empire*.[66] In his analysis of *Lost Highway*, Brophy paradoxically locates the film's heavy soundscape with absence: 'When we first enter Madison's apartment, a strange aura occupies the cinema: it is the sound of nothing, the texture of silence. That humming tone that says nothing is occurring, that ringing rumble of space itself. ... Like room temperature, it is a palpable nothingness'.[67] This 'texture of silence' seeps not only across Lynch's cinematic worlds but also across platforms; it hums during his DVD menus and, as we have seen, unites the cameos in *Interview Project*. In fact, although each soundscape is different, prolonged acousmatic sound is one of Lynch's most consistent aural tropes. And unlike the punctuating moments of audiovisual rupture prompted by the gramophone or scenes of miming, these noises persist. They do not suggest a catastrophic rupture, but more a world that is, and remains, ontologically strange.

The yearning for an audiovisual resolution is activated during the gramophone scenes of *Eraserhead*, as we have seen. But the rest of the film forges an even greater sensory disturbance. Saturated by an almost continuous wash of warped industrial sound, the film is incredibly – even distractingly – noisy. Although the ambience of the noise changes as Henry moves through different spaces, the sounds remain implausible. The exterior landscape is desolate, almost ruinous, and yet reverberates with deafening whooshes and crashes, howls and shrieks that remain visually unresolved. This, combined with a peculiar absence of natural ambient sound, suggests that we aren't necessarily hearing what we are seeing; or rather, we aren't seeing what we are hearing. Where are these sounds coming from? K. J. Donnelly refers to the cacophony 'as acousmatic sound effects: seemingly the sounds emanating from some dreadful but indistinct industrial machines somewhere in the distance'.[68] For him, these sounds point towards physical objects that exist in the film's world but are never revealed to us. But unless the industrial wasteland is juxtaposed with monstrous working factories and a plethora of wild animals, this seems unlikely. While Donnelly seeks the implied source of the sounds, Chion, in a reading reminiscent of Lynch's desire for a *beautiful* borderline between aural planes, finds an 'absence of any separation between the music and its overall atmosphere', using a particular edit where the sound of an electronic organ dissolves into the drone of a boiler to support his argument.[69] This slippage troubles the nature of the *acousmêtre* altogether. The mixture of implausible soundscape, a lack of realistic ambience and the creative convergence of noise and music points towards a refreshed role for sound in film. Here, soundtrack exists on the border between dramatic music and ambient sound. Real-world sounds are not used to substantiate and flesh out the film's world, either through audiovisual synchronicity or sonic ambience. Rather, they are creatively stretched into the space normally occupied by dramatic music; and here, instead of forging an illusory realism, the sounds are remediated in real time to comment on the action and on Henry's psychological state as he undergoes his strange adventure. In this sense, they clearly belong to the diegesis's aesthetic. And yet, the decision of Lynch and Splet to retain the original nature of the noises as sound effects rather than as music troubles this unity. Writing about autonomous acousmatic noise in a way that evokes the eerie, Brian Kane has argued that the 'sound object is never quite autonomous' as it generates a longing for the absent source: 'one central, replicated feature of acousmatic listening appears to be that under-determination of the sonic source encourages imaginative supplementation'. This, in turn, can lead to a subjective and highly imaginative form of re-visualization, often driven by a 'surplus-meaning'.[70] *Eraserhead*'s sounds-effects are clear enough that Donnelly's 'imaginative supplementation' locates them in a factory just beyond sight. While this may or may not be a plausible interpretation, his process is important. The desire of audiovisual resolution encourages a 'surplus-meaning' to manifest as imagined images and locations that may appear at odds with those given to us on screen.

When discussing the sustained acousmatic sounds of *Twin Peaks: Fire Walk with Me*, Chion evokes something that comes close to the weird: the film, he writes,

> contains a whirligig of stressed sound effects, like the reverse-playback in which words are spoken back to front preceded by their end reverberations, so that the words pop up like little bubbles, low held sounds, dizzying slides and so on. This constant sound activity, the source and nature of which often remain obscure, is one of the film's most original aspects. It creates a sense of the screen as a fragile membrane with a multitude of currents pressing on it from behind.[71]

Chion's imagery here is important. However, I want to suggest a different reading predicated not on a weird intrusion from beyond – a 'multitude of currents' trying to get in – but rather by a movement outwards towards an eerie absence. If we think transmedially across texts and through media, we can suggest instead that sound also, and paradoxically, takes us *beyond* the 'fragile membrane'. While drawing us in, it simultaneously creates a fissure in our viewing experience, asking us to split our attention between inside and out; on what is there, but also on what is not. And herein lies the eerie power of Lynch's sound. In all of the examples above, an audiovisual aporia – by which sound and image rub against each other without colliding – arises as sound constantly directs our attention elsewhere: beyond the frame or behind the technology. As we've seen, Fisher's understanding of absence is predicated on what it is that is missing: 'Behind all of the manifestations of the eerie, the central enigma at its core is the problem of agency.'[72] What is so eerie about Lynch's soundscapes is his constant refusal to identify a sonic agency: Who or what is making these noises? Where are they coming from and what do they point to? What kind of entity can leave such a troubling sonic remnant? What has just left the image? In the examples above, the eerie rarely dissipates. van Elferen has described Lynch's sonic worlds as 'nostalgic and sweet, yet empty, disturbing and ominous', but they are more than this.[73] Lynch's acousmatic soundscapes continually signify away from themselves. They point towards peripheral places that lie beyond the threshold and behind the curtain; areas that cannot rationally be located in the off-screen space but bristle with an eerie 'sense of alterity'.

(c) Music re-voiced

The eerie does not arise simply through the liminalities of noise music – through audiovisual rupture that is left to gape, or through the lateralization of sound – however. It is also embodied in the remediated structures, tones and textures of Lynch's more traditionally conceived music collaborations with Badalamenti. Like his sound design, their dramatic music and songs point elsewhere, never fully engaging with the present, or at least preventing a fully historical location for current events. During a discussion of the music for *Twin Peaks*, Mark Frost reads Badalamenti's mixture of styles and timbres in terms of historical displacement: 'If the show was a boat moving along, Angelo's music was the river that carried it. It gave you a very specific sense of time and place that felt outside of real time and real place. It helped elevate the show into the mythological realm.'[74] This mythological ambiguity arises in several ways. The first is at the level of musical structure and texture. Badalamenti's drone-based dramatic music often resists the pull of closure, refusing common tonal progressions and cadences, which results in an unusual teleological stasis that enables the fluid confluence of sound effects and music identified by Lynch above. Unbound by tonality, its open-ended forms strain towards something else, reaching upwards and outwards as well as forwards. In his analysis of Laura Palmer's theme, John Richardson suggests that the harmonically mysterious music works together with the image to create ambiguity:

> The vision of Laura fashioned is fragmentary, internally inconsistent and unfathomable. We catch glimpses but never do we get a sense that we are seeing and hearing the whole picture. The presence of excessive, and therefore parodic, gestures in the music is one way of creating instability,

of implying that this version of Laura is not the whole truth and thus creating a vacuum where knowledge concerning Laura ought to be.[75]

It is easy to find the audiovisual eerie at work within the resisted tonal closures and thwarted melodic expectations that continually direct our attention elsewhere.

Second, and connected to this harmonic stasis, are hybrid sonic textures that combine Golden Hollywood and music hall timbres with echoes of 1980s dream-pop, shoe-gaze and ambient, 1940s noir jazz and 1950s rockabilly to resist any easily discernible historical setting. In her analysis of Badalamenti's references 'to the music hall (*Eraserhead*), to classical Hollywood film music (*Blue Velvet*) or to popular music of the 1950s (*Twin Peaks, Wild at Heart*)', van Elferen interprets these references as creating 'modes of nostalgia for times that lie eternally locked in the past'.[76] This sonic mytholigization is most prevalent in the songs that pepper Lynch's audiovisual work, both pre-existent and original. His choice of pre-existing music continually highlights an absent past; or, in hauntological terms, a nostalgia for lost futures (Simon Reynolds, Fisher).[77] This is clearly seen in the skewed cultural nostalgia that emerges when Sailor Ripley (Nicolas Cage) sings his two Elvis songs ('Love Me' (1956), with the Hurricane Club's heavy metal band as the backing band and 'Love Me Tender' (1956)) in *Wild at Heart* (1990) and when Dorothy Vallens (Isabella Rossellini) performs her slippery rendition of the title track, 'Blue Velvet', at the Slow Club. Returning again to Fisher, this type of troubled retro-aesthetics can be read as a postmodern melange that disrupts nostalgia and convolutes time.[78] Often manifesting in front of curtains at moments of narrative confusion and audiovisual rupture, these moments of retro-aesthetics suggest physical or emotional thresholds.

Lynch's original songs promote this connective nostalgia even more clearly. Retro organs, 1950s guitar riffs and dreamy girls' voices spill forth through analogue microphones and record players. Yet, like his visual obsession with vintage cars and diners, Lynch's songs expose the sinister, twisted and freaky undercurrents that lie beneath the bubble-gum innocence of teeny-bop-driven 1950s culture. Characterized by extremely slow, ethereal, reverb-heavy vocal lines that float above guitar-driven textures, Lynch's collaboratively written songs remediate and make strange the familiar qualities of 1950s and 1960s rock 'n' roll. While this surrealist reconfiguration is particularly apparent in his work with Julee Cruise, it also infuses *Inland Empire*, Lynch's first film for which he wrote most of the music alone. In 'Ghost of Love' (2007), for instance, Lynch's own voice strains and shuffles around the heartbeat pulse; he stays too long on one chord, the melodic line obsesses over too small a range and refuses the refuge of the rockabilly chorus. As we hear the song, the images distort, stretching and pulling with the music's rhythmic lope to give a highly disorienting feel.

This form of subversive musical nostalgia, which is analysed in detail in McGrath's chapter, is very different from van Elferen's reading of styles that are 'locked in the past'. Rather, it folds time together: this is not nostalgia but rather listening across voids; it's embracing the disembodied textures to create a weird montage. But this form of audiovisual timelessness is also closely linked to the idea of the eerie. Infused with absence, nostalgia and remembrance, the music evokes the same sort of eerie as his empty corridors, unpopulated rooms and badly lit roads.

The transmedial eerie

The idea of listening to and across voids is significant. Lynch's soundscapes, dramatic scores and scenes of performance are unique to each project. These sonic components often manifest from multiple and sustained collaborations and operate in specific ways within the diegesis. Nevertheless, Lynch's 'signature style' materialized during his earliest projects and has continued throughout his career. To return to the idea of the assemblage auteur, it becomes clear that Lynch fully integrates the voices of his long-term collaborators – Badalamenti, Splet and Cruise among others – into his style, creating a sonic quality that continues to develop even when those collaborators are no longer involved. Like his visual style, this sonic quality is pervasive. Friedberg noted above that the 'types of images' on various moving image platforms are 'losing their medium-based specificity': in Lynch's work, this dissolution is also signalled by an aural constancy across the mediums of television, film, music video, internet and albums which even bleeds into various sonic off-shoots, ancillary projects and fan-based variations.

Lynch's sonic style, then, is immediately apparent. But when does style give way to more tangible semantic connections between projects? While Lynch's collaboratively conceived soundworlds produce a distinct quality that spreads across projects, his tight investment in the visual and the audio components of his projects, and his desire to leave threads hanging loosely in the spaces beyond the frame, creates flashes of conspicuous flavour at pertinent moments across numerous projects. As we have seen, Lynch's remediated sonic textures and disembodied sounds are knitted tightly into his visual fabric. In particular, his diffuse and expansive noises signal in the same way as the recurrence of confined visual spaces, curtains, chiaroscuro lighting and fog, all of which impair or obstruct vision. Both give rise to the sense that vital information is being withheld. And yet, this unity is troubled when audiovisual synchronicity stumbles and cracks in one of the three ways outlined above. First, secure audiovisual connections are vexed. The audiovisual fractures apparent in the recurring trope of the gramophone, for instance, point not only towards an audiovisual rupture at the filmic level but also towards the continual deferral of semiotics inherent in recording media. The scenes of singing and miming, where image and sound are torn apart entirely, enact this 'failure of presence' even more emphatically. Second, the defamiliarizing strategies of *musique concrète* and the acousmatic noises that refuse de-mythologization continually emphasize the 'failure of absence'. And third, the fusion of styles and textures in the dramatic music and diegetic songs destabilizes common sonic vocabularies, folding together different textures in a way that highlights the eerie absence of bygone eras and cultures. It is in these distinct *audiovisual* moments that more substantial links between discrete projects can arise.

Yet, what makes these audiovisual disjunctions a case of transmedial flow rather than simply a continuity of style? The key here lies in the destination of the sounds. If we return to Jenkins's identification of transmedia arising through the augmentation of certain aspects of a text to form 'a point of entry into a different story or a portal into exploring another aspect of the world', it is clear to see that, in much of Lynch's work, the focus lies less on the point of entry, and rather on the point of exit as attention is continually drawn to the edge of the screen.[79] In sonic terms, the disembodied and de-visualized sounds encourage us to listen beyond what is shown, a process that decentres the work by emphasizing the eerie absent. This spread outwards initiates a fundamental transgression of cinematic convention, whereby attention is drawn into the frame both visually and aurally, and acousmatic sound serves primarily to reinforce the validity of the filmed world. In Lynch's worlds, sound and music do just the opposite. They press beyond the frame but rarely become visually substantiated: 'Sometimes sound even overplays the visual.' In this sense, the ontological strangeness of Lynch's worlds persists, as Fisher reminds us: 'Once the questions and enigmas are resolved, the eerie immediately dissipates.'[80] And yet, these moments of audiovisual rupture are striking and when they recur in other projects – usually at moments of similar emotional upheaval – an immediate aesthetic thrum is generated that crosses diegetic borders. As the disembodied sounds of Lynch's film, TV and internet worlds press outwards, in other words, they reach for each other. If we follow these sonic portals, connections and reverberations between projects, it becomes clear that Lynch's incorporeal soundscapes and remediated songs suggest more than a strong sense of style: rather, they are intertextual echoes and transmedial extensions that flow into the eerie void before reappearing in other projects reinvested with accumulated aesthetic significance. Geoffrey Long reminds us that transmedia stories should include 'passing references to external people, places, or events' that can be picked up as 'potential migratory cues' for further exploration.[81] In Lynch's work, these migratory cues can be clearly defined (as they are in the transmedial spread of *Twin Peaks*), but they can also be abstract, aesthetic and expansive, based not on places or events or characters but on audiovisual textures, gaps and contradictions.

With this in mind, we can attempt to articulate a form of transmedial deconstruction. The eerie in Lynch's soundworlds results in a paradox: the sounds strain beyond the frame, never succumbing to a state of de-acousmaticization. And yet this same eerie state arises in numerous films. Returning to the metaphor of the hyperlink, we can see that it is a useful starting point to understanding Lynch's cross-media references. Yet while hyperlinks may not always take us somewhere that makes sense, they do take us somewhere concrete. The audiovisual eerie, on the other hand, takes us to a nebulous aural space whose re-visualization requires our own individual process of 'imaginative supplementation'. Because the obscurity of Lynch's texts already abound with surplus and slippery meanings and because his *concrète* sounds often lack a specificity, any attempt to (re)fabricate a source leads to further conundrum. It is this process that generates the 'sense of alterity' – a 'sensation that lie[s] beyond common experience'. Significantly, though, these moments recur across texts at similar moments of narrative and emotional upheaval. These pockets of audiovisual dissonance can be read as portals that link together projects in terms of affect, emotion and anxiety. Lynch's form of transmedia, then, is based not on augmentation but on discontinuity, ambiguity and repetition. It requires an unstable relationship between sound and image, or a shudder in the audiovisual fabric, to fully manifest – either through disembodied sound, ruptured or de-synchronized noise or through remediated textures replete with hauntological absence and a longing for times past.

It is immediately clear that Lynch's cross-media echoes are different to the ideas that underpin Jenkins's formative understanding of a transmedia story as that which 'unfolds across multiple media platforms, with each new text making a distinctive and valuable contribution to the whole'. Beyond the *Twin Peaks* group of films and artefacts, Lynch rarely indulges in sequels, spin-offs, novels and comics that extend fictional worlds or the pre-screening artefacts that preceded films such as *The Blair Witch Project* to extend and blend real and fictional worlds. Lynch's work operates in a less tangible way, with connections arising through a shared aesthetic condition rather than specific narrative occurrences or characters. This condition is apparent at both a physical level – through the interaction of sound with image – and at the level of affect – through the continual deferral of resolution.

While Lynch and his team have played with traditional forms of transmedial storytelling, then, they have also embraced more open-ended, eerie types of connections that lie beyond clear narrative gap-filling. Van Elferen goes some way towards this idea:

In this sense it is not surprising that the leitmotifs in Lynch's films are not tied to single characters or situations; they are designed to haunt diegetic, meta-diegetic, and extra-diegetic spaces alike, thereby loosening the boundaries between them. His soundtracks traverse the boundaries between these levels of narration, perception, and experience, and they can most accurately be described as *trans-diegetic.*[82]

While I agree with her reading, I want to end by going one step further to think beyond and between the boundaries of each cinematic representation to become transmedial. In fact, when taken together, the three layers of aurality that drive these worlds – room tone, Badalalemti's composed score and covers or lip-syncs of pre-existent songs – confute the notion of the diegetic altogether and offer instead an extended form of transmedial world-undoing. This refreshed form of transmedia, dominated by what remains unseen and unsaid, repositions attention from visual modes of storytelling to *audio*visual ones.

CHAPTER 17

When is a door not a door? Transmedia to the *n*th degree in David Lynch's multiverse

Greg Hainge[1]

May 21, 2017. A digital streaming platform. Laura Palmer (last seen in the analogue realm of 35mm and, before that, via terrestrial television or, perhaps, via the transmission of a magnetic imprint decoded via a helical scan dependent on a precise calibration of the differential speeds of the linear progression of VHS tape and the spin rate of the rotating playback head such that when the latter accelerates the former by a factor of 165, electromagnetic signals are transduced into the realm of perception) says to Agent Cooper (in the compound backmasking syntax of the inhabitants of the Black Lodge that bends time's arrow back on itself multiple times, sending us round the bend), from a point in time twenty-five years prior to now, 'I'll see you again in 25 years. Meanwhile...'. Fade to credits that begin with a fog-filled screen that seems to embody the very idea of the mists of time as through the haze there emerge images familiar from long ago, Douglas firs and Laura's prom photo. This though is not a simple redux, since, as the credit sequence continues, there is an uncanny sense generated out of the defamiliarization of nostalgia as well-known theme music slides over images that resonate strongly with their forebears but are at the same time very different, marked by the distinctly contemporary aesthetic of drone shots and HD. Cut to the Black Lodge, shot in the tones of another time as ?????? (later identified as the Fireman) tells Agent Cooper to 'listen

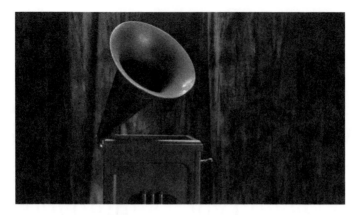

FIGURE 17.1 *Is it a gramophone or is it a portal? Image from* Twin Peaks: The Return, *Part 1 (David Lynch, 2018).*

to the sounds' and we cut to a shot of a gramophone from whose horn issue sounds that are not those of the technology that we witness (Figure 17.1).

While the opening of David Lynch's third season of *Twin Peaks* tells us very little that might elucidate the mystery left hanging twenty-five years prior that left an entire generation suspended in the meanwhile, less than five minutes into this new iteration, *Twin Peaks: The Return* tells us much about itself as a transmedia form, about all transmedia forms that speak always not only to their media but also to their time and the time of the media that they both supplant and prefigure. As Friedrich Kittler puts it, 'Media cross one another in time, which is no longer history.'[2] For Kittler, this has been the case since 6 December 1877 when Edison first presented a prototype of his phonograph to the public. 'Ever since that epochal change', Kittler writes, 'we have been in possession of storage technologies that can record and reproduce the very flow of acoustic and optical data'.[3] In doing so, what these technologies did was to render explicit a particular relationship of art to time:

> What phonographs and cinematographs, whose names not coincidentally derive from writing, were able to store was time: time as a mixture of audio frequencies in the acoustic realm and as the movement of single-image sequences in the optical. Time determines the limit of all art, which first has to arrest the daily data flow in order to turn it into images or signs.[4]

Yet what Kittler's analysis ultimately shows is not only the way that different media forms overlap in time, building on each other according to an evolutionary logic that adheres to the unidirectionality of time's arrow, but also the way that this engagement with time enables a reconceptualization of the very nature of time itself, from the time axis reversal enabled by the phonograph to the fission of pitch from length in Willis's experiments.[5] Kittler writes,

> Willis made a decisive discovery in 1829. He connected elastic tongues to a cogwheel whose cogs set them vibrating. According to the speed of its rotation, high or low sounds were produced that sounded like the different vowels, thus proving their frequency. For the first time pitch no longer depended on length, as with string or brass instruments; it became a variable dependent on speed and, therefore, time. Willis had invented the prototype of all square-curve generators, ranging from the bold verse-rhythm experiments of the turn of the century to *Kontakte*, Stockhausen's first electronic composition.[6]

The logic of this tight, symbiotic relationship between media forms and time that might be said to convert all media forms into transmedia forms is perhaps extended to its furthest extreme 100 years after this, however, as is explained by Norbert Wiener in his article 'Spatio-temporal Continuity, Quantum Theory and Music'. This is a major work in the history of a new approach towards composition and the production of musical sound that was to come to be known by the name of granular synthesis, but the primary aim of Wiener's article is to suggest that his own interventions into the field of harmonic analysis (as expounded at a talk in Göttingen in 1925, at a time when 'the world was clamoring for a theory of quantum effects which would be a unified whole and not a patchwork'[7]) pre-empted by some five years the development of quantum theory when Werner Heisenberg 'formulated his principle of duality or indeterminism'.[8] As Wiener explains:

> The classical physics of Newton is one in which a particle may have at the same time a position and a momentum – or, what is not very different, a position and a velocity. Heisenberg eventually observed that under the conditions under which a position can be measured with high precision, a momentum or velocity can be measured only with low precision, and vice versa. This duality is of exactly the same nature as the duality between pitch and time in music, and in fact Heisenberg came to explain it through the same harmonic analysis which I had already presented to the Göttingers at least five years before.[9]

If Wiener was himself more concerned with showing how it was he, rather than Heisenberg, who had formulated a quantum theory of the universe, what is of more interest for our purpose here is the fact that the phenomenon described by Wiener, because of the wave-particle duality of quantum entities or grains and the uncertainty principle that this brings into being, effectively splits apart position and momentum, time and space and this, in the musical realm of granular synthesis, means that time and pitch can be treated as independent variables – a discovery which, in turn, opens the way for the development of pitch shifting and autotune technologies.

Granular synthesis is a sound synthesis method similar to sampling but operating on a micro-time scale that consists of combining grains of sound together in different forms to produce sounds that could not be produced via conventional, analogue means (even if granular synthesis can produce sounds that closely resemble such sounds). In the musical realm, a grain is a microinterval of acoustic content, typically five to fifty milliseconds in duration, generally moulded into a number of envelope shapes intended to reduce the perceptions of 'clicks' when these grains are combined in sequence in granular synthesis. In descriptions of granular synthesis techniques, one often finds diagrams of triangular sound envelopes that are shown as either discrete grains (in an arrangement that produces a rhythmic effect) or else as regularly spaced overlapping grains. It is the latter configuration that forms the basis of pitch-synchronous granular synthesis, a technique that gives a temporal impression of a continuous pitch duration that can, as the density of grains used is increased, in effect compressing time, increase the amplitude such that we have the impression of a rise in pitch. In diagrammatic form, this looks something like this:

Spooky. This impossible confluence is not a simple gimmick with which to begin this short piece on Lynch's *Twin Peaks*, however, for I want to take seriously the transmedia possibility of finding in the heavily autotuned voice of Rebekah del Rio singing 'ya no hay estrellas' ['there are no more stars'] in part 10 of *The Return* everything that we need to know about Lynch's universe and, in doing so, to continue on in the transmedial spirit of Wiener, bringing together into one narrative space theoretical physics and artistic creation. Indeed, to start at the end – which is always the best place to start – what I want to suggest here is that when del Rio's autotuned voice sings 'ya no hay estrellas' it is, in both its content and form, giving voice to the fundamental principle of the Lynchian universe, its core operational and transmedial logic that has to do with a quantum view of existence in which time and space are produced out of the relations between particles dispersed throughout an entropic universe that is heading, inexorably, towards the heat death that will come when there are no more stars.

But let us now fast forward to the start.

If the concept of transmedia is taken to signify a certain continuity or recurrence that would be present across different media forms, then such can perhaps only be so at the expense of a consideration of the media itself in contradistinction to the content carried by those forms – which is to say their thematics. For, as I have argued elsewhere, if we turn our attention to a constant that is present across all forms of expression no matter the medium via which that expression is carried, namely noise, then this will tell us something specific about the particular medial configuration via which this expression is carried, which is to say something singular rather than constant. To put the argument in its most condensed form, far from being an external form of interference that enters into a communications channel to trouble the clear transmission of the desired semantic content of any expression (and taking all ontology to be relational, I take this term to apply to all Being), noise reveals to us something of the singular nature of the particular assemblage that gives rise to any expression, pointing us, then, to the medium out of which expression is contracted (be this technological or otherwise).[10] This is not to disavow the possibility of there existing something resembling a directorial signature that would be present across the work of distinct individuals in a transmedia landscape, or a consistent stylistics as well as thematics, but simply to suggest that this signature will itself always be determined in part by the specificity of the medium. This is perhaps nowhere more apparent than across the career and media forms of Lynch whose work has always been characterized by a deep reflection on the material specificity of the media in which he works – as he makes wonderfully explicit as *Twin Peaks* undergoes its media metamorphoses, *Twin Peaks: Fire Walk with Me* (1992) beginning with a television set being smashed with a bat and *Twin Peaks: The Return* emulating at key moments the buffering glitches that can disrupt the viewing of streamed content.

While moments such as these (and the recurrent trope of vinyl noise that we hear throughout Lynch's filmic output) are explicit avowals of this principle carried into the thematics of the work, the more general operation in play here is that media forms can but express something of their material specificity in the transmission of their manifest content. This point, if we pause to reflect on it, is both self-evident and entirely unsurprising. What is perhaps more surprising is that we can say precisely the same thing of these different media forms' *time*, which is to say that media forms are not situated in an objective temporal constant, universal time but, rather, that they produce their own time. On one level this idea is once more entirely unsurprising and, when we think about it, self-evident and intimately related to what we have said about the material specificity of different technological configurations.

The most obvious instantiation of this principle can be found not in the serial form of *Twin Peaks* or the feature-length running time of Lynch's films – which have to do in both cases with genre convention rather than technological conditions and capacities – but, rather, in Lynch's 1995 contribution to the collective project conceptualized and curated by

Philippe Poulet, *Lumière and Company* (1995). For this project, Poulet restored the Lumière Brothers' original hand-cranked Cinematograph, created film stock replicating the formula used by the Lumières and invited directors from around the world to make a short film under a set of constraints conforming to those under which the Lumières were obliged to work given the technological limitations of their set-up, namely, a single sequence shot of fifty-two seconds, no synchronous sound and a maximum of three takes. Lynch's short for this project, *Premonition Following an Evil Deed*, does not completely conform to this first constraint, coming in at fifty-six seconds. He *does*, however, fully respect the requirement to film in a single take, even if the techniques and multi-set set-up that Lynch uses could easily lead us to believe that this were not so. Cristina Álvarez López has expertly analysed the ways in which Lynch's short contravenes not only the temporal constraint of the cinematograph but also the spatio-temporal signification of the sequence shot as understood by critics such as André Bazin, for whom it is associated with a realist tendency in the cinema. For Bazin, heightened depth of field and long takes, in the work of directors such as Welles and Renoir, imbue film with the kind of objectivity that always, for him, necessarily inhabits the photographic image while enabling this logic to be extended out across time also.[11] Bazin's argument relies on the existence of there being such a thing as objective, universal time, of the space-time continuum being, precisely, continuous and self-identical across the entire universe. But, as Álvarez López points out, Lynch's short contests this version of reality and 'puts in crisis the very idea of reality as defined by its space-time unity'.[12] Going on to note the multiple and (from a common-sense perspective) illogical temporalities of Lynch's title, Álvarez López concludes her article with a vital insight:

> Lynch does indeed pulverize the sequence-shot, but only because his universe is one in which linear chronology and spatial succession have already been pulverized. From this destruction, something new emerges: the sequence-shot as expression of a (meta-)physical continuity between multiple times and spaces, as a perceptual short-circuit with its blackouts and whiteouts – an uncertain site where impossible connections happen.[13]

If Álvarez López's insight here is so crucial, it is precisely because it enables us to intuit something about Lynch's work that applies not only to this particular short but to many other works of his across many different media forms. This commingling of different temporalities, indeed, takes us back to Lynch's very first work, *Six Figures Getting Sick* (1966), in which he found the means to fulfil his desire to create 'a moving painting' – as explained in many interviews over the course of his career – and thereby liberate the Baroque art of painting from what Bazin would scathingly call its 'convulsive catalepsy'.[14] This commingling of different temporalities also, however, thrusts us into stranger, more discombobulating territory still.

Carlo Rovelli, in a book that sets out to explain quantum time and, in doing so, why we have been so mistaken for so long in our understanding of the nature of time, notes that

> the grammar of many modern languages conjugates verbs in the 'present', 'past' and 'future' tenses. It is not well adapted for speaking about the real temporal nature of reality, which is more complex. [...]
>
> What confuses us when we seek to make sense of the discovery that no objective universal present exists is only the fact that our grammar is organized around an absolute distinction – 'past/present/future' – that is only partially apt, here in our immediate vicinity. The structure of reality is not the one that this grammar presupposes. We say that an event 'has been' in relation to me but 'is' in relation to you.[15]

While this may be true in relation to language, Lynch's grammar across the diverse range of media he works in is resolutely not of this kind – and whether this grammar is inherent to these different media forms and only intensified by Lynch or else generated out of his particular treatment of them ultimately matters little. Take, for instance, his mixed-media painting *This Man Was Shot 0.9502 Seconds Ago* (2004), the title of which is painted onto the canvas on which we also see a man, arms spread as wide as his mouth, a crimson red explosion where his chest should be from which emanates a strange, bandaged protuberance labelled 'spirit'. The man's eyes are two voids in the middle of his face that interpolate us directly and in so doing the painting suspends us between two different perspectives, each of which exists in its own time. From the point of view of the figure before us, the catastrophic event of 0.9502 seconds prior has accelerated the entropic principle of all things in the universe to the point that time can no longer be said to exist at all, whereas for us, looking at this figure, time exists infinitely suspended between these two discrete moments, experienced not as a duration flowing across and between these moments but, rather, as the coexistence of two times 0.9502 seconds apart.

The kind of temporality that I am gesturing towards here is beautifully evoked by Marina Warner who writes that 'the plot of *Lost Highway* binds time's arrow into time's loop, forcing Euclidian space into Einsteinian curves where events lapse and pulse at different rates and everything might return eternally'.[16] What has perhaps not been fully appreciated up until the present time, however, is the implication of this for our broader understanding of the Lynchian universe.[17] For (and we are in the space available only able – fittingly – to rush over this far too quickly) if what Lynch presents us with is, in effect, akin to a post-Einsteinian vision of quantum time, then this is the case not only in relation to the temporalities at play in the diegetic content of his work but also the relations deployed across the works' plastic treatment of time. While the intervals at play are, of course, nowhere even remotely near the miniscule scale of Planck time (which is to say 10^{-44} seconds) 'at which quantum effects become visible', the *treatment* of time in Lynch's universe requires us to conceptualize time in terms of granularity which, in turn, requires us fundamentally to recalibrate our understanding of the concept of duration.[18] As Rovelli explains:

> The 'quantization' of time implies that almost all values of time *t do not exist*. If we could measure the duration of an interval with the most precise clock imaginable, we should find that the time measured takes only certain discrete, special values. It is not possible to think of duration as continuous. We must think of it as discontinuous: not as something which flows uniformly but as something which in a certain sense jumps, kangaroo-like, from one value to another.[19]

There is in what Rovelli writes here and elsewhere in this volume a great deal of similarity with those theories of the cinematic apparatus formulated by Henri Bergson and others in his wake intended, via a consideration of this prosthetic technology of perception, to enable us to intuit a different relation to time than that of our everyday common-sense apprehension of it. Take, for instance, the following pronouncement by Gilles Deleuze from the preface to the English translation of the second volume of his work on the cinema, *The Time-Image*:

> What we call temporal structure, or direct time-image, clearly goes beyond the purely empirical succession of time – past-present-future. It is, for example, a coexistence of distinct durations, or of levels of duration; a single event can belong to several levels: the sheets of past coexist in a non-chronological order.[20]

On closer inspection, however, it quickly becomes apparent that there is a crucial difference between what is suggested by Bergson and Deleuze's redeployment of the latter for his own ends and what is suggested by Rovelli. For Deleuze (and Bergson), indeed, there is something called time in which we are situated, that constitutes, in fact, our subjectivity, that is quite simply 'the interiority in which we are, in which we move, live and change' and that 'makes the present pass and preserves the past in itself'.[21] It is precisely out of this movement that the relations between the virtual and the actual are contracted, but here, once again, all is dependent on the *a priori* existence of sheets of time.[22] For Rovelli, however, and other proponents of the loop theory that he works on (or loop quantum gravity theory, to use its full name), time can never be imagined to pre-exist a relation but is, rather, generated out of the non-commutativity of physical variables in relation with each other.[23] At the root of theories such as this is the contention that there is no such thing as a time variable that would exist at the fundamental level and thus operate as a constant – a theory supported by the simple fact of the differential speed of clocks at different altitudes. As Rovelli opens the first chapter of his book, 'let's begin with a simple fact: time passes faster in the mountains than it does at sea level.'[24] At the quantum scale, this is to say – which is precisely the scale at which the evental nature of everything is made apparent such that we are no longer distracted by the surface effect of apparent fixed form ('*Everything* in the world becomes blurred when seen close up') or, indeed, by the limitations of our own temporal perception which simply cannot register phenomena deployed in the microintervals upon which such theories depend – time and space are not phenomena in which we are situated but produced only out of the relations between physical variables in a system.[25] Rovelli explains:

> The variables of [loop] theory describe the fields that form matter, photons, electrons, other components of atoms and the gravitational field – all on the same level [...]. The fields manifest themselves in granular form: elementary particles, photons and quanta of gravity – or rather 'quanta of space'. These elementary grains do not exist immersed in space; rather, they themselves form that space. The spatiality of the world consists of the web of their interactions. They do not dwell in time: they interact incessantly with each other, and indeed exist only in terms of these incessant interactions. And this interaction is the happening of the world: it *is* the minimum elementary form of time that is neither directional nor linear.[26]

This, I would argue, is far closer to the operational logic that we find in Lynch's universe than the formulations of Deleuze and Bergson, for it is a logic in which a non-chronological presentation of time is produced not out of 'the pre-existence of a past in general: the coexistence of all the sheets of the past; and the existence of a most contracted degree', all of these coming to constitute subjectivity itself, but, rather, from the generation of different times out of every different assemblage or set of relations such that a scene viewed from a different viewing position produces not simply a different perspective on the same scene but an entirely different scene taking place in its own space and time and, what is more, at its own speed – speed being nothing but the relation between time and space.[27] It is this logic that enables us to understand how it is that so much of Lynch's universe seems to be (for all of its coherence on many levels) split between two worlds.

Oftentimes this logic seems, indeed, to rend the world in two, into separate parts, but – as per the logic of granular synthesis which enables pitch to be fissured from time, for time to be stretched and pitch shifted independently and simultaneously – these two worlds can overlap or, perhaps better, be overlaid on each other, with the result that the different times produced by each of these worlds are connected and incommensurables commingle. The clearest example of this phenomenon comes with the instantaneously infamous 'gotta light?' sequence from *Twin Peaks: The Return*'s part 8 in which the Woodsman repeats this mantra in his time as the couple in a car he has accosted for a light scream in theirs, this scene taking place across the threshold of their car door. In this sequence (credited as taking place on 5 August 1956 in a small town near the New Mexico Desert where a nightmarish creature, part insect part amphibian, has just hatched from an egg), from inside the cab of a car driving down a road at night we see a series of figures shuffling across the road, stopping the oncoming traffic in its tracks. The driver of our car similarly brakes so as not to hit one of these lumberjack-clad figures, allowing one of them to make his way to the side of the car, lean in through the driver's side window, cigarette in hand, and say, repeatedly, 'gotta light?'. Distracted by him, the driver of the car and his wife have not noticed another of these figures creep up to the front of their car, making an already threatening scene all the more so as they seem to be surrounded. The driver's wife in the passenger seat starts to scream, but to scream and move at a different speed than the woodsmen outside, the pitch of her voice slowed and lowered to a horrific drawn out bellowing howl as the woodsman's gravelly voice continues to sound in 'real' time, which is to say his time and that is presumably here, then, also our time (Figure 17.2).

This ability to bend time into different speeds in the one space seems to be an innate characteristic of the woodsmen, as we see in an earlier sequence from this same episode after Mr C (aka Evil Cooper) has been double-crossed and shot by Ray Monroe.[28] Mr C falls to the ground and Ray goes to deliver the final, fatal shot but is distracted by a group of ghost-like, diaphanous woodsmen who emerge from the trees in the background, seeming to move

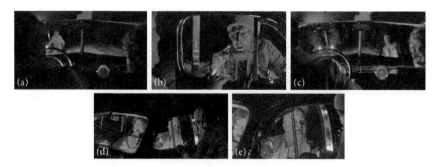

FIGURE 17.2 *The woodsman talks in his time, which is not that of the couple, over the threshold of the car door. Images from* Twin Peaks: The Return, *Part 8 (David Lynch, 2018).*

too quickly (and later too slowly). They gather around Mr C's body and grab at it obsessively, gradually covering him in blood and revealing an orb in which we see Killer BOB's face. From the moment the woodsmen emerge from the darkness, this entire scene is accompanied by a strange piece of music that is pitched so low and moves so slowly that it seems to resemble one of the droning industrial soundscapes found throughout Lynch's work more than anything we might classically recognize as music, yet careful attention (and videos of reverse pitch shifting on many a *Twin Peaks* fansite) reveals this to be nothing other than Beethoven's 'Moonlight Sonata' slowed down multiple times and consequently pitched down multiple octaves – a technique already deployed on Lynch's 'remix' of the Muddy Magnolia's song 'American Woman' (2017) that accompanies the first appearance of Mr C in part 1. Through a remarkable economy of form, Lynch's suggestion here seems to be that time is nothing other than the artefact of different realities, a suggestion that takes on enormous significance when viewed in the context of *Twin Peaks: The Return* which, according to Timothy Galow, is predicated on 'an unbridgeable temporal gap'[29] and which, if it is about anything, is surely (for both Lynch, his characters and his audience) about the temporal disjunct between different stages of life, about the different times produced not only by our media forms but the technologies of our own bodies which, it is now widely accepted, also entertain a different relation to time as they age.[30]

While made most explicit in these instances of temporal pitch shifting, the operational logic at play here is in fact present throughout this episode (and many other places besides). For Joel Hawkes, *The Return* repeatedly 'looks to make viewers conscious of the effect of [its] framing techniques [...] by emphasizing the dominance of the screen as a reality-mediating device (that bends time and space)'.[31] In this particular episode, however, the principle is far more fundamental, for the two sequences described above come either side of the extended sequence showing the explosion and aftermath of the Trinity Test that, according to the commentary on this episode that exploded all over the internet in the minutes, hours, days, weeks and months following its first airing, can be read as the genesis story of BOB. While this event is undoubtedly figured to be precisely this, given the transmedial logic of Lynch's work that I am attempting to unpack, it is also, at the same time, so much more than this, for it places us face to face with the highest expression of this operational logic out of which his entire universe is formed. As Michael Light explains in a note on the photographs of the 216 nuclear tests that the United States conducted between July 1945 and November 1962 (and published in a volume called *100 Suns*), a nuclear explosion is an event produced from a reaction at the atomic scale that generates incommensurate times, scales and speeds: 'In a hundred-millionth of a second, the temperature at its core builds to several hundred million degrees, many times the temperature of the Sun, and pressures reach a hundred million atmospheres, creating initial expansion speeds of about five million miles an hour'[32] (Figure 17.3).

The code name Trinity was chosen by J. Robert Oppenheimer in reference to John Donne's *Holy Sonnet XIV*, 'Batter my heart, three-person'd God'. In the context of Lynch's universe or, more specifically, *Twin Peaks*, this is an apposite reference point because this sonnet speaks to the struggle between good and evil, darkness and light that always coexist in Lynch's worlds. More than this, however, the very concept of Trinity speaks to a coexistence of different realities, of different forms of Being and, crucially, of the deep mystery that issues from reality thus conceived – a deep sense of irreducible mystery being an essential element of Lynch's imaginary. As he has said to Kristine McKenna:

> I love child things because there's so much mystery when you're a child. When you're a child, something as simple as a tree doesn't make sense. You see it in the distance and it looks small, but as you go closer, it seems to grow – you haven't got a handle on the rules when you're a child. We think we understand the rules when we become adults but what we really experienced is a narrowing of the imagination.[33]

As counterintuitive as it may sound, here also we come across a strange, impossible confluence, for what Lynch is suggesting is remarkably close to the view of theoretical physicist Richard Feynman, known primarily for his contributions to the field of quantum electrodynamics for which he

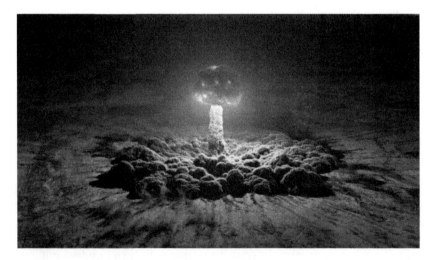

FIGURE 17.3 *The production of incommensurate scales and phenomena produced by Trinity. Figure from* Twin Peaks: The Return, *Part 8 (David Lynch, 2018).*

won the Nobel Prize in Physics in 1965. Across the course of his career, indeed, Feynman stressed again and again the vitally important role of the imagination as a necessary element of the scientific method in the face of the indisputable fact that we can have no access to an absolute understanding of the world around us. If this is so, it is quite simply because 'Nature's imagination far surpasses our own',[34] with the result that our imagination must stretch itself 'to the utmost, not, as in fiction, to imagine things which are not really there, but just to comprehend those things which *are* there'.[35] As much as Feynman seems to be at pains here to clearly demarcate different discursive practices, to delineate the world into two cultures in a manner not dissimilar to other contemporaries of his, the implication of his suggestion can be read in fact to take us in the very opposite direction and create a transdiscursive resonance that imbues scientific observation of the physical world with a metaphysical dimension and vice versa. 'We must frankly admit that *we do not know*,' says Feynman, before continuing: 'But in admitting this, we have probably found the open channel. [...] If we want to solve a problem that we have never solved before, we must leave the door to the unknown ajar.'[36] In saying this, Feynman provides us with what is perhaps the clearest description of Lynch's own methodology ever expressed in a work not about Lynch as well as a wonderfully lucid indication of the hermeneutic strategy that his work demands of us. And perhaps this is precisely what Lynch has been telling us all along, for, as John Alexander notes: 'Only in the American noir films of Fritz Lang do doors feature as significantly as an icon of intrigue as in the Lynch film; half-opened doors, slightly opened doors, doors ajar [...].'[37] More than this, however, and to return to our main concern here, doors – as Johan Fornäs has argued (with the help of Benjamin and Simmel) in relation to multimodality, intermediality and intertextuality (and thus, we can infer, transmediality) – are markers not only of intrigue but also (especially when they are ajar) of thresholds, of the transgression of boundaries, of passages towards other spaces, other times and other media.[38]

So let us now go to the end, which is, let us remember, where we started, and in doing so necessarily find ourselves somewhere else, not now at the start but at the end, the final part of *Twin Peaks: The Return* where doors (even though they have always played a crucial role in Lynch's universe) have perhaps never been so openly on display, never occupied so much screen time, never figured so blatantly as portals not so much to different spaces as different times, with characters on either side of their threshold cohabiting what appears to be a continuous space in different times (Figure 17.4).

Towards the start of this episode, it is MIKE who, in the compound backmasking syntax of the Black Lodge, asks the crucial question, namely, 'Is it future or is it past?'. This, though, as happens so often in Lynch's work, is somewhat of a red herring (or a blue key that won't open the lock before us) because for the question to make any sense it would be necessary for time's

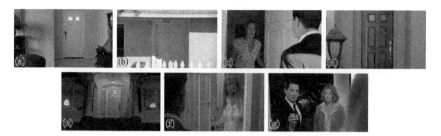

FIGURE 17.4 *Doors and thresholds. Images from* Twin Peaks: The Return, *Part 18 (David Lynch, 2018).*

arrow to remain intact and the entirety of this episode seems not so much to snap time's arrow in two or bend it back on itself as to pulverize it into grains, into microintervals that, when recombined, as in granular synthesis, produce an entirely new reality never seen or heard before. Nonetheless, having taken Carrie Page (who bears a more than uncanny resemblance to Laura Palmer) back to what he believes to be the Palmer household, Agent Cooper takes the bait and asks (attempting to understand how it can be that the inhabitants of this house know nothing of Sarah Palmer), 'Wait, what year is this?'. Carrie turns to look back at the house and we pause for a long beat. Faintly, as though an echo through time, we hear Sarah Palmer calling out 'Laura', which triggers a blood curdling scream from Carrie/Laura that echoes long after the lights in the house have gone out and the screen cuts to black.

These dying seconds of *Twin Peaks: The Return* function according to the same operational logic talked of throughout this discussion, an echo having much in common with granular synthesis insofar as it repeats and recombines a discrete interval of sound, this recursivity tearing a rift in the dominant logic of chronological time according to which any such return is impossible at the same time as it recalibrates the tight confluence of space and time that seems so immutable in our everyday experience.[39] And here also we return to the transmedia logic of all of our contemporary media forms which, from that historical moment pinpointed by Kittler, have always fought against the entropic principle of life and sought to give us access to an entirely different relation to time and, indeed, space. As we might expect by now, however, there is no such thing as a return to the same and so, finally, we must reformulate Kittler's formulation according to which 'time determines the limit of all art' to suggest instead that art, no matter the media form through which it passes into expression, determines its own time and that, as a consequence, we must never approach it through a hermeneutic framework formulated in advance but, rather, only ever through a constantly renewed contact that will itself generate the only sufficient reason possible, this meaning, of course, that a door is never just a door.

CHAPTER 18

On (vari-)speed across David Lynch's work

John McGrath

He [Lynch] said so much music [in general] would sound better if it were played slower.

– BADALAMENTI[1]

The glitchy post-classical editing of David Lynch's images is often matched with music that barely moves. We are treated to a store of visual symbols and tropes that have invited a great deal of critical engagement; yet the prevalence of sonic slowness is just as persistent and, when experienced in conjunction with the images, salient. This aesthetic of slowness and sonic immobility has been hitherto little discussed until now. In this module, Elena del Río investigates the ways in which Lynch's fascination with the sensibility of the formless enables differential energy to flow through various systems, while Greg Hainge draws on granular synthesis to show how Lynch's worlds trouble our understanding of duration and encourage the coexistence of different temporal and narrative planes. Holly Rogers understands such temporal disturbances and spatial concurrences as evoking a sense of the eerie, noting that moments of audiovisual dissonance open a space for formless granularity to arise. Building on these ideas, I focus in on Lynch's recurrent choice of sound and music that highlight slowness and 'slowing' across his work with film, TV and advertising.

Although having worked with music, music video, adverts, film and TV, Lynch's style is always recognizable. Directors who work with music video (such as Fincher and Gondry) learn to press musical elements into the foreground in order to create a sonically driven audiovisual flow.[2] By contrast, those who work in long-form format and film develop the skill of suggestion, which allows them to create the sense of before and after necessary for successful world-building. Often directors with experience in both forms are able to bring together techniques gleaned from these disparate formats and build an extended multimodal vocabulary. Although Lynch shares various techniques between projects, his preference for sonic slowness allows him to surpass formal and aesthetic boundaries almost entirely. Using recording techniques from mid-twentieth-century studio practice, the director extends variations in sonic speed and pitch to his audiovisual work to form a transmedial practice that allows his film and TV work to take on musical form.

By all accounts Lynch works fast, making quick decisions in order to tap into the particular audiovisual frisson and flow that comes with on-set spontaneity, as Dean Hurley, his long-time sound editor/collaborator (*Inland Empire* (2006), *The Air Is on Fire* (2007), *Twin Peaks: The Return* (2017)), notes:

> David likes fast. You'll hear him in interviews talk about action, reaction – in a perfect world, that time is close down to nil. That's why he likes digital, because he can act and react, and he can manipulate close to real time.[3]

While maintaining spontaneity on set is central to Lynch's working process, his sonic content is less hurried and many of his projects are awash with extremely slow pre-existent and/or newly composed music. A brief primer might include Chris Isaak's 'Wicked Game' (1989) that plays a central role in *Wild and Heart* (1990) and for which Lynch also directed the music video; the slow, ethereal singing of Julee Cruise that stretches across several of Lynch's projects; Roy Orbison's 'In Dreams' (1963) that drives the pivotal miming scene in *Blue Velvet* (1986) and 'Crying' (1961) in *Mulholland Drive* (2001); Lynch's ominous ambient compositions in *Inland Empire*; the 6/8 space-rockabilly and vibrato guitar swells of his diners and roadhouse joints; the musical collaboration with Lykke Li; and the slow Badalamenti drones of *Twin Peaks*.

Working with slow music and sound is one thing, but physically slowing down a pre-existent recording takes this penchant for slowness to another level of affect. Hurley's account of a recording session for *Twin Peaks* gives a good sense of how the vari-speed technique formed a fundamental part of their collaborations:

> That's how a lot of how 'Twin Peaks' sound was done. For example, Cooper getting shot in Part Eight and the Woodsmen coming out of the

black. There's this bassy plume of tones that are happening in slow-mo. It's a very dark track. He wanted to take Vladimir Horowitz's 'Moonlight Sonata', which is a composition he loves, and slow that down ... the equivalent of dropping it two octaves.[4]

Vari-speed is the process of speeding up or slowing down the recording (tape initially, now predominantly done through digital emulation). Like tape, an emulator (such as that included with Logic Pro X or Avid) will also manipulate the pitch at the same time so that speeding up makes the pitch frequency higher as a result of increasing the rate of oscillation and vice versa.

Developed in the late 1950s, vari-speed presented a solution to technical problems in the studio. It might enable a singer to sound younger, for instance, a possibility explored by David Seville when he recorded 'Witch Doctor' in 1958; recorded at half speed, the track delivered his quintessential chipmunk effect when returned to normal speed.[5] A few years later, the vari-speed technique became synonymous with the Beatles – in 'Strawberry Fields Forever' (1967), it enabled two very different takes to be combined, for instance. The dreamy mood evoked by the speed and pitch matching is fundamental to the sound of the record, while the unique vocal timbres on other songs like 'Lucy in the Sky with Diamonds' (1967) are the result of the same technique.[6] Many subsequent pop musicians have employed vari-speed along similar lines: Prince, The Beach Boys and Led Zeppelin to name a few.

The ability to manipulate speed and maintain the same pitch is a much more recent technology as Alexander Rehding writes: this new ability 'has effectively severed the connection between the temporal aspect of sonic frequency and the temporality of sound duration'.[7] Steve Reich first strove for such a technology (though not yet available) in *Slow Motion Sound* (1967), a composition that included 'direction to slow down recorded sound while retaining the original pitch'.[8] We can now easily achieve this via digital audio workstations (DAWs) – such are the evolving affordances of music technology.

Despite his access to modern technology, Lynch shows a continual preference for techniques taken from mid-century music recording practice. During an interview on his sound work with Lynch, for instance, Hurley recalls the director's request for the 'John Lennon vocal effect'.[9] Beyond the influence of Lennon's signature vocal doubling and use of automatic double tracking ((ADT) – pioneered at Abbey Road), perhaps this request also points to the Beatles as formative in Lynch's penchant for vari-speed. The director doesn't appear concerned with preserving the pitch when he slows things down; in fact, he uses the strangeness of pitch manipulation as an essential compositional tool: 'It's a mood – you slow things down for a feeling,' he explains.[10] This taste for older tech is echoed by the often lo-fi aesthetic of the cinematography and video footage employed in his visual work.

Lynch has experimented with vari-speed throughout his career – manipulating tapes and relishing slowing time. Chris Isaak's 'In the Heat of the Jungle' (1989) is slowed down to half speed for the backyard motel sequence in *Wild at Heart*, for instance. In *Twin Peaks: The Return*, the technique appears at several pivotal moments: 'American Woman' by Muddy Magnolias (2017) is slowed down and mixed with eerie noise when Cooper's evil doppelganger is first introduced (episode 1), allowing the low, stretched lyric 'Do I look like' to assume a new and uncanny meaning, while Beethoven's drastically slowed down 'Moonlight' Sonata (1801) is juxtaposed with images of the woodsmen 'healing' a shot Mr C. in the moonlight of episode 8 – mentioned by Hurley above.[11]

Lynch's creative world is a collaborative one and his relationships with sound designers and composers are often long-standing. It is significant that tempo manipulation manifests differently through various collaborations. Besides Hurley, we see Lynch's aesthetic of slowness echo through Angelo Badalamenti's drone-based soundscapes. Recalling the making of *Twin Peaks*, the composer describes how he initially provided what he terms 'firewood' – clips of sounds and musical material – that Lynch would then manipulate and experiment with before adding into scenes alongside the score. When working with his 'firewood', the director would sometimes reduce the speed ×2 or even ×4 not only to better match the visual rhythm but also to determine the audiovisual affect.[12] Rather than focusing primarily on audiovisual syncs or rhythmic coincidences, instead an affective connection between sound and image is built upon through this slow mood aesthetic.

In the long form of a TV series or feature film we often see Lynch slowing down material and stretching time – the temporal canvas allowing for certain emotions to subtly manifest. This filmic expansive gesture often needs long periods to establish. In the short form of adverts however, message and delivery are sped up. An example of Lynch speeding up a motif transmedially occurs in the score for the 1991 Public Service Announcement (PSA) for 'Clean Up New York', an anti-littering campaign. Here, Lynch's black-and-white avant-garde noir style is augmented by a vari-sped iteration of *Twin Peaks* material – the 'Stair/Danger Theme'.[13] This leitmotif generally adumbrates a sinister event in the series, a lurking threat, something hiding in the bushes (episode 17); it itself appears vari-sped within *Twin Peaks* on a number of occasions, sounded at half speed as Cooper lays out the evidence in episode 8 and again as Leland plays golf in his office in episode 15 for instance.[14] The PSA advert is set in a dark and gloomy New York City overrun by out-of-control vermin. A series of cuts portray various careless and irresponsible citizens dropping food wrappers and waste onto the street while a subterranean ominous presence lurks (Figures 18.1 and 18.2). The music begins with a bass melody reminiscent of Bernard Herrmann's opening leitmotif for *Citizen Kane* (1941). Thirty-six seconds in and we begin to hear the 'Stair/Danger Theme', but sped up so as to match the frantic pace

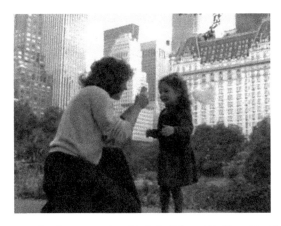

FIGURE 18.1 *A mother litters in New York in 'Clean Up New York' (Lynch, Public Service Announcement, 1991).*

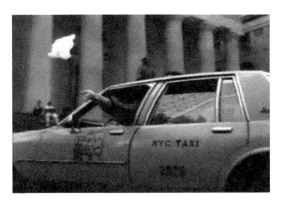

FIGURE 18.2 *A New York cab driver throws litter from the cab window in 'Clean Up New York' (Lynch, Public Service Announcement, 1991).*

and terror caused by the depicted rats. This is distorted intertextuality. The familiar bass ostinato and two-note string and brass motif have increased in pitch while the percussive clicks and hits are shriller and unsettling as a result. The sudden shriek of the advert's climax is a direct vari-speed manipulation of the 'Stair/Danger Theme'. Music is foregrounded here; the timbre of the vari-sped brass glissandi is particularly eerie due to the uncanny and unique nature of the manipulated frequencies.

Lynch has worked on various adverts, as Holly Rogers discusses in this volume, but what marks out this particular advert is the fact that that its music is something we've heard before. The powerful PSA imagery of a city overrun with rats as a result of littering is matched with the frantic high speed of the vari-sped 'Stair/Danger Theme'. This works in two ways. First, the vari-sped music is perfect for the advert, as its fast pace and high pitch signal an appropriate frenzied terror. Second, it also operates on a meta, intertextual level. While the audiovisual pairing delivers a nightmarish dystopian vision of an eerie cityscape, it is one that is uncannily familiar. The dark, foreboding tension where mysterious forces lurk under the surface, so apparent in the worlds of *Twin Peaks* is here transplanted to the murky cityscape. Where once there was mist, now there is smog. Do these intertextual references colour the audiovisual harmony, forcing us to find parallels between the two locations, or does the interaction of familiar sounds with new images render a dissonance? While the audiovisual success of the advert does not rely on recognition of the leitmotif, it certainly adds layers of signification that operate at various levels for those aware of its resonances. Yet the audience must listen hard. Because the shorter canvas of the advert contrasts with the vast time-frame of the *Twin Peaks* world, the sped-up theme is condensed, concise and powerful. Thus heightened, the vari-speed version retains its associations while forcing a new level of urgency necessary for the limited canvas of the commercial. As the leitmotif from one format is altered and transplanted into another, might this reiteration also colour our reinterpretation of *Twin Peaks*? As the world-building spills into other forms – across the internet, through releases of archived footage and sound material, even into branded coffee – the anti-teleological or anti-linear narrative theme of Lynch's work is well suited to this play with vari-speed and of sound worlds without end.

CHAPTER 19

Journeying into the land of the formless real with Lynch and Simondon

Elena del Río

A door is not a door but a threshold. If doors separate distinct, adjoining spaces, thresholds join spaces and render them communicable by facilitating the passage of energies and forces between them. If a topology of thresholds appropriately describes the dissolution of identities and the bending of the space-time continuum/linearity in David Lynch's cinema, one may ask if a strictly formalist lens is still the most conducive to understanding how this cinema operates. By putting into question the usefulness of a straightforward formalist approach to Lynch's films, it is not my intention to invalidate the auteurist argument that attributes a directorial signature to a series of works sharing a recurrent and recognizable series of motifs, iconic objects, themes and so on. Yet, in this case formal recurrence alone is not as important to the ontology of this cinema as is the transitory or fluctuating mode in which forms appear and operate therein. In this sense, morphology/formalism may be less productive a method here than morphogenesis/ontogenesis, the process that traces the emergence and mutability of forms. This brief discussion of Lynch's work in the context of transmedia is therefore aimed at proposing two ideas that run counter to traditional scholarship, although they are hinted at to varying degrees in all of the Lynch chapters in this collection: First, I want to draw attention to Lynch's films as direct engagements with the real in their attempts at enacting the ways in which reality itself operates; and second, over and against formalist assessments of his cinema, I want to stress the formless as the ontogenetic force behind it.

Drawing attention to the formless is not to dismiss form altogether, but to pinpoint its mutable, provisional state. The formless is indeed invoked in this very sense in the other Lynch chapters in this volume. Holly Rogers alludes to it in her account of the weird intrusions in Lynch's cinema as 'marked by an exorbitant presence, a teeming which exceeds our capacity to represent it'.[1] Greg Hainge's allusion to doors-as-thresholds, one that inspires the opening sentence in this chapter, and his reference to Cristina Álvarez López's description of Lynch's sequence shot as an 'expression of metaphysical continuity between multiple times and spaces'[2] again hints at this cinema's fluidity of form, as does John McGrath's technical discussion of overlaid, poly-rhythmical soundtrack composition in Lynch's transmedial work.[3] Obviously, the category of the formless is still dependent on form, as form and the formless are but two phases in a dynamic and relational activity that traverses the real down to its invisible, infinitesimal levels. But my choice to favour the formless is meant directly as a critique of late capitalism and the media culture we inhabit in their overwhelming fetishization and oversaturation of form. Such obsessive attention to form, I would argue, occurs at the expense of an account of in-formation as process, the taking on of form as constant variation. In this regard, I propose a reading of Lynch's transmedia cinematic practice as an effort to revalorize the force of the formless. Indeed, the transmedia impetus in Lynch's cinema is key to activating the operations that enable the constant variability and instability of form as implied in my privileging of the formless.

To describe Lynch's cinema as a cinema of the real and to see it as an instantiation of the formless is to state the same thing. For all its alleged distortions and contortions of reality, Lynch's transmedia practice does not betray the real, but rather only a certain narrow tradition of cinema realism. In point of fact, I would suggest that this cinema offers us one of the closest and most complex views of reality as it unfolds below the surface level of formed substances. If the real cannot be encompassed by the latter (and only someone very naïve would think so), hence cannot simply be accessed through visual/formal representation, one has to find ways to 'render visible forces that are not themselves visible' (Anne Sauvagnargues).[4] This is not a matter of rescuing a depth that connotes subjective interiority, but a matter of mimicking an operational model of reality primarily attuned with affects and forces that push forms into becoming otherwise, and more than they are, at each instant. It is in its rejection of substantialism that Lynch's cinema intimately resonates with Gilbert Simondon's philosophy of individuation and in-formation. My contribution to the section on Lynch in this volume will therefore suggest a few ways in which Simondon's conceptual apparatus helps us understand the operational force of Lynch's transmedia cinema, an affective-performative cinema that actually makes things happen, hence modelling the ontogenesis of the real itself. Specifically, I will be discussing the transmedial qualities of Lynch's films in reference to Simondon's conceptualization of the operation of individuation and the corollary concepts of the pre-individual, transindividual, metastability, information and transduction.

A great number of scholars have found Deleuzian film theory and philosophy to be productive tools in assessing Lynch's cinema, this author included. Simondon's philosophy, which Deleuze found intensely resonant with his own, provides us with yet another set of conceptual tools whose specificity matches the media operations in Lynch's cinema to an uncanny degree. Given the well-documented relations between Deleuze and Simondon, it may be germaine at this point to address these relations and to consider what exactly Simondon's conceptual apparatus adds to Deleuze's notion of becoming. While Deleuze's philosophy, and in particular his work on cinema, have by now been considerably integrated into film and media scholarship, film scholars have not yet engaged with Simondon's philosophy of individuation to a comparable degree.[5] Yet, as Anne Sauvagnargues has observed, Deleuze was significantly indebted to Simondon, from whom he borrowed the concepts of disparation, modulation and crystallization, all of which became decisive in Deleuze's analysis of art.[6] The two philosophers shared a strong opposition to substantialist approaches (where being is governed by notions of substance, form and matter) and a firm understanding of being as becoming. The uniqueness of Simondon's perspective, in my view, lies in the way he looks to the scientific field, especially thermodynamics and cybernetics,[7] to fashion concepts that can operate transversally across different existential territories and can offer rather concrete models for understanding the operations that take place in any process of individuation, be it human or non-human, individual or collective.

On the assumption, therefore, that Simondon's thought may be relatively unfamiliar to film and media scholars, I would like to start by offering a summation of some of his key ideas relevant to this discussion. First and foremost, Simondon's notion of individuation-as-process is meant to overturn substantialist views of the individual, self or subject. His concept of metastability is central to individuation as perpetual ontogenetic process. Metastability addresses 'a type of equilibrium no longer situated at the level of stability, but implying the transformations operating in a system which has not exhausted its potential difference'.[8] Second, the individual is 'incompatible with itself', as it is 'always more-than-individual'.[9] Simondon conceives this 'more-than-individual' as an 'excess of pre-individual being' in the individual subject.[10] The pre-individual belongs to the collective and constitutes the latent presence of the collective within the individual. It is this impersonal, yet intimate, dimension of the collective that is addressed in Simondon's notion of the transindividual. The transindividual thus expresses a form of individuation neither synonymous with isolation nor with sociability/socialization; rather, it involves an experience of solitude that is simultaneously a 'milieu densely populated with relations'.[11] The transindividual surpasses social functions (it is not an expression of social taste or opinion) as well as outright individual isolation. Indiscernible qua individual, the transindividual shares an impersonal affective life with others in its milieu.

When we look at Lynch's transmedia cinema through a Simondonian lens, we can detect a shared rejection of substantialism and hylomorphism in both their respective domains of cinema and philosophy. The hylomorphic doctrine is based on the Aristotelian distinction between form and matter.[12] Hylomorphism assumes that form is generated through the imposition upon inert, passive matter of a pregiven abstract form.[13] By contrast, for Simondon, form and matter do not relate through static opposition or hierarchy, but they are both 'made present as forces' that inform each other in mutual tension and modulation.[14] The Simondonian example Muriel Combes uses to explain this mutuality of force is the relation between the mould and a piece of clay. The clay brick individuates as an energetic system that brings into contact the clay's own 'potential for deformations' and the mould's function as a 'limit imposed on these deformations'.[15] Thus, form and matter emerge as co-constituted by the same flow of 'energetic materiality in movement' in which they are equally caught.[16]

For Simondon, then, being is not about identity, but about a transductive operation perpetually in the making: the exchange of information as differential energy between systems. Here I'd like to emphasize the importance of the prefix trans- to both Simondon and Lynch. For now, I'd like to connect this prefix to the idea of the formless by way of the constant variability of form: its transitory or transitional nature. Rogers's discussion of Lynch's 'audiovisual eerie' in this volume touches on this elusiveness of form and identity when she writes that in Lynch's cinema, 'rather than the substantiation of specific character, plot or ... event, connections between works can manifest at a more elusive, conceptual level'.[17] The idea of an individual person possessing a fixed or permanent identity is equally ludicrous to Lynch as it is to Simondon. An unfinished, continuous process of individuation gives rise to successive individuated phases of the self. To understand the energetics and psychosomatics involved in Lynch's transmedia cinema, we'll begin by examining how the process of individuation works in his films: as a relational operation continuously in flux.

For Simondon, the process of individuation entails a joined configuration of individual and collective. Individual and collective do not pre-exist their relations. The individual cannot gain a sense of self through pure psychic interiority, and, inversely, the collective does not consist of pure exteriority detached from the psyche. Individual and collective undergo successive individuations, and, furthermore, they individuate simultaneoulsy in a thoroughly co-constitutive, relational manner. Simondon does not consider the group as an ensemble of individuals, but pure relationality. What constitutes the basis for this relationality is a surplus of being that at any given moment makes the individuated body or group more-than-individual, more than itself – a pre-individual, pre-personal zone of potential that is never exhausted as individual or group pass through successive individuations. This pre-individual share is indeed the non-structured field of potential that pushes both individual and collective towards further individuations.

Take, for example, the account of individuation enacted in *Inland Empire* (2006), a film that foregrounds the collective to an unprecedented degree in Lynch's work. As I've argued elsewhere through the prism of Leibniz's philosophy of the fold,[18] in this film, the individual (or rather, an unfolding series of individuated individuals played by actress Laura Dern) becomes individuated in relation to a collective field of affects. These affects are experienced by, and circulate among, many other, in this case female, individuals (Nikki/Sue/Lost Girl/chorus of female prostitutes). In this process of individuation, the individual encounters a pre-individual zone of unstructured potential. The outlines of a particular individual are of less consequence to the film than is the pre-individual affective potential that moves and is exchanged among many. The prominence of this pre-individual unstructured share of potential is such that it dissolves a coherent, identifiable individuated subjectivity. Yet the price of incoherence is well worth paying for achieving a surplus of energy and creativity that surpasses and annuls the distinction between individual and collective. *Inland Empire* activates this surplus of vitality afforded by the pre-individual in order to carry out a transformation of pain into joy, paralysis into movement. Insofar as the pre-individual is a force of immanence that disrupts the self-other dialectic, the film does not feature Dern/self versus others, but Dern's many individuations/instantiations of self in relation to a collectivity of women with which her own experience amply resonates.

How is Dern, through her several incarnations of women differently positioned with regard to class and cultural background, capable of reaching and inhabiting this suprapersonal psychosomatic intuition of the collective? By discovering the transindividual, 'the mode of relation to others constitutive of collective individuation'.[19] Although the collective is latent within the individual in the form of a pre-individual excess, the individual has to pass 'through an ordeal of solitude'[20] in order to effectuate this pre-individual potential and to reach the transindividual collective. Paradoxically, this ordeal of solitude, which in *Inland Empire* emerges out of a hair-raising experience of violence and pain, is not about narcissistic isolation. Instead, solitude coexists with the forging of a dense network of relations with a multiplicity of others. The transindividual relations that bind Dern to an unquantifiable collectivity of women are not of the order of an intersubjective sociality based on socio-economic functions or interests. Instead, we find an affective collective with a strong energetic affinity – a similar experience of having lived through and beyond an affective ordeal of violence and abuse by men. Such affective collectivity revolves around the differential movement between a diminishing and an augmentation of the body's powers/affects in a Spinozan sense.[21] Dern's discovery of the transindividual manifests itself in an augmented capacity to feel and is thus an active/performative actualization of the more-than-individual each individual bears with itself. In this regard, the concept of transindividuality runs counter Maurice Merleau-Ponty's premise that the self cannot fully feel for or in place of the other, insofar as an unbridgeable chasm separates each individual's affective experience:

> Paul suffers because he has lost his wife, or is angry because his watch has been stolen, whereas I suffer because Paul is grieved ... and our situations cannot be superimposed on each other. If ... we undertake some project in common, this common project is not one single project, it does not appear in the selfsame light to both of us ... simply because Paul is Paul and I am myself. Although his consciousness and mine ... may contrive to produce a common situation in which they can communicate, it is nevertheless from the subjectivity of each of us that each one projects this 'one and only' world.[22]

In contradistinction with the phenomenological irreducibility of individual subjectivity, Simondon's transindividual posits the 'intimacy of the common' as a structuration of emotion that coincides with the emergence of the collective. As Combes notes, for Simondon, 'Intimacy arises less from a private sphere than from an impersonal affective life, which is held immediately in common.'[23] Among the multiplicity of the pack, or the collective in Simondon's sense, Dern is the anomalous or exceptional individual who, having discovered the transindividual, effectuates the power of the pack by becoming both its most intense instantiation of pain and 'its most active site of transformation'.[24]

The way in which a diversity of media in Lynch's films are shown to coexist and reverberate with each other is not substantially different from the operations of individuation just outlined: 'There is an individuation of modes of thought, by the same token by which there is an individuation of modes of physical, technical and vital individuation.'[25] As we shall see, the fact that we think of media as apparatuses/technologies of enunciation does not strictly differentiate their process of individuation from human individuation as such. I alluded earlier to the importance of the prefix 'trans' to both Simondon and Lynch's departure from substantialism. Just like Dern as transindividual refers to a zone of potential that can only achieve effectuation in the relational, collective field of existence, the concept of 'transmedia' leads us beyond a consideration of media as isolated, independent modes/systems of expression, communication or information.

A transmedial cinema, especially in the non-substantialist version practised by Lynch, thus points to the becoming of media as 'more-than-themselves'. The 'more-than' charge here arises when we stop thinking of media merely as physical objects or communicational tools and we attend to the pre-individual zone of potential or energy activated and shared by different media when they are brought into a relation of affective proximity. In this zone of transmedial affectivity, a medium does not coincide with itself, nor with another medium it relates to; rather, their relationality suggests a qualitative leap that creates something new and oddly incorporeal, which, I would suggest, is precisely what is involved in the concept of transmedia.

As has been said in the other Lynch chapters in this volume, this transmedial quality in Lynch is inseparable from the undoing of the world,[26] the dismantling of fixed notions of interiority, exteriority and of the space-time linear continuum. A vivid example of the indivisible ties between transmedia and transpatiality/transtemporality occurs in *Inland Empire*'s final scene when the Lost Girl is finally liberated from her imprisonment – her imprisonment not so much by Phantom Man as a physical being that keeps her captive as by affective forces that she alone cannot transform. The Lost Girl sits in a hotel room looking at a TV set where images of the film itself unfold. This TV that does not function as such, but more as an affective screen, transmedially resonates in these closing moments with images that recall the kinaesthetics and the blurring of the line between individual and collective typically enacted in the music video. Images of Dern coming into the room and kissing the Lost Girl as a handsome prince would kiss a beautiful princess held hostage against her will are overlaid with 'Polish Poem', a song composed by Lynch and Chrysta Bell (2006) and imbued with a heightened sense of relief and tenderness. The force of love in the song is then visibly transducted into a potent blue light that holds the women's bodies in its embrace. A couple of girls are seen joyfully running in the hallway somewhere near or perhaps far, but certainly in close affective proximity. What matters here is not this particular inscription of music video aesthetics nor the TV presence, but rather the co-systemic, transpatial and transtemporal functioning of these media as catalysts and relays of energy. As Rogers puts it in her thorough discussion of Lynch's transmedia cinema and its audiovisual eerie in particular, 'As sound is wrestled from the image, it is allowed to take on a life of its own ... *we are asked to question whether this life was ever dependent on the physical apparatus at all.*'[27] The crucial operation involves one of two things: either linking the unlinkable/incongruous or unlinking that which we expect to be linked. Just as identity in this cinema is dissolved beyond recognition, the media forms that are showcased lose their distinctive contours to become disparate, yet resonant, modulations of energy. Media become transparent, translucent, incorporeal, pure threshold or passage, in Rogers's words, 'ethereal forms of transmedia'.[28] As both Rogers and Hainge suggest, transmedia here entail a loss of medium-based specificity,[29] an idea that reaffirms the prominence of the formless in Lynch's cinema.

This formlessness, of course, extends to the affects themselves, which in Lynch are always in a state of fluid agitation/vibration, not in the solid, stable forms we call emotions. This state of affective agitation is sometimes felt by the spectator as cognitively arresting and disorienting, experienced more as Artaud's visceral shock than as Brechtian alienation. Take, for example, the scene in *Blue Velvet* (1986) where Ben (Dean Stockwell) lipsyncs Roy Orbison's 'In Dreams' (1963). This performance, like all performances in Lynch's cinema, functions as a 'disorganizing force' in the film, not only because 'it disables the narrative inertia toward coherence', but also because 'it functions as a whirlpool of affective energies' that are connecting disparate worlds and values. These unwieldy energies 'disrupt the rigid moral patterns that structure our emotional and affective experiences'[30] and generate 'emotions for which we do not have a name'[31] – notably here by forcing a coexistence between Ben's moral perversion and the affective intensity that nonetheless radiates from his performance of the song. In Simondon, the coexistence or proximity of disparate affective zones is the very catalyst of individuation. Such disparation of energies functions here not only within the scene but it also extends into the relation between consecutive scenes. Thus, towards the end of the song, Frank (Dennis Hopper), who has been mesmerized and transported by the song beyond his sadistic self – momentarily bringing in the potential for a new individuation – swiftly shifts back to his usual mode of active aggression.

To finish this incursion into Lynch's world of the formless real, I will give a brief account of the ways in which several interrelated concepts that Simondon finds in the sciences – thermodynamics and cybernetics in particular – concepts such as metastability, information and transduction can further elucidate the ontogenetic operations of Lynch's transmedial cinema. It is because of the quality of metastability – a system's 'provisional equilibrium subject to constant perturbation'[32] – that Nikki in *Inland Empire* can turn into affluent Sue into white-trash Sue and on into a proximity with the Lost Girl and the chorus of prostitutes. This constant mutation is not rooted in psychological contents or processes, but in an exchange of forces experienced as affective contagion. Thus, we can now relate metastability to Lynch's practice of transmedia as described above – a transmedial approach that wrests importance away from the specificity of media apparatuses and instead uses these simply as catalysts of transformational energy. This understanding of transmedia transcends the discursive levels of allusion and self-referentiality to involve a performative model of reality as event-in-the-making, or ontogenesis.

Take, for example, the Lynchian convention of the film-within-the-film in *Inland Empire*. Besides stretching the theme of female abuse by men across temporal and cultural divides, the film-within-the-film serves as the material support for the activation of metastability, as it provides a stage for Dern's mutating identity from Nikki into Sue and so forth. Something akin in terms of the protagonist's metastable identity, yet also drastically different in tone, takes place in the film-within-the-film as it plays out in *Mulholland Drive*. Here, we are given clues as to Betty's (Naomi Watts) potential individuations, ones that are visualized, yet never actualized, by the film. Elsewhere I have discussed the unforeseeable intertwining of looks and faces between Betty and Adam (Justin Theroux) in the scene in *Mulholland Drive* when Betty walks onto the set where Adam is pretending to audition several girls for the leading role in his film. I have described this intense meeting of gazes as 'a moment straight out of the virtual', an affective force that is incommensurate with the 'rules of reproductive/repetitive coherence that classical narrative is compelled to follow'.[33] In Simondonian terms, this virtual affective force would remain a part of the unstructured ground of pre-individual potential, which, like Frank's unactualized potential in *Blue Velvet*, is not to become a part of Betty's individuations in the film. Yet, these moments are of vital importance for signalling the primacy of operation and potential over structure, of the formless over form.

Simondon divorces information from anthropocentrism and ties it into a philosophy of nature. (As Juho Rantala says, 'There can be information without consciousness, but not without a system.')[34] Energetic, affective circulation is what Simondon understands as information: the passage of energy between disparate systems that enter into a dynamic relation or synergy. In-formation, in Simondon's philosophy, has nothing to do with the distribution of data or the acquisition of knowledge, and everything to do with a system taking on of (new) form through an energetic process whereby a signal/energy is exchanged between heterogeneous systems. Virtually all of Lynch's films enact the process of 'propagation of energy within a domain', explicitly materialized in Lynch's propensity for featuring flickering, unstable sources of light that are operative rather than decorative, that is, actively engaged in the activation and circulation of differential forces. We can see a highly elaborate and prolonged instance of the activation of information in the discombobulating series of sensations that takes hold of Betty and Rita's (Laura Elena Harring) bodies at the Club Silencio in *Mulholland Drive*. As in Simondon's notion of information, an overhauling of these women's former selves propels them into a new individuation, a new level of material existence. This upheaval is spectacularly staged as a dynamic relation of energies circulating between stage and audience and provoking an affective experience beyond the tolerable. In this scene, an MC conducts a performative/ontogenetic event where he conjures up sounds and affects out of the virtual. The transmedia backdrop of the scene – the stage performance, the emphasis on recorded sound and lipsyncing – is entirely incorporeal and is not reliant on the specificity of physical apparatuses, but rather on their suitability to becoming immaterial catalysts for an exchange of energies. It is this effective and operative immateriality that the recorded status of the sound gestures towards and not its illusory or deceiving quality. What matters is the real, in-formational power of these energies and the qualitative leap that their coming together can activate. As Massumi explains, 'The moment of invention is when the two sets of potentials click together, coupling into a single continuous system. A synergy clicks in. A new "regime of functioning" has suddenly leapt into existence. A threshold has been crossed, like a quantum leap to a qualitatively new plane of operation.'[35]

Information in this sense is closely related to the concept of transduction, which involves 'the operation whereby a domain undergoes information … a physical, biological, mental or social operation, through which an activity operates from point to point within a domain'.[36] The formation of a crystal provides a clear illustration of transduction. As Sauvagnargues explains it, 'Beginning with a very small seed, [the crystal] grows in every direction within its pre-individual milieu, each already formed layer serving as the structuring basis of the next molecular stratum in the process of being constituted through an amplifying reticulation.'[37] Transduction thus refers to the processual, continual folding and unfolding of individuation. We can find this transductive quality of individuation ostensibly at work in any Lynch film that 'pick[s] up on an earlier detail seeded in the original film'.[38] A motif, image or sound is thus extended or transformed so that it becomes otherwise while still retaining its original formative seed/impulse. Such endless layering and elaboration upon an original impulse can also be referred to Lynch's habit of working with an ensemble of actors that have been featured in his films for decades. Likewise, his transmedial penchant for stages, red curtains, lipsyncing performances, just to name a few of his formal attachments, involves a desire to keep inventing an interminable series of fluid, metastable forms. It should also be noted that this process of doing while undoing, undoing while doing, takes place at a high speed, that is, it is intensely affective and discomfiting, since the flow of information does not encounter visible, and even less audible, obstructions that might impede its passage. We are thus back into the realm of thresholds. That is partly why scholars have found sound in Lynch to be an even more compelling site of this undoing of form, given sound's ability to escape any and all frames. While the image presents a greater proclivity towards form, a non-anchored sound or a sound coming from unseen worlds can enhance the ephemerality of the image or intensify the speed of its mutation.

Transduction is thus at the heart of the mutating powers of individuation. This transitory, formless quality of identity, which I have developed here in terms of Simondon's theory of individuation, is also evoked in Deleuze's emphasis on difference over identity. As he puts it in *Difference and Repetition*, clearly inspired by Simondon, 'when the identity of things dissolves … things are reduced to … all the differences … through which they pass'.[39] This constant movement that passes unimpeded through thresholds is crucial to understanding the thrilling and disquieting effects of Lynch's cinema. The proximity of this cinema to life and to the real lies precisely in its perpetual state of perturbation. Just like 'life lives on a moving threshold of metastability',[40] so do Lynch's films. Still, Simondon, like Deleuze, can only provide us with a method that approximates, without ever capturing, the movement of continuous transformation in Lynch's cinema. As all the chapters in the Lynch segment of this volume attest to, we may even be able to explain the process of this movement, but its eeriness is left for us to feel in largely unexplainable ways.

PART SEVEN

Multi-vocality, synchronicity and transcendent cinematics: Barry Jenkins

'Let me show you what that song really is': Nicholas Britell on the music of *Moonlight*

Dale Chapman

In the 'diner' sequence of Barry Jenkins's 2016 film *Moonlight*, Chiron, the film's quiet protagonist, has driven from Atlanta to meet up with Kevin, a friend from his youth, who now runs a greasy spoon in their childhood home city of Miami. Their reunion is charged, given a moment of intimacy that they shared in an earlier time in their lives; this is especially true for Chiron, an African American man whose awakening of gay male desire had rendered him vulnerable to bullying and abuse during that earlier time.[1] The Chiron that returns from Atlanta now goes by the name 'Black', 'trapping' (dealing drugs) in the wake of the prison term he served for confronting his high school tormentor.

In the midst of the diner scene, Kevin punches in a song on the jukebox, and then looks meaningfully over at Chiron as the opening strains of Barbara Lewis's 'Hello Stranger' (1963) saturate the aural space of the scene. The sequence is given a tremendous assist by Lewis's song itself. As a song, it's happy to reside at length in its own textures: at the beginning of the first verse, where we expect to hear Lewis's lead vocal entry, the sonic space is occupied by a fulsome male doo-wop harmonization; Lewis takes her time with the song's greeting ('He-ello stranger...'), as if allowing the song's protagonist to revel in the felicity of reunion. Everything about the song reinforces the overall *slowness* of the scene, its own willingness to linger.

The pace of the diner scene is anticipated by the length of the sequence preceding it, where Chiron shuts off the car (and its music), changes his shirt, brushes his hair, adjusts himself – and then the tracking shot follows behind him for the entirety of his walk across the parking lot to the diner. What further intensifies the quiet of Chiron's walk is the reverberant sub-bass of the track that bookends the diner scene, a 'chopped and screwed' setting of Jidenna's 2015 song 'Classic Man', deploying the distended, elongated sonic manipulation specific to this Houston-based production style.

This mix of 'Classic Man' is held in tension between its lyrical content and its musical setting: the lyrics emphasize the singer's gentlemanly qualities, his fashion sense, his politeness with women, his generosity with his friends – all of which, in the *Moonlight* version, is packaged in a thunderous trap aesthetic, with crisp hi-hats, shuddering sub-bass, vocals saturated with autotune pitch correction. The 'chopped and screwed' production in the song's *Moonlight* version pitches Jidenna's vocals down by an interval of a third, giving them a hardened aspect, even as it gives the listener more time to absorb their message of gentlemanly virtue.[2] There is a contradiction in the song that seems to embody Chiron in his act three persona as Black: encased within a hard, streetwise, impenetrable self, hiding in plain sight, is another Chiron, one that hasn't been granted an opportunity to fully realize itself.[3]

* * *

Moonlight mobilizes music, image and cinematic form in the service of a story that must be understood as irreducibly intersectional: as Michael Gillespie argues, *Moonlight*'s attention to temporality necessarily refuses the easy congealing of its characters into essentialist tropes, and dramatizes the inescapably *dynamic* means through which its characters navigate blackness, masculinity, queerness and their mutual constitution.[4]

Music and sound serve as privileged points of entry to the distinctive temporality of *Moonlight*. Beyond the film's exquisite use of source music, the underscore provided by composer Nicholas Britell – whose other recent film credits include *12 Years a Slave* (2013), *The Big Short* (2015) and Jenkins's adaptation of James Baldwin's *If Beale Street Could Talk* (2018) – serves as an especially vital touchstone for understanding *Moonlight*'s aesthetic range and emotional power.

In *Moonlight*, Britell alters the terms of conventional non-diegetic film scoring, subjecting the score's classical tropes to the hyper-real digital manipulations available to hip-hop producers. The end result is a ground-breaking application of a 'chopped and screwed' aesthetic to the processes of film composition, an approach to production that allows Britell to radically foreground the dynamic fluidities of the characters' subject positions: in the film's three chapters, chronicling the transformation of quiet 'Little' through the brittle, vulnerable 'Chiron' to the emotionally opaque 'Black', we hear a sonic manipulation of the emotional textures underlying these shifts in character and their constitutive masculinities.

Britell's underscore punctuates the film's long moments of quietude with a searing, fragile beauty. In the first chapter of *Moonlight*, following Chiron as 'Little', Chiron is taken under the wing of Juan, a local drug dealer who sees in Little something vulnerable and precious; their relationship is crystallized in a scene where Juan takes Chiron to the beach to teach him how to swim. As Juan teaches Little how to float on his back, tenderly cradling his head, the two actors are shot with the camera next to them in the water, from beneath the level of the horizon, with waves sloshing over the camera's point of view; we feel ourselves to be there with Juan and Little, in the turbulence of the waves.[5] We hear a delicately arpeggiated violin solo emerge from the drone figure in the score. As the arpeggios unfold, becoming more virtuosic in their realization, Britell's choice of harmonic language becomes ever more deeply expressive, moving from a reinforcement of the tonic to an exquisite passage of chromatic voice-leading, the descending bass line held in tension with suspensions in the violin's upper voices. As Britell notes, arpeggiation has the effect of individuating notes, and it is only the *unfolding of time itself* that reassembles them as harmonic progressions; in this way, the violin figuration of this sequence brings us close to the immediacy of time, in all its intimacy and dynamism. Jenkins understood this scene to be enacting a moment of 'spiritual transference' between Juan and Little, an intensification of their relationship (Figure 20.1).[6]

The arpeggiated violin cue from Juan and Little's swimming scene reappears in two other crucial moments in the film, near the breaks between the Little/Chiron chapters and the Chiron/Black chapters. In the first of these two instances, Paula, Chiron's mother, has returned home following a

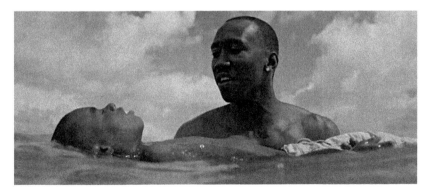

FIGURE 20.1 *Juan and Little in the waves: from the opening chapter of* Moonlight *(Barry Jenkins 2016), scored by Nicholas Britell.*

confrontation with Juan, where he condemned her for her ever-increasing drug use (which his own product made possible) and the harm that that portended for Chiron. Standing opposite each other in the hallway of their apartment, Paula and Little stare at one another in silent mutual antagonism; the reverb-laden fragments of the arpeggiated violin cue shimmer in the background here as Paula suddenly screams at Little, her words inaudible as all sound in the diegesis is cut out. A variant of this scene returns at the beginning of the third chapter of the film, now a memory manifested as nightmare: in the sequence, as a distorted, pitched-down version of the violin figuration undulates in the background, a buzzing hum intensifies to a point of arrival. In a reversal of the first hallway sequence, the buzzing peaks and abruptly cuts out, and this time we actually hear Paula's shout in all of its raw fury, screaming at Little, 'Don't look at me!' Chiron, now fully grown as 'Black', wakes from the dream.

Britell notes that part of the beauty of the swimming lesson sequence resides in its precariousness: during the shooting, as a serendipitous accident, a storm had begun to gather, casting a shadow across Juan and Little's moment of shared joy. For Jenkins, according to Britell, the swimming lesson presages all that was to come for Little – the joy of Chiron's life, as embodied in the moment of Juan and Chiron's communion; and intimations of difficulty and despair, as indexed by the storm clouds and the roiling chromatic turbulence, the shifts of major and minor, inscribed in the musical setting of the sequence. By extension, Britell suggests that the *return* of this musical material – filtered, distorted, digitally time-stretched and partially pitched down, in accordance with the remix aesthetic of 'chopped and screwed' – casts a different sort of shadow: it arrives at a moment of traumatic import for Little, a moment in which the shadows of unrealized possibilities linger in his mind as he faces his mother's frustration and rage. Here, too, music becomes a powerful vector of temporal connections, linking the immediacy of the charged moment to past memory and future possibility.

* * *

The following conversation with Britell, which has been edited for length and clarity, took place by phone on 14 March 2019. Our discussion ranged across a variety of issues salient to Britell's score for *Moonlight*, extending from his collaboration with director Barry Jenkins to the importance of hip-hop aesthetics and production methods in his approach to film composition.

People have mentioned in interviews the use of the 'chopped and screwed' aesthetic, particularly in the context of 'Little's Theme'. One of the things that occurs to me – and this has I guess more to do with the use of Jidenna's 'Classic Man' as a bookend symmetrically on either side of the diner scene – is the way in which it teaches us a kind of *slowness*: there's an aesthetic posture built into 'chopped and screwed' that's about a general slowing

down, it seems to be a way of training the viewer to approach that diner scene and that dimension of the movie in a particular way. I wonder if that was something that you had thought about in terms of the music of *Moonlight* in general or your contribution to it.

I think that with 'chopped and screwed', that was something that, literally the first time I met Barry, he talked about his love of 'chopped and screwed' music. He knew that he had wanted *Moonlight* to have a score that had potentially a 'classical' sound, where you could really feel that this was real people playing instruments, that there was a sense of *humanity* in that. He knew that he didn't want an electronic score, for example. So right away, I had a sense from Barry that he wanted a classical score, but at the same time he was talking about how much he loved 'chopped and screwed' music, and pretty quickly we came upon this discussion of, well, is there a way to actually do *both* of those things? What if I were to write pieces of music, that maybe were, say, more in a classical idiom, but what if I were to take my own recordings, and 'chop and screw' those? And I think what was so exciting for us was these early experiments [with the 'chopped and screwed' sound] immediately felt like they were connected to the picture. They just felt like they were telling us something about not just the *ideas* in the movie but the *progression* of the ideas in the movie and the way that the story would develop.

I think to your point about slowing things down, there's a *deepening* that happens over the course of the film. As we learn more, there's maturation that's happening, the ideas themselves are growing and getting deeper, and the *music itself* is getting deeper. And the music isn't just going down [in pitch], it's actually being chopped and screwed. So, 'Little's Theme' in chapter one is in D major, Chiron's theme in chapter two is in B major – so we're lower; Black's theme in chapter three is in A major, which is again lower, and the cello version of it, which is Black's theme, was actually recorded in the same key as chapter one, but it was screwed down so you're now in A major. You're not just hearing cellos playing lower, they actually were playing higher, and I'm [digitally] *moving* them. I'm *making* them sound lower. So we had this wonderful result. That was wonderful for us, that feeling of this classical music that basically had more *low end*, this classical music that has this almost hip-hop feeling, it's almost hip-hop production. And yet, internally, these are cellos and pianos.

I think that one of the things that we [Britell and Jenkins] were both fascinated by was how much potential this felt like there was right away with this idea. Because, as you've already mentioned, Black is *listening* to 'chopped and screwed music' [just before the diner scene]. So there's also a connectivity between the diegetic music and the process we're following in our non-diegetic score – the audience is very much linked with the characters almost across the screen. They're linked through the screen, because there's this connection between what is essentially source and what is actually score. We're saying there's a link between us in the audience and this world.

In the press, I'm seeing less discussion of this incredibly beautiful cue that first appears when Juan is teaching Little to swim, and it's this arpeggiated, partita-like figure. It struck me almost as analogous to a Bach partita, in the sense that it's this mixture of arpeggiation, and just this beautiful set of suspensions that are pulling you into the scene, into the world of Juan and Little. Then we see it again later, at those two crucial moments where Paula is confronting Little in the hallway, where we're looking straight on with Paula, she's framed symmetrically in the doorway, and at a certain moment she screams at Little. In the first one, her voice is blocked out of the diegesis, and in the second one, the score cuts out and *she* is what we hear. I wonder if you can talk a little bit about that cue and what you think it's doing emotionally in the context of the film.

I remember with this scene, this was something that, actually my initial instinct was *not* right. [Laughs] My first take when I saw the swimming sequence was that, I had been thinking, okay, let's take 'Little's theme', let's take this idea – there's this perfect fourth that's going back and forth, this – [sings the perfect fourth] – and I was saying, what if I modulate this, what if I do this in F major, what if it's more of a string orchestra cue – so I was already feeling a little bit more of the large scope of this moment, but the emotional landscape where I was saying to myself, okay, this is a beautiful moment in Little's childhood. He's learning to swim, this is the one father figure in his life, this is something memorable and something very special. And I played this [version of 'Little's theme'] for Barry, and he was basically like, 'Nope!' [laughs] He said, 'this isn't at all what I'm feeling'.

Barry said to me, here's the way I see this: this is a spiritual baptism. He's in the water, this is the beginning of the rest of Little's life. We have to understand here a sense of where we're going in Little's life: all that is to come, presaging that in some sense, and how in the arc of the storytelling it's really crucial that he felt *that* way, *there*. So that sense where he said a sort of spiritual baptism there, for me, I think immediately I changed the tonality of what I was experimenting with. I was like, you know what? This is D *minor*. This isn't F major. [laughs] And I think one of the things that I did – I had always been fascinated with the idea of arpeggios, especially on a monophonic instrument; a lot of string instruments are essentially playing one note at a time, even if they can do double-stops. And it's *time itself* with arpeggios that creates harmonies. I feel that's something so beautiful that the notes are individuated, and yet it is our experience of time that puts it together in our mind that creates these harmonies. There was something about the sense of arpeggios and time and feeling – you mentioned those suspensions – just feeling the complexity of that moment. I started exploring that sound of these arpeggios, and I just started writing the piece.

So I created an instrumental demo of that for Barry. And then I notated out [the] music, and I actually notated out [what is] essentially a violin cadenza, in a lot of ways. It's almost this concerto-like cadenza texture, so soloistic and [to record the part], I called up Tim Fain, who had recorded 'Little's Theme'. He recorded it, and I actually did it separately, I recorded the violin separate from the orchestra, in two parts, and then I mixed them together. By recording them separately I actually had a lot of control over the mix. Because it was really important to be able to control how the violin sat in relation to the orchestra. What that also did was help me answer the *rest* of your question [laughs], because by recording the violin separately I had control where I could 'chop and screw' it.

So that's what I did, if you notice in the scene with Paula in the hallway, which I believe on the soundtrack was called 'The Spot', because it comes from there, that moment and there's also the 'don't look at me!' moment. Basically, I 'chopped and screwed' that violin. But the idea in that [cue], I remember initially, that was an experiment. Once we had that idea for the swimming sequence, once this was there, it immediately opened this door of like, wow, this is a crucial musical idea, and how does it play into the rest of the film? The way it plays is that it actually continues on in a morphed form. I guess you could almost say that there's sort of this *shadow* of this idea, which is being cast over and linked with Paula.

I think that was how that happened, but also it's a very orchestral moment, and as you know, there's a lot of *Moonlight* that's very intimate, very *consciously* intimate. There's also a lot of *Moonlight* that is solemn. The big moments ... it's very clear why they need to be big moments to us, because there's such a heightened level of feeling. And the music is there to basically reaffirm that, in a lot of ways. But similarly, all the silences are incredibly conscious silences on our part, where *the world* is the score at that point, where we want to be alone with the characters.

Actually, when you are alone with those characters it's the silences that are even more powerful and [that] speak louder. And it makes you appreciate or hopefully understand why the score exists some places in life, doesn't it? I always feel for me personally at the end of the film, when it's Black and Kevin in the apartment, the silence there for me is just so powerful, and I remember experimenting with, you know, where do we put the music? Is there music here? And it just felt like, no, there's no music here. They're finally together; let's just let their togetherness speak for itself. And it's only once we have had that experience that those very individual notes of Kevin's theme come back right before the ending credits.

Yeah. And it occurs to me, too, that there's elements of the sound design that seem really to kind of accentuate that. So as Black is walking closer to the diner door, it's this incredibly long sequence, but I could swear that that they're ramping up the street sounds, that it's intensifying the street sounds during that moment.

I will often meld [extramusical] sounds in with my music. For example, there's a couple of places where the sea sounds that you hear at the beginning and the end of the movie are actually sounds that I was creating. I actually almost sort of performed those sounds, which had this ocean-and-sea kind of experimental stuff that I was doing. Because there was a certain crescendo that we wanted to have happen at certain moments, I was actually able to play those in, in addition to the actual ocean sounds that may be in the sounds there. I think that the sounds are really a big part of *Moonlight*, because the ocean has a *meaning* in *Moonlight*. It's almost this other realm, where truths are revealed and told. If you think about these moments that happen on the beach – with Juan, with Kevin and then at the very end, the final shot – the ocean is a very special place in the film, and there's also a musical correspondence that, when we're near the ocean, oftentimes there's the sound of that tremolo string, the sort of shaking of the bow on the string that you hear in the piece [from the swimming sequence]. That's the thing that you hear [in] the 'Metro Rail Closing' track, when Chiron is walking to the beach, the last thing that you hear is that shaking of the bow. It's actually the same exact [thing].

I think Barry and I have almost these musical symbols that we think about when we're working. We even weave stuff in, like the sequence when Chiron goes into the school to fight back, the hi-hat sound that you're hearing in that piece is actually the sound of him and Kevin 'high-fiving' at the beach. I basically sampled the sound and started using it as an instrument. Then when you see him put his hand on the doorknob, to go into that actual classroom, that last thing you hear is the 'slap'. That is the sound of them high-fiving, from that more beautiful time in their lives. It's speaking to, I think, this idea that the musical world that we're trying to create is something where we're not trying to tell you *what* to feel. We're hoping to try to evoke the actual *experience* of feeling some of these things. So by for example weaving in the sound of those hands connecting, in a beautiful moment, it's almost like you can imagine the swirling ideas and emotions that are going through Chiron's head at that moment. We were thinking, what if that memory [of the high-fiving], that moment, is almost ricocheting in his head? Because that's how emotion actually works. I feel that's how those moments [are] in our lives, when something is really crazy like that, you feel those things swirling.

This process that you talk about in terms of 'chopping and screwing', and pitching down 'Little's Theme' and this arpeggiated cue that we hear on the beach and then subsequently in the two encounters with Paula, it also reappears with a slightly different setting, with Kevin cooking at the diner. That's a moment where we get him and this almost ritualistic kind of attention that he's putting into the preparation of the meal. I guess that seems like another resonance of that same moment that's continuing through Little's life in that way.

There's this motif, this descending three notes that's like [sings motif], that sort of an idea – which is the 'Chef's Special' track that I think you're talking about when he's cooking. That, actually, for me, was distinct from the Juan-oriented or the Paula-oriented stuff. For me, that scene was actually linked to the ending of the movie, which is both the end credits, and also the music that you hear at the end of the beach sequence, and the music when he and Kevin are in the apartment at the very end, that I think we called 'Who Is You?'. For me, those are very linked, and also linked with Kevin's smoking: that night-time scene that comes in the dream, the Kevin dream, basically. I think when I was writing that idea, Kevin's theme itself had elements of Little's theme connected to it. [The] top of the melody, it descends, it has this [sings motif], which is actually Little's theme up top – the fourth, the perfect fourth going up and down.

I guess it's just an aesthetic thought [of mine] that, I often feel that a direct leitmotif is not always the best usage of thematic material. Because stories are complex, and we understand that characters are complex. I think sometimes the notion of a leitmotif is almost too 'on the nose': I see this person, so I hear their identification. [laughs] We don't need that! 'Little's Theme' is Little's theme, of course. But, the ways in which I think about these sorts of thematic ideas is that they're always somehow in relation to other things happening. So 'Little's theme' is Little's theme, it's his theme in relation to the world, and his theme *in relation to* the other characters. Even with the Kevin motif, the Kevin motif does tend to happen around Kevin, but it's also about Kevin and Chiron. You know, it's Kevin *with* Chiron.

You were a member of the hip-hop group the Witness Protection Program, you remarked that this was an especially productive time of your life for musical creation, that you were cranking out two or three different beats a day, that you were playing synths and keyboards with the group on the road, and working intensely during that period on audio studio production techniques. We were wondering how that particular moment may have shaped your later approach to film production, on the other work that you're doing or in *Moonlight* specifically.

I deeply believe that hip hop is the most significant art form to emerge in the past fifty years. I think that it's this summation of a continuum across history of how music can relate to *other* music. If you look back at the continuum of music over the past one hundred years, there were so many beautiful original jazz compositions, but actually a lot of jazz was also improvisations, for example, on American songbook Broadway songs. So jazz is already taking on this kind of metaperspective of music *about* music, in a way. You know, it's, 'I know you know that song, but let me *show you* what that song really is.' And I think hip hop is saying, 'oh, you know these songs *and* you know these recordings, but let me show you what these are.' [laughs] I think that's just mind-blowingly amazing.

I was always fascinated with why hip hop *sounded* the way that it did. So those years when I was in my band, I would spend pretty much every waking hour just experimenting with hip-hop production techniques and trying to understand how these tracks were made, what made them sound that way, what made the drums sound that way – how *were* these tracks being sampled, and what was the nature of that sound? I think that on a musical form level, I think there's something about the way in which the elements within a hip-hop track are introduced. Oftentimes there's a sample that gets introduced, and then maybe a bass comes in, and *then* the drums come in. Or, maybe there's just an a cappella vocal – and then the beat just drops. Or this sort of *staggered* nature of the form and how it all kind of builds and all comes together as one. I don't know why, but that's just always been something that I found really powerful on a musical level.

As far as your question about audio production in particular, I think one of the reasons that I was able to immediately approach this question of 'chopping and screwing' classical music with Barry [in *Moonlight*] was because I knew immediately how to do it! When he started talking about it, I was like, 'Oh, I can do this *right now*.' There was not even a hesitation in my mind about how to approach that. It felt like this amazing opportunity to use this knowledge and this experience that I had, which was just, thousands of hours by myself in a room, you know. [laughs]

I feel very strongly that music isn't just about the notes. Music is about the sounds as well. It's about the feeling of the sounds, and the storytelling that the sounds themselves have. I think that in particular on *Moonlight*, when Barry was saying to me this idea of real instruments with humans – and it feels almost *tactile* – I purposely kept in the recordings the sounds of the musicians *breathing*. You can actually hear Tim [Fain] taking breaths. We kept those noises in, and that's not a mistake. That was a conscious choice. I *want* to hear that because for me that's so much more evocative, and I think if I go back and I listen to some of my favourite hip-hop tracks – if I'm listening, let's say, to like, Gang Starr, for example, if I'm listening to 'Moment of Truth' and hearing these samples, it's not just a beautiful Ellis Marsalis track being sampled, it's also the *sound* of that. It's not just the sound of the recording, but also the process of sampling itself, like you're hearing record player sounds, you're hearing the vinyl sounds. And again, these are all of our own personal responses to these things, but I just think that's so powerful, and so evocative that, you all hear the story of the music when you hear those tracks, you hear the *many* stories in the music. It's almost like you're going through time when you hear these tracks.

CHAPTER 21

If Beale Street Could Talk, what'd be playing in the background? First notes on music, film, time and memory

Kwami Coleman

Film and sound recordings are illusory temporal media that require elapsed, clock time[1] for playback and consumption. They are illusory in that each medium sets forth with unfolding events that may be nonlinear, cyclical and otherwise abstracted: in film, a scene sequence that distorts or fractures the chronology of the narrative or perhaps the frame rate of a particular scene (i.e. slow motion); and, in music, tempo, metre (incremental or fluid), strong accents against a uniform metric pulse (syncopation) and architectonic recurrences or transformations of motivic material in formal structure (i.e. *sonata allegro* form). Film and recorded music creators understand that their craft, in one way or another, requires the manipulation of at least two senses of time: that of the interior world of an art piece, which unfolds against the unyielding incremental ticking of exterior, 'real world' clock time.[2]

This somewhat adversarial phenomenon invests in these media forms a layered temporal texture, where the standardized clock time – the primary means by which the modern subject conceives of quantified, passing time (which is spent travelling to work, earning a day's salary at work or watching a film and listening to an audio recording – an act that accompanies the workday commute, or happens during social leisure time afterwards and in between work) – parallels and intersects with the more fluid and malleable dreamlike time in film and recorded music. In fact, it is this latter more pliable time that makes film, for the French philosopher Henri Bergson, who was perhaps the first serious cinema theorist, a medium for realizing temporal flow, except for Bergson, whose *Matter and Memory* (1896) came at the precipice of the twentieth century, the flipbook-like artifice of early film had not yet matched the flexibility of the mind in recalling the past (memory) and envisioning the future (imagination).[3] However, as we know, cinematography in the last century is if anything an achievement in temporal multiplicity and dislocation. I want to suggest that these discrete layers of temporality and the play in between them propels the intersubjective drama of Jenkins's *If Beale Street Could Talk*, and music in the film opens up the possibility of conjuring for the viewer more than memories from the characters' past but their ideation of themselves in an epochal moment. My point is that clock-time quantification – the objective 'exterior' duration – of the sound recording played back, diegetically, in the film measures time in the narrative and evokes a historical moment when black music, in the form of late-1950s and early-1960s jazz and rhythm and blues, speaks to the subjectivity of the film's characters' as they relate to themselves and their external world.

In the 2018 film adaptation of James Baldwin's novel *If Beale Street Could Talk*, written for the screen and directed by Barry Jenkins, with an original score by Nicholas Brittell and music supervision by Gabe Hilfer, play between musical time (interior world) and music-in-clock-time (exterior world) is a means by which an important dimension of the narrative drama is conveyed. In the former, which is Britell's score, the viewer is able to grasp, by his use of leitmotiv, perhaps the most important narrative trope: the ardent inner emotional world of the two protagonists, Tish and Fonny – one that is held steadfast by their seemingly eternal love for each other (in the novel, as in the film, Tish is the narrator, and the plot of both is composed of her recollection of memories which, perhaps due to the media, unfolds more linearly in the novel than in the film). The outer world of clock-time duration is folded into the plot via diegetic jazz recordings,[4] like Webster Young's 'The Lady' (1957), which appears forty-six minutes – almost halfway – into the film; its playback accompanying Fonny's reunion with an old, recently jailed friend, Daniel Carty.[5] The folding-in of durational clock time (via music) is something possible in the film, and not in the novel. Young's track is then followed quickly by Miles Davis and Bill Evans's dolorous 'Blue in Green' (1959), which supports Carty's climactic and foreshadowing testimony of events leading up to his unspeakable incarceration, and plays through Tish's returns to the scene. At no point does any character change the record on the phonograph; these two recordings blend from one to the other, elapsing without interruption in the scene (and with only post-production cuts). They work to time the dialogue by measuring its length and pace, echoing the tone and mood of the conversation (as Fonny may have subconsciously intended when he put the record on, before the scene begins), and they convey to the viewer an important facet of the characters' identities as young black New Yorkers enveloped in a discussion of the issues most central in their lives.

The records that play underneath and around Fonny and Daniel's dialogue, as they sit around the kitchen table smoking cigarettes and drinking beer, situate the viewer in an early 1960s New York City where these recordings, especially for its African American residents, in Harlem and around the city, completed the aural dimension of social life. For sure, the late-1950s jazz recordings used in Jenkins's *Beale Street* are meant to evoke a young, bohemian and multi-racial Greenwich Village counterculture, yes, but also its specifically black subculture; one that was connected to Harlem, but also miles away – miles from the parents and maybe even the world view of their pre-war generation of migrants, as both of Tish's parents were.[6] As much as jazz influenced the post-war white hipsters of the Village,[7] it was still a black vernacular culture, one part of the continuum of black American music, not completely excised from rhythm-and-blues and more ancient forms.[8] These jazz records are part of the material culture of these three young black adults: objects vested with a power to articulate how or what they want to feel, and their playing of the phonograph in the film constitutes an act that is both ephemeral and permanent in its repeatability.[9] What 'sounds' is a dimension of their identity: their (inter-)subjectivity; how they understand themselves, each other, and their world, at roughly three minutes a track and thirty minutes a side per LP.[10]

The most parturient moment is when Fonny and Tish's first make love, at 32:50 minutes in. This scene is one of Tish's memories, appearing in the film just after her deeply unsettling encounter with Fonny's mother and two sisters who, called over to Tish's family apartment in Harlem to learn that she's expecting, curse her and the unborn child. The camera cuts to Fonny's basement apartment on Bank Street after their magical wander through Greenwich Village, and follow the two protagonists as they walk in, both timid, knowing fully well where their hearts are leading them. They slowly disrobe and kiss each other carefully; here, Britell's score divulges the trembling warmth felt by each with a soaring cello melody floating atop tremolo strings ('Eros'), but this commentary fades to the scene's rain-pattered silence as an almost-nude Fonny, sitting with Tish on the bed, with both ardor and fear, stares plungingly into her eyes. After a moment, he lovingly covers her newly bare body with a blanket, kisses her another time, then stands, walking over to his phonograph in just his trousers. He then guides the stylus onto the platter, shuts off a light, and unbuckles his belt; as this happens, a rhapsodic piano passage introduces them (and the viewer) to the John Coltrane Quartet's profoundly tender interpretation of 'I Wish I Knew', from their 1963 album *Ballads* (Impulse A [S] 32). This, the first track of side two, plays as Fonny walks to the bed, kneels into Tish's embrace, and joins her for the first time (gently whispering, before he does: 'Don't be scared. Just remember that I belong to you. Just remember that I wouldn't hurt you for anything in this world. You're just gonna have to get used to me. And we got all the time in the world. Hold onto me.'). The title alone, for viewers who recognize the song, is too suggestive to be insignificant. We hear Tish gasp, and the track, with Coltrane not yet at the ending phrase of the melody, fades out with reverb as the camera begins to pan away to respectfully give the lovers their privacy.

The next image the viewer sees, tellingly, is the needle coasting the lock groove – the inner-most ring of a vinyl record – that spins in perpetuity until a listener manually lifts the stylus. A record manufacturing convention, it's meant to signal, with low static, that the end of the side has been reached, the sound experience is over and further action is required for the musical sound to resume. For the concerned viewer, this detail means that roughly fifteen minutes have elapsed, since that's how much music is on Side 2 of *Ballads*, except that we don't know how long the record has been spinning after its final audible notes. What we do know is that their profound experience had at least fifteen minutes if expressive commentary by John Coltrane, McCoy Tyner, Jimmy Garrison and Elvin Jones, and, conceivably, the characters will remember their first bond each time this record is played. At least fifteen minutes of a sound memory, plus infinity.

If jazz records grant the characters agency to sound how they feel or want to feel, Britell's leitmotivic score unearths their deepest desires and misgivings. On the film's soundtrack, which is commercially available, one finds titles attached to the two recurrent motifs that accompanies Fonny and Tish throughout their most vulnerable and challenging moments in the plot – 'Eden (Harlem)' and 'Agape', each a passacaglia in the same key, with the same melodic material carried in the former by the strings and, in the latter, by the brass. A third recurrent motif in the film, 'Eros' – the soaring cello melody and tremolo strings passage that follows the lovers into Fonny's basement apartment – is also anchored by a cyclical ground bass ostinato. Britell's articulates his use of leitmotif indirectly when discussing his generative process with Jenkins:

So I actually wrote a piece of music – the first thing I wrote for the film – exploring the sound of mixing trumpets and flügelhorns and cornets and French horns. Jenkins really loved it, but when we put it up against some early sequences of the movie, it just felt like it was missing something. It didn't feel quite right yet for the film. And that led us to, *What was it missing?* And we realized that the musical landscape was missing strings. For us, the strings became like a musical exploration or expression of love. What's remarkable about the way Jenkins made the film is that it explores so many different *kinds* of love. It explores the love of parents for their children, it explores romantic love, it explores this divine, pure kind of love that exists between people. The strings came to symbolize that for us in a lot of ways.

One of the main [musical] themes in the film is the notes from that first piece that I'd written for brass, [even though] that actual brass piece is not in the movie. It's like the mold of a sculpture. We included it as one of the bonus tracks on the score album – it's called 'Harlem Aria'.[11]

Here, Britell describes how even a theme orchestrated differently better captures and amplifies an object of the imagination and heart's emotion, as the track titles of the score soundtrack make clear. This possibility is the thesis Matthew Bribitzer-Stull's *Understanding the Leitmotif: From Wagner to Hollywood Films*, which makes an argument for how this compositional tool, which crudely translates to 'leading motive' in English, serves to enhance and protract the more interior and ineffable psycho-emotional dimension of opera and film, both 'musico-dramatic constructs'.[12] This is accomplished by three means, which I quote in full:

1   Leitmotifs are bifurcated in nature, comprising both a musical physiognomy and an emotional association.

2   Leitmotifs are developmental in nature, evolving to reflect and create new musico-dramatic contexts.

3   Leitmotifs contribute to and function within a larger musical structure.[13]

On point three, I see the leitmotivic pieces of Britell's score as supporting the film's malleable temporality by threading fundamental abstract ideas or emotions together across disparate scenes, which would otherwise be discrete moments in the chronology of the plot. They are a sonic window into how the characters feel, yes, but also their memories, and these memories, like our own, are induced by different events and appear slightly altered each time. And, given the durational constraints of the film (it's just shy of two hours), these memories, which are actually Tish's, as she's the narrator, are in aggregate a vivid glimpse into a rich epochal moment.

I've suggested that music's multipurpose significance in *If Beale Street Could Talk* can be understood as a matter of time in two ways: if the frame of the film's temporal aperture is its duration, its film score projects the memories and imagined futures of the characters, and the jazz recordings the quantifiable expressions of the characters' subjectivities in the course of the narrative plot. I admit that these are all preliminary ideas that deserve more thinking, but I support this particular framework for music's role in invoking both quantifiable and experiential time in the drama from

Baldwin's own language from the novel; here, for Tish, music helps her mark the time and remember:

> I sat on the hassock, leaning on Daddy's knee. Now it was seven o'clock and the streets were full of noises. I felt very quiet after my long day, and my baby began to be real to me. I don't mean that it hadn't been real before; but, now, in a way, I was alone with it. Sis had left the lights very low. She put on a Ray Charles record and sat down on the sofa.
>
> I listened to the music and the sounds from the streets and Daddy's hand rested lightly on my hair. And everything seemed connected – the street sounds, and Ray's voice and his piano and my Daddy's hand and my sister's silhouette and the sounds and the lights coming from the kitchen. It was as though we were a picture, trapped in time: this had been happening for hundreds of years, people sitting in a room, waiting for dinner and listening to the blues. And it was as though, out of these elements, this patience, my Daddy's touch, the sounds of my mother in the kitchen, the way the light fell, the way the music continued beneath everything, the movement of Ernestine's head as she lit a cigarette, the movement of her hand as she dropped the match into the ashtray, the blurred human voices rising from the street, out of this rage and a steady, somehow triumphant sorrow, my baby was slowly being formed.[14]

CHAPTER 22

The shot and the cut: Joi McMillon's and Barry Jenkins's artistry

Carol Vernallis

Carol: Hi, Joi! Thank you for finding time for me.

Joi: You're so welcome!

Carol: I like to run ideas by directors and artists and they say 'Yeah, I see it this way' or 'No, I don't see what you're seeing.' I want to show how Barry Jenkins and all of you are transmedial artists. Can I start with some things I've noticed?

Joi: Sure!

Carol: Okay, so – I've been watching *If Beale Street Could Talk*. And I've been wondering about what makes your and Nate's editing styles so interesting? Let me point out several interlocking aspects of your work. When you're cutting between two actors in medium close-up, most editors would spend roughly equal time with both, but I like that you take your time – I think it's risky – to hone in on one person, and then have us as viewers do the cognitive work of building around the shots. I think that's really good.

And then there are aesthetic choices within larger sections, too. When Tish's mom, Sharon, for example, converses with Pietro Alvarez, Victoria's (brother?), in Puerto Rico, the scene begins with him in long shot, to gradually move in closer, with little time on Sharon. Uneven weighting happens in *Moonlight*, too, when Black and his mother hold a conversation at the rehab centre's patio (she's given much weight and Black's given little).

In *Beale Street*, this scene between Sharon and Pietro is part of a larger section. Sharon tries on her wig in preparation for her meetings, so she may not need to be as present for us later. This section closes with an encounter between Sharon and Victoria. Most shots are filmed on an angle, with one or both women out of focus. As we move in closer, we've only got one woman, so there's a sense of disorientation. After Victoria is whisked away, Sharon's alone, crumpled with her hands tightening, murmuring, 'What have I done? Idiot!' Yet we can remain with her for such a long time at this moment, because we were with her before we drifted away – and her presence projects.

In addition (at a larger scale), *Beale Street*'s second half becomes more impressionistic, both with sound and image, than its first. The film has already started letting itself out a bit (like Tish's dress – a film is always talking about itself). There's a recent long black extended frame, for example, or the moment when Tish just sits there and the sound comes up. Sharon's extended scene with her trying on her wig has an impressionistic soundscape. I don't get as strong a sense of these cycles and multi-layered interactions in *Lemon*, but there are other things to celebrate about that film. Do you have thoughts about this? A lot of Jenkins's material emerges in its timing, and our ability to remember, right?

Joi: You know, working on these films with Barry, a lot of what we do is, across the board, a collaboration. So a lot of times, the way something is shot influences the way we cut it together. And the way something is shot is influenced by how it was written, or how Barry envisions the scene coming together. So I think a lot of these choices, be it how long we linger on someone, or how we put together a scene that, even though it's focused on one person, the frame is containing both characters, is mostly dependent on how the footage is speaking to us. And what type of emotion the moment is calling for.

In *Beale Street*, I cut the section where Fonny's friend (Fonny – played by Stephan James) – his friend Daniel Carty (played by Brian Tyree Henry) – comes over. And throughout the stages of their time together, each beat of that moment in Fonny's apartment is different. The first beat is kind of like 'How's it going?' It's jovial. They're interchanging, they're laughing and then they start to slowly but surely reveal each other and what they're going through. And as each person starts to reveal more of what's lying underneath, in the edits, we start to spend time more on each character, and they're slowly, but surely, starting to be more vulnerable with each other.

Carol: As I remember, as we move through that section, Daniel's in darkness, and he talks about the white devil. Daniel's statement here is the main beat for me, but that might not be as true for other viewers. I wonder why it wouldn't feel threatening for European-American audiences? Perhaps there are a lot of moments soon to come that will take us out of this one. The friends have a wonderful dinner, and food is shared at the film's close too. There's a sense of grace and gratitude for both food and community. There's Levi, who's generous. And also the older woman in the store, who speaks up and protects the young couple from Officer Bell. So there's kind a breaking away from, or in some way, out of – but that's a long drive after this moment.

Joi: I think one of the things that that moment was conveying is that, oftentimes, in black communities, the good and the bad go hand in hand. I think we don't shy away from, or have a hard time, finding the good in the bad. We're able to come together and celebrate the life that we have been given, despite how many obstacles or despite the oppression that we feel in day-to-day life. Our home is our sanctuary.

And so, you know, it's like the juxtaposition of that darkness that Daniel talks about directly coming up against them having a moment where they can laugh and talk and commune together. It's kind of like a celebration of how we keep going. And that's why they come so closely together.

Carol: Perhaps another quick moment like that in *Beale Street* is when Fonny says – '"A munchin" in your belly'? And then the couple starts laughing. Fonny and Tish, across the glass. It's very grim, and –

Joi: Oh! Yeah, he said 'A midget in your belly.' That was a moment Barry was adamant we kept in, because I think one of the things someone said was 'In the moment, they realized how young they were.' And I think sometimes – my friend was telling me they did a study among cops, and they showed them images of young black kids, and the cops saw those kids as adults. But then when they showed them pictures of young white children, they oftentimes saw them younger than how old they were. And so, I think in that moment, them laughing at the visitation area of the prison is just a moment for you to realize that these kids are so young. They've barely gotten started, and this is what they're up against.

Carol: Yes. Do you know the studies that show teachers are hardest on African American boys? I think Fonny is depicted as at risk for unmerited punishment. He stole from the trade school. He slept in the park. He smokes pot. He's an artist. His family has disinherited him. So one wonders about lingering things that might have made him vulnerable to be picked off by the police.

Joi: Yeah, it's sad, but most young black men growing up in this America are always on the edge of going one way or the other, just by one bad choice. Second chances aren't often given, so you have to make good with that one chance that you get.

Carol: Yeah, I have a close friend whose brother was sentenced to prison. He and his spouse got into an altercation and the police were brought in. The evidence was dodgy, the wife took it back, and even friended my friend on Facebook, but the court doesn't have time to hear cases. I didn't know that you only have one shot, really. They're a mixed-race couple. We've all pondered how much this is a piece. The grandmother's raising the son, and the family's destroyed, so *Beale Street* still seems true today. There's some question of whether the film's contemporary or historical – because the problems are still unfolding. The mass incarceration of so many young men…

Joi: Exactly. It's a cycle that's really hard to be broken.

Carol: Yet Tish's family is very strong. Here's an example – Tish tells her mother 'I'm pregnant,' and then you don't see the mother's reaction, but then, somehow, the father, for me – I feel he's cut into the scene with Fonny's family so that he serves as a fulcrum. There's some weight on him.

Joi: One of the things I find so interesting about the film-making process is that oftentimes when a film is adapted from a novel, the novel has done a lot of, I would say, the research that one would have to do about a character. One of the things our screenwriting teacher challenged us to do in film school was to give each character in our script a history. You know, what's their family like? With this family that James Baldwin created, the book established their history and their conflicts, and what makes them tick, how they try to present themselves to the world and how they are internally. A lot of times in films, scenes that we shot but don't end up keeping still influence the actors, because they still had to act that section out; their previous performance still informs their acting in the current scene. We shot the scene where Tish tells her mom, and of course her mother's so understanding about it, but what came to be very evident to us is that how she acted in that scene was also obviously there when the whole family was together. So we don't need to see that, because we're clearly seeing that once again when all the family's together. And the same for Joseph – played by Coleman Domingo – with his whole arc and that whole situation of coming to terms with the pregnancy and still feeling like 'You're my little girl.' Some of his lines got cut, but you can still feel the warmth from that family in that scene, which I think is good.

Carol: Later, Tish is wearing her mother's sweater, right? And the kind of patterns on the sweater – there's paisley, there's also an African kente cloth-like design that runs through everything. But that's a subtle kind of memory.

Joi: Yeah, one of the things that I think is so cool about collaborations among everyone on the crew. These subtle details show that the family still prides themselves on presenting themselves like they're like – you know, because my mom would also tell me this about how, back in the day, the way you presented yourself to the world was so, so important.

Tisch borrows her mom's sweater, and then also the lipstick that the mom wears in Puerto Rico is the thing that she wears to work. So they share makeup.

Carol: Oh, yeah – wow! I noticed in the script, the mom tries on hats in front of the mirror in Puerto Rico, but in the film she puts on a wig and takes it off again. And then sounds come in – I read online that you help with sound design – and maybe those sounds connect to when the baby is born. But, at the time, it's very impressionistic. Do you know the moment I'm talking about, where she's getting ready to meet…

Joi: Yeah! Mm-hmm. So, one of the things that Barry talked about in putting this movie together is how a lot of the story is a woman's story, and so for him, he says, during the whole process, he definitely listened to the women that were helping him and collaborating with him in making this film. And so, when Regina read the scene – a lot of who Sharon Rivers is, she based on her mom and her grandmother. And, to her, she said she didn't feel it would have been a scarf. To her, in her mind, it makes more sense that it would be a wig; wigs were kind of like their armour when they went out into the world. So Barry was like 'Okay, let's switch to a wig.'

Carol: But then she takes it off. And then she, of course, puts it on again, so she has some ambivalence.

Joi: Exactly. It's basically uncertainty of what version of Sharon Rivers does she feel like would help her get this information from this man she's meeting. Does he want to see the Sharon Rivers that she presents to the world, or does he want to see the Sharon Rivers who's the mom at home that's trying to take care of her daughter and keep her family together? So it's basically the battle of what version of herself she wants to present to this person that she's meeting.

Carol: That makes sense. I think it's true in *Moonlight*, and also in *Beale Street*, that the greater space for shots and for emotion and just … for people being – it isn't as available at the beginning of the film, but later the film opens out.

Earlier in the film, before the baby is born, I find there are a few moments that create a space for more open film-making approaches. There's a long frame of black, as well as the montage sequence where

Tish narrates the baby's and her negotiating its kicks in her womb. She enumerates this discussion. And there's a long shot of Tish just sitting there, before her child's born. And that's something that doesn't seem as possible earlier. In the second half of the film, we have other more impressionistic moments, like the frame's division into quadrants, when Fonny's and Tish's fathers are stealing from the garment district, which is reminiscent of *Superfly* and *Shaft*. Or there's multiple overlapping dissolves of Tish later on. Perhaps there's more freedom in the second half, and that's true for *Moonlight*, too, in some ways?

Joi: Yeah, it's interesting, because oftentimes, when you're setting up the world that people are about to enter, you want them to become accustomed to the space.

Carol: But you do have one moment early in the film when the two families get together, with Fonny's family learning about Tish's pregnancy. That's a good juxtaposition, with the sense of quiet of the family's taking in Tish's news, and the broader, more raucous scene with the in-laws. There's a wipe-by where the mother moves before Tish, and then Tish thinks about Fonny's and her visit to the Italian restaurant. I didn't have trouble with the flashback in the theatre, but when I saw on my iPad, it felt a little more...

Joi: Yeah, it's one of those things where when we put together a film, sound is influential on how the world comes together. And so I think when we're going in and out of Tish's flashbacks, I think a lot of it is cued by the sound creeping in on the frame that's about to come up. And so, visually, if you're just looking at it and can't quite hear it as well, it might affect you differently than seeing it in the theatre and being able to hear all of the sound design that we did with the surround.

Carol: That's a good point. Let me try another! Ernestine turns around with a brief extreme close-up, and calls Tish a jezebel. This follows soon with a shot in long duration of Tish at the Dior counter. These irregular shot lengths heighten the stakes for Tish and her customers' encounters. (How long will they stay? How intimate will this be?)
  And I just found one special music video-like moment!

Joi: Yeah! [laughs]

Carol: It's so helpful to try this stuff out. ... So I believe visual contour and musical contour are important. You can set up what viewers might experience as interlocking shapes. Fonny and Tish hold hands while walking along the sidewalk, and our eyes may be tempted to pan up to the kids who are jumping on the cars' roofs adjacent to them. Next, in the bathtub, a young Tish reaches up to Fonny with a handful of soap bubbles. And then there's a third arcing contour in the following shot. The trumpet's melodic line leaps up – and the couple stands together on the subway, and we feel as if they might wear crowns. That's a lot of arcing! Later in the film, the baby's born, and he in his grandmother's arms and the camera arc up. At the film's close, the young son emerges from the bottom of the frame, seemingly out of the repressive black-and-white photos. It's as if the next generation might endure and transcend these great limitations. These are hopeful gestures that span the film.

Joi: Yeah, I think that one of the things Barry does well is he creates these films that are, to me, the overarching theme is 'love in spite of'. And that was the message in *Moonlight*, and that's definitely the message in *Beale Street*. It's finding hope where oftentimes you'll feel like it might be hopeless. It's understanding that love is one of the things that can endure these circumstances. And it's how people come out on the other side. All of those are areas where we can heighten the fact that these people are just hopeful and immersed in each other's worlds. And oftentimes, they're surrounded by people and they're only really seeing each other.

Carol: What is it like – affectively – working with such heart-breaking content? *Lemon, Moonlight* and *Beale Street* are heart breaking in different ways.

Joi: It's interesting because *Lemon*, being a dark comedy, and *Moonlight* and *Beale Street* being dramas, ultimately I feel like I'm just a storyteller. For me the genre of the film doesn't really truly affect the editing. I like to tell stories that I feel are impactful, that are honest and authentic. I like stories that I know telling them will be essential but also challenging. *Moonlight* was the first feature that I ever edited, and so to some people I might be a newbie, but I've been working in this industry for fifteen years now, and I've been in a lot of different cutting rooms, and I've worked with a lot of different directors and editors, and I feel so grateful being in the industry at this time, and being able to collaborate with some of the most fluent film-makers working in the industry.

Carol: I'd like to know more about the 'transmedia' angle. You've edited reality TV, documentaries and comedies. You've been able to sweep across. These all have been from the world of film-making, right? It's not like you've done commercials or stuff like that, right? Do you want to do that?

Joi: Well, actually, when Barry did *Medicine for Melancholy*, he did a lot of writing, and then he was a partner in a company called Strike Anywhere. There I edited a lot of commercials for him.

Carol: Oh, wonderful! And he did some commercials. That's good to know.

Joi: Yeah, and I edited a short for Barry. So I feel like I've kind of done a little bit of everything. I've done television, I've done reality television and I've done films and commercials. And I feel like this, for me, I think a lot of times people want to figure you out and put you in boxes and go 'You are a drama – a film editor,' you know? Or 'You're a comedy film editor.' But I think right now, because there's so much content, and people are allowing television to be more like film, right now – what I was on the call about – we're getting ready to do *Underground* for Amazon, the limited series. Right now I'm working with Janicza again on a film called *Zola*, which is, again, another dark comedy. Basically, right now, the world is allowing the boxes to be broken open, and people are allowed to work in just about any field that they would like to, which I feel like is refreshing.

Carol: I like that the European and Asian directors he likes are the ones I like too, so... *Moonlight* feels more like an art film to me.

Joi: Yeah.

Carol: Yeah. Was it easier to edit *Moonlight* partly just because of its colour palette? Which felt easier to edit?

Joi: [laughs] You know, I feel like each film holds its own challenges. There's always a moment that you spend time on because it just takes a little bit longer to click. I feel like with *Moonlight*, structure wise, it was chapters one, two and three, and these were contained. *Moonlight* was probably easier than *Beale Street*, when we're dipping in and out of the past and present. The audience needs to keep track of what's past, what's present and what's happening to the characters at each moment – it's trying to create a film that appears to be seamless. It's challenging and takes a lot of work to get there. We really spent time so that, for an audience member, the film didn't take you out of it as we dipped in and out of the past.

Carol: Thinking about how viewers are putting pieces together – part of it is we're given less about what's going on with marriage, or why Fonny's really been put in prison. We don't know enough about 'the powers that be' and their unspeakable machinations. So we're dipping back and forth; there has to be some trust, I guess. Right?

Joi: Exactly, yeah.

PART EIGHT

Community, identity and transmedial aspirations across the web

CHAPTER 23

Multimodal and transmedia subjectivity in animated music video: Jess Cope and Steven Wilson's 'Routine' from *Hand. Cannot. Erase.* (2015)

Lori Burns

Videographer Jess Cope's animated music videos are celebrated for their carefully crafted storyworlds, powerful narratives, expressive subjectivities and finely wrought environments.[1] In Cope's treatment of Steven Wilson's 'Routine' (2015), her visual aesthetics and stop-motion animation techniques intersect sensitively with Wilson's musical content to bind storyworld and human experience to musical form and performance.[2] The meaning and expressivity of 'Routine', however, is only fully received through a thorough engagement with the transmedia materials of Wilson's *Hand. Cannot. Erase.* (2015, hereafter *H.C.E.*) concept album.[3] While Cope's video certainly stands on its own as an engaging and thoughtful treatment of the song, an understanding of its role in the larger transmedia storyworld enhances spectator appreciation of the depth and significance of the human tragedy being presented. By creating a subject who embodies the imagination and experience of the *H.C.E.* protagonist, Cope's video treatment of 'Routine' offers a significant contribution to Wilson's transmedia work.

Cope and Wilson have developed a rich and profound artistic partnership, beginning with the 2012 music video for 'Drag Ropes', a musical collaboration between Steven Wilson and Mikael Åkerfeldt of Opeth for their *Storm Corrosion* (2010–12) project. Cope and Wilson continued their partnership with two music videos for his 2013 album, *The Raven That Refused to Sing (and Other Stories)*, a collection of eerie tales. For the two videos from that album ('The Raven' and 'Drive Home'), Cope featured stop-motion animation puppets in scenery created on layers of multi-planed glass. Her work with the song 'Routine' began when Wilson shared an article on a woman who lost her family to a school shooting; the resulting stop-motion video, which took eight months to shoot, conveys the female subject's tragic experience in a miniature domestic setting.[4] Launched on the 2015 *Hand. Cannot. Erase.* tour (Figure 23.1), the video was not released on YouTube until 29 October 2015. Their most recent music video collaboration, 'People Who Eat Darkness' (released on the 2018 *To the Bone* tour), continues with the melancholy themes that characterize their growing body of work.[5]

In the fields of literary and film studies, transmedia storytelling is the focus of a burgeoning scholarly area[6] and music scholars are recognizing tremendous potential for transmedia approaches to popular music.[7] Since the 1960s, rock artists have developed diverse media materials to shape cultural messages, create artistic identities and explore human subjectivities. As media technologies have advanced, artistic strategies for developing the complete album package have expanded from album artwork and promotional clips to cinematic and animated films, illustrated books and comics, music videos, concert films, staged musicals, video games and

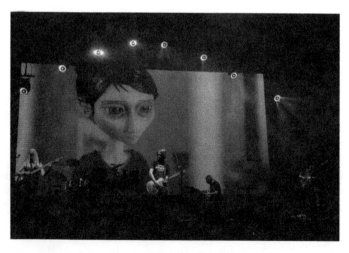

FIGURE 23.1 H.C.E. *tour 2015, Photo Lasse Hoile. Available at http://stevenwi lsonhq.com/sw/hand-cannot-erase-uk-tour-update-from-sw/#!prettyPhoto.*

internet blogs. For music creators, such materials are designed to promote the album and to contribute particular narrative elements to the storyworld. These materials have the potential to build powerful stories about human experience that play out in our textual, sonic and visual imaginations.

In addition to the insights that can emerge from being attentive to transmedia storytelling, it is equally important for the analyst of such materials to address their multimodal nature.[8] Media narratologists Marie-Laure Ryan and Jan-Noël Thon explain that multimodality is characterized by the integration of different types of signs (e.g. moving images, spoken language and music) within the same media object. In keeping with their understanding, I consider multimodality to comprise the artistic integration of multiple semiotic modes or channels within one media text. The term 'multimodal' must be carefully distinguished from the term 'multimedia', which connotes an artistic work that features the simultaneous presentation of different media texts, such as the screening of a film and/or delivery of a spoken narrative during a live music concert.[9] In an analysis of a multimedia performance, the analyst might address the ways in which the different media texts intersect, whereas an analyst of a multimodal work would focus on the layers of expression across a range of semiotic channels that are integrated within a single artefact.[10] The analysis presented in this chapter is meant to provide the reader-spectator with an experience of narrative immersion by delivering the interpretive materials of this transmedia artefact in a dynamic, multimodal platform.

Steven Wilson's *H.C.E.* comprises an elaborate transmedia storyworld through the multimodal intersection of the lyrics, music, video images, artwork, artefacts, texts and performances. In interviews, Wilson describes his compositional aims to communicate album narratives through these multidimensional materials in order to portray more vividly the experiences of his narrative subjects.[11] The limited special edition of the album includes a hardcover 'scrapbook' featuring images and texts that elaborate the narrative and offer contexts and perspectives from the subject's life. Taking these materials to the realm of social media, Wilson also launched a blog with entries dating from 2008 to 2015.[12] No longer available, the blog was launched in January 2015 as part of the promotional lead-up to the album release in February.[13] Four of the album's songs were given music video treatments, with Cope's 'Routine' standing out as the only animated video for the album.

Wilson declares that *H.C.E.* is 'driven by narrative' and that the materials account for 'all of the curves of someone's life'.[14] The story was inspired by the true story – captured in the drama-documentary film, *Dreams of a Life* (2011) – of Joyce Carol Vincent, who died in a London apartment, but whose body was not found for three years.[15] In Wilson's creative response to that story, his protagonist (only known as 'H') is an alienated subject who cannot sustain relationships and who is fascinated by 'stories of the disappeared'. 'Routine' steps out of H's biographical narrative, and offers what narratologists refer to as a character focalization, as H enters the tragic situation of another woman – Madeline Hearne – whose story she notices in the news.[16]

Adopting Henry Jenkins's concern for how each text makes its own 'distinctive and valuable contribution' to the convergence of media materials, my goal is to illuminate how transmedia storytelling operates in and through Cope's video treatment of Wilson's 'Routine'.[17] Cope's challenge with this video would have been to convey two levels of narrative:

(1) the immediate story about the subject, Madeline, who is coping with loss.

(2) the larger narrative of H, from whose perspective Madeline's story emerges.

Cope could not merely develop a video treatment that respected the values of the individual song, 'Routine', but was also creatively obliged to align and integrate that video treatment within the broader *H.C.E.* transmedia platform. The analysis below demonstrates how Cope's contribution aligns with Wilson's collection of transmedia materials. For the spectator-listener of the *H.C.E.* narrative, Wilson provided many clues to the meanings and messages of this profound human story and Cope's video treatment contributes significantly to our understanding of H's experience. My objective is to examine how these narrative levels emerge in the musical expression as well as in the video performance.

Wilson and Cope's transmedia treatment of the *H.C.E.* narrative extends beyond the album materials, as the song 'Routine' was also featured in the musical soundtrack to the animated game, 'Last Day of June' (released in 2017). The video game is based on Cope's animated video treatment of 'Drive Home',[18] a song belonging to the set of transmedia materials connected to the album *The Raven That Refused to Sing (And Other Stories)* (Kscope, 2013).[19] With the 'Drive Home' video, which was based on Hajo Müller's artwork and stories from the limited edition of that album, Wilson and Cope take music production to another level of transmedia engagement and exploit the potential of a single video to generate an extended narrative about a tragic tale (Burns 2016). Although the music of the song 'Drive Home' does not actually appear in the video game soundtrack, Wilson includes another song from the same album – 'The Raven' (which also has a video treatment by Jess Cope) – as well as songs from *Grace for Drowning* (Kscope, 2011), *Insurgentes* (Kscope, 2008) and *H.C.E.*[20]

When I refer to the music video as a 'performance', I have Donald Crafton's notion of the animator as performer in view.[21] Adopting his analytic perspective, we can attribute the portrayal of embodied subjectivity to Jess Cope as the performer, since she is responsible for the capturing of minute gestures in careful synchronization with musical nuances. In the analysis below, I examine how Cope's animated character is rendered to express profound aspects of the subject's consciousness, emotions and experience. Cope builds a distinctly humanized subject, endowing her with strong senses (visual, auditory, olfactory and haptic), the capacity for thoughtful reflection and intense emotions. My analysis aims to illuminate the attributes of her subject as her appearance, gestures and motivations are portrayed through Cope's eminently sensitive portrayal of Wilson's lyrics and music. Following the analytic presentation, I will return to reflect on Cope's portrayal of human subjectivity in this endearing character.

Mapping the multimodality of 'Routine' within the transmedia storyworld of *H.C.E.*

'Routine' expresses cogent human emotions through the musical vehicle of a searching progressive rock arrangement and the visual vehicle of a delicately animated storyworld. My close reading of 'Routine' examines visual-musical intersections to illuminate the multi-layered performativity of the expressive subject. Both artists work at the micro level with their materials, timing, spatial treatment, gestures and intensity, thus providing many parameters to pursue in the consideration of subjectivity and storyworld.

In order to respond to Wilson and Cope's call for narrative immersion in the transmedia storyworld, while recognizing the limitations of print media, I offer here an innovative approach to music video analysis that incorporates word, sound and image in a dynamic platform. I have mapped the textual, musical and visual narrative of 'Routine' using a digital storymapping tool (https://storymap.knightlab.com/) and a digital content management platform (https://omeka.org/). The reader of this chapter is invited to visit the 'Musical Storyworlds' webpage (http://biblio.uottawa.ca/omeka1/tr ansmedia/) in order to explore my interpretive curation of both *H.C.E.* more broadly and 'Routine' more specifically, through three storymap timelines:[22]

> The *Narrative Timeline* follows the temporal narrative of *events* in H's life, *not* in the order of the album materials, but rather in the order of H's experience.

> The *Musical Timeline* maintains the album order and offers a musical analysis of the full tracklist.

> The *'Routine' Timeline* maps the lyrical, musical and visual elements of the music video.

The background 'storymap' for the *'Routine' Timeline* is an image derived from the music analysis tool *Sonic Visualiser*, extracted with three layers of sonic information: the top layer offers a 'peak frequency' spectrogram, showing pitch frequency (low to high) on the y axis (with the colours green, yellow and red indicating degrees of sonic intensity from quieter to louder, respectively) and linear temporality on the x axis; the middle layer offers a full spectrogram of the song, again with green, yellow and red indicating degrees of intensity; and the bottom layer is the amplitude (loudness) wave form of left and right channels.

The annotations in the wave form identify the formal analysis of the song structure: Verse 1 – Verse 2 – Chorus – Verse 3 – Instrumental link – Bridge – Verse 4 – Instrumental link – Chorus – Chorus – Postlude. The annotations in the spectrogram layer offer an analysis of the visual narrative, which moves through a twenty-four-hour temporal period, aligned to the musical formal structure. And the annotations in the top spectrogram layer offer descriptions of instrumental and vocal gestures. These annotations will be explained in the analytic commentary that follows.

With the aim of creating an immersive analytic experience that adopts the multimodal discourse of my object of inquiry, the following interpretive account invites the reader to engage immediately in the musical and visual dialogue and thus to confirm the analytic claims immediately while the material intersections are illustrated in an interpretive curation or exhibit. Thus the *'Routine' Timeline* is meant to serve as a visual complement to the discussion, which illustrates the multimodal intersections of word, sound and image as the spectator would experience it in an immersive viewing and listening session.

The storymap is organized as a series of events (Event 0 through Event 12) that correspond to the musical and visual form. On a methodological note, it is worth mentioning here that in my initial readings of the video, while I had always observed a seamless connection between sound and image, it was only through this detailed mapping process that I discovered Jess Cope's extraordinary attention to musical form: every section of Wilson's song structure is treated to a complementary temporal setting in the video, moving from the morning of one day to the morning of the next.[23] While Wilson's song captures the emotional perspectives of the narrative subject, Cope's temporal treatment pursues her lived experience in time, space and place.

Event 0 (Transmedia contexts): The first gathering of materials provides some important connections to the *H.C.E.* scrapbook and blog. H's fascination with the story of 'Routine' lies in its focus on 'the disappeared'. The music video conveys the subject's loss of her husband and two children to a school shooting; we learn this implicitly in the lyrics of the song, such as, 'what should I do with all the children's clothes?' and explicitly in the video, when a newspaper clipping flutters to the floor. At the broader level, H's collection of news clippings about lost women includes one report about Madeline Hearne herself going missing. The spectator understands

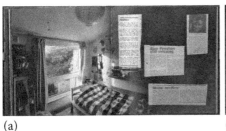
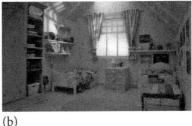

(a)   (b)

FIGURE 23.2 *(a) Photo of H's bedroom in the* H.C.E. *special edition book (pp. 42–3); and (b) Cope's video treatment of the children's bedroom [00:13] (*H.C.E. *Jess Cope / Stephen Wilson, 2015).*

H's fascination with disappearance to emerge at a critical moment in her life when her adopted sister enters her life for six months, but then 'disappears' when she is placed with another family. Thereafter, H does not succeed in forming successful attachments and gradually alienates herself from society, aiming towards her own disappearance. The *H.C.E.* spectator receives 'Routine' as a moment when H identifies with Madeline Hearne's story, immersing and inserting herself into that narrative.

Cope's design of the children's bedroom setting has much in common with the bedroom that is pictured in the materials of *H.C.E.*: the sloped ceilings, the window adjacent to a single bed, the shelves on the wall filled with artwork and memorabilia all connect to the children's bedroom scene (Figures 23.2a and 23.2b). With this subtle visual reference, Cope establishes a strong link to the *H.C.E.* storyworld, communicating to the spectator that Madeline Hearne's world is coming to us through H, who infuses the story with her own experiences. As the album reaches the darkest point in H's social alienation, with the song 'Ancestral', one of the blog entries connected to that track says, 'I dream of … Madeline Hearne.' In this blog entry, she also asks why she stays, revealing her own desire to 'disappear'. These contexts are important for the spectator to receive the focalized narrative of 'Routine', as Madeline Hearne's story is embedded within H's narrative of alienation.

Event 1: Morning light

[video timecode 00:00] [audio clip 1: 00:00–00:12]

As we enter Event 1, please note the following features of the digital curation: the numbered clips are embedded in the *'Routine' Timeline* Storymap; each 'event' begins with the analytic snapshot, and then proceeds with sound clips, screenshots and, in some instances, brief video clips.

Wilson's Verse 1 creates a reflective sonic backdrop, with his warm, airy and dark vocal accompanied by quiet piano in a lilting 5/4 metre. The vocal production is detailed and articulate, but not harsh, highlighting the higher frequencies of his voice as he asks what will become of the children's clothes and their 'footprints in the hallway'. The verse closes with the ambient sounds of an ocean wave. Just as Wilson treats this opening verse like an introduction, Cope presents the establishing shots of her film: a warm, but sombre morning light first shines through the children's bedroom window and the hallway where their boots and other personal items are stowed; an outdoor shot then exposes the full morning sky, with the subject standing in front of her house at the cliff's edge. Cope exploits the moment of ambient sound to show the subject's moment of reflection: when the shot changes to reveal her face, we see an anguished woman with tears around her eyes and a distant regard.

It is worth taking a moment here to comment on Cope's handling of Wilson's lyrical content. She responds to specific words in a subtle treatment in which the lyrical reference is echoed in the image several seconds later. In Verse 1, when Wilson sings, 'and the footprints in the hallway' [00:12–00:16], the scene is the children's bedroom, and it is only after an intervening shot of the hallway that the camera moves to the boot rack [00:21–00:24] to signal a connection to the lyrical story. Cope's lyrical-visual echo is a strategy that occurs throughout the video.

Event 2: Kitchen routines

[00:41] [audio clips 2 and 3: 00:40–00:49 and 01:01–01:07]

Verse 2 is characterized by a pushed vocal delivery and more dynamic piano, creating a greater sense of urgency to the question, 'how to be of use/ make the tea and the soup'. Cope's visual treatment responds to Wilson's intensification of the voice and piano by focusing on the kitchen breakfast table set for four, with nobody seated and the subject washing dishes at the sink. The music of the verse closes with a linking passage in which a high-pitched boy falsetto soars above the continuing pattern of the piano and carries seamlessly into the subsequent Chorus. Cope again takes advantage of the brief instrumental passage to concentrate on the subject's distressed face and distant expression before she begins to move from the kitchen to the hallway (see Figure 23.1, which features the image at 00:59). The subject's movement out of the kitchen is sensitively linked to the transitional function of the musical passage. The boy falsetto gesture not only represents her thoughts and memories but also seems to motivate her to continue on to another routine. In this gesture, we can understand her to be both locked in the memory and wanting to escape.

Event 3: Sensory memory

[01:09] [audio clip 4: 01:10–01:15]

The linking passage leads seamlessly into Ninet Tayeb's delivery of the chorus in an ethereal vocal, with the boy falsetto continuing high in the distance. Compared to Wilson's very centred vocal, Tayeb's voice is given a spacious treatment. Cope complements the musical link with a smooth scene transition, following the subject from the kitchen to the hallway. The female singer's vocal now seems to represent the subject's thoughts, as she pauses to breathe in the scent of her husband's coat jacket and then moves upstairs to fold the children's clothing [Video Clip 1: 01:13–01:21]. At the cadence of the Chorus, Cope once again closes the section with a moment of concentration on the subject's expression as she handles and breathes in the scent of a child's sweater, exploring her olfactory memory.

Event 4: Domestic routines

[1:40] [audio clip 5: 01:41–01:47]

During the more effected vocal delivery of Verse 3, which now features a rich reverberation on Wilson's vocal and a bright guitar, the subject continues to tidy the children's room, taking time to look at their artwork on the wall. Again, creating visual echoes of the lyrics, she responds to 'making beds' [1:41–1:42] with the physical action starting a few seconds later [1:45]. Cope captures her gaze towards the wall as she is making the bed, then reveals that her gaze is directed at the children's drawings by framing the image from behind the subject. As the verse continues towards the close, Cope captures three hand gestures that bring us into an awareness of the subject's haptic memories, showing her sense of touch to be connected to her domestic routines as a wife and mother (smoothing the bedding, scrubbing the floor and wiping the kitchen counters). The lyrical reference to 'paintings … stuck to the fridge' [1:55–1:59] is echoed visually with a sequence featuring a child's artwork fluttering to the floor and the subject then taking the time to put it back and touch it fondly [2:06–2:07].

Event 5: Passing time

[2:19] [audio clip 6: 02:19–02:29]

The instrumental link from Verse 3 to the Bridge is more extensive than the brief passages that close Verses 1, 2 and the Chorus. The piano and acoustic guitar continue, now with a high string sound filling out the texture. During this passage, Cope conveys the subject's passing of time in the living room by superimposing her image while she moves from one position to another. Here she is surrounded by the aesthetic symbols of their activities as a family in the heart of the home: the piano, the seating area with cozy cushions, her knitting materials and so on. With the sun streaming in the window, it seems a place filled with contentment, however the subject is alone.

Event 6: Midday

[02:39] [audio clip 7: 02:38–02:43]

When Wilson's lengthy Bridge section begins, the busy piano and guitar texture fades away to open the space for a boy soprano, who enters with a solo passage characterized by indiscernible words and musical metre. Cope treats this passage as a midday moment, when the subject steps outside to witness the impending arrival of a storm. She once again exploits a non-texted passage to create an episode of reflection and memory. In this case, it is a sonic memory, with the distant boy soprano solo representing her lost children.

Event 7: Darkening sky

[03:18] [audio clip 8: 03:33–03:47]

The boy solo fades out to silence, after which the metre changes to a calming 6/4 and an acoustic guitar, flute and mellotron occupy an expansive texture with breadth, depth and height. Much of the sonic information is panned rather than centred, and the instruments are produced and mixed to suggest intimacy (i.e. we hear the breath of the flute and the guitar transients), creating a heightened sense of awareness. During this musical evocation of the alertness one might feel at dusk, Cope casts the clouds, the house and the rooms with a gloomy light. She shows the subject to be moving through her end of day routine of tidying the hallway again and sorting the mail, some of which she places in a large storage container of unopened letters. While the flute solo closes, the subject sits down at the kitchen table and sees a moving toy on the floor. The subject's gestures here create a powerful transmedia connection to the *H.C.E.* storyworld: first, Madeline's refusal to read the letters from friends and family resonates with H's movement towards total alienation from society; and second, her vision of the moving toy is revealed to be a figment of her imagination, which also resonates with H's challenges discerning the real from the imaginary.

Event 8: Imagining routines

[4:12] [audio clip 9: 04:40–04:50]

The Bridge section continues with a bass solo in 5/4 metre, followed by the electric guitar [4:31], which is accompanied by the full drum kit for the first time in the song. Cope signals this increase in musical intensity with a number of visual strategies: first, the moving toy that had approached during the close of the flute section is confirmed to be an illusion, since there is nothing on the floor. This imagined event seems to trigger a series of memories represented as a series of her routines, most of which we have already seen, now edited in a montage style: smoothing the bedding, dusting the piano, scrubbing the floor, smelling the jacket and handling the children's toys. The fragmented, discontinuous style of the image sequence suggests that these routines are being imagined by the subject while she remains seated at the table and, once again, Cope shows her memories to be attached to sensorial experiences of sight, touch and smell. By enhancing the sensory experience for the audience, Cope vitalizes the materials that are used throughout the set.

Event 9: Solitary evening meal

[5:10] [audio clips 10 and 11: 05:20–05:39 and 05:40–05:52]

The music of Verse 4 stands out for a number of musical effects: the texture cuts back from the dynamic Bridge instrumentation to voice and piano; Tayeb delivers the verse for the first time; the melody pitched is one full step higher than the first three verses; the verse is extended in a descending line as a spacious reverb gradually increases to augment the effect of her deepening voice; and Tayeb's vocals are overdubbed in a richly layered texture for the final phrase. In her visual treatment of this distinctive verse, Cope shows the subject to be moving through the motions of a solitary evening meal, although the table is set and the food is prepared for the full family. Losing appetite when she regards the empty places, the subject begins to wash the dishes. This represents yet another of Cope's visual echoes as the lyrics say, 'keep washing' [05:21] and it is several seconds later [05:31] when the gesture appears.

The verse is followed by an instrumental linking passage [5:40] (to the subsequent chorus) that features a sudden textural shift from simple bass and piano to a loud, heavy texture with full kit, bass and guitars. During this instrumental passage, the subject's act of scrubbing a plate leads to drops of her own blood falling into the sink – the critical moment in the narrative when her obsessive repetition of routine gestures is shown to cause physical harm. Cope responds to the sudden dynamic and textural shift in the music with the peak of anxiety for the subject, who now imagines an alarming amount of blood in the sink, only to realize that it was merely a drop [Video Clip 2: 05:41–05:44].

Event 10: Destructive sequence

[5:56] [audio clip 12: 06:11–06:19]

While the rock instrumentation continues to deliver at full force, the subject begins a sequence of destruction in the kitchen, breaking a plate, knocking over a chair, pounding the table and spilling the food. The Chorus [6:11] then features Tayeb's voice in a powerful and dynamic presentation an octave higher than the earlier Chorus sections, with heavy instrumental backing. During the lyrical declaration, 'routine keeps me in line', the subject careens through the house, breaking things, knocking things over and tearing apart all of the order that she had created during her completion of the daytime domestic routines. All of the personal items she had so lovingly handled during the day are now treated to rough, damaging behaviour: she tears the mail, knocks the magazines to the floor, throws the children's toys and pulls the clothes from the neat cupboard. Returning to the hallway, breathing hard and in a distraught state, she knocks over the bucket of water, picks up the scrub brush and throws it violently, knocking the child's lunchbox to the floor. Cope takes this opportunity to return to the image of the fallen magazines. When that print material moves into focus, the spectator sees and understands, for the first time, the true source of her pain and emotion: a newspaper clipping with the headline, 'Father and Two Sons Killed in School Shooting.' The subject runs from the house, heading outside again, now into the night sky, while the last strains of the chorus are heard. With her reference to the newspaper clipping, Cope once again creates a subtle but powerful connection to the *H.C.E.* transmedia storyworld, in which H collects news stories about people who have disappeared or experienced loss (Figures 23.3a and 23.3b).

Event 11: Night scream

[7:15] [audio clip 13: 07:15–07:23]

Following the two heavy and dynamic statements of the Chorus, Wilson interjects a musical section, lying outside of the common form, which can only be described as a primal scream.[24] Shaking and overcome with her

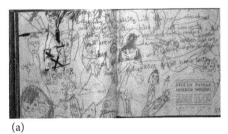
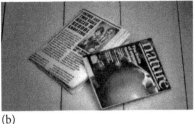

(a)   (b)

FIGURE 23.3 *(a) Photo of newsclippings in* H.C.E. *special edition book (pp. 44–5); and (b) Cope's video treatment of the newspaper report of Madeline's lost family [07:05] (*H.C.E. *Jess Cope / Stephen Wilson, 2015).*

emotion, the subject stands at the cliff's edge and screams into the night sky, before bending forward, clutching her abdomen in evident physical pain [Video Clip 3: 07:09–07:23]. Notably, it is the only moment in Cope's video that features diegetic vocal music.[25] The scene is uncluttered with any physical objects; we see only the subject, the moon and sky, and the ground upon which she stands. Cope enhances the darkness of the scene with clouds and fog that surround the subject, seeming to place her directly within the night sky and atmospheric conditions. With this image, Cope makes another strong link to the larger transmedia storyworld of *H.C.E.* (Figures 23.4a and 23.4b), communicating subtly to the reader-spectator that this primal cry does represent not only Madeline's pain but also H's experience in her own confrontation with pain and loss.

Event 12: Postlude/morning light

[7:25] [audio clip 14: 08:01–08:21]

The intensity of Wilson's primal scream is followed by a calm musical postlude. A bright guitar with a warbly tone accompanies Wilson's gentle and relaxed vocal. His reflective lyrics, 'don't ever let go / try to let go' are overdubbed by Tayeb at the upper octave. With this tortured expression, Wilson represents the double bind of the grieving mother, who desperately wants to retain every nuanced memory of her family, but also recognizes her need to move on with her life. The harmonic progression of this peaceful passage repeats a simple teleological progression that resolves previous harmonic tensions. Cope complements Wilson's formal postlude by reprising the images of morning light streaming through the bedroom window, the kitchen and the living room, with the subject now bearing a peaceful expression. The colour of the morning light is warmer than in the opening

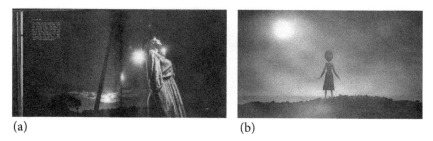

(a)   (b)

FIGURE 23.4 *(a) Image of H gazing at the night sky in* H.C.E. *special edition book (pp. 48–9); and (b) Cope's video treatment of Madeline's night scream [07:19] (*H.C.E. *Jess Cope / Stephen Wilson, 2015).*

scene, with pink hues, as compared with the grey tones of the establishing shots. Cope now portrays her subject in a quiet mood, appearing to have found a positive avenue and possibly a resolution. In the living room, as she reads letters from the mail basket that she had previously hidden away in the hallway cupboard, her face has a calm appearance and the redness of her eyes is gone. When she returns outside into the warm light, she experiences a gentle breeze in her hair and clothing [Video Clip 4: 08:40–08:51]; with this simple movement of air – its effect heightened by its delivery through stop-motion animation – Cope reminds the spectator again that this is a subject with haptic sensibilities.

Interpretive conclusions

The analytic and presentational methodology adopted here offers great potential for transmedia curation and multimodal narratology. The *'Routine' Timeline* immerses the spectator within the multimodal materials of words, music and images in order to facilitate the curation of artistic and performative gestures that are otherwise challenging to receive. An empirical approach to each expressive event across the multimodal channels (lyrics, music and images) allows the spectator to understand the cultural and artistic workings of each domain. As I began my own interpretation, I had gathered the word-sound-image analytic data, but I had not yet formed a thorough understanding of the ways in which these elements intersect. After analysing the lyrics, conducting a thorough formal and timbral analysis of the song and studying the video images, I put these analytic layers into dialogue, progressing gesture by gesture, in order to realize a deeper understanding of Wilson's and Cope's artistic processes.

This detailed study reveals Cope's remarkable sensitivity to the musical structure of Wilson's progressive rock song. In her handling of the formal design, each scene in the video corresponds precisely to a section in his musical form and her sophisticated handling of linking passages allows her to create seamless visual transitions. She maximizes these transitions for their potential to portray the subject's determined attempts to keep her emotions under control. We witness her emotional struggle, as she staves off the outburst until darkness comes, just as Wilson maintains musical control until the release of the primal scream. The animated subject is made all the more compelling by Cope's manifestation of human attributes through her sensorial responses and psychological conflict. Cope responds to Wilson's musical moods, gestures, timbres and dynamics by creating an animated subject who is infused with human emotions, senses, motivations and consciousness.

Discussing subjectivity as expressed and developed in film contexts, film theorist Dominique Chateau defines subjectivity in the following ways:

1 Subjectivity as consciousness: the ability to connect our mind to the environment, to be aware of our feelings or ideas and also to be aware of our own existence.

2 Subjectivity as internal representations of various kinds: sensations, perceptions, feelings, mental images, dreams and ideas.

3 Subjectivity as the position of the subject: the identity of the human being as a unified source of external and internal representations, and also as a source of self-representation (and self-consciousness).[26]

With this definition of subjectivity in mind, we can understand Cope's subject to fulfil all of these aspects:

1 The subject of the video, Madeline, is fully connected to and situated within her environment and appears to be wrapped up in her feelings and ideas as she contemplates a new existence without her family.

2 Madeline's subjective experiences are represented through her memories, feelings, physical senses and perceptions.

3 Madeline is represented as an embodied subject, but her subjectivity is limited by the constrained scope of the representation; focusing on a very immediate period of memory engagement, the only place where Madeline's larger world contexts appear is the newspaper clipping that reports the heinous shooting. However, due to the transmedia contexts of *H.C.E.* – through which H's struggles are projected onto Madeline – we gain a fuller understanding of Madeline as an embodied subject, coherently represented within a larger storyworld. Ultimately, we view Madeline's experiences of memories and sensations through H's eyes: it is H's subjectivity and

her longing for a connection to environment and family that the
H.C.E. transmedia spectator is meant to identify.

Let us return to Wilson's transmedia storyworld in order to understand how
the video 'Routine' operates within its broader contexts. The song steps out
of the immediate *H.C.E.* narrative, allowing H to connect with Madeline
Hearne's story. It is H who brings us this story, and it is only through the
transmedia materials that we learn about Madeline's disappearance after
the tragic loss of her family. 'Routine' slots into the narrative of H's own
battle with loss and disappearance, a battle that leads her along the path
of alienation and self-imposed 'disappearance'. Madeline's expression of
mental anguish brings to life an emotion that is nowhere expressed in the
H.C.E. narrative other than through this story. Madeline allows us to witness
the pain of lost love, while H denies her engagement with that experience.
Within the 'Routine' story, the subject comes to grips with her loss, while in
the broader *H.C.E.* narrative, H descends deeper and deeper into alienation
and self-destruction. 'Routine' is thus pivotal in its presentation of the
emotional narrative of *H.C.E.*: a subject who is experiencing the loss of her
loved ones; who hangs onto the memories, not wanting to let go; who finds
escape and peace in sleep/night; and who – in the continuation of the story
through the transmedia materials – eventually disappears herself.

Musically, 'Routine' stands out from the other tracks for its formal
coherence and classic progressive rock aesthetics. However, it connects to
several tracks on the album through specific sonic and gestural references.
The intensity of the guitar solo during the bridge section links the song
to other tracks on the album that reveal guitar solos to be moments of
deep internal reflection and impending 'disappearance': Tracks 2 ('3 Years
Older'), 7 ('Regret #9'), 9 ('Ancestral') and 10 ('Happy Returns'). The
interjection of Tayeb's voice, especially as an overdub to Wilson's voice,
adds an element of female reflection to the sonic design of 'Routine' just as
it does in Tracks 3 ('Hand Cannot Erase'), 9 ('Ancestral') and 10 ('Happy
Returns'). The entry of the choir in the postlude creates a strong intertextual
link to the choral effects in Tracks 10 ('Happy Returns') and 11 ('Ascendant
Here On...'), where the choir signals that H has truly stepped out of life on
earth. Finally, the harmonic progression of the postlude in 'Routine' points
clearly to a progression first heard in Track 4 ('Perfect Life') and later in
Track 11 ('Ascendant Here On...'), although in both of those tracks the
progression is left in an unresolved state.

For the reader interested in musical structure, the harmonic progression in
question is a strongly directional predominant – dominant – tonic progression
(ii – V – I) that is the hallmark of common-practice tonality. In 'Routine', the
postlude repetition of the progression is an important part of what makes
the music sound so calm and resolved. Remarkably, the same progression
does not lead to a satisfying resolution during the entire remainder of the

album. Track 11 ('Ancestral') repeats a predominant – dominant – tonic progression, although in a key (G sharp minor) chromatically removed from the album's tonal centre of G major, while the G-major treatments of ii – V – I in Tracks 4 ('Perfect Life') and 11 ('Ascendant Here On...') are left hanging on the unresolved dominant harmony. Ultimately, it is 'Routine' that provides the cathartic resolution, although in the key of the dominant (D major), which conveys a degree of distance from the broader tonal scheme. Within the tonal structure of the album, the harmonic resolution of 'Routine' in the dominant (a key that is clearly removed from the tonic) offers a musical analogy to H's focalization of Madeline's story – an otherworldly place (removed from reality) where H can come to terms with her own feelings of loss. In her real world, however, such catharsis is not achieved; instead, the final track of the *H.C.E.* album ('Ascendant Here On...') simply lets go of the search for resolution.

Concluding remarks

In her animated visual treatments of Wilson's transmedia stories ('Drive Home', 'The Raven', 'Routine' and 'People Who Eat Darkness') Cope has created unique animated subjects whose stories emerge through her engagement with the memories, emotions, senses and social contexts of her characters. Under the laborious effort of stop-motion animation, Cope performs these characters as credible subjects that belong coherently and integrally within transmedia storyworlds. With this study, it has been my objective to immerse the reader in the finely crafted multimodal discourse of the Wilson-Cope music video, as well as to situate this artefact within the contexts of its broader transmedia platform. Both Wilson and Cope make evident their own commitment to multimodal and transmedia subjectivity by enriching 'Routine' with nuanced intersections across the expressive channels of words, music and images, thus making a 'distinctive and valuable contribution' to the *H.C.E.* transmedia storyworld.[27]

Popular music artists have engaged with a variety of transmedia materials throughout the twentieth century, with the nature of these materials and their dissemination changing with the advances of technology. We can identify many antecedents to contemporary transmedia musical discourse, including the concept album and rock opera, film clips and videos, concert spectacles, as well as literary adaptations and other textual developments. With the concept album as the basis for *H.C.E.*, Steven Wilson mobilizes a significant antecedent and ongoing component of the transmedia musical work.[28] Interest in the concept album is not unique to the progressive rock genre, but rather extends across musical styles, revealing its potential for artistic expression that is grounded in specific musical contexts, cultures and aesthetics. In recent times, music critics have pointed to an increase in the popularity of the concept album across a wide scope of genres.[29] It is certainly to be expected that music scholars look primarily to the song content (words and music) in order to interpret the concept album. As they receive and interpret these works, music analysts use a variety of methods to account for musical and lyrical connections, as well as to explore the overall messages and meanings that are communicated. Although the musicological inclination is to place the greatest analytic emphasis upon the music of the concept album, the *transmedia* content of the concept album is vital to the production of meaning. For instance, Tim Smolko (2013) spends considerable energy on the lyrical content, artistic packaging and live performances of Jethro Tull's *Thick as a Brick* in order to offer a more thorough examination of the concept album materials. Taking that approach even further, Phil Rose (2015) analyses Pink Floyd's concept albums as multimedia artefacts and applies a range of theoretical techniques from literary, film and psychology studies in order to illustrate how the album materials work together to promote meanings and messages. My larger aim is to bridge these two worlds by bringing both the musical and the transmedia materials into dialogue with one another.

For the albums he has produced as a solo artist, Steven Wilson has dedicated himself to the construction of transmedia recordings, beginning with *Insurgentes* (2008) and *Grace for Drowning* (2011), both of which feature the photography and filmwork of Lasse Hoile. *The Raven That Refused to Sing (And Other Stories)* (2013) continues with Hoile's photography, but adds the stories and illustrations by Hajo Mueller and the two animated videos by Jess Cope. With *H.C.E.*, the collaborative team of Wilson, Hoile, Mueller and Cope reach a peak of creativity, in the production of the scrapbook, the blog, music videos and the concert tour, which together build a complex convergence of transmedia storytelling. That complex convergence – which Carol Vernallis has named the 'media swirl' (2013) – challenges and calls upon the spectator-consumer to develop new analytic modalities in order to understand and interpret the compelling stories of human experience and subjectivity that emerge.

CHAPTER 24

Jay Versace's Instagram empire: Queer black youth, social media and new audiovisual possibilities

Gabrielle Veronique

I don't use Instagram except to watch Jay Versace. One night my friend sent me a video of him dancing, and I was hooked. Who was this guy? Was he a genius of dance, comedy, the entire genre of extremely miniature cinema? Captioned 'Mood ✌️🌀// TAG YOUR DAY ONES', the video shows Versace and two friends dancing to upbeat R&B on what seems to be a suburban street. I probably watched it twenty times in the first sitting. I have watched it countless times since and still I cannot resist it. It has become a mainstay in my life. If I feel glum, 'Mood ✌️🌀' is there for me. I cannot get enough of it; it still makes me laugh.

It also brings up many questions. For instance:

1 What is the meaning of these cryptic emojis? What is their relationship to actually anything that's happening, including the broader themes of friendship and Mood? How do a Vulcan greeting and a fuming face come together to make meaning?
2 Where are these people?
3 Where is the music coming from??

4a   And when are they? In their personal timelines and in the broader march of history, how old are they? When is the specificity of Versace's extremely high flat-top? Given that his hair is always on his head, is he always bringing this kind of '90s nostalgia in a low to high grade way? (He's about twenty and has since changed his hair, but this was, when 'Mood 🌿 🐾made, many months off).

4b   When is the nostalgia of their clothes? Versace's friends are hitting more contemporary notes of updated '90s trends, but Versace is in full period costume.

4c   When are they in their process? Are we catching them in media res? The video is clearly composed and staged, and the camera seems to be held by a person instead of a tripod. Is this what this group does for fun? The garage and basketball hoop strongly imply youth in suburbia. Maybe they're just doing this because it's the best idea they could come up with on an idle day. There's a sense of the matter of fact, of creativity in passing.

5   Do Versace's friends also create huge amounts of content in ostensible solitude? If so, how did this transcendent exception come into being?

The key to the joke lies somewhere in the whens. The thumbnail already gives a summative glimpse of the three movement languages at work. Versace's is all lines, wingspan and angles, flanked on the left by one friend low to the ground with a hidden face and rounded back, and on the right by another friend upright, open and dancing to the sunshine. The thumbnail is drawn from somewhere in the middle of the video, a curated and compressed snapshot of the forces at play.

One arc in this video is the transition of movement languages – the eye draws around from dancer to dancer. Versace starts off in the foreground, dancing with excess power and purpose. It feels like there is a circular hinge in the very middle of his body around which everything else can torque if he wants it to. Like his clothes, his dancing is often a note beyond vintage: low squats, tutting with the entire length of his arm, Harlem shaking not so much with his shoulders as with anything that will come along for the ride. His friends present contrast in shape and pace. Versace is fast and furious, with a seriousness of intention and a stoicness of purpose, while one friend is serving up laid back, effortless cool with lateral slides and an occasional shake of the shoulder, and the other is giving the world's most exuberant cabbage patch.

About halfway through, they rotate and the sunshine friend takes centre stage. The transition is extremely (even infuriatingly) musical – Versace rounds his until now straight back and leaps away, while his friend kicks down and forward exactly when we hear a gummy percussion hit in the music. He's off to the races with an energetic Harlem shake, angular, vervy and tight to the body, in contrast to Versace's comically wide base. As Versace becomes a back-up dancer, he also plays around with the youthfulness of his movement. While in the beginning, he offered a virtuosic show of powerful, flailing abandon, he locks his torso and his hip joints as he leaps away and starts to do someone's great-uncle's two-step, topped with a curved upper-back. In the final beats of the video, the third friend completes the rotation, casually and calmly shimmying off.

As is often the case in Versace's work on Instagram, there is an aesthetic of abrupt starts and stops. Versace, like many social media influencers his age, started out on Vine, where the time constraint was so tight that abruptness was built into the format. Instagram is more flexible, but the convention remains. Something about this video feels like it passes by too fast to catch all the beats of the joke. On Instagram, there's no way to drop the needle. The only option is to re-watch and pause over and over to catch a frame and pick up the details. Having tried this many times, I can attest that every pause is its own revelation. There's is a density of motion, commitment and comedic spark that is irrepressibly seductive.

Versace's movement language in 'Mood 👢🐵' is very much of a type for him – it's wide, passionate and aggressive. He seems to max out the stretches of limbs in space, usually just a bit outside the music, but punctuated by moments of unnervingly inspired musicality. He often maintains over-focused eye contact with the camera. Sometimes he makes it all the way to the ground and, with varying degrees of matter-of-factness, humps the floor. There's often a strong sense of character and story. Paradigmatic examples include the following:

- *'Me popping up at my ex house on Christmas for a plate'* (5 December 2017) Versace dances in his dancing room, familiar from many of his videos. Somehow he ends up in plough position. As my friend put it recently, 'He seems to barely have control of this one.'

- *'This will be my extra ass all black history month'* (18 January 2018) Through movement, Versace expresses black pride in a park.

- *'This for my future bae just Incase he watchin 👵👵👵💜👵👵👵'* (4 March 2018) Versace dances in the middle of a neighbourhood street. He shows off a full range of relationships to the ground – standing, hopping and crawling with great rhythmic purpose.

- *'Wait for it … smh 👤'* (4 May 2018) Versace dances so passionately in his dancing room that he almost breaks his ceiling lamp.

- *'when computer love come on bitches be feeling robotic asf'* (2 July 2018) Versace, wearing his wig, embodies a robot.

- *'me at all the cookouts this summer'* (5 July 2018) – Wearing his wig, Versace dances in a public lot. He is confident and will not let anyone kill his sunshine. For a brief and casual moment, he humps the ground.

- *'guess what ima be for halloween* 😉*'* (1 October 2018) – Versace dresses as a diaphanous roach.

- *'ITS MY FATASS BIRTHDAY'* (24 January 2019) – Versace celebrates his fatass birthday.

Sometimes his intensity of commitment and laser focus at the camera morphs into a one-sided dance fight, lampooning an arbitrarily confrontational posture in the architecture of the subject. 'MAGAAAAAAAAAAAAAAAAA GAAAAAAAAAAAAAAAAAAAAA' (20 April 2018) is, in its choreographic arc, very similar to 'This for my future bae'. In a preamble, Versace paces and provokes. Who is he provoking? Anyone? Everyone? It's unclear. Someone is holding the camera and tracks him as he walks back and forth. He's hot and dares you to try it. Before the beat drops, he assumes the position. And he's off – he begins to dance powerfully. He is not to be messed with. Or maybe he is and he isn't at the same time.

'MAGAAAAAAAAAAAAAAAAAAGAAAAAAAAAAAAAAAAAAAA' is nearly a music video. Versace lipsyncs, and the music is overdubbed. It has strong narrative drive and arc, with a story that aligns with the song's lyrics. Two commenters come to a similar conclusion:

> **neferinka**
>
> @sandwichnyamu prof is being so petty about grading. Should just send him this.

> **sandwichnyamu**
>
> @neferinka oh my gosh. Why is this a whole music video 😂

There is something in this, though, that resists clear semantic sense. The song, DJ Blaqstarr's 'Get My Gun' remix (2018), is already in the caption being turned from a provocative image into a series of evocative syllables. The sonic detail that Versace leads with is the abstracted idea of aggressive singing. Versace's movement also explodes beyond the bounds of what a music video could earnestly contain. That he doesn't take the narrative seriously is effervescent in his commitment to the abstraction of surplus movement.

This is also true in 'KEEP MY NAME OUT YOUR MOUTH' (8 June 2018), where his dancing reminds me of Josephine Baker. Unlike 'MAGAGA', this video is a selfie, even more disconnected from the affect of the dance fight. He starts rolling before he's fully ready in face and energy, so his eyes aren't with the rest of him when he begins. We get to see the shaky and vulnerable second it takes between pressing play and getting into character. Versace has pointed control of the camera and the editing. Typically, when filming himself in the dance room, the camera is already set-up and fixed, so the editing here is a specific choice. Perhaps the character is an inspired dancer, a genius undiscovered! But in the end knows not what he says or how a person goes about saying it. When words and the camera fail, dance takes over.

The camera is a potent tool for character development in Versace's work. For instance, in 'black, messy and carefree 🎶💜' (30 August 2018), the movement of the camera mirrors and amplifies the character-defining elements of Versace's walk, which is exuberant, jaunty and elastic. Everything seems to spring from the bounciness of the music's timbral palette – the video swings on a bungee cord. Versace gradually approaches the swaying, parambulating camera, held by someone walking backwards, and the elasticated bounce becomes more and more fully all-consuming.

In '2018 we lying all year' (2 March 2018), Versace films himself with his camera in one hand, which diagonally mirrors the gestures he makes with the other as he delivers a treatise on the merits of new-age post-truth. Sometimes, he says,

> lying is good. Most of the time lying is actually more good quality, like the fabric is more good of a texture when you lie than when you tell the truth. See me, I'm deep, I'm woke, I'm spiritual; so I learned that when you lie, you're actually manifesting your life; when you lie you're creating your life; when you lie, you're speaking it into existence. We need, in 2018 we need to speak more shit into existence.

Somehow the character he's playing has fundamentally misunderstood the core of manifesting the life you want. He's got the shape of the sentiment but has landed, maybe inadvertently, on an insidious interpretation of its spirit. His hands are integral to his rhetorical instincts, which are over-done and a bit contrived. After this part of the speech, there's an extra beat and angular rotation of the camera, to show him in the profile of a thinker, at an angle and from below. In general, there's a rhythm to his speech and to the framing – something of the spoken word launched at complete inanity.

Funny as it is, this video is somehow about the distortion of the subject position. The character is delusional about his propheticism but can fully indulge in the fantasy of speaking his philosophy to the masses. The subject position, which in the analogue world can come into being through the social, falls through the prism of the camera made into a mirror. The phone camera is a conduit for mass communication, but in the moment of content production, is a reflecting medium that allows us to communicate alone.

The collapse of the camera and mirror is a running theme in Versace's work. The camera and the mirror often face each other and are absorbed into one another. There is a confusion of which is which. Versace uses mirrors to stage dialogues with himself. The tone that he takes is often somewhere between confrontational, playful and acerbic. This is generally true of his rhetorical style, but when he turns it on himself, it produces a tension between the need to laugh (it is comedy, after all) and the hum of genuine concern. His work is often skating on the line between parody and autobiography, and it's hard to avoid the feeling that someone we know and love is treating himself ungently.

In 'MORNING ROUTINE' (23 July 2017), which he reposted on its one-year anniversary, Versace is filming himself going through a manically energetic set of self-affirmations in his bathroom mirror. He starts: 'Listen here, bitch! You are that bitch; you're cute as fuck, you're bomb as fuck, personality on motherfuckin fleek!' The camera is fixed far enough behind him that we can clearly see the mirror, which is decorated with fish decals, as a distinct object.

Because the video has a manic edge, there is a sense that maybe Versace doesn't fully believe himself and is actually staging a persuasive argument by barrage with his self-esteem. By the end, he starts fully leaning into the conceit that the person in the mirror is separate from himself. He tells the face in the mirror that he has to go, but to keep shining and, 'Remember: you. that. bitch. Say it with me.'

'Getting ready for valentines day 😌😌💜🐱' (11 February 2018) ends similarly. Here, Versace uses the mirror, whose frame is only fleetingly visible, to create two versions of himself. The face in the mirror is stern, severe and direct, doling out tough love to the person outside the mirror, tremulous, insecure and unsure. The tough love character begins his speech calmly: 'Jay, you got the game fucked up – you have it fucked up, your man? He's coming! He's on his way!'

The video is uncut and Versace has to switch characters quickly in the short and disorienting turn of his phone from the mirror to himself. By the end, the two versions of Jay have gone through a round of conflict and the tremulous character has been cowed into quiet submission.

> 'Say it with me,' says the face in the mirror, 'Your man comin'
>
> 'My man comin,' is the unsteady echo.
>
> 'Okay,' says the face, nodding its head. 'Now get the fuck up, and go on Tinder'

Versace uses a similar set-up in 'I think I'm on my period' (2 August 2018), where the dialogue between two versions of himself leads to a crisis of subjectivity. If the eyes are the window to the soul, the mirror is, in this case, a window to the very existence of the self. Versace begins by addressing the image in the mirror:

'Let's talk.'
'Ummm ... ok?'
'Who are you?'
'I'm the person ... I'm your body, Jay's body.'

But, we learn, Jay wants to talk to the person inside his body. The two figures don't understand who the other is. The mirror knows somehow that it can only reflect form, and even to say that it's Jay's body is a little too concrete. Later Jay asks, 'So, who am I inside this body, because I don't feel like it's me.' After a beat of bewildered silence from the mirror, he continues: 'Bitch, I don't know who I am anymore.' Jay needs to know who he is, but the tools he has available are a mirror and a camera, both of which deal in the ephemera of light. The mirror is not exactly visible in this video, but we know it's there only because the image flips from character to character and we can see the person in the mirror holding a phone. As the identity crisis heats up, both characters start to break down and the distinctions between them begin to evaporate.[1]

Early on, the mirror image points out that he didn't even choose to be there. There's a feeling here of not being able to escape the mirror. It's a fixture in Versace's house, so in the fabric of the setting that we can't fully see it's there. It creates light effects which give the illusion of solid forms, vessels for a physically contained understanding of the person. But light, an uncontained chaos, breaks in on a stable sense of self.

The mirror is one of many items in Versace's house that recur. The house is almost a character in its own right, if only because so much of Versace's work seems to be produced on his own, at home. And he's not just producing content for Instagram – he's also deeply invested in making creative work for SoundCloud and YouTube, while maintaining a career as an actor with major ad campaigns, which capitalize on the first-person nature of his celebrity.[2] In 2018, he was on a Sprite can and was the face of a curated '90s inspired capsule collection of vintage pieces for Reebok. In a long-form ad for the Reebok campaign, Versace visits Shaq, one of the iconic celebrity faces of Reebok in the 1990s. The ad begins with Versace calling his mom, weaving in an autobiographical strand. Shaq lets Versace raid his closet, and the mantle of celebrity is passed from generation to generation through the gift of fashion. These are not just actors representing a brand – they are cast as two ordinary, charismatic people forming a genuine connection across generational lines inside the home, which for both of them is a capsule for the markers of public facing personality: Shaq has an accolades room,

Versace has his own portrait on the wall and both see personal wardrobe as an extension of identity.[3]

On Versace's Instagram, it's not clear where the Reebok campaign begins and ends. When he reposts photos or videos from the campaign, he's clearly representing the brand. But what if he's just wearing the clothes? When he wears his purple Reebok sweatshirt while stress-recovery eating on his kitchen floor, is he still working for them? Maybe? The video, published in November 2018 is playing on '90s nostalgia, which is at the core of his campaign for Reebok. His sweatshirt is vintage, as is the music, and his Disney Pochantas cup, a favorite nostalgic detail in the comments – apparently it came as a collectible from either Burger King or McDonald's. Who can say which. Either way, it transports people to their childhood, which is where, Versace tells us in one of his Reebok ads, he discovered and began to carry the '90s culture with him always.

When he's eating on the floor, the parody seems to eddy, along with the song and the smoke from his incense. Versace isn't just eating, he's feeding his soul. The whole thing is hitting him deep. It's sad and blissful, pleasure and pain. His whole body is in it. This experience moves him. In the climax, the music jolts and takes him over. The eddying of the joke spins suddenly to a moment of greatest turbulence. What this has to do with Reebok is unclear, but it's satisfying to watch.

Ambivalence about Instagram is, oddly enough, foregrounded in the Reebok campaign. In an interview published by the company, Versace meditates on his love for the '90s:

> The thing I appreciate most about the '90's is ... the fact that there was no social media, there was nobody going on Instagram to see what else somebody else is doing so they can copy them. I feel like right now we're all trying to do what everyone else is doing because of social media, and we're trying to base our lives off of other people. But I feel like in the 90's it was more free of creativity, and we're still trying to be as creative as they were.[4]

The tug is salient in Versace's work. For one, it feels like he can't possibly have time off. So much of his work is about leisure that it's hard to imagine what actual leisure would look like for him. On his personal Instagram, Versace has also expressed disappointment that comedy is the heart of his professional brand. He wants to be followed as more than a comedian, a serious artist who has more to offer. Perhaps he feels caught in the entrapping web of a life on social media.

Even without four million followers, it feels near-impossible to opt out either marginally or completely. And with such a large following, there must be intense pressure to produce content which is often a labour of one.

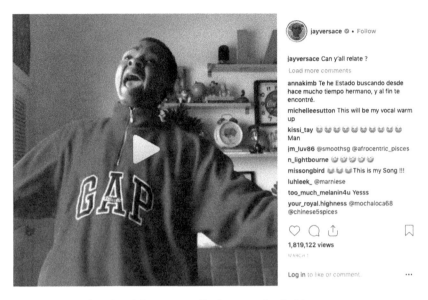

FIGURE 24.1 *Thumbnail for 'Can y'all relate?', uploaded by @jayversace (1 March 2019).*

In April 2019, he uploaded a video as a 'reminder to tell the people in your life that you are proud of them'; 'Sometimes', he says, 'people don't even know that they touch people.' Many people have tagged friends in the comments, and what unfolds is an outpouring of loveliness, so many people professing love and support for each other in public. The comments are their own essay on friendship. Versace's work on Instagram is often a virtuosic exercise in contradictions, but as a fan, I am proud of him, and grateful. Life is ambivalent, but laughter is a gift. And it honestly moves me. In 'Can y'all relate?' (March 2018), we catch him in the middle of what might be an interminable riff, where he's singing with his whole comic being (Figure 24.1). It's pure grain and sometimes, kind of, the word 'yeah'. On many days when I've needed it, this is how his work has made me feel. What more could be better?

PART NINE

Diagramatic, signaletic and haptic unfoldings across forms and genres: Lars von Trier

The demonic quality of darkness in *The House That Jack Built*: Haptic transmedial affects throughout the work of Lars von Trier

Bodil Marie Stavning Thomsen

Each new film directed by Lars von Trier sets expectations high among audiences who have come to anticipate intriguing explorations of film media, in which technological innovations are generally developed as a response to aesthetic issues that carry wider ethical-political implications. Von Trier's oeuvre is full of transmedia explorations, pushing the limits of genre film and mixing traits from film noir, horror and melodrama. He has widened the criteria of filmic composition by seeking inspiration in other technologies (electronic and digital video, digital programming and animation) and art forms (music, theatre, literature and figurative art). In the majority of his films, pathos and irony, comedy and tragedy, gothic and grotesque coexist in chiasmatic crossings. These things collectively have widened the spectrum of what a film can do.

The following short presentation of von Trier's ongoing work with haptic compositions will exemplify how each film,[1] in different ways, provokes the audience into shifting attention from a simple decoding of narration to an awareness of the 'signaletic materiality' of pixels, signals and diagrams provided by celluloid strips, electronic images and digital programming.[2] The many examples of haptic composition in von Trier's work could be seen as a transmedial 'signaletic material' affecting audiences across projects. Von Trier's interest in scrutinizing the signaletic materiality of film, video and digitalization has consistently highlighted the transmedial quality and ability of haptic compositions to affect audiences in non-representational ways. Affect reactions such as horror, pain or anguish are felt physically, and impacted by haptic perceptions of blurred or noisy images and sounds. Haptic compositions might just as well bring about sensations of joy as the opposite – simply because they can inspire an awareness towards the signaletic materiality of film.

Von Trier has produced haptic compositions in numerous ways. The Europe trilogy (*The Element of Crime*, 1984; *Epidemic*, 1987; and *Europa*, 1991) represents innovative explorations of the iconic qualities of film noir. The trilogy reintroduced the expressionistic technique of back-projection, as well as sepia toning and a focus on water, in order to negate depth in favour of foregrounding the pulsating movement of the film image, forcing the audience to inspect modulations of the image rather than the story or the narrative structure. Von Trier's preference for underlining the strange and uncanny in this first trilogy by use of haptic compositions is explored in depth in his following works. For instance, in the TV production *Medea* (1988), which followed Carl Th. Dreyer's manuscript based on Euripides's play of the same name, the artificial colours of TV were used as an affective tonality to underscore Medea's moods before and after her decision to repay Jason's betrayal by killing their sons. The use of water in the introduction, flooding first Medea and then the camera, is another haptic element underscoring the affective tonality of the figure of Medea. Dwelling on the waves in this way, as they slowly cleanse her face, covering her body as well as the camera lens, which in effect blurs the TV-viewers' sight, underscores how Medea's acts should not be judged by the ethical parameters used in, for instance, watching a melodrama. By utilizing the haptic surface of the image as a near-sighted inspection (or rather touch) of the realm of emotion or affect, von Trier succeeded – here and in many subsequent films – in questioning classical filmic and societal criteria for ethical and political judgement.

Apart from this, it can be seen as a general trait that main actors are bereft of one or more faculties, means or capabilities. In *The Kingdom* (1994) the girls, Mary and Mona, are silenced (killed and brain-damaged), producing a haptic overload of ghosts and evil spirits whose messages are interpreted by the odd detective Mrs. Drusse. But the ghosts were also 'given' a real existence as edited layers of shadows within the very materiality of the signal. This is partly attributable to the salt-and-pepper noise of the video signal, which the editor, Molly Malene Stensgaard, worked with in various ways; often working with three to four layers of videotape, and adding a 'ghost' into a blow-up of a recording. The ghosts were thus seen as if they inhabited the signaletic material, and as such they, in a material sense, could affect the TV viewer directly. In *The Kingdom II* (1997), the haptic surface modulation even materializes in the form of a huge green eye staring back from the TV set.

This association of von Trier's haptic compositions with uncanny or grotesque elements was brought into a more realistic scenario in *Breaking the Waves* (1996), where Bess's head is put through tests of psychological and religious judgement in response to the deprivation of Jan's faculties from the neck down. Her intuition and actions could be judged as both 'insane' and 'good' depending on whether or not the spectator accepts the pathos attributed to the haptic tonality of her moods. The aesthetics of the electronic signal that worked so well in *The Kingdom* were brought into this film by transmitting the 35-mm film recordings to video and back again, making the images grainy-haptic. With clear references to Carl Th. Dreyer's *The Passion of Joan of Arc* (1928), which depicted the clairvoyance of Joan as apprehensible, the haptic aesthetic underscores Bess's passionate affect rather than her actions. Meanwhile, as the chapter sections of picturesque romantic landscapes (along with a bird's-eye view from above) establish an optical aesthetic that counters the haptic-grainy realism, the spectator's negotiation between seeing with a register of pathos connected to Bess's face, rather than a romantic mastering of the depths of the landscape, becomes a matter of preferring a haptic rather than an optic orchestration. The often-dramatic shifts between a haptic and an optic orchestration of vision come to a miraculous conclusion in the film's ending, when bells in heaven suddenly materialize, indicating the resurrection of Bess. This pathetic ending was interpreted by many as offensive, while others saw the scene as an ironic twist to the whole idea of depicting 'goodness'. In my view, both readings are viable, just as a haptic vision does not oppose but merely alternates an optic vision. The quality of the film is that it succeeds in putting the audience into an echoing zone of indecision after leaving the theatre. In the chapter sections, which are underlined with rock classics from the 1970s, the assuring optical stills of romantic landscapes are slowly decomposed by the haptic movements of fog and water within these images. The film's generally realistic and haptic portrayal of the Scottish Highlands, which includes close-ups, handheld camera and jump cuts, could only find rest during these sections in Bess's face in close-up. Thus, haptic and optic are intertwined like pathos and irony. Unlike Dreyer's interpretation in *Joan of Arc*, this film is far from religious in a metaphysical sense, because it keeps underlining the affective tonalities – even in visual superiority.

In the second film of the Golden Heart Trilogy, *The Idiots* (1998), which also happens to be the second film produced under the Dogme 95 manifesto, jump-cut aesthetics are made physically sensuous. That haptic compositions can induce a 'touching with the eyes' of the object seen is in the extensive use of handheld camera emphasized to such a degree that the audience's settling of affect reactions of dizziness or nausea became apparent. When, towards the end of the film, Karen (Bodil Jørgensen) is slapped in the face, and the camera follows the movement of the hand, it feels as if the spectator is slapped too. In this film it becomes obvious that haptic sensations are granted equal status with the usual employment of perception in making sense of moving images. In my reading of *The Idiots,* I point out how the ten rules of Dogme 95 are used in an efficient way to diagrammatically brace the signaletic materiality of film.[3] By using small handheld DV technology with sound recording functions, more impetus was placed on catching live expressions than on the realistic coherence prevalent in Hollywood cinema. This haptic-affective form of realism characterized most of the Dogme films that were successfully produced from 1995 to 2005.

The theme of the third film in the Golden Heart Trilogy, *Dancer in the Dark* (2000), was deprivation of vision. Selma (Björk) substitutes her increasing lack of vision with joyful music sequences based on rhythms from the sounds of bodies, machines and buildings belonging to the diegetic world. When these sounds gather a rhythmic pace, other instruments join the music. Contrary to the dream sequences of a classical musical, these sequences of music and vivid colour work towards making the spectator become more aware of Selma's lack of vision. Musical production, so to speak, takes over where vision runs out – as a cover for this lack. The 100 cameras and the attempt to fuse image and sound digitally also placed an emphasis on the haptic, myopic reality of Selma's reduced vision compared to the full-blown musical melodrama of her imagination. This reality carries the spectator's impetus towards an affective involvement that might prove to have a different outcome than the trial against Selma. In the end, the music abruptly stops with her heart as a zoom focuses on her son's spectacles falling to the floor. Combining the silenced voice of Selma and the myopic glasses braces the synaesthetics of sound and vision to an event of blinded silence that is bound to affect the audience when leaving the theatre.[4]

In the following planned America trilogy, which eventually only consisted of *Dogville* (2003) and *Manderlay* (2005), von Trier deals with the highly praised indexical realism of film and photography. In creating a kind of mash-up or composite of the characteristics of theatre, literature and digital media in the two films, the signaletic material of film is highlighted. All shoots took place indoors, as in a theatre space, and the spectator was equipped with a bird's-eye view, as in a computer game, while an extra-diegetic voiceover explained the thoughts of the actors, as in a book. The ability of readers to peep into brains and houses alike was induced in the setting of the two films, where chalk lines serve as walls and doors, inspired by Bertolt Brecht's play, *The Caucasian Chalk Circle* (1948). His alienation theory, which prevents the audience from getting lost in illusions by depriving them a perspective of depth and hindering empathy with actors, is utilized by von Trier to underscore how easily we imagine things that are not actually seen or heard. In spite of von Trier's use of predominant traits from other media and the stripping of filmic indexicality, spectators reported that they clearly watched the movie as a film once they got used to its style.

Whereas one might consider Brecht's directions for creating alienation a guiding diagrammatic principle for the study of indexicality and what is recorded on film in *Dogville* and *Manderlay*, the following film, *The Boss of It All* (2006), was an absurd comedy reminiscent of the plays of Samuel Beckett and Luigo Pirandello. All the diagrammatic instructions that were part of the setting and the instructions for the actors in the America films (staying on the set during the entire shoot, for instance) were in this film managed by the software that instructed the camera's movements and centring. From a visual point of view, this film is ugly but hilarious, since it often leaves the actors outside the frame while, for instance, zooming into a kitchen roll or the backside of a computer. Another clearly diagrammatic film is von Trier's co-production with Jørgen Leth, *The Five Obstructions* (2003), in which von Trier creates rules for Leth's production of short films in order to force him to leave his comfort zone (since the 1960s) of modernistic aesthetics.

Below, I will go into more detail concerning the Depression trilogy, which consists of *Antichrist* (2009), *Melancholia* (2011) and *Nymphomaniac* (2014). Apart from making the haptic – in especially the fast-speed preludes of *Antichrist* and *Melancholia* along with the digitally manipulated sounds of 'nature' – the centre of demonic attraction, the spectator was included in *Nymphomaniac* in a clearly diagrammatic way. Here, von Trier's consistent work with the diagrammatic layer of narration functions as gestures of irony as well as of humour, as digressions occur referencing art, his own oeuvre and snippets of musical scores. This is developed in his most recent films to a degree where his tutoring tends to dominate everything. Meanwhile, he still invites the audience to use the faculties of seeing and listening, and the diagrammatic method thus becomes another way to make audiences aware of sensation being intertwined with sense-making.

Overall, von Trier's many transmedia experiments with video, computer animation, digital sound and transferences between forms of analogue and digital media assist the spectator in paying attention to the seeing and listening modes applied to film. Themes and stories might work as framings to von Trier's filmic explorations of the possibility of sensing in other ways. In other words: once the spectator has experienced the affective level of sensory perception offered in von Trier's films, the narrational content represented becomes secondary. In the following I will focus on the director's most recent film, *The House That Jack Built* (2018), with a view to how the above-mentioned affective sensory perception is mediated in yet another transference between sight and sound.

Serial killing and chasing images

The House That Jack Built provides five versions of serial murderer Jack's (Matt Dillon) one-dimensional point of view. The film's depiction of Jack's gruesome deeds throughout twelve years is accompanied with an equally thorough explanation of his lack of empathy for his victims. The film was originally planned as a TV series and some spectators might experience the film as absurd due to the frenetic speed and leaps between incidents and evasive explanations. No effort is spared in underlining that this is a dissection of all the well-known characteristics of a psychopath. Meanwhile, audiences are likely to also feel abhorrence towards violence as such, and film violence in particular, while watching the film. Just like Michael Haneke's stated ambition with *Funny Games* (1997), von Trier raises the question of the use of violence as a force to stimulate voyeurism at all costs.

In Laura Mulvey's famous article 'Visual Pleasure and Narrative Cinema', Hitchcock's pairing of violence and voyeurism as a fuelling of narrative drive at the expense of women is key. In *Rear Window* (1954) the female counterpart, Lisa (Grace Kelly), to the voyeuristic protagonist and 'stand in' for the spectator, Jeff (James Stewart), is only able to capture his attention when she acts as a stand in for him *and* is in danger of becoming the next victim.[5] In this situation, she shows him a wedding ring hidden from the view of the apparent murderer Lars Thorwald (Raymond Burr). The ring on her finger becomes the visual proof of Thorwald murdering his wife *and* at the same time of Lisa's proposed marriage to Jeff. Her act makes Jeff come to realize that voyeuristic, narrative desire is not the only desire possible, and that women have active powers besides being the trigger or the excuse for male action. In *Psycho* (1960), Hitchcock famously uncovers the boundless voyeuristic drive of spectators following the narrative thread to its bitter end. The point of view switches to that of Norman Bates (Anthony Perkins), when he peeps through a hole in the wall and the camera allows the spectator to also watch the female protagonist, Marion Crane (Janet Leigh), undressing. The frantic shower scene shows neither the murderer nor the murder as such. The scene's focus is on underscoring the unconscious force of voyeuristic desire – to see more in order to reach narrative closure.

In the accompanying poster to *The House That Jack Built* von Trier comments directly on the voyeuristic gaze in turning the perspective back onto the perpetrator, Jack. He is seen as if through the semi-translucent shower curtain in *Psycho*, and the film follows his narrative, murderous quest to the very end, which in this case is hell. In the epilogue or *Katabasis,* Jack's descent into hell is followed in images that might best be compared with Peter Jackson's fantasy film *Lord of the Rings* (2001). This framing of Jack as an already damned soul in a bigger epos refers directly to Dante Alighieri's *The Divine Comedy*, where Dante in its first part is escorted by Vergil into hell.[6] The epilogue thus also functions as an unwinding of the film's vicious spiral of violence at a slower pace. In this way, von Trier certainly dissociates himself from the narrative, voyeuristic 'drive' as material for entertainment. However, the film – in the usual manner of von Trier – is philosophically engaged in the study of why violence and the quest for the sublime are intertwined in Western art tradition. This quest even includes his own film oeuvre, and thus von Trier 'becomes' Jack. The voyeuristic gaze is, so to speak, looking inwards or backwards, to also include the director peeping through the camera lens.

The thing that links this film especially to what I see as his general pursuit of using haptic imagery and exploring the signaletic materiality of film is the inspection of what Jack expresses as 'the demonic quality of darkness'. This statement applies both to his psychopathic drive to kill and to his attraction towards the filmic and photographic negative. The film's overall question of why artists strive to create iconic works of art is thus linked to Jack's acts of killing, shunning the light as well as the dark or haptic side of visual mastery. But whereas the icon in *Breaking the Waves* (Bess's face) was scrutinized along with a psychiatric evaluation of her head and passed as 'good' due to a haptic-affective layer, *The House That Jack Built* is devoid of haptic-affective engagement in Jack, who practices facial mime in order to act in a convincing manner. However, well-known iconic artworks are displayed to a great extent, as is also seen in *Melancholia*, which has striking similarities to this film, especially in the preference for the circular form of a haptic negative 'energy'. And whereas the filmic indexicality (of the diegetic world) of *Dogville* and *Manderlay* was evaluated against a mash-up of other media forms and survived as a convincing signaletic material, the indexicality of *The House That Jack Built* is not in the least convincing. Besides, Jack's killing and cover-up actions are portrayed as accidental and increasingly impulsive, which on the other hand makes the audience more aware of his mental state. In that respect it clearly resembles *Nymphomaniac*, which also displays a compulsive drive towards repetitive patterns of serial segmentation. But unlike in *Nymphomaniac*, there is no escape for Jack. His actions are not excused even though the audience are granted access to his emotions at the end. He disappears into the abyss of the haptic materiality of blood with the iconic colour of red.

There is no end to the cross-referential diagrammatic connections that can be drawn across von Trier's works when it comes to his different uses of the haptic imagery accentuating the signaletic materiality of film. A unifying statement to what attracts the director as well as the audience to his haptic imagery might actually be Jack's statement: 'Through the negative, you could see the inner demonic quality of light – the dark'. Von Trier's search into what a haptic quality could look like and might bring about could be seen as a quest into the signaletic materiality of film – and as such is prior to his transmedia experiments.

Who is Jack?

The film's opening scene makes a pun on the name 'Jack' by linking it to a jack used for jacking up cars. Jack, in his red van, encounters a woman in distress (Uma Thurman) standing next to a car. She has a puncture and convinces him to drive her to the nearest repair shop to get her red jack fixed. During the drive to and from the garage, he is calm and silent, while she keeps talking about how she might become the victim of assault and murder if he turned out to be a serial killer. She claims safety, however, by referring to her red jack placed between their seats in his red van. The scene illustrates the obvious killing scene by poking fun at expectations of gruesome violence, as Jack with the red van smacks the red jack right into her face – ending her flow of speech. The suspense composition of this 'shut up' gesture is conflated in the scene: red attracts red and creates bloody red. The face of beauty is decomposed as an icon in favour of an icon with even more attraction, as the scene fades into a cubist composition of a woman's head, probably by Picasso. This transmedia composition in which a filmic icon of beauty is decomposed into the primary icon of red only to quickly dissolve into an iconic modern artwork, where personal traits have disappeared, might be seen as von Trier's first comment on the drive towards iconicity despite media forms. Notwithstanding the expectation that she is bound to be murdered, and despite the escape out of the narrative to a painting, this gruesome scene is likely to create an affect caused by rupture. Through this first murder incident the audience is introduced to a violence beyond entertainment, thus alluding to von Trier's alternative reflection on what it takes to create iconic art.

Before this first incident, a zoom onto Jack's feet in a circular field of water brings a certain awareness to the haptic layer of the film, and Jack's question to Verge (Bruno Ganz) if there are any rules[7] has introduced hell as the film's framing – without further filmic representation during the first five incidents of murder. Nevertheless, sound – the rumbling sounds of something that might be connected to a power plant, a grinding mill or a waterfall – is heard and commented upon throughout the film. In the epilogue, the rumbling sound turns out to be the sound of hell.[8] Another thing that opens for the wider question of what it takes to produce iconic art is the musical score. On numerous occasions documentary footage of Glenn Gould playing Bach *Prelude in C Minor* is seen and heard, and after more than one of Jack's successful killings, snippets are heard of David Bowie's 'Fame' (1975). The song emphasizes that fame both reduces the famous person's option to escape (in insanity) and to access future (as blank). The access to the flame of fame thus also induces to crime, since the curse of fame is that, as Bowie sings, it 'makes a man take things over'. Apart from these recurring snippets of music, only diegetic sound is heard.[9] The use of truncated snippets of music was explored to a large extent in *Antichrist* with excerpts from Händel's *Rinaldo* (1711), and in *Melancholia* with excerpts from Wagner's *Tristan und Isolde* (1859). In making snippets of Almira's lamentation and the Tristan accord recur throughout the films, Trier strikes a melancholic chord and, by accentuating again and again the sombre tones, he seems to evoke a haptic tonality of music.[10]

The main character, Jack, is presented as an engineer with aspirations to be considered an architect. His building project for a house leads him into an extended search for the right material for his planned 'artistic masterpiece'. Porous concrete, wood and stone are discarded one by one in favour of human bodies that in the end become his building material. These bodies have piled up alongside his serial killings, and have been stored in a freezer. This materiality has, however, throughout the film first and foremost been evaluated in its visual capacity, and almost like Norman's treatment of his mother-mummy in *Psycho*, Jack forms and manipulates his victims into different positions and expressions to reflect his own artistic mood. In one scene, Jack stages two of his victims – one frozen in a grotesque posture and another still bleeding – for a photo shoot. Following this, he explains his interest (since childhood) in the visual materiality of the negative. The scene shows him with his first camera, looking at the light that pours through a circular opening. But in its negative version this ingress of light becomes dark, an impenetrable surface eliminating insight – and this is, in fact, what arouses interest in Jack. When looking closer at his statement: 'Through the negative, you could see the inner demonic quality of light – the dark,' it becomes clear that the opaqueness of the surface (of the negative) has a quality surpassing that of light. This scene is, as stated above, one of von Trier's most explicit unifying statements about his elaboration of haptic quality throughout his films. It relates perfectly to the use of haptic compositions in his Depression trilogy, but it differs in many ways from the use of the haptic to produce sympathetic insight in *Medea* or affective empathy in *Breaking the Waves*. The grotesque haptic quality of the ghosts and demons in *The Kingdom* that encourage laughter is recognizable in *The Idiots*, as the spectator must acknowledge that the laughter first and foremost revolves around herself and her idiocy. The excessive possibilities of what the haptic could signify or denote in *The House That Jack Built* seem to have been distilled to an attraction towards a demonic quality of the dark. Jack's almost scientific illustration of the dark matter of the negative leads immediately to further exploration of the dark quality of light, only now related to Jack's depression as an adult. This is illustrated by a monochrome black-and-white drawing of a stick man and his shadow walking from one lamppost to the next in the night (Figure 25.1). Jack explains that the densest shadow under the lamppost marks where the pain is at its deepest. When the shadows in front and behind him are of equal length between two lampposts, he is at ease, but when the shadow behind

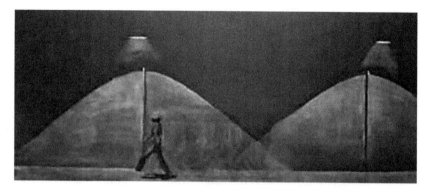

FIGURE 25.1 *Drawing of a stick man and his shadow walking from one lamppost to the next.* The House That Jack Built *(Lars von Trier, 2019).*

him grows bigger and approaches its zenith under the lamp, the pain grows and the compulsion to murder becomes irresistible.

What is key to this explanatory section and to the film in general is that the attraction towards the opaque, black surface of the negative exceeds the attraction of the positive version of the image to which the voyeuristic drive of narration also belongs. What is more, the dark quality of light is shown as a haptic, impenetrable – and unqualified – surface, which leaves no room for laughter, irony or humour. The question then becomes not what a narrative impetus shows, but what it hides. What von Trier proposes is that the quality of darkness is productive of great art (illustrated as murder) since its function is to endure the intervals of anxiety between (the delusion of) optic mastery.

A diagrammatic approach

The structure of *The House That Jack Built* comes rather close to the composition used in *Nymphomanic*. Here, the audience follows Joe (Charlotte Gainsborough), whose sexual compulsion is laid out as a visual, Dionysian force commented on verbally by the virgin Seligman (Stellan Skarsgård), who acts as an Apollonian interpreter.[11] A visual, negotiating layer of explorative diagrams between the two positions is an innovative feature of this film. As a result, it has – despite its theme – not the least power to sexually arouse the audience. All visual explorations of positions and so-called perversions of the (lust and death) drives of sexuality are immediately explained away. Any dwelling on close sexual encounters is obstructed, and thus narrative pleasure is gone. The ambition of this film, like the other two films in the depression trilogy, *Antichrist* and *Melancholia*, is clearly to explore the creativity of what are nowadays considered mental illnesses and thus bereft of significance. They are clearly productive in artistic production, but they are often interpreted as violent, offensive and negative, and thus do not really 'count' as creative forces in relation to artistic productivity.

In *Nymphomaniac* the diagrammatic layers of visual comments sometimes accompany Seligman's evasive explanations of Joe's escapades, while sometimes they become a track for the indirect speech of the implied author, inspired by Marcel Proust's *In Search of Lost Time*. This diagrammatic layer addresses the audience directly in a similar way as Jean-Luc Godard's comments (often whispered or written on the filmic material). Examples are the pedagogical explanation showing when the stream of a river is better suited for fishing, or how the Fibonacci sequence of numbers should be counted. The diagrams are informative, annoyingly pedantic or funny, but they certainly direct the attention of the audience to what it means to be bereft of narrative pleasure. Thus, Mulvey's point that voyeuristic superiority and narrative pleasure are intertwined is, so to speak, commented on by von Trier, as he encourages the audience to explore the negative or haptic side of creativity, namely self-destruction, death and the eternal recurrence embedded in Dionysian creativity.

In *The House That Jack Built* diagrams are first and foremost connected to von Trier's general meta-comment on what is considered art in a Western tradition. Documentary footage on genocide in the concentration camps of Hitler, Stalin or Mao form diagrammatic assemblages with the masterpieces of modern art. They seem to ask the question of why annihilation and mass murder in politics, and wreckage and ugliness in modern art, is seen as iconic – and why this is not applicable to film art.[12] Contrary to what is the case in *Nymphomaniac*, this diagrammatic layer by which Trier approaches the audience directly is not exactly funny. Humour has left the scene, unless the whole film is viewed as an absurd comedy. However, another kind of diagrammatic composition is at work throughout the whole film, only this time it takes place in layers of sound rather than visuals. This needs an explanation: Verge (like Seligman in *Nymphomaniac*) voices an Apollonian interpretation, but his body is hidden from vision until the epilogue. Even though he introduces himself as Verge and Jack's henchman from the film's very beginning, and even though Jack is continuously in dialogue with him, the task of the audience to follow Jack's violent deeds makes the reference to *The Divine Comedy* fade into the background. But, as was the case in *Dancer in the Dark*, sound and haptic imagery take over the visuals in the end. Verge appears in person when Jack's failed ambitions to open a locked door in his freezer's storage room is suddenly successful. In that moment, just as policemen are about to work their way through the outer metal door with blowtorches to arrest him, he manages to escape. But escape is not the issue here. Jack desperately needs the extra space to obtain a perfect distance to the five men he aims at with his gun.[13]

The gun's blurry camera vision introduces the audience to the haptic space for real – again (as in the hunting scene) through a circular field of vision. The decent to hell through a circular well cover is placed at the centre of Jack's quickly built and messy house of corpses.[14] Until this scene Verge was an acousmêtre only, a voice speaking from behind a veil.[15] After Verge has introduced Jack to all the levels of the Inferno, the film ends with Jack falling into the pit of hell, as he tries to escape his fate by crawling around to the 'other side'. At the very end, a negative image of hell is 'taken', projected and is the last vision seen by the audience. This is a negative imprint of Sandro Botticelli's *The Abyss of Hell* (c. 1485), which originally illustrated the nine levels of the Inferno in *The Divine Comedy*. In the following I will relate this 'negative image' of hell with the acousmatic instance in *The House That Jack Built* in order to further explore Jack's (and von Trier's) pursuit of the 'right material' for the production of iconic art (or architecture).

Diagramming the acousmêtre

What has been known since Dionysius the Areopagite (ca. 500 CE) as the *via negativa* of theology is related to giving a negative or mystical form of appreciation to God, because 'God' goes beyond human perception. In relating this to *The House That Jack Built,* one could say that Jack (von Trier), in his expelled exodus, pursues his aim of negotiating how art relates to ideas of immortal images or iconic signs. This aim is uttered by Jack when he, as a child, watches a photographic negative for the first time and determines that the dark is 'the inner demonic quality of light'. As mentioned previously, the circular form, which also applies to the approaching planet in *Melancholia*, should be seen as a haptic ingress in the narrative flow. It is noteworthy as well that Verge's body is actually – at a rewinding speed – inserted into the murder scenes in the epilogue in circular and haptically blurry frames, after Jack asks why he never noticed him. Something similar was also seen in *Antichrist*, where a false flashback of the woman's (Charlotte Gainsbourg's) open eyes during intercourse indicates that she has seen their son walk around and that she – as seen from the man's (Willem Dafoe's) point of view – is guilty of their son's death.[16]

In the following murder crimes Jack's 'insight' into dark matter teaches him how to cast or project shadows onto his victims. One victim (Sofie Gråbøl) is in search of masculine power in order to bring strength and endurance to her two boys (Rocco and Cohen Day), who don't believe in male superiority. As a hunter, he gives them a lesson in obedience and subjection and kills the two boys – and finally their mother, like a jackrabbit on the run. They are later exhibited as tokens of a traditional hunt, displaying the superiority of the hunter. In the following murder incident, Jack seems to have found a soulmate. Her name, Jackeline (Riley Keough) is a female form of his. She deliberately exposes herself to his moods, and he plays with her like a cat with a mouse. In one significant scene, he calms her while he talks to her through a red toy phone from behind a wall. She fears that he will leave her – and later she desperately tries to escape. During the scene, he makes her dwell on the feeling of anxiety, provoking her to scream for help.

Here the lack of response to her screams calls for the acousmêtre in two different ways, as explained by Michel Chion in reference to Hitchcock, de Palma and *King Kong*: 'The man's shout delimits a territory, the woman's scream has to do with limitless. The scream gobbles up everything into itself – it is centripetal and fascination – while the man's cry is centrifugal and structuring. The screaming point is where speech is suddenly extinct, a black hole, the exit of being'.[17] Anxiety takes Jackeline over, while Jack concludes: 'In this hell of a town, country, world – no one wants to help!' Anxiety caused and widened by loneliness and isolation seems to be the 'dark matter' that makes him 'take over' and proceed to murder.

This episode ends with diagramming the cultivation of grapes in order to obtain a sublime taste. The cultivation of taste in wine production includes decay and putrefaction, in processes where grapes are exposed to frost, to drying-up or to becoming mouldy. This dark secret – of the connection of decay and sublimity, of mass murder and iconic art – gains another twist when the noble art of rot is connected to the 'perfect ruins' of architecture and the mortal sound of the sirens of the German Stuka airplane. As von Trier explains in a diagrammatic way with documentary footage from the Second World War, the intrinsic screeching sound of the Stuka's sirens, which even made pilots pass out, was known as the killing sound, as it appeared even before the airplane was visible in the sky. Thus, the sound anticipating the sight of the Stuka becomes, for Trier, an iconic sign of the sublime combination of art and death, mastered so well by the Nazi regime. Trier is, so to speak, talking to his audience from behind a veil, explaining that the acousmêtre is able to kill, especially when it is bereft of its visual representation.

In the film's fifth incident of serial murder another reference is made to the mass killings of war. A story about a lack of ammunition on the Eastern Front of the Second World War, which allegedly resulted in experiments with regard to killing more men with less ammunition, sets Jack's ambition to kill a group of men with one 'full metal jacket'. This technical term, from which an absurd thread of narration spins off, turns out to become a play on words that again broadens the meaning of 'Jack'.[18] When Jack meets Verge and follows him to the underworld for the last section of the film, he has been fully equipped wearing a red cloak, similar to the one on Botticelli's portrait of Dante

In the film's epilogue or *Katabase*, visuals are fully fledged, starting with Verge and Jack's swim through narrow caves, apparently filmed with

GoPro cameras. The representation of hell takes on a ground colour palette dominated by ochre, yellow and red – iconic red. This section is very different from the rest of the film, even though some of the childhood images also shimmered with warm colours. In the description of the fields of Elysium that Jack is denied access to, a vision of the meadows of grass reaped with a scythe makes him shed tears. It is explained, however, that it is neither a remembrance of childhood nor the well-known representation of death that touches him. He is, rather, affected by the very sound of reaping – another acousmêtre that he used to listen to – turned away from the actual reaping men. Similarly, it is the materiality of water felt on his skin or the corrosive smell of dead, decaying bodies, which seems to transgress Jack's filter. His affected condition makes him want to escape his fate of descending into the red substance of hell.

Affects and ethical concerns on the acousmêtre and the haptic

If an ethical demand is to be applied to this film, it might be that the production of great art needs to get into a close encounter with the materiality of sight, sound and physical sensation. Apart from the accentuation of sound via the acousmêtre, the amount of diagrammatic assemblages of iconic artworks is striking. A significant example is Trier's filmic remake of Eugène Delacroix's *The Barque of Dante* (1822), which presents the struggle of agitated bodies to embark on the small boat of Dante and Vergil (Figure 25.2).[19] With

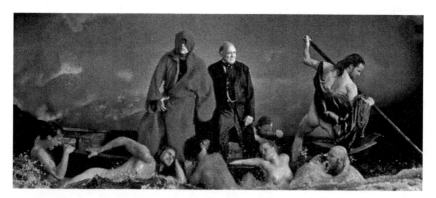

FIGURE 25.2 *Jack and Verge (Virgil from Dante's* Inferno *(1317)) are depicted into a tableaux of Delacroix's* The Barque of Dante *(1722) in* The House That Jack Built *(Lars von Trier, 2019).*

high-speed cameras, which were also used in *Antichrist* and *Melancholia* to highlight details in haptic images, the effect of an ultimate slow motion is obtained. Dying bodies and almost drowned corpses struggle to stay alive and to avoid the unavoidable. This extended scene of a nightmare becoming real might be von Trier's image of 'the demonic quality of darkness', an image of living on the edge that, in its high-speed motion, has been induced with similar qualities of repetition and monotony as the reaping sound of the scythe or the killing sound of the Stuka.

In dealing with reverberations of well-known literature, film and painting, von Trier makes his point clear: great art must affect (not entertain) the public at all costs. And this point comes through to everyone, including those who cannot cope with violence on film. *The House That Jack Built* is neither entertaining nor funny, and the violence does indeed affect the audience with abhorrence. Its reference to Dante's masterpiece of the early renaissance makes his point clear, that all effort must be put into a convincing illustration of death – which is so difficult to imagine. This said, Jack's illustration is rather poor. As in the nursery rhyme, his house cannot shelter anything and it is by no means sublime. The house that Hitchcock built for Norman Bates and his mummified mother had deliberate associations to gothic novels. Jack's house is less convincing, and deliberately so. As previously explained, von Trier distances himself from using violence as a voyeuristic drive for entertainment, while at the same time underscoring how the impact of murder on a large scale often competes with works of art in impressing an audience. Both can become icons in scale, number or composition, if they are able to stand alone, like the colour red. As with Karlheinz Stockhausen's grotesque remarks on the events of 9/11, von Trier's study shows that great works of art in Western culture often compete with mass murder in giving words, images and sound to the 'demonic quality of darkness'.

As von Trier allows Jack to die in the last scene in his unsuccessful effort to reach the 'other side', which in *The Divine Comedy* would lead to Purgatory, repentance and further on to Paradise, the audience is left with no utopia, no hope for resurrection. Jack's descent into the iconic hell of red that mirrors the first 'smack in the face' might have real iconic impact on audiences. Notwithstanding this, the rhythm, vocal and lyrics to Ray Charles's 'Hit the Road Jack' (1961), which accompany the audience leaving the cinema, seem to offer another perspective of leaving subjectivity behind. Overall, the film could be seen as a wake-up call for art and technology to build houses that are neither merely entertaining nor aspiring to sublimity in the classical Kantian sense. And it even seems to say from behind a veil – adding to what it is showing – that one place to start is to listen to the 'demonic quality of darkness' in the acousmêtre and haptic visuality, since death is the fate we all share.

Concluding remarks

The House That Jack Built can certainly be seen as an accentuation of von Trier's visual strategy that I have termed 'haptic', following Riegl's coining of the concept as well as Deleuze and Guattari's writings. In a rather sombre way, this film leaves no doubt that haptic imagery in this stage of his career equals the dark matter without which we cannot appreciate light – and that it has to be acknowledged as a significant power in the production of art.

In the first ten years of von Trier's career, haptic images – especially connected to water, fog and sepia toning – were clearly present in the film noir aesthetics of the Europe trilogy. In the 1990s, transmedia explorations of how video might take on a new kind of realism and vivify film proved to be quite successful. In the case of *The Kingdom* and *The Idiots* especially it became noticeable that this exploration exceeded stylistic traits, as the dwelling on uncanny, grotesque or abject haptic elements became integrated parts of the signaletic material (e.g. the electronic signal in *The Kingdom* and the 'spastic jesting' of the handheld camera, jump cuts and mash-up of colours in *The Idiots*). Imbedded in and stressing the signaletic material, haptic layers and compositions at the time directly impacted the audience to laugh, feel disgust and even vomit. This creation of non-representational encounters, which can create affective events behind narration has since become mainstream. Anthony Dod Mantle, cinematographer on the first Dogme 95 production, Thomas Vinterberg's *Festen* (1998), and many of von Trier's films have propagated the handheld method as a style that would not obstruct narration. With the ten rules of Dogme 95, von Trier experimented in *The Idiots* with a diagrammatic approach to such a degree that the non-representational encounters could only be missed if the whole film was disregarded.

In *Breaking the Waves*, the question of what a film can do in terms of remediating other media was posed in relation to visual perception. The privileging of illusory depth, as in landscape painting, and the connection of beauty to the face as an icon were deconstructed and given a renewed impetus due to the haptic form of realism explored in *The Idiots* and Dogme 95. In *Dancer in the Dark,* the musical was renewed in the same way, as the film's focus on the myopic Selma, who senses through rhythm and music, succeeds in making the music haptic to the audience. This layer of haptic music composed of diegetic rhythms reversed the narrative story in musical intermissions, and in the end the abrupt cessation of music felt like sensing the beat of a heart – due to the absence of rhythm.

In the America films the exploration of haptic imagery played a minor role, since the diagrammatic structure controlled by a grid of cameras was more in focus here, mixing different media to a digitally mastered mash-up. The diagrammatic layer was further developed in *The Five*

Obstructions, where directing rules were forced upon Jørgen Leth to make him appreciate haptic compositions, whereas digital programming secured random camera movements and absurd haptic imagery in *The Boss of It All*, which deconstructed narration altogether. In the Depression trilogy, the diagrammatic structure almost formed a texture with the haptic, which allowed von Trier to create a second layer of comments and even arguments, which again superimposed the story. Von Trier himself has referred to these films – into which *The House That Jack Built* should be included – as symbolic. Their manifestation of ideas and political comments are surely more explicit than in his films from the 1990s. Also, haptic imagery has also increased and sometimes seems to take over the whole scene, like water or blood seeping into the field of optic perception.

Von Trier's films are thus in many ways able to affect us on another level than the level of narration, style and genre. His focus on the creation of affective haptic encounters often makes the event of seeing a von Trier film linger for days and weeks. In this exploration of the potentialities of the signaletic materiality of film, the media of the body are sharpened: the capacity to see, talk, listen and sense.

CHAPTER 26

Diamonds, Wagner, the *Gesamtkunstwerk* and Lars von Trier's depression films

Linda Badley

A twelve-carat white double diamond, cut out of two raw stones, sits on a black pedestal in a large white space at the M HKA Museum (Museum of Modern Art), in Antwerp. The visitor, wearing a virtual reality helmet, is invited to enter its scintillating centre. This is Lars von Trier's most recent project, *Melancholia: The Diamond*, an exhibition running from 8 February until 5 May 2019 that brings together 'the oldest material that exists on Earth and an absolutely new material,' as the exhibit's co-producer Leonid Ogarev explained.[1] The first of thirteen planned, one for each of his films, *Melancholia: The Diamond* suggests the 2011 film's apocalyptic conclusion, in which two planets collide, merging into one. Senior curator Anders Kreuger explains the project's goal: to transmute one medium into another, a film into a microscopic crystalline sculpture designed to make us think 'about how you can reformulate reality from one form and language into another'.[2]

Melancholia: The Diamond epitomizes the transmedial impulse that has driven von Trier's career. With a brilliant cut on one side and rough on the other, it further embodies the extreme dialectical oppositions, both conceptual and stylistic, from which his films are composed. His four most recent films, *Antichrist* (2009), *Melancholia* (2011), *Nymphomaniac* (2013 and 2014) and *The House That Jack Built* (2018), for example, dialogue between two opposing characters and juxtapose a raw, handheld camera style with a highly polished, technically virtuosic aesthetic. They are also self-confessed psychodramas marketed as the product of his experience of clinical depression in 2006 through 2007. On one level therapeutic exercises in which his psychological dysfunctions are confessed, projected and grappled with, the first three have been aptly dubbed (by fans and bloggers) his 'Depression trilogy'.[3] Pivotal in the theorization of the New Extreme Cinema, all four convert 'low'/exploitation genres – in von Trier's case, horror, apocalyptic disaster/sci-fi and pornography – into high art while incorporating an array of media into cinema and vice versa. Embracing theatre, painting, music, literature, architecture, philosophy and politics while returning to the more controversial inspirations from his youth – Strindberg, Munch, Nietzsche, the Marquis de Sade, Albert Speer and, yes, Hitler – von Trier's post-depression films push narrative cinema to its limits, much as Wagner's *Gesamtkunstwerk*, or 'total work of art', was conceived as an ideal encompassing all arts – theatre, music, dance, painting, sculpture and literature. At the same time, they sustain ironic, post-Brechtian critiques of their own and Western culture's excesses to express a central dichotomy throughout Trier's cinematic practice: an equal passion for 'Wagnerian' operatics and anti-Wagnerian distantiation and critique.

   Antichrist signalled this shift to transmediality with its stunning black-and-white prologue choreographed to Handel's 'Lascia ch'io pianga' (from *Rinaldo*, 1711) followed by naturalistic handheld domestic scenes alternating with painterly slow-motion dream sequences, haptic evocations of natural processes accompanied by Lynchian drones (composed of sound mixes taken from nature), Boschian grotesquery and allusions to Tarkovsky, Dreyer and Bergman. But *Melancholia* was the first of the post-depression films wholly to embrace the Wagnerian, leading to his alleged 'Nazi outburst' during the 2011 Cannes film festival critics' screening interview. When *The Times* journalist Kate Muir asked von Trier about his German background, *Melancholia*'s gothic elements and his fascinations with the Nazi aesthetic, von Trier responded:

> 'I thought I was a Jew for a long time, and I was very happy being a Jew ... but it turned out that I was not a Jew. ... But anyway, I really wanted to be a Jew, and then I found out that I was really a Nazi, because my family was German ... which also gave me some pleasure ... what can I say? I understand Hitler ... and I sympathize with him a little bit. ... I'm a Nazi.'[4]

Compelling the Cannes board of directors to declare him 'persona non grata', these remarks cemented his status as the most controversial world film-maker. I believe they are best understood however as his attempt to explain, via his signature droll self-mockery, two issues that have informed his foundational myth and life's work: his complicated Jewish and German background and his lifelong fascination with and alienation from the German Romantic aesthetic.[5]

While allegedly expressing 'sympathy' with Hitler, von Trier went on to suggest that any empathy and admiration lay more with Hitler's architect Albert Speer – for having 'some talent' that the Reich had supported. Then, to the final question from another journalist about whether *Melancholia* was his equivalent of a Hollywood blockbuster and whether he would ever attempt a more ambitious film, he answered with his usual drollery: 'Yeah … we Nazis have a tendency to … do things on a grander scale.' In part, this chapter is about such a 'grander' – and overtly transmedial – scale as it pertains to the post-depression films.

Pundits who realized von Trier was joking pronounced the remarks merely 'stupid'. But as Andrew O'Hehir astutely noted, what he 'was actually trying to say wasn't stupid at all'; it related 'directly' to the 'artistic method and themes' of *Melancholia*, which 'may be the ultimate cinematic expression of the German Romantic aesthetic … [and] an enormous source of inspiration for Adolf Hitler and the Third Reich – the thread that leads from Goethe and Schubert to the worst crimes of the 20th century'.[6] A fascination with Germany, German Romanticism and Wagner have in fact informed a great many of von Trier's choices: from his student film *Befrielsesbilleder* (*Images of Liberation*, about the end of the Nazi occupation of Denmark) to his Holocaust-haunted Europe Trilogy (1984–91), the first two films of which are influenced by and/or permeated with Wagner's music[7] along with 'the charged aura of evil that hangs over Wagner since the Holocaust', as *New York Times* music critic John Rockwell describes it,[8] and to his (commissioned and subsequently abandoned) plan for directing the 2006 Bayreuth performance of Wagner's Ring Cycle (*Der Ring des Nibelungenlied*, 1848–74).

Even Dogme 95's collaborative minimalism, which he marketed as a corrective to the excesses of globalized Hollywood blockbusters, von Trier has explained as a personal limitation on his 'Wagnerian' obsession with the technical aspects and manipulative powers of film-making, to the neglect of the actors. Meanwhile, the *Golden Heart Trilogy* (1996–2000), which began concurrently with Dogme, shifted from von Trier's earlier 'masculine' concern with the post-Second World War Germany to tragic female melodramas with soaringly emotional performances from actresses, films that Rockwell describes as the expressive equivalent of music, evoking 'a new kind of hyper-emotional artistic experience'.[9] Although nominally a musical, with a four-minute 'Overture' and final aria cut off by the heroine's death, *Dancer in the Dark* aspired to the emotional reaches of opera, to the extent that composer Poul Ruders was moved to adapt it as the opera *Selma Jezková* (2010), and Missy Mazzoli's brilliant *Breaking the Waves* (2016) won the inaugural Best New Opera Award from the Music Critics Association of North America. It should be no surprise then that von Trier told an interviewer in 1999 that 'to film Wagner ... would be the ultimate goal of my life. ... I could die happy,'[10] or that in 2001, he was commissioned by Wagner's grandson to direct the 2006 Bayreuth *Ring*. He withdrew in 2004, however, after recognizing that despite two years of 'excellent progress', the 'dimensions and requirements' of the stage production would 'exceed his powers'.[11]

In a 'Deed of Conveyance' that he subsequently posted on Zentropa's website, von Trier publicly shared his key ideas for the aborted *Ring* project: a fascinating blend of Wagnerian 'monumentalism' with a 'less is more' aesthetic that, on the surface, recalls the powerful minimalism of Dogme 95. The document devotes most of its attention to the aesthetic practice of 'enriched darkness', which employed obscurity, videos and fluid scenery to guide the audience's vision and revealed its origins in cinema by referring to horror movies' reliance on darkness to create suspense and fear. To this end, von Trier argues against lighting the stage 'democratically', stressing the importance of 'conceal[ing] the technology' and 'manipulating to the extreme'.[12] Von Trier's ideas reveal a director 'dedicated to a Wagnerian aesthetic of overwhelming emotional intensity and willing to pull out all the stops to achieve it', Ryan Minor contends. Enriched darkness moreover required '(hidden) human labor on an extraordinarily Wagnerian scale ... armies of stagehands equipped with night-vision goggles, continuously moving the sets' – validating Adorno's charge that Wagner 'strives unceasingly to spirit away its own origins in human labor'.[13]

While impossible to engineer for a live production, von Trier's ideas were realized variously in all four of his post-depression films.[14] The Bayreuth project bears most directly on *Melancholia*, however, which von Trier described in his 'Director's Statement' as a headlong 'dive' into the 'abyss of German Romanticism. Wagner in spades'.[15] With its spectacular cinematography, costumes and Wagner's famous, hypnotic, infinitely unresolving 'Tristan chord' from the orchestral prelude to *Tristan and Isolde* (1865) as its sole motif, the second film in the trilogy is his most operatic, soaring and falling with Justine's emotions and prophetic visions. In achieving this, it aspires to sumptuous transmediality, interweaving music with animated paintings, melodrama and allusions from literature and modernist art cinema – to a 'total' work of art.

Melancholia's themes and style also bear comparison to the Nazi aesthetic as Frederic Spotts discusses it by way of overlapping themes including monumentalism, sacrifice and destruction.[16] Hitler's obsession with monumental or massively oversized neoclassical architecture is legendary. Also, think of the Nuremberg Rallies engineered by Speer whose 'cathedral of light' – 130 searchlights at 40 foot intervals – shot beams into the sky to 25,000 feet, producing an illusion of columns ascending into infinity. On another level, Speer's sublimely atmospheric illumination drew on the aesthetic power of darkness venerated by the Romanics,[17] and may have influenced von Trier's aesthetic of 'enriched darkness'. As for 'monumentalism', von Trier uses the term broadly in the DVD commentaries to refer to grandiose or transcendental images, icons and affects, such as *Antichrist*'s massive trees and *Melancholia*'s looming castle. But what could be more monumental than aspiring to Wagner's *Gesamtkuntswerk* itself?

Transcendence through sacrifice is the concept central to the *Golden Heart Trilogy* – in Bess's sexual martyrdom and Selma's sacrifice of her life to save her son's eyesight. In *Melancholia* the theme is modulated through the 'Liebestod', German Romanticism's keynote – especially in *Tristan*, where love's consummation is sublimated in death (Figure 26.1). In an important distinction, however, Justine is in love with annihilation itself, embodied in the approaching planet. Hitler experienced destruction as aesthetic pleasure and death as purification or cleansing, and Speer reports having seen him ecstatic while watching a documentary of London in flames after German air raids.[18] In Wagner, death is not tragic but redemptive. In *Melancholia*, the moment when the Tristan chord merges with the roar of the consuming planet marks the redemptive reconnection of Justine, Claire and Leo. Or consider the sequence in which Justine gazes with infinite longing at the death planet while bathing in its blue light – providing what von Trier in the audio commentary naughtily pronounced 'a picture ... Adolf would have liked'.[19] In the prologue, after repeated images of falling, sinking, looming and circling, the two planets perform a dance of magnetic attraction, ending as Melancholia sucks the earth sensually into its bosom. No wonder audiences sat stunned throughout the end credits and more than one critic claimed to have left the theatre 'light, rejuvenated and unconscuinably happy'[20] or soaring 'in a state of ecstasy'.[21]

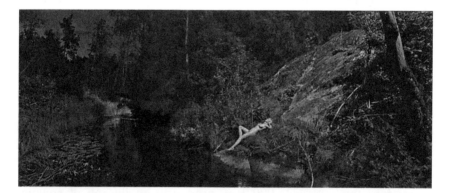

FIGURE 26.1 *In an homage to* Tristan and Isolde's *'Liebestod', Kirsten Dunst's Justine offers herself to the planet Melancholia.* Melancholia *(Lars von Trier, Richard Wagner, 2011).*

In short, von Trier is 'embracing all of [German Romanticism], the Eros and the Thanatos, the sensuality and the mannered artfulness and the love of destruction', O'Hehir asserts. Yet, at the same time, the film argues 'that the tendency that leads to magnificent art and poetry and the one that leads to totalitarianism and the cheesiest grade of 1990s music videos are all essentially the same'. After seeing the completed film, von Trier found it excessively opulent and emotional, joking in the press notes that it was like 'cream on cream'.[22] Yet if *Melancholia* represents the director at his most Wagnerian, it is equally informed by a post-Brechtian deconstruction of its own pretentions, announcing that its 'total' embrace of intermediality – of the *Gesamtkunstwerk* – is, like the massive faux castle (Sweden's Tjolöholm Slott, near Gothenborg, posing as an American tycoon's palace) and absurd wedding rituals of the caustically satirical Part I, a grandiose performance. Thus associating the film's aesthetic and production design with the values of globalized American capitalism, this critique aligns it with the overtly political US duology.

As several critics noted, Part I was a heavy-handed, sarcastic variation on Thomas Vinterberg's Dogme #1, *Festen* (1998), and allegory and stage directions are proffered throughout with a similar obviousness. The title is a quadruple reference to (1) the director's widely publicized clinical depression, represented in (2), the heroine, a case study of the same, (3) the rogue planet absurdly ten times the size of Earth, a projection of same and (4) Albrecht Dürer's famous engraving, *Melencholia I* (1514) figured as woman meditating on what appears to be a planet. The film's high cultural pretentions are announced in a slo-mo stream of allusions to treasures of Western art and culture – music, painting (Bruegel's *Hunters in the Snow* (1565), Millais's *Ophelia* (1852)), literature (Shakespeare's *Hamlet* (1599–1602)) cinema (the Bruegel pays homage to a quote in Tarkovsky's *Solaris* (1971), the falling horse to *Andrei Rublev* (1966), the burning house to *Mirror* (1975) and *The Sacrifice* (1986)). In the film proper, which focuses on the sisters' relationship, Claire nurses Justine until their roles blend and reverse, referencing Bergman's *Persona* (1966). The prologue's second shot, a lawn flanked by parallel rows of teardrop-shaped bushes and doubled shadows, evokes the famous garden, topiary and frozen sculptures of Alain Resnais *Last Year at Marienbad* (1961), the ultimate European art film.

Like its castle (and several Nazis' residences), *Melancholia* is a repository for plundered art that audiences are invited to appreciate and analyse in reference to context. The result is that instead of simply becoming immersed in a spectacle of destruction (per the apocalyptic genre formula or Hitler's vision of London burning) we are distantiated through processing the allusions, quotations and transmutations. Then von Trier proffers spoilers, depicting the collision of the planets near the prologue's beginning, styling the title card as a tombstone rubbing (eventually concluding the film with a black screen). The wedding ritual sequence quotes, alludes to and plays off European art cinema's most decadent and apocalyptic party scenes in films that epitomize modernist alienation: Buñuel's *The Exterminating Angel* (1962), Renoir's *The Rules of the Game* (1939), Antonioni's *La Notte* (1961) and Visconti's *The Leopard* (1963). Satire on capitalist acquisition is epitomized in the subplot concerning Justine's promotion to art director of an advertising company whose latest design, displayed on a screen, embodies her protest in a *Vogue*-style send-up of *The Land of Cockaigne* (1567, Bruegel's anatomy of gluttony) in high art reduced to marketing (Figure 26.2). Most obviously, however, commentary is embodied in the monumental castle from which Justine repeatedly flees and which, like Disney World or Xanadu, expresses power and capital by amalgamating past styles within a modern structure. 'Superkitsch! Absolutely perfect!' von Trier pronounced it: 'a tremendously rustic box full of different styles.'[23] For Adorno, kitsch exemplifies the false consciousness inherent in capitalism, with 'superkitsch' suggesting a post-postmodern awareness through which kitsch becomes provisionally 'cool'.[24]

Justine's melancholia stems not from trauma in the conventional sense but from consumerist desire or having too much, as Abbas Ackbar suggests.[25] Hence, in the overture's clinging yarn and slow-motion sinking images, her movement is weighted down by the materialization of lack expressed simultaneously by Wagner's 'Tristan chord', which builds the tension of desire without resolution. Hence, *Melancholia*'s monumental setting stands for Western aspiration, art and culture doomed to extinction – yet in the hugely diminished sense of kitsch about to become space dust (or, more accurately, cyber dust), and in the end, it is replaced by the simple eloquence of a teepee of stripped branches that speaks simultaneously of the

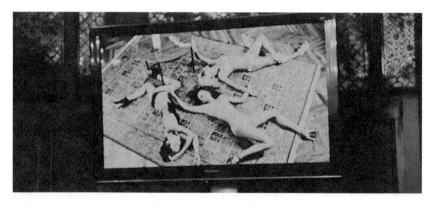

FIGURE 26.2 *High art reduced to marketing: Justine's latest ad design embodies her protest against capitalist consumerism in a* Vogue-*style send-up of* The Land of Cockaigne *(1567, Pieter Bruegel the Elder's anatomy of gluttony).* Melancholia *(Lars von Trier, 2011).*

emptiness of monuments, America's original inhabitants and Earth before modernization.[26]

Trier's next film, *Nymphomaniac*, which debuted what he has christened a new form, 'Digressionism', had a completely different (and notably unmusical) aesthetic and tone: staged as a Socratic dialogue between the eponymous Joe, who narrates her picaresque sexual adventures, and her interlocutor Seligman, an erudite sixty-year-old virgin. On one level a comical inversion of Sade's verbose libertines, Seligman provides the film's post-Brechtian variation on the *Verfremdungseffekt*. Where *Melancholia* was lushly cinematic and emotional, *Nymphomaniac* was calculatedly ugly and talky, with the frame narrative taking place in Seligman's shabby, poorly lit apartment off an alley somewhere in Europe. Yet with its literary narrative frame, episodic structure and encyclopedic reach, it was intended as von Trier's magnum opus, and even more obviously aspired to be a 'total' work of art.

Running five and a half hours and consisting of two volumes and eight chapters with elaborate title cards, *Nymphomaniac* dissects and theorizes Joe's picaresque porn narrative through Seligman's abstruse digressions and von Trier's Baroque visual, aural and haptic illustrations. Von Trier's most flamboyantly transmedial film, it features quotes from and/or alludes to a surfeit of musical, literary, religious, historical and cinematic texts: early music and rad heavy metal (Bach, Handel, Mozart and Rammstein), Izaac Walton (*The Compleat Angler*, 1653), Marcel Proust, Thomas Mann, Dostoevsky, Poe, *1001 Nights*, Brecht and Godard, along with most of von Trier's own previous works. 'Digressionism' assured that the film would be in no way erotic, Manuel Claro, von Trier's cinematographer, proud to have been associated with such a 'literary' work, told me in December 2014.[27]

Arguably, *Nymphomaniac* is less concerned with what Peter Schepelern calls the 'summing up of the woman' at the centre of most of von Trier's films since 1988s *Medea*[28] than its own discourse of encyclopedic excess, a compulsion to say and be everything. In this respect, it likely draws on Sade, as Lowry Pressly observes, noting that 'the site of the film's eroticism is [like Sade's] in its discourse, in the telling of the story'.[29] As Joe narrates her sexual escapades, competing for narrative dominance, Seligman comments, analyses and catechizes through elaborately digressive analogies: with fly fishing, Fibonacci sequences, Zeno's paradox, knot tying, cake forks, the Western versus Eastern church and so on, Joe responding in turn with bits on parallel parking, eight-cylinder engine spark plug caps, James Bond's Walther PPK automatic and the like. These digressions/analogies are illustrated through title cards, set pieces and collages from various media: from fly fishing maps and underwater footage to diagrams, superimposed numbers, archival photographs and film clips, and elaborately choreographed musical illustrations. Searching for a musical equivalent for

Sade's writing, scholar Philippe Sollers seizes on Bach's contrapuntalism,[30] and it is no accident that Chapter 5 embraces an analogy between Joe's sexual experience (which she limits for the sake of illustration to three men) and 'Ich ruf zu dir, Herr Jesu Christ' from *The Little Organ Book* (1708–17), Bach's Baroque organ music, illustrated and dissected through a three-way split-screen (Figure 26.3). Articulating the multisensory and polyphonic nature of Joe's cumulative sexual experience, this is the film's most expressive sequence. 'A Gargantuan hybrid' crossing cinema, novel, encyclopedia and treatise, as I noted in 2015, 'the film itself most closely resembles anatomy or novel of ideas, a genre favored by Sade's greatest (and longest) hits'.[31]

Nymphomaniac's 'digressions' are wickedly funny deployments of post-Brechtian (and/or Sadeian) alienation effect. Von Trier's digressionist *The House That Jack Built* is likewise the blackest of comedies – while pointedly featuring the late Bruno Ganz, who played Hitler in *Der Untergang/Downfall* (2004), as the eponymous serial killer/engineer/architect's confessor Verge (from Dante's *Inferno*, 1472). Arguing that murder is art and art is murder, and in a direct allusion to Albert Speer, Jack performs the violence he believes is inherent in human creativity, theorizing murder via 'the noble rot' of wine making and Speer's aesthetic of 'ruin value'. His 'artful' murders and architectural efforts are erected against (and blight) a pristine natural backdrop of Mount St. Helens.

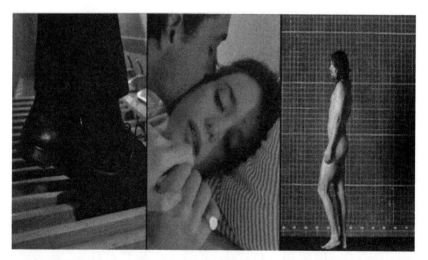

FIGURE 26.3 *Stacy Martin as Joe in an analogy between Bach's contrapuntalism and her sexual experience with multiple men, illustrated through a three-way split-screen scored to 'Ich ruf zu dir, Herr Jesu Christ' from* The Little Organ Book *(1708–17).* Nymphomaniac *(Lars von Trier, Johann Sebastian Bach, 2013).*

If the film is controversial for Jack's victimization of women, what is truly provocative is the way the film takes on Western art and culture with reference to the Nazi aesthetic, damning it all, together with Jack and von Trier himself, to hell, as Bodil Marie Stavning Thomsen has similarly suggested in her section of this module. Jack's blood-soaked confessions are accompanied by lectures and illustrated with a bricolage of aural and visual layers, from gothic architecture to the engravings of William Blake and the paintings of Picasso and Eugène Delacroix, to the piano virtuoso Glenn Gould and David Bowie's 'Fame' (1975), to diagrams and paintings of hunting rituals and trophy displays, to archival photographs of Speer's monster dome, mountains of Nazi concentration camp bodies, documentary footage of screeching Stuka dive bombers, and clips from nine of von Trier's own films. The heritage and iconography of the Third Reich is juxtaposed with Jack's architectural efforts and models (which he ponders in poses reminiscent of photos of Hitler and Speer with models of Berlin) and his most ambitious 'works', his attempt to execute five men with one full metal jacket cartridge, an homage to the Nazis and the frozen bodies he moulds into a grotesquely 'monumental' sculpture (Figure 26.4). The film ends in twenty minutes of enriched darkness and monumentalism in reverse, as Jack descends through a watery cavern to the River Styx, where Jack and Verge are merged into a tableaux of Delacroix's *The Barque of Dante* (1822), eventually reaching the circles of Dante's hell, whose streaming lava refers back to the eruption of Mt. St. Helens.

After watching Leni Riefenstahl's Nuremberg rally film *Triumph of the Will* (1935) with Mick Jagger fifteen times, David Bowie, one of von Trier's formative influences said (in a line that Jack might have uttered), 'Hitler was one of the first great rock stars. ... He was no politician, he was a great

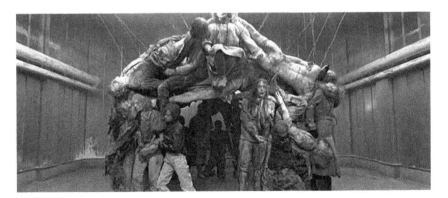

FIGURE 26.4 *Jack's 'monumental' house of corpses, reminiscent of hunting trophy displays and Holocaust images, in* The House That Jack Built *(Lars von Trier, 2019).*

media artist. How he worked his audience. … He made an entire country a stage show'[32] – one that Speer turned into something approximating Wagner's total work of art. *Melancholia, Nymphomaniac* and *The House That Jack Built* acknowledge this basic understanding, albeit in radically different ways, offering lessons from art and music, history and the present. Gagged after saying as much on a Cannes interview platform, von Trier has taken to confessing this paradox more and more directly in his darkest and most outrageously transmedial works.

CHAPTER 27

Lars von Trier, Brecht and the Baroque gesture

Donald Greig

Lars von Trier's *Dogville* (2003) and *Manderlay* (2005), the first two of an abandoned Land of Opportunities trilogy, are of interest not just for a broadly transmedial strategy of theatrical presentation but also for their more specific invocation of Bertolt Brecht's theory of drama, particularly that of his epic theatre.[1] Contrary to the generally accepted line on these films and for reasons that will become apparent, I do not subscribe to the Brechtian line of argument, an opinion prompted in part by the use of Baroque music, which, I will argue, is part of an integrationist strategy that runs counter to the premises of Brechtian theatre.

A very cine-literate director, von Trier's films are characterized by an eclectic and magpie-like approach to allusion, recycling images, tropes and citations from his favourite directors – Andrei Tarkovsky, Carl Theodor Dreyer, to name but two. However, the adoption in *Antichrist* (2009) of Tarkovsky's alternation of monochromatic film with muted colour, a feature of *The Mirror* (1975), *Stalker* (1975) and *Nostalgia* (1983), is no more a transmedial act than making *Medea* (1988) from Dreyer's original script. Rather, these acts of *hommage* are instances of intertextuality and to make more of them does nothing to advance the claim that von Trier is a transmedial director.[2]

Similar care must be taken when we consider his use of music, which, in the case of early music, is long and knowing, despite some of his later cursory comments on the subject. For example, of the Requiem mass written in the early 1500s by the late medieval composer, Pierre de la Rue, used in his student film, *Befrielsesbilleder* (*Images of a Liberation*, 1982), von

Trier is almost indifferent, describing it simply 'a choral piece'.[3] In the same context he claims that he mainly listens to 'disposable pop music', though he admits to having been a more serious listener in the past.[4] If, though, we are to take the disquisition on the Renaissance composer Palestrina, polyphony and Bach in *Nymphomaniac* (2013) as his own rather than that of a friendly musicologist, his understanding of technical musical terms such as polyphony and *cantus firmus* is assured.[5]

With *Dogville* and *Manderlay*, von Trier makes a contribution to Baroque music's particular history in film. In the silent era, if we are to judge by the compendiums of music cues made available to theatre musical directors, such repertoire was used sparingly, a clear exception being *Anna Boleyn* (Ernst Lubitsch, 1920, released as *Deception* in the United States), which included music by J. S. Bach, Rameau, Vivaldi, Handel and Corelli among others.[6] Thirty years later, the film historian Lo Duca pasted an all-Baroque score onto his sonorized version of Dreyer's *La Passion de Jeanne d'Arc* (1928, re-released in 1952), after which, though not necessarily consequentially, Vivaldi and Bach make regular appearances in the art-house films of Pier Paolo Pasolini, Andrei Tarkovsky and Ingmar Bergman.

Returning to von Trier's early career, in *Befrielsesbilleder*, the polyphonic extracts provide an accompaniment to red-saturated images of Nazi soldiers contemplating a return to their devastated homeland, followed by documentary footage of the retribution visited upon Danish collaborators. Von Trier jettisons the plainchant incipits of the requiem text and retains only the choral sections, which serve as a lament for the futility of war.[7] However, any argument for textual alignment between music and image rests on an assumption of the spectator's ability to recognize the style of late medieval music and discern the softly enunciated text. This encapsulates some of the problems that confront film music theory over the issue of pre-existent music: how it operates with the moving image – exactly how and what it means – and how any interpretation depends in part on familiarity with the musical repertoire in question. My reading of the extract from De La Rue's mass, for example, reaches towards the marshy terrain of intentionality, claiming an authorial source for something which von Trier's casual dismissal (or merely convenient amnesia) undermines. Alternatively, we take the a cappella rendition merely as an instance of sonic beauty, an assertion of the sublime to counterpoint the brutality of fascist occupation and its aftermath in much the same way that a fragment of the first movement of Mozart's String Quartet in C Major (1785) operates elsewhere in the same film. Again, though, individual response is determined by recognition, which might range from a basic knowledge of art music gleaned from television and adverts, on the one hand, to an expert's ability to cite the Köchel number (K465) of the specific string quartet. In the case of the latter, we rub up against what Anahid Kassabian describes as the 'immediate threat of history', where pre-existent music brings personal knowledge to bear, potentially throwing the spectator out of the fiction, back towards the music's origins as courtly or civic entertainment, or, in the case of De La Rue's Requiem mass, as liturgical drama.[8] This problem is exacerbated in the case of early music; medieval music has only very recently taken its place on the concert stage.[9] As such, its unfamiliarity challenges the idea of the parallelism of art music with image advanced by Royal S. Brown. After all, how sure is the spectator that this is even art music that they are hearing?[10]

Taken together, the use of De La Rue in *Befrielsesbilleder* and the references in *Nymphomaniac* serve as a primer on early music, and also as a prelude and pointer to the director's use of Baroque repertoire in *Dogville* and *Manderlay*.[11] Through the experiences of Grace (played in the first film by Nicole Kidman and by Bryce Dallas Howard in the second), these wry critiques examine respectively the place of the outsider in the United States and the country's inheritance of slavery. The presentation of both films is theatrically stylized, broken into clear chapters with punctuating narration, shot on a minimalist soundstage with white lines to indicate the streets and buildings of small communities, and the frequent use of jittery handheld camera lends a compensating sense of verisimilitude through the deployment of *cinéma verité* codes (Figure 27.1).

Wearing the tag of 'historically informed' on its sleeve, the music in both films is a confection of works by Vivaldi, Albinoni and Handel played by the English Concert on original instruments and at Baroque pitch (where the standard of A at 440Hz becomes 415Hz). Given the vast repertoire of instrumental music of the eighteenth century, it is probably only the specialist who would be able to identify all of the compositions; what operates here is a more generalized consciousness of musical style. Save for the use of David Bowie's 'Young Americans' (1975), heard over montages of provocative images of economic and racial oppression in both films, the music is seemingly disengaged from proceedings, occupying the same inaccessible, omniscient non-diegetic world of the narrator. Restraint, not a word often associated with

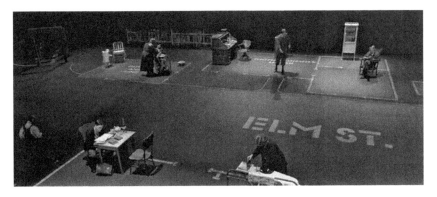

FIGURE 27.1 *The staging of* Dogville *(Lars von Trier, 2003).*

the Danish enfant terrible, is the surprising dramatic trope of the music despite the films' harrowing subject matter. It does so in distinct yet interrelated ways: first, it provides a detached commentary through an intrinsic cultural and historical distance from the depicted events – what, after all, have Italian and German court and church composers of the eighteenth century got to do with the New World? and second, it presents a mode of elegant self-containment through the less-inflected performance practices of early music. Furthermore, the original music is edited so as to ensure that cues begin with firmly stated themes and end on clear cadences, distilling the formality of eighteenth-century musical design into musical vignettes, as clear and clear-cut as the occasional chapter titles which they often accompany (Figure 27.2).

The introduction of *Manderlay*, for example, begins not at the rather undefined *tutti* of the first movement of Vivaldi's Bassoon Concerto in A minor (RV 498, unknown date, probably spurious) but at bar 14 with the first solo intervention. Similarly defined is the ending, a closure onto the related major key of C on the first beat of bar 37 in the strings. Likewise, a short sequence in *Dogville* wherein Grace finds happiness in work is accompanied by the first movement of Albinoni's Concerto for Oboe and Strings in D minor (op.9, no.2, 1722), which is brought to a premature cadence on Bb rather than the home key. Such harmonic shifts are barely noticed, not least because the music is always played very much beneath the voice-over, and a smooth narrative organization prevails.

This formal circumscription is in obvious contrast to the 'infinitely unresolving "Tristan chord"' from the orchestral prelude to *Tristan and Isolde* (1865) in *Melancholia* (2011), as Linda Badley argues elsewhere in this collection. But while *Melancholia*'s musical strategy is different from that of *Dogville* and *Manderlay* the genesis of these earlier films can be traced to von Trier's specific experience of working on Wagner's *Ring* for a production at Bayreuth:

> While working on the Ring, von Trier was also involved in work on his next film, *Dogville*, and there is no doubt that the one had an influence on

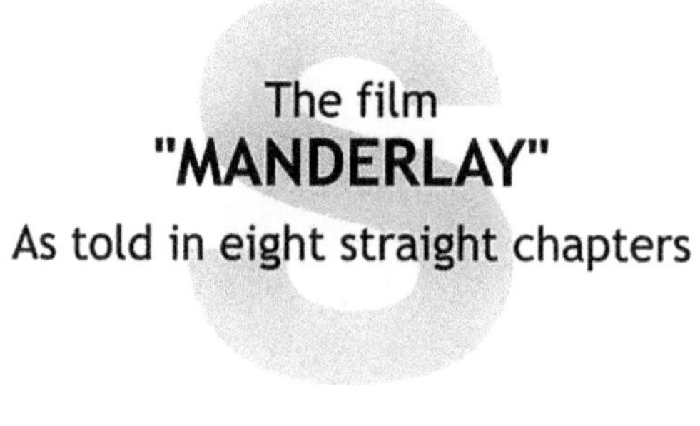

The film
"MANDERLAY"
As told in eight straight chapters

FIGURE 27.2 *Manderlay introduced (Lars von Trier, 2005).*

the other, not least in the exchange of genre-typical aesthetics. *Dogville*, with its radical, minimalistic style, its chalk lines on the floor instead of walls, doors and other objects, is one of the most uncinematic, Brechtian films in recent history, and von Trier's fascination with Harry Kupfer's and Wieland Wagner's minimalistic sets may well have prompted this theatricalisation of the modern film medium.[12]

There are, though, other precedents for von Trier's 'theatricalisation of the modern film medium': the theatricalized audiences of the camp/cult singalong/actalong screenings of *The Sound of Music* (Robert Wise, 1965) and *Rocky Horror Picture Show* (Jim Sharman, 1975), for example, and the hybridized form of filmed plays and operas broadcast live in cinemas. The Metropolitan Opera of New York initiated *Opera Live* in 2006 and The National Theatre of Great Britain began similar broadcasts of theatrical productions in 2009. Such displacements of cinematic audiences for those of the theatre also apply to *Dogville* and *Manderlay*, but filmed theatricality also invites comparison with television dramas. Key here are the historical dramas made by the BBC in the 1970s, such as *The Six Wives of Henry VIII* (Naomi Capon and John Glenister, 1970), remade as the film *Henry VIII and His Six Wives* (Waris Hussein, 1972), *Elizabeth R* (various directors, 1971) and, in particular, *I, Claudius* (Herbert Wise, 1976), all of which had worldwide distribution. The specific intertextual links to von Trier's work that distinguish these productions from others like them: the two Tudor productions featured historically appropriate music arranged and performed by the brilliant early music proponent and practitioner David Munrow; and though the (very occasional) incidental music of *I, Claudius* consisted mainly of bogus arrangements of fanfares, it was arranged by the musicologist David Wulstan and sung by members of his group, the Clerkes of Oxenford. While high production values extended to costume design and location shooting in the cases of *The Six Wives of Henry VIII* and *Elizabeth R*, the set-bound *I, Claudius*, which looked creaky even in 1975, shares with *Dogville* and *Manderlay* an aesthetic of theatrical minimalism and thespian distinction.[13] Beyond (Sir) John Hurt, who played the part of Caligula in *I, Claudius* (a role that launched his film career), and who plays the narrator in the Land of Opportunities films, a cast of British thespian royalty – (Sir) Derek Jacobi, (Sir) Patrick Stuart, and (Dame) Siân Phillips – is answered by *Dogville* and *Manderlay*'s parallel regal international cast of Nicole Kidman, Lauren Bacall, Ben Gazzara, James Caan, Willem Dafoe, Danny Glover, Udo Kier and so on.

None of these productions, though, invite comparisons with Brecht's epic theatre in the way that *Dogville* and *Manderlay* do. Brecht is the name heard most often when the norms of narrative film and illusionist theatre are challenged, though in contrast to rigorous debates in film theory, Brecht's evolving theory is often set loose from its pressing political moorings.[14] Similar appeasement infects the Land of Opportunities films. The denouements of both films present the resolution of contradictions as being contingent on human nature rather than social and political realities. In *Dogville*, for example, Grace's debasement at the hands of the small community leads her reluctantly to exert the power she enjoys as a gangster's daughter and accept that her belief in humanity was merely misplaced faith in the possibility of change. And in *Manderlay*, where at the beginning of the film Grace has recovered her optimism, she is once again forced to admit that the suffering of oppressed former slaves is self-willed. When she finally and literally wields the whip hand, we are presented with an image of immutable human instinct. Given the obvious racial division between Grace as a white woman who, furthermore, entertains cliched fantasies of black male sexuality, this film and *Dogville* trace disturbingly racist and misogynistic trajectories that von Trier unconvincingly justifies by a glib quasi-Christian sleight of hand that protests his own suffering as the source: 'Those characters are not women. They are self-portraits.'[15] Brecht's Marxist politics are resolutely opposed to the assertion of unchangeable human nature – Brecht's 1941 play is, after all, *The Resistible Rise of Arturo Ui* – and his plays are the demonstration of the construction of that human nature by economic, ideological and social forces. Von Trier's dramas do not present contradictions for the spectator to resolve; von Trier has already resolved them, as surely as the Baroque vignettes resolve. Such fatalism is not post-Brechtian; it is anti-Brechtian. A comment by Brecht about concert music may equally apply to the use of Baroque music in the Land of Opportunities films:

> Music is cast in the role of Fate. As the exceedingly complex whole unanalysable fate of this period of the grisliest, most deliberate exploitation of man by man. Such music has nothing but purely culinary ambitions left. It seduces the listener into an enervating, because unproductive, act of enjoyment.[16]

To be fair, von Trier only cites the German playwright as the 'second-hand inspiration' derived from an Oedipal attachment – his mother was keen on Brecht – and, more specifically, inspired by Pirate Jenny's song from Brecht's 1928 play, *The Threepenny Opera*, composed by Kurt Weill.[17] Von Trier is, though, at least complicit. The design of both *Dogville* and *Manderlay* – the chalked floor, the fabular narrative, the detached narrator, the episodic structure and so on – certainly echo some of Brecht's productions, but there is a huge gulf between mere non-naturalism and Brecht's politics of form. *Verfremdungseffekt*, his term for the various theatrical means by which the audience is encouraged to discern the production of illusion, provides the critical distance necessary to comprehend the social and political conditions beyond the confines of the theatre itself, '[leaving its] spectators productively disposed after the spectacle is over'.[18]

Making the Brechtian argument for acting and music in *Dogville* and *Manderlay*, and for the performances involved in both, is difficult to sustain. Acting is far from the gestic approach that Brecht advocates, where the actor signals their status as both performer and character. A documentary about the film included with the DVD release reveals Dallas describing a very method approach that distinctly American reorientation of Stanislavskyan principles which Brecht opposed: when filming *Manderlay*, all Dallas thought about was 'Grace, and what Grace thinks and what Grace wants, and how Grace feels about the situation … and I haven't really zoomed out yet and looked at the situation as a movie'.[19] Brecht preferred that music take the form of song, with musicians visible at the back of the stage where the drama's chapters are chalked on boards. While *Dogville* and *Manderlay*'s music asserts a temporal and geographical distance, such repertoire and the similarly non-diegetic narrator owe more to the literary conventions of the eighteenth-century novel. Von Trier himself cites as inspiration *Barry Lyndon* (Stanley Kubrick, 1975), a film also with a narrator and Baroque music in the main, re-orchestrated by Leonard Rosenman presumably for fear that it would otherwise be unpalatable to the mass audience. Schubert is added to the mix because, according to Kubrick, he could not discover a single 'love theme' in the entire Baroque repertoire.[20] More recently, the various chapters of *The Favourite* (Yorgos Lanthimos, 2019) are announced in similar fashion (sans narrator), with historically appropriate music (Vivaldi, Bach, Purcell).[21] In the case of *Dogville* and *Manderlay*, Baroque music's elegance and gravity are coordinated with the distinct gravelly diction of John Hurt, the sardonic narrator, narrowing the range of connotations of the repertoire, which Kassabian identifies as 'intricacy, excess, ornamentation, restraint, calculation, and lack of emotion'.[22]

Sound more generally acts as an illusionist supplement: Foley sounds resolutely complete the illusion of the otherwise simple miming of opening and closing of doors, rendering the visual and acoustic realms the recto and verso of a unified dimension. Cinematic codes such as wobbly reframings, sudden zooms and breaking of eyelines – inherited from the *nouvelle vague*, implicit in the Dogme '95 manifesto and manifest in von Trier's films from *Breaking the Waves* (1996) onwards – had by 2003 become familiar tropes of reality television and its parodic cousins: the mockumentary and its fourth-wall-breaking sitcom avatars (*The Larry Sanders Show*, USA, 1992–8; *The Office*, UK, 2001–3).[23] Illusionism is thus ensured rather than disrupted; a window is opened onto the fictional world while self-reflexive gestures are refound as filmic style rather than signalling form itself, a fulfilment of Brecht's frequent warning that repetition blunts distancing effects. As Jan Simons puts it, 'The simulacrum of [the town] Dogville presents itself as just that, a simulacrum. Baudrillard will probably feel more at home in *Dogville* than Bazin or Brecht would.'[24]

The musical line from *Breaking the Waves* to *Dogville* and *Manderlay* is also instructive. In *Breaking the Waves*, the second movement of the Sonata for Flute or Recorder and Harpsichord in E♭ major, probably by Bach (BWV 1031), is heard not in the body of the film but over the final credits.[25] Arguably, this inverts the common Hollywood device of featuring a specially written pop song over the final credits to serve as a promotional tool. The separate chapters of the film meanwhile are accompanied by hits from the 1970s, the period in which the film is set, played over the distinctive contributions of video artist Per Kirkeby, who provided slow-moving/still landscape images. *Dogville* and *Manderlay* invert this approach: as mentioned, Bowie's 'Young Americans' plays over the final credits, implementing the audiovisual aesthetic of the pop video, while Baroque music supplements the film's absence of cinematic vistas with the musical 'beauty' of stately eighteenth-century instrumental music at chapter breaks.

All three films also use their preferred repertoire to accompany montage sequences: Grace is put to work at various tasks in *Dogville* to the strains of Albinoni's Oboe Concerto in D minor; in *Manderlay*, the same character observes the (lack of) changes in behaviour of the newly freed slaves to the opening bars of Vivaldi's aforementioned bassoon concerto; and in *Breaking the Waves*, Jan is brought home from the hospital to the sound of T. Rex's 'Hot Love'. The interchangeability of instrumental Baroque music and pop music highlights their similarities; both are organized according to a fixed musical beat – in the case of Baroque concerti movements, either a tempo (*Allegro, Andante*, etc.) or dance form (Gavotte, Minuet, etc.) – responsible for what Roy M. Prendergast describes as the repertoire's 'rather square phrasing', while pop music eschews metrical variance and foregrounds a rigid beat usually through drum patterns.[26] Both repertoires serve well as punctuational markers, their temporal self-determinism halting narrative flow and providing an effective aural anchor to the temporal and topographical ellipses of the montage sequences.

Perhaps more than anything else, it is this shared functionality of pop music and music of the eighteenth century that undermines any seeming claim of early music to any subversive role, at least through and across von Trier's films. But then that was probably always the fate of early music once it had taken its place on the concert stage, whence Brecht thought it was impossible 'to make any political or philosophical use of music'.[27] That is not to say that more involved readings of the mediations of early music and its performance are not valid, as Carlo Cenciarelli has convincingly shown with regard to the figuring of the 'Goldberg' Variations in the Hannibal Lecter franchise, but that the efficacy of any extant music in film to be either subversive or immersive is inevitably contingent upon individual familiarity and shifting historical knowledge.[28] And such knowledge is not necessarily learned in the classroom but through encounters with repertoire across and within other media.

NOTES

Chapter 1

1 David Bordwell, 'Intensified Continuity: Visual Style in Contemporary American Film', *Film Quarterly* 55, no. 3 (Spring 2002): 16–28; Jeff Smith, *The Sounds of Commerce: Marketing Popular Film Music* (New York: Columbia University Press, 1998), 199–205; Carol Vernallis, *Experiencing Music Video: Aesthetics and Cultural Context* (New York: Columbia University Press, 2004), 35–7; Carol Vernallis, 'Music Video, Songs, Sound: Experience, Technique and Emotion in *Eternal Sunshine of the Spotless Mind*', *Screen* 49, no. 3 (2008): 277–97.

2 Vernallis, conversations with directors: Åkerlund, Spring 2016; Abteen Bagheri, Spring 2018; Joseph Kahn, Spring 2018.

3 Interview with director, winter 2019.

4 Henry Jenkins, 'The Reign of the "Mothership": Transmedia's Past, Present and Possible Futures', in *Wired TV: Laboring Over an Interactive Future*, ed. Denise Mann (New Brunswick: Rutgers University Press, 2014), 244.

5 Claudia Gorbman, 'Auteur Music', in *Beyond the Soundtrack: Representing Music in Cinema*, eds. Daniel Goldmark, Lawrence Kramer and Richard Leppert (Berkeley: University of California Press, 2007), 149.

6 Richard Dyer, *Only Entertainment* (New York: Routledge, 1992), 18.

7 Joe Tompkins, 'The Makings of a Contradictory Franchise: Revolutionary Melodrama and Cynicism in *The Hunger Games*', *Journal of Cinema and Media Studies* 58, no. 1 (2018): 70–90.

8 In a piece entitled 'Beyoncé, New Technologies, Politics, and Our Unclaimed Futures' (accepted to JSAM, pending revisions), I draw from Marx, Rawls, Appiah, Kimberley Crenshaw to discuss social justice in relation to new technologies.

9 Meyers is incredibly inventive, fast, hardworking and engaged with many forms (including hip hop), so perhaps this could have been foreseen.

10 Dyer, *Only Entertainment*, 20–1. I would wish our contributors and subjects might share my impulses, which go something like this: We, at least in America, are incredibly wealthy. Our lives are contingent, shaped by what's been bequeathed to us, our gifts and inheritances. We might give some, yet still less than commonly granted authority to free will, and, instead, through a sense of gratitude, and an embrace of the world, wish that we all might matter. We might strive for everyone to have good lives, and for the world's flourishing. Flourishing as a baseline for people might include freedom from precarity (healthcare, education, housing, employment, respect, community, etc.). With incredible resources (the world's best soil, rich cultural capital, etc.), we have enough to support us all.

11 Richard Dyer and Paul MacDonald, *Stars* (London: British Film Institute, 1979); Carl Plantinga, *Passionate Views: Film, Cognition, and Emotion* (Maryland: Johns Hopkins University Press, 1999).
12 Interview with producer, winter 2019.
13 I've claimed that this relation can emulate human ones.
14 For theory that works towards this audiovisual fusion, see the work of Claudia Gorbman, Richard Dyer, Nicholas Cook, Michel Chion, Carol Vernallis and Holly Rogers.
15 Gorbman, 'Auteur Music', 149.
16 Mark Fisher, *The Weird and the Eerie* (London: Repeater Books, 2016).
17 David Bordwell, 'Observations in Film Art: Now Leaving Platform 1' (2009), at http://www.davidbordwell.net/blog/2009/08/19/now-leaving-from-platform-1/ (accessed 12 December 2018).
18 Jenkins, 'The Reign of the "Mothership"', 244.
19 Henry Jenkins, *Convergence Culture: Where Old and New Media Collide* (New York: New York University Press, 2006), 95–6.

Chapter 2

1 Raymond Williams, *Marxism and Literature* (Oxford: Oxford University Press, 1977), 132.
2 'A radical form of an appropriation, enhanced agency, fandom, self-rule and identitarian practice is "cosplay" (costume + role playing), i.e. the practice of dressing up and pretending to be a fictional character.' Adriano D'Aloia, Marie-Aude Baronian and Marco Pedroni, 'Fashionating Images: Audiovisual Media Studies Meet Fashion', *Comunicazioni Sociali* 1 (2017): 12.
3 David Herman, *Basic Elements of Narrative* (Oxford: Wiley-Blackwell, 2009), 119.
4 Christian Metz, 'The Imaginary Signifier', *Screen* 16, no. 2 (1975): 14–76; Jean-Pierre Oudart, 'Cinema and Suture', *Screen* 18, no. 4 (1977/78): 35–47; Stephen Heath, 'Notes on Suture', *Screen* 18, no. 4 (1977/78): 48–76.
5 See, for example, Murray Smith, *Engaging Characters: Fiction, Emotion, and the Cinema* (Oxford: Clarendon Press, 1995); Carl Plantinga and Greg M. Smith, eds., *Passionate Views: Film, Cognition, Emotion* (Baltimore: Johns Hopkins University Press, 1999); Amy Coplan, 'Caring About Characters: Three Determinants of Emotional Engagement', *Film and Philosophy* 10, no. 1 (2006): 1–19; Carl Plantinga, '"I Followed the Rules, and They All Loved You More": Moral Judgment and Attitudes Toward Fictional Characters in Film', *Midwest Studies in Philosophy* 34, no. 1 (2010): 34–51; Margrethe Bruun Vaage, 'Fiction Film and the Varieties of Empathic Engagement', *Midwest Studies in Philosophy* 34, no. 1 (2010): 158–79.
6 Mario Bunge, *Treatise on Basic Philosophy. Volume IV: Ontology – A World of Systems* (Amsterdam: Reidel, 1979).
7 Renira Rampazzo Gambarato, 'Signs, Systems and Complexity of Transmedia Storytelling', *Estudos em Comunicação* 12 (2012): 74.

8 Carole Lyn Piechota, 'Give Me a Second Grace: Music as Absolution in The Royal Tenenbaums', *Senses of Cinema* 38 (2006): http://sensesofcinema.com /2006/on-movies-musicians-and-soundtracks/music_tenenbaums/ (accessed 8 March 2019); James MacDowell, 'Notes on Quirky', *Movie: A Journal of Film Criticism* 1 (2010): 1–16; James MacDowell, 'Wes Anderson, Tone and Quirky Sensibility', *New Review of Film and Television Studies* 10, no. 1 (2012): 6–27; Elena Boschi and Tim McNelis, '"Same Old Song": On Audio-Visual Style in the Films of Wes Anderson', *New Review of Film and Television Studies* 10, no. 1 (2012): 28–45; Lara Rose Hrycaj, 'What Is This Music? Auteur Music in the Films of Wes Anderson', unpublished PhD thesis, Wayne State University (2013); Sunhee Lee, 'Wes Anderson's Ambivalent Film Style: The Relation between *Mise-en-scène* and Emotion', *New Review of Film and Television Studies* 14, no. 4 (2016): 409–439. Peter Kunze also points out that 'Robert Yeoman's cinematography has immeasurably impacted the visual style we too often credit to Wes Anderson alone'. 'Introduction: The Wonderful Worlds of Wes Anderson', in *The Films of Wes Anderson: Critical Essays on an Indiewood Icon*, ed. Peter C. Kunze (New York: Palgrave Macmillan, 2014), 4.

9 MacDowell, 'Wes Anderson, Tone and Quirky Sensibility', 9. See also Lee, 'Wes Anderson's Ambivalent Film Style', 414–17.

10 Jeffrey Sconce, 'Irony, Nihilism, and the New American "Smart" Film', *Screen* 43, no. 4 (2002): 360.

11 Donna Peberdy, '"I'm Just a Character in Your Film": Acting and Performance from Autism to Zissou', *New Review of Film and Television Studies* 10, no. 1 (2012): 48, 50; Lee, 'Wes Anderson's Ambivalent Film Style', 431–7.

12 MacDowell, 'Notes on Quirky', 5; Lee, 'Wes Anderson's Ambivalent Film Style', 417–20 and 431–7. Francesco Casetti calls this the 'unreal objective shot'. *Inside the Gaze: The Fiction Film and Its Spectator*, trans. Nell Andrew and Charles O'Brien (Bloomington: Indiana University Press, 1998), 50. This type of shot is 'unreal' because it refers to unusual camera angles and is 'objective' or omniscient because it takes a God's eye viewpoint and cannot be attributed to any character in the diegesis (the spectator identifies with the camera's look).

13 Piechota, 'Give Me a Second Grace'; Boschi and McNelis, '"Same Old Song"'.

14 Claudia Gorbman, 'Auteur Music', in *Beyond the Soundtrack: Representing Music in Cinema*, eds. Daniel Goldmark, Lawrence Kramer and Richard Leppert (Berkeley: University of California Press, 2007), 149–62; Hrycaj, 'What Is This Music?'

15 Kogonada, 'Wes Anderson//Centered' (2014): http://vimeo.com/89302848 (accessed 9 March 2019).

16 Kim Wilkins, 'The Sounds of Silence: Hyper-Dialogue and American Eccentricity', *New Review of Film and Television Studies* 11, no. 4 (2013): 412–13.

17 Ibid., 417.

18 Adrian Martin, '*Mise-en-scène* Is Dead, or the Expressive, the Excessive, the Technical and the Stylish', *Continuum* 5, no. 2 (1992): 87–140.

19 Peter Bradshaw, 'Come Together Review – Wes Anderson's H&M Christmas Ad Is Short and Sweet', *The Guardian* (28 November 2016), at https://www. theguardian.com/film/2016/nov/28/come-together-review-wes-anderson-h-and-m-christmas-ad-adrien-brody (accessed 9 March 2019).

20 Mark Wolf, *Building Imaginary Worlds: The Theory and History of Subcreation* (New York: Routledge, 2014), 246.

21 Arthur Melzer, 'Rousseau and the Modern Cult of Sincerity', *The Harvard Review of Philosophy* 5, no. 1 (1995): 5.

22 'Masses of people are concerned with their single life histories and particular emotion as never before; this concern has proved to be a trap rather than a liberation.' Richard Sennett, *The Fall of Public Man* (New York: Alfred A. Knopf, 1977), 5.

23 Melzer, 'Rousseau and the Modern Cult of Sincerity', 5.

24 Jay Magill, *Sincerity: How a Moral Ideal Born Five Hundred Years Ago Inspired Religious Wars, Modern Art, Hipster Chic, and the Curious Notion That We All Have Something to Say (No Matter How Dull)* (New York: W.W. Norton, 2012), 225.

25 Landers, in Magill, *Sincerity*, 190.

26 Linda Hutcheon, *Irony's Edge: The Theory and Politics of Irony* (London and New York: Routledge, 1994), 66.

27 Peter Wollen, *Signs and Meaning in the Cinema*, revised edition (London: Secker and Warburg/British Film Institute, 1972), 94.

28 Ibid., 96.

29 Greg Smith, *Film Structure and the Emotion System* (Cambridge: Cambridge University Press, 2003), 14.

30 Ibid., 14.

31 The lyrics of the third song on the album, 'Little Sister' (not used in the film) suggest incest between a brother and a sister, one of the main themes in *The Royal Tenenbaums* (although Margot is Richie's adopted sister).

32 Hrycaj, 'What Is This Music?' 117.

33 David Brooks, *Bobos in Paradise: The New Upper Class and How They Got There* (New York: Simon & Schuster, 2000), 66.

34 Wes Anderson and Owen Wilson, *The Royal Tenenbaums* (London: Faber and Faber, 2001), 101.

35 David S. Miall and Don Kuiken, 'A Feeling for Fiction: Becoming What We Behold', *Poetics* 30 (2002): 221–41.

36 The painting is currently available at https://spoke-art.com/collections/vendors?q=Matt%20Linares (accessed 27 July 2018).

37 Other artworks from the 'Bad Dads' exhibitions are available on the Spoke website: https://spoke-art.com/collections/bad-dads-prints (accessed 27 July 2018).

38 Plantinga, '"I Followed the Rules"', 43.

39 Ibid., 46.

40 Nicholle Lamerichs, *Productive Fandom: Intermediality and Affective Reception in Fan Cultures* (Amsterdam: Amsterdam University Press, 2018), 211.

41 Claude Lévi-Strauss, 'The Effectiveness of Symbols', in *Structural Anthropology*, trans. C. Jacobson and B. G. Schoepf (London: Allen Lane, 1972), 186–205.

42 Peter Berger and Thomas Luckmann, *The Social Construction of Reality: A Treatise in the Sociology of Knowledge* (Garden City, NY: Anchor Books, 1966).

Chapter 3

1   See Lisa Schwarzbaum, 'Take a Tour of Wes Anderson's World', *BBC* (7 March 2014), at http://www.bbc.com/culture/story/20140307-wes-andersons-tiny -world-a-tour; and Anna Peele, 'The Wonderful World of Wes Anderson', *GQ* (22 March 2018), at https://www.gq.com/story/the-wonderful-world-of-we s-anderson (both accessed 15 April 2019).

2   Henry Jenkins, *Convergence Culture: Where Old and New Media Collide* (New York: New York University Press, 2006), 114.

3   Peter Kunze, 'From the Mixed-Up Films of Mr. Wesley W. Anderson: Children's Literature as Intertexts', in *The Films of Wes Anderson: Critical Essays on an Indiewood Icon*, ed. Kunze (New York: Palgrave Macmillan, 2014), 103.

4   See James MacDowell, 'The Andersonian, the Quirky, and 'Innocence', in *The Films of Wes Anderson*, 154.

5   Michel Chion, *Audio-Vision: Sound on Screen*, ed. and trans. Claudia Gorbman (New York: Columbia University Press, 1994), 8.

6   See James MacDowell, *Irony in Film* (New York: Palgrave Macmillan, 2016), 100.

7   See Paul Weedon, 'Mark Mothersbaugh on Shaping Wes Anderson's Sound', *Little White Lies* (10 December 2016), at http://lwlies.com/articles/mark-mot hersbaugh-on-working-with-wes-anderson/ (accessed 15 April 2019).

8   See Rachel Dean-Ruzicka, 'Themes of Privilege and Whiteness in the Films of Wes Anderson', *Quarterly Review of Film and Video* 30, no. 1 (2013): 25–40.

9   See, for example, Carole Lyn Piechota, 'Give Me a Second Grace: Music as Absolution in *The Royal Tenenbaums*', *Senses of Cinema* 38 (2006), http://sen sesofcinema.com/2006/on-movies-musicians-and-soundtracks/music_tenenba ums/ (accessed 15 April 2019); Elena Boschi and Tim McNelis, '"Same Old Song": On Audio-Visual Style in the Films of Wes Anderson', *New Review of Film and Television Studies* 10, no. 1 (2012): 28–45; and Arved Ashby, 'Wes Anderson, Ironist and Auteur', in *Popular Music and the New Auteur: Visionary Filmmakers After MTV*, ed. Arved Ashby (New York: Oxford University Press, 2013), 180–201.

10 Adam Lerner, ed., *Mark Mothersbaugh: Myopia* (New York: Princeton Architectural Press, 2014), 34.

11 The 'mutato' part of Mutato Muzika was a direct link to Mothersbaugh's roots in Devo. Mutato was a fusion of 'mutant' and 'potato', which related to the band's absurdist reasoning that we are all devolving, and no more special than the common potato, or spud.

12 Simon C. Jones and Thomas G. Schumacher, 'Muzak: On Functional Music and Power', *Critical Studies in Mass Communication* 9, no. 2 (1992): 156.

13 In the early 1980s, Mothersbaugh and the members of Devo even rearranged and recorded some of the band's best-known songs as muzak versions that were eventually released in 1987 as the *E-Z Listening Disc*.

14 Mothersbaugh quoted in Matthew Klickstein, *Slimed! An Oral History of Nickelodeon's Golden Age* (New York: Plume, 2013), 131–2.

15 Mothersbaugh quoted in Chris Garcia, 'Oral History of Mark Mothersbaugh', Filmed November 2017 at Los Angeles, CA. Video, 1:23:51. https://www.you tube.com/watch?v=YfeLBV3J6NI&t=3896s (accessed 15 April 2019).

16 Donna Kornhaber, *Wes Anderson* (Urbana: University of Illinois Press, 2017), 19.

17 On Mothersbaugh's activities as an 'inveterate collector', see Robert Koehler, 'Mothersbaugh: The Collector', *Variety* (15 January 2014), at https://variety .com/2014/music/features/mothersbaugh-the-collector-1201059076/ (accessed 15 April 2019); on his Mae Zedong memorabilia and Hitler-era collection, see Randall Roberts, 'Are You Not Devo? You are Mutato', *LA Weekly* (5 December 2007), at http://www.laweekly.com/music/are-you-not-devo-you -are-mutato-2151061 (accessed 15 April 2019); on his 'eccentric sounds and noisemakers', see Harley Brown, 'Interview: Mark Mothersbaugh', *Red Bull Music Academy Daily* (12 June 2017), at http://daily.redbullmusicacademy.co m/2017/06/interview-mark-mothersbaugh (accessed 15 April 2019).

18 Kornhaber, *Wes Anderson*, 13.

19 Ibid., 45.

20 Jason Diamond, 'Devo's Mark Mothersbaugh on Growing Up Blind, Carving Ruby Turds', *Rolling Stone* (6 June 2017), at https://www.rollingstone.com/ culture/culture-news/devos-mark-mothersbaugh-on-growing-up-blind-carvin g-ruby-turds-200623/ (accessed 15 April 2019).

21 Richard Brody, 'Wild, Wild Wes', *The New Yorker* (2 November 2009), at https://www.newyorker.com/magazine/2009/11/02/wild-wild-wes (accessed 15 April 2019).

22 Whitney Crothers Dilley, *The Cinema of Wes Anderson: Bringing Nostalgia to Life* (New York: Wallflower Press, 2017), 12–15.

23 Ibid., 26.

24 Annette Lareau, *Unequal Childhoods: Class, Race, and Family Life*, Second edition (Berkeley: University of California Press, 2011), 1.

25 Ibid., 3.

26 Ibid., 5.

27 Philip Norman, *Paul McCartney: The Life* (New York: Little, Brown and Company, 2016), 335.

28 G. Barry Golson, *The Playboy Interviews with John Lennon and Yoko Ono*, conducted by David Sheff (New York: Playboy Press, 1981), 157–8.

29 Another Beatles song that includes a 'simulated' harpsichord (played on a Lowery organ) is 'Lucy in the Sky with Diamonds' (1967), which specifically evokes the imaginative imagery of wonderment of childhood.

30 Ben Winters, '"It's All Really Happening": Sonic Shaping in the Films of Wes Anderson', in *Music, Sound and Filmmakers: Sonic Style in Cinema*, ed. James Wierzbicki (New York: Routledge, 2012), 52.

31 See Jen Hedler Phillis, '"I Always Wanted to be a Tenenbaum": Class Mobility and Neoliberal Fantasy in Wes Anderson's *The Royal Tenenbaums*', in *The Films of Wes Anderson*, 173–4.

32 Cash also holds a position as an 'Assistant Professor of English Literature' at the fictional Brooks College. Given that Cash is the only character in the film to hold an academic position, one wonders if this is in some way a larger critique or spoof of academic institutions and their specific canon of taste.

33 Sunhee Lee, 'Wes Anderson's Ambivalent Film Style: The Relation Between *Mise-en-scène* and Emotion', *New Review of Film and Television Studies* 14, no. 4 (2016): 431.

34 Maura Kelly, 'Mark Mothersbaugh', *The Believer* (1 September 2005), at https://www.believermag.com/issues/200509/?read=interview_mothersbaugh (accessed 15 April 2019).

35 Anderson quoted in Lerner, *Mark Mothersbaugh*, 17.

36 Ibid.

37 See Jonathan Dornbush, 'Wes Anderson Wants to Build a Theme Park with Devo's Mark Mothersbaugh', *Entertainment Weekly* (5 November 2014), at http://ew.com/article/2014/11/05/wes-anderson-devo-mark-mothersbaugh-t heme-park/; and Joe Berkowitz, 'These are Rides from that Wes Anderson Theme Park That's Definitely Happening', *Fast Company* (5 November 2014), at https://www.fastcompany.com/3038073/these-are-the-rides-from-that -wes-anderson-theme-park-thats-definitely-happening (both accessed 15 April 2019).

Chapter 4

1 See the museum website at https://www.khm.at/en/visit/exhibitions/wesanderso nandjumanmalouf2018/ (accessed 6 February 2019).

2 Cody Delistraty, 'Wes Anderson, Curator? The Filmmaker Gives It a Try', *New York Times* (7 November 2018), at https://www.nytimes.com/2018/11/07/arts/ design/wes-anderson-vienna-kunsthistorisches-museum.html (accessed 6 February 2019).

3 Theodor W. Adorno, *Minima Moralia: Reflections on a Damaged Life*, trans. E. F. N. Jephcott (London: Verso, 2005).

4 Martin Jay, 'Taking on the Stigma of Inauthenticity', in *Essays from the Edge: Parerga and Paralipomena* (Charlottesville: University of Virginia Press, 2011), 28.

5 Ibid.

6 I explore this idea further in my chapter '"It's All Really Happening": Sonic Shaping in the Films of Wes Anderson', in *Music, Sound and Filmmakers: Sonic Style in Cinema*, ed. James Wierzbicki (New York: Routledge, 2012), 45–60.

7 See, for example, Kate McQuiston, 'Some Assembly Required: Hybrid Scores in *Moonrise Kingdom* and *The Grand Budapest Hotel*', in *The Routledge Companion to Screen Music and Sound*, eds. Miguel Mera, Ronald Sadoff and Winters (New York: Routledge, 2017), 477.

Chapter 5

1 Alexandre Desplat quoted in Eric Kelsey, 'A Minute With: Composer Alexandre Desplat on the Art of Scoring Film', *Reuters* (5 February 2014), at https://www.reuters.com/article/us-alexandredesplat-idUSBREA140XO20140 205 (accessed 24 April 2019).

2 Lara Hrycaj, 'What Is This Music? Auteur Music in the Films of Wes Anderson' (2013), at https://digitalcommons.wayne.edu/oa_dissertations/662 (accessed 24 April 2019).

3 Claudia Gorbman, 'Auteur Music', in *Beyond the Soundtrack: Representing Music in Cinema*, ed. Daniel Goldmark, Lawrence Kramer and Richard Leppert, 1st edition (University of California Press, 2007), 149.

4 Hrycaj, 'What Is This Music?', 240.

5 See for instance https://www.pond5.com/music/1/wes-anderson.html (accessed 24 April 2019).

6 Desplat quoted in 'Harry Potter Composer Alexandre Desplat and the Shadow of John Williams', *Classic FM* (2015), at https://www.classicfm.com/composers /desplat/news/john-williams-influence/ (accessed 24 April 2019).

7 See Matt Zoller Seitz and Anne Washburn, *Wes Anderson Collection: The Grand Budapest Hotel* (New York, NY: Harry N. Abrams, 2015), 117.

8 See Warren Buckland's chapter in this book: 'The Wes Anderson Brand: New Sincerity Across Media', 27.

9 Mothersbaugh quoted in Paul Weedon, 'Mark Mothersbaugh on Shaping Wes Anderson's Sound', *Little White Lies* (2016), https://lwlies.com/articles/ma rk-mothersbaugh-on-working-with-wes-anderson/ (accessed 24 April 2019).

10 Theo Cateforis, "The World of Wes Anderson and Mark Mothersbaugh: Between Childhood and Adulthood in *The Royal Tenenbaums*", in *Transmedia Directors: Artistry, Industry and New Audiovisual Aesthetics*, eds. Carol Vernallis, Holly Rogers and Lisa Perrott (New York: Bloomsbury, 2019), 38.

11 Desplat quoted in Seitz and Washburn, *Wes Anderson Collection: The Grand Budapest Hotel*, 135.

12 See, for example, his score for David Fincher's *The Curious Case of Benjamin Button* (Warner Bros., 2009).

13 For more on this, see Lawrence M. Zbikowski, *Conceptualizing Music: Cognitive Structure, Theory, and Analysis* (Oxford University Press, 2005), 67–8.

14 Cateforis, "The World of Wes Anderson and Mark Mothersbaugh", 47.

15 Schulwerk began in Germany in the 1930s and is still widespread globally. It originally taught children to play 'recorders, xylophones, and metallophones of all ranges, glockenspiels, kettledrums, small drums, tomtoms, gongs, various kinds of cymbals, triangles, [and] tune bells'. Carl Orff and Arnold Walter, 'The Schulwerk: Its Origin and Aims', *Music Educators Journal* 49, no. 5 (1963): 72.

16 Juan Chattah, 'Semiotics, Pragmatics, and Metaphor in Film Music Analysis', *Electronic Theses, Treatises and Dissertations* (1 February 2006): 111, at http://diginole.lib.fsu.edu/etd/3874 (accessed 24 April 2019).

17 All cue titles correspond to track titles used in the film's original soundtrack album.

18 Lara Hrycaj, 'What Is This Music?' 139.

19 Warren Buckland, "The Wes Anderson Brand: New Sincerity Across Media", in *Transmedia Directors*, 19.

20 Hrycaj, 'What Is This Music?', 65.

21 Ibid., 103.

22 Ibid., 62.

23 Sleigh bells are heard during their travel by train ('Daylight Express to Lutz'), on foot ('No Safe House'), by taxi ('M. Ivan'), by cable car ('Cantus at Gabelmeister's Peak') and by sled (later in 'Cantus').

24 See Matt Grobar, 'Composer Alexandre Desplat On The Booming Taiko Drums & Barking Saxophones of "Isle of Dogs"', *Deadline* (blog: 9 January 2019), at https://deadline.com/2019/01/alexandre-desplat-isle-of-dogs-wes-anderson-composer-interview-1202520992/ (accessed 24 April 2019).

25 An example of the pitch organization is a bitonality that juxtaposes two implied pentatonic scales. The double bass establishes the tonic as E♭ with a looping bass line of E♭–B♭–D♭–B♭. Over this, one of the recorders plays a melody on D, E and G. While the G makes a major third against the E♭ tonic, suggesting positive affect, the other two pitches could not be more dissonant or strange against E♭, forming a chromatic cluster around it. Elsewhere in the cue, the celeste arpeggiates a G♭ augmented triad, which implies the dissonant minor-major-seventh chord against the E♭ tonic (E♭–G♭–B♭–D). Bernard Herrmann heavily used this chord type in his scores for Hitchcock's suspense films; see Royal S. Brown, *Overtones and Undertones: Reading Film Music*, 2nd Printing (University of California Press, 1994), 151.

26 Ewan Clark, 'Harmony, Associativity, and Metaphor in the Film Scores of Alexandre Desplat' (Victoria University of Wellington, 2018), 277.

27 Ibid.

28 Jeff Smith, *The Sounds of Commerce: Marketing Popular Film Music* (Columbia University Press, 1998), 4.

29 Ibid., 11.

30 See Harvey Kubernik, *Hollywood Shack Job: Rock Music in Film and on Your Screen* (UNM Press, 2006), 195.

31 Smith, *The Sounds of Commerce*, 5 (emphasis mine).

32 Hrycaj, 'What Is This Music?', 44.

33 Ibid., 38.

34 Rhythms from popular styles other than jazz are also occasionally played by brushed drum kit, such as the bluegrass in *Fantastic Mr. Fox*.

35 This includes the cues 'And Also Because He Fired Me', 'No Lifeguard on Duty', 'Snowflake Music/Mr Henry's Chop Shop' and 'You're Breaking His Heart'.

36 Tagg and Robert Clarida, *Ten Little Title Tunes: Towards a Musicology of the Mass Media* (Mass Media Music Scholars' Press, 2003), 566–73.

37 A brief history of these kinds of jazz-influenced scores is provided in Mervyn Cooke, *A History of Film Music* (New York: Cambridge University Press, 2008), 223–4. Desplat has cited Mancini as one of his influences in an interview with Max Max Covill, 'Composer Alexandre Desplat on Choosing Luc Besson Over "Star Wars"', *Film School Rejects* (21 November 2017), at https://filmschoolrejects.com/composer-alexandre-desplat-choosing-luc-besson-star-wars/ (accessed 24 April 2019).

38 Tagg and Clarida, *Ten Little Title Tunes*, 580–8.

39 Hefti, *Batman*. RCA Victor LPM 3573, 1966.

40 Hrycaj, 'What Is This Music?', 234.

41 See Kate McQuiston, 'Some Assembly Required: Hybrid Scores in Moonrise Kingdom and The Grand Budapest Hotel', in *The Routledge Companion to Screen Music and Sound*, eds. Miguel Mera, Ronald Sadoff and Ben Winters (London: Routledge, 2017), 481.

42 An extensive commentary on the influence of existing music on Desplat's scores for *Moonrise Kingdom* and *The Grand Budapest Hotel* may be found in McQuiston, 'Some Assembly Required.' This has highlighted to me the importance of curated existing music as an influence on the Desplat/Anderson scores.

43 For more on this see Yi-Hsin Cindy Liu, 'The Examination of the Appearance and Use of French Horn in Film Scores from 1977 to 2004' (D.M.A. Thesis, University of Cincinnati, 2005), 17.

44 For more in-depth discussions of this theme, see Clark, 'Harmony, Associativity, and Metaphor in the Film Scores of Alexandre Desplat', 286–8; McQuiston, 'Some Assembly Required', 489–90; and Mark Richards, 'Oscar Nominees 2015, Best Original Score (Part 1 of 6): Alexandre Desplat's *The Grand Budapest Hotel* I Film Music Notes' (2015), at http://www.filmmusic notes.com/oscar-nominees-2015-best-original-score-part-1-of-6-alexandre-des plats-the-grand-budapest-hotel/ (accessed 24 April 2019).

45 The concept of intradiegesis is introduced in Ben Winters, 'The Non-Diegetic Fallacy: Film, Music, and Narrative Space', *Music and Letters* 91, no. 2 (1 May 2010): 224–44.

46 Grobar, 'Composer Alexandre Desplat On the Booming Taiko Drums & Barking Saxophones Of "Isle Of Dogs"'.

Chapter 6

1 Coppola quoted in Guy Lodge, 'Sofia Coppola: "I Never Felt I Had to Fit into the Majority View"', *The Guardian* (2 July 2017), https://www.theguardian. com/film/2017/jul/02/sofia-coppola-beguiled-i-never-felt-i-had-to-fit-into-t he-majority-view-interview (accessed 12 February 2019).

2 Coppola quoted in David Faraci, 'Interview: Sofia Coppola (*Marie Antoinette*)', *CHUD.com* (12 October 2006), https://chud.com/interview-sof ia-coppola-marie-antoinette/ (accessed 12 February 2019).

3 Merle Ginsberg, 'Launching Sofia', *W Magazine* (1 September 1994), https://www.wmagazine.com/story/sofia-coppola-milk-fed (accessed 12 February 2019).

4 Derek Blasberg, 'The Dreamy Team', *Harper's Bazaar* (13 August 2014), https://www.harpersbazaar.com/fashion/designers/a3169/marc-jacobs-sofia-cop pola-0914/ (accessed 12 February 2019).

5 Carol Vernallis, *Unruly Media: YouTube, Music Video, and the New Digital Cinema* (New York: Oxford University Press, 2013), 22.

6 For a sampling of this work, see Anna Backman Rogers, *Sofia Coppola: The Politics of Visual Pleasure* (New York: Berghahn Books, 2018); Fiona Handyside, *Sofia Coppola: A Cinema of Girlhood* (I.B. Tauris, 2017); Diana Diamond, 'Sofia Coppola's *Marie Antoinette*: Costumes, Girl Power, and Feminism', in *Fashion in Film*, ed. Adrienne Munich (Bloomington: Indiana University Press, 2011), 203–31; Belinda Smaill, 'Sofia Coppola: Reading the Director', *Feminist Media Studies* 13, no. 1 (2013): 148–62; and Todd Kennedy, 'Off With Hollywood's Head: Sofia Coppola as Feminine Auteur', *Film Criticism* 35, no. 1 (Fall 2010): 37–59.

7   See Tim Anderson, 'Lost in Transition: Popular Music, Adolescence, and the Melodramatic Mode', in *Popular Music and the New Auteur: Visionary Filmmakers After MTV*, ed. Arved Ashby (New York: Oxford University Press, 2012), 63–83; and Justin Wyatt, *The Virgin Suicides: Reverie, Sorrow, and Young Love* (New York: Routledge, 2018).

8   Anderson, 'Lost in Transition', 66.

9   Ibid., 68.

10 Wyatt, *The Virgin Suicides*.

11 Scott quoted in Michael Dempsey, "Review of Blade Runner", *Film Quarterly* 36, no.2 (Winter 1983): 34.

12 Scott quote in Scott Bukatman, *Blade Runner*, (London: British Film Institute, 1997), 18.

13 'Sofia Coppola's Commercials: 6 Stunning Ads by Director Sofia Coppola', *Bold Content* (23 January 2015), https://boldcontentvideo.com/2015/0 1/23/sofia-coppolas-commercials-6-stunning-ads-by-director-sofia-coppola/ (accessed 28 January 2019).

14 Jacob Swinney, 'Watch: A Video Essay About Sofia Coppola's Dreamlike Aesthetic', *Indiewire.com* (11 February 2015), https://www.indiewire.com/ 2015/02/watch-a-video-essay-about-sofia-coppolas-dreamlike-aesthetic-133103/ (accessed 28 January 2019).

15 Steff Yotka, 'Marc Jacobs's Fragrance Gets the "Virgin Suicides" Treatment', *Fashionista* (26 June 2014), at https://fashionista.com/2014/06/sofia-coppola -daisy-dream-video (accessed 30 January 2019).

16 Jessie David Fox, 'Theories on What Bill Murray Whispered at the End of *Lost in Translation*', *Vulture* (3 October 2013), https://www.vulture.com/2013/10/ lost-in-translation-whisper-theories.html (accessed 1 February 2019).

17 Zack Sharf, '"Lost in Translation" 15 Years Later: Sofia Coppola on ending the Film on Her Terms and the Year it Took to Get Bill Murray', *Indiewire* (27 August 2018), https://www.indiewire.com/2018/08/lost-in-translation- 15th-anniversary-sofia-coppola-interview-ending-whisper-meaning-1201998 010/ (accessed 1 February 2019).

18 A couple of videos suggest that Bob quietly urges Charlotte to 'tell the truth' to her emotionally distant husband. See Fox, 'Theories on What Bill Murray Whispered'.

19 'Production Notes: *The Virgin Suicides*', *Cinema Review*, http://www.cine mareview.com/production.asp?prodid=959 (accessed 2 February 2019).

20 Ibid.

21 Ibid.

22 Dennis Lim, 'It's What She Knows: The Luxe Life', *New York Times* (10 December 2010), https://www.nytimes.com/2010/12/12/movies/12sofia.html (accessed 2 February 2019).

23 Ibid.

24 Anderson, 'Lost in Transition', 64.

25 Ibid., 80.

26 Dennis Bechor, '*A Very Murray Christmas* Director Sofia Coppola: "I Wanted to Do Something Joyful"', *Time* (4 December 2015), http://time.com/4132069/ sofia-coppola-a-very-murray-christmas/ (accessed 5 February 2019).

27 For more on the concept of a *melomane*, see Claudia Gorbman's 'Auteur Music', in *Beyond the Soundtrack: Representing Music in Cinema*, eds. Daniel Goldmark, Lawrence Kramer and Richard Leppert (Berkeley: University of California Press, 2007), 149–62.

28 Quoted in Bechor, 'Something Joyful'.

29 Allan Scully, 'The Flaming Lips Will Share Bizarre, Absurd Musical Moments Saturday in Eugene', *The Register-Guard* (31 May 2018), https://www.register guard.com/entertainmentlife/20180531/flaming-lips-will-share-bizarre-absurd -musical-moments-saturday-in-eugene (accessed 6 February 2019).

Chapter 7

1 Bruce Bennett, 'The Cinema of Michael Bay: An Aesthetic of Excess', *Senses of Cinema* 75 (June 2015), at http://sensesofcinema.com/2015/michael-bay-do ssier/cinema-of-michael-bay/ (31 January 2017).

2 Ibid.

3 'Michael Bay', https://en.wikipedia.org/wiki/Michael_Bay (27 February 2019).

4 Scott D. Lipscomb, 'The Perception of Audio-Visual Composites: Accent Structure Alignment of Simple Stimuli', *Selected Reports in Ethomusicology* 12 (2005): 37–67.

5 Scott D. Lipscomb and Roger A. Kendall, 'Perceptual Judgment of the Relationship Between Musical and Visual Components in Film', *Psychomusicology* 13, no. 1 (1996): 60–98.

6 Mark Kerins, *Beyond Dolby (Stereo): Cinema in the Digital Sound Age* (Bloomington, IN: Indiana University Press, 2010), 232–40.

7 Lutz Koepnick, *Michael Bay* (Urbana, IL: University of Illinois Press, 2018), 96.

8 Kerins, *Beyond Dolby*, 92.

9 'The Sound of Transformers Age of Extinction' (2 July 2014), at https://ww w.michaelbay.com/2014/07/02/the-sound-of-transformers-age-of-extinction/ (accessed 27 February 2019).

10 Roger Ebert, 'Review: *Transformers: Dark of the Moon*' (28 June 2011), at https://www.rogerebert.com/reviews/transformers-dark-of-the-moon-2011 (accessed 27 February 2019).

11 'Sound of Transformers Age of Extinction'.

12 Noel Murray, 'Six Michael Bay Music Videos that Help Explain the Art of Michael Bay', *The Dissolve* (27 June 2014), at https://thedissolve.com/featur es/interdisciplinary/637-six-michael-bay-music-videos-that-help-explain-the/ (accessed 1 March 2019).

13 It's hard to imagine a better pairing of sonic and visual style than hiring Michael Bay to direct videos for the over-the-top, everything-to-the-extreme operatic bombast of a Jim Steinman/Meat Loaf album.

14 This progression does not necessarily hold for some of Bay's later music videos done for artists (Aerosmith and Faith Hill) who were contributing songs to his feature films. But by the time he was making these he had a couple of feature

films under his belt and likely was no longer trying to develop a style through his music video work.

15 Carol Vernallis, 'The New Cut-Up Cinema: Music, Speed, and Memory', paper presented at annual *Screen* Studies Conference, Glasgow, Scotland, 4–6 July 2008.

16 Smith quoted in Sean Fennessey, 'An Oral History of Michael Bay, the Most Explosive Director of All Time', *GQ* (27 June 2011), https://www.gq.com/story/michael-bay-oral-history (accessed 28 February 2019). Emphasis in original.

17 Carol Vernallis, *Unruly Media: YouTube, Music Video, and the New Digital Cinema* (New York; Oxford: Oxford University Press, 2013), 33.

18 'Michael Bay – What Is Bayhem?' *Every Frame a Painting* (3 July 2014), at https://www.youtube.com/watch?v=2THVvshvq0Q (accessed 28 February 2019).

19 Murray, 'Six Michael Bay Music Videos that Help Explain the Art of Michael Bay'.

20 Koepnick, *Michael Bay*, 112.

21 Brian Tallerico, 'Review: *Transformers: The Last Knight*' (20 June 2017), at https://www.rogerebert.com/reviews/transformers-the-last-knight-2017 (accessed 28 February 2019).

22 Bay is in the minority of contemporary film-makers in this way; while many people are concerned with content playing well across multiple formats/venues to maximize ancillary revenue streams, Bay is still making movies designed to be seen and heard in a theatre.

23 Kate Kenny, 'Michael Bay: A New Kind of Director', *The Atlantic* (1 July 2014), at https://www.theatlantic.com/entertainment/archive/2014/07/once-and-for-all-michael-bay-is-not-an-auteur/373715/ (accessed 26 February 2019).

24 Bennett, 'The Cinema of Michael Bay'.

Chapter 8

1 For Marvel Phase 3, see Rebecca Ford and Borys Kitt, 'Marvel Reveals Complete Phase 3 Plans, Dates "Black Panther", "Inhumans", "Avengers: Infinity War"', *The Hollywood Reporter* (28 October 2014), at https://www.hollywoodreporter.com/heat-vision/marvel-reveals-complete-phase-3-plans-dates-black-panther-inhumans-avengers-infinity-war-744455. For Star Wars, see Marc Graser, '"Star Wars": The "Sky's the Limit" for Disney's Spinoff Opportunities', *The Hollywood Reporter* (12 September 2013), at https://variety.com/2013/biz/news/star-wars-skys-the-limit-for-disney-when-it-comes-to-opportunities-1200609291/. For the DCEU: Darren Franich, 'Warner Bros. Announces 10 DC Movies Including "Wonder Woman"', *Entertainment Weekly* (15 October 2014), at https://ew.com/article/2014/10/15/justice-league-green-lantern-wonder-woman-flash-movies/. All accessed 23 April 2019.

2 While most characters speak English in the movie, the Koreans speak Korean. Their speech is sometimes subtitled, sometimes left untranslated, sometimes translated on screen via a machine. When the movie screened in

non-Anglophone territories, it was dubbed or subtitled according to local convention.

3   This pieced-together funding system is widespread. What makes *Snowpiercer* a model is the combination of that system – described in more detail below – with the auteurist account of the movie's development and style.

4   Mark Betz, *Beyond the Subtitle: Remapping European Art Cinema* (Minneapolis: University of Minnesota Press, 2009), 83.

5   See John Hill and Nobuko Kawshima, ed., 'Film Policy in a Globalised Cultural Economy', special issue of *International Journal of Cultural Policy* 22, no. 5 (2016). In particular, Brian Yecies, 'The Chinese-Korean Coproduction Pact: Collaborative Encounters and the Accelerating Expansion of Chinese Cinema', 770–86.

6   '*Le Transperceneige: From the Blank Page to the Black Screen*' (dir. Jésus Castro-Ortega, 2015), on *Snowpiercer* (RadiusTWC/Starz/Anchor Bay, 2015; Blu-Ray).

7   Jerome Baron, Skype interview with the author, 7 August 2018.

8   See Nicolas Finet, *Histoires du Transperceneige* (Paris: Casterman, 2013), 70. My translation.

9   Baron interview.

10 Ibid.

11 Finet, *Histoires*, 71. Italics added; my translation.

12 Matthew Kirschenbaum, *Track Changes: A Literary History of Word Processing* (Cambridge, MA: Belknap, 2016). But for a round-up of what history there is, see also Stayci Taylor and Craig Batty, 'Script Development and the Hidden Practices of Screenwriting: Perspectives from Industry Professionals', *New Writing* 13, no. 2 (2016): 204–17.

13 Julian Hoxter, 'The New Hollywood, 1980–1999', in *Screenwriting*, eds. Hoxter and Andrew Horton (New Brunswick, NJ: Rutgers University Press, 2014), 101–26, 122.

14 Masterson, phone interview with the author, 13 July 2018. See also ScreenCraft Staff, 'Exclusive: Interview with *Snowpiercer* Screenwriter Kelly Masterson', *ScreenCraft* (28 July 2014), at https://screencraft.org/2014/07/28/interview-snowpiercer-screenwriter-kelly-masterson/ (accessed 24 April 2019).

15 Choi, phone interview with the author, 31 July 2018.

16 Data from KOFIC, *Status & Insight: Korean Film Industry 2013* (2014), 25. Later volumes of KOFIC's *Korean Cinema* series are available at http://www.koreanfilm.or.kr/eng/publications/books.jsp (accessed 23 April 2019).

17 I want to thank Keith B. Wagner for his input on this discussion of CJ and highlight his forthcoming essay, 'Systematizing Contemporary Korean Cinema in the Age of Asian Globalization: Out from Hollywood's Shadow to the Rise of Hallyuwood', in *From Postwar to Contemporary Korean Art (1953-Present): Conflicts, Innovations and Interactions*, eds. Yeon Shim Chung, Sunjung Kim and Kimberly Chung (forthcoming). As different as CJ and other Korean studios are from their Hollywood counterparts, they are still subject to the pull of self-allegorization. So in the abandoned animated introduction to *Snowpiercer*, the camera tracks through a still CG representation of a city on the verge of freezing. Among the stores that line the street is an outpost of Bibigo!, a Korean barbeque restaurant chain owned by CJ's parent company.

18 The Czech rules can be found here: https://www.filmcommission.cz/incentives/
    eligibility-and-amount/ (accessed 23 April 2019).
19 Claussova, phone interview with the author, 9 August 2018.
20 Ibid.
21 Data from 'Film incentives paid in 2010–2015', at https://fondkinematografi
    e.cz/english/film-incentives.html, 'Film incentives paid in 2010–2015' (accessed
    23 April 2019).
22 For an account of the interaction between state funding and taxation schemes,
    see J. D. Connor, 'Independence and the Consent of the Governed: The Systems
    and Scales of *Under the Skin*', *Jump Cut* 57 (Fall 2016), at http://ejumpcut.org/
    archive/jc57.2016/-ConnorSkin/index.html (accessed 23 April 2019).
23 I discuss the shift from phases to sites in 'The Modern Entertainment
    Marketplace, 2000–the present', in *Directing*, ed. Virginia Wright Wexman
    (New Brunswick, NJ: Rutgers University Press, 2017), 137–53.
24 For a differing approach to the material deposits left by 'immaterial', global
    motion picture production, see Hye Jean Chung, *Media Heterotopias: Digital
    Effects and Material Labor in Global Film Production* (Durham, NC: Duke
    University Press, 2018).
25 Nikki Lee and Julian Stringer, 'From *Screenwriting for Sound* to Film Sound
    Maps: The Evolution of Live Tone's Creative Alliance with Bong Joon Ho',
    The New Soundtrack 8, no. 2 (2018): 145–59, 153. A fuller reading of
    Snowpiercer appears in their essay '*Snowpiercer*: Sound Designable Voices
    and the South Korean Global Film', in *Locating the Voice in Film: Critical
    Approaches and Global Practices*, eds. Tom Whittaker and Sarah Wright
    (Oxford: Oxford University Press, 2017), 263–77.
26 Lee and Stringer, 'From *Screenwriting for Sound* to Film Sound Maps', 153–4.
27 For production design, see the discussion of Patrizia von Brandenstein in
    Dorothy Heisner, *Production Design in the Contemporary American Film:
    A Critical Study of 23 Films and Their Designers* (Jefferson, NC: McFarland,
    2004), 156. For VFX supervisors see Barbara Robertson, 'VFX Supervisor
    Ken Ralston on *Alice in Wonderland*', *Studiodaily* (21 February 2011), at
    http://www.studiodaily.com/2011/02/vfx-supervisor-ken-ralston-on-alice-in-
    wonderland/ (accessed 23 April 2019). For composers, see the entry on Rupert
    Gregson Williams in Chris Jones and Genevieve Jolliffe, *The Guerilla Film
    Makers Handbook*, 3rd ed. (New York: Continuum, 2006), 368. For sound, in
    addition to Lee and Stringer, see Gianluca Sergi, *The Dolby Era: Film Sound in
    Contemporary Hollywood* (Manchester: Manchester University Press, 2004),
    118.
28 Q&A with Kevin Feige and Jon Favreau, USC (17 May 2018), at https://www.
    youtube.com/watch?v=HWGf3aRX4-o (accessed 23 April 2019).
29 Quoted in '*Le Transperceneige*'.
30 The translation device that occasionally serves an important role in the movie
    is one materialization of that.
31 Choi interview. He is referring to Peter Biskind, *Down and Dirty Pictures:
    Miramax, Sundance, and the Rise of Independent Film* (New York: Simon &
    Schuster, 2005).
32 Choi interview.

33 Data from Boxofficemojo.com (accessed 23 April 2019).
34 Dorothy Pomerantz, 'What the Economics of "Snowpiercer" Say about the Future of Film', *Forbes* (9 August 2014), at https://www.forbes.com/sites/dorothypomerantz/2014/09/08/what-the-economics-of-snowpiercer-say-about-the-future-of-film/#4ff09ca76bb1 (accessed 23 April 2019). A second aspect of this agreement requires more space than I can give it: the conversion of the movie into a television series and the chaos that surrounded its production. See Katie Kilkenny, 'Fired "Snowpiercer" Showrunner Calls replacement an "Idiot" for Not Reaching Out', *The Hollywood Reporter* (17 May 2018), at https://www.hollywoodreporter.com/live-feed/fired-snowpiercer-showrunner-calls-replacement-an-idiot-not-reaching-1112964 (accessed 23 April 2019).

Chapter 9

1   Ben Radatz, '*Se7en*', *Art of the Title* (10 July 2012), at http://www.artofthetitle.com/title/se7en/ (accessed 28 March 2019).
2   Ibid.
3   Fincher quoted in Mark Salisbury, 'David Fincher: British Film Institute Interview', in *David Fincher: Interviews*, ed. Laurence Knapp (Jackson: University Press of Mississippi, 2014), 148.
4   Jan-Christopher Horak, *Saul Bass: Anatomy of Film Design* (Lexington: University Press of Kentucky, 2014).
5   Guy Julier, *The Culture of Design*, 3rd ed. (Los Angeles: Sage Publications, 2014), 24.
6   J. D. Connor, *The Studios After the Studios: Neoclassical Hollywood (1970–2010)* (Palo Alto: Stanford University Press, 2015), 190.
7   For one example of this argument, see Stephen Metcalf, 'How Superheroes Made Movie Stars Expendable', *New Yorker* (28 May 2018), at https://www.newyorker.com/magazine/2018/05/28/how-superheroes-made-movie-stars-expendable (accessed 28 March 2019).
8   Ignatiy Vishnevetsky, 'What is the 21st Century?: Revising the Dictionary', *Mubi* (1 February 2013), at https://mubi.com/notebook/posts/what-is-the-21st-century-revising-the-dictionary (accessed 28 March 2019).
9   Julier, *Culture of Design,* 40.
10 Ibid., 38.
11 John Pavlus, 'Why David Fincher is the Best Design Thinker in Hollywood', *Fast Company* (28 February 2011), at https://www.fastcompany.com/1663318/why-david-fincher-is-the-best-design-thinker-in-hollywood (accessed 28 March 2019).
12 Alexander R. Galloway, *Protocol: How Control Exists After Decentralization* (Cambridge: MIT Press, 2004).
13 Fincher quoted in Michael Goldman, 'With Friends Like These…', *American Cinematographer* (October 2010), at https://www.theasc.com/ac_magazine/October2010/TheSocialNetwork/page1.php (accessed 28 March 2019).
14 Salisbury, 'David Fincher: British Film Institute Interview', 154–5.
15 Michael Cioni and Ian Vertovec, interview by Debra Kaufman, *Creative COW* (2011), at https://library.creativecow.net/kaufman_debra/The-Girl-with-the-Dragon-Tattoo/1 (accessed 16 February 2019).

16 Fincher quoted in Bill Desowitz, 'Fincher Talks '*Benjamin Button*' and VFX', *VFXWorld* (9 January 2009), at http://www.awn.com/vfxworld/fincher-talk s-benjamin-button-and-vfx (accessed 28 March 2019).

17 Baxter quoted in Ian Failes, 'Maintaining the Mystery: Editor Kirk Baxter on *Gone Girl*', *FXGuide* (2 October 2014), at https://www.fxguide.com/featured/ maintaining-the-mystery-editor-kirk-baxter-on-gone-girl/ (accessed 28 March 2019).

18 Galloway quoted in Eugene Thacker, 'Protocol is as Protocol Does', foreword to *Protocol*, xix.

19 See David Geffner, 'To Catch a Killer', *ICG Magazine* (March 2007), at http://www.icgmagazine.com/2007/march/march07.html (accessed 28 March 2019).

20 Nelson quoted in Oliver Peters, 'Crime Scenes: Evolving the Postproduction Process on "Mindhunter"', *Digital Video* (November 2017), 13–15.

21 Fincher quoted in Ryan Dombal, 'Trent Reznor and David Fincher', *Pitchfork* (27 September 2010), at https://pitchfork.com/features/interview/7862-trent-reznor-and-david-fincher/ (accessed 28 March 2019).

Chapter 10

1 I've interviewed color grader Aubrey Woodiwiss. Speaking with him has given me a sense of color's power and its close relations with music. Woodiwiss says he wants to take viewers on a ride. We can see this in 'This Is What We Came For,' as color is dampened and brought up. The effect is similar to a composer or conductor working with a symphony's instrumentalists. Aubrey and Emil want people to feel color, and many of their choices are made right on set. Calvin Harris's 'Feels' (ft. Pharrell Williams, Katy Perry, and Big Sean) is a video that pays homage to Gilligan's Island and Tim Burton's Ed Wood. In this clip, Emil and Aubrey continuously "spun the color wheel," which nicely fits with the song's psychedelic-sounding backward guitar. It also seems to fit the loping feel of the rhythm guitar, which emphasizes the offbeats. (The color wheel can offer a spin-the-bottle-like game, since it's comprised of a circle made up of analogous and complementary relationships). Some intermediary touches were added later, like a lavender bearded dragon.

Chapter 11

1 See Kat Bein, 'Calvin Harris Tops the "Forbes" Highest-Paid DJ List for Sixth Straight Year', *Billboard Magazine* (31 July 2018), at https://www.billboar d.com/articles/news/dance/8467942/calvin-harris-top-paid-dj-forbes (accessed 18 March 2019).

2 Most EDM tracks in this style feature a recurring lyric halfway through the verse (e.g. 0:24, 1:39 in 'Outside') that behaves somewhat like a pre-chorus. But with little to no contrast in accompaniment material or texture, the similarities to a true pre-chorus end there. In any case, the presence or absence

of this feature in no way detracts from the broader three-part (verse, riser and drop) sonic trajectory.

3   The difference between the chorus and the drop can be expressed neatly as the difference between two different kinds of climax: syntactical and statistical (respectively); see Brad Osborn, 'Subverting the Verse/Chorus Paradigm: Terminally Climactic Forms in Recent Rock Music', *Music Theory Spectrum* 35, no. 1 (2013): 23. Choruses fulfil their role within the syntax of verse/chorus forms as the memorable lyrical-melodic hook. Drops present the highest value in several measurable parameters, especially loudest volume and thickest texture.

4   See Jason Summach, 'The Structure, Function, and Genesis of the Pre-chorus', *Music Theory Online* 17, no. 3 (2011), at http://www.mtosmt.org/issues/ mto.11.17.3/mto.11.17.3.summach.html (accessed 1 March 2019).

5   See especially David Bordwell, *Film Art: An Introduction*, 11 ed. (New York, NY: McGraw-Hill Education, 2016).

6   See Brad Osborn, 'Music Videos as Music Theory: Teaching MTV's Buzz Clips', Paper presented at the Teaching and Learning Popular Music Symposium, Ann Arbor, MI, 18–21 November 2015.

7   Asaf Peres labels the sections of a three-part EDM design as verse, chorus and post-chorus rather than verse–riser–drop or the conventional system of verse– pre-chorus–chorus; see Asaf Peres, 'The Sonic Dimension as Dramatic Driver in 21th-Century Pop Music', PhD dissertation, University of Michigan (2016). The 'post-chorus' was popularized first by Mark Spicer to account for the presence of four distinct sections (verse, pre-chorus, chorus and post-chorus) in tracks like Lady Gaga's 'Alejandro'. See Mark Spicer, '(Per)Form In(g) Rock: A Response', *Music Theory Online* 17 March (2011), at http://www.mtosmt.org/issues/m to.11.17.3/mto.11.17.3.spicer.html (accessed 3 April). However, recent EDM forms almost never contain the sort of explicitly contrasting pre-chorus heard in 'Alejandro'. This can be seen as part of a larger trend to remove 'filler' sections such as intros, bridges and solos (it is no coincidence that more songs are now beginning directly on the chorus). With the second section of a four-part design removed, several scholars have opted to stick with section names one, three and four for EDM songs (verse, chorus and post-chorus); see Jeff Ensign, 'Form in Popular Song, 1990–2009', PhD dissertation, University of North Texas (2015); Harding, 'Pop Drop'; Peres, 'The Sonic Dimension'; and Alyssa Barna, 'The Dance Chorus in Recent Top-40 Music', paper presented at Music Theory Midwest (2018).

8   Harding christens the popdrop 'the sound of 2016', finding it in hits by Justin Bieber, The Chainsmokers, Selena Gomez and others; see Charlie Harding, 'How the Pop-Drop Became the Sound of 2016', *Switched on Pop* blog (2016), at https://www.billboard.com/articles/columns/pop/7625628/pop-drop-sound- of-2016-chainsmokers-justin-bieber-switched-on-pop (accessed 3 April 2019).

9   Two issues complicate this formal design even further. First, Harris *begins* the track with quiet versions of both the chorus and post-chorus, devoid of the EDM functions (riser, build and drop) they will eventually contain. Second, quite unusually for either pop or EDM songs, this track contains only one full rotation of its verse–riser-chorus–drop 'core' (1:32ff), making its constituent sections even harder to identify; see Mark Butler, *Unlocking the Groove: Rhythm, Meter, and Musical Design in Electronic Dance Music* (Bloomington, IN: Indiana University Press, 2006). Harris and Rihanna have previously used a remarkably similar formal arrangement in their 2011 collaboration 'We Found Love' (1:22ff).

10 The only example in these videos that comes close to splitting the difference between drop and chorus so closely is heard in 'How Deep Is Your Love', in which the song title is initially presented alongside a quiet riser, but then reappears at the end of each phrase of the drop, giving the latter section a chorus-esque quality.

11 Nine Inch Nails' video for 'Hurt' (1995) ends with an instructive example of this (4:20), in which the musical track's volume climax coincides perfectly with a fish being speared by a diving bird, creating a combined multimedia stimulus. Every time I hear that music, I picture the dive-bombing bird and that poor fish.

12 While music is perceived *metrically* – four beats form a phrase, four phrases form a verse and so on – cinematography is less predictable. Cuts are, of course, rhythmic, but do not follow a predictable metre, though important phrase and formal breaks tend to be sufficient (yet not necessary) conditions for a cut. Music video cuts are notoriously quick, relative to film. For more on the similarities and differences between musical rhythm and the rhythm of cuts, see Carol Vernallis, *Experiencing Music Video: Aesthetics and Cultural Context* (New York: Columbia University Press, 2004).

13 This typical formal process neatly blends Spicer's 'cumulative' beginnings with his 'accumulative' endings; see Mark Spicer, '(Ac)Cumulative Form in Pop-Rock Music', *Twentieth-Century Music* 1 (2004): 29–64.

14 See Emily Caston, '"The First Cut Is the Deepest" Excerpts from a Focus Group on Editing Music Videos, with Explanatory Historical and Theoretical Notes', *Music, Sound, and the Moving Image* 11, no. 1 (2017): 99–118.

15 See Vernallis' interview with Nava elsewhere in this book.

16 See Gillian Rose, *Visual Methodologies: An Introduction to the Interpretation of Visual Materials* (London: Sage, 2007), 46.

17 See Tim Carter, 'Word Painting', *Grove Music Online*, at https://doi.org/10.1093/gmo/9781561592630.article.30568 (accessed 3 April 2019).

18 See Lori Burns, 'Multimodal Analysis of Popular Music Videos', in *Coming of Age: Teaching and Learning Popular Music in Academia*, ed. Carlos Xavier Rodriguez (Ann Arbor, MI: University of Michigan Press, 2017), 81–110.

19 See Vernallis, *Experiencing Music Video*, 190.

20 See Michel Chion, *Audio-Vision: Sound On Screen* (New York: Columbia University Press, 1990), 223.

21 See Vernallis' interview with Nava elsewhere in this book.

Chapter 12

1 Carol Vernallis writes that digital intermediate (DI) 'functions like Photoshop's processes for altering images, but it works with real-time moving media. You can tweak an individual pixel's colour, isolate it and modulate it, thereby fracturing the moving image, pulling it away from its referent in the world': *Unruly Media: YouTube, Music Video, and the New Digital Cinema* (New York, Oxford University Press 2013), 333. Brown and Kutty continue: 'The technique (which is sometimes referred to as 'bleeding pixel effect') involves using compression artifacts as a visual style', a pioneering example of which is Takeshi Murata's *Monster Movie*

(2005) (168). Too, 'not being structured so overtly around character and action', datamoshing 'lends itself to being understood as a spectacle of colour with little or no narrative' (169); William Brown and Meetali Kutty, 'Datamoshing and the Emergence of Digital Complexity from Digital Chaos', *Convergence: The International Journal of Research into New Media Technologies* 18, no. 2 (2012): 165–76.

2 John Belton, 'Painting by the Numbers: The Digital Intermediate', *Film Quarterly* 61, no. 3 (Spring 2008): 58–65.

3 For more information on Fischinger's work, see William Moritz's *Optical Poetry: The Life and Work of Oskar Fischinger* (Bloomington, IN: Indiana University Press, 2004).

4 Maura McDonnell, 'Visual Music', in 'Videomusic: Overview of an Emerging Art Form', *eContact!* 15, no. 4 (April 2014), at https://www.econtact.ca/15_4/mcdonnell_visualmusic.html (accessed 22 March 2019). I am also reminded of Daniel Albright's useful take on remediation, which he calls *pseudomorphosis*: something that occurs when, 'in a work in a single artistic medium, the medium is asked to ape, or do the work of some alien medium. This typically involves a certain wrenching or scraping against the grain of the original': Albright, *Panaesthetics: On the Unity and Diversity of the Arts* (New Haven: Yale University Press, 2014), 212.

5 See Lisa Perrott, 'Zig Zag: Reanimating Len Lye as Improvised Theatrical Performance and Immersive Visual Music', in *The Oxford Handbook of New Audiovisual Aesthetics*, eds. John Richardson, Claudia Gorbman and Carol Vernallis (New York and Oxford: Oxford University Press, 2013), 233–48.

6 My thoughts here are informed in part by what Belton has written of digital intermediate: 'We know that the relationship of a digital image to what it is an image of involves forms and/or stages of mediation potentially far greater than those involved in the typical photographic image. DI represents a perfect instance of such mediation – the mediation of image data during the post-production process. For the most part, it is difficult for us to perceive this manipulation. To the extent that digital imaging, in general, effectively simulates photochemical imagining, it does not effect our psychology of the image – *that is, not until it becomes visible* – as in spectacular digital special-effects sequences or in digital image break-up': 'Painting by the Numbers', 61 (emphasis added). In addition, and building on Perrott's reading of Len Lye's work, I believe that what Nava is accomplishing with his colour magic is similar to what Lye was doing with, for example, the scratching of film – that is, drawing special attention to the materiality (or, for Nava, the digitality) of the work: Perrott, 'Zig Zag', 240.

7 What I am seeing as colour magic is not necessarily, as in visual music, a set of pitch-colour correspondences, musico-formal representations or analogical traces. Rather, in Nava's work, the approach feels different: added to the complex workings of colour signification is an indexical relationship to digitality.

8 Teju Cole, *Known and Strange Things* (New York: Random House, 2016), 154.

9 Ibid.

10 Emil Nava, 'Emil Nava: "I Want to Shut Down the Internet"', *52 Insights* (28 November 2018), at https://www.52-insights.com/music-video-emil-nava-i-want-to-shut-down-the-internet/ (accessed 15 February 2018).

11   Bruce Sterling, 'An Essay on the New Aesthetic', *Wired* (2 April 2012), at https://www.wired.com/2012/04/an-essay-on-the-new-aesthetic/ (accessed 15 February 2019).

12   Cole, *Known and Strange Things*, 156.

13   Charles Baudelaire, *Artificial Paradises*, transl. and introduced by Stacy Diamond (Secaucus, NJ: Citadel Press, 1996), 63.

14   Emil Nava, *Snorkeling, Instagram* (8 May 2018), at https://www.instagra m.com/p/BiiyTYUBO7I/?hl=en (accessed 12 March 2019). Also: it is worth noting that Ammolite, Nava's '360 Creative' company, is named after an organic gemstone known for its brilliant iridescence.

15   As Nava mentioned in an unpublished interview with Vernallis, 'I love colors. So much of it is through feeling. I didn't go to film school and I didn't study film. I started as a PA runner to get coffee, so everything I know is based on emotion and feeling, and for me, colors are a huge part of that … interjecting big punches of color is like injecting punches of feeling.'

16   On such matters, especially within the domain of music video studies, Fred Moten's recent thoughts on 'chromatic saturation' lend special guidance: 'In the literature of color vision, chromatic saturation refers to the relative amount of hue perceived in a colored stimulus. Black is generally understood as an unsaturated or achromatic color that, on the other hand, increases the apparent saturation or brightness of colors paired or juxtaposed with it. Now we might achieve some accurate sense of the differences between the uses of the terms *chromaticism* and *chromatic saturation* in music and the visual arts and sciences. In music the accent is on difference; in the visual the accent is on purity': *The Universal Machine* (Durham, NC: Duke University Press, 2018), 156.

17   Cole, *Known and Strange Things*, 156.

Chapter 13

1   I discuss the binding of sound and image in greater detail in my book, *Experiencing Music Video: Aesthetics and Cultural Context* (New York: Columbia University Press, 2008). Hitchcock's composer Bernard Herrmann has also made this claim.

2   This is a good example of how hard it is to track a director's oeuvre. Only a small handful of showpieces tend to be on directors' websites. I'm almost certain I came across this clip on the Getty site. I liked it so much that I googled to find out about the director, sure enough, it was Meyers.Subsequent to writing this chapter, I discovered that artist Lina Iris Viktor successfully sued Dave Meyers for using her work without permission. I've requested interviews with Viktor and Meyers, and I plan to include my thoughts and feelings about this event in my forthcoming monograph, *Embracing the Media Swirl: Politics, Audiovisuality, and Aesthetics*. Viktor discusses her reasons for not granting permission in a lecture she gave at the University of Michigan on December 8th, 2018. Lina Iris Viktor – Materia Prima https://www.youtube.com/watch?v=FOsyOcG1JVU

3   I'm grateful to Lea Pao for drawing my attention to Lamar's stressed and unstressed syllables here.

Chapter 14

1 Tony Oursler, 'David Bowie', *Artforum* (March 2016), at: https://www.art
   forum.com/print/201603/david-bowie-58102 (accessed 15 March 2018).
2 Henry Jenkins, 'The Reign of the "Mothership": Transmedia's Past,
   Present and Possible Futures', in *Wired TV: Laboring Over an Interactive
   Future*, ed. Denise Mann (New Brunswick: Rutgers University Press,
   2014), 244.
3 Lisa Perrott, 'The Animated Music Videos of Radiohead, Chris Hopewell
   and Gastón Viñas: Fan-participation, Collaborative Authorship and Dialogic
   World-building', in *The Bloomsbury Handbook to Popular Music Video
   Analysis*, eds. Lori Burns and Stan Hawkins (New York: Bloomsbury, 2019),
   47-68.
4 Mikhail Bakhtin, 'Discourse in the Novel', in *The Dialogic Imagination: Four
   Essays*, ed. Michael Holquist (Austin: The University of Texas Press, 1981),
   294–457.
5 David Bordwell, 'Observations in Film Art: Now Leaving Platform 1' (2009),
   at http://www.davidbordwell.net/blog/2009/08/19/now-leaving-from-pla
   tform-1/ (accessed 12 December 2018).
6 Henry Jenkins, *Convergence Culture: Where Old and New Media Collide*
   (New York: New York University Press, 2006), 95–6.
7 Henry Jenkins, 'The Aesthetics of Transmedia: In Response to David Bordwell
   (Part 3)' (2009), at http://henryjenkins.org/blog/2009/09/the_aesthetics_of_
   transmedia_i.html (accessed 12 December 2018).
8 William Boyd, 'William Boyd: How David Bowie and I Hoaxed the
   Artworld', *The Guardian* (12 January 2016), https://www.theguardian.com/
   music/2016/jan/12/art-david-bowie-william-boyd-nat-tate-editor-critic-mo
   dern-painters-publisher (accessed 15 November 2018).
9 For more on this see Mark Wolf, 'Transmedia World-Building: History,
   Conception, and Construction', in *The Routledge Companion to Transmedia
   Studies*, eds. Matthew Freeman and Renira Rampazzo Gambarato (New
   York: Routledge, 2019), 141–7.
10 Švankmajer's work is analysed in Peter Hames, ed., *Dark Alchemy: The Films
   of Jan Švankmajer* (Wiltshire: Flicks Books, 1995).
11 *Détournement* is a strategy of reusing cultural items, interrupting
   conventional signifying systems by altering their familiar coding, and
   rerouting their dominant or intended meanings. For more on *détournement*
   and automatism see Jeremy Stubbs, 'Surrealism's Book of Revelation: Isadore
   Ducasse's *Poésies, Détournement* and *Automatic Writing*', *Romantic Review*
   87, no. 4 (1996): 493–510; Guy Debord and Gill J. Wolman, 'Methods of
   Détournement', *Les Lèvres Nues* no. 8 (May 1956), *Nothingness.org*,
   http://library.nothingness.org/articles/SI/en/display/3.
12 For more on *Gesamtkunstwerk*, see Chapter 26 in this volume.
13 Kristztina Lajosi, 'Wagner and the (Re)mediation of Art:
   Gesamtkunstwerk and Nineteenth Century Theories of Media', *Frame* 23,
   no. 2 (2010): 43.
14 Ibid., 46.

15 Michael Goddard, 'Audiovision and Gesamtkunstwerk: The Aesthetics of First and Second Generation Industrial Music Video', in *Music/Video: Histories, Aesthetics, Media*, eds. Gina Arnold, Daniel Cookney, Kirsty Fairclough and Michael Goddard (London: Bloomsbury Academic, 2017), 163–80.

16 Mehdi Derfoufi, 'Embodying Stardom, Representing Otherness: David Bowie in "Merry Christmas Mr. Lawrence"', in *David Bowie: Critical Perspectives*, eds. Eoin Devereux, Aileen Dillane and Martin Power (London: Routledge, 2015), 160.

17 See, for example, Ana Mendes and Perrott, 'Introduction: Navigating with the Blackstar: The Mediality of David Bowie', *Celebrity Studies* 10, no. 1 (2019): 4–13.

18 Bowie, David, interview extract from 'Changes: The David Bowie Story'. Interview by Stuart Grundy. *BBC Radio*, 1 May 1976. BBC Sound Archive. Quoted in Kathryn Johnson, 'David Bowie Is', in *David Bowie: Critical Perspectives*, 9.

19 Ibid., 14.

20 Bowie quoted in Jean Rook, 'Waiting for Bowie and Finding a Genius Who Insists He's Really a Clown', *Daily Express* (5 May 1976), cited in Aileen Dillane, Eoin Devereux and Martin Power, 'Culminating Sounds and (En) Visions: *Ashes to Ashes* and the case for Pierrot', in *David Bowie: Critical Perspectives*, 35.

21 Johnson, 'David Bowie is', 15.

22 Will Brooker, *Forever Stardust: David Bowie Across the Universe* (London: I B Taurus, 2017), iii.

23 October, 'Transition Transmission: Media, Seriality, and the Bowie-Newton Matrix', *Celebrity Studies* 10, no. 1 (2019): 104.

24 Ibid., 104; *The Man Who Fell to Earth* (1976), [Film] Dir. Nicholas Roeg, based on the 1963 book of the same title, by Walter Tevis. In this film David Bowie acted as Thomas Newton, a humanoid alien who comes to Earth to get water for his dying planet.

25 October, 'Transition Transmission', 104.

26 Nick Reilly, 'Is Jodie Whittaker channelling David Bowie in her "Dr Who" Reveal?', *NME* (17 July 2017), https://www.nme.com/news/tv/is -jodie-whittaker-channelling-david-bowie-2112168 (accessed 10 November 2018).

27 Mairi McKenzie, 'Football, Fashion and Unpopular Culture: David Bowie's Influence on Liverpool Football Club Casuals 1976–79', *Celebrity Studies* 10, no. 1 (2019): 38.

28 See Christopher Mcquade, '"I loathed it". What David Bowie Learnt From His Brief Spell in Adland', *The Drum* (11 January 2016), https://www.the drum.com/news/2016/01/11/i-loathed-it-what-david-bowie-learned-his-bri ef-spell-adland (accessed 10 November 2018).

29 *The Mask* (1969) [Film] Dir. Malcolm J. Thomson, Thomasso Film, London. Filmed in 1969 as part of the promotional film *Love You Till Tuesday*, which was initially shelved and only reached a screen audience when it was released on video in 1984. Available online at: https://vimeo.com/249177125 (accessed 5 August 2018).

30 Chris O'Leary, 'The Mime Songs', *Pushing Ahead of the Dame* (21 October 2009), https://bowiesongs.wordpress.com/tag/the-mask/ (accessed 15 August 2018).

31 *Pierrot in Turquoise or the Looking Glass Murders* (1968), [Pantomime performance] Dir. Brian Mahoney, London.

32 *Pierrot in Turquoise or the Looking Glass Murders* (1970), [Television show], BBC.

33 Toija Cinque, Angela Ndalianis and Sean Redmond, 'David Bowie On-Screen', *Cinema Journal* 57, no. 3 (2018): 126.

34 Jacques Derrida, *Specters of Marx: The State of the Debt, the Work of Mourning and the New International* (New York: Routledge, 1994), 20.

35 Mark Fisher, *Ghosts of My Life: Writings on Depression, Hauntology and Lost Futures* (Alresford: Zero Books, 2014); Fisher, 'What is Hauntology?' *Film Quarterly* 66, no. 1 (2012): 16–24.

36 Lisa Perrott, 'Time is Out of Joint: The Transmedial Hauntology of David Bowie', *Celebrity Studies* 10, no. 1 (2019): 119–39.

37 Jackie Mallon, 'Designer Kansai Yamamoto Talks All Things David Bowie', *Fashion United* (21 May 2018), https://fashionunited.uk/news/fashion/designer-kansai-yamamoto-talks-all-things-david-bowie/2018052129750 (accessed 15 August 2018).

38 Camille Paglia explores this in 'Theatre of Gender: David Bowie at the Climax of the Sexual Revolution', in *David Bowie Is*, eds. Victoria Broackes and Geoffrey Marsh (London: V&A Publishing, 2013), 69–92.

39 Ibid.

40 Devereux, Dillane and Power examine Bowie's reiteration of Pierrot 'as an avatar for everyman, for creativity and for the struggles over identities'. Devereux, Dillane and Power, 'Saying Hello to the Lunatic Men: A Critical Reading of "Love is Lost"', *Contemporary Music Review* 37, no. 3 (2018): 257.

41 This is discussed by Shelton Waldrep, *Future Nostalgia: Performing David Bowie* (New York: Bloomsbury, 2015), 49–69.

42 Angela Ndalianis, 'Bowie and Science Fiction/Bowie as Science Fiction', *Cinema Journal* 57, no. 3 (2018): 140.

43 Bowie collaborated with fashion designers Yamamoto, Freddi Burretti, Natasha Korniloff, Peter Hall, Diana Moseley, Georgio Armani, Alexander McQueen, Hedi Slimane and Michael Fish (see Broakes and Marsh, *David Bowie Is*).

44 Roeg quoted in Josh Weiss, 'Nicholas Roeg, Director of The Man Who Fell to Earth with David Bowie, Dead at 90', *SYFYWIRE* (24 November 2018), https://www.syfy.com/syfywire/nicolas-roeg-director-of-the-man-who-fell-to-earth-with-david-bowie-dead-at-90 (accessed 5 January 2019).

45 October, 'Transition Transmission', 107.

46 *The Elephant Man* (1980–1), [Theatrical Play] Dir. Jack Hofsiss, Broadway, Booth Theatre. Available online at: https://dangerousminds.net/comments/extended_footage_of_david_bowie_as_the_elephant_man (accessed 5 February 2019).

47 For more on this, see Angus MacKinnon, 'The Future Isn't What It Used To Be', *New Musical Express* (13 September 1980), http://www.bowiegoldenyea rs.com/press/80-09-13-nme.html (accessed 5 November 2018).

48 *Vittel,* ibid.

49 Chris O'Leary, 'Love Is Lost', *Pushing Ahead of the Dame* (1 September 2015), https://bowiesongs.wordpress.com/2015/09/01/love-is-lost/ (accessed 2 December 2018).

50 Devereux, Dillane and Power, 'Saying Hello to the Lunatic Men', 262.

51 *Faust* (1994) [Film] Dir. *Jan Švankmajer*, Czech Republic: Athanor.

52 Tom Hawking, 'Deconstructing David Bowie's DIY Video for "Love Is Lost"', *Flavorwire* (31 October 2013), http://flavorwire.com/422969/deconstruct ing-david-bowies-diy-video-for-love-is-lost (accessed 10 December 2018).

53 'A Soulful Art Legacy: 25 David Bowie Paintings', *Very Private Gallery*, https://veryprivategallery.com/david-bowie-paintings/ (accessed 5 April 2019).

54 Boyd, 'William Boyd'.

55 See Broackes and Marsh, *David Bowie Is*, 138–43.

56 *Heroes* (1977), album by David Bowie, RCA Victor, PL 12522, UK.

57 *Roquairol* (1917) [Painting] Painter. Erich Heckel.

58 For more information see 'Inside David Bowie's Private Collection', *Sotheby's*, at https://www.sothebys.com/en/slideshows/inside-david-bowies-private-col lection?slide=romuald-hazoume-alexandra-1995-estimate-5-000-7-000 (accessed 15 December 2018).

59 Oursler, 'David Bowie'.

60 Boyd, 'William Boyd'.

61 Damien Hirst, 'Damien Hirst with David Bowie', *Sotheby's*, Catalogue note (2016), http://www.sothebys.com/en/auctions/ecatalogue/2016/bowie-co llector-part-i-modern-contemporary-art-evening-auction-l16142/lot.5.html (accessed 15 December 2018).

62 Sales, quoted in Alecia Adejobi, 'The Truth about David Bowie and Damien Hirst's Friendship and Their 755k Art Masterpiece', *International Business Times* (15 November 2016), https://www.ibtimes.co.uk/truth-about-david-b owie-damien-hirsts-friendship-their-755k-art-masterpiece-1591622 (accessed 15 December 2018).

63 See Colin Marshall, 'David Bowie and Brian Eno's Collaboration on "Warszawa" Reimagined in a Comic Animation', *Open Culture* (16 September 2014), http://www.openculture.com/2014/09/david-bowie-brian-enos-collaboration-on-warszawa-reimagined-in-comic-animation.html (accessed 15 December 2018).

64 Andy Gibson, 'Flight of the Conchords: Recontextualizing the Voices of Popular Culture', *Journal of Sociolinguistics* 15, no. 5 (2011): 603–26.

65 Kevin Holm-Hudson, "Who Can I Be Now?': David Bowie's Vocal Personae', *Contemporary Music Review* 37, no. 3 (2018): 216.

66 Idiosyncratic qualities are traceable to specific time periods and albums, such as the slippage in Bowie's voice between working-class cockney and highly educated British dialects and phrases, and its canny resemblance to the 'light entertainer' voice of Anthony Newly, which is particularly apparent on Bowie's album *Love You Till Tuesday* (1967).

67 For instance, Anthony Newly, Jacques Brel and Scott Walker. See Perrott, 'Time is Out of Joint', 124–5.

68 Examples include the film *Velvet Goldmine*, Peter Capaldi's performance in the series *Doctor Who* and Gillian Anderson's performance in the series *American Gods*. Glenn D' Cruz, 'He's Not There: Velvet Goldmine and the Spectres of David Bowie', in *Enchanting David Bowie: Space/Time/Body/ Memory,* eds. Toija Cinque, Christopher Moore and Sean Redmond (New York: Bloomsbury, 2015), 259–73; Jaymi Mccan, 'The Thin White Doc: New Doctor Who Based on David Bowie', *Express* (29 June 2014), https:// www.express.co.uk/celebrity-news/485534/The-Thin-White-Doc-New-Doct or-Who-based-on-David-Bowie (accessed 2 November 2018).

69 Winston Cook-Wilson, '*Twin Peaks* Brought Back David Bowie's Character in the Most Insane Way Possible', *Spin* (21 August 2017), https://www.spin.com /2017/08/twin-peaks-episode-15-recap-david-bowie/ (accessed 22 September 2017).

70 Denis Flannery, 'Absence, Resistance and Visitable Pasts: David Bowie, Todd Haynes, Henry James', *Continuum: Journal of Media and Cultural Studies* 31, no. 4 (2017): 542–51.

71 Michael Hogan, 'David Bowie got a Fitting Farewell from his Favourite Show', *The Telegraph* (2 June 2016), https://www.telegraph.co.uk/tv/2016 /06/02/peaky-blinders-david-bowie-got-a-fitting-farewell-plus-8-more-th/ (accessed 4 January 2019).

72 See, for instance, figures 1 and 2 in Mendes and Perrott, 'Introduction: Navigating with The Blackstar', 5–6.

73 Lisa Perrott, 'Bowie the Cultural Alchemist: Performing Gender, Synthesizing Gesture and Liberating Identity', *Continuum: Journal of Media & Cultural Studies* 31, no. 4 (2017): 528–41.

74 Ayun Halliday, 'David Bowie Songs Reimagined as Pulp Fiction Book Covers: Space Oddity, Heroes, Life on Mars and More', *Open Culture* (1 April 2019), http://www.openculture.com/2019/04/david-bowie-songs-re imagined-as-pulp-fiction-book-covers.html?fbclid=IwAR3WLFylt1y7CL EQGkW2FRxEoPWQEKMLDfy8qjjFJ5v9Co44CGboCPCTGP0 (accessed 2 April 2019).

75 Tanja Stark, 'Crashing Out with Sylvian: David Bowie, Carl Jung, and the Unconscious', *Tanja Stark: Art Words Ideas* (22 June 2015), https://tanjast ark.com/2015/06/22/crashing-out-with-sylvian-david-bowie-carl-jung-and -the-unconscious/ (accessed 5 August 2018).

76 Adam Campbell-Schmitt, 'A Ziggy Stardust Bar Lands in London this Fall', *Food & Wine* (27 August 2018), https://www.foodandwine.com/news/ziggy-stardust-bar-hotel-cafe-royal-london-david-bowie?utm_campaign=foodand wine&utm_medium=social&utm_source=facebook.com&xid=soc_social flow_facebook_fw (accessed 10 December 2018).

77 Floria Sigismondi, *Facebook*, 14 January 2016, https://www.facebook.com/ floria.sigismondi/posts/the-passing-of-david-bowie-has-affected-me-in-ways-i-have-never-experienced-he-c/451732985031106/ (accessed 20 January 2016).

78 Floria Sigismondi, 'Floria Sigismondi Discusses her Dark Aesthetic', *MTV News* (4 April 1997), http://www.mtv.com/news/1426430/floria-sigismondi-discusses-her-dark-aesthetic/ (accessed 10 August 2018).

79 Taryn Nobil, 'Director Floria Sigismondi talks David Bowie, "The Handmaid's Tale", "Fleshy Love" and Fellini', *Variety* (12 October 2017), https://variety.com/2017/music/news/director-floria-sigismondi-discusses-mu sic-and-film-red-bull-music-academy-1202588494/ (accessed 10 August 2018).

80 For instance, time appears anthropomorphically in the lyrics from Bowie's song 'Rock 'n' Roll Suicide' (1972): 'time takes a cigarette, puts it in your mouth'; and his song 'Time' (1973): 'time, he flexes like a whore, falls wanking to the floor.'

81 Lisa Perrott, 'Floria Sigismondi as Gestural Animator and Puppeteer', *Animation: An Interdisciplinary Journal* 10, no. 2 (2015): 119–40.

82 Carol Vernallis and Hannah Ueno, 'Interview with Music Video Director and Auteur Floria Sigismondi', *Music, Sound and the Moving Image* 7, no. 2 (2013): 167–94.

83 Sigismondi's blurring of film and music video conventions are evident in *Leaning Towards Solace,* created in 2012 for the Sigur Rós *Valtari Mystery Film Experiment* (see Chapter 15 of this volume).

84 *Scene 360,* http://www5.csudh.edu/dearhabermas/ARTdirect_FloriaSigi smondi.html (accessed 2 March 2018).

85 Oliver Kupper, 'Activating the Vehicle of Ascension: An Interview of Filmmaker and Artist Floria Sigismondi', *Autre* (18 July 2016), https://autre. love/interviewsmain/2016/7/18/activating-the-vehicle-of-ascension-an-intervi ew-of-filmmaker-and-artist-floria-sigismondi (accessed 10 December 2018).

86 Vernallis and Ueno, 'Interview with Music Video Director and Auteur Floria Sigismondi', 176.

87 Aylish Wood, 'Re-Animating Space', *Animation: An Interdisciplinary Journal* 1, no. 2 (2006): 135.

88 Bowie used this 'cut-up' technique to create lyrics for his album *Diamond Dogs* (1974).

89 Chris O'Leary, 'Little Wonder', *Pushing Ahead of the Dame* (7 August 2013), https://bowiesongs.wordpress.com/2013/08/07/little-wonder/ (accessed 5 May 2018).

90 Ibid.

91 Ibid.

92 Sigismondi, 'Floria Sigismondi Discusses her Dark Aesthetic', ibid.

93 Tanja Stark, '"Crashing Out with Sylvian" David Bowie, Carl Jung, and the Unconscious', in *David Bowie: Critical Perspectives*, eds. Aileen Dillane, Eoin Devereux and Martin Power (New York: Routledge, 2015), 84.

94 http://tildastardust.tumblr.com

95 Jackie Stacey, 'Crossing Over With Tilda Swinton-The Mistress of "Flat Affect"', *International Journal of Politics, Culture and Society* 28, no. 3 (2015): 267.

96 Nicole Kidman plays a neurotic housewife, Saoirse Ronan wakes to discover she's a reanimated mannequin and Andy Serkis channels a sad clown; see:

'Great Performers', *The New York Times* magazine, https://www.nytimes. com/interactive/2017/12/07/magazine/great-performers-horror-show.html# daniel-kaluuya (accessed 2 March 2019).

97   Carl Jung, *The Archetypes and the Collective Unconscious* (England: Routledge and Keegan Paul, 1959).

98   Stark, 'Crashing Out with Sylvian', 93.

99   For example, see: 'The Incubus and Succubus', *Ferrebeekeeper* (30 October 2014), https://ferrebeekeeper.wordpress.com/2014/10/30/the-incubus-and-s uccubus/ (accessed 5 April 2019).

100 Jung, *The Archetypes and the Collective Unconscious*, 25–6.

101 Lesley Stern, 'Putting on a Show, or the Ghostliness of Gesture', *Lola* (July 2002), http://www.lolajournal.com/5/putting_show.html (accessed 10 October 2018).

102 October, ibid.

103 Carl Jung, 'The Syzygy: Anima and Animus', in *Collected Works of C. G Jung*, Vol. 9 (London: Routledge and Kegan Paul, 1951), 11–22.

104 For more on this, see: Nancy M. Reale, 'Boccaccio's Decameron: A Fictional Effort to Grapple with Chaos' (2005), 3. At: http://www.nyu.edu/projects/me diamosaic/literature/BoccaccioDecameronEssay.pdf (accessed 5 April 2019).

105 *Saint Lucy* (1521) [Painting] Artist: Domenico Beccafumi, https://commons. wikimedia.org/wiki/File:St_lucy_1521_Domenico_Beccafumi.jpg (accessed 13 February 2019).

106 https://www.adforum.com/talent/81772858-floria-sigismondi/work/34460926

107 https://www.adforum.com/talent/81772858-floria-sigismondi/work/34494721

108 Marshall McLuhan, *Understanding Media: The Extensions of Man* (Cambridge: MIT Press, 1964), 7–23.

109 Chris O'Leary, 'The Next Day', *Pushing Ahead of the Dame* (10 August 2015), https://bowiesongs.wordpress.com/2015/08/10/the-next-day/ (accessed 5 May 2018).

110 'Conversations with Bowie', *Capital Radio Studio Recording* (Bootleg), Recorded 14 May 1979, Joe Coscarelli, '"Black Star": David Bowie's Connection to Elvis Presley', *The New York Times* (14 January 2016), https:// www.nytimes.com/live/david-bowie-in-memoriam/black-star-david-bowies-connection-to-elvis-presley (accessed 7 July 2018).

111 William Smythe, 'Jungian Dialogism and the Problem of Depth', *Journal of Analytical Psychology* 63, no. 4 (2018): 453.

112 Boshier, first quoted in Sarah Cascone, 'Take a Peek at David Bowie's Idiosyncratic Art Collection', *Artnet* (12 January 2016), https://news.artnet. com/art-world/take-peek-david-bowies-art-collection-405296 (accessed 2 May 2018).

Chapter 15

1   Lawson Fletcher, 'The Sound of Ruins: Sigur Rós' *Heima* and the Post-rock Elegy for Place', *Interference: A Journal of Audio Culture* 2 (2011): 1–11.

2 Sigur Rós, "Valtari Mystery Film Experiment", at https://sigur-ros.co.uk/valtari/videos/invite/ (accessed 8 January 2019).

3 Sigur Rós, *Valtari,* recorded at Sundlaugin, Greenhouse Studios, Air Studios 2009–12, Parlophone, 2012.

4 Sigur Rós, 'About', *Liminal*, at https://liminal.la/ (accessed 1 March 2019).

5 Henry Jenkins, 'Transmedia Storytelling 101'. *Confessions of an Aca-Fan*, at http://henryjenkins.org (accessed 1 March 2019).

6 Henry Jenkins, *Convergence Culture: Where Old and New Media Collide* (New York: New York University Press, 2006), 95–6.

7 Sigur Rós, 'The Valtari Music Experiment', at https://sigur-ros.co.uk/valtari/videos/ (accessed 1 March 2019).

8 Jenkins, *Confessions of an Aca-Fan*, 21 March 2007.

9 Radha O'Meara and Alex Bevan, 'Transmedia Theory's Author Discourse and its Limitations', *Media/Culture Journal* 21, no. 1 (2018), at http://journal.media-culture.org.au/index.php/mcjournal/article/view/1366 9 (accessed 4 March 2019).

10 Anna L. Tsing, Heather A. Swanson, Elaine Gan, and Nils Bubandt, *Arts of Living on a Damaged Planet: Ghosts and Monsters of the Anthropocene* (Minneapolis, MN: University of Minnesota Press, 2017), 1.

11 Peter M. Vitousek, Harold A. Mooney, and Melillo J. Lubchenco, 'Human Domination of Earth's Ecosystems', *Science* 277 (1997): 494–9.

12 Anna Storm, *Post-Industrial Landscape Scars* (New York: Palgrave Macmillan, 2014).

13 Jenkins, *Confessions of an Aca-Fan*, 21 March 2007.

14 Amanda Roscoe Mayo, 'Mystery Revealed: Sigur Rós' Valtari Film Experiment', *KQED Arts* (17 March 2013), at https://www.kqed.org/arts/117962 (accessed 1 March 2019).

15 Jenkins, *Confessions of an Aca-Fan*, 21 March 2007.

16 Peter Doyle, 'From "My Blue Heaven" to "Race with the Devil": Echo, Reverb and (Dis)ordered Space in Early Popular Music Recording', *Popular Music* 23, no. 1 (2004): 31–49.

17 Edward D. Miller, 'The Nonsensical Truth of the Falsetto Voice: Listening to Sigur Rós', *Popular Musicology* 2 (2003), at http://www.popular-musicology-online.com/issues/02/miller.html (accessed 1 March 2019).

18 Collin Davis, 'Hauntology, Spectres and Phantoms', *French Studies* 59, no. 3 (2005): 373–9.

19 Arit John, '*Varúð* Exhibit Channels the Airy Non-gravity of the *Valtari* Cover Art', *The Reykjavík Grapevine* (29 October 2012), at https://grapevine.is/culture/art/2012/10/29/proceed-with-caution/ (accessed 1 October 2018).

20 Ibid.

21 Ibid.

22 Ibid.

23 Icelandic Arts Centre, 'Ingibjörg Birgisdóttir', at https://icelandicartcenter.is/people/artists/ingibjorg-birgisdottir/ (accessed 1 March 2019).

24 Carol F. Sawyer and David R. Butler, 'The Use of Historical Picture Postcards as Photographic Sources for Examining Environmental Change: Promises and Problems', *Geocarto International* 3 (2006): 73–80.

25 Ibid.

26 Jeffery Meikle, *Postcard America: Curt Teich and the Imaging of a Nation, 1931–1950* (Austin: University of Texas Press, 2016).

27 John, '*Varúð* Exhibit'.

28 Jeffery Meikle, 'A Paper Atlantis: Postcards, Mass Art, and the American Scene, The Eleventh Reyner Banham Memorial Lecture', *Journal of Design History* 13, no. 4 (2000): 267–86.

29 Nicolas Whybrow, 'Watermarked: "Venice Really Lives Up to Its Postcard Beauty"', *Performance Research: Journal of Performing Arts* 20, no. 3 (2015): 50–7.

30 Brian Massumi, 'The Future Birth of the Affective Fact: The Political Ontology of Threat', in *The Affect Theory Reader*, eds. Melissa Gregg and Gregory J. Seigworth, 52–70 (Durham, NC: Duke University Press, 2010), 53.

31 Robert Kirkman, 'A Little Knowledge of Dangerous Things: Human Vulnerability in a Changing Climate', in *Merleau-Ponty and Environmental Philosophy: Dwelling on the Landscapes of Thought*, eds. Suzanne L. Cataldi and William S. Hamrick, 19–35 (Albany: State University of New York Press, 2007), 27.

32 Guggenheim Museum, 'Ryan McGinley Tree #1', at https://www.guggenheim.org/artwork/20711 (accessed 20 October 2018).

33 Team Gallery (New York), 'I Know Where the Summer Goes', at https://www.artsy.net/show/team-gallery-ryan-mcginley-i-know-where-the-summer-goes (accessed 1 March 2019).

34 Luca Panaro, 'Ryan McGinley', *Around Photography International* 13 (2008): 30–4.

35 Rory Satran, 'The Endless Road Trip of Ryan McGinley', *i-D* (28 August 2015), at https://i-d.vice.com/en_us/article/kz8pa9/the-endless-road-trip-of-ryan-mcginley (accessed 2 October 2019).

36 Ibid.

37 Ibid.

38 Jan Zalasiewicz, Colin Waters, and Mark Williams, 'City-strata of the Anthropocene', *Annales. Histoire, Sciences Sociales* 2 (2017): 329–51.

39 Numéro Cinq, 'Ryan McGinley's "Varúð" Introduced by R.W. Gray', at http://www.teamgal.com/exhibitions/131/i_know_where_the_summer_goes (accessed 1 September 2018).

40 Jonathan Berger, 'How Music Hijacks Our Perception of Time', *Nautilus* (23 January 2014), Issue 9, at http://nautil.us/issue/9/time/how-music-hijacks-our-perception-of-time (accessed 1 September 2018).

41 Gia Kourlas, 'Making Words Dance on Screen', *The New York Times* (23 November 2012), at https://www.nytimes.com/2012/11/24/arts/dance/sidi-larb i-cherkaouis-choreography-for-anna-karenina.html?pagewanted=all&_r=1& (accessed 1 September 2018).

42 Sheril Dodds, *Dance Screen. Genres and Media from Hollywood to Experimental Art* (New York: Palgrave, 2001); Melanie Kloetzel, 'Bodies in Place: Location as Collaborator in Dance Film', *International Journal of Performance Arts and Digital Media* 11, no. 1 (2015): 18–41; Douglas Rosenberg, 'Video Space: A Site for Choreography', *Leonardo* 33, no. 4 (2000): 275–80.

43 Kourlas, 'Making Words Dance'.
44 Karen Barbour, Vicky Hunter and Melanie Kloetzel *(Re)Positioning Site Dance: Local Acts, Global Perspectives* (Bristol: Intellect Books, 2019); Sally Mackey and Nicolas Whybrow, 'Taking Place: Some Reflections on Site, Performance and Community', *Research in Drama Education: The Journal of Applied Theatre and Performance* 12 (2007): 1–14.
45 Erin Brannigan, *Dancefilm: Choreography and the Moving Image* (New York: Oxford University Press, 2011), 44.
46 Kloetzel, 'Bodies in Place', 22.
47 Emma Green, 'Dancers Bend the Laws of Physics in a Mesmerizing Video for Sigur Rós', *The Atlantic* (11 March 2013), at https://www.theatlantic.com/video/archive/2013/03/dancers-bend-the-laws-of-physics-in-a-mesmerizing-video-for-sigur-r-oacute-s/466236/ (accessed 1 September 2018).
48 Matt Edgeworth, 'Human Impact has Created a "Plastic Planet": Anthropocene Study into Lasting Effects of Plastic on Land and Oceans', *ScienceDaily* (27 January 2016) at https://www.sciencedaily.com/releases/2016/01/160127083854.htm (accessed 1 September 2018).
49 Glenn Albrecht, Gina Marie Sartore, Linda Conor, Nick Higginbotham, Sonia Freeman, Brian Kelly, Helen Stain, Anne Tonna and Georgia Pollard, 'Solastalgia: The Distress Caused by Environmental Change', *Australasian Psychiatry* 15, no. 1 (2007): 95–8.
50 Yi-Fu Tuan, *Escapism* (Baltimore, MA: Johns Hopkins University Press, 1998).
51 Brett Ashley Kaplan, *Unwanted Beauty: Aesthetic Pleasure in Holocaust Representation* (Chicago: University of Illinois Press, 2007).
52 Denis Smalley, 'Spectromorphology: Explaining Sound-shapes', *Organised Sound* 2, no. 2 (1997): 107–26.

Chapter 16

1 David Bordwell, 'Observations on Film Art: Now Leaving from Platform 1' (2009), at http://www.davidbordwell.net/blog/2009/08/19/now-leaving-from-platform-1/ (accessed 30 August 2018).
2 Henry Jenkins, *Convergence Culture: Where Old and New Media Collide* (New York and London: New York University Press, 2006), 95–6.
3 Jenkins, 'The Aesthetics of Transmedia: In Response to David Bordwell (Part Three)' (2009), at http://henryjenkins.org/blog/2009/09/the_aesthetics_of_transmedia_i_2.html (accessed 30 August 2018).
4 Bordwell, 'Observations on Film Art'.
5 Mark Fisher, *The Weird and the Eerie* (London: Repeater Books, 2016), 53.
6 Anne Friedberg, 'The End of Cinema: Multimedia and Technological Change', in *Reinventing Film Studies*, eds. Christine Gledhill and Linda Williams (New York: Oxford University Press, 2000), 439.
7 Jenkins quoted in Dan Harries, *The New Media Book* (London and New York: British Film Institute, 2002), 171.

8 Lynch quoted in Scott Thill, 'David Lynch Interviews – Uncut' (2007), *Wired*, at https://www.wired.com/2007/01/david-lynch-interviews-uncut/ (accessed 30 August 2018).

9 Dennis Lim, 'David Lynch Goes Digital' (2007), *Slate*, at http://www.slate.com/articles/arts/dvdextras/2007/08/david_lynch_goes_digital.html (accessed 30 August 2018).

10 Lynch speaking in his video introduction to the project at http://interviewproj ect.davidlynch.com/www/ (accessed 30 August 2018).

11 The video is available at https://www.youtube.com/watch?v=3bgoRGqHwBE (accessed 30 August 2018).

12 Michel Chion, *David Lynch* (London: British Film Institute, 1995), 41.

13 Marina Warner, 'Voodoo Road: *Lost Highway* by David Lynch', *Sight and Sound* 7, no. 8 (August 1997): 6.

14 Brian Jarvis, *Postmodern Cartographies: The Geographical Imagination in Contemporary American Culture* (London: Pluto Press, 1998), 178.

15 Michel Chion, 'Chapter Five – Lynch-Kit: From Alphabet to Word', *David Lynch*, 161–98.

16 Zoran Samardzija, 'DavidLynch.com: Auteurship in the Age of the Internet and Digital Cinema', (2010), *Scope*, at https://www.nottingham.ac.uk/scope/docum ents/2010/february-2010/samardzija.pdf (accessed 30 August 2018).

17 Lynch cited in Chion, *David Lynch*, 10.

18 Dorian Lynskey explains how Badalamenti began the scoring process for *Twin Peaks*, for example: 'He scored the pilot episode before seeing a single frame, translating Lynch's descry options into music, which the director than used to inform the mood and rhythm of scenes and performances'; Dorian Lynskey, '"Make it Like the Wind, Angelo": How the *Twin Peaks* Soundtrack Came to Haunt Music for Nearly 30 Years', *Guardian* (Friday, 24 March 2017), at https://www.theguardian.com/music/2017/mar/24/twin-peaks-soundtrack-da vid-lynch-angelo-badalamenti (accessed 30 August 2018).

19 Lynch speaking in 'The Monster Meets … Filmmaker David Lynch', *Monster Cable* (Fall 1998), at http://www.lynchnet.com/monster.html (accessed 30 August 2018).

20 I've looked at the aesthetics of rupture in various other genres, including experimental film and avant-garde theatre: see, for instance, Holly Rogers, 'Audiovisual Dissonance in Found Footage Film', in *The Music and Sound of Experimental Film*, eds. Holly Rogers and Jeremy Barham (New York and Oxford: Oxford University Press, 2017), 185–204; and Holly Rogers, 'Audio-Visual Collisions: Moving Image Technology and the Laterna Magika Aesthetic in New Music Theatre', in *New Music Theatre in Europe: Transformations between 1955–1975*, ed. Robert Adlington (New York: Routledge, 2019), 79–100.

21 Jenkins, 'The Aesthetics of Transmedia'.

22 Fisher, *The Weird and the Eerie*.

23 Annette Davidson, '"Up in Flames": Love, Control and Collaboration in the Soundtrack to *Wild at Heart*', in *The Cinema of David Lynch: American Dreams, Nightmare Visions*, eds. Erica Sheen and Davison (London and New York: Wallflower Press, 2004), 120.

24 Andrew Sarris, 'Notes on the Auteur Theory in 1962', *Film Culture* 27 (1962–3): 6–7.

25 Timothy Corrigan, 'The Commerce of Auteurism: A Voice Without Authority', *New German Critique* 49 (1990): 44.

26 Chion wrote, 'More than ever, Lynch took part in the construction of the soundtrack of *Fire Walk with Me*. He singlehandedly took on the film's sound design and, in addition, collaborated in the mixing, being credited as sound designer and as one of the three "re-recorders"'; Chion, *David Lynch*, 150.

27 Roberta Pearson, 'The Writer-Producer in American Television', in *Contemporary Television Series*, eds. Michael Hammond and Lucy Mazdon (Edinburgh: Edinburgh University Press, 2005), 18.

28 Jason Mittell, *Complex TV: The Poetics of Contemporary Television Storytelling* (New York: New York University Press, 2015), 298 (italics his).

29 Frost, *The Secret History of Twin Peaks* (2016) formed from notes, clippings, documents and letters by someone known mysteriously only as 'The Archivist'; and *Twin Peaks: The Final Dossier* (2017) that provides context and insight on events between the second and third series.

30 *Soundtrack from Twin Peaks* (1990), *Twin Peaks: Fire Walk with Me* (1992) and *Twin Peaks Music: Season Two Music and More* (2007). The third series had two soundtracks, both released on 8 September 2017 by Rhino Records: *Twin Peaks: Limited Event Series Original Soundtrack* and *Twin Peaks: Music from the Limited Event Series*.

31 Jenkins, *Convergence Culture*, 3.

32 Jenkins, 'The Aesthetics of Transmedia'.

33 Matt Hill, *Fan Cultures* (London and New York: Routledge, 2002), 101.

34 Henry Jenkins, 'If It Doesn't Spread, It's Dead (Part One): Media Viruses and Memes' (2009), at http://henryjenkins.org/blog/2009/02/if_it_doesnt_spread_its_dead_p.html (accessed 30 August 2018).

35 See http://www.enterthelodge.com/about/ (accessed 30 August 2018).

36 Smith quoted in Lynskey, '"Make it Like the Wind, Angelo"'.

37 Ibid.

38 The quote continues: 'Yet if the entity or object *is* here, then the categories which we have up until now used to make sense of the world cannot be valid. The weird thing is not wrong, after all: it is our conceptions that must be inadequate'; Fisher, *The Weird and the Eerie*, 15.

39 Ibid., 61.

40 Herbert Graves, *Making Strange: Beauty, Sublimity and the (Post) Modern 'Third' Aesthetic* (New York and Amsterdam: Rodopi, 2008), 10–11.

41 Fisher uses *Mullholland Drive* as an example of weirdness arising from thwarted expectation by which 'the film feels like a "wrong" version of a recognizable Hollywood film-type'; Fisher, *The Weird and the Eerie*, 57.

42 Chion, *David Lynch*, 109.

43 Some of these transitions are noted in Isabella van Elferen, 'Dream Timbre: Notes on Lynchian Sound Design', in *Music, Sound and Filmmakers: Sonic Style in Cinema*, ed. James Wierzbicki (New York and London: Routledge, 2012), 178.

44 David Lynch in 'David Lynch Interview: "There is Something So Incredibly Cosmically Magical About Curtains"', at https://www.timeout.com/london/art/david-lynch-interview-there-is-something-so-incredibly-cosmically-magical-about-curtains (accessed 30 August 2018).

45 Fisher, *The Weird and the Eerie*, 53.

46 Ibid., 57.

47 Greg Hainge, *Noise Matters: Towards an Ontology of Noise* (New York, London: Bloomsbury, 2013), 190, 191.

48 Fisher, *The Weird and the Eerie*, 61.

49 Ibid.

50 Ibid., 62.

51 Philip Brophy, 'Parties in Your Head: From the Acoustic to the Psycho-Acoustic', in *The Oxford Handbook of New Audiovisual Aesthetics*, eds. John Richardson, Claudia Gorbman and Carol Vernallis (New York and Oxford: Oxford University Press, 2013), 317–18.

52 van Elferen, 'Dream Timbre', 176.

53 David Toop, *Sinister Resonance: The Mediumship of the Listener* (New York and London: Continuum, 2010), 115.

54 Walter Murch, 'Stretching Sound to Help the Mind See', *New York Times* (1 October 2000), at http://www.nytimes.com/2000/10/01/arts/01MURC.html?pagewanted=all (accessed 30 August 2018).

55 van Elferen, 'Dream Timbre', 183.

56 Chion notes that 'Henry is back at home and turns on the phonograph. He places the needle on different grooves of a jazz record, carving out little islands of swing music separated by silence'; Chion, *David Lynch*, 44.

57 Hainge, *Noise Matters*, 182.

58 Mark Fisher, 'The Metaphysics of Crackle', *Dancecult: Journal of Electronic Dance Music Culture* 5, no. 2 (2013): 42–55.

59 I have written about audiovisual aporia in Holly Rogers, 'Sonic Elongation and Sonic Aporia: Soundscape Composition in Film', in *Oxford Handbook of Cinematic Listening*, ed. Carlo Cenciarelli (New York and Oxford: Oxford University Press, forthcoming for 2019).

60 Lynch quoted in Tom Kenny, *Sound for Picture: Film Sound Through the 1990s* (Vallejo, CA: MixBooks, 2000), 133.

61 Lynch quoted in Chris Rodley, *Lynch on Lynch* (London: Faber and Faber, 1997), 242.

62 Alan Splet quoted in 'Interview: Alan Splet', *Cagey Films* (17 December 1981), at https://web.archive.org/web/20121201060512/http://www.cageyfilms.com/links/eraserhead/interviews/other-eraserhead-crew/alan-splet/ (accessed 30 August 2018).

63 David Hughes explains further: 'Lynch experimented with recording techniques, just as he had during his innovative sound work on *Eraserhead*, placing microphones inside bottles and lengths of plastic tubing to try and capture a unique sound'; *The Complete Lynch* (London: Virgin, 2001), 211.

64 Schaeffer quoted in Brian Kane, *Sound Unseen: Acousmatic Sound in Theory and Practice* (New York: Oxford University Press, 2014), 3.

65 Chion, *Audio-Vision*, 72, 73.

66 Chion, *David Lynch*, 38.
67 Philip Brophy, 'Lost Highway: Booms, Drones and Other Dark Waves', at http://www.philipbrophy.com/projects/cnsncs/LostHighway.html (accessed 30 August 2018).
68 K. J. Donnelly, '*Saw* Heard: Musical Sound Design in Contemporary Cinema', in *Film Theory and Contemporary Hollywood Movies*, ed. Warren Buckland (New York and London: Routledge, 2009), 111.
69 Chion, *David Lynch*, 43–4.
70 Kane, *Sound Unseen*, 148, 9, 209.
71 Chion, *David Lynch*, 150.
72 Fisher, *The Weird and the Eerie*, 63.
73 van Elferen, 'Dream Timbre', 175.
74 Frost quoted in Lynskey, '"Make It Like the Wind, Angelo"'.
75 John Richardson, 'Laura and Twin Peaks: Postmodern Parody and the Musical Reconstruction of the Absent Femme Fatale', in *The Cinema of David Lynch*, 87.
76 van Elferen, 'Dream Timbre', 181.
77 Simon Reynolds, *Retromania: Pop Cultures Addiction to Its Own Past* (London: Faber and Faber, 2011); Mark Fisher, *Ghosts of My Life: Writings on Depression, Hauntology and Lost Futures* (Alresford: Zero Books, 2014).
78 As Chion explains with reference to *Blue Velvet*, 'Neither of these two worlds are quite cotemporaneous with ours. The author succeeds in mixing the atmosphere of the '50s with that of today, so that we no longer know where we are.' Chion, *Lynch*, 1995, 84.
79 Jenkins, 'The Aesthetics of Transmedia'.
80 Fisher, *The Weird and the Eerie*, 62.
81 Geoffrey Long, 'Transmedia Storytelling: Business, Aesthetics, and Production at the Jim Henson Company' PhD Thesis: Massachusetts Institute of Technology, Department of Comparative Media Studies, 2007, 60.
82 van Elferen, 'Dream Timbre', 184. Italics hers.

Chapter 17

1 For two very different but equally important conversations, I would like to thank Lawrence English and Aidan Byrne who know far more than I about granular synthesis and quantum physics, respectively.
2 Friedrich Kittler, *Gramophone, Film, Typewriter*, trans. Geoffrey Winthrop-Young and Michael Wutz (Stanford: Stanford University Press, 1999), 115.
3 Ibid., 3.
4 Ibid.
5 Ibid., 35–6.
6 Ibid., 26. To illustrate Willis's experiment, Kittler includes in his book an uncredited illustration that could easily be thought to represent what is described here but is more likely to be, in fact, an illustration of a mechanism that has more in common with Christian Gottlieb Kratzenstein's resonators for the synthesis of vowel sounds that are activated by the passage of air through a

combination of pipes and reeds (and the image is indeed credited as such in the only image of it circulating on the internet). Fittingly, perhaps, this illustration of disembodied mouths attached to a machine provides us with a nightmarish image that resonates strongly with the kinds of visions found across the many media forms of Lynch's universe.

7   Norbert Wiener, 'Spatio-temporal Continuity, Quantum Theory and Music', in *The Concepts of Space and Time: Their Structure and Their Development*, ed. Milič Čapek (Dordrecht: Springer-Science+Business Media, 1976), 544.

8   Ibid., 545.

9   Ibid., 545–6.

10 See Greg Hainge, *Noise Matters: Towards an Ontology of Noise* (New York: Bloomsbury Academic, 2013).

11 See André Bazin, 'The Ontology of the Photographic Image', trans. Hugh Gray, *Film Quarterly* 13, no. 4 (1960): 4–9.

12 Álvarez López, 'Foreplays #6: David Lynch's "Premonition Following an Evil Deed"', *Mubi Notebook* (2018), at https://mubi.com/notebook/posts/foreplay s-6-david-lynch-s-premonition-following-an-evil-deed (accessed 21 December 2018).

13 Ibid.

14 Bazin, 'The Ontology of the Photographic Image', 8.

15 Carlo Rovelli, *The Order of Time* (London: Penguin Books, 2017), 98–9.

16 Marina Warner, 'Voodoo Road: *Lost Highway* by David Lynch', *Sight and Sound* 7, no. 8 (1997): 6–10.

17 I must at this point remind the reader that the core project of Martha Nochimson's second book on Lynch, *David Lynch Swerves: Uncertainty from Lost Highway to Inland Empire* (Austin: University of Texas Press, 2013), is an attempt to revise her previous readings of Lynch by bringing to his work insights from quantum physics intended to unpack an interest in the field that Nochimson had gleaned from conversations with him over the years (x). As well as forming a major component of her own analyses, the volume also contains an interview with Lynch where she tries to draw him explicitly on the link between quantum physics and his vision (173–82), as well as an interview with quantum physicist and David Lynch fan David Z. Albert in which she tries to do the same from the other side of the door (183–214). In her own readings, Nochimson focuses primarily on the concepts of non-locality, superpositionality, entanglement and decoherence, rather than the concept of quantum time that is my focus here. My contribution to this investigation here should therefore be considered more of a companion piece to Nochimson's work rather than a rebuttal or corrective.

18 Rovelli, *The Order of Time*, 74.

19 Ibid., 74–5.

20 Gilles Deleuze, *Cinema 2: The Time-Image*, trans. Hugh Tomlinson and Robert Galeta (Minneapolis: University of Minnesota Press, 1997), xii.

21 Ibid., 82, 98.

22 Ibid., 99.

23 Rovelli, *The Order of Time*, 122.

24 Ibid., 9.

25 Ibid., 117. It is in relation to this understanding of quantum time that my study diverges most significantly from that of Nochimson whose discussion of temporality in Lynch's work conceptualises time in terms of a circularity in which becomes possible the phenomenon of time reversal symmetry (23) – an understanding which runs the risk of assuming that we are still dealing with a conception of time as a fundamental albeit one whose directionality is not fixed, rather than time as something that is produced only out of relations.

26 Ibid., 108.

27 Deleuze, *Cinema 2*, 99.

28 More generally, of course, different temporalities, speeds and directionalities of time are a characteristic of the Black Lodge and all that resides in or emerges from that space.

29 Timothy William Galow, 'From *Lost Highway* to *Twin Peaks*: Representations of Trauma and Transformation in Lynch's Late Works', in *Critical Essays on Twin Peaks: The Return*, ed. Antonio Sanna (London: Palgrave Macmillan, 2019), 217.

30 For a layperson's explanation of this phenomenon, see Bob Holmes, 'Why Time Flies in Old Age', *New Scientist*, at https://www.newscientist.com/article/mg15220571.700-why-time-flies-in-old-age/ (accessed 25 January 2019); and Christian Yates, 'Why Time Seems To Go By More Quickly As We Get Older', *The Conversation*, at https://theconversation.com/why-time-seems-to-go-by-more-quickly-as-we-get-older-63354 (accessed 25 January 2019).

31 Joel Hawkes, 'Movement in the Box: The Production of Surreal Social Space and the Alienated Body', in *Critical Essays on Twin Peaks: The Return*, ed. Antonio Sanna (London: Palgrave Macmillan, 2019), 149–68.

32 Michael Light, *100 Suns* (New York: Alfred A. Knopf, 2003).

33 Lynch quoted in Richard Barney, ed., *David Lynch Interviews* (Jackson: University Press of Mississippi, 2009), 126.

34 Richard Feynman, *The Character of Physical Law* (Cambridge, MA: MIT Press, 1985), 162.

35 Richard Feynman, *What Do You Care What Other People Think? Further Adventures of a Curious Character* (New York: Norton & Company, 1988), 127–8.

36 Ibid., 247.

37 John Alexander, *The Films of David Lynch* (Dalkeith: Charles Letts & Co, 1993), 26–7.

38 See Jonas Fornäs, 'Passages Across Thresholds: Into the Borderlands of Mediation', *Convergence* 8, no. 4 (2002): 89–106.

39 What is being suggested here is close to Matthew Ellis and Tyler Theus's suggestion that this final scene demonstrates that '*The Return* effectively narrates its own relationship to the earlier series as one in which *any* form of comprehension is called into question, the untenable link between past and present a mere construction like Benjamin's angel whisked backwards into the future': Matthew Ellis and Tyler Theus, 'Is it Happening Again? *Twin Peaks* and *"The Return"* of History', in *Critical Essays on Twin Peaks: The Return*, ed. Antonio Sanna (London: Palgrave Macmillan, 2019), 34.

Chapter 18

1   Daniel Dylan Wray, 'The Discomfort Zone: Exploring the Musical Legacy of David Lynch', at https://pitchfork.com/features/article/9958-the-discomfort-zone-exploring-the-musical-legacy-of-david-lynch/ (accessed 15 November 2018).

2   For more on musically driven film, see Holly Rogers, 'Introduction', in *The Music and Sound of Experimental Film*, eds. Rogers and Jeremy Barham (New York and Oxford: Oxford University Press, 2017), 1–22.

3   Chris O'Falt, 'Sound Comes First', at https://www.indiewire.com/2018/05/twin-peaks-the-return-sound-design-david-lynch-hidden-studio-process-dean-hurley-1201965234/ (accessed 15 November 2018).

4   Ibid.

5   Karl Pedersen and Mark Grimshaw-Aagaard, eds., *The Recording, Mixing, and Mastering Reference Handbook* (New York: Oxford University Press, 2019), 223.

6   Pete, 'Beatles Production Tricks Part II – VariSpeed', at https://ofbuckleyandbeatles.wordpress.com/2010/12/05/beatles-production-tricks-part-ii-varispeed/ (accessed 15 November 2018).

7   Alexander Rehding, 'The Discovery of Slowness', in *Thresholds of Listening: Sounds, Technics, Space,* ed. Sander Van Maas (New York: Fordham University Press, 2015), 220.

8   Ibid.

9   Rhino, 'Twin Peaks: An Interview with Music Director Dean Hurley', at https://www.rhino.com/article/twin-peaks-an-interview-with-music-director-dean-hurley (accessed 15 November 2018).

10   Mark Cousins, 'Scene by Scene with David Lynch', transcription available at https://sphinx.mythic-beasts.com/~mark/random/david-lynch/ (accessed 15 November 2018).

11   Emma Griffiths, 'Q&A with David Lynch's Music Collaborator Dean Hurley', at https://www.synchtank.com/blog/qa-with-david-lynchs-music-collaborator-dean-hurley-part-1-working-on-and-protecting-the-experience-of-twin-peaks-the-return/; and Pieter Dom, 'To Score The Haunting Woodsmen Scene', at https://welcometotwinpeaks.com/music/woodsmen-beethoven-moonlight-sonata/ (accessed 15 November 2018).

12   Angelo Badalamenti, 'Angelo Badalamenti On Working with David Lynch', at https://www.youtube.com/watch?v=a_9D5PiOjog (accessed 15 November 2018).

13   Pieter Dom, 'Slow Speed Orchestra Bundle & David Lynch's Clean Up New York PSA', at https://welcometotwinpeaks.com/music/slow-speed-orchestra-clean-up-new-york/ (accessed 15 November 2018). To hear the theme in its original form, see Angelo Badalamenti, 'Angelo Badalamenti Stair Music Danger Theme', at https://www.youtube.com/watch?v=ffhTeSHLozY (accessed 15 November 2018).

14   Ross Dudle, 'Twin Peaks Soundtrack Design', at http://twinpeakssoundtrackdesign.blogspot.com/p/twin-peaks-music-scene-guide.html (accessed 15 November 2018).

Chapter 19

1   Holly Rogers, 'The Audiovisual Eerie: Transmediating Thresholds in the
    Work of David Lynch', in *Transmedia Directors: Artistry, Industry and New
    Audiovisual Aesthetics*, eds. Carol Vernallis, Holly Rogers and Lisa Perrott
    (New York and London: Bloomsbury, 2019), 253.

2   Cristina Álvarez López, quoted in Greg Hainge, 'When Is a Door Not a Door?
    Transmedia to the nth Degree', in *Transmedia Directors*, 276.

3   John McGrath, 'On (Vari-)Speed in David Lynch's Work', in *Transmedia
    Directors*, 285–90.

4   Anne Sauvagnargues, *Artmachines: Deleuze, Guattari, Simondon*, trans.
    Suzanne Verderber with Eugene Holland (Edinburgh: Edinburgh University
    Press, 2016), 73.

5   Among the few available film and media contributions drawing on Simondon's
    thought to date, the following are worth noting, ranging from sustained
    analyses of his philosophy to sporadic mentions: Elena del Río, '*La Grande
    Bellezza*: Adventures in Transindividuality', *Necsus: European Journal of Media
    Studies* (Autumn 2017), at https://necsus-ejms.org/la-grande-bellezza-adventu
    res-in-transindividuality/ (accessed 3 March 2019); Tom Gunning, 'Animation
    and Alienation: Bergson's Critique of the Cinématographe and the Paradox
    of Mechanical Motion', *The Moving Image* 14, no. 1 (Spring 2014): 1–9;
    Jon Hackett, 'The Ontogenesis of Cinematic Objects: Simondon, Marx and
    the Invention of Cinema', *Platform: Journal of Media and Communication*
    6 (2015): 11–21; Mark Hansen, 'Body Times', in *New Philosophy for New
    Media* (Cambridge, MA: MIT Press, 2006), 235–68; Bruno Lessard, '"It's the
    End of the World!": The Paradox of Event and Body in Hitchcock's *The Birds*',
    Film-Philosophy 14, no. 1 (2010): 144–67; Tyler Fox, 'Prehensive Transduction:
    Techno-Aesthetics in New Media Art', *Platform: Journal of Media and
    Communication* 6 (2015): 96–107.

6   Sauvagnargues, *Artmachines*, 75.

7   The scientific accent that Hainge's chapter in this volume brings to bear on
    his analysis of Lynch's transmedial cinema via Norbert Wiener's cybernetics
    also extends to a Simondonian perspective. In fact, Simondon's theory of
    individuation was influenced by Wiener's theory of information, which he
    develops in a new direction. This new direction, for Brian Massumi, involves
    a qualitative approach clearly differentiated from Wiener's quantitative
    formalization. Massumi writes: 'Although a quantum leap does coincide
    with the discharge of a measurable amount of energy, it also coincides
    with the passing of a threshold to a qualitatively new level of existence.
    That qualitative crossing is the crucial point for Simondon': '"Technical
    Mentality" Revisited: Brian Massumi on Gilbert Simondon', in *Gilbert
    Simondon: Being and Technology*, eds. Arne de Boever, Alex Murray, Jon
    Roffe and Ashley Woodward (Edinburgh: Edinburgh University Press, 2013),
    32.

8   Anne Sauvagnargues, 'Crystals and Membranes: Individuation and
    Temporality', in *Gilbert Simondon: Being and Technology* (Edinburgh:
    Edinburgh University Press, 2013), 58.

9 Muriel Combes, *Gilbert Simondon and the Philosophy of the Transindividual*, trans. Thomas LaMarre (Cambridge, MA and London: MIT Press, 2012), 32.

10 Ibid., 35.

11 Ibid., 37.

12 Sauvagnargues, *Artmachines*, 68.

13 Massumi, 'Technical Mentality', 24.

14 Gilbert Simondon, *L'indviduation à la lumière des notions de forme et d'information* (Grenoble: Éditions Jérôme Millon, 2005), 44, quoted in Combes, *Gilbert Simondon*, 5.

15 Combes, *Gilbert Simondon*, 5.

16 Sauvagnargues, *Artmachines*, 71.

17 Rogers, 'The Audiovisual Eerie'.

18 Elena del Río, *The Grace of Destruction: A Vital Ethology of Extreme Cinemas* (New York and London: Bloomsbury, 2016), 138–55.

19 Combes, *Gilbert Simondon*, 35.

20 Ibid.

21 Following Deleuze and Spinoza, Massumi defines affect as 'the passage from one experiential state of the body to another ... implying an augmentation or diminution in that body's capacity to act' ('Notes on the Translation and Acknowledgments', in Gilles Deleuze and Félix Guattari, *A Thousand Plateaus: Capitalism and Schizophrenia*, trans. Massumi (Minneapolis: University of Minnesota Press, 1987), xvi. The following is Deleuze and Guattari's more challenging, yet fascinating, definition of affect in *A Thousand Plateaus*: 'To every relation of movement and rest, speed and slowness grouping together an infinity of parts, there corresponds a degree of power. To the relations composing, decomposing, or modifying an individual there correspond intensities that affect it, augmenting or diminishing its power to act' (256). Without going into too much depth about it, Deleuze here establishes some significant parallels between Spinoza's affective becomings and Simondon's theory of individuation. As Combes also stresses, Simondon 'situat[es] the center of individuality in affectivity and emotivity' and is indeed 'quite close to the Spinozan understanding of the subject of ethics as a site of perpetual variation, in its power to act, which is a function of its capacity to affect other subjects ... and to be affected by them': Combes, *Gilbert Simondon*, 30.

22 Maurice Merleau-Ponty, *The Phenomenology of Perception* (New York: Routledge, 2002), 415.

23 Combes, *Gilbert Simondon*, 51.

24 del Río, *The Grace of Destruction*, 146.

25 Massumi, 'Technical Mentality', 31.

26 Rogers, 'The Audiovisual Eerie'.

27 Ibid., 258 (emphasis added).

28 Ibid., 252.

29 Ibid., 242; Hainge, 'When Is a Door Not a Door?' 273.

30 Elena del Río, *Deleuze and the Cinemas of Performance: Powers of Affection* (Edinburgh: Edinburgh University Press, 2008), 194.

31 Ibid., 196.

32 Massumi, 'Technical Mentality', 30.

33 del Río, *Deleuze and the Cinemas of Performance*, 190.

34 Juho Rantala, 'The Notion of Information in Early Cybernetics and in Gilbert Simondon's Philosophy', paper presented at Doctoral Congress in Philosophy, 22–24 October 2018, University of Tampere, Finland, 6.

35 Massumi, 'Technical Mentality', 25.

36 Combes, *Gilbert Simondon*, 6.

37 Sauvagnargues, 'Crystals and Membranes', 59.

38 Henry Jenkins quoted in Rogers, 'The Audiovisual Eerie', 242.

39 Gilles Deleuze, *Difference and Repetition*, trans. Paul Patton (New York and London: Continuum, 2004), 80.

40 Massumi, 'Technical Mentality', 30.

Chapter 20

1 Michael Gillespie, 'One Step Ahead: A Conversation With Barry Jenkins', *Film Quarterly* (posted 28 February 2017), at https://filmquarterly.org/2017/02/28/one-step-ahead-a-conversation-with-barry-jenkins/ (accessed 27 March 2019).

2 For Jidenna's reaction to having the song incorporated in the film, see Jidenna, in Lauren Nostro, 'Jidenna Reacts To His Song "Classic Man" Appearing in *Moonlight*', *Genius.com* (posted 24 February 2017), at https://genius.com/a/jidenna-reacts-to-his-song-classic-man-appearing-in-moonlight (accessed 26 March 2019).

3 On this point, see Jenkins, in Matthew Schnipper, 'Director Barry Jenkins on the Music That Made *Moonlight*', *Pitchfork.com* (posted 29 November 2016), at https://pitchfork.com/thepitch/1377-director-barry-jenkins-on-the-music-that-made-moonlight/ (accessed 26 March 2019).

4 Gillespie, 'One Step Ahead'. On this same point, as it applies to black film writ large, see Michael Gillespie, *Film Blackness: American Cinema and the Idea of Black Film* (Durham, NC: Duke University Press, 2016), 2.

5 Jenkins, in Devan Coggin, 'Barry Jenkins Deconstructs The Swimming Lesson Scene From Moonlight', *Entertainment Weekly* (posted 6 December 2016), at https://ew.com/article/2016/12/06/moonlight-barry-jenkins-swimming-lesson-scene/ (accessed 6 April 2019).

6 Ibid.

Chapter 21

1 I use this term in the way provided by Tamar Avnet and Anne-Lauer Sellier, 'Clock Time vs. Event Time: Temporal Culture or Self-regulation?' *Journal of Experiential Social Psychology* 47 (2011): 665–7.

2 Helen Powell identifies three layers of temporality in film: the time of registration (i.e. filming, editing and otherwise production), that of narration (storytelling) and that of consumption (viewing). For the purposes of this essay, I focus on the latter two, since they are, out of the three, the most perceptible and registerable for the viewer. These two temporal levels 'storytelling' and

'viewing' I analogize as the media object's interior and exterior worlds, respectively. For more on this, see: Helen Powell, *Stop The Clocks!: Time and Narrative in Cinema* (London: I. B. Taurus & Co., 2012), 3.

3   Ibid., 17–20.

4   Michel Chion makes the distinction between the film score (which in *Beale Street* operates leitmotivically), what he calls 'pit music' after the orchestra's place near the opera stage, and diegetic music which he less abstractly names 'screen music'. He focuses on the former, commenting on how pit music can swing from a non-diegetic to diegetic function seamlessly in Chion, 'Music as Spatiotemporal Turntable', in *Audio-Vision: Sound on Screen*, ed. Claudia Gorbman (New York: Columbia University Press, 1994). I consider in this short chapter the dramatic function and temporal multiplicity of screen music in the form of a vinyl record, which is a material object wielded by the characters that seems to articulate in a durationally finite way, a mood or feeling that the characters themselves may be less explicit about.

5   This track, from the album *For Lady* (1957), is in tribute to Billie Holiday and features pieces made famous by her, adapted for an instrumental sextet of trumpet/cornet (Webster Young), tenor saxophone (Paul Quinichette), piano (Mal Waldron), guitar (Joe Puma), bass (Earl May) and drums (Ed Thigpen).

6   Tish's parents, in the novel, met in Albany, New York. Her mother, called Sharon throughout Tish's first-person narrative, migrated to New York State from Birmingham, Alabama, leaving at nineteen as a singer 'running away with a traveling band, but, more especially, with the drummer...'. Joseph, Tish's father, a merchant seaman originally from Boston who was now a porter at a bus station, met Sharon in Albany, in the bus station, and followed her, in love, to New York City, marrying her within a week after their arrival. James Baldwin, *If Beale Street Could Talk* (New York: Vintage International, 1974/2002), 27–30.

7   See Norman Mailer, 'The White Negro: Superficial Reflections on the Hipster', *Dissent* (20 June 2007), https://www.dissentmagazine.org/online_articles/the-white-negro-fall-1957 (accessed 28 April 2019). More importantly, see: Ingrid Monson's dissection of Mailer's piece, which interrogates the celebratory tone by which Mailer describes the nihilistic appropriation of black jazz and vernacular culture by white hipsters in the name of subverting their social privilege, in Monson, 'The Problem with White Hipness: Race, Gender, and Cultural Conceptions in Jazz Historical Discourse', *Journal of the American Musicological Society* 48, no. 3 (Autumn 1995): 396–422.

8   For the most historically significant exploration of this connection', see Amiri Baraka, 'The Changing Same (R&B and the New Black Music)', *Black Music* (1966/2010), 180–211.

9   Jonathan Sterne, *The Audible Past: Cultural Origins of Sound Production* (Durham: Duke University Press, 2003), 288.

10 Chion understands sound as influencing the perception of time in the (moving) image in three ways: (1) it bestows an element of temporal animation onto an image, especially a static one (i.e. still or 'freezeframe'); (2) it endows shots with temporal linearization (temporal succession); and (3) it vectorizes, 'or

dramatizes shots, orienting them toward a future, a goal and creation of a feeling of imminence and expectation. The shot is going somewhere and it is oriented in time': *Audio-Vision*, 13–14. I see the sound disc and phonograph as, in addition to Britell's film score, allowing for the third entry in Chion's list.

11 Hannah Giorgis and Britell, 'How If Beale Street Could Talk Translates Joy and Terror Into Sound', *The Atlantic* (19 December 2018), at https://www.the atlantic.com/entertainment/archive/2018/12/if-beale-street-could-talk-nicho las-britell-composer-music-score/577879/ (accessed 25 April 2019).

12 Matthew Bribitzer-Stull, *Understanding the Leitmotif: From Wagner to Hollywood Film Music* (New York: Cambridge University Press, 2015), 1.

13 Ibid., 10.

14 Baldwin, *If Beale Street Could Talk*, 41.

Chapter 23

1 Cope's videos are featured at the Owl House Studios website, at www. owlhousestudios.com (accessed 19 January 2019).

2 Cope, 'Steven Wilson: Routine', *Owl House Studios* music video (10:04), at https://www.owlhousestudios.com/index.php/films/81-films-row-3-1/84-ro utine (accessed 28 May 2018).

3 Steven Wilson, *Hand. Cannot. Erase.* (Deluxe Edition). Kscope, KSCOPE522, 2015.

4 See Stephen Humphries, 'An Interview with Jess Cope', *Steven Wilson*, at http: //stevenwilsonhq.com/sw/an-interview-with-jess-cope/ (accessed 15 November 2018).

5 Jess Cope, 'Steven Wilson: People Who Eat Darkness', YouTube video (6:03), at https://www.youtube.com/watch?v=MPcoUCFAVcQ (accessed 15 November 2018).

6 See, for instance, Elizabeth Evans, *Transmedia Television: Audiences, New Media, and Daily Life* (New York and London: Routledge, 2011); Matthew Freeman, *Historicising Transmedia Storytelling: Early Twentieth-Century Transmedia Story Worlds* (London: Routledge Press, 2017); Marie-Laure Ryan, 'Transmedial Storytelling and Transfictionality', *Poetics Today* 34, no. 3 (2013): 361–88; Marie-Laure Ryan and Jan-Noël Thon, eds., *Storyworlds Across Media* (Lincoln: Universtiy of Nebraska Press, 2014); Jan-Noël Thon, *Transmedial Narratology and Contemporary Media Culture* (Lincoln: University of Nebraska Press, 2016); and Kelly McErlean, *Interactive Narratives and Transmedia Storytelling: Creating Immersive Stories Across New Media Platforms* (Abingdon: Routledge, 2018).

7 See Lori Burns, 'The Concept Album as Visual – Sonic – Textual Spectacle: The Transmedial Storyworld of Coldplay's Mylo Xyloto', *iaspm@Journal* 6, no. 2 (2016): 91–116; Lori Burns, 'Transmedia Storytelling in Steven Wilson's "The Raven That Refused to Sing"', in *The Routledge Companion to Popular Music Analysis: Expanding Approaches*, ed. Ciro Scotto (New York and London: Routledge Press, 2018), 95–113; Nicola Dibben, 'Visualizing the App

Album with Björk's *Biophilia*', in *The Oxford Handbook of Sound and Image in Digital Media*, eds. Carol Vernallis, Amy Herzog and John Richardson (Oxford: Oxford University Press, 2013), 682–706; Christofer Jost, 'Popular Music and Transmedia Aesthetics: On the Conceptual Relation of Sound, Audio-Vision and Live Performance', in *Reinventing Sound: Music and Audiovisual Culture*, ed. Enrique Encabo (Newcastle upon Tyne: Cambridge Scholars Publishing, 2015), 2–13; and Carol Vernallis, *Unruly Media: YouTube, Music Video, and the New Digital Cinema* (Oxford and New York: Oxford University Press, 2013).

8 Multimodal analysis is explored in the following writings: Lori Burns, 'Multimodal Analysis of Popular Music Video: Genre, Discourse, and Narrative in Steven Wilson's "Drive Home"', in *Coming of Age: Teaching and Learning Popular Music in Academia*, ed. Carlos Rodrigues (Ann Arbor: University of Michigan Press, 2016), 81–110; Lars Elleström, ed., *Media Borders, Multimodality and Intermediality* (Basingstoke: Palgrave Macmillan, 2010); Gunther Kress and Theo van Leeuwen, *Multimodal Discourse* (London: Bloomsbury Academic, 2001); David Machin, *Analysing Popular Music: Image, Sound, Text* (Thousand Oaks: Sage Publications, 2010); Ruth Page, ed., *New Perspectives On Narrative and Multimodality* (Abingdon: Routledge, 2010); Jennifer Rowsell, *Working with Multimodality: Rethinking Literacy in a Digital Age* (London and New York: Routledge Press, 2013); Carey Jewitt, Jeff Bezemer, and Kay O'Halloran, eds., *Introducing Multimodality* (Abingdon: Routledge, 2016); Clemens Wöllner, ed., *Body, Sound and Space in Music and Beyond: Multimodal Explorations* (Abingdon: Routledge, 2017); Elise Seip Tønnessen and Frida Forsgren, eds., *Multimodality and Aesthetics* (Abingdon: Routledge, 2018).

9 See Nicholas Cook, *Analysing Musical Multimedia* (New York: Oxford University Press, 1998); Andrew Blake, *Popular Music: The Age of Multimedia* (London: Middlesex University Press, 2007); Jamie Sexton, ed., *Music, Sound and Multimedia: From the Live to the Virtual* (Edinburgh: University of Edinburgh Press, 2007); and Julie McQuinn, ed., *Popular Music and Multimedia* (Abingdon: Routledge, 2011).

10 See Theo Van Leeuwen, 'Multimodality', in *The Handbook of Discourse Analysis*, eds. Deborah Tannen, Heidi E. Hamilton and Deborah Schiffrin (John Wiley and Sons, 2015), 447–65; and Machin, *Analysing Popular Music*.

11 Jordan Blum, 'Genius. Doesn't. Fade. A Conversation With Steven Wilson', *PopMatters* (12 March 2015), at https://www.popmatters.com/genius-doesnt -fade-a-conversation-with-steven-wilson-2495558585.html (accessed 28 May 2018).

12 For an exploration of social media storytelling and narrative development, see Ruth Page, 'The Narrative Dimensions of Social Media Storytelling', in *The Handbook of Narrative Analysis*, eds. Anna De Fina and Alexandra Georgakopoulou (Hoboken: John Wiley & Sons, 2015), 329–47.

13 The interested reader can visit the following site to view an archived version of the blog: https://web.archive.org/web/20160410132301/http://handcannot erase.com:80/ (accessed 19 January 2019).

14 Blum, 'Genius. Doesn't. Fade'.

15 Carol Morley, *Dreams of a Life* (London: Dogwoof Ltd, 2011).

16 The term 'character focalization' was first used by Gérard Genette in *Discours du Récit* (Paris: Seuil, 1972).

17 Henry Jenkins, *Convergence Culture: Where Old and New Media Collide* (New York: New York University Press, 2006), 95.

18 Cope, 'Steven Wilson: Drive Home', *Owl House Studios* music video (8:24), at https://www.owlhousestudios.com/index.php/films/80-films-row-3-2/81-dr ive-home (accessed 28 May 2018).

19 Steven Wilson, *The Raven that Refused to Sing*. Kscope, KSCOPE241, 2012.

20 Cope and Simon Cartwright, 'Steven Wilson: The Raven That Refused To Sing', *Owl House Studios* music video (7:48), at https://www.owlhouse studios.com/index.php/films/77-the-raven-that-refused-to-sing (accessed 28 May 2018). For a discussion of this video, see Burns, 'Transmedia Storytelling'.

21 Donald Crafton, Shadow of a Mouse: Performance, Belief, and World-Making in Animation *(Berkeley: University of California Press, 2013)*.

22 Lori Burns and Laura McLaren, 'Interpreting the Materials of a Transmedia Storyworld: Word-Music-Image in Steven Wilson's *Hand. Cannot. Erase.* (2015)', in *The Bloomsbury Handbook of Music Production*, eds. Simon Zagorski-Thomas and Andrew Bourbon (London: Bloomsbury Publishing, 2019), forthcoming.

23 Vernallis explores how music videos often reflect song form through a range of visual strategies, including editing and use of colour. See Carol Vernallis, *Experiencing Music Video: Aesthetics and Cultural Context* (New York: Columbia University Press, 2004), 163–5.

24 This gesture is reminiscent of the high vocalize in 'The Great Gig in the Sky' [1:08] from Pink Floyd's *The Dark Side of the Moon* (SHVL 805, Harvest Records, 1973), although the gesture here is short, intense and charged with grief.

25 For a discussion of diegetic sound in film, see Claudia Gorbman, *Unheard Melodies: Narrative Film Music* (Bloomington and Indianapolis: Indiana University Press, 1987).

26 Dominique Chateau, ed., *Subjectivity: Filmic Representation and the Spectator's Experience* (Amsterdam: Amsterdam University Press, 2011), 12.

27 Jenkins, *Convergence Culture, 95.*

28 Music analysts have addressed the progressive rock concept album in a number of key writings. See, for instance, Allan Moore, *Aqualung* (New York: Continuum, 2004); Kevin Holm-Hudson, *Genesis and the Lamb Lies Down on Broadway* (Aldershot: Ashgate Press, 2008); Marianne Tatom Letts, *Radiohead and the Resistant Concept Album: How To Disappear Completely* (Bloomington and Indianapolis: Indiana University, 2010).

29 See Gareth Shute, *Concept Albums* (Scotts Valley, CA: CreateSpace Publishing Company, 2015); Ben Wener, 'Concept Albums are Once Again in Vogue in the Digital Age', *Pop Matters* (7 December 2006), at http://www.popmatter s.com/pm/feature/concept-albums-are-once-again-in-vogue-in-the-digital-age/ (accessed 15 November 2018).

Chapter 24

1 Katlego Disemelo has written on queer, black South-African Instagram celebrities in a way that is very relevant to this analysis of Versace's work. In a piece on queer image making and identity construction on Instagram, Disemelo writes the following about a portrait of the South-African duo FAKA: 'The juxtapositions at work in the image – masculinity/femininity, male/female, pragmatism/ethereality, toughness/softness – suggest a playful ambivalence. Nothing is stable or fixed – even the floor is a kind of optical illusion. There is an interplay, too, of different temporalities. The image is a still digital photograph, but not inanimate; it stretches forward with each moving second and appears, therefore, in constant motion. Using one of Instagram's latest features, this Instagram Stories image was only meant to last for 24 hours – a moment captured in time but reproduced as a fleeting, ephemeral performance of gender fluidity and ambivalence.' Disemelo's also argues lyrically for the importance of doing this kind of work about queer black creators on social media: 'We should busy ourselves with looking to the seemingly quotidian experiences, representations and lives of young and old black queer people who are everywhere marginalized because of their race, class, sexuality, physical ability and gender non-conformity. Keguro Macharia cautions that we must constantly question the materiality and contestations of established notions of the queer archive. We should, therefore, interrogate and take seriously popular cultural online trends, musical tastes, colloquialisms and self-styling – the everyday performances of marginalized queer subjectivities. We must take careful stock of those disidentificatory practices of meaning-making undertaken by marginalized queer subjectivities in order to archive *their* stories and realities.' Katlego Disemelo, 'Performing the Queer Archive: Strategies of Self-Styling on Instagram', in *Acts of Transgression: Contemporary Live Art in South Africa*, eds. Jay Pather and Catherine Boulle (Johannesburg: Wits University Press, 2019), 231, 238.

2 In the epilogue for a book on 'anxious labour' in social media, Greg Goldberg close reads a famous moment in the Communist Manifesto to meditate on the cultural anxiety over the erosion of the 'real' as we gradually become more and more involved with the digital as a site for the social. Goldberg writes: 'Despite the awkwardness of transposing "all that is solid [melts into air]" into a contemporary context, there is something about the sentence that still appeals to me and that I would like to preserve, through a willful misreading. I have played around with this clause in order to propose that the solid now serves as a discursive proxy for valued forms of relationality, such that the desire for the solid can be interpreted as a desire for the collective, the collaborative, the communal – [...] In other words, the loss of the real/material dollar bill, or embodied other, or tangible commodity is distressing insofar as the real/material is tied symbolically to valued forms of relationality; it is the undoing of these forms that motivates the desire for the solid. Conversely, the immaterial is tied to devalued forms of relationality: the irresponsible, the promiscuous, the self-serving, and the self-destructive.' Greg Goldberg, *Antisocial Media: Anxious Labor in the Digital Economy* (New York: New York University Press, 2018), 165.

3 Versace also regularly posts portraits of himself on Instagram. Often these are not selfies, but carefully composed studies in his personal fashion. Their tone is often more serious than his videos. When linking out to work on other platforms like SoundCloud and YouTube, he sometimes effaces himself completely, posting images of cartoons, vintage photographs or sometimes just his hands. For more on self-portraiture, auteurism and art photography on Instagram, see Laura Cornell, 'Self-Portraiture in the First-Person Age', *Aperture* 221 (Winter 2015): 34–41. Cornell asks: 'Now that we are at the end of the *only for me era,* what strategies of artistic self-portraiture are viable? How to distinguish art from selfies in the *big scroll*?' (36).

4 Versace quoted in Danielle Rines, 'Jay Versace Curated a '90s Inspired Capsule for Reebok', *Reebok* (posted October 2018), at https://www.reebok.com/us/blog/303185-jay-versace-curated-a-90s-inspired-capsule-for-reebok (accessed 4 May 2019).

Chapter 25

1 According to Alois Riegl, 'haptic' vision permits emotion, or a 'touching with the eyes', when studying surfaces like carvings, ornaments and fabrics in detail. In film, the plane of pixels and signal noises or surface modulations can activate a sense of the virtual. Haptic compositions thus deprive the spectator of a habitual voyeuristic and narrative superiority. For more on this, see: Alois Riegl, *Late Roman Art Industry* (Rome: Georgio Bretschneider (1902) 1985); Bodil Marie Stavning Thomsen, *Lars von Trier's Renewal of Film 1984–2014. Signal, Pixel, Diagram* (Aarhus: Aarhus University Press, 2018); Gilles Deleuze, *Cinema 1: The Movement-Image* (Minneapolis: University of Minnesota Press, 1986); Gilles Deleuze and Félix Guattari, *A Thousand Plateaus. Capitalism and Schizophrenia* (New York: Bloomsbury Academic, 2013); Brian Massumi, *Parables for the Virtual. Movement, Affect, Sensation* (London: Duke University Press, 2002).

2 For more on 'the signaletic material', see: Gilles Deleuze, *Cinema 2: The Time-Image* (Minneapolis: University of Minnesota Press, 1989), 265; Bodil Marie Stavning Thomsen, 'Signaletic, Haptic and Real-time Material', *Journal of Aesthetics and Culture* 4, no. 1 (2012): 1–11.

3 To diagram means to schematically or graphically represent or illustrate something, often used for statistical purposes or in architecture. In the following I refer to C. S. Peirce's definition: 'The greatest point of art consists in the introduction of suitable abstractions. By this I mean such a transformation of our diagrams that characters of one diagram may appear in another as things': Charles Sanders Peirce quoted in *The Rule of Reason: The Philosophy of Charles Sanders Peirce*, eds. Jacqueline Brunning and Paul Forster (Toronto: University of Toronto Press, 1997), 226. Brian Massumi's use of Peirce to pinpoint the diagrammatic traits of Marcel Proust's *In Search of Lost Time* has inspired me to make a diagrammatic reading of *The Idiots* and later films: Marcel Proust, *In Search of Lost Time* (New York: The Modern Library, 2003); Brian Massumi, *Semblance and Event. Activist Philosophy and*

the Occurrent Arts (Cambridge, MA & London: The MIT Press, 2011), 99; Thomsen, *Lars von Trier's Renewal of Film*.

4 In the extra DVD material, von Trier states that he wanted Björk's music to take over from the visuals and vice versa in order to obtain a sort of digital fusion of sound and image. An example is his idea that a mic onto her heart in the death-by-hanging scene should be the real-time rhythm of the music – and its arrest. According to him, quarrelling over whether or not music should take the lead over film was one of the main disagreements between the two artists.

5 Laura Mulvey, 'Visual Pleasure and Narrative Cinema', in Laura Mulvey, *Visual and Other Pleasures* (London: Macmillan (1975) 1989), 14–26.

6 Dante Alighieri, *The Divine Comedy* (Everyman's Library (1320; 1472) 1995): in this first example of a first-person narrator, Vergil, who wrote about the underworld in *The Aeneid* between 29 and 19 BC (cf. Virgil, *The Aeneid* (Vintage, 1995)), is Dante's omniscient companion.

7 This question has meta-filmic significance, since von Trier in many interviews has stated that the flaw of his upbringing was that there were no borders and no rules. He has often returned to this want and call for rules, the purpose of which are to be broken nevertheless.

8 A similar movement of sound from the background to becoming the interstice of musical sequences that provide comment – and thus move to the foreground of perception – is also applicable to *Dancer in the Dark*.

9 Snippets of Vivaldi's 'The Four Seasons' (1723) are heard in relation to the hunting scene, and a small section of Wagner's 'Tristan und Isolde' is also heard. Ray Charles's song 'Hit the Road, Jack' (1961) is played repeatedly at the ending. I see this as a kind of remembrance of the expulsion, dismissal or banishment from society. Trier himself experienced being banned from the Cannes society of directors in 2011 after his poorly phrased attempt to use irony at a press conference, where he compared the aesthetic beauty of *Melancholia* and the aesthetics of Hitler's regime.

10 For more on this, see Thomsen, *Lars von Trier's Renewal of Film*, 284–91.

11 Ibid.

12 The wider structure of the film adds to this. The structure of Jack's final house of corpses in the film was made by Danish architect Bjarke Ingels, and as an appendix to the film, it was exhibited in full size at Kunsthal Charlottenborg in Copenhagen from 21 September 2018 to 13 January 2019.

13 The escape through the (until then) closed door has a similarity to Franz Kafka's novel *Before the Law*, since it means that the entrance is meant for Jack only at this moment; *Before the Law* (1915), at *Franz Kafka Online*, http://www.kafka-online.info/before-the-law.html (accessed 5 April 2019).

14 This might be a reference to David Lynch's widespread use of holes as escape routes into other worlds or universes.

15 The word 'acousmatic' comes from a name for the disciples of Pythagoras, *akousmatikoi*, who listened to the philosopher's lectures from behind a curtain in order to better focus on his discourse. Pierre Schaeffer uses the concept in order to isolate the listening mode to modern audio technology (cf. Brian Kane, *Sound Unseen. Acousmatic Sound in Theory and Practice* (Oxford: Oxford University Press, 2014), 4). In a film context, Michel Chion

uses the concept of 'acousmêtre' as a way of placing focus on sound and the sound object, dissociated from, but living within, visual representation like a 'hidden monster, or the Big Boss, or the evil genius, or on rare occasions a wise man. [...] He must, even if only slightly, have one foot in the image, in the space of the film; he must haunt the borderlands that are neither the interior of the filmic stage nor the proscenium – a place that has no name, but which the cinema forever brings into play' (cf. Michel Chion, *The Voice in Cinema* (New York: Columbia University Press (1982) 1999), 24). Lynch is famous for his use of empathy and detachment in relation to the acousmêtre (e.g. in *Blue Velvet* (1986) and in *Mulholland Drive* (2001)), but it is also famously used in *Singing in the Rain* (1952). In *Breaking the Waves* (1996) von Trier pokes fun at God's voice from above by letting Bess produce the male voice herself.

16 For the full analysis of *Antichrist*, see Thomsen, *Lars von Trier's Renewal of Film*, 235–61.
17 Chion, *The Voice in Cinema*, 79.
18 And it certainly brings to mind Stanley Kubrick's *Full Metal Jacket* (1987).
19 The painting was inspired by Théodore Gericault's *The Raft of the Medusa* (1819), which shocked the art public due to its realistic portrayal of the flesh of the dying and dead bodies.

Chapter 26

1   Ogarev quoted in Nina Siegal, 'Lars von Trier Wants to Turn All His Films into Diamonds', *New York Times* (11 February 2019), at https://www.nytimes.com/2019/02/11/arts/design/lars-von-trier-diamond-melancholia.html (accessed 14 February 2019).
2   Kreuger quoted in Ibid.
3   See, for example, Jacob Matikainen, 'A Closer Look at Lars von Trier's Depression Trilogy', *Screen Robot* (27 February 2014), at https://screenrobot.com/closer-look-lars-von-triers-depression-trilogy/ (accessed 15 February 2019).
4   Lars von Trier – '"I Understand Hitler"', at https://www.youtube.com/watch?v=QpUqpLh0iRw (accessed 14 February 2019).
5   See Linda Badley, *Lars von Trier* (Urbana and Chicago: University of Illinois Press, 2011), 7–10.
6   Andrew O'Hehir, 'Pick of the Week: Lars von Trier's Spectacular *Melancholia*', *Salon* (10 November 2011), at https://www.salon.com/2011/11/11/pick_of_the_week_lars_von_triers_spectacular_melancholia/ (accessed 15 February 2019).
7   See Badley, *Lars von Trier*, 21–47.
8   John Rockwell, 'FILM: Von Trier and Wagner, a Bond Sealed in Emotion', *New York Times* (8 April 2001), at https://www.nytimes.com/2001/04/08/movies/film-von-trier-and-wagner-a-bond-sealed-in-emotion.html (accessed 14 February 2019).
9   Ibid.
10 Quoted in Ibid.

11　Von Trier paraphrased by the festival website and quoted in John Rockwell, 'REVERBERATIONS; Maybe Lars von Trier's Vision Was Just What Wagner Needed', *New York Times* (11 June 2004), at https://www.nytimes.com/2004/0 6/11/movies/reverberations-maybe-lars-von-trier-s-vision-was-just-what-wagn er-needed.html (accessed 14 February 2019).

12　Von Trier, '"Deed of Conveyance": Lars von Trier on the Nibelungen Ring – The Enriched Darkness', *Mostly Opera* (4 October 2007), at https://mostlyo pera.blogspot.com/2007/10/lars-von-trier-on-nibelungen-ring.html (accessed 14 February 2019).

13　Ryan Minor, 'Introduction to Lars von Trier's "Deed of Conveyance"', *The Opera Quarterly* 23, nos. 2–3 (Spring–Summer 2007): 338–40.

14　In fact, the audio commentary for *Antichrist* and *Melancholia* references 'monumental' images (von Trier and Murray Smith, Audio Commentary, *Antichrist* [Criterion Collection, DVD, 2009]; von Trier and Peter Schepelern, Audio Commentary, *Melancholia* [Artificial Eye, Blu-Ray, 2011]), and *Nymphomaniac* and *The House That Jack Built* open with protracted scenes of 'enriched darkness'. In *Jack,* this is literally a black screen, with the echo of distant voices and a hollow dripping sound, and the film concludes with the epilogue's darkly elegiac, slow-motion descent into hell.

15　Von Trier, 'Director's Statement – Lars von Trier', in 'Production Notes', in *Melancholia* (Official Movie Site) (Magnolia Pictures, 2011), at http://www. magpictures.com/presskit.aspx?id=bbcb733d-8d0e-495a-ba6d-be9a79453d1c (accessed 14 February 2019).

16　Frederic Spotts, *Hitler and the Power of Aesthetics* (New York: Overlook Press, 2003), 71–2, 98–100, 105–6, 114–17, 321–9, et passim.

17　Ibid., 57.

18　Speer cited in Saul Friedländer, *Reflections of Nazism: An Essay on Kitsch and Death*, trans. Thomas Weyr (New York: Harper and Row, 1982), 70.

19　Trier and Schepelern, *Melancholia.*

20　J. Hoberman, 'Cannes 2011: Lars von Trier's *Melancholia.* Wow', *VoiceFilm* (18 May 2011), at http://www.voicefilm.com/2011/05/cannes_2011_lars_von_t riers_melancholia_wow.php (accessed 14 February 2019).

21　Lisa Schwarzbaum, 'Cannes Film Festival: Lars von Trier's Stunning *Melancholia* – The End of the World (and a Challenge to *The Tree of Life*)', *EW*.com (18 May 2011), at http://www.ew.com/ (accessed 14 February 2019).

22　Von Trier, 'Director's Statement', Press Kit, Cannes Film Festival, *Melancholia* (Magnolia Pictures & Zentropa Entertainments, 2011), at http://www.magp ictures.com/presskit.aspx?id=bbcb733d-8d0e-495a-ba6d-be9a79453d1c (accessed 14 February 2019).

23　Von Trier quoted in Nils Thorsen, *Geniet – Lars von Triers Liv, Film og Fobier* (Copenhagen: Politken, 2011), 386–7. Passage translated by Anders Marklund.

24　Theodor Wiesengrund Adorno, *The Culture Industry* (New York: Routledge, 2001; 1972, 1976; repr.).

25　Abbas Akbar, 'Junk Space, *Dogville*, and Poor Theory', Lecture: Film Theory and Visual Culture Seminar, Vanderbilt University (6 December 2013).

26　Linda Badley, 'The Transnational Politics of Lars von Trier's and Thomas Vinterberg's *Amerika*', in *Cinemas of Elsewhere: A Globalized History of*

Nordic Film Cultures, eds. Arne Lunde and Anna Stenport (Edinburgh: Edinburgh University Press, 2019), forthcoming.

27 Manuel Alberto Claro, Skype interview conducted by Linda Badley (11 December 2014).

28 Peter Schepelern, '"Forget about Love": Sex and Detachment in Lars von Trier's *Nymphomaniac*', *Kosmorama* no. 259 (11 March 2015), at www.kosmorama.org/ (accessed 14 February 2019).

29 Lowry Pressly, '*Nymphomaniac: Vol. 1*: Fishers of Men, Meaning', *The Los Angeles Review of Books* (21 March 2014), at https://lareviewofbooks.org/essay/nymphomaniac-vol-1-fishers-men-meaning (accessed 14 February 2019).

30 Philippe Sollers, *Sade's Way. ParisLike* (2013), Video Documentary (20 December 2015), at http://www.parislike.com/EN/snoopy-philippe-sollers-video.php (accessed 14 February 2019).

31 Linda Badley, '"Fill All My Holes": *Nymphomaniac*, Sade, and the (Female) Libertine Body', *Cinema as Provocation. Ekphrasis: Images, Cinema, Media, Theory* 2 (2015): 21–38.

32 Spotts, *Hitler and the Power of Aesthetics*, 56.

Chapter 27

1 The final part of the trilogy *Wasington* [*sic*] was never made. Brecht's theory of theatre was constantly evolving, but it is generally accepted that epic theatre marks a move away from his earlier didactic plays (*Lehrstücke*). Its principles, synthesized in 'A Short Organum for the Theatre' published in 1949, argue for a mode of theatrical presentation that eschew theatre's traditional reliance on character and human psychology. The aim is to engage the audience cognitively rather than emotionally in order to encourage political action. Traditional theatre, by contrast, induces a passive, hand-wringing acceptance of the way things are and evermore will be. Central to Brecht's approach is the foregrounding of theatrical artifice through alienation techniques – the famous *Verfremdung*. This constitutes a politics of form, which Roland Barthes describes as semiotic, to produce 'a theatre of consciousness, not of action, of problems not of answers'. See Roland Barthes, 'Literature and Signification', in *Critical Essays*, trans. Richard Howard (Evanston: Northwester University Press, 1972), 263. For Brecht's 'Short Organum' see *Brecht on Theatre*, trans. John Willett (London: Methuen, 1964), 179–205.

2 Von Trier inherited Dreyer's dinner jacket. See 'A Tale of Tailoring', by Torsten Grunwald, at https://www.carlthdreyer.dk/en/carlthdreyer/about-dreyer/biography/tale-tailoring (accessed 20 February 2019).

3 Stig Björkman, ed., *Trier on von Trier*, trans. Neil Smith (London: Faber and Faber, 2003), 47. The mass is performed by Ars Nova, directed by Bo Holten, who would write the score for *The Element of Crime* (1984). At the time, Holten was teaching in the music department of the National Film School of Denmark. He described von Trier as a student with 'a keen interest in music'. Private correspondence, 29 January 2019. At one time, von Trier was to have was to have provided the scenic conceptual design of Holten's opera on Martin

Luther, *Schlagt sie tot!*, the world premiere of which is on 11 May 2019 at the Malmö Opera.

4　See Björkman, *Trier*, 47.

5　Bach's organ choral-prelude, 'Ich ruf zu dir, Herr Jesu Christ' (BWV 639) is the ostensible subject of Stellan Skarsgård's mini-lecture, a piece which notably figures in *Solaris* (Tarkovsky, 1972), forming one of von Trier's familiar intertextual homages to other film-makers (he had already dedicated *Antichrist*, his 2009 film, to the Russian director).

6　For more on *Anna Boleyn*, see Rick Altman, *Silent Film Sound* (New York: Columbia University Press, 2004), 315–16.

7　Plainchant sections are indicated in square brackets: *[Requiem aeternam] dona eis, Domine, et lux perpetua luceat eis. [Te decet hymnus, Deus in Sion] et tibi redetur votum in Jerusalem;exaudi orationem meam, ad te omnis caro veniet.* [Eternal rest] grant them, O Lord, and let eternal light shine upon them. [A hymn to you is fitting, O God in Zion,] and a vow made to you in Jerusalem; hear my prayer, all flesh comes to you.

8　Anahid Kassabian, *Hearing Film: Tracking Identifications in Contemporary Hollywood Film Music* (London: Routledge, 2001), 3.

9　For more on the position that medieval music is a twentieth-century construction, see Daniel Leech-Wilkinson, *The Modern Invention of Medieval Music* (Cambridge: Cambridge University Press, 2002).

10　Brown writes that 'the music, rather than supporting and/or coloring the visual images and narrative situations, stands as an image in its own right, helping the audience read the film's other images as such rather than as a replacement for an imitation of objective reality'. Royal S. Brown, *Undertones and Overtones: Reading Film Music* (Berkeley: University of California Press, 1994), 239–40.

11　Peter Schepelern makes the same point and extends it to later periods of music, arguing that *Nymphomaniac* (2014) present 'a nearly encyclopedic survey of Western music from baroque to modernism', Peter Schepelern, '"Forget About Love": Sex and Detachment in Lars von Trier's *Nymphomaniac*', *Kosmorama* # 259 (11 March 2015), at www.kosmorama.org/ (accessed 23 February 2019).

12　Nila Parly, 'Lars von Trier's Lost Ring', *Cambridge Opera Journal* 30, no. 1 (2018): 20.

13　The series' set-bound orientation was not dictated by budgetary constraints but for 'artistic reasons'. See http://www.bbc.co.uk/blogs/genome/entries/2d0 39235-8a57-4265-a607-7f534af7950f (accessed 21 February 2019).

14　Nenad Jovanovic presents a cogent summary of the various appropriations of Brechtian theory in film studies in 'Introduction: Revisiting Brecht and Cinema', in *Brechtian Cinemas: Montage and Theatricality in Jean-Marie Straub and Danièle Huillet, Peter Watkins, and Lars von Trier* (Albany: State University of New York Press, 2017), 1–32. The term 'post-Brechtian', a concept from which Brecht would surely have insisted his name was removed, is summed up by Angelos Koutsourakis: 'Very schematically, the term "post-Brechtian" describes a postmodern rethinking of Brecht which shares his preference for a fragmented representation and formal abstraction, but not his political certainties.' *Politics as Form in Lars von Trier: A Post-Brechtian Reading* (London: Bloomsbury Academic, 2015), 12.

15 Dana Thomas, 'Meet the Punisher: Lars von Trier Devastates Audiences – and Actresses'. Interview with Lars von Trier in *Newsweek* 5 April 2004, cited in Badley, *Lars von Trier* (Urbana: University of Illinois Press, 2011), 70.

16 Bertolt Brecht, 'On the Use of Music in an Epic Theatre', in Willett, *Brecht* (London: Methuen, 1964), 89.

17 Björkman, *Trier*, 245.

18 Brecht, 'A Short Organum', 205.

19 'The Road to *Manderlay*', in *Manderlay*, DVD (Denmark: Zentropa, 2005).

20 The piece that stood in as a love theme was the second movement of Schubert's E flat major Piano Trio, which John Baxter describes as the soundtrack's 'most evocative piece': *Stanley Kubrick: A Biography* (London: Harper Collins, 1997), 293.

21 Like *Barry Lyndon*, *The Favourite* also uses more contemporary music – Olivier Messiaen, Luc Ferrari and Anna Meredith – and like *Dogville* and *Manderlay*, has a pop song running over the credits, Elton John's 'Skyline Pigeon' (1968).

22 Kassabian, *Hearing Film*, 70. Interestingly, Kassabian makes no reference to composer George Fenton's contributions, simply saying that 'most of the score consists of Baroque period music'. For more detailed consideration of the splicing of period music with Fenton's music, see Mervyn Cooke, 'Baroque à la Hitchcock: The Music of *Dangerous Liaisons*', in *Recomposing the Past: Representations of Early Music on Stage and Screen*, eds. James Cook, Alexander Kolassa and Adam Whittaker (Abingdon: Routledge, 2018), 32–50; and Miguel Mera, 'Representing the Baroque: The Portrayal of Historical Period in Film Music', *The Consort: Journal of the Dolmetsch Foundation* 57 (2001): 3–21.

23 For more details, see Mette Hjort and Scott MacKenzie, 'Introduction', in *Purity and Provocation: Dogma 95*, eds. Mette Hjort and Scott MacKenzie (London: Palgrave Macmillan, 2003), 1–29.

24 Jan Simons, *Playing the Waves: Lars von Trier's Game Cinema* (Amsterdam: Amsterdam University Press, 2014), 157.

25 It is played on modern trumpet with organ, arranged by Joachim Holbeck, who would arrange all the music for *Dogville* and *Manderlay*.

26 Roy M. Prendergast, *Film Music: A Neglected Art* (New York: Norton, 1977), 151.

27 Brecht, 'On the Use of Music', 85.

28 See Carlo Cenciarelli, 'Dr Lecter's Taste for "Goldberg", or: The Horror of Bach in the Hannibal Franchise', *Journal of the Royal Musical Association* 137, no. 1 (2012): 107–34.

BIBLIOGRAPHY

Chapter 1

Bordwell, David. 'Intensified Continuity: Visual Style in Contemporary American Film' *Film Quarterly* 55, no. 3 (2002): 16–28.

Bordwell, David. 'Observations in Film Art: Now Leaving Platform 1' (2009), at http://www.davidbordwell.net/blog/2009/08/19/now-leaving-from-platform-1/ (accessed 12 December 2018).

Dyer, Richard. *Only Entertainment*. New York: Taylor and Francis, 2005.

Dyer, Richard and Paul MacDonald. *Stars*. London: BFI Publishing, 1979.

Gorbman, Claudia. 'Auteur Music'. In *Beyond the Soundtrack: Representing Music in Cinema*, edited by Daniel Goldmark, Lawrence Kramer and Richard Leppert, 149–62. Berkeley: University of California Press, 2007.

Jenkins, Henry. 'The Reign of the "Mothership": Transmedia's Past, Present and Possible Futures." In *Wired TV: Laboring Over an Interactive Future*, edited by Denise Mann, 244–68. New Brunswick: Rutgers University Press, 2014.

Jenkins, Henry. *Convergence Culture: Where Old and New Media Collide*. New York: New York University Press, 2006.

Plantinga, Carl. *Passionate Views: Film, Cognition, and Emotion*. Baltimore: Johns Hopkins University Press, 1999.

Smith, Jeff. *The Sounds of Commerce: Marketing Popular Film Music*. New York: Columbia University Press, 1998.

Tompkins, Joe. 'The Makings of a Contradictory Franchise: Revolutionary Melodrama and Cynicism in *The Hunger Games*'. *Journal of Cinema and Media Studies* 58, no. 1 (2018): 70–90.

Vernallis, Carol. *Experiencing Music Video: Aesthetics and Cultural Context*. New York: Columbia University Press, 2004.

Vernallis, Carol. 'Music Video, Songs, Sound: Experience, Technique and Emotion in *Eternal Sunshine of the Spotless Mind*'. *Screen* 49, no. 3 (2008): 277–97.

Chapter 2

Anderson, Wes and Owen Wilson. *The Royal Tenenbaums*. London: Faber and Faber, 2001.

Berger, Peter and Thomas Luckmann. *The Social Construction of Reality: A Treatise in the Sociology of Knowledge*. Garden City: Anchor Books, 1966.

Boschi, Elena and Tim McNelis. '"Same Old Song": On Audio-Visual Style in the Films of Wes Anderson'. *New Review of Film and Television Studies* 10, no. 1 (2012): 28–45.

Bradshaw, Peter. 'Come Together Review – Anderson's H&M Christmas Ad Is Short and Sweet'. *The Guardian* (28 November 2016), at https://www.theguardian.com/film/2016/nov/28/come-together-review--anderson-h-and-m-christmas-ad-adrien-brody (accessed 27 July 2018).

Brooks, David. *Bobos in Paradise: The New Upper Class and How They Got There*. New York: Simon & Schuster, 2000.

Bunge, Mario. *Treatise on Basic Philosophy. Volume IV: Ontology – A World of Systems*. Amsterdam: Reidel, 1979.

Casetti, Francesco. *Inside the Gaze: The Fiction Film and Its Spectator*, translated by Nell Andrew and Charles O'Brien. Bloomington: Indiana University Press, 1998.

Coplan, Amy. 'Caring About Characters: Three Determinants of Emotional Engagement'. *Film and Philosophy* 10, no. 1 (2006): 1–19.

D'Aloia, Adriano, Marie-Aude Baronian, and Marco Pedroni. 'Fashionating Images: Audiovisual Media Studies Meet Fashion'. *Comunicazioni Sociali* 1 (2017): 3–12.

Gambarato, Renira Rampazzo. 'Signs, Systems and Complexity of Transmedia Storytelling'. *Estudos em Comunicação* 12 (2012): 69–83.

Gorbman, Claudia. 'Auteur Music'. In *Beyond the Soundtrack: Representing Music in Cinema*, edited by Daniel Goldmark, Lawrence Kramer and Richard Leppert, 149–62. Berkeley: University of California Press, 2007.

Heath, Stephen. 'Notes on Suture'. *Screen* 18, no. 4 (1977/8): 48–76.

Herman, David. *Basic Elements of Narrative*. Oxford: Wiley-Blackwell, 2009.

Hrycaj, Lara Rose. 'What Is This Music? Auteur Music in the Films of Anderson'. Unpublished PhD thesis, Wayne State University, 2013.

Hutcheon, Linda. *Irony's Edge: The Theory and Politics of Irony*. London: Routledge, 1994.

'Wes Anderson // Centered'. *Vimeo* video, 2:23. Posted by 'kogonada', 17 March 2014, at http://vimeo.com/89302848 (accessed 27 July 2018).

Kunze, Peter. 'Introduction: The Wonderful Worlds of Anderson'. In *The Films of Anderson: Critical Essays on an Indiewood Icon*, edited by Peter C. Kunze, 1–9. New York: Palgrave Macmillan, 2014.

Lamerichs, Nicholle. *Productive Fandom: Intermediality and Affective Reception in Fan Cultures*. Amsterdam: Amsterdam University Press, 2018.

Lee, Sunhee. 'Anderson's Ambivalent Film Style: The Relation between *Mise-en-scène* and Emotion'. *New Review of Film and Television Studies* 14, no. 4 (2016): 409–39.

Lévi-Strauss, Claude. 'The Effectiveness of Symbols'. *Structural Anthropology*, translated by Claire Jacobson and Brooke Grundfest Schoepf, 186–205. London: Allen Lane, 1972.

MacDowell, James. 'Anderson, Tone and Quirky Sensibility'. *New Review of Film and Television Studies* 10, no. 1 (2012): 6–27.

MacDowell, James. 'Notes on Quirky'. *Movie: A Journal of Film Criticism* 1 (2010): 1–16.

Magill, Jay. *Sincerity: How a Moral Ideal Born Five Hundred Years Ago Inspired Religious Wars, Modern Art, Hipster Chic, and the Curious Notion That We All Have Something to Say (No Matter How Dull)*. New York: W. W. Norton, 2012.

Martin, Adrian. '*Mise-en-scène* Is Dead, or the Expressive, the Excessive, the Technical and the Stylish'. *Continuum* 5, no. 2 (1992): 87–140.

Melzer, Arthur. 'Rousseau and the Modern Cult of Sincerity'. *The Harvard Review of Philosophy* 5, no. 1 (1995): 4–21.

Metz, Christian. 'The Imaginary Signifier'. *Screen* 16, no. 2 (1975): 14–76.

Miall, David and Don Kuiken. 'A Feeling for Fiction: Becoming What We Behold'. *Poetics* 30 (2002): 221–41.

Oudart, Jean-Pierre. 'Cinema and Suture'. *Screen* 18, no. 4 (1977/8): 35–47.

Peberdy, Donna. '"I'm Just a Character in Your Film": Acting and Performance from Autism to Zissou'. *New Review of Film and Television Studies* 10, no. 1 (2012): 46–67.

Piechota, Carole Lyn. 'Give Me a Second Grace: Music as Absolution in The Royal Tenenbaums'. *Senses of Cinema* 38 (February 2006), at http://sensesof cinema.com/2006/on-movies-musicians-and-soundtracks/music_tenenbaums/ (accessed 27 July 2018).

Plantinga, Carl. '"I Followed the Rules, and They All Loved You More": Moral Judgment and Attitudes toward Fictional Characters in Film'. *Midwest Studies in Philosophy* 34, no. 1 (2010): 34–51.

Plantinga, Carl and Greg Smith, eds. *Passionate Views: Film, Cognition, Emotion*. Baltimore: Johns Hopkins University Press, 1999.

Sconce, Jeffrey. 'Irony, Nihilism, and the New American "Smart" Film'. *Screen* 43, no. 4 (2002): 349–69.

Sennett, Richard. *The Fall of Public Man*. New York: Alfred A. Knopf, 1977.

Smith, Greg. *Film Structure and the Emotion System*. Cambridge: Cambridge University Press, 2003.

Smith, Murray. *Engaging Characters: Fiction, Emotion, and the Cinema*. Oxford: Clarendon Press, 1995.

Vaage, Margrethe Bruun. 'Fiction Film and the Varieties of Empathic Engagement'. *Midwest Studies in Philosophy* 34, no. 1 (2010): 158–79.

Wilkins, Kim. 'The Sounds of Silence: Hyper-Dialogue and American Eccentricity'. *New Review of Film and Television Studies* 11, no. 4 (2013): 403–23.

Williams, Raymond. *Marxism and Literature*. Oxford: Oxford University Press, 1977.

Wolf, Mark. *Building Imaginary Worlds: The Theory and History of Subcreation*. New York: Routledge, 2014.

Wollen, Peter. *Signs and Meaning in the Cinema*. Revised edition. London: Secker and Warburg/British Film Institute, 1972.

Chapter 3

Ashby, Arved. 'Wes Anderson, Ironist and Auteur'. In *Popular Music and the New Auteur: Visionary Filmmakers After MTV*, edited by Arved Ashby, 180–201. New York: Oxford University Press, 2013.

Berkowitz, Joe. 'These Are The Rides From That Wes Anderson Theme Park That's Definitely Happening'. *Fast Company* (5 November 2014), at https://www.fastcompany.com/3038073/these-are-the-rides-from-that-wes-anderson-theme-park-thats-definitely-happening (accessed 14 April 2019).

Boschi, Elena and Tim McNelis. '"Same Old Song": On Audio-Visual Style in the Films of Wes Anderson'. *New Review of Film and Television Studies* 10, no. 1 (2012): 28–45.

Brody, Richard. 'Wild, Wild Wes'. *The New Yorker* (October 26, 2009), at https://www.newyorker.com/magazine/2009/11/02/wild-wild-wes (accessed 14 April 2019).

Brown, Harley. 'Interview: Mark Mothersbaugh'. *Red Bull Music Academy Daily* (12 June 2017), at http://daily.redbullmusicacademy.com/2017/06/interview-mark-mothersbaugh (accessed 14 April 2019).

Chion, Michel. 1994. *Audio-Vision: Sound on Screen*. Edited and translated by Claudia Gorbman. New York: Columbia University Press.

Dean-Ruzicka, Rachel. 'Themes of Privilege and Whiteness in the Films of Wes Anderson'. *Quarterly Review of Film and Video* 30, no. 1 (2013): 25–40.

Diamond, Jason. 'Devo's Mark Mothersbaugh on Growing Up Blind, Carving Ruby Turds'. *Rolling Stone* (6 June 2017), at https://www.rollingstone.com/culture/culture-news/devos-mark-mothersbaugh-on-growing-up-blind-carving-ruby-turds-200623/ (accessed 14 April 2019).

Dilley, Whitney Crothers. *The Cinema of Wes Anderson: Bringing Nostalgia to Life*. New York: Wallflower Press, 2017.

Dornbush, Jonathon. 'Wes Anderson Wants to Build a Theme Park with Devo's Mark Mothersbaugh'. *Entertainment Weekly* (5 November 2014), at http://ew.com/article/2014/11/05/wes-anderson-devo-mark-mothersbaugh-theme-park/ (accessed 14 April 2019).

'Oral History of Mark Mothersbaugh'. YouTube video, 1:23:51. Posted by 'Computer History Museum,' 12 February 2018, at https://www.youtube.com/watch?v=YfeLBV3J6NI&t=3896s (accessed 14 April 2019).

Golson, Barry. *The Playboy Interviews with John Lennon and Yoko Ono*. Interviews conducted by David Sheff. New York: Playboy Press, 1981.

'Mark Mothersbaugh'. *IMDb*, at https://www.imdb.com/name/nm0006205/ (accessed 27 June 2018).

Jenkins, Henry. *Convergence Culture: Where Old and New Media Collide*. New York: New York University Press, 2006.

Jones, Simon and Thomas Schumacher. 'Muzak: On Functional Music and Power'. *Critical Studies in Mass Communication* 9, no. 2 (1992): 156–69.

Kelly, Maura. 'An Interview with Mark Mothersbaugh'. *The Believer* (1 September 2005), at https://believermag.com/an-interview-with-mark-mothersbaugh/ (accessed 14 April 2019).

Klickstein, Mathew. *Slimed! An Oral History of Nickelodeon's Golden Age*. New York: Plume, 2013.

Koehler, Robert. 'Mothersbaugh: The Collector'. *Variety* (15 January 2014), at https://variety.com/2014/music/features/mothersbaugh-the-collector-1201059076/ (accessed 14 April 2019).

Kornhaber, Donna. *Wes Anderson*. Champaign: University of Illinois Press, 2017.

Kunze, Peter. 'From the Mixed-Up Films of Mr. Wesley W. Anderson: Children's Literature as Intertexts'. In *The Films of Wes Anderson: Critical Essays on an Indiewood Icon*, edited by Kunze, 91–107. New York: Palgrave Macmillan, 2014.

Lareau, Annette. *Unequal Childhoods: Class, Race, and Family Life*. Second Edition. Berkeley: University of California Press, 2011.

Lee, Sunhee. 'Wes Anderson's Ambivalent Film Style: The Relation Between *Mise-en-scène* and Emotion'. *New Review of Film and Television Studies* 14, no. 4 (2016): 409–39.

Lerner, Adam. *Mark Mothersbaugh: Myopia*. New York: Princeton Architectural Press, 2014.

MacDowell, James. 'The Andersonian, the Quirky, and 'Innocence'. In *The Films of Wes Anderson: Critical Essays on an Indiewood Icon*, edited by Peter Kunze, 153–69. New York: Palgrave Macmillan, 2014.

MacDowell, James. *Irony in Film*. New York: Palgrave Macmillan, 2016.

Norman, Philip. *Paul McCartney: The Life*. New York: Little, Brown and Company, 2016.

Peele, Anna. 'The Wonderful World of Wes Anderson'. *GQ* (22 March 2018), at https://www.gq.com/story/the-wonderful-world-of-wes-anderson (accessed 14 April 2019).

Phillis, Jen Hedler. '"I Always Wanted to Be a Tenenbaum": Class Mobility and Neoliberal Fantasy in Wes Anderson's *The Royal Tenenbaums*'. In *The Films of Wes Anderson: Critical Essays on an Indiewood Icon*, edited by Peter Kunze, 171–80. New York: Palgrave Macmillan, 2014.

Piechota, Carole Lyn. 'Give Me a Second Grace: Music as Absolution in *The Royal Tenenbaums*'. *Senses of Cinema* 38 (February 2006), at http://sensesof cinema.com/2006/on-movies-musicians-and-soundtracks/music_tenenbaums/ (accessed 14 April 2019).

Roberts, Randall. 'Are You Not Devo? You are Mutato'. *LA Weekly* (5 December 2007), at http://www.laweekly.com/music/are-you-not-devo-you-are-mutato-215 1061 (accessed 14 April 2019).

Schwarzbaum, Lisa. 'Take a Tour of Wes Anderson's World'. *BBC* (7 March 7 2014), at http://www.bbc.com/culture/story/20140307-wes-andersons-tiny-world-a-tour (accessed 14 April 2019).

Weedon, Paul. 'Mark Mothersbaugh on Shaping Wes Anderson's Sound'. *Little White Lies* (10 December 2016), at http://lwlies.com/articles/mark-mothersb augh-on-working-with-wes-anderson/ (accessed 14 April 2019).

Winters, Ben. '"It's All Really Happening": Sonic Shaping in the Films of Wes Anderson'. In *Music, Sound and Filmmakers: Sonic Style in Cinema*, edited by James Wierzbicki, 45–60. New York: Routledge, 2012.

Chapter 4

Adorno, Theodor W. *Minima Moralia: Reflections on a Damaged Life*. Translated by E. F. N. Jephcott. London: Verso, 2005.

Delistraty, Cody. 'Wes Anderson, Curator? The Filmmaker Gives It a Try'. *New York Times* (7 November 2018), at https://www.nytimes.com/2018/11/07/arts/design/wes-anderson-vienna-kunsthistorisches-museum.html.

Jay, Martin. *Essays from the Edge: Parerga and Paralipomena*. Charlottesville: University of Virginia Press, 2011.

McQuiston, Kate. 'Some Assembly Required: Hybrid Scores in *Moonrise Kingdom* and *The Grand Budapest Hotel*'. In *The Routledge Companion to Screen Music and Sound*, ed. Miguel Mera, Ronald Sadoff and Ben Winters, 477–93. New York: Routledge, 2017.

Winters, Ben. '"It's All Really Happening": Sonic Shaping in the Films of Wes Anderson'. In *Music, Sound and Filmmakers: Sonic Style in Cinema*, ed. James Wierzbicki, 45–60. New York: Routledge, 2012.

Chapter 5

Bordwell, David. 'Wes Anderson Takes the 4:3 Challenge'. In *The Wes Anderson Collection: The Grand Budapest Hotel*, edited by Matt Zoller Seitz, 235–50. New York: AbramsBooks, 2015.

Brown, Royal. *Overtones and Undertones: Reading Film Music*. Second Edition. Berkeley: University of California Press, 1994.

Clark, Ewan. 'Harmony, Associativity, and Metaphor in the Film Scores of Alexandre Desplat'. PhD dissertation. Victoria University of Wellington, 2018.

Cooke, Mervyn. *A History of Film Music*. New York: Cambridge University Press, 2008.

Covill, Max. "Composer Alexandre Desplat on Choosing Luc Besson Over 'Star Wars'." *Film School Rejects* (21 November 2017), at https://filmschoolrejects.com/composer-alexandre-desplat-choosing-luc-besson-star-wars/ (accessed 22 April 2019).

Goldwasser, Dan. 'The New Sound of Hollywood'. *Soundtrack.net* (19 January 2006), at http://www.soundtrack.net/content/article/?id=183 (accessed 22 April 2019).

Grobar, Matt. 'Composer Alexandre Desplat on the Booming Taiko Drums & Barking Saxophones Of 'Isle Of Dogs'." *Deadline* (9 January 2019), at https://deadline.com/2019/01/alexandre-desplat-isle-of-dogs-wes-anderson-composer-interview-1202520992/ (accessed 22 April 2019).

Liu, Yi-Hsin Cindy. 'The Examination of the Appearance and Use of French Horn in Film Scores from 1977 to 2004'. Thesis. University of Cincinnati, 2005, at https://etd.ohiolink.edu/pg_10?0::NO:10:P10_ACCESSION_NUM:ucin1116000974 (accessed 22 April 2019).

Martens, Todd. 'Pop & Hiss Goes to the Movies: Alexandre Desplat Gets Rootsy for "Fantastic Mr. Fox"'. *Los Angeles Times* (8 December 2009), at https://latimesblogs.latimes.com/music_blog/2009/12/pop-hiss-goes-to-the-movies-alexandre-desplat-gets-rootsy-for-fantastic-mr-fox.html (accessed 22 April 2019).

McQuiston, Kate. 'Some Assembly Required: Hybrid Scores in *Moonrise Kingdom* and *The Grand Budapest Hotel*'. In *The Routledge Companion to Screen Music and Sound*, edited by Miguel Mera, Ronald Sadoff and Ben Winters, 477–93. New York: Routledge, 2017.

'DP/30: Alexandre Desplat, Isle of Dogs'. YouTube video, 35:17. Posted by 'DP/30: The Oral History of Hollywood', 11 December 2018, at Hollywood. https://www.youtube.com/watch?v=1g9Lkpw7rRg&t=300s (accessed 22 April 2019).

Richards, Mark. 'Oscar Nominees 2015, Best Original Score (Part 1 of 6): Alexandre Desplat's the Grand Budapest Hotel'. *Film Music Notes* (21 January 2015), at http://www.filmmusicnotes.com/oscar-nominees-2015-best-original-score-part-1-of-6-alexandre-desplats-the-grand-budapest-hotel/ (accessed 22 April 2019).

Chapter 6

Anderson, Tim. 'Lost in Transition: Popular Music, Adolescence, and the Melodramatic Mode of Sofia Coppola'. In *Popular Music and the New Auteur: Visionary Filmmakers After MTV*, edited by Arved Ashby, 63–83. New York: Oxford University Press, 2012.

Bachor, Kenneth. '*A Very Murray Christmas* Director Sofia Coppola: I Wanted to Do Something "Joyful"'. *Time* (4 December 2015), at http://time.com/4132069/sofia-coppola-a-very-murray-christmas/ (accessed 5 February 2019).

Blasberg, Derek. 'Marc and Sofia: The Dreamy Team'. *Harper's Bazaar* (13 August 2014), at https://www.harpersbazaar.com/fashion/designers/a3169/marc-jacobs-sofia-coppola-0914/ (accessed 12 February 2019).

Bukatman, Scott. *Blade Runner*. London: British Film Institute, 1997.

Dempsey, Michael. 'Review of Blade Runner'. *Film Quarterly* 36, no. 2 (1983): 34.

Diamond, Diana. 'Sofia Coppola's *Marie Antoinette*: Costumes, Girl Power, and Feminism'. In *Fashion in Film*, edited by Adrienne Munich, 203–31. Bloomington: Indiana University Press, 2011.

Faraci, Devin. 'Interview: Sofia Coppola (Marie Antoinette)'. *CHUD.com* (12 October 2006), at https://chud.com/interview-sofia-coppola-marie-antoinette/ (accessed 12 February 2019).

Fox, Jesse David. 'Theories on What Bill Murray Whispered at the End of *Lost in Translation*'. *Vulture* (3 October 2013), at https://www.vulture.com/2013/10/lost-in-translation-whisper-theories.html (accessed 1 February 2019).

Ginsberg, Merle. 'Launching Sofia'. *W Magazine* (1 September 1994), at https://www.wmagazine.com/story/sofia-coppola-milk-fed (accessed 12 February 2019).

Gorbman, Claudia. 'Auteur Music'. In *Beyond the Soundtrack: Representing Music in Cinema*, edited by Daniel Goldmark, Lawrence Kramer and Richard Leppert, 149–62. Berkeley: University of California Press, 2007.

Handyside, Fiona. *Sofia Coppola: A Cinema of Girlhood*. London: I.B. Tauris, 2017.

Kennedy, Todd. 'Off With Hollywood's Head: Sofia Coppola as Feminine Auteur'. *Film Criticism* 35, no. 1 (Fall 2010): 37–59.

Lim, Dennis. 'It's What She Knows: The Luxe Life'. *The New York Times* (10 December 2010), at https://www.nytimes.com/2010/12/12/movies/12sofia.html (accessed 2 February 2019).

Lodge, Guy. 'Sofia Coppola: "I never felt I had to fit into the majority view"'. *The Guardian* online (2 July 2017), at https://www.theguardian.com/film/2017/jul/02/sofia-coppola-beguiled-i-never-felt-i-had-to-fit-into-the-majority-view-interview (accessed 12 February 2019).

'Production Notes: *The Virgin Suicides*'. *Cinema Review*, at http://www.cinemareview.com/production.asp?prodid=959 (accessed 2 February 2019).

Rogers, Anna Backman. *Sofia Coppola: The Politics of Visual Pleasure*. New York: Berghahn Books, 2019.

Sharf, Zack. '"Lost in Translation,"15 Years Later: Sofia Coppola on Ending the Film on Her Terms and the Year It Took to Cast Bill Murray'. *IndieWire* (27 August 2018), at https://www.indiewire.com/2018/08/lost-in-translation-15th-anniversary-sofia-coppola-interview-ending-whisper-meaning-1201998010/ (accessed 1 February 2019).

Smaill, Belinda. 'Sofia Coppola: Reading the Director'. *Feminist Media Studies* 13, no. 1 (2013): 148–62.

'Sofia Coppola's Commercials –6 Stunning Ads by Director Sofia Coppola'. *Bold Content* (23 January 2015), at https://boldcontentvideo.com/2015/01/23/sofia-coppolas-commercials-6-stunning-ads-by-director-sofia-coppola/ (accessed 28 January 2019).

Swinney, Jacob. 'Watch: A Video Essay About Sofia Coppola's Dreamlike Aesthetic'. *IndieWire* (11 February 2015), at https://www.indiewire.com/2015/02/watch-a-video-essay-about-sofia-coppolas-dreamlike-aesthetic-133103/ (accessed 28 January 2019).

Vernallis, Carol. *Unruly Media: YouTube, Music Video, and the New Digital Cinema*. New York: Oxford University Press, 2013.

Wyatt, Justin. *The Virgin Suicides: Reverie, Sorrow, and Young Love*. New York: Routledge, 2018.

Yotka, Steff. 'Marc Jacobs's Fragrance Gets the "Virgin Suicides" Treatment'. *Fashionista* (26 June 2014), at https://fashionista.com/2014/06/sofia-coppola-daisy-dream-video (accessed 30 January 2019).

Chapter 7

Bennett, Bruce. 'The Cinema of Michael Bay: An Aesthetic of Excess'. *Senses of Cinema* 75 (June 2015), at http://sensesofcinema.com/2015/michael-bay-dossier/cinema-of-michael-bay/ (accessed 31 January 2017).

Ebert, Roger. 'Reviews: Transformers: Dark of the Moon'. *Roger Ebert.com* (28 June 2011), at https://www.rogerebert.com/reviews/transformers-dark-of-the-moon-2011 (accessed 27 February 2019).

Fennessey, Sean. 'An Oral History of Michael Bay, the Most Explosive Director of All Time'. *GQ* (27 June 2011), at https://www.gq.com/story/michael-bay-oral-history (accessed 28 February 2019).

Kilkenny, Katie. 'Michael Bay: A New Kind of Director'. *The Atlantic* (1 July 2014), at https://www.theatlantic.com/entertainment/archive/2014/07/once-and-for-all-michael-bay-is-not-an-auteur/373715/ (accessed 26 February 2019).

Kerins, Mark. *Beyond Dolby (Stereo): Cinema in the Digital Sound Age.*
Bloomington: Indiana University Press, 2010.

Koepnick, Lutz. *Michael Bay.* Urbana: University of Illinois Press, 2018.

Lipscomb, Scott. 'The Perception of Audio-Visual Composites: Accent Structure
Alignment of Simple Stimuli'. *Selected Reports in Ethnomusicology* 12 (2005):
37–67.

Lipscomb, Scott and Roger Kendall. 'Perceptual Judgment of the Relationship
Between Musical and Visual Components in Film'. *Psychomusicology: A Journal
of Research in Music Cognition* 13, nos. 1–2 (1994): 60–98.

'Michael Bay – What Is Bayhem?' YouTube video, 8:41. Posted by 'Every Frame a
Painting' (3 July 2014), at https://www.youtube.com/watch?v=2THVvshvq0Q
(accessed 28 February 2019).

Murray, Noel. 'Six Michael Bay Music Videos That Help Explain the Art of
Michael Bay'. *The Dissolve* (27 June 2014), at https://thedissolve.com/featur
es/interdisciplinary/637-six-michael-bay-music-videos-that-help-explain-the/
(accessed 1 March 2019).

'The Sound of Transformers Age of Extinction'. *Michael Bay.com* (2 July 2014), at
https://www.michaelbay.com/2014/07/02/the-sound-of-transformers-age-of-exti
nction/ (accessed 27 February 2019).

Tallerico, Brian. 'Reviews: Transformers: The Last Knight'. *Roger Ebert.com* (20
June 2017), at https://www.rogerebert.com/reviews/transformers-the-last-
knight-2017 (accessed 28 February 2019).

Vernallis, Carol. 'The New Cut-Up Cinema: Music, Speed, and Memory'. Academic
paper. Screen Studies Conference, Glasgow. 4–6 July 2008.

Chapter 8

Betz, Mark. *Beyond the Subtitle: Remapping European Art Cinema.* Minneapolis:
University of Minnesota Press, 2009.

Biskind, Peter. *Down and Dirty Pictures: Miramax, Sundance, and the Rise of
Independent Film.* New York: Simon & Schuster, 2005.

Chung, Hye Jean. *Media Heterotopias: Digital Effects and Material Labor in
Global Film Production.* Durham: Duke University Press, 2018.

Connor, J. D. 'Independence and the Consent of the Governed: The Systems and
Scales of *Under the Skin*'. *Jump Cut* 57 (Fall 2016), at http://ejumpcut.org/
archive/jc57.2016/-ConnorSkin/index.html (accessed 12 March 2019).

Connor, J. D. 'The Modern Entertainment Marketplace, 2000–The Present."
In *Directing (Behind the Silver Screen)*, edited by Virginia Wright Wexman,
132–54. New Brunswick: Rutgers University Press, 2017.

'Exclusive: Interview with *Snowpiercer* Screenwriter Kelly Masterson'. *ScreenCraft*
(28 July 2014), at https://screencraft.org/2014/07/28/interview-snowpiercer-
screenwriter-kelly-masterson/ (accessed 12 March 2019).

Finet, Nicolas. *Histoires du Transperceneige.* Paris: Casterman, 2013.

Ford, Rebecca and Borys Kitt. 'Marvel Reveals Complete Phase 3 Plans, Dates
"Black Panther," "Inhumans," "Avengers: Infinity War"'. *The Hollywood*

Reporter (28 October 2014), at https://www.hollywoodreporter.com/heat-vision/marvel-reveals-complete-phase-3-plans-dates-black-panther-inhumans-avengers-infinity-war-744455 (accessed 12 March 2019).

Franich, Darren. 'Warner Bros. Announces 10 DC Movies Including "Wonder Woman"'. *Entertainment Weekly* (15 October 2014), at https://ew.com/article/2014/10/15/justice-league-green-lantern-wonder-woman-flash-movies/ (accessed 12 March 2019).

Graser, Marc. '"Star Wars": The "Sky's the Limit" for Disney's Spinoff Opportunities'. *The Hollywood Reporter* (12 September 2013), at https://variety.com/2013/biz/news/star-wars-skys-the-limit-for-disney-when-it-comes-to-opportunities-1200609291/ (accessed 12 March 2019).

Heisner, Dorothy. *Production Design in the Contemporary American Film: A Critical Study of 23 Films and Their Designers*. Jefferson: McFarland, 2004.

Hill, John and Nobuko Kawashima. 'Introduction: Film Policy in a Globalised Cultural Economy'. *International Journal of Cultural Policy* 22, no. 5 (2016): 667–72.

Hoxter, Julian. 'The New Hollywood, 1980–1999'. In Screenwriting, edited by Julian Hoxter and Andrew Horton, 101–26. New Brunswick: Rutgers University Press, 2014.

'IRON MAN Marvel Studios 10th Anniversary Q&A with Jon Favreau & Kevin Feige - May 17, 2018.' YouTube video, 1:11:57. Posted by 'TheMovieReport.com' (18 May 2018), at https://www.youtube.com/watch?v=HWGf3aRX4-o (accessed 12 March 2019).

Jones, Chris and Genevieve Jolliffe. *The Guerilla Film Makers Handbook*. Third edition. New York: Continuum, 2006.

Kilkenny, Katie. 'Fired "Snowpiercer" Showrunner Calls Replacement an "Idiot" for Not Reaching Out'. *The Hollywood Reporter* (17 May 2018), at https://www.hollywoodreporter.com/live-feed/fired-snowpiercer-showrunner-calls-replacement-an-idiot-not-reaching-1112964 (accessed 12 March 2019).

Kirschenbaum, Matthew. *Track Changes: A Literary History of Word Processing*. Cambridge: Belknap, 2016.

Lee, Nikki and Julian Stringer. 'From *Screenwriting for Sound* to Film Sound Maps: The Evolution of Live Tone's Creative Alliance with Bong Joon Ho'. *The New Soundtrack* 8, no. 2 (2018): 145–59.

Lee, Nikki and Julian Stringer. '*Snowpiercer*: Sound Designable Voices and the South Korean Global Film'. In *Locating the Voice in Film: Critical Approaches and Global Practices*, edited by Tom Whittaker and Sarah Wright, 263–79. Oxford: Oxford University Press, 2017.

Pomerantz, Dorothy. 'What the Economics of "Snowpiercer" Say about the Future of Film'. *Forbes* (8 September 2014), at https://www.forbes.com/sites/dorothypomerantz/2014/09/08/what-the-economics-of-snowpiercer-say-about-the-future-of-film/#4ff09ca76bb1 (accessed 12 March 2019).

Robertson, Barbara. 'VFX Supervisor Ken Ralston on *Alice in Wonderland*'. *Studiodaily* (21 February 2011), at http://www.studiodaily.com/2011/02/vfx-supervisor-ken-ralston-on-alice-in-wonderland/ (accessed 12 March 2019).

Sergi, Gianluca. *The Dolby Era: Film Sound in Contemporary Hollywood*. Manchester: Manchester University Press, 2004.

'Summary of Status & Insight: Korean Film Industry 2013'. *KOFIC* (10 July 2014), at http://kofic.org/eng/news/kofic_news.jsp?pageIndex=1&blbdComCd=60 1007&seq=1622&mode=VIEW&returnUrl=&searchKeyword= (accessed 12 March 2019).

Taylor, Stayci and Craig Batty. 'Script Development and the Hidden Practices of Screenwriting: Perspectives from Industry Professionals'. *New Writing* 13, no. 2 (2016): 204–17.

Wagner, Keith B. 'Systematizing Contemporary Korean Cinema in the Age of Asian Globalization: Out from Hollywood's Shadow to the Rise of Hollywood'. In *From Postwar to Contemporary Korean Art (1953–Present): Conflicts, Innovations and Interactions*, edited by Yeon Shim Chung, Sunjung Kim and Kimberly Chung (Forthcoming).

Yecies, Brian. 'The Chinese-Korean Coproduction Pact: Collaborative Encounters and the Accelerating Expansion of Chinese Cinema'. *International Journal of Cultural Policy* 22, no. 5 (2016): 770–86.

Chapter 9

Connor, J. D. *The Studios After the Studios: Neoclassical Hollywood (1970–2010)*. Redwood City: Stanford University Press, 2015.

Desowitz, Bill. 'Fincher Talks "Benjamin Button" and VFX'. *AWN.com* (9 January 2009), at http://www.awn.com/vfxworld/fincher-talks-benjamin-button-and-vfx (accessed 31 March 2019).

Dombal, Ryan. 'Trent Reznor and David Fincher'. *Pitchfork* (27 September 2010), at https://pitchfork.com/features/interview/7862-trent-reznor-and-david-fincher/ (accessed 31 March 2019).

Geffner, David. 'To Catch a Killer'. *ICG Magazine* (March 2007), at http://www.icgmagazine.com/2007/march/march07.html (accessed 31 March 2019).

Failes, Ian. 'Maintaining the Mystery: Editor Kirk Baxter on *Gone Girl*'. *FXGuide* (2 October 2014), at http://www.fxguide.com/featured/maintaining-the-mystery-editor-kirk-baxter-on-gone-girl/ (accessed 31 March 2019).

Galloway, Alexander. *Protocol: How Control Exists After Decentralization*. Cambridge: MIT Press, 2004.

Goldman, Michael. "With Friends Like These…" *American Cinematographer* (October 2010), at https://www.theasc.com/ac_magazine/October2010/The SocialNetwork/page1.php (accessed 31 March 2019).

Horak, Jan-Christopher. *Saul Bass: Anatomy of Film Design*. Lexington: University Press of Kentucky, 2014.

Julier, Guy. *The Culture of Design*. Third edition. London: Sage Publications, 2014.

Kaufman, Debra. '4K DI on The Girl With The Dragon Tattoo'. *Creative COW* (2011), at https://library.creativecow.net/kaufman_debra/The-Girl-with-the-Dragon-Tattoo/1 (accessed 31 March 2019).

Pavlus, John. 'Why David Fincher Is the Best Design Thinker in Hollywood'. *Fast Company* (28 February 2011), at https://www.fastcompany.com/1663318/why-david-fincher-is-the best-design-thinker-in-hollywood (accessed 31 March 2019).

Peters, Oliver. 'Crime Scenes: Evolving the Postproduction Process on "Mindhunter"'. *Creative Planet Network* (26 October 2017), at https://www.creativeplanetnetwork.com/news-features/crime-scenes-evolving-postproduction-process-mindhunter-619626 (accessed 31 March 2019).

Radatz, Ben. 'Se7en (1995)'. *Art of the Title* (10 July 2012), at http://www.artofthetitle.com/title/se7en/ (accessed 31 March 2019).

Salisbury, Mark. 'David Fincher: British Film Institute Interview'. In *David Fincher: Interviews*, ed. Laurence Knapp, 145–58. Jackson: University Press of Mississippi, 2014.

Vishnevetsky, Ignatiy. 'What Is the 21st Century?: Revising the Dictionary'. Mubi (1 February 2013), at https://mubi.com/notebook/posts/what-is-the-21st-century-revising-the-dictionary (accessed 31 March 2019).

Chapter 11

Barna, Alyssa. 'The Dance Chorus in Recent Top-40 Music'. Academic Paper. Annual Conference of Music Theory Midwest, London, ON, 18–19 May 2018.

Bein, Kat. 'Calvin Harris Tops the "Forbes" Highest-Paid DJ List For Sixth Straight Year'. *Billboard Magazine* (31 July 2018), at https://www.billboard.com/articles/news/dance/8467942/calvin-harris-top-paid-dj-forbes (accessed 23 March 2019).

Burns, Lori. 'Multimodal Analysis of Popular Music Videos: Genre, Discourse, and Narrative in Steven Wilson's "Drive Home"'. In *Coming of Age: Teaching and Learning Popular Music in Academia*, edited by Carlos Xavier Rodriguez, 81–110. Ann Arbor: University of Michigan Press, 2017.

Butler, Mark. *Unlocking the Groove: Rhythm, Meter, and Musical Design in Electronic Dance Music*. Bloomington: Indiana University Press, 2006.

Ensign, Jeffrey. 'Form in Popular Song, 1990–2009'. PhD dissertation. University of North Texas, December 2015.

Harding, Charlie. 'How the Pop-Drop Became the Sound of 2016'. *Billboard* (19 December 2016), at https://www.billboard.com/articles/columns/pop/7625628/pop-drop-sound-of-2016-chainsmokers-justin-bieber-switched-on-pop (accessed 2 February 2019).

Osborn, Brad. 2013. 'Subverting the Verse-Chorus Paradigm: Terminally Climactic Forms in Recent Rock Music'. *Music Theory Spectrum* 35, no. 1 (2013): 23–47.

Osborn, Brad. 2015. 'Music Videos as Music Theory: Teaching MTV's Buzz Clips'. Paper presented at the Teaching and Learning Popular Music Symposium, Ann Arbor, MI, November 18–21.

Peres, Asaf. 'The Sonic Dimension as Dramatic Driver in 21st-Century Pop Music'. PhD dissertation. University of Michigan, 2016.

Spicer, Mark. 2004. '(Ac)cumulative Form in Pop-Rock Music'. *Twentieth-Century Music* 1, no. 1 (2004): 29–64.

Spicer, Mark. '(Per)Form in(g) Rock: A Response'. *Music Theory Online* 17, no. 3 (2011), at http://www.mtosmt.org/issues/mto.11.17.3/mto.11.17.3.spicer.html (accessed 23 March 2019).

Summach, Jay. 'The Structure, Function, and Genesis of the Prechorus'. *Music Theory Online* 17, no. 3 (2011), at http://www.mtosmt.org/issues/mto.11.17.3/mto.11.17.3.summach.html (accessed 23 March 2019).

Vernallis, Carol. *Experiencing Music Video: Aesthetics and Cultural Context*. New York: Columbia University Press, 2004.

Chapter 12

Baudelaire, Charles. *Artificial Paradise*. Translation, Introduction, and Notes by Stacy Diamond. Secaucus: Citadel Press, 1996.

Belton, John. 2008. 'Painting by the Numbers: The Digital Intermediate'. *Film Quarterly* 61, no. 3 (2008): 58–65.

Brown, William and Meetali Kutty. 'Datamoshing and the Emergence of Digital Complexity from Digital Chaos'. *Convergence: The International Journal of Research into New Media Technologies* 18, no. 2 (2012): 165–76.

Cole, Teju. *Known and Strange Things*. New York: Random House, 2016.

McDonnell, Maura. 'Visual Music'. *eContact!* 15, no. 4: 'Videomusic: Overview of an Emerging Art Form' (April 2014), at https://www.econtact.ca/15_4/mcdonnell_visualmusic.html (accessed 22 March 2019).

Moritz, William. *Optical Poetry: The Life and Work of Oskar Fischinger*. Bloomington: Indiana University Press, 2004.

Moten, Fred. *The Universal Machine*. Durham: Duke University Press, 2018.

Nava, Emil. 'Emil Nava: "I Want to Shut Down the Internet"'. *52 Insights* (28 November 2018), at https://www.52-insights.com/music-video-emil-nava-iwant-to-shut-down-the internet/ (accessed 15 February 2018).

Nava, Emil. '#snorkeling #ammolite #ammoliteinc #director #colour'. *Instagram* (9 May 2018), at https://www.instagram.com/p/BiiyTYUBO7I/?hl=en (accessed 12 March 2019).

Sterling, Bruce. 'An Essay on the New Aesthetic'. *Wired* (2 April 2012), at https://www.wired.com/2012/04/an-essay-on-the-new-aesthetic/ (accessed 15 February 2019).

Vernallis, Carol. *Unruly Media: YouTube, Music Video, and the New Digital Cinema*. New York: Oxford University Press, 2013.

Chapter 13

Vernallis, Carol. *Experiencing Music Video: Aesthetics and Cultural Context*. New York: Columbia University Press, 2004.

Chapter 14

Adejobi, Alecia. 'The Truth About David Bowie and Damien Hirst's Friendship and Their 755k Art Masterpiece'. *International Business Times* (15 November 2016), at https://www.ibtimes.co.uk/truth-about-david-bowie-damien-hirsts-friendship-their-755k-art-masterpiece-1591622 (accessed 15 December 2018).

Bakhtin, Mikhail. 'Discourse in the Novel'. In *The Dialogic Imagination: Four Essays*, edited by Michael Holquist, 294–457. Austin: The University of Texas Press, 1981.

Bordwell, David. 'Observations in Film Art: Now Leaving Platform 1' (19 August 2009), at http://www.davidbordwell.net/blog/2009/08/19/now-leaving-from-platform-1/ (accessed 12 December 2018).

Boshier, Derek. Quoted in Cascone, Sarah. 'Take a Peek at David Bowie's Idiosyncratic Art Collection' *Artnet* (12 January 2016), at https://news.artnet.com/art-world/take-peek-david-bowies-art-collection-405296 (accessed 2 May 2018).

Boyd, William. 'William Boyd: How David Bowie and I Hoaxed the Artworld'. *The Guardian* (12 January 2016), at https://www.theguardian.com/music/2016/jan/12/art-david-bowie-william-boyd-nat-tate-editor-critic-modern-painters-publisher (accessed 15 November 2018).

Broackes, Victoria, and Geoffrey Marsh, eds. *David Bowie Is*. London: V&A Publishing, 2013.

Brooker, Will. *Forever Stardust: David Bowie Across the Universe*. London: I. B. Tauris, 2017.

Campbell-Schmitt, Adam. 'A Ziggy Stardust Bar Lands in London This Fall'. *Food & Wine* (27 August 2018), at https://www.foodandwine.com/news/ziggy-stardust-bar-hotel-cafe-royal-london-david-bowie?utm_campaign=foodandwine&utm_medium=social&utm_source=facebook.com&xid=soc_socialflow:facebook_fw (accessed 10 December 2018).

Cinque, Toija, Angela Ndalianis and Sean Redmond. 'David Bowie On-Screen'. *Cinema Journal* 57, no. 3 (2018): 126–30.

Cook-Wilson, Winston. '*Twin Peaks* Brought Back David Bowie's Character in the Most Insane Way Possible'. *Spin* (21 August 2017), at: https://www.spin.com/2017/08/twin-peaks-episode-15-recap-david-bowie/ (accessed 22 September 2017).

Coscarelli, Joe. '"Black Star": David Bowie's Connection to Elvis Presley'. *The New York Times* (14 January 2016), at https://www.nytimes.com/live/david-bowie-in-memoriam/black-star-david-bowies-connection-to-elvis-presley (accessed 7 September 2017).

D'Cruz, Glenn. 'He's Not There: *Velvet Goldmine* and the Spectres of David Bowie'. In *Enchanting David Bowie: Space / Time / Body / Memory*, edited by Toija Cinque, Christopher Moore and Sean Redmond, 259–73. New York: Bloomsbury, 2015.

Debord, Guy and Gill J. Wolman. 'Methods of *Détournement*'. *Les Lèvres Nues*, no. 8 (May 1956), Nothingness.org, at http://library.nothingness.org/articles/SI/en/display/3 (accessed 1 April 2019).

Derfoufi, Mehdi. 'Embodying Stardom, Representing Otherness: David Bowie in "Merry Christmas Mr. Lawrence"'. In David Bowie: *Critical Perspectives*, edited by Eoin Devereux, Aileen Dillane and Martin Power, 160–77. London: Routledge, 2015.

Derrida, Jacques. *Specters of Marx: The State of the Debt, the Work of Mourning and The New International*. New York: Routledge, 1994.

Devereux, Eion, Aileen Dillane and Martin J. Power. 'Saying Hello to the Lunatic Men: A Critical Reading of "Love Is Lost"'. *Contemporary Music Review* 37, no. 3 (2018), 257–71.

Fisher, Mark. *Ghosts of My Life: Writings on Depression, Hauntology and Lost Futures*. Alresford, Hants: Zero Books, 2014.

Fisher, Mark. "What Is Hauntology?" *Film Quarterly* 66, no. 1 (2012): 16–24.

Flannery, Denis. "Absence, Resistance and Visitable Pasts: David Bowie, Todd Haynes, Henry James." *Continuum: Journal of Media and Cultural Studies* 31, no. 4 (2017): 542–51.

Gibson, Andy. "Flight of the Conchords: Recontextualizing the Voices of Popular Culture." *Journal of Sociolinguistics* 15, no. 5 (2011): 603–26.

The New York Times Magazine 'Great Performers', https://www.nytimes.com/interactive/2017/12/07/magazine/great-performers-horror-show.html#daniel-kaluuya (accessed 2 March 2019).

Goddard, Michael. 'Audiovision and Gesamtkunstwerk: The Aesthetics of First and Second Generation Industrial Music Video'. In *Music/Video: Histories, Aesthetics, Media*, edited by Gina Arnold, Daniel Cookney, Kirsty Fairclough and Michael Goddard, 163–80. London: Bloomsbury Academic, 2017.

Halliday, Ayun. 'David Bowie Songs Reimagined as Pulp Fiction Book Covers: Space Oddity, Heroes, Life on Mars and More'. *Open Culture* (1 April 2019), at http://www.openculture.com/2019/04/david-bowie-songs-reimagined-as-pulp-fiction-book-covers.html?fbclid=IwAR3WLFylt1y7CLEQGkW2FRxEoPWQEKMLDfy8qjjFJ5v9Co44CGboCPCTGP0 (accessed 2 April 2019).

Hames, Peter, ed. *Dark Alchemy: The Films of Jan Švankmajer*. Flicks Books: Wiltshire, 1995.

Hawking, Tom. 'Deconstructing David Bowie's DIY Video for "Love Is Lost"'. *Flavorwire* (31 October 2013), at http://flavorwire.com/422969/deconstructing-david-bowies-diy-video-for-love-is-lost (accessed 10 December 2018).

Hirst, Damien. 'Damien Hirst with David Bowie'. *Sotheby's*, Catalogue note, 2016, at http://www.sothebys.com/en/auctions/ecatalogue/2016/bowie-collector-part-i-modern-contemporary-art-evening-auction-l16142/lot.5.html (accessed 15 December 2018).

Hogan, Michael. 'David Bowie Got a Fitting Farewell from His Favourite Show'. *The Telegraph* (2 June 2016), at https://www.telegraph.co.uk/tv/2016/06/02/peaky-blinders-david-bowie-got-a-fitting-farewell-plus-8-more-th/ (accessed 4 January 2019).

Holm-Hudson, Kevin. '"Who Can I Be Now?": David Bowie's Vocal Personae'. *Contemporary Music Review* 37, no. 3 (2018): 214–34.

'Inside David Bowie's Private Collection'. *Sotheby's*, at https://www.sothebys.com/en/slideshows/inside-david-bowies-private-collection?slide=romuald-hazoume-alexandra-1995-estimate-5-000-7-000 (accessed 15 December 2018).

Jenkins, Henry. 'The Reign of the "Mothership": Transmedia's Past, Present and Possible Futures'. In *Wired TV: Laboring Over an Interactive Future*, edited by Denise Mann, 244–68. New Brunswick: Rutgers University Press, 2014.

Jenkins, Henry. 'The Aesthetics of Transmedia: In Response to David Bordwell (Part 3)'. (2009), at http://henryjenkins.org/blog/2009/09/the_aesthetics_of_transmedia_i.html (accessed 12 December 2018).

Jenkins, Henry. *Convergence Culture: Where Old and New Media Collide*. New York: New York University Press, 2006.

Johnson, Kathryn. 'David Bowie Is'. In David Bowie: *Critical Perspectives*, edited by Aileen Dillane, Eoin Devereux and Martin Power, 1–18. New York: Routledge, 2015.

Jung, Carl. *The Archetypes and the Collective Unconscious*. England: Routledge and Keegan Paul, 1959.

Jung, Carl. 'The Syzygy: Anima and Animus'. *Collected Works of C. G Jung*, vol 9. London: Routledge and Kegan Paul, 1951.

Kupper, Oliver. 'Activating the Vehicle of Ascension: An Interview of Filmmaker and Artist Floria Sigismondi'. *Autre* (18 July 2016), at https://autre.love/interv iewsmain/2016/7/18/activating-the-vehicle-of-ascension-an-interview-of-film maker-and-artist-floria-sigismondi (accessed 10 December 2018).

Lajosi, Kristztina. 'Wagner and the (Re)mediation of Art: Gesamtkunstwerk and Nineteenth Century Theories of Media'. *Frame* 23, no. 2 (2010): 42–60.

MacKinnon, Angus. 'The Future Isn't What It Used to Be'. *New Musical Express* (13 September 1980), at http://www.bowiegoldenyears.com/press/80-09-13-nme .html (accessed 5 November 2018).

Mallon, Jackie. 'Designer Kansai Yamamoto Talks All Things David Bowie'. *Fashion United* (21 May 2018), at https://fashionunited.uk/news/fashion/designe r-kansai-yamamoto-talks-all-things-david-bowie/2018052129750 (accessed 15 August 2018).

Marshall, Colin. 'David Bowie and Brian Eno's Collaboration on "Warszawa" Reimagined in a Comic Animation.' *Open Culture* (16 September 2014), at http://www.openculture.com/2014/09/david-bowie-brian-enos-collaboration-on-warszawa-reimagined-in-comic-animation.html (accessed 15 December 2018).

McCan, Jaymi. 'The Thin White Doc: New Dr Who Based on David Bowie'. *Express* (29 June 2014), at https://www.express.co.uk/celebrity-news/485534/ The-Thin-White-Doc-New-Doctor-Who-based-on-David-Bowie (accessed 2 November 2018).

McKenzie, Mairi. 'Football, Fashion and Unpopular Culture: David Bowie's Influence on Liverpool Football Club Casuals 1976–79'. *Celebrity Studies* 10, no. 1 (2019), 25–43.

McLuhan, Marshall. *Understanding Media: The Extensions of Man*. Cambridge: MIT Press, 1964.

Mcquade, Christopher. '"I Loathed It" – What David Bowie Learnt From His Brief Spell in Adland." *The Drum* (11 January 2016), at https://www.thedrum.com/ news/2016/01/11/i-loathed-it-what-david-bowie-learned-his-brief-spell-adland (accessed 10 November 2018).

Mendes, Ana and Lisa Perrott. "Introduction: Navigating with the Blackstar: The Mediality of David Bowie." *Celebrity Studies* 10, no. 1 (2019): 4–13.

Ndalianis, Angela. 'Bowie and Science Fiction / Bowie as Science Fiction'. *Cinema Journal* 57, no. 3 (2018): 139–49.

Nobil, Taryn. 'Director Floria Sigismondi Talks David Bowie, "The Handmaid's Tale", "Fleshy Love" and Fellini." *Variety* (12 October 2017), at https://variety .com/2017/music/news/director-floria-sigismondi-discusses-music-and-film-red-bull-music-academy-1202588494/ (accessed 10 August 2018).

October, Dene. 'Transition Transmission: Media, Seriality, and the Bowie-Newton Matrix'. *Celebrity Studies* 10, no. 1 (2019): 104–18.

O'Leary, Chris. 'The Next Day'. *Pushing Ahead of the Dame* (10 August 2015), at https://bowiesongs.wordpress.com/2015/08/10/the-next-day/ (accessed 5 May 2018).

O'Leary, Chris. 'The Mime Songs'. *Pushing Ahead of the Dame* (21 October 2009), at https://bowiesongs.wordpress.com/tag/the-mask/ (accessed 15 August 2018).

O'Leary, 'Love Is Lost'. *Pushing Ahead of the Dame* (1 September 2015), at https://bowiesongs.wordpress.com/2015/09/01/love-is-lost/ (accessed 2 December 2018).

O'Leary, Chris. 'Little Wonder'. *Pushing Ahead of the Dame* (7 August 2013), at https://bowiesongs.wordpress.com/2013/08/07/little-wonder/ (accessed 5 May 2018).

Oursler, Tony, 'David Bowie'. *Artforum* (March 2016), at https://www.artforum.com/print/201603/david-bowie-58102 (accessed 15 March 2018).

Paglia, Camille. 'Theatre of Gender: David Bowie at the Climax of the Sexual Revolution'. In *David Bowie Is*, edited by Victoria Broackes and Geoffrey Marsh, 69–92. London: V&A Publishing, 2013.

Perrott, Lisa. 'The Animated Music Videos of Radiohead, Chris Hopewell and Gastón Viñas: Fan-participation, Collaborative Authorship and Dialogic World-building'. In *The Bloomsbury Handbook to Popular Music Video Analysis*, edited by Lori Burns and Stan Hawkins. New York: Bloomsbury, 2019.

Perrott, Lisa. 'Time Is Out of Joint: The Transmedial Hauntology of David Bowie'. *Celebrity Studies* 10, no. 1 (2019): 119–39.

Perrott, Lisa. 'Bowie the Cultural Alchemist: Performing Gender, Synthesizing Gesture and Liberating Identity'. *Continuum: Journal of Media & Cultural Studies* 31, no. 4 (2017): 528–41.

Perrott, Lisa. 'Floria Sigismondi as Gestural Animator and Puppeteer'. *Animation: An Interdisciplinary Journal* 10, no. 2 (2015): 119–40.

Reale, Nancy M. 'Boccaccio's *Decameron*: A Fictional Effort to Grapple with Chaos' (2005, 3), at http://www.nyu.edu/projects/mediamosaic/literature/BoccaccioDecameronEssay.pdf (accessed 5 April 2019).

Reilly, Nick. 'Is Jodie Whittaker Channelling David Bowie in Her 'Dr Who' Reveal?' *NME* (17 July 2017), at https://www.nme.com/news/tv/is-jodie-whittaker-channelling-david-bowie-2112168 (accessed 10 November 2018).

Rook, Jean. 'Waiting for Bowie and Finding a Genius Who Insists He's Really a Clown'. *Daily Express* (5 May 1976).

Saint Lucy (1521) [Painting] Artist: Domenico Beccafumi. Available online at: https://commons.wikimedia.org/wiki/File:St_lucy_1521_Domenico_Beccafumi.jpg (accessed 13 February 2019).

Scene 360, at http://www5.csudh.edu/dearhabermas/ARTdirect_FloriaSigismondi.html (accessed 2 March 2018).

Sigismondi, Floria. *Facebook* (14 January 2016), at https://www.facebook.com/floria.sigismondi/posts/the-passing-of-david-bowie-has-affected-me-in-ways-i-have-never-experienced-he-c/451732985031106/ (accessed 20 January 2016).

Sigismondi, Floria. 'Floria Sigismondi Discusses Her Dark Aesthetic'. *MTV News* (4 April 1997), at http://www.mtv.com/news/1426430/floria-sigismondi-discusses-her-dark-aesthetic/ (accessed 10 August 2018).

Smythe, William. 'Jungian Dialogism and the Problem of Depth'. *Journal of Analytical Psychology* 63, no. 4 (2018): 453.

Stacey, Jackie. 'Crossing Over With Tilda Swinton-The Mistress of 'Flat Affect''. *International Journal of Politics, Culture and Society* 28, no. 3 (2015): 243–71.

Stark, Tanja. '"Crashing Out with Sylvian" David Bowie, Carl Jung, and the Unconscious'. In David Bowie: *Critical Perspectives*, edited by Aileen Dillane, Eoin Devereux and Martin Power, 82–110. New York: Routledge, 2015.

Stark, Tanja. 'Tanja Stark: Art Words Ideas', 22 June 2015, at https://tanjastark.com/2015/06/22/crashing-out-with-sylvian-david-bowie-carl-jung-and-the-unconscious/ (accessed 5 August 2018).

Stern, Lesley. 'Putting on a Show, or the Ghostliness of Gesture'. Lola (July 2002), at http://www.lolajournal.com/5/putting_show.html (accessed 10 October 2018).

Stubbs, Jeremy. 'Surrealism's Book of Revelation: Isadore Ducasse's *Poésies*, *Détournement* and *Automatic Writing*'. *Romantic Review* 87 (4): 493–510.

Vernallis, Carol and Hannah Ueno. 'Interview with Music Video Director and Auteur Floria Sigismondi'. *Music, Sound and the Moving Image* 7, no. 2 (2013): 167–94.

Very Private Gallery. 'A Soulful Art Legacy: 25 David Bowie Paintings'. https://veryprivategallery.com/david-bowie-paintings/ (accessed 5 April 2019).

Waldrep, Shelton. *Future Nostalgia: Performing David Bowie*. New York: Bloomsbury, 2015.

Weiss, Josh. 'Nicholas Roeg, Director of the Man Who Fell to Earth with David Bowie, Dead at 90'. *SYFYWIRE* (24 November 2018), at https://www.syfy.com/syfywire/nicolas-roeg-director-of-the-man-who-fell-to-earth-with-david-bowie-dead-at-90 (accessed 5 January 2019).

Wolf, Mark. 'Transmedia World-Building: History, Conception, and Construction'. In *The Routledge Companion to Transmedia Studies*, edited by Matthew Freeman and Renira Rampazzo Gambarato, 141–7. New York: Routledge, 2019.

Wood, Aylish. 'Re-animating Space'. *Animation: An Interdisciplinary Journal* 1, no. 2 (2006): 133–52.

Chapter 15

Albrecht, Glenn, Gina Marie Sartore, Linda Conor, Nick Higginbotham, Sonia Freeman, Brian Kelly, Helen Stain, Anne Tonna and Georgia Pollard. 'Solastalgia: The Distress Caused by Environmental Change'. *Australasian Psychiatry* 15, no. 1 (2007): 95–8.

Barbour, Karen, Vicky Hunter and Melanie Kloetzel. *(Re)Positioning Site Dance: Local Acts, Global Perspectives*. Bristol: Intellect Books, 2019.

Beggs, Scott. '"Seraph" Is a Powerful Tragedy from John Cameron Mitchell, Dash Shaw and Sigur Ros'. *Film School Rejects* (1 October 2012), at https://filmschoolrejects.com/sfotd-seraph-is-a-powerful-tragedy-from-john-cameron-mitchel l-dash-shaw-and-sigur-ros-e077eca3dd92/.

Berger, Jonathan. 'How Music Hijacks Our Perception of Time'. *Nautilus* 9 (23 January 2014), at http://nautil.us/issue/9/time/how-music-hijacks-our-perception-of-time.

Brannigan, Erin. *Dancefilm: Choreography and the Moving Image*. New York: Oxford University Press, 2011.

Costa, Maddy. 'GY!BE: Interview'. *The Guardian* (11 October 2012), at https://www.theguardian.com/music/2012/oct/11/godspeed-you-black-emperor-interview.

Crutzen, Paul. 'The Geology of Mankind: The Anthropocene'. *Nature* 415 (2002): 23.

Davis, Colin. 'Hauntology, Spectres and Phantoms'. *French Studies* 59, no. 3 (2005): 373–9.

Dodds, Sheril. *Dance Screen*. Genres and Media from Hollywood to Experimental Art. New York: Palgrave, 2001.

Doyle, Peter. 'From "My Blue Heaven" to "Race with the Devil": Echo, Reverb and (Dis)ordered Space in Early Popular Music Recording'. *Popular Music* 23, no. 1: 31–49.

Duerden, Nick. 'Jon Thor Birgisson: "I Like Being a Social Outcast"'. *The Independent* (14 March 2010), at https://www.independent.co.uk/arts-entertainment/music/features/jon-thor-birgisson-i-like-being-a-social-outcast-1919278.html.

Edgeworth, Matt. 'Human Impact Has Created a "Plastic Planet": Anthropocene Study into Lasting Effects of Plastic on Land and Oceans'. *ScienceDaily* (27 January 2016). www.sciencedaily.com/releases/2016/01/160127083854.html.

Elsdon, Peter. 'Embodied Listening and the Music of Sigur Rós'. *Popular Musicology* 2 (2015), at http://www.popular-musicology-online.com/issues/02/elsdon.html.

Green, Emma. 'Dancers Bend the Laws of Physics in a Mesmerizing Video for Sigur Rós'. *The Atlantic* (11 March 2013), at https://www.theatlantic.com/video/archive/2013/03/dancers-bend-the-laws-of-physics-in-a-mesmerizing-video-for-sigur-r-oacute-s/466236/.

Fletcher, Lawson. 'The Sound of Ruins: Sigur Rós' Heima and the Post-rock Elegy for Place'. *Interference: A Journal of Audio Culture* 2 (2012): 1–11.

Guggenheim Museum. 'Ryan McGinley Tree #1', https://www.guggenheim.org/artwork/20711 (accessed 20 October 2018).

Jazairy, El Hadi. 'Cinematic landscapes in Antonioni's *L'Avventura*'. *Journal of Cultural Geography* 26, no. 3 (2009): 349–67.

Jenkins, Henry. 'Transmedia Storytelling 101'. *Confessions of an Aca-Fan* (21 March 2007). http://henryjenkins.org/blog/2007/03/transmedia_storytelling_101.html.

Jenkins, Henry. *Convergence Culture: Where Old and New Media Collide*. New York: New York University Press, 2006.

John, Arit. '*Varúð* Exhibit Channels the Airy Non-gravity of the *Valtari* Cover Art'. *The Reykjavík Grapevine* (29 October 2012), at https://grapevine.is/culture/art/2012/10/29/proceed-with-caution/.

Johnson, Mark and Steve Larson. '"Something in the Way She Moves:' Metaphors in Musical Motion'. *Metaphor and Symbol* 18, no. 2 (2003): 63–84.

Kaplan, Brett Ashley. *Unwanted Beauty: Aesthetic Pleasure in Holocaust Representation*. Chicago: University of Illinois Press, 2007.

Kirkman, Robert. 'A Little Knowledge of Dangerous Things: Human Vulnerability in a Changing Climate'. In *Merleau-Ponty and Environmental Philosophy: Dwelling on the Landscapes of Thought*, edited by Suzanne L. Cataldi and William S. Hamrick, 19–35. Albany: State University of New York Press, 2007.

Kloetzel, Melanie. 'Bodies in Place: Location as Collaborator in Dance Film'. *International Journal of Performance Arts and Digital Media* 11, no. 1 (2015): 18–41.

Knight, David. 'Sigur Rós 'Ekki Múkk' by Nick Abrahams'. *Promo News* (28 September 2012), at http://www.promonews.tv/videos/2012/09/28/sigur-r%C3%B3s-ekki-m%C3%BAkk-nick-abrahams.

Kourlas, Gia. 'Making Words Dance on Screen'. *The New York Times* (23 November 2012), at https://www.nytimes.com/2012/11/24/arts/dance/sidi-larb i-cherkaouis-choreography-for-anna-karenina.html?pagewanted=all&_r=1&.

Mackey, Sally and Nicolas Whybrow. 'Taking Place: Some Reflections on Site, Performance and Community'. *Research in Drama Education: The Journal of Applied Theatre and Performance* 12 (2007): 1–14.

Magnússon, Haukur Sigurbjörn. 'Nico And Jónsi GO ALL IN!'. *The Reykjavík Grapevine* (9 April 2010), at https://grapevine.is/culture/music/2010/04/09/nico -and-jonsi-go-all-in/.

Massumi, Brian. 'The Future Birth of the Affective Fact: The Political Ontology of Threat'. In *The Affect Theory Reader*, edited by Melissa Gregg and Gregory J. Seigworth, 52–70. Durham: Duke University Press, 2010.

Mayo, Amanda Roscoe. 'Mystery Revealed: Sigur Rós' Valtari Film Experiment'. *KQED Arts*(17 March 2013), at https://www.kqed.org/arts/117962.

Meikle, Jeffery. 'A Paper Atlantis: Postcards, Mass Art, and the American Scene, The Eleventh Reyner Banham Memorial Lecture'. *Journal of Design History* 13, no. 4 (2000): 267–86.

Meikle, Jeffery. *Postcard America: Curt Teich and the Imaging of a Nation, 1931–1950*. Austin: University of Texas Press, 2016.

Miller, Edward. 'The Nonsensical Truth of the Falsetto Voice: Listening to Sigur Rós'. *Popular Musicology* 2 (2003), at http://www.popular-musicology-onlin e.com/issues/02/miller.html.

O'Meara, Radha and Alex Bevan. 'Transmedia Theory's Author Discourse and Its Limitations'. *Media/Culture Journal* 21, no. 1 (2018): 1–6.

Panaro, Luca. 'Ryan McGinley'. *Around Photography International* 13 (2008): 30–4.

Paynes, Steph. 'Robin Guthrie'. *Guitar Player* (February 1991).

Reynolds, Simon. 'Insides: Interview'. *Melody Maker* (27 November 1993).

Reynolds, Simon. 'The Ambient Pool'. *The Wire* (May 1996).

Rosenberg, Douglas. 'Video Space: A Site for Choreography'. *Leonardo* 33, no. 4 (2000): 275–80.

Satran, Rory. 'The Endless Road Trip of Ryan McGinley'. *i–D* (27 August 2015), at https://i-d.vice.com/en_us/article/kz8pa9/the-endless-road-trip-of-ryan-mcginley.

Sawyer, Carol F. and David R. Butler. 'The Use of Historical Picture Postcards as Photographic Sources for Examining Environmental Change: Promises and Problems'. *Geocarto International* 3 (2006): 73–80.

Schwagerl, Christian. 'How We Must Adjust our Lifestyles to Nature: Welcome to the "Anthropocene" the Human Epoch'. *The Independent* (24 February 2015), at https://www.independent.co.uk/environment/how-we-must-adjust-our-lifes tyles-to-nature-welcome-to-the-anthropocene-the-human-epoch-10068001.html.

Schwartz, David. *Listening Subjects: Music, Psychoanalysis, Culture*. London: Duke University Press, 1997.

Smalley, Denis. 'Spectromorphology: Explaining Sound-Shapes'. *Organised Sound* 2, no. 2 (1997): 107–26.

Steffen, Will, Wendy Broadgate, Lisa Deutsch, Owen Gaffney and Cornelia Ludwig. 'The Trajectory of the Anthropocene: The Great Acceleration'. *The Anthropocene Review* 2, no. 1 (2015): 81–98.

Storm, Anna. *Post-industrial Landscape Scars*. New York: Palgrave Macmillan, 2014.

Tsing, Anna Lowenhaupt, Heather Anne Swanson, Elaine Gan and Nils Bubandt. *Arts of Living on a Damaged Planet Ghosts and Monsters of the Anthropocene*. Minneapolis, MN: University of Minnesota Press, 2017.

Tuan, Yi-Fu. *Escapism*. Baltimore: Johns Hopkins University Press, 1998.

Vitousek, Peter Morrison, Harold Mooney, Jane Lubchenco and Jerry Melillo. 'Human Domination of Earth's Ecosystems'. *Science* 277 (1997): 494–9.

Whybrow, Nicolas. 'Watermarked: "Venice Really Lives Up to Its Postcard Beauty"'. *Performance Research: Journal of Performing Arts* 20, no. 3 (2015): 50–7.

Wulf, Tim, Diana Rieger and Josephine Schmitt. 'Blissed by the Past: Theorizing Media-Induced Nostalgia as an Audience Response Factor for Entertainment and Well-Being'. *Poetics* 69 (2018): 70–80.

Zalasiewicz, Jan, Colin Waters and Mark Williams. 'City-Strata of the Anthropocene'. *Annales. Histoire, Sciences Sociales* 2 (2017): 329–51.

Chapter 16

Bordwell, David. 'Observations on Film Art: Now Leaving from Platform 1', 19 August 2009, at http://www.davidbordwell.net/blog/2009/08/19/now-leaving-from-platform-1/ (accessed 30 August 2018).

Brophy, Philip. 'Lost Highway: Booms, Drones and Other Dark Waves' (1997), at http://www.philipbrophy.com/projects/cnsncs/LostHighway.html (accessed 30 August 2018).

Brophy, Philip. 'Parties in Your Head: From the Acoustic to the Psycho-Acoustic'. In *The Oxford Handbook of New Audiovisual Aesthetics*, ed. Claudia Gorbman, John Richardson and Carol Vernallis, 309–22. Oxford: Oxford University Press, 2013.

Chion, Michel, *David Lynch*. London: British Film Institute, 1995.

Corrigan, Timothy. 'The Commerce of Auteurism: A Voice Without Authority'. *New German Critique* 49 (1990): 43–57.

Davidson, Annette. '"Up in Flames": Love, Control and Collaboration in the Soundtrack to *Wild at Heart*'. In *The Cinema of David Lynch: American Dreams, Nightmare Visions*, ed. Annette Davison and Erica Sheen, 119–35. New York: Wallflower Press, 2004.

Donnelly, K. J. '*Saw* Heard: Musical Sound Design in Contemporary Cinema'. In *Film Theory and Contemporary Hollywood Movies*, ed. Warren Buckland, 103–23. New York and London: Routledge, 2009.

Fisher, Mark. 'The Metaphysics of Crackle'. *Dancecult: Journal of Electronic Dance Music Culture* 5, no. 2 (2013): 42–55.

Fisher, Mark. *Ghosts of My Life: Writings on Depression, Hauntology and Lost Futures*. Alresford: Zero Books, 2014.

Fisher, Mark. *The Weird and the Eerie*. London: Repeater Books, 2016.

Friedberg, Anne. 'The End of Cinema: Multimedia and Technological Change'. In *Reinventing Film Studies*, ed. Christine Gledhill and Linda Williams, 438–52. New York: Oxford University Press, 2000.

Graves, Herbert. *Making Strange: Beauty, Sublimity and the (Post) Modern 'Third' Aesthetic*. New York: Rodopi, 2008.

Hainge, Greg. *Noise Matters: Towards an Ontology of Noise*. New York, London: Bloomsbury, 2013.

Harries, Dan. *The New Media Book*. London: British Film Institute, 2002.

Hill, Matt. *Fan Cultures*. New York: Routledge, 2002.

Hughes, David. *The Complete Lynch*. London: Virgin, 2001.

Jarvis, Brian. *Postmodern Cartographies: The Geographical Imagination in Contemporary American Culture*. London: Pluto Press, 1998.

Jenkins, Henry. 'If It Doesn't Spread, It's Dead (Part One): Media Viruses and Memes'. *Confessions of an Aca-Fan* (11 February 2009), at http://henryjenkins.org/blog/2009/02/if_it_doesnt_spread_its_dead_p.html (accessed 30 August 2018).

Jenkins, Henry. 'The Aesthetics of Transmedia: In Response to David Bordwell (Part Three)'. *Confessions of an Aca-Fan* (15 September 2009), at http://henryjenkins.org/blog/2009/09/the_aesthetics_of_transmedia_i_2.html (accessed 30 August 2018).

Jenkins, Henry. *Convergence Culture: Where Old and New Media Collide*. New York: New York University Press, 2006.

Kane, Brian. *Sound Unseen: Acousmatic Sound in Theory and Practice*. New York: Oxford University Press, 2014.

Kenny, Tom. 'Cruising with David Lynch Down the "Lost Highway"'. In *Sound for Picture: Film Sound Through the* 1990s, 128–36. Vallejo: MixBooks, 2000.

Lim, Dennis. 'David Lynch Goes Digital'. *Slate* (23 August 2007), at http://www.slate.com/articles/arts/dvdextras/2007/08/david_lynch_goes_digital.html (accessed 30 August 2018).

Long, Geoffrey. *Transmedia Storytelling: Business, Aesthetics, and Production at the Jim Henson Company*. PhD thesis. Department of Comparative Media Studies, Massachusetts Institute of Technology, 2007.

Lynch, David. 'David Lynch Interview: "There Is Something so Incredibly Cosmically Magical about Curtains'. *Time Out* (13 January 2014), at https://www.timeout.com/london/art/david-lynch-interview-there-is-something-so-incredibly-cosmically-magical-about-curtains (accessed 30 August 2018).

Lynch, David. 'Spira'. *Davidlynch.com* (27 May 2010), at http://interviewproject.davidlynch.com/www/ (accessed 30 August 2018).

Lynch, David. 'The Monster Meets…Filmmaker David Lynch'. *Monster Cable* (Fall 1998), at http://www.lynchnet.com/monster.html (accessed 30 August 2018).

Lynskey, Dorian. '"Make it Like the Wind, Angelo': How the *Twin Peaks* Soundtrack Came to Haunt Music for Nearly 30 Years'. *The Guardian* (24 March 2017), at https://www.theguardian.com/music/2017/mar/24/twin-peaks-soundtrack-david-lynch-angelo-badalamenti (accessed 30 August 2018).

Malkinson, Agnes. "Damn Fine Coffee' Advertising: David Lynch's TV Commercial Adaptation of *Twin Peaks*'. *Senses of Cinema* (July 2016), at http://sensesof cinema.com/2016/twin-peaks/26839/ (accessed 30 August 2018).

Mittell, Jason. *Complex TV: The Poetics of Contemporary Television Storytelling*. New York: New York University Press, 2015.

Murch, Walter. 'Stretching Sound to Help the Mind See'. *The New York Times* (1 October 2000), at http://www.nytimes.com/2000/10/01/arts/01MURC.html? pagewanted=all (accessed 30 August, 2018).

Pearson, Roberta. 'The Writer-Producer in American Television'. In *The Contemporary Television Series*, ed. Michael Hammond and Lucy Mazdon, 11–26. Edinburgh: Edinburgh University Press, 2005.

Reynolds, Simon. *Retromania: Pop Cultures Addiction to its Own Past*. London: Faber and Faber, 2011.

Richardson, John. 'Laura and Twin Peaks: Postmodern Parody and the Musical Reconstruction of the Absent Femme Fatale'. In *The Cinema of David Lynch: American Dreams, Nightmare Visions*, ed. Annette Davidson and Erica Sheen, 77–92. London: Wallflower Press, 2004.

Rodley, Chris. *Lynch on Lynch*. London: Faber and Faber, 1997.

Rogers, Holly. 'Audio-Visual Collisions: Moving Image Technology and the Laterna Magika Aesthetic in New Music Theatre'. In *New Music Theatre in Europe: Transformations between 1955–1975*, ed. Robert Adlington, 79–100. New York: Routledge, 2019.

Rogers, Holly. 'Audiovisual Dissonance in Found Footage Film'. In *The Music and Sound of Experimental Film*, ed. Holly Rogers and Jeremy Barham, 185–204. New York and Oxford: Oxford University Press, 2017.

Rogers, Holly. 'Sonic Elongation and Sonic Aporia: Soundscape Composition in Film'. In *The Oxford* Handbook *of Cinematic Listening*, edited by Carlo Cenciarelli. Oxford: Oxford University Press, forthcoming in 2019.

Samardzija, Zoran. 'DavidLynch.com: Auteurship in the Age of the Internet and Digital Cinema'. *Scope* (February 2010), at https://www.nottingham.ac.uk/ scope/documents/2010/february-2010/samardzija.pdf (accessed 30 August 2018).

Sarris, Andrew. 'Notes on the Auteur Theory in 1962'. In *Film Theory and Criticism*, ed. Leo Brandy and Marshall Cohen, 451–70. Oxford: Oxford University Press, 2009.

Splet, Alan. 'Interview: Alan Splet'. *Cagey Films* (17 December 1981), at https:// web.archive.org/web/20121201060512/http://www.cageyfilms.com/links/erase rhead/interviews/other-eraserhead-crew/alan-splet/ (accessed 30 August 2018).

Thill, Scott. 'David Lynch Interviews – Uncut'. *Wired* (1 February 2007), at https://www.wired.com/2007/01/david-lynch-interviews-uncut/ (accessed 30 August 2018).

Toop, David. *Sinister Resonance: The Mediumship of the Listener*. New York: Continuum, 2010.

van Elferen, Isabella. 'Dream Timbre: Notes on Lynchian Sound Design'. In *Music, Sound and Filmmakers*, ed. James Wierzbicki, 175–88. New York: Routledge, 2012.

Warner, Marina. 'Voodoo Road: *Lost Highway* by David Lynch'. *Sight and Sound* 7, no. 8 (August 1997): 6–10.

Chapter 17

Alexander, John. *The Films of David Lynch*. Dalkeith: Charles Letts & Co, 1993.

Álvarez López, Cristina. 'Foreplays #6: David Lynch's "Premonition Following an Evil Deed"'. *Mubi Notebook*, at https://mubi.com/notebook/posts/foreplays-6-david-lynch-s-premonition-following-an-evil-deed (accessed 21 December 2018).

Barney, Richard, ed. *David Lynch Interviews*. Jackson: University Press of Mississippi, 2009.

Bazin, André. 'The Ontology of the Photographic Image,' translated by Hugh Gray. *Film Quarterly* 13, no. 4 (1960): 4–9.

Deleuze, Gilles. *Cinema 2: The Time-Image*, translated by Hugh Tomlinson and Robert Galeta. Minneapolis: University of Minnesota Press, 1997.

Ellis, Matthew and Tyler Theus. 'Is It Happening Again? *Twin Peaks* and *"The Return"* of History'. In *Critical Essays on Twin Peaks: The Return*, edited by Antonio Sanna, 23–36. London: Palgrave Macmillan, 2019.

Feynman, Richard. *The Character of Physical Law*. Cambridge, MA: MIT Press, 1985.

Feynman, Richard. *What Do You Care What Other People Think? Further Adventures of a Curious Character*. New York: Norton & Company, 1988.

Fornäs, Jonas. 'Passages Across Thresholds: Into the Borderlands of Mediation'. *Convergence* 8, no. 4 (2002): 89–106.

Galow, Timothy William. 'From *Lost Highway* to *Twin Peaks*: Representations of Trauma and Transformation in Lynch's Late Works'. In *Critical Essays on Twin Peaks: The Return*, edited by Antonio Sanna, 201–20. London: Palgrave Macmillan, 2019.

Hainge, Greg. *Noise Matters: Towards an Ontology of Noise*. New York: Bloomsbury Academic, 2013.

Hawkes, Joel. 'Movement in the Box: The Production of Surreal Social Space and the Alienated Body'. In *Critical Essays on Twin Peaks: The Return*, edited by Antonio Sanna, 149–68. London: Palgrave Macmillan, 2019.

Holmes, Bob. 'Why Time Flies in Old Age'. *New Scientist*, at https://www.new scientist.com/article/mg15220571.700-why-time-flies-in-old-age/ (accessed 25 January 2019).

Kittler, Friedrich. *Gramophone*, Film, *Typewriter*, translated by Geoffrey Winthrop-Young and Michael Wutz. Stanford, CA: Stanford University Press, 1999.

Light, Michael. *100 Suns*. New York: Alfred A. Knopf, 2003.

Lynch, David. *Images*. New York: Hyperion, 1994.

Nochimson, Martha. *David Lynch Swerves: Uncertainty from Lost Highway to Inland Empire*. Austin: University of Texas Press, 2013.

Rovelli, Carlo. *The Order of Time*. London: Penguin Books, 2017.

Warner, Marina. 'Voodoo Road: *Lost Highway* by David Lynch'. *Sight and Sound* 7, no. 8 (1997): 6–10.

Wiener, Norbert. 'Spatio-Temporal Continuity, Quantum Theory and Music'. In *The Concepts of Space and Time: Their Structure and Their Development*, edited by Milič Čapek, 539–46. Dordrecht: Springer-Science+Business Media, 1976.

Yates, Christian. 'Why Time Seems to go by More Quickly as We Get Older'. *The Conversation*, at https://theconversation.com/why-time-seems-to-go-by-more-quickly-as-we-get-older-63354 (accessed 25 January 2019).

Chapter 18

Badalamenti, Angelo. 'Angelo Badalamenti on Working with David Lynch', at https://www.youtube.com/watch?v=a_9D5PiOjog (accessed 15 November 2018).
Badalamenti, Angelo. 'Angelo Badalamenti Stair Music Danger Theme', at https://www.youtube.com/watch?v=ffhTeSHLozY (accessed 15 November 2018).
Cousins, Mark. 'Scene by Scene with David Lynch', at https://sphinx.mythic-beasts.com/~mark/random/david-lynch/ (accessed 15 November 2018).
Dom, Pieter. 'Slow Speed Orchestra Bundle & David Lynch's Clean Up New York PSA', at https://welcometotwinpeaks.com/music/slow-speed-orchestra-clean-up-new-york/ (accessed 15 November 2018).
Dom, Pieter. 'To Score The Haunting Woodsmen Scene', at https://welcometotwinpeaks.com/music/woodsmen-beethoven-moonlight-sonata/ (accessed 15 November 2018).
Dudle, Ross. 'Twin Peaks Soundtrack Design' at http://twinpeakssoundtrackdesign.blogspot.com/p/twin-peaks-music-scene-guide.html (accessed 15 November 2018).
Griffiths, Emma. 'Q&A with David Lynch's Music Collaborator Dean Hurley', at https://www.synchtank.com/blog/qa-with-david-lynchs-music-collaborator-dean-hurley-part-1-working-on-and-protecting-the-experience-of-twin-peaks-the-return/ (accessed 15 November 2018).
O'Falt, Chris. 'Sound Comes First', at https://www.indiewire.com/2018/05/twin-peaks-the-return-sound-design-david-lynch-hidden-studio-process-dean-hurley-1201965234/ (accessed 15 November 2018).
Pedersen, Karl and Mark Grimshaw-Aagaard (eds.). 2019. *The Recording, Mixing, and Mastering Reference Handbook*. New York: Oxford University Press.
Pete (blogger). 'Beatles Production Tricks Part II – VariSpeed', at https://ofbuckleyandbeatles.wordpress.com/2010/12/05/beatles-production-tricks-part-ii-varispeed/ (accessed 15 November 2018).
Rehding, Alexander. 'The Discovery of Slowness', in *Thresholds of Listening: Sounds, Technics,* Space, ed. Sander Van Maas, 206–25. New York: Fordham University, 2015.
Rhino. 'Twin Peaks: An Interview with Music Director Dean Hurley', at https://www.rhino.com/article/twin-peaks-an-interview-with-music-director-dean-hurley (access date 13 November 2018).
Rogers, Holly. 'Introduction'. In *The Music and Sound of Experimental Film*, edited by Rogers and Jeremy Barham, 1–22. New York and Oxford: Oxford University Press, 2017.
Wray, Daniel Dylan. 'The Discomfort Zone: Exploring the Musical Legacy of David Lynch', at https://pitchfork.com/features/article/9958-the-discomfort-zone-exploring-the-musical-legacy-of-david-lynch/ (accessed 15 November 2018).

Chapter 19

Combes, Muriel. *Gilbrt Simondon and the Philosophy of the Transindividual*. Translated by Thomas LaMarre. Cambridge: MIT Press, 2013.

Deleuze, Gilles. *Difference and Repetition*. Translated by Paul Patton. New York: Continuum, 2004.

Deleuze, Gilles and Félix Guattari. *A Thousand Plateaus: Capitalism and Schizophrenia*. Translated by Brian Massumi. Minneapolis: University of Minnesota Press, 1987.

del Río, Elena. *Deleuze and the Cinemas of Performance: Powers of Affection*. Edinburgh: Edinburgh University Press, 2008.

del Río, Elena. *The Grace of Destruction: A Vital Ethology of Extreme Cinemas*. New York: Bloomsbury, 2016.

del Río, Elena. '*La Grande Bellezza*: Adventures in Transindividuality'. *Necsus: European Journal of Media Studies* (Autumn 2017), at https://necsus-ejms. org/la-grande-bellezza-adventures-in-transindividuality/ (accessed 3 March 2019).

Fox, Tyler. 'Prehensive Transduction: Techno-Aesthetics in New Media Art'. *Platform: Journal of Media and Communication* 6 (2015): 96–107.

Gunning, Tom. 'Animation and Alienation: Bergson's Critique of the Cinématographe and the Paradox of Mechanical Motion'. *The Moving Image* 14, no. 1 (Spring 2014): 1–9.

Hackett, Jon. 'The Ontogenesis of Cinematic Objects: Simondon, Marx and the Invention of Cinema'. *Platform: Journal of Media and Communication* 6 (2015): 11–21.

Hansen, Mark. 'Body Times'. In *New Philosophy for New Media*, 235–68. Cambridge: MIT Press, 2006.

Lessard, Bruno. "It's the End of the World!': The Paradox of Event and Body in Hitchcock's *The Birds*'. *Film-Philosophy* 14, no. 1 (2010): 144–67.

Massumi, Brian. '"Technical Mentality" Revisited: Brian Massumi on Gilbert Simondon'. In *Gilbert Simondon: Being and Technology*, edited by Arne de Boever, Alex Murray, Jon Roffe, and Ashley Woodward. Edinburgh: Edinburgh University Press, 2013.

Merleau-Ponty, Maurice. *The Phenomenology of Perception*. New York: Routledge, 2002.

Rantala, Juho. 'The Notion of Information in Early Cybernetics and in Gilbert Simondon's Philosophy'. Paper presented at Doctoral Congress in Philosophy, University of Tampere, Finland, October 2018.

Sauvagnargues, Anne. 'Crystals and Membranes'. In *Gilbert Simondon: Being and Technology*, edited by Arne de Boever, Alex Murray, Jon Roffe and Ashley Woodward, 57–70. Edinburgh: Edinburgh University Press, 2013.

Sauvagnargues, Anne. *Artmachines: Deleuze, Guattari, Simondon*. Translated by Suzanne Verderber with Eugene Holland. Edinburgh: Edinburgh University Press, 2016.

Simondon, Gilbert. *L'individuation à la lumière des notions de forme et d'information*. Grenoble: Éditions Jérôme Millon, 2005.

Chapter 20

Coggin, Devan. 'Barry Jenkins Deconstructs the Swimming Lesson Scene from *Moonlight*'. In *Entertainment Weekly* (6 December 2016), at https://ew.com/article/2016/12/06/moonlight-barry-jenkins-swimming-lesson-scene/ (accessed 6 April 2019).

Gillespie, Michael. *Film Blackness: American Cinema and the Idea of Black Film*. Durham, NC: Duke University Press, 2016.

Gillespie, Michael. 'One Step Ahead: A Conversation With Barry Jenkins'. *Film Quarterly* (28 February 2017), at https://filmquarterly.org/2017/02/28/one-step-ahead-a-conversation-with-barry-jenkins/ (accessed 27 March 2019).

Nostro, Lauren. 'Jidenna Reacts to His Song 'Classic Man' Appearing In *Moonlight*'. In *Genius.com* (24 February 2017), at https://genius.com/a/jidenna-reacts-to-his-song-classic-man-appearing-in-moonlight (accessed 26 March 2019).

Schnipper, Matthew. 'Director Barry Jenkins on the Music That Made *Moonlight*'. In *Pitchfork.com* (29 November 2016), at https://pitchfork.com/thepitch/1377-director-barry-jenkins-on-the-music-that-made-moonlight/ (accessed 26 March 2019).

Chapter 21

Avnet, Tamar and Anne-Lauer Sellier. 'Clock Time vs. Event Time: Temporal Culture or Self-Regulation?' *Journal of Experiential Social Psychology* 47 (2011): 665–7.

Baldwin, James. *If Beale Street Could Talk*. New York: Vintage International, 1974/2002.

Baldwin, James. *James Baldwin: The Last Interview and Other Conversations*. Brooklyn: Melville House, 2014.

Baraka, Amiri. *Black Music*. New York: Akashic Classics, 2010.

Jones, LeRoi. *Blues People: Negro Music in White America*. New York: William Morrow & Co., 1963.

Bribitzer-Stull, Matthew. *Understanding the Leitmotif: From Wagner to Hollywood Film Music*. New York: Cambridge University Press, 2015.

Chion, Michel. *Audio-Vision: Sound on Screen*. Edited by Claudia Gorbman. New York: Columbia University Press, 1994.

Doane, Mary Ann. *The Emergence of Cinematic Time: Modernity, Contingency, and the Archive*. Cambridge: Harvard University Press, 2002.

Giorgis, Hannah and Nicholas Britell. 'How If Beale Street Could Talk Translates Joy and Terror into Sound'. *The Atlantic* (19 December 2018). https://www.theatlantic.com/entertainment/archive/2018/12/if-beale-street-could-talk-nicholas-britell-composer-music-score/577879/ (accessed April 25 2019).

Mailer, Norman. 'The White Negro: Superficial Reflections on the Hipster'. *Dissent* (20 June 2007), at https://www.dissentmagazine.org/online_articles/the-white-negro-fall-1957 (accessed 28 April 2019).

Monson, Ingrid. 'The Problem with White Hipness: Race, Gender, and Cultural Conceptions in Jazz Historical Discourse'. *Journal of the American Musicological Society* 48, No. 3 (Autumn 1995): 396–422.

Powell, Helen. *Stop The Clocks!: Time and Narrative in Cinema*. London: I.B. Tauris & Co., 2012.

Sterne, Jonathan. *The Audible Past: Cultural Origins of Sound Production*. Durham: Duke University Press, 2003.

Chapter 23

Blake, Andrew. *Popular Music: The Age of Multimedia*. London: Middlesex University Press, 2007.

Blum, Jordan. 'Genius. Doesn't. Fade: A Conversation with Steven Wilson'. *PopMatters*. https://www.popmatters.com/genius-doesnt-fade-a-conversation -with-steven-wilson-2495558585.html. Accessed 12 March 2015.

Burns, Lori. 'The Concept Album as Visual–Sonic–Textual Spectacle: The Transmedial Storyworld of Coldplay's *Mylo Xyloto*'. *IASPM@Journal* 6, no. 2 (2016): 91–116.

Burns, Lori. 'Multimodal Analysis of Popular Music Video: Genre, Discourse, and Narrative in Steven Wilson's "Drive Home"'. In *Coming of Age: Teaching and Learning Popular Music in Academia*, edited by Carl Rodrigues, 81–110. Ann Arbor: University of Michigan Press, 2017.

Burns, Lori. 'Transmedia Storytelling in Steven Wilson's "The Raven That Refused to Sing"'. In *The Routledge Companion to Popular Music Analysis: Expanding Approaches*, edited by Ciro Scotto, 95–113. New York and London: Routledge Press, 2018.

Burns, Lori and Laura McLaren. 'Interpreting the Materials of a Transmedia Storyworld: Word-Music-Image in Steven Wilson's *Hand. Cannot. Erase.* (2015)'. In *The Bloomsbury Handbook of Music Production*, edited by Simon Zagorski-Thomas and Andrew Bourbon, forthcoming. London: Bloomsbury Publishing, 2019.

Chateau, Dominique, ed. *Subjectivity: Filmic Representation and the Spectator's Experience*. Amsterdam: Amsterdam University Press, 2011.

Cook, Nicholas. *Analysing Musical Multimedia*. New York: Oxford University Press, 1998.

Crafton, Donald. *Shadow of a Mouse: Performance, Belief, and World-Making in Animation*. Berkeley: University of California Press, 2013.

Dibben, Nicola. 'Visualizing the App Album with Björk's *Biophilia*'. In *The Oxford Handbook of Sound and Image in Digital Media*, edited by Carol Vernallis, Amy Herzog, and John Richardson, 682–706. Oxford: Oxford University Press, 2013.

Elleström, Lars, ed. *Media Borders, Multimodality and Intermediality*. Basingstoke: Palgrave Macmillan, 2010.

Evans, Elizabeth. *Transmedia Television: Audiences, New Media, and Daily Life*. New York and London: Routledge Press, 2011.

Freeman, Matthew. *Historicising Transmedia Storytelling: Early Twentieth-Century Transmedia Story Worlds*. London: Routledge Press, 2017.

Genette, Gérard. *Discours du récit*. Paris: Seuil, 1972.

Gorbman, Claudia. *Unheard Melodies: Narrative Film Music*. Bloomington and Indianapolis: Indiana University Press, 1987.

Herman, David. 'Word-Image/Utterance-Gesture: Case Studies in Multimodal Storytelling'. In *New Perspectives on Narrative and Multimodality*, edited by Ruth Page, 78–98. Abingdon: Routledge Press, 2009.

Holm-Hudson, Kevin. *Genesis and The Lamb Lies Down on Broadway*. Aldershot: Ashgate Press, 2008.

Humphries, Stephen. 'An Interview with Jess Cope'. *Steven Wilson*, http://stevenwilsonhq.com/sw/an-interview-with-jess-cope/. Accessed 15 January 2019.

Jenkins, Henry. *Convergence Culture: Where Old and New Media Collide*. New York: New York University Press, 2006.

Jewitt, Carey, Jeff Bezemer and Kay O'Halloran, eds. *Introducing Multimodality*. Abingdon: Routledge Press, 2016.

Jost, Christofer. 'Popular Music and Transmedia Aesthetics: On the Conceptual Relation of Sound, Audio-Vision and Live Performance'. In *Reinventing Sound: Music and Audiovisual Culture*, edited by Enrique Encabo, 2–13. Newcastle upon Tyne: Cambridge Scholars Publishing, 2015.

Kelly, Jem. 'Pop Music, Multimedia and Live Performance'. In *Music, Sound and Multimedia: From the Live to the Virtual*, edited by Jamie Sexton, 105–20. Edinburgh: Edinburgh University Press, 2007.

Kress, Gunther, and Theo van Leeuwen. *Multimodal Discourse*. London: Bloomsbury Academic, 2001.

Letts, Marianne Tatom. *Radiohead and the Resistant Concept Album: How to Disappear Completely*. Bloomington and Indianapolis: Indiana University Press, 2010.

Machin, David. *Analysing Popular Music: Image, Sound, Text*. Los Angeles: Sage, 2010.

McErlean, Kelly. *Interactive Narratives and Transmedia Storytelling: Creating Immersive Stories Across New Media Platforms*. Abingdon: Routledge Press, 2018.

McQuinn, Julie. *Popular Music and Multimedia*. Aldershot: Ashgate, 2011.

Moore, Allan F. *Aqualung*. New York: Continuum, 2004.

Page, Ruth. 'Seriality and Storytelling in Social Media'. In *Storyworlds: A Journal of Narrative Studies* 5, no. 1 (2013): 31–54.

Page, Ruth, ed. *New Perspectives on Narrative and Multimodality*. Abingdon: Routledge Press, 2010.

Rose, Phil. *Roger Waters and Pink Floyd: The Concept Albums*. Madison: Fairleigh Dickinson University Press, 2015.

Rowsell, Jennifer. *Working with Multimodality: Rethinking Literacy in a Digital Age*. London and New York: Routledge Press, 2013.

Ryan, Marie-Laure. 'Transmedial Storytelling and Transfictionality'. In *Poetics Today* 34, no. 3 (2013): 361–88.

Ryan, Marie-Laure and Jan-Noël Thon. 'Storyworlds Across Media: Introduction'. In *Storyworlds Across Media: Toward a Media-Conscious Narratology*, edited by Marie-Laure Ryan and Jan-Noel Thon, 1–21. Lincoln: University of Nebraska Press, 2014.

Sexton, Jamie, ed. *Music, Sound and Multimedia: From the Live to the Virtual.* Edinburgh: University of Edinburgh Press, 2007.

Shute, Gareth. *Concept Albums.* California: Investigations Publishing, 2013.

Smolko, Tim. *Thick as a Brick and A Passion Play: Inside Two Long Songs.* Bloomington and Indianapolis: Indiana University Press, 2013.

Thon, Jan-Noël. *Transmedial Narratology and Contemporary Media Culture.* Lincoln: University of Nebraska Press, 2016.

Tønnessen, Elise Seip and Frida Forsgren, eds. *Multimodality and Aesthetics.* Abingdon: Routledge, 2018.

Van Leeuwen, Theo. *Speech, Music, Sound.* Houndmills: Palgrave Macmillan, 1999.

Van Leeuwen, Theo. 'Multimodality'. In *The Handbook of Discourse Analysis*, edited by Deborah Tannen, Heidi E. Hamilton and Deborah Schiffrin, second edition, 447–65. Hoboken: John Wiley and Sons, 2015.

Vernallis, Carol. *Unruly Media: YouTube, Music Video, and the New Digital Cinema.* Oxford and New York: Oxford University Press, 2013.

Wener, Ben. 'Concept Albums are Once Again in Vogue in the Digital Age'. *Pop Matters* (7 December 2006). Accessed 19 January 2019, at http://www.popm atters.com/pm/feature/concept-albums-are-once-again-in-vogue-in-the-digital -age/.

Wöllner, Clemens, ed. *Body, Sound and Space in Music and Beyond: Multimodal Explorations.* Abingdon: Routledge Press, 2017.

Chapter 24

Cornell, Laura. 'Self-Portraiture in the First-Person Age'. *Aperture* 221 (Winter 2015): 34–41.

Disemelo, Katlego. 'Performing the Queer Archive: Strategies of Self-Styling on Instagram'. In *Acts of Transgression: Contemporary Live Art in South Africa*, ed. Jay Pather and Catherine Boulle, 219–42. Johannesburg: Wits University Press, 2019.

Goldberg, Greg. *Antisocial Media: Anxious Labor in the Digital Economy.* New York: New York University Press, 2018.

Rines, Danielle 'JAY VERSACE CURATED A '90S INSPIRED CAPSULE FOR REEBOK'. *Reebok* (posted October 2018), at https://www.reebok.com/us/blog /303185-jay-versace-curated-a-90s-inspired-capsule- for-reebok (accessed 4 May 2019).

Chapter 25

Alighieri, Dante. *The Divine Comedy.* Translated by Allen Mandelbaum. London: Everyman's Library, 1995.

Brunning, Jacqueline and Paul Forster (eds). *Peirce, Charles Sanders 1997: The Rule of Reason: The Philosophy of Charles Sanders Peirce.* Toronto: University of Toronto Press, 1997.

Chion, Michel. *The Voice in Cinema*. New York: Columbia University Press, 1999.

Deleuze, Gilles. *Cinema 1: The Movement-Image*. Translated by Hugh Tomlinson and Barbara Habberjam. Minneapolis: University of Minnesota Press, 1986.

Deleuze, Gilles. *Cinema 2: The Time-Image*. Translated by Hugh Tomlinson and Robert Galeta. Minneapolis: University of Minnesota Press, 1989.

Deleuze, Gilles and Félix Guattari. *A Thousand Plateaus*. New York: Bloomsbury Academic, 2013.

Kafka, Franz. 'Before the Law'. Translated by Ian Johnston. *Frank Kafka online*, at http://www.kafka-online.info/before-the-law.html (accessed 5 April 2019).

Kane, Brian. *Sound Unseen: Acousmatic Sound in Theory and Practice*. Oxford: Oxford University Press, 2014.

Manovich, Lev. 'New Media from Borges to HTML'. In *The New Media Reader*, edited by Noah Wadrip-Fruin and Nick Montfort, 13–25. Cambridge: The MIT Press, 2003.

Massumi, Brian. *Parables for the Virtual. Movement, Affect, Sensation*. Durham: Duke University Press, 2002.

Massumi, Brian. *Semblance and Event: Activist Philosophy and the Occurrent Arts*. Cambridge: The MIT Press, 2011.

Mulvey, Laura. 'Visual Pleasure and Narrative Cinema'. In *Visual and Other Pleasures*. London: Macmillan, 1989.

Proust, Marcel. *In Search of Lost Time*. Translated by Charles Kenneth Scott Moncrieff. New York: The Modern Library, 2003.

Riegl, Alois. *Late Roman Art Industry*. Translated by Rolf Winkes. Rome: Georgio Bretschneider, 1985.

Spinoza, Baruch de. *Ethics*. Translated by Edwin Curley. London: Penguin Books Limited, 1996.

Thomsen, Bodil Marie Stavning. 'Signaletic, Haptic and Real-Time Material'. *Journal of Aesthetics and Culture* 4, issue 1 (2012): 1–11.

Thomsen, Bodil Marie Stavning. *Lars von Trier's Renewal of Film 1984–2014. Signal, Pixel, Diagram*. Aarhus: Aarhus University Press, 2018.

Wills, David, ed. *Jean-Luc Godard's* Pierrot le fou. Cambridge: Cambridge University Press, 2000.

Chapter 26

Adorno, Theodor Wiesengrund. *The Culture Industry: Selected Essays on Mass Culture*. New York: Routledge, 2001.

Akbar, Abbas. 'Junk Space, "Dogville", and Poor Theory'. Lecture, Film Theory and Visual Culture Seminar, Vanderbilt University, 6 December 2013.

Badley, Linda. 'Fill All My Holes': *Nymphomaniac*, Sade, and the (Female) Libertine Body'. Special Issue: *Cinema as Provocation. Ekphrasis: Images, Cinema, Media, Theory* 2 (2015): 21–38.

Badley, Linda. *Lars von Trier*. Chicago: University of Illinois Press, 2011.

Badley, Linda. 'The Transnational Politics of Lars von Trier's and Thomas Vinterberg's "Amerika"'. In *Cinemas of Elsewhere: A Globalized History of*

Nordic Film Cultures, edited by Arne Lunde and Anna Stenport. Edinburgh: Edinburgh University Press, 2019.

Claro, Manuel Alberto. Skype interview conducted by Linda Badley, 11 December 2014.

Debruge, Peter. 'Film Review: "Nymphomaniac"'. *Variety*, 17 December 2013, at https://variety.com/2013/film/reviews/film-review-lars-von-triers-nymphoman iac-1200964948/.

Fazio, Giovanni. 'The Antichrist, Melancholia and Nymphomania According to Lars von Trier'. *The Japan Times* (29 October 2014), at https://www.japantim es.co.jp/culture/2014/10/29/films/film-reviews/antichrist-melancholia-nymph omania-according-lars-von-trier/#.

Friedländer, Saul. *Reflections of Nazism: An Essay on Kitsch and Death*. Translated by Thomas Weyr. New York: Harper and Row, 1982.

Hoberman, J. 'Cannes 2011: Lars von Trier's *Melancholia*. Wow'. *VoiceFilm* (18 May 2011). http://www.voicefilm.com/2011/05/cannes_2011_lars_von_triers_melancholia_wow.php.

'Lars von Trier – "I understand Hitler"'. YouTube video, 4:25. Posted by 'Hammid,' 18 May 2011, at https://www.youtube.com/watch?v=QpUqpLh0iRw.

Matikainen, Jacob. 'A Closer Look at Lars von Trier's Depression Trilogy'. *Screen Robot* (27 February 2014), at https://screenrobot.com/closer-look-lars-von-triers-depression-trilogy/.

Minor, Ryan. 'Introduction to Lars von Trier's "Deed of Conveyance"'. In *The Opera Quarterly* 23, nos. 2–3 (2007): 338–40.

O'Hehir, Andrew. 'Pick of the Week: Lars von Trier's spectacular 'Melancholia". Salon (10 November 2011), at https://www.salon.com/2011/11/11/pick_of_the_week_lars_von_triers_spectacular_melancholia/.

Pressly, Lowry. '"Nymphomaniac: Vol. 1": Fishers of Men, Meaning'. *The Los Angeles Review of Books* (21 March 2014), at https://lareviewofbooks.org/ar ticle/nymphomaniac-vol-1-fishers-men-meaning/.

Rockwell, John. 'FILM; Von Trier and Wagner, a Bond Sealed in Emotion'. *The New York Times* (8 April 2001), at https://www.nytimes.com/2001/04/08/movie s/film-von-trier-and-wagner-a-bond-sealed-in-emotion.html.

Rockwell, John. 'REVERBERATIONS; Maybe Lars von Trier's Vision Was Just What Wagner Needed,' *The New York Times* (11 June 2004), at https://www.nytimes.com/2004/06/ 11/movies/reverberations-maybe-lars-von-trier-s-vision-was-just-what-wagner-needed.html.

Schepelern, Peter. '"Forget about Love": Sex and Detachment in Lars von Trier's *Nymphomaniac*'. *Kosmorama* 259 (11 March 2015), at https://www.kosmorama.org/en/ kosmorama/artikler/forget-about-love-sex-and-detachment -lars-von-triers-nymphomaniac.

Schwarzbaum, Lisa. 'Cannes Film Festival: Lars von Trier's Stunning "Melancholia" – The end of the World (and a challenge to 'The Tree of Life')'. *Entertainment Weekly* (18 May 2011), at https://ew.com/article/2011/05/18/cannes-film-fest ival-lars-von-trier-melancholia-terrence-malick/.

Siegal, Nina. 'Lars Von Trier Wants to Turn All His Films into Diamonds'. *The New York Times* (11 February 2019), at https://www.nytimes.com/2019/02/11/arts/ design/lars-von-trier-diamond-melancholia.html.

'Sollers, Philippe. *Sade's Way'*. *ParisLike*. Video Documentary, 31:26. 2013, at http://www.parislike.com/EN/snoopy-philippe-sollers-video.php.

Spotts, Frederic. *Hitler and the Power of Aesthetics*. New York: Overlook Press, 2003.

Thorsen, Nils. *Geniet – Lars von Triers Liv, Film Og Fobier*. Copenhagen: Politiken, 2011.

van Joeij, Boyd. '"Nymphomaniac" Is Lars von Trier's Epic Attempt at a Sex-With-Brains Magnum Opus'. *Indiewire* (17 December 2013), at https://www.indie wire.com/2013/12/review-nymphomaniac-is-lars-von-triers-epic-attempt-at-a-sex-with-brains-magnum-opus-32096/.

von Trier, Lars. 'Lars von Trier on the Nibelungen Ring – The Enriched Darkness'. *Mostly Opera* (4 October 2007), at https://mostlyopera.blogspot.com/2007/10/lars-von-trier-on-nibelungen-ring.html.

von Trier, Lars. 'Director's Statement'. In 'Complete Press Kit', PDF Download. Cannes Film Festival, *Melancholia*. Magnolia Pictures & Zentropa Entertainments, 2011, at http://www.magpictures.com/presskit.aspx?id=bbcb73 3d-8d0e-495a-ba6d-be9a79453d1c.

von Trier, Lars and Murray Smith. Audio Commentary. *Antichrist*. DVD. Directed by Lars von Trier. New York: Criterion Collection, 2009.

von Trier, Lars and Peter Schepelern. Audio Commentary. *Melancholia*. Blu-Ray. Directed by Lars von Trier. London: Curzon Artificial Eye, 2011.

Chapter 27

Altman, Rick. *Silent Film Sound*. New York: Columbia University Press, 2004.

Baxter, John. *Stanley Kubrick: A Biography*. London: Harper Collins, 1997.

Björkman, Stig. *Trier on von Trier*. Translated by Neil Smith. London: Faber and Faber, 2003.

Brecht, Bertolt. 'On the Use of Music in an Epic Theatre'. In *Brecht on Theatre*, translated by John Willett, 84–90. London: Methuen, 1964.

Brown, Royal S. *Undertones and Overtones: Reading Film Music*. Berkeley: University of California Press, 1994.

Cenciarelli, Carlo. 'Dr Lecter's Taste for 'Goldberg', or: The Horror of Bach in the Hannibal Franchise'. *Journal of the Royal Musical Association* 137, no. 1 (2012): 107–34.

Cooke, Mervyn. 'Baroque à la Hitchcock: the music of *Dangerous Liaisons*'. In *Recomposing the Past: Representations of Early Music on Stage and Screen*, edited by James Cook, Alexander Kolassa and Adam Whittaker, 32–50. Abingdon: Routledge, 2018.

Hjort, Mette and Scott MacKenzie, eds. *Purity and Provocation: Dogma 95*. London: Palgrave Macmillan, 2003.

Jovanovic, Nenad. *Brechtian Cinemas: Montage and Theatricality*, edited by Jean-Marie Straub and Danièle Huillet, Peter Watkins and Lars von Trier. Albany: State University of New York Press, 2017.

Kassabian, Anahid. *Hearing Film: Tracking Identifications in Contemporary Hollywood Film Music*. London: Routledge, 2001.

Koutsourakis, Angelos. *Politics as Form in Lars von Trier: A Post-Brechtian Reading*. London: Bloomsbury Academic, 2015.

Leech-Wilkinson, Daniel. *The Modern Invention of Medieval Music*. Cambridge: Cambridge University Press, 2002.

Mera, Miguel. 'Representing the Baroque: The Portrayal of Historical Period in Film Music'. *The Consort: Journal of the Dolmetsch Foundation* 57 (2001): 3–21.

Prendergast, Roy M. *Film Music: A Neglected Art*. New York: Norton, 1977.

Simons, Jan. *Playing the Waves: Lars von Trier's Game Cinema*. Amsterdam: Amsterdam University Press, 2014.

INDEX